C0-AOS-122

One God – One Cult – One Nation

Beihefte zur Zeitschrift für die alttestamentliche Wissenschaft

Band 405

De Gruyter

One God – One Cult – One Nation

Archaeological and Biblical Perspectives

Edited by
Reinhard G. Kratz and Hermann Spieckermann

In cooperation with
Björn Corzilius and Tanja Pilger

De Gruyter

ISBN 978-3-11-022357-6
e-ISBN 978-3-11-022358-3
ISSN 0934-2575

Library of Congress Cataloging-in-Publication Data

Kratz, Reinhard Gregor, 1957–
One God, one cult, one nation : archaeological and biblical perspectives / Reinhard G. Kratz, Hermann Spieckermann.
p. cm. – (Beihefte zur zeitschrift fuer die alttestamentliche wissenschaft)
Includes bibliographical references and index.
ISBN 978-3-11-022357-6 (hardcover 23 × 15,5 : alk. paper)
1. Bible. O.T. – Antiquities. 2. Bible. O.T. – Criticism, interpretation, etc. 3. Excavations (Archaeology) – Israel. 4. Israel – Antiquities. I. Spieckermann, Hermann. II. Title.
BS1196.5.K73 2010
221.9'3–dc22
2010021655

Bibliographic information published by the Deutsche Nationalbibliothek

The Deutsche Nationalbibliothek lists this publication in the Deutsche Nationalbibliografie; detailed bibliographic data are available in the Internet at http://dnb.d-nb.de.

Printing: Hubert & Co. GmbH & Co. KG, Göttingen
∞ Printed on acid-free paper

Printed in Germany

www.degruyter.com

Preface

The present volume contains the updated versions of lectures delivered during two events of the Göttingen research training group (*Graduiertenkolleg*) "Götterbilder – Gottesbilder – Weltbilder: Polytheismus und Monotheismus in der Welt der Antike". One of the events was an international and interdisciplinary symposium in Jerusalem during September 2008. This symposium was organized by the research training group in co-operation with the *Centrum Orbis Orientalis* (CORO) and the Hebrew University of Jerusalem. The topic of the meeting also provided the title for the present volume: "One God, One Nation, One Cult". Under this heading we tried to bring Biblical Studies into conversation with Archaeology. The second meeting originated in a field trip that was originally part of the 2008 meeting. Here we visited – amongst other sites – Beth Shean/Nysa-Scythopolis. As a result we continued the interdisciplinary conversation now at a meeting in Göttingen in July 2009 and focussed on a specific case-study. In addition to the essays published here several important papers were delivered and discussed at the two meetings by both, invited participants (e.g. Prof. Gunnar Lehmann, Ben-Gurion University, Beersheba) and doctoral students of the research training group. For various reasons we were unable to publish theses papers in the present volume but some of the insights from them were incorporated in the various essays presented here.

The idea, planning and execution of the two meetings go back to the initiative of two doctoral students and members of the research training group: Björn Corzilius and Tanja Pilger. Before joining the doctoral programme in Hebrew Bible at Göttingen both spent part of their undergraduate education in Jerusalem – Björn Corzilius studied at the Dormition-Abbey and Tanja Pilger at the Hebrew University of Jerusalem. Tanja Pilger completed her doctoral thesis on the Elihu speeches in the Book of Job during the *Wintersemester* 2009/10 and Björn Corzilius will submit his thesis on the composition of the Book of Micah during the *Wintersemester* 2010/11. When the two students approached us floating the idea of holding one of our symposia in Jerusalem we were immediately taken by that idea but quite frankly did not see how to put it into reality. It is due to the tireless commitment of the two doctoral students that we were able to realize the plan. Both were not only responsible for the organisation of the meetings and their smooth execution but also in charge of the scholarly programme. Here they proposed and invited the speakers and ensured that the present volume was copy-edited and made ready for publication. Thus it was only natural that Björn Corzilius and Tanja Pilger should write the introduction to the volume. All in all it was a great achievement and we are very grateful for two unforgettable highlights of academic work and personal exchange as part of our research training group.

Furthermore we would like to thank the participants of the two conferences as well as the contributors to the present volume for their encouraging participation in every sense. We thank the Hebrew University for their splendid hospitality as well as for its trust and interest in the work of our research training group. The continued exchange with colleagues from Israel is very important to us – professionally and personally. The *Deutsche Forschungsgemeinschaft* (DFG) not only funds our research training group but also contributed significantly towards the costs of the symposium in Jerusalem – we are very grateful for the support! Next to Björn Corzilius and Tanja Pilger several people were involved in the production of the camera-ready copy of the present volume: we thank Gerd Krumbiegel for his assistance in proof-reading and for the compilation of the indexes; Franziska Ede and PD Dr. Anselm C. Hagedorn helped to produce English versions of contributions originally written in German. Finally we record our thanks to the publisher de Gruyter and especially to Sabina Dabrowski for the usual excellent support.

Göttingen, June 2010
Reinhard G. Kratz and Hermann Spieckermann

Table of Contents

Introduction

BJÖRN CORZILIUS AND TANJA PILGER

Gustaf Dalman (1854-1941), the first director of the German Protestant Institute of Archaeology in Jerusalem (1902-1917), was a notable pioneer in research of Ancient Israelite history.[1] In order to shed light upon the social, cultural and religious reality of Ancient Israel he intensely observed and portrayed the social life, the religious practice and the geographical and climatic living conditions in then contemporary Palestine. The main fruits of his passionate observation and meticulous description are *Palästinischer Diwan* (1901) and *Jerusalem und sein Gelände* (1930), but first of all his monumental life's work *Arbeit und Sitte in Palästina* (1928–1942).[2]

„Nicht nur die Bibel selbst, sondern ganz besonders auch das nachbiblische jüdische Schrifttum, das er [sc. Gustaf Dalman] so gründlich kannte, wies ihn durch eine Fülle verstreuter Angaben auf diese Dinge hin und reizte den ihm

The authors would like to thank to PD Dr. Anselm C. Hagedorn for his help with the English of the Introduction.

1 Our commemoration of Gustaf Dalman and his lifework exclusively aims at honoring him for his meaningful contribution to the exploration of Ancient Israelite history on the basis of his remarkable knowledge of the biblical and rabbinic sources as well as his sensitive observations during years of research. Admittedly, at that time German research on contemporary Jewish life and Israelite history has been interwoven with the disastrous rise of Anti-Semitism. Although Dalman fought against anti-Semitic tendencies, in his personal piety he was deeply convinced by a Christian superiority, which caused a missionary interest. The general topic of the problematic interrelation between German research and emerging Anti-Semitism has been depicted by CHRISTIAN WIESE, Wissenschaft des Judentums und protestantische Theologie im wilhelminischen Deutschland, SchrLBI 61, Tübingen 1999, esp. 88–99; on Dalman in particular see the critical acclaim of JULIA MÄNNCHEN, Gustaf Dalman als Palästinawissenschaftler in Jerusalem und Greifswald 1902–1941, ADPV 9/II, Wiesbaden 1993, 259–272.

2 GUSTAF DALMAN, Palästinischer Diwan. Als Beitrag zur Volkskunde Palästinas gesammelt und mit Übersetzung und Melodien herausgegeben, Leipzig 1901; id., Jerusalem und sein Gelände, Gütersloh 1930; id., Arbeit und Sitte in Palästina, vol. I–VII, Gütersloh 1928–1942. Since completing his *Arbeit und Sitte* was not granted to him in lifetime, Dalman's fragments on domestic life, birth, marriage and death have been published by JULIA MÄNNCHEN (ed.), Arbeit und Sitte in Palästina: Das häusliche Leben, Geburt, Heirat, Tod, vol. VIII, Berlin/New York 2001.

angeborenen Realismus, den er in der Selbstdarstellung seines Lebens ein mütterliches Erbteil nennt, auch von den Realien her das Verständnis der Bibel zu vertiefen […] So entstand in ihm – wir wissen nicht seit wann, wenn auch die letzten Wurzeln offenbar schon in den Träumen seiner Kindheit lagen – der Plan einer neuen Biblischen Archäologie, die sich von den älteren und gleichzeitigen Werken desselben Namens zunächst durch die volle Heranziehung des Stoffes aus dem nachbiblischen jüdischen Schrifttum und ferner vor allem dadurch unterscheiden sollte, daß sie die Naturverhältnisse, Arbeitsweisen und Lebensgewohnheiten des gegenwärtigen Palästina und seiner Bevölkerung als reale und noch erforschbare Wirklichkeit in allen Einzelheiten zur Grundlage der Rekonstruktion des fernen biblischen Altertums machte."[3]

In his obituary Albrecht Alt honoured Gustaf Dalman for his meaningful contribution to the exploration of Ancient Israel. Alt particularly emphasizes Dalman's plan of a 'new biblical archaeology' which differs significantly from similar previous attempts insofar as a reconstruction of Ancient Israel may not solely be based upon the biblical testimony itself. Rather, Dalman's concept requires to draw on the biblical scriptures as well as the extra biblical material, the literary, epigraphical and archaeological sources and his beloved *Landeskunde.* The present venture follows in Dalman's footsteps, relating the different source material and trying to renew the fruitful discourse between Archaeology, Biblical and Ancient Near Eastern Studies.

The contributions collected in this volume originated as lectures delivered during an international and interdisciplinary conference entitled 'One God – One Nation. One God – One Cult' (Jerusalem, September 2008). The conference was directed by the Graduate Programme 'Concepts of the Divine and of the World. Polytheism and Monotheism in the Ancient World' in cooperation with the 'Centrum Orbis Orientalis' (CORO) at the Georg-August-University Goettingen. Eminent scholars of the Ancient Near East, Archaeology, Biblical and Religious Studies joined the debate on current research issues concerning the historiography of Ancient Israel and the development of Ancient Israelite religion. The conference questioned in particular the historicity of the early Monarchy under the reign of David and Solomon ('One Nation'), the reliability of the biblical portray about the drastic cult reforms, undertaken by the Judean kings Hezekiah and Josiah ('One Cult'), and the corresponding implications for changes of divine concepts in the Hebrew Bible ('One God'). Due to the success of the first meeting, 'The Ancient City: Beth Shean/Nysa-Scythopolis' (Goettingen, July 2009) continued the interdisciplinary discourse. On the basis of

3 ALBRECHT ALT, Gustaf Dalman, PJ 37 (1941), 5–6; cf. similarly MARTIN NOTH, Gustaf Dalman, ZDPV 65 (1942), 1–5.

ancient Beth Shean the socio-cultural and religious interdependencies in the Levant have been exemplarily expounded in order to illustrate the *longue durée* within the history of an ancient city.

The controversial dispute about the reconstruction of ancient Israelite history, i.e. a reconstruction that simultaneously takes into consideration the biblical testimony on the one hand and the archaeological, iconographical and epigraphical material on the other hand, forms the background of our attempt. The debate has been initiated by recent archaeological challenges against the historicity of the biblical narrative, especially regarding the United Monarchy and the cult reform programme in Judah during the 8th and 7th century. The complexity of both issues revealed the insight, that a reliable reconstruction of ancient Israelite history requires an intensive interdisciplinary cooperation, especially between Archaeology and Biblical Studies. The present volume, stressing the discourse of both disciplines on the basis of the recent results of research, aims at combining the various perspectives on the topics in question and embedding them into the broader horizon of Ancient Near Eastern and Religious studies. The interdisciplinary interest of our enterprise, inspired by the work of Gustaf Dalman, shapes the structure of the four chapters, that constitute the present volume.

The first chapter 'The Great Monarchy: Biblical and Archaeological Perspectives on David and Solomon' deals with the rise of statehood and the character of early day kingship in Israel. Israel Finkelstein and Amihai Mazar open the discussion on the historicity of the biblical account on David and Solomon and their kingdom, relating the time in question to the results of archaeological research. Has the biblical testimony, depicting 10th century Israel as the 'Golden Era' of Israelite kingship, been proven wrong by the archaeological data? ISRAEL FINKELSTEIN initiated the debate with his popular and widely read monographs *The Bible unearthed* (2001) and *David and Solomon* (2006).[4] His re-evaluation of the archaeological material led Finkelstein to a divergent dating of the transition from Iron Age I to Iron Age IIA. Accordingly, he differentiates between the literary view of the early days of Israelite kingship, as portrayed in the Hebrew Bible, and the historical reality in Ancient Israel. Finkelstein connects the change from chiefdom to statehood in Israel with the political and historical events at the end of the 9th century BCE and affirms his 'low chronology' against the conventional theory, that is – in his view – mainly based on the biblical

4 Cf. ISRAEL FINKELSTEIN/NEIL A. SILBERMAN, The Bible unearthed: Archaeology's new vision of ancient Israel and the origin of its sacred texts, New York 2001; id., David and Solomon: In Search of the Bible Sacred Kings and the Roots of Western Tradition, New York 2006.

report itself. "If there was a historical United Monarchy, it was that of the Omride dynasty and it was ruled from Samaria." (23) In the present study Finkelstein defends his theses against objections recently raised in archaeological research, again arguing for the reliability of the biblical testimony.

While Israel Finkelstein radically doubts the historicity of David's and Solomon's United Monarchy, AMIHAI MAZAR comes to a more tentative assessment in his analysis of the archaeological material. "The United Monarchy can be described as a state in an early stage of evolution, far from the rich and widely expanding state portrayed in the biblical narrative ... [T]he evidence brought here calls for balanced evaluation of the biblical text, taking into account that the text might have preserved valuable historical information based on early written documents and oral traditions that retained long-living common memory." (52) Walking "in the middle of the road" (29) between the conventional, biblically inspired view of David and Solomon and Finkelstein's radical position, Mazar argues for a 'modified conventional chronology' which regards the transition from 10th to the 9th century BCE as the beginning of statehood in Israel.

Following Mazar's call for a balanced exploration of the biblical testimony, the evaluation of the archaeological data regarding the early period of the monarchy is complemented by a critical analysis of the relevant literary sources, narrating the supposedly glorious era of early Israelite kingship. ERHARD BLUM devotes his study to the Succession Narrative, which describes Solomon's ascension to the throne as well as the stabilization of his rule over Israel and Judah. Analyzing the milieu of the David story and Solomon's family background Blum points out "that essential features of the narrative plot and of the overall tendency fit either the 10th century or the beginning of the 9th century BCE." (70) In stark contrast to Finkelstein's challenge against the historicity of the biblical account Blum concludes that "there can be little doubt that both kings reigned on Judah and on the northern tribes called 'Israel' with Jerusalem as residence and capital." (73) While Blum has dealt with the rise of Israelite kingship the studies by Alexander Rofé and Markus Witte focus their attention on the downfall of the United Monarchy. In his critical remarks on 'The Assembly at Shechem' ALEXANDER ROFÉ offers a careful literary analysis of 1 Kings 12, narrating the division into a northern Israelite and a southern Judean kingdom. With regard to its literary genre and the date of composition he disagrees with the background of the 10th century BCE. In his opinion the narrative was influenced by late biblical wisdom literature and has to be characterized as "a paradigmatic legend emanating from wisdom circles" (81).

Therefore, he alternatively assumes a historical setting in the late Persian period. Following Rofé's critical observations the first part of the volume is completed by MARKUS WITTE'S portrayal of the reception history of 'The Share in David' in later Wisdom literature, particularly in the Book of Ben Sira. From Ben Sira's point of view, as Witte concludes, the events narrated in 1 Kings 12 are regarded as historical. Ben Sira "sees them as a paradigm, as far as they are a proof for the validity of wisdom-sentences. Finally, Ben Sira looks at the events on the typological level as far as they reflect his experience of the opposition between Jerusalem and Samaria." (109) As the tenor of the first part of our volume shows, the understanding of the rise of statehood in Israel as well as the historical evaluation of the literary characters David and Solomon is far from clear and necessarily requires the continuation of the initiated discourse.

The second part expounds the problems of 'The Cult Centralization in its Near Eastern Context' and focuses on the reform programme attributed to the Judean kings Hezekiah and Josiah. Does the biblical testimony about the reforms, intending to purify and unify the YHWH cult in Jerusalem, contain reliable historical information about cultic changes in 8th and 7th century Judah? Two issues are related to the topic under investigation. The idea of centralization forms the background of the reform programme according to the biblical testimony in Deuteronomy and 2 Kings. Furthermore such a radical reform should have left its marks in the archaeological remains of the time in question. Both, the literary and the archaeological evidence, are to be discussed in close relation to each other.

Regarding the literary evidence REINHARD G. KRATZ discusses the idea of centralization in the Book of Deuteronomy and asks for valuable Ancient Near Eastern analogies, such as the Vassal Treaties of Esarhaddon, the Mesopotamian concept of a capital city or the epigraphic evidence of Nabonidus' cultic reform. The result of his religio-historical comparison is ambivalent. Though the external evidence surveyed illuminates the cultural background of Deuteronomy all supposed analogies do not serve as a direct parallel for the idea of an exclusive cultic centralization because it "is so special and singular in the world of the ancient Near East" (136). Subsequently, Kratz queries inner Judean reasons which may have caused the idea of centralization. He assumes that it might be a reaction to the downfall of Samaria or the end of the Judean kingdom, clearly favouring the latter possibility. On the basis of the Mesopotamian literary sources, HANSPETER SCHAUDIG similarly asks for comparable concepts of centralization in the Ancient Near Eastern world and concentrates his study on the Mesopotamian concepts of cultic places and the ideal capital city as part of the divine order of the world. "Temples and cults were regarded as parts of the divine layout of civilization as revealed by the gods to humankind at the beginning of history" (151). Therefore, it was hard to found, replace or remove a sanctuary. Referring to the current issue Schaudig states "in Babylonia 'a cultic reform' like those undertaken by Hezekiah and Josiah would seem incompatible with major concepts of the divine" (152). Solely the reforms of Nebuchadrezzar II who transformed Babylon into the centre of his empire and of the whole world, established "a religious-political programme 'Marduk alone', – henotheistically focusing on Marduk as the king of the gods, the most important god, and in fact the only god who matters, – produced the closest parallel to the 'Yahweh alone' movement in Judah in the 7th and 6th century BCE" (163). From different points of view Kratz and Schaudig congenial conclude that there is no reliable analogy for the biblical concept of cultic centralization within the Ancient Near Eastern world. If the cult reforms really happened according to the biblical testimony they have certainly been a unique phenomena.

Furthermore, such a drastic reform programme should have left obvious marks within the material culture, if it was really carried out. Evaluating the presumed evidence for cultic changes in Judah ZE'EV HERZOG presents the archaeological data unearthed at Tel Arad and Tel Beer-sheba. Both sites indicate an abolishment of sanctuaries in the kingdom of Judah and have been used as to proof for the biblical testimony about the cult reforms of Hezekiah and Josiah. Recent scholarship, however, has questioned the connection between the marks of destruction and the biblical testimony. On the basis of archaeological evidence and biblical statements Herzog argues for an intentional abolishment of the Southern cult centres which can only be dated to the 8th century BCE. "It justifies the conclusion that the acts of abolishment of cult discovered in the archaeological record of Arad and Tel Beer-sheba are a result of Hezekiah's cultic reform. [...] Furthermore, the archaeological data raises doubts about the biblical description of the abolishment of temples by King Josiah." (196–197)

Subsequent to Herzog's archaeological evaluation JUHA PAKKALA focuses again on the literary sources. Although both scholars intend to shed light upon the question whether the cult reforms under Hezekiah and Josiah took place, both arrive at different conclusions. On the basis of his analysis of the biblical sources in 2 Kings 18:4 and 2 Kings 22–23 Pakkala states that there has not been a cult reform in Judah before 587/586 BCE at all. "Many features in the texts and the broader historical context suggest that the cult reforms, in any form intended by the biblical authors, did not take place. It is more probable that they are literary inventions and projections of later ideals into the monarchic period." (229) Pakkala regards the destruction of Jerusalem in 587/586 BCE with its disastrous consequences for state, monarchy and cult as a turning point in Israelite history and he doubts any significant change in religious and cultic practices before the catastrophe in Judah because of missing solid evidences. Similar to the debate on the United Monarchy, the discussion on the prominent Judean cult reform programme, presented in the second part of the volume, again leads to an heterogeneous conclusion, requesting further examination of the source material.

While the first two parts of the present volume deal with two highly disputed topics of biblical history in general the third part 'The Ancient City: Perspectives on the political and cultural interrelations at Beth Shean' concentrates on the history of one city in particular, well-attested in ancient literary sources and carefully investigated by archaeological research. Beth Shean, identified with Tel Beth-Shean (arab. Tel Ḥosn) in Northern Israel, is situated in a fertile, water-rich valley and located at the junction of two important roads, that follow the Jordan valley and connect the coastal plain with the inland. Both factors assigned a great strategic and political importance to the city and caused their heterogeneous cultural prosperity. Accordingly, Tel Beth Shean has been inhabited almost continuously from the late Neolithic period to the Bronze and Iron Ages. Later, the city moved from the summit of Tel Beth Shean to the valley, and continued to exist under the name Nysa-Scythopolis, flourishing as an impressive Hellenistic Polis during the Greco-Roman and Byzantine period.

As a case study the focus on Beth Shean aims at depicting the *longue durée* of an ancient city's history in order to point out its political development as well as its religious and cultural interrelations. Its central location and continuous settlement within an environment of cultural diversity and political change qualifies Beth Shean/Nysa-Scythopolis as an ideal case for examination. How can the city be characterized in political and cultural respect? This part of the volume again correlates material and literary evidence to illuminate the profile of Beth Shean and Nysa-Scythopolis.

The portrayal of the ancient city from its early foundation in the late Neolithic times to its devastation during the Early Islamic period is opened by the contributions of AMIHAI MAZAR and GABRIEL MAZOR. Both scholars guide through the history of Beth Shean and Nysa-Scythopolis in light of the archaeological remains and the results of recent explorations, which have been discovered during years of archaeological research under their direction. Mazar conducted numerous excavation seasons on Tel Beth Shean between 1989 and 1996, Mazor in collaboration with Rachel Bar Nathan directed several expeditions at Roman-Byzantine Nysa-Scythopolis between 1986 and 2000. According to their respective research interest, Mazar "provides an overview of the textual sources and archaeological data relating to all periods of occupation at the site through the end of the Iron Age" (239), stressing the close interaction between Egyptian and Canaanite culture at Beth Shean. Mazor continues the survey throughout the "Hellenistic and Roman-Byzantine era" paying special attention to "the rather complicated issues of ethnicity and religious affiliation and their influential impact over culture and history" (273).

The archaeological portrait of the ancient city is completed by the contribution of KATHARINA HEYDEN who traces the history of Nysa-Scythopolis according to the literary sources. Heyden's study is the first attempt to carefully examine the literary material on Nysa-Scythopolis in regard to the city's political and cultural history and to relate the archaeological data to the literary and epigraphic sources. What was the status of Nysa-Scythopolis in Late Antiquity amidst various religious and cultural influences and political change? Heyden's analysis of the rich literary material leads her "to differentiate between *cultic* and *cultural* changes" (331). Accordingly, Heyden concludes that "Scythopolis remained a Greek city until the Islamic conquest […] only in cultural, not in cultic respect. After the disappearance of official pagan cults, the urban Hellenistic culture in late antique Scythopolis was the common ground on which every religious community (Christians, Jews and Samaritans) could practice its own cult" (332).

The final part of our volume headed 'The One and The Only: Perspectives on the Development of a Divine Concept' deals with the implications for concepts of the Divine corresponding to the debate about early Israelite kingship and Cult Centralization in Judah. The results of research on both topics are discussed in regard to the developing monotheism on the basis of literary and archaeological sources and theoretically reviewed from the perspective of Religious Studies.

HERMANN SPIECKERMANN as a Biblical scholar concentrates on the concept of kingship and cult in the religio-political context of the Ancient Near East. He outlines a unique relationship between one god and his people in the Northern and Southern kingdom, which is comparable to the concept of kingship in the Ancient Near East. In Mesopotamia kingship "is closely linked with divine will which aims at establishing dominion, order, and welfare for the land and the 'four regions' […] of the world." (351) In respect to the singular relationship between

YHWH and his people in the North and the South from the late 8th century BCE onwards Spieckermann concludes, "that the concept of kingship in pre exilic Israel and Judah was by and large similar to the Mesopotamian" (352). This close similarity is reflected by the prophetic traditions within the Hebrew Bible and first of all in the Book of Deuteronomy which characterizes God's people as 'holy people' chosen by love. Lastly, Spieckermann considers the post-exilic period where the understanding of Israel's election and Israel's regarding as 'a great nation' among all nations in the ancient world has been developed depending on the changes of dominion. Complementing Spieckermann's study MATTHIAS KÖCKERT concentrates on the concepts of YHWH in the Northern and the Southern Kingdoms in pre-exilic time by offering a critical evaluation of the biblical and non-biblical sources. In his profound analysis Köckert arrives at the following conclusion: In both kingdoms "YHWH is the royal as well as the state god […]. Cultic poetry praises him as a divine king […]. The heavenly king exercises his rule via the earthly king, his agent on earth." (388) YHWH is worshipped at different sanctuaries with Asherah as his female partner who is subordinate to him. Furthermore, this yahwistic religion supports "prophetic opposition that dissolves the automatism of a national-religious connection of God, king and sanctuary." (389) The main difference concerns YHWH's cultic representation as the bull-image in the North, which is the traditional symbol of the storm-god, and the cherub-throne in the South, which originated in Phoenician city culture. "Both items are symbols of the presence of the divine that are specifically connected with the king […]. It is probable not a coincidence that only Judah and not Israel developed a royal ideology comparable to the other states in the ancient Near East. Since Judah outlived the Northern kingdom it also becomes the place of new developments that took shape in the Book of Deuteronomy. In the end they moved beyond those aspects that connected Israel with Judah: YHWH became the one and only god." (389)

Aiming at completing the picture from an archaeological perspective, EPHRAIM STERN is interested in cult practices in the Judean kingdom from the 7th century BCE until the exilic period. His contribution is entirely based on the archaeological finds. By evaluating the Judean cultic objects, especially the numerous male and female clay figurines Stern suggests that they are "pagan representations of the national Judean god, Yahweh and his consort Ashtart or Asherah." This prompts his conclusion "that a cult existed between the foreign pagan practices and the pure monotheism of Jerusalem, which may be called 'Yahwistic Paganism', common to all other Judean settlements." (400)

Since nothing is known about cult practices during the Babylonian period on the basis of archaeological data, Stern stresses the complete absence of sanctuaries and cultic figurines and assumes the emergence of monotheism among the Babylonian exiles. The "change from many gods to one god in Judah was established by the Jews in Babylon, and from there it was brought back to Judah." (402)

While Spieckermann, Köckert and Stern argue for an exilic or post-exilic shift towards Monotheism in Israel and Judah, MICHAEL SEGAL draws attention to a divine concept from late post-exilic times as exemplified in the debate about Monotheism and Angelology in the Book of Daniel. In his contribution Segal offers an accurate description of both theological aspects by being aware of the textual and literary development of the Book of Daniel which reached, in his opinion, its final form in the 2nd century BCE. Segal concentrates on Daniel's visions interpreted by an angelic intermediary in Dan. 10–12 and argues for a later addition of those texts related to angelology and monotheism. Segal reasons that these later references were influenced by "the theological and cosmological worldview expressed in Daniel 7" (418) in order to unify the views presented throughout the second part of the Book of Daniel.

From a theoretical perspective in Religious Studies, CHRISTOPH AUFFARTH introduces the Greek philosophical tradition into the current debate on Monotheism. His comparison between Israel and Greece leads Auffarth to differentiate between the concepts of relative and absolute monotheism. Both cultures show tendencies towards a relative monotheism, characterized by a plurality of gods, but providing a specific relationship between one god and his people or one nation and her god/goddess. "In Israel, thinking about monotheism became possible and necessary due to the fact that traditional cultic behaviour had been destroyed and its practice prevented by the destruction of the temple by the Babylonians." (445) The lack of a cult supported a form of non-cultic religion and the establishment of a relative monotheism. In Greek cultural history, absolute monotheism was constructed by Plato. During the Roman Empire monotheism became the great vision of justice in cooperation with imperial power and Platonic superhuman monotheism. According to Auffarth the platonic concept forms the background of the modern debate on monotheism.

These contributions illuminate the special relationship between YHWH and his people in Israel and Judah taking into consideration the Ancient Near Eastern background of biblical culture. They trace the development from many gods to one god in Judah and towards a (relative) monotheistic concept of the divine. The downfall of the monarchy in Judah and the Babylonian exile serve as the main factors for understanding the shift towards a monotheistic concept of the divine.

The overview on background, intention and contents of the present volume was opened with the reminiscence of Gustaf Dalman and his meaningful contribution to the exploration of Ancient Israelite history. By relating the various source material and renewing the important discourse between Archaeology, Biblical and Ancient Near Eastern Studies, we follow in Dalman's footsteps in order to shed light upon currently disputed topics in Israelite historiography. Although decades of research have passed since Dalman's expedition through Palestine his 'concept of a new biblical archaeology' appears to be a quite modern challenge. Recognizing the heterogeneous source material and relating the various results of research a 'New Biblical Archaeology' encompasses an interdisciplinary, metainstitutional and cooperative discourse, that will enable us create a reliable illumination of Ancient Israelite history.

I. The Great Monarchy: Biblical and Archaeological Perspectives on David and Solomon

A Great United Monarchy?

Archaeological and Historical Perspectives*

ISRAEL FINKELSTEIN

Twelve years have passed since I first presented – to the German Institute in Jerusalem – my ideas on the chronology of the Iron Age strata in the Levant and how it impacts on our understanding of the biblical narrative on the United Monarchy of ancient Israel.[1] I was naïve enough then to believe that the logic of my 'correction' was straightforward and clear. Twelve years and many articles and public debates later, however, the notion of Davidic conquests, Solomonic building projects, and a glamorous United Monarchy – all based on an uncritical reading of the biblical text and in contradiction of archaeological finds – is still alive in certain quarters. This paper presents my updated views on this matter, and tackles several recent claims that archaeology has now proven the historicity of the biblical account of the great kingdom of David and Solomon.

The Traditional Theory

The quest for the United Monarchy has been the most spectacular venture of 'classical' biblical archaeology.[2] The obvious place to begin the search was Jerusalem. Yet Jerusalem proved elusive: the nature of the site made it difficult to peel away the layers of later centuries and the Temple Mount has always been beyond the reach of archaeologists.

The search was therefore diverted to other sites, primarily Megiddo, specifically mentioned in 1 Kings 9:15 as having been built by Solomon. Starting over a century ago, Megiddo became the focus of the

---

* This study was supported by the Chaim Katzman Archaeology Fund and the Jacob M. Alkow Chair in the Archaeology of Israel in the Bronze and Iron Ages, both at Tel Aviv University.

1 Finkelstein (1996).

2 E.g., Yadin (1970); Dever (1997).

endeavor to make flesh and bones of the great Solomonic kingdom. As a prologue and homage to German scholarship, let me say that as far as I can judge, regarding Megiddo the closest to the truth was Carl Watzinger, who published the finds from the Schumacher excavations – the first investigation of the site in the early days of the 20th century. In a relatively early stage of research Watzinger suggested that the late Iron I stratum at Megiddo was destroyed by Pharaoh Shishak in the late 10th century BCE.[3] This proposal was not far from today's Low Chronology for the Iron Age strata, now backed by several hundred radiocarbon measurements.[4]

Nevertheless, this correct notion was forgotten two years later, when the University of Chicago team began promoting its ideas regarding Solomon at Megiddo. Based on the Solomon-Megiddo link in 1 Kings 9:15 and on the mention in 1 Kings 9:19 of Solomon's cities for chariots and horses, P.L.O. Guy identified a set of pillared buildings found close to the surface of the mound as stables built by Solomon.[5] The 'stables' paradigm dominated scholarship for almost 30 years, until Yigael Yadin started excavating at Hazor. Yadin noticed the similarity between the six-chambered city-gate that he uncovered at Hazor, the one at Megiddo that the University of Chicago's team had uncovered, and the one at Gezer unearthed by Macalister. Based on 1 Kings 9:15, Yadin described the three gates as blueprint architecture of the Solomonic era.[6] Yadin proceeded to carry out soundings at Megiddo and revised the Oriental Institute team's stratigraphy and historical interpretation.[7] He proposed that in addition to the gate, Solomonic Megiddo is represented by two palaces built of ashlar blocks – one discovered in the 1920s and the other partially traced by him in the 1960s (and almost fully excavated in the course of the renewed excavations at Megiddo in recent years[8]). Two additional finds at Megiddo seemed to support Yadin's interpretation: The major city that had existed before the city of the palaces – the last layer that features 'Canaanite' material culture – was destroyed by a massive conflagration, and the next city, built over the palaces, featured the famous Megiddo stables. Yadin's interpretation seemed to fit the biblical testimony perfectly:

---

3 Watzinger (1929).
4 Sharon et al. (2007).
5 Guy (1931).
6 Yadin (1958; 1970).
7 Yadin (1970).
8 Cline (2006).

1) Late Iron I (Canaanite) Megiddo was devastated by King David ca. 1000 BCE;[9]
2) The palaces represent the Golden Age of King Solomon; their destruction by fire should be attributed to the campaign of Pharaoh Sheshonq I (Shishak) in the late 10th century BCE (Megiddo is mentioned in Sheshonq I's list at Karnak and a fragment of a stele placed by him at the site was found by the University of Chicago team);
3) The stables date to the days of King Ahab in the early 9th century BCE; Ahab is reported by Shalmaneser III to have faced the Assyrian army at Qarqar with a mighty force of 2000 chariots.

Yadin's interpretation became the standard theory on the United Monarchy.[10] It matched the view expressed by most biblical scholars of his time, who argued that the (much later) biblical author had access to archival material from the 10th century BCE.[11] After all, they said, the Bible refers to a palace scribe and other administrators at the time of David and Solomon.

Why The Traditional Theory Was Wrong

The idea of a Solomonic archive in Jerusalem was a mirage. First, it was caught in a circular argument: There is genuine information about the 10th century > because there was an archive in Jerusalem > because a court-scribe is mentioned in the Bible. Second, it has now been dismissed by archaeology; a century and half of excavations in Jerusalem and all other major Judahite sites has provided no evidence for meaningful scribal activity before the late 8th century BCE. Recently found 10th and 9th century BCE late proto-Canaanite and Philistian inscriptions at Khirbet Qeiyafa and Tel Zayit in the Shephelah seem to belong to a lowland polity of the time (below).[12]

Yadin's archaeology paradigm on the United Monarchy has also been proven wrong. It was entangled in a web of serious problems from the outset. First, the city-gate at Megiddo must have been built later than the gates at Hazor and Gezer, as it connects to a wall that

9 Cf. recently Harrison (2004), 108.
10 E.g., Mazar (1997); Dever (1997); Ben-Tor (2000); Stager (2003).
11 E.g., Na'aman (1997a) and bibliography.
12 Garfinkel/Ganor (2008); Tappy et al. (2006).

runs over the two palaces;[13] Megiddo does not have an Iron IIA fortification. Second, similar city-gates have been discovered at other places, among them sites that date to late monarchic times, centuries after Solomon (e.g., Tel Ira in the Beer-sheba Valley), and sites built outside the borders of the great United Monarchy even according to the maximalist view (Ashdod and Khirbet Mudayna eth-Themed in Moab).

No less important, all three pillars of Yadin's theory do not withstand thorough scrutiny. Yadin described the identification of Solomonic architecture as follows:

> "Our decision to attribute that layer to Solomon was based primarily on the 1 Kings passage, the stratigraphy and the pottery. But when in addition we found in that stratum a six-chambered, two-towered gate connected to a casemate wall identical in plan and measurement with the gate at Megiddo, we felt sure we had successfully identified Solomon's city."[14]

We need to deal, then, with stratigraphy, chronology, and the biblical passage. Needless to say, stratigraphy provides only relative chronology and the same holds true for pottery. Regarding the latter, archaeologists have committed the ultimate mistake. William Dever argued that the Solomonic strata at Megiddo, Hazor, and Gezer were not dated because of the association with the biblical text, but according to a well-defined family of vessels – red slipped and burnished – which dates to the 10th century BCE.[15] He based this statement on Holladay's study of the Gezer pottery:

> "The key stratum seems to be Gezer Field III Phase UG3A, which is both very short and historically exceptionally well positioned. It comes after the Solomonic building period, richly documented by biblical and historical data and secured by comparative regional archaeological and architectural criteria combined with comparative pottery criteria."[16]

In simpler words, the key stratum was dated by the pottery > the pottery was dated by its relationship to the six-chambered gate > which was, in turn, dated according to the biblical testimony to the days of Solomon – another clear example of circular reasoning.

So, we are back to square one. Stratigraphy and pottery tell us nothing when it comes to absolute chronology. In order to reach a date according to traditional archaeology we need a find that would anchor the archaeology of Israel to the well-dated dating systems of Egypt and Assyria. The problem is, there is no such anchor for the 10th century BCE; in fact, no such anchor exists between the mid 12th and the late

---

13 Ussishkin (1980).

14 Yadin (1970), 67.

15 For instance, Dever (1997), 237–239.

16 Holladay (1990), 62–63.

8th century BCE – over four centuries in the Iron Age. The fragment of the Shoshenq I stele found in the 1920s at Megiddo could have given us such an anchor had it been found in-situ and the same holds true for the Mesha stele from Dibon in Moab and the Hazael Inscription from Tel Dan. Yet, all three were found out of context. This means that the traditional connection between the remains on the ground and the historical sequence is based on a single biblical reference (1 Kings 9:15). In other words, the entire reconstruction of the great Solomonic state – by Yadin and others – has been based on a single verse.

Let us take a look at this verse. I will argue later, based on archaeology, that in the 10th century BCE the early Davidides could not have ruled beyond the central highlands and its immediate vicinity. But even if they had, with no archival material, how could the late 7th century BCE author know about building activities in the mid-10th century BCE? One possibility is that the author projected a recollection of a situation closer to his days into the distant past in order to advance his ideology. He could have deployed a memory of the three important administrative cities of the Northern Kingdom in the lowlands in the first half of the 8th century BCE – Megiddo, Hazor, and Gezer – in order to convey his Pan-Israelite notion that the great Solomon ruled from Jerusalem over the entire country, including the lands of the Northern Kingdom (in his time already long destroyed), and that ruling over these territories was, thereby, not only the legitimate right of kings in his own era but also the right of future Davidic Kings.

To sum-up this point, Yadin's affiliation of the Megiddo palaces to the days of Solomon based on 'the 1 Kings passage, the stratigraphy and the pottery' does not withstand modern archaeological and biblical scrutiny.

The traditional dating system raises additional historical and archaeological problems:

1. The rise of territorial states in the Levant was an outcome of the westward expansion of the Assyrian empire in the early 9th century BCE. Extra-biblical sources leave little doubt that all major states in the region – Aram Damascus, Moab, and northern Israel – emerged in the 9th century BCE. It is difficult to envision a great empire ruled from the marginal region of the southern highlands a century before this process.

2. Affiliating the destruction of the Megiddo palaces with the campaign of Pharaoh Sheshonq I leaves no destruction layers in the north

for the well-documented assault of Hazael, king of Aram Damascus, on the Northern Kingdom in the mid-9th century BCE.[17]

3. The traditional dating of the Iron Age strata in the Levant raises serious problems in any attempt to synchronize the archaeology of the Levant with that of northern Syria and the Aegean basin.[18]

4. Local inconsistencies also exist and are best manifested by the Kefar Veradim tomb. This tomb, in the north of Israel, yielded an Assyrian-shaped bronze bowl with a late-Proto-Canaanite inscription and Iron IIA pottery assemblage.[19] Such bowls do not appear before the 9th century BCE. As noted by Benjamin Sass, applying the traditional chronology results in an absurd situation in which the inscription is dated to the 11th century, the pottery to the 10th and the bowl (by comparison) to the 9th century BCE.[20]

5. Most annoying, over a century of archaeological explorations in Jerusalem – the capital of the glamorous biblical United Monarchy – failed to reveal evidence for any meaningful 10th-century building activity. The famous stepped stone structure – usually presented as the most important United Monarchy remain[21] – demonstrates continuous construction effort which aimed at supporting the steep eastern slope of the City of David. Pottery dating to the 9th century BCE was found between the courses of its earliest sector, while its upper part was probably reconstructed in Hellenistic times, in order to support the First Wall of the Hasmonean period.[22] The common pretext for the absence of 10th century remains in Jerusalem – that they were eradicated by later activity – should be brushed aside: monumental fortifications from both the Middle Bronze and late monarchic times (that is, the 16th and 8th centuries BCE) did survive later occupations. This means that 10th-century Jerusalem was no more than a small, remote highlands village, not the exquisitely decked out capital of a great empire.[23] Recent attempts to save a Solomonic empire ruled from a poor capital in Jerusalem by comparing it to the Zulu in Africa or to Ghenghis Khan in Mongolia[24] show nothing else than the absurd in such comparisons. For temporal, geographical, and functional reasons, Solomonic Jerusalem

---

17 Na'aman (1997b).

18 Mazzoni (2000), 121; Coldstream (2003) respectively.

19 Alexander (2002).

20 Sass (2005), 39.

21 For instance, Cahill (2003); Mazar (2006).

22 Finkelstein et al. (2007); the building identified by Eilat Mazar as the palace of King David will be dealt with below.

23 Finkelstein (2001); Ussishkin (2003).

24 Faust (2004).

may be compared to Omride Samaria, to Hammah, or to Zincirli – not to the Zulu.

To sum-up this point, a brief contemplation of the circular argumentations behind the traditional theory and the difficulties that I have just mentioned is sufficient for understanding that something was fundamentally wrong with the conventional dating, and thereby conventional theory regarding the United Monarchy.

Fixing Iron Age Chronology

So much for the negative evidence. Other straightforward clues come from two sites related to the Omride dynasty – Samaria in the highlands and Jezreel in the valley.

Ashlar blocks uncovered in the foundations of one of the so-called 'Solomonic' palaces at Megiddo carry unique masons' marks, found in one other building in Israel: the 9th century palace of Omri and Ahab at Samaria. As noted long ago by Fisher, Crowfoot and recently by Franklin,[25] these masons' marks are so distinctive that they must have been executed by the same group of masons. But one palace was dated to the 10th century (Megiddo) and the other to the 9th century BCE (Samaria). There are only two alternatives here: either to push the Megiddo building ahead to the 9th century, or to pull the Samaria palace back to the 10th century BCE. The biblical source on the building of Samaria by King Omri must be a reliable one, since it is supported by Assyrian texts that relate to the Northern Kingdom as *bit omri* – the typical genre of relating to a kingdom after the founder of its capital. Therefore, down-dating Megiddo is the only option.

The excavations at Jezreel, located less than ten miles to the east of Megiddo, revealed equally surprising results: The destruction layer of the royal compound there, dated to the mid-9th century BCE, yielded a rich collection of vessels identical to a Megiddo assemblage that was conventionally dated to the late 10th century BCE.[26] Ben-Tor suggested that the restorable pottery found in the casemates of the Jezreel compound in fact date to an earlier layer there.[27] Yet, this means that the upheaval of large scale leveling operations, transportation of fills, and the construction of the casemates left an earlier assemblage of restorable vessels intact exactly in the lines of the later casemates; needless to

25 Fisher (1929), 58; Crowfoot (1940), 146; Franklin (2005).

26 Zimhoni (1997), 25–26, 38–39.

27 Ben-Tor (2000).

say, this is difficult to comprehend. So here again, one can either push the Megiddo assemblage or pull the Jezreel one. Since the Jezreel compound is architectonically identical to that of Samaria, it must date to the 9th century BCE. In this case, too, only one option remains: down-dating the Megiddo palaces to the 9th century BCE.

Another clue may come from Egypt. Stephan Münger has dealt with a group of 'mass produced' Egyptian amulets found in large numbers in the Levant.[28] They seem to have been mass-produced in the Delta in the time of Pharaohs Siamun and Sheshonq I. Yet, in Israel these amulets appear for the first time in late-Iron I layers, which were previously dated to the 11th century BCE. At Dor, five such amulets were found in one room with a late Iron I pottery assemblage.[29] Some objections to this idea may be sound,[30] but Münger's theory remains a valid (if not the preferable) possibility for dating these amulets.

Radiocarbon Results

In recent years a large number of samples from Iron Age strata have been subjected to ^{14}C dating procedures. In order to resolve the debate on the dating of the Iron Age strata in the Levant, two questions needed to be dealt with: When did the Iron IIA – the ceramic phase which characterize the strata which have traditionally been affiliated with the time of Solomon – begin and when did it end (traditionally the Solomonic period is dated to 970–931 BCE and the Iron IIA to ca. 1000–925 BCE)?

A short while after the introduction of ^{14}C dating to the Iron Age debate, it became clear that the Iron IIA continued at least until the second half of the 9th century BCE – a century later than the traditional dating.[31] In other words, destruction layers that were conventionally dated to the late 10th century and associated with the campaign of Pharaoh Sheshonq I, provide ^{14}C dates in the mid-to-late 9th century BCE and should therefore be linked to Hazael's assault on the Northern Kingdom.[32] The Megiddo palaces, which constituted the backbone of the traditional approach to the United Monarchy, belong to the late

28 Münger (2003).

29 Gilboa et al. (2004).

30 Brandl in a lecture at an Oxford 2004 conference.

31 Mazar/Carmi (2001); Sharon (2001); this is in line with the initial, pre-radiocarbon low chronology proposal, which was based on archaeological and historical considerations – Finkelstein (1996).

32 Na'aman (1997b); Finkelstein/Piasetzky (2007a).

Iron IIA ceramic phase.[33] In absolute chronology terms this means that they date to the first half of the 9th century BCE.

This left only one question to be resolved: the beginning of the Iron IIA, or, in other words, the date of the transition from the late Iron I to the early Iron IIA. In a recent publication, Sharon et al. have dealt with this transition,[34] which was put by the traditionalists in 1000 BCE, by Mazar's Modified Conventional Chronology in 980 BCE[35] and by me in the second half of the 10th century BCE. Based on 385 measurements, from 21 sites, measured in three laboratories by three different methods, Sharon et al. put the transition in the second half of the 10th century BCE. According to them, of the 36 possible statistical interpretations of these results, 35 fit the Low Chronology and one falls in between, without supporting the traditional chronology. A few years earlier Eliezer Piasetzky and I estimated a less than 1% probability that the High Chronology hypothesis is correct.[36] In a recent article, Mazar and Bronk Ramsey have attempted to retain a date for the Iron I/IIA transition in the first half of the 10th century BCE.[37] But their selection of data for the study can be disputed. According to their own numbers, it is sufficient to exclude the charcoal samples (which introduce the 'old wood effect') and run the numbers with the short-lived samples (that is, grain seeds, olive pits, etc.) in order to place this transition in the second half of the 10th century BCE. To sum-up this point, all 12 Bayesian models (using only short-lived samples) available today put the Iron I/IIA transition in the late 10th century BCE (Table 1); they support the Low Chronology for the Iron Age strata and negate Mazar's Modified Conventional Chronology as well as the proposal by Herzog and Singer-Avitz to put this transition in the mid-10th century BCE.[38]

33 Herzog/Singer-Avitz (2006).
34 Sharon et al. (2007).
35 Mazar (2005).
36 Finkelstein/Piasetzky (2003).
37 Mazar/Bronk Ramsey (2008).
38 Mazar (2005); Herzog/Singer-Avitz (2004; 2006).

Model	Dates [68% range]	Reference
Focused/combined	925–885	Sharon et al. 2007
Focused/uncombined	900–870	
Focused/cautious	935–895	
Composite/combined	925–895	
Composite/uncombined	915–900	
Composite/cautious	925–900	
Coarse/combined	955–925	
Coarse/uncombined	930–910	
Coarse/cautious	940–905	
Model B3*	940–917	Mazar/Bronk Ramsey 2008
Model C3*	948–919	
New, unpublished work	916–900	Finkelstein/ Piasetzky, in press
* Using only short-lived samples		

Table 1: All available Bayesian models for the Iron I/IIA transition

To sum-up this point, the radiocarbon results support what I have suggested over the last twelve years: 1) The supposed time of the United Monarchy is covered by the late Iron I, which, in the north, is still influenced by Late Bronze (that is, 'Canaanite') material culture;[39] 2) The Israelite expansion into the northern valleys took place in the late 10th century BCE;[40] and 3) The so-called 'Solomonic' monuments were in fact built by the Omrides.[41]

Excursis I: Arguments Raised Against The Alternative Dating

Some have tried to gain a moment of fame by attempting to participate in the fiery chronology debate, with results that are quite amusing and that demonstrate a misunderstanding of the issue. Harrison's long discussion of the Megiddo evidence is meaningless, as it is based on the traditional arguments: King David destroyed Megiddo VIA; Solomon built Megiddo VA–IVB, etc.[42] And Gal's statement that "the identifica-

39 Finkelstein (2003).

40 Finkelstein/Piasetzky (2007b).

41 Finkelstein (2000).

42 Harrison (2003).

tion of Horvat Rosh Zayit with biblical Cabul [...] and its association with the 'Land of Cabul' relate it to both King Solomon and Hiram of Tyre [...] thus providing it with an appropriate historical-geographical basis"[43] (he means chronological basis) is a clear manifestation of circular reasoning.

But there have also been serious challenges, which needed to be addressed:

1. The *Taanach* argument of Lawrence Stager:[44] Pharaoh Sheshonq I, who campaigned in Palestine in the second half of the 10th century BCE, mentions Taanach in his Karnak list. According to Stager, Taanach features only one destruction layer – the one corresponding to a Megiddo stratum, which is traditionally dated to the 10th century BCE. Yet, a reevaluation of the Taanach finds points to an earlier stratum that was also destroyed in a fierce fire.[45] This provides a conflagration layer at Taanach for whoever is seeking a Sheshonq destruction.

2. The *density of strata* argument, raised by Mazar and Ben-Tor.[46] If the date of 10th century strata is lowered to the early 9th century BCE, too many strata are left in northern Israel for the relatively short period of time until the Assyrian takeover in 732 BCE. There are several answers to this argument: First, the traditional dating does the same to earlier strata; second, the number of strata depends on the quality of excavations; third, the history of border sites (such as Hazor – the subject of Ben-Tor's complaint) was more turbulent than that of inland sites (such as Megiddo).

3. The *how can you accept one biblical testimony and reject another* argument.[47] Put simply, the question is, how can one reject the historicity of the biblical testimony on the building activities of Solomon and at the same time accept the historicity of the verses on the construction of Samaria by Omri. There are two answers to this question: First, accepting the historicity of one verse and rejecting another is exactly the nature of two centuries of biblical scholarship. Second, the biblical description of the Solomonic state is idealized, with many references to realities of much later times in Israelite history,[48] while the description of the Omride state is far more accurate historically – and this includes, of course, the important Elijah and Elishah cycles in Kings.

---

43 Gal (2003), 149.

44 Stager (2003), 66.

45 Finkelstein (1998).

46 Mazar (1997), 163; Ben-Tor (2000).

47 E.g., Mazar (1999), 40, n. 38; Ben-Tor (2000), 12, 14.

48 For instance, Knauf (1991).

4. Several scholars, primarily William Dever, suggested that the Low Chronology camp is a minority.[49] The truth is, I am far from being troubled by the idea of being part of a minority that defends a case which, so I believe, is supported by the evidence. Just to set the record straight, however, among the small group of scholars who understand the intricate archaeological arguments behind the debate, the supporters of the Low Chronology make an impressive group.[50] Looking at the Dream Team on my side I can only hope to always be able to stand with a similar minority. Incidentally, all defections are from the traditional 'majority' to the Low Chronology 'minority'. Dever himself has recently started his long, cold voyage of defection: "Caution is indicated at the moment; but one should allow the possibility of slightly lower 10th–9th centuries BCE dates."[51]

Excursus II: Traditional Biblical Archaeology Strikes Back

Several scholars have recently come forward with new revelations, which ostensibly support the traditional interpretation of the biblical material on the time of David and Solomon.

A King David Palace in Jerusalem

A few massive walls recently unearthed in the City of David have been dated by excavator Eilat Mazar to the 10th century BCE and interpreted as the remains of the palace of King David; Mazar connected these remains to the Stepped Stone Structure on the eastern slope of the City of David.[52] She bases her identification of the building on a few Iron IIA pottery items found in one spot in her dig area and on a highly literal reading of the biblical text: Melchizedek of Genesis 14 was a Middle Bronze ruler of Jerusalem; Adonizedek of Joshua 10 was a Late Bronze monarch there; and David's palace is identified according to the topography in 2 Samuel 5. Not only is this an uncritical reading of biblical texts, archaeology does not support Mazar's interpretation:[53]

---

49 Dever (2001), 68.

50 See temporary and far from complete list in Finkelstein/Silberman (2002), 66–67.

51 From the abstract of his lecture at a 2004 Oxford conference.

52 E. Mazar (2007a).

53 Cf. in detail Finkelstein et al. (2007); moreover, the palace of the early Davidides must have been located – in line with all capitals of the ancient Near Eastern territorial kingdoms – in the ruling compound, that is, on the Temple Mount.

- The walls unearthed by Mazar do not connect into one coherent plan and seem to belong to more than one building.
- Since the entire area had been excavated in the past, the dating of the remains is difficult. Some of the walls may be affiliated with the Iron IIA, in the 9th century BCE; others may date as late as the Hellenistic period.
- The Iron IIA pottery items found in one spot are not necessarily in situ and in any event date to the 9th century BCE.
- The Stepped Stone Structure on the slope has at least two construction phases: one in the Iron IIA or early Iron IIB (9th or early 8th centuries BCE) and the second in the Hellenistic period.

The Iron IIA construction effort in the City of David – the early stage of the Stepped Stone Structure and possibly some of the walls unearthed by Eilat Mazar – indeed manifest a phase in the development of the state in Judah, but this phase dates to the 9th rather than 10th centuries BCE and has nothing to do with the biblical United Monarchy.

Khribet en-Nahas and King Solomon's Mines

Levy et al. have recently suggested affiliating the copper production site of Khirbet en-Nahas in the Araba valley south of the Dead Sea with biblical Edom and dating the large square fortress there to the 10th century BCE.[54] Accordingly, they argued that Edom emerged to statehood as early as the 10th century BCE, thereby seeing the verses in Gen. 36:31 and 2 Sam. 8:14 as historical. They also hinted that the copper production at Khirbet en-Nahas may be linked to the biblically-described King Solomon's mines.[55] This is not so, because:

- Khirbet en-Nahas is not located in Edom. Production at Nahas is radiocarbon-dated between the late 12th and late 9th centuries BCE,[56] that is, in the Iron I and Iron IIA. In the Iron IIA – the peak period of production – there was not a single settlement on the Edomite plateau. All sites there date later, from the late 8th and 7th centuries BCE.[57] The Khirbet en-Nahas phenomenon connects to the settlement history of the Beer-sheba Valley to its west – along the roads that carried the copper to the Mediterranean ports, international roads of the coastal plain, and Egypt. The most significant

54 Levy et al. (2004; 2008).

55 Levy et al. (2008), 16465.

56 Levy et al. (2004; 2008); Finkelstein/Piasetzky (2008).

57 Bienkowski (1992).

site in the Beer-sheba Valley that may be mentioned in relation to the copper production at Khirbet en-Nahas is Iron I and IIA Tel Masos, which yielded evidence for copper production and trade.[58]
- Based on comparison to the forts of En Hatzeva on the western side of the Araba and Tell el-Kheleifeh at the head of the Gulf of Aqaba, the fort at Khirbet en-Nahas seems to date to the late 8th or 7th century BCE.
- Regarding the biblical material, Levy et al. take the list of the kings "who reigned in the land of Edom, before any king reigned over the Israelites" in Gen. 36:31 as historical testimony of the existence of a territorial polity there in the 12th and 11th centuries BCE; and the reference in 2 Sam. 8:14 to garrisons put by King David in Edom as reflecting a 10th century BCE reality.[59] It is true that some scholars accepted the list in Genesis 36 as containing genuine historical information,[60] yet, the list may represent a post-monarchic situation in Edom,[61] a late Iron II reality,[62] or may altogether refer to Aramean (rather than Edomite) kings.[63] And the reference to Edom in 2 Samuel 8 most likely depicts an 8th century BCE reality, reflected back to the time of the founder of the Jerusalem dynasty.[64]

Therefore, Khirbet en-Nahas is not connected to the biblically narrated United Monarchy of ancient Israel.

The Tel Zayit Abecedary and Literacy in 10th century BCE Jerusalem

The recently discovered Tel Zayit abecedary has been dated to the 10th century BCE and interpreted as evidence for literacy in Jerusalem at that time:

> "In view of the well-established archaeo-paleographic chronology of the Tel Zayit inscription [...] and the clear cultural affiliation of its archaeological context with the Judaean highlands, we may reasonably associate it with the nascent kingdom of Judah [...] the appearance of an abecedary in an outlying town some distance from the capital city of Jerusalem demon-

58 See in details, Finkelstein (2005).
59 Levy et al. (2005), 158–159.
60 For instance Westermann (1986), 561.
61 Knauf (1985).
62 Bartlett (1989), 94–102.
63 Lemaire (2001).
64 Na'aman (2002), 214.

strates a movement toward literacy in the extreme western frontier of the kingdom during the mid-tenth century B.C.E."[65]

This is not so, because:[66]

- The archaeological context of the abecedary puts it no earlier than the late 10th century BCE and more likely in the course of the 9th century BCE.
- The pottery and other finds from Tel Zayit cannot help in establishing the territorial affiliation of the site – with Judah or with the coastal plain.
- The Tel Zayit abecedary belongs to a group of Late Proto-Canaanite and Philistian inscriptions from the southern coastal plain and the Shephelah, which continue Late Bronze III Egyptian administrative tradition in this region. Not a single inscription of this type has ever been found in the territory of Judah.
- Tel Zayit was a peripheral town in the territory of the strong Iron I-Iron IIA kingdom of Gath.

Therefore, the Tel Zayit abecedary is important for the study of the history and culture of the southern lowlands; it has nothing to do with the rise of Judah or with literacy in Judah in the Iron IIA.

Khirbet Qeiyafa and the David and Goliath Tradition

Garfinkel and Ganor have recently dated a casemate wall which they excavated at Khirbet Qeiyafa in the valley of Elah in the Shephelah to the early Iron IIA. Based on ^{14}C samples they put this phase in the Iron Age sequence in the early part of the 10th century BCE. Garfinkel and Ganor labeled a late proto-Canaanite inscription found at the site as the earliest Hebrew inscription known thus far, interpreted the finds at this site as supporting the biblical description of the United Monarchy, and connected the site to the David and Goliath story in 1 Samuel.[67]
This is far more complicated, because:

- The pottery assemblage from Khirbet Qeiyafa seems to belong to the late Iron I/early Iron IIA transition.
- The four ^{14}C determinations from Qeiyafa provide an average uncalibrated date of 2844±15 BP, which translates to 1026–944 BCE (68% probability). This date fits the results for the late Iron I strata in

---

65 Tappy et al. (2006), 42.

66 Cf. in detail Finkelstein et al. (2008).

67 Garfinkel/Ganor (2008).

both the north (e.g., Megiddo VIA) and the south (Qasile X). Note that the latest Iron I destructions in the north provide an uncalibrated date of 2794±10, which translates to 941–915 BCE,[68] while several early Iron IIA sites both in the north and in the south provide still later dates.[69]

- The date of the casemate wall depends on its association with this late Iron I pottery found on bedrock, inside the fortification line, and on Hellenistic pottery found in several locations related to the fortification system. One should wait for additional results in order to reach an accurate dating. Even if the fortification indeed dates to the late Iron I/early Iron IIA, this phenomenon is not unique: contemporary or even somewhat earlier fortifications are known at Khirbet el-Umeiri in Ammon, several sites in Moab, and Khirbet ed-Dawwara a few kms northeast of Jerusalem.
- In the late Iron I/early Iron IIA the site could have been the westernmost outpost of Judah or the easternmost outpost in the territory of nearby (nearer than Jerusalem) Philistine Gath, which was the largest and most important city-state in southern Israel at that time.[70]
- Any proposal regarding the 'ethnic', or territorial affiliation of Qeiyafa should weigh many factors, such as the culinary practices as revealed by the faunal assemblage, the typology of the pottery, the provenance of the pottery, the nature of the ostracon (below), etc. All this should be compared to the finds in other contemporary lowlands sites.[71]
- Plotting all late proto-Canaanite and Philistian inscriptions from southern Canaan on a map, it becomes evident that they are all concentrated in the southern coastal plain and the Shephelah, mainly in or near the territory of Philistine Gath.[72] These include the inscriptions from Qubur el-Walaidah, Tell es-Safi/Gath, Tel Zayit, Khirbet Qeiyafa, Beth-shemesh, Gezer and Izbet Sartah. Not a single one was found in Judah proper. This territory was the hub of the Late Bronze III Egyptian administration in Canaan and the concentration of the inscriptions may reflect a lasting administrative and cultural tradition in this region.
- Making straight forward connection between this site and the biblical tradition on the duel between David and Goliath takes archaeo-

68 Finkelstein/Piasetzky (2007b).

69 See, e.g., Boaretto et al. (in press); Finkelstein/Piasetzky (in press).

70 Uziel/Maeir (2005).

71 Na'aman (2008).

72 For instance, Finkelstein et al. (2008).

logy back a century, to the days when archaeologists roamed the terrain with the Bible in one hand and a spade in the other. The story of David and Goliath is a complex one. There could have been an ancient memory on conflicts between Judah and Philistine Gath in this region and the story of the slaying of Goliath by a hero named David or Elhanan (2 Sam. 21:19) may be related to this ancient tradition. But the text in 1 Samuel 17 is Deuteronomistic in its language, and it seems to depict Homeric influence.[73] It is clear therefore that the story could not have been put in writing before the late 7th century BCE. More than anything else the story portrays the theological goals of the authors and the historical reality of the time of the authors – centuries after the high days of Khirbet Qeiyafa.

A final note on this issue: This eruption of the traditional biblical archaeology, characterized by a highly literal interpretation of the biblical text, should not come as a surprise. It is an unavoidable phase in the now two-centuries-long battle between the advocators of a critical history of ancient Israel and the supporters of a conservative approach that tells a basically biblically narrated history of ancient Israel in modern words. Following every high-tide of critical studies comes a 'counter-revolution' of the conservative school.

In fact, this is an old branch in the study of ancient Israel, which I would label 'wishful thinking archaeology.' It is spectacularly manifested in the case of Jerusalem. Some scholars reconstruct 10th century Jerusalem as an elaborate city surrounded by heavy fortifications.[74] Asked once if evidence for such a fortification has ever been found – even a single course of a few stones – the answer was in the negative, but with a comment that 10th century Jerusalem 'must have been surrounded by such a fortification.'

Back To History

What is the meaning of all this for reconstructing the history of ancient Israel?

Regarding dating, the biblical figure of 40 years for David's reign and 40 years for Solomon are typological and mean no more than 'many years' – the author did not know exactly how many – and the

73 Goliath is even dressed in the armor of a 7th century BCE or later Greek mercenary – Finkelstein (2002).

74 E.g., Cahill (1998); E. Mazar (2007b, Fig. 1).

Saul-David-Solomon sequence is a later literary construct. In reality, the House of Saul and the founder of the Jerusalem dynasty could have been contemporaries. Hence, there is no way to know exactly when in the general framework of the 10th century BCE each of these figures reigned.[75]

Regarding territory, the early monarchs in Jerusalem could have dominated a small territory in the southern highlands – about the size of the territory ruled by Abdi-Heba in the Amarna period. Or, if they manage to take over the early north Israelite, Saulide entity which stretched to their north,[76] they could have ruled over larger territories in the highlands. But the early Davidides' rule did not extend into the northern valleys (characterized in much of the 10th century BCE by late-Canaanite material culture and late-Canaanite city-states system[77]), or into the lower Shephelah in the west (ruled at that time by powerful Ekron and then Gath). The kingdom of David and Solomon was ruled from a humble settlement in Jerusalem.

Geopolitically, the beautiful Megiddo palaces – until recently the symbol of Solomonic splendor – date to the time of the Omride Dynasty of the Northern Kingdom. This should come as no surprise: Archaeology – especially at Samaria – attests to their extraordinary building ability,[78] and texts written by contemporary monarchs all attest to the great power of 9th century Israel. The story of the reign of the Omride princess Ataliah in Jerusalem, the reference for the participation of a Judahite king in the conflict of Israel with the Arameans, and archaeology all indicate that the Omrides dominated the marginal, weaker Judah to their south. The great, powerful and glamorous Israelite state was the Northern Kingdom, not the small, isolated and poor territory dominated by 10th century Jerusalem.

Literally, the David and Solomon material in Samuel and Kings should be pealed away stratigraphically, layer by layer, with archaeology and ancient Near Eastern texts providing the evidence. In other words, in this and other cases, archaeology provides vital evidence for incorporating biblical texts into an historical context. In what follows I wish to briefly summarize the stratigraphy of the texts:[79]

Layer A. The first layer is comprised of the description of David's life as an outlaw challenging authority. This account fits the reality of

75 E.g., Handy (1997), 101–102; Ash (1999), 24–25.

76 I believe that there is enough evidence – archaeological, extra-biblical and biblical to argue for the existence of such polity – Finkelstein (2006).

77 Finkelstein (2003).

78 Finkelstein (2000).

79 For details cf. Finkelstein/Silberman (2006a).

an Apiru band active on the fringe of the settled land – a reality that must have disappeared with the growth of Judah in the 9th century BCE. It therefore seems to contain germs of genuine early history. Needless to say, these were not put in writing before the late 8th century BCE and therefore could have absorbed later realities during the long period of oral transmission.

Layer B. Other texts may reflect 9th century BCE realities. I refer to certain details in the description of David's wars,[80] and to the reference to Geshur and Gath. The latter is described as the most important Philistine city in the Shephelah; it was destroyed in the second half of the 9th century BCE and is not mentioned in late monarchic prophetic works and in 7th century Assyrian sources.[81]

Layer C. The first compilation of texts – the early version of the units that had been described long ago as the History of David Rise and the Succession History – may be related to the time shortly after the collapse of the Northern Kingdom. Archaeology has shown an unprecedented population growth in a short period of a few decades, in the late 8th century BCE, in both Jerusalem and the highlands of Judah. This growth can only be explained as the result of a torrent of Israelite refugees who settled in the south.[82] The compilation of the early texts could have aimed at establishing an early pan-Israelite history – pan-Israelite within Judah – in an attempt to accommodate the two populations and their traditions: northern (negative) and southern (positive) traditions regarding the founders of the Jerusalem dynasty. As I have argued (with Neil Silberman) elsewhere, the main question regarding the famous *apologia* in Samuel[83] should be: at what time was it impossible for a Judahite writer to erase the negative northern traditions.

Layer D. The positive description of Solomon as a great monarch must predate the Deuteronomistic negative reference to him in 1 Kings 11. The account of the great Solomon in 1 Kings 3–10 as the cleverest and richest of all monarchs, a great builder and the one who traded with far-off lands, including Arabia, is based on 8th and 7th centuries BCE realities. Some of them can be interpreted as memories of the later days of the Northern Kingdom. I have already mentioned the Megiddo, Hazor, and Gezer verse in 1 Kings 9. In addition, I would refer to the stories of Solomon's cities of chariots and horsemen, which probably reflect a memory of the great horse breeding and training facilities of

80 Na'aman (2002).
81 Maeir (2004).
82 Finkelstein/Silberman (2006b); for a different view cf. Na'aman (2007).
83 McCarter (1980); Halpern (2001), 73–103.

the Northern Kingdom at Megiddo,[84] and to King Hiram of Tyre, who should probably be identified with the only Hiram known from reliable extra-biblical texts – the contemporary of Tiglath-pileser III in the late 8th century BCE. These stories were intended to equate the grandeur of Solomon with that of the great monarchs of the Northern Kingdom. Other materials on Solomon perfectly fit the Assyrian century, specifically the first half of the 7th century BCE. The lavish visit of Solomon's trading partner, the Queen of Sheba, in Jerusalem must reflect the participation of late 8th- and 7th-century Judah, under Assyrian domination, in the lucrative Arabian trade. The same holds true for the description of the trade expeditions to distant lands that set off from Ezion-geber on the Gulf of Aqaba – a site which was not inhabited before late-monarchic times.[85] These Solomon stories (and the whole stature of Solomon, which reminds one of a great Assyrian monarch) depict a positive approach to the incorporation of Judah into the Assyrian global economy and as such, they seem to echo realities of the days of King Manasseh, in the first half of the 7th centuries BCE.

Layer E. Finally, there are the Deuteronomistic materials of the late 7th century BCE. Among them I would refer to the post-Assyrian pan-Israelite ideas, aimed at the Israelite population outside of Judah, in the northern highlands. No less obvious are materials about the Philistines that depict realities related to the presence of Greek mercenaries in the region in late monarchic times. In this I refer to the mention of *seranim*, the Cherethites and Pelethites, a league of Philistine cities, etc. Above all, I would refer to the dressing of Goliath as a Greek hoplite and to the Homeric nature of the David and Goliath duel.[86] This was a time when tiny Judah faced mighty Egypt and the victory of David over the giant Goliath – the description of his attire symbolizing the power of Egypt's mercenary forces – could have depicted the hopes of Judah, which faced a dramatic conflict with the 26th Dynasty.

The final late-monarchic text is therefore a product of late 7th century Judah. At a time when the Northern Kingdom was no more than a memory and the mighty Assyrian army had faded away, a new David – the pious Josiah – came to the throne in Jerusalem, intent on 'restoring' the glory of his distant ancestors. He was about to 'recreate' a great and devout United Monarchy, 'regain' the territories of the vanquished Northern Kingdom, and rule from Jerusalem over all Israelite territories and all Israelite people. The description of the glamorous United Monarchy served these goals.

---

84 Cantrell (2006); Cantrell/Finkelstein (2006).

85 Pratico (1993).

86 Finkelstein (2002).

All this may seem to belittle the stature of the historical David and Solomon. But in the same breath we gain a glimpse into the glamor of the Northern Kingdom – the first true, great Israelite state. If there was a historical United Monarchy, it was that of the Omride dynasty and it was ruled from Samaria. And no less important, we are given a glimpse into the fascinating world of late-monarchic Judah.

Bibliography

Alexandre, Y. (2002), A Fluted Bronze Bowl with a Canaanite–Early Phoenician Inscription from Kefar Veradim, in: Z. Gal (ed.), Eretz Zafon: Studies in Galilean Archaeology, Jerusalem, 65–74.

Ash, P.S. (1999), David, Solomon and Egypt: A Reassessment, JSOT.S 297, Sheffield.

Bartlett, J.R. (1989), Edom and the Edomites, JSOT.S 77, Sheffield.

Ben-Tor, A. (2000), Hazor and Chronology of Northern Israel: A Reply to Israel Finkelstein, BASOR 317, 9–15.

Bienkowski, P. (1992), The Date of Sedentary Occupation in Edom: Evidence from Umm el-Biyara, Tawilan and Buseirah, in: P. Bienkowski (ed.), Early Edom and Moab: The Beginning of the Iron Age in Southern Jordan, Sheffield Archaeological Monigraphs 7, Sheffield, 99–112.

Boaretto, E./Finkelstein, I./Shahack-Gross, R. (in press), Radiocarbon Results from the Iron IIA Site of Atar Haroa in the Negev Highlands and Their Archaeological and Historical Implications, forthcoming in Radiocarbon.

Cahill, J.M. (1998), David's Jerusalem: Fiction or Reality? It is There: The Archaeological Evidence Proves It, BArR 24/4, 34–41, 63.

– (2003), Jerusalem at the Time of the United Monarchy: The Archaeological Evidence, in: A.G. Vaughn/A.E. Killebrew (eds.), Jerusalem in Bible and Archaeology: The First Temple Period, SBL Symposium Series No. 18, Atlanta, 13–80.

Cantrell, D.O. (2006), Stable Issues, in: I. Finkelstein/D. Ussishkin/B. Halpern (eds.), Megiddo IV: The 1998–2002 Seasons, vol. 2, Tel Aviv, 630–642.

– /Finkelstein, I. (2006), A Kingdom for a Horse: The Megiddo Stables and Eighth Century Israel, in: I. Finkelstein/D. Ussishkin/B. Halpern (eds.), Megiddo IV: The 1998–2002 Seasons, vol. 2, Tel Aviv, 643–665.

Cline, E.H. (2006), Area L (The 1998–2000 Seasons), in: I. Finkelstein/D. Ussishkin/B. Halpern (eds.), Megiddo IV: The 1998–2002 Seasons, vol. 1, Tel Aviv, 104–123.

Coldstream, N.J. (2003), Some Aegean Reactions to the Chronology Debate in the Southern Levant, Tel Aviv 30, 247–258.

Crowfoot, J.W. (1940), Megiddo – A Review, PEQ 72, 132–147.

Dever, W.G. (1997), Archaeology and the "Age of Solomon": A Case Study in Archaeology and Historiography, in: L.K. Handy (ed.), The Age of Solomon: Scholarship at the Turn of the Millennium, Studies in the History and the Culture of the Ancient Near East, vol. 11, Leiden, 217–251.

– (2001), Excavating the Hebrew Bible, or Burying It Again? BASOR 322, 67–77.

Faust, A. (2004), The United Monarchy and Anthropology: A Note on the Debate over Jerusalem's Possible Status as a Capital, in E. Baruch/A. Faust (eds.), New Studies on Jerusalem 10, 23–36 (in Hebrew).

Finkelstein, I. (1996), The Archaeology of the United Monarchy: An Alternative View, Levant 28, 177–187.

– (1998), Notes on the Stratigraphy and Chronology of Iron Age Ta'anach, Tel Aviv 25, 208–218.

– (2000), Omride Architecture, ZDPV 116, 114–138.

– (2001), The Rise of Jerusalem and Judah: The Missing Link, Levant 33, 105–115.

– (2002), The Philistines in the Bible: A Late-Monarchic Perspective, JSOT 27/2, 131–167.

– (2003), City-States to States: Polity Dynamics in the 10th–9th Centuries B.C.E., in: W.G. Dever/S. Gitin (eds.), Symbiosis, Symbolism, and the Power of the Past: Canaan, Ancient Israel, and Their Neighbors from the Late Bronze Age through Roman Palestina: Proceedings of the Centennial Symposium W.F. Albright Institute of Archaeological Research and American Schools of Oriental Research: Jerusalem, May 29–31, 2000, Winona Lake, 75–84.

– (2005), Khirbat en-Naḥas, Edom and Biblical History, Tel Aviv 32, 119–125.

– (2006), The Last Labayu: King Saul and the Expansion of the First North Israelite Territorial Entity, in: Y. Amit/E. Ben Zvi/I. Finkelstein/O. Lipschits (eds.), Essays on Ancient Israel in Its Near Eastern Context: A Tribute to Nadav Na'aman, Winona Lake, 171–177.

– /Herzog, Z./Singer-Avitz, L./Ussishkin, D. (2007), Has King David's Palace in Jerusalem Been Found? Tel Aviv 34, 142–164.

– /Piasetzky, E. (2003), Recent Radiocarbon Results and King Solomon, Antiquity 77, 771–779.

– /Piasetzky, E. (2007a), Radiocarbon, Iron Age Destructions and the Israel-Aram Damascus Conflicts in the 9th Century BCE, UF 39, 261–276.
– /Piasetzky, E. (2007b), Radiocarbon Dating and the Late-Iron I in Northern Canaan: A New Proposal, UF 39, 247–260.
– /Piasetzky, E. (2008), Radiocarbon and the History of Copper Production at Khirbet en-Naḥas, Tel Aviv 35, 82–95.
– /Piasetzky, E. (in press), Radicarbon Dating the Iron Age in the Levant: A Bayesian Model for Six Ceramic Phases and Six Transitions, (forthcoming in Antiquity).
– /Sass, B./Singer-Avitz, L. (2008), Writing in Iron IIA Philistia in the Light of the Tel Zayit Abecedary, ZDPV 124, 1–14.
– /Silberman, N.A. (2002), The Bible Unearthed: A Rejoinder, BASOR 327, 63–73.
– /Silberman, N.A. (2006a), David and Solomon: In Search of the Bible Sacred Kings and the Roots of Western Tradition, New York.
– /Silberman, N.A. (2006b), Temple and Dynasty: Hezekiah, the Remaking of Judah and the Rise of the Pan-Israelite Ideology, JSOT 30/3, 259–285.
Fisher, C.S. (1929), The Excavation of Armageddon, OIC 4, Chicago.
Franklin, N. (2005), Correlation and Chronology: Samaria and Megiddo Redux, in: T.E. Levy/T. Higham (eds.), The Bible and Radiocarbon Dating: Archaeology, Text and Science, London, 310–322.
Gal, Z. (2003), The Iron Age 'Low Chronology' in Light of the Excavations at Horvat Rosh Zayit, IEJ 53, 147–150.
Garfinkel, Y./Ganor, S. (2008), Khirbet Qeiyafa: Sha'arayim, Journal of Hebrew Scriptures 8, art. 22, 1–10.
Gilboa, A./Sharon, I./Zorn, J.R. (2004), Dor and Iron Age Chronology: Scarabs, Ceramic Sequence and ^{14}C, Tel Aviv 31, 32–59.
Guy, P.L.O. (1931), New Light from Armageddon: Second Provisional Report (1927–29) on the Excavations at Megiddo in Palestine, OIC 9, Chicago.
Halpern, B. (2001), David's Secret Demons: Messiah, Murderer, Traitor, King, Grand Rapids.
Handy, L.K. (1997), On the Dating and Dates of Solomon's Reign, in: L.K. Handy (ed.), The Age of Solomon: Scholarship at the Turn of the Millennium, Studies in the History and the Culture of the Ancient Near East, vol. 11, Leiden, 96–105.
Harrison, T.P. (2003), The Battleground: Who Destroyed Megiddo? Was it David or Shishak? BArR 29/6, 28–35, 60, 62.
– (2004), Megiddo 3: Final Report on the Stratum VI Excavations, OIP 127, Chicago.

Herzog, Z./Singer-Avitz, L. (2004), Redefining the Centre: The Emergence of State in Judah, Tel Aviv 31, 209–244.

– /Singer-Avitz, L. (2006), Sub-Dividing the Iron Age IIA in Northern Israel: A Suggested Solution to the Chronological Debate, Tel Aviv 33, 163–195.

Holladay, J.S. (1990), Red Slip, Burnish, and the Solomonic Gate-way at Gezer, BASOR 277/278, 23–70.

Knauf, E.A. (1985), Alter und Herkunft der edomitischen Königsliste Gen 36, 31–39, ZAW 97, 245–253.

– (1991), King Solomon's Copper Supply, in: E. Lipinski (ed.), Phoenicia and the Bible, Leuven, 167–186.

Lemaire, A. (2001), Les premiers rois araméens dans la tradition biblique, in: P.M.M. Daviau/J.W. Wevers/M. Weigl (eds.), The World of the Aramaeans I: Biblical Studies in Honour of Paul-Eugène Dion, JSOT.S 324, Sheffield, 113–143.

Levy, T.E./Adams, R.B./Najjar, M./Hauptmann, A./Anderson, J.D./Brandl, B./Robinson, M.A./Higham, T. (2004), Reassessing the Chronology of Biblical Edom: New Excavations and ^{14}C Dates from Khirbet en-Naḥas (Jordan), Antiquity 78, 865–879.

– /Najjar, M./van der Plicht, J./ Higham, T./ Bruins, H.J. (2005), Lowland Edom and the High and Low Chronologies: Edomite State Formation, the Bible and Recent Archaeological Research in Southern Jordan, in: T.E. Levy/T. Higham (eds.), The Bible and Radiocarbon Dating: Archaeology, Text and Science, London, 129–163.

– /Higham, T./Bronk Ramsey, C./ Smith, N.G./Ben-Yosef, E./Robinson, M./Münger, S./ Knabb, K./Schulze, J.P./Najjar, M./Tauxe, L. (2008), High-Precision Radiocarbon Dating and Historical Biblical Archaeology in Southern Jordan, Proceedings of the National Academy of Sciences 105/43, 16460–16465.

Maeir, A.M. (2004), The Historical Background and Dating of Amos VI 2: An Archaeological Perspective from Tell Eṣ-Sâfī/Gath, VT 54, 319–334.

Mazar, A. (1997), Iron Age Chronology: A Reply to I. Finkelstein, Levant 29, 157–167.

– (1999), The 1997–1998 Excavations at Tel Reḥov: Preliminary Report, IEJ 49, 1–42.

– (2005), The Debate over the Chronology of the Iron Age in the Southern Levant: Its History, the Current Situation, and a Suggested Resolution, in: T.E. Levy/T. Higham (eds.), The Bible and Radiocarbon Dating: Archaeology, Text and Science, London, 15–30.

– (2006), Jerusalem in the 10th Century B.C.E.: The Glass Half Full, in: Y. Amit/E. Ben Zvi/I. Finkelstein/O. Lipschits (eds.), Essays on An-

cient Israel in Its Near Eastern Context: A Tribute to Nadav Na'aman, Winona Lake, 255–272.
– /Bronk Ramsey, C. (2008), ^{14}C Dates and the Iron Age Chronology of Israel: A Response, Radiocarbon 50, 159–180.
– /Carmi, I. (2001), Radiocarbon Dates from Iron Age Strata at Tel Beth Shean and Tel Reḥov, Radiocarbon 43, 1333–1342.
Mazar, E. (2007a), Preliminary Report on the City of David Excavations 2005 at the Visitors Center Area, Jerusalem.
– (2007b), Jerusalem – 4000-Year-Old Capital in the Light of Recent Archaeological Excavations, Eretz-Israel 28, 125–133 (in Hebrew).
Mazzoni, S. (2000), Syria and the Chronology of the Iron Age, Revista sobre Oriente Próximo y Egipto en la antigüedad 3, 121–138.
McCarter, K.P. (1980), The Apology of David, JBL 99/4, 489–504.
Münger, S. (2003), Egyptian Stamp-Seal Amulets and their Implications for the Chronology of the Early Iron Age, Tel Aviv 30, 66–82.
Na'aman, N. (1997a), Sources and Composition in the History of Solomon, in: L.K. Handy (ed.), The Age of Solomon: Scholarship in the Turn of the Millennium, Studies in the History and the Culture of the Ancient Near East, vol. 11, Leiden, 57–80.
– (1997b), Historical and Literary Notes on the Excavations of Tel Jezreel, Tel Aviv 24, 122–128.
– (2002), In Search of Reality Behind the Account of David's Wars with Israel's Neighbours, IEJ 52, 200–224.
– (2007), When and How Did Jerusalem Become a Great City? The Rise of Jerusalem as Judah's Premier City in the Eighth-Seventh Centuries B.C.E., BASOR 347, 21–56.
– (2008), In Search of the Ancient Name of Khirbet Qeiyafa, Journal of Hebrew Scriptures 8, art. 21, 1–8.
Pratico, G.D. (1993), Nelson Glueck's 1938–1940 Excavations at Tell el-Kheleifeh: A Reappraisal, American Schools of Oriental Research Archaeological Reports, Number 03, Atlanta.
Sass, B. (2005), The Alphabet at the Turn of the Millennium: The West Semitic Alphabet ca. 1150–850 BCE: The Antiquity of the Arabian, Greek and Phrygian Alphabets, Journal of the Institute of Archaeology of Tel Aviv University, Occasional Publications No. 4, Tel Aviv.
Sharon, I. (2001), 'Transition Dating' – A Heuristic Mathematical Approach to the Collation of Radiocarbon Dates from Stratified Sequences, Radiocarbon 43, 345–354.
– /Gilboa, A./Jull, T.A.J./Boaretto, E. (2007), Report on the First Stage of the Iron Age Dating Project in Israel: Supporting A Low Chronology, Radiocarbon 49, 1–46.

Stager, L.E. (2003), The Patrimonial Kingdom of Solomon, in: W.G. Dever/S. Gitin (eds.), Symbiosis, Symbolism, and the Power of the Past: Canaan, Ancient Israel, and Their Neighbors from the Late Bronze Age through Roman Palestina: Proceedings of the Centennial Symposium W.F. Albright Institute of Archaeological Research and American Schools of Oriental Research: Jerusalem, May 29–31, 2000, Winona Lake, 63–74.

Tappy, R.E./McCarter, P.K./Lundberg, M.J./Zuckerman, B. (2006), An Abecedary of the Mid-Tenth Century B.C.E. from the Judaean Shephelah, BASOR 344, 5–46.

Ussishkin, D. (1980), Was the "Solomonic" City Gate at Megiddo Built by King Solomon? BASOR 239, 1–18.

– (2003), Solomon's Jerusalem: The Text and the Facts on the Ground, in: A.G. Vaughn/A.E. Killebrew (eds.), Jerusalem in the Bible and Archaeology: The First Temple Period, SBL Symposium Series No. 18, Atlanta, 103–116.

Uziel, J./Maeir, A.M. (2005), Scratching the Surface of Gath: Implications of the Tell eṣ-Sâfī /Gath Surface Survey, Tel Aviv 32, 50–75.

Watzinger, K. (1929), Tell el-Mutesellim II. Bericht über die 1903 bis 1905 mit Unterstützung sr. Majestät des Deutschen Kaisers und der Deutschen Orient-Gesellschaft vom Deutschen Verein zur Erforschung Palästinas veranstalteten Ausgrabungen. Die Funde, Leipzig.

Westermann, C. (1986), Genesis 12–36: A Commentary, London.

Yadin, Y. (1958), Solomon's City Wall and Gate at Gezer, IEJ 8, 80–86.

– (1970), Megiddo of the Kings of Israel, BA 33/3, 66–96.

Zimhoni, O. (1997), Studies in the Iron Age Pottery of Israel: Typological, Archaeological and Chronological Aspects, Tel Aviv.

Archaeology and the Biblical Narrative: The Case of the United Monarchy

AMIHAI MAZAR

Of the various approaches to the historicity of the biblical narratives, the most justified one is in my view the claim that the so-called 'Deuteronomistic History' preserved kernels of ancient texts and realities. This core included components of geo-political and socio-economic *realia*, as well as certain information on historical figures and events, although distorted and laden with later anachronisms, legends and literary forms added during the time of transmission, writing and editing of the texts and inspired by the authors' theological and ideological viewpoint. The authors and redactors must have utilized early source materials, such as temple and palace libraries and archives, monumental inscriptions perhaps centuries old, oral transmissions of ancient poetry and folk stories rooted in a remote historical past, and perhaps even some earlier historiographic writings[1].

This general approach to the biblical text also dictates the evaluation of the historical reality of those narratives relating to David and Solomon. The views are considerably divided: revisionist historians (the so-called 'minimalists') and several archaeologists pointed out the infeasibility of the biblical description of the United Monarchy. Conservatives continue to maintain the biblical narrative as a general framework for historical reconstruction, and those who are 'in the middle of the road' search for possible alternative historical reconstructions.[2] The

---

1 Cf. Miller/Hayes (1986); Halpern (1988); Na'aman (1997; 2002); (2007), 399–400; Dever (2001); Liverani (2005); various papers in Williamson (2007).

2 Among the vast literature on this subject published during the last two decades I would mention the collection of essays reflecting a wide variety of views edited by Handy (1997). For conservative approaches defining the United Monarchy as a state "from Dan to Beer Sheba" including "conquered kingdoms" (Ammon, Moab, Edom) and "spheres of influence" in Geshur and Hamath cf. e.g. Ahlström (1993), 455–542; Meyers (1998); Lemaire (1999); Masters (2001); Stager (2003); Rainey (2006), 159–168; Kitchen (1997); Millard (1997; 2008). For a total denial of the historicity of the United Monarchy cf. e.g. Davies (1992), 67–68; others suggested a 'chiefdom' comprising a small region around Jerusalem, cf. Knauf (1997), 81–85; Niemann (1997), 252–299;

archaeological paradigm concerning the United Monarchy as formulated mainly by Yadin[3] was attacked by several scholars,[4] while others continue to support this archaeological paradigm.[5]

In this paper, I summarize my previous views on this subject, respond to a recent critique relating to 10th century Jerusalem, and add comments on several new archaeological discoveries relating to this subject.

Summary of My Previous Views

In several papers published during the last years I expressed my views concerning the United Monarchy.[6] Some of the points are summarized below (without references) and the general conclusions are cited at the end of this paper.

1. The mentioning of *btdwd* 'The house of David' as a title of Judah in the Tel Dan stele, probably erected by Hazael, king of Damascus, should be given the weight it deserves. It means that about 140 years after the presumed end of David's reign, in the region David was well-known as founder of the dynasty that ruled a kingdom centered in Jerusalem.
2. The Shoshenq I raid to the Land of Israel ca. 925/920 BCE matches the mentioning of this event in 1 Kings 14:25–28. This is the only existing correlation between a biblical reference and an external written source relating to the 10th century BCE, and it means that the biblical writer must have utilized earlier documents, rooted in 10th century BCE reality. The only plausible explanation for choosing a route for this raid through the cen-

---

and Finkelstein (1999). For a 'middle of the road' approach suggesting a United Monarchy of larger territorial scope though smaller than the biblical description cf. e.g. Miller (1997); Halpern (2001), 229–262; Liverani (2005), 92–101. The latter recently suggested a state comprising the territories of Judah and Ephraim during the time of David, that was subsequently enlarged to include areas of northern Samaria and influence areas in the Galilee and Transjordan. Na'aman (1992; 1996) once accepted the basic biography of David as authentic and later rejected the United Monarchy as a state, cf. id. (2007), 401–402. For recent theoretical discussions of the emergence of the Israelite state, cf. Masters (2001); Joffe (2002).

3 Cf. Yadin (1972), 135–164, summarized in A. Mazar (1990a), 375–387.

4 Cf. Wightman (1990), Jamieson–Drake (1991) and esp. Finkelstein (1996); Finkelstein/Silberman (2006); Finkelstein (2007).

5 Cf. e.g. A. Mazar (1997); Dever (1997); Meyers (1998), 243–256; Lemaire (1999), 116–120; Ben-Tor (2000); Halpern (2001), 427–478; Masters (2001); Stager (2003).

6 Cf. A. Mazar (1997; 2003; 2007a; 2007b; 2008).

tral hill country north of Jerusalem must have been the existence of a substantial political power in the central hill country. The most obvious candidate for such a polity is the Solomonic kingdom, and Shoshenq's goal was perhaps to terminate the rising Israelite state which threatened Egyptian economic interests. The archaeological research relating to Shoshenq I should not concentrate on looking for destruction layers in each of the sites mentioned in his list, since it is unknown whether the Egyptian army indeed violently destroyed them. Rather, the very fact that a place is mentioned in this list means that it was occupied at the time of the raid and was well-known to the Egyptians. Such an approach provides an important chronological anchor for several excavated sites throughout the country, such as Arad and Taanach, among others. The mention of Reḥov and Beth-Shean in the list fits the archaeological evidence at those sites.

3. The list of ca. 70 names in the Negev mentioned in Shoshenq's list, some of them clearly Hebrew names, fits the unusual phenomenon of short-lived settlements known in the Negev Highlands and in the Beer-Sheba-Arad region. The material culture in these settlements represents a cultural symbiosis by the inhabitants – probably people who came from Judah or the southern coastal plain who were joined by local desert nomads. The motivation for this settlement wave must have been economic, perhaps related to the contemporary large-scale copper smelting activity at Feinan (see below). The goal of Shoshenq's southern branch of his campaign was perhaps to put an end to the extensive settlement in this region, which perhaps was considered by the Egyptians as competing with or threatening their own interests.[7]
4. The date of the transition from Iron I to Iron IIA is important for defining the material culture of the alleged time of the United Monarchy in the 10th century BCE (based on inner biblical chronology). The results of radiocarbon dates relating to this transition can be interpreted in various ways: while Sharon et

7 The concept of a 'Tel Masos Chiefdom' centered at Tel Masos and including the Negev Highland sites, as suggested by Finkelstein, is highly questionable. Tel Masos is located in a different geographic zone (Arad-Beer-Sheba valley) than the Negev Highland sites, its ceramic repertoire seems to be earlier than that of the Negev Highland sites and it lacks the hand-made pottery (probably produced by local nomads) which comprises about 50% of the pottery in the Negev Highland sites.

al. insist on dating the transition to ca. 900 BCE,[8] Finkelstein, who since 1996 dated the transition to Shoshenq's time, now corrected his view (at least in relation to the end of Megiddo VIA) and claims an earlier date in the 10th century BCE for that violent destruction, which marks the end of the Iron Age I at Megiddo.[9] Utilizing the data published by Sharon et al., Bronk Ramsey and myself calculated that the transition must have occurred during the first half of the 10th century BCE, which would fit with Finkelstein's recent view.[10] This enables us to determine the alleged date of the archaeological evidence related to the United Monarchy to the transition of Iron I/IIA and to the early part of Iron IIA.[11]

5. Demographic assessments of 10th century BCE Judah are questionable, since they are based on surface surveys of sites which in many cases were settled continuously for most of the Iron Age. Both temporal and spatial aspects of the development of such sites remain enigmatic in such surveys, and thus calculations of the numbers of sites and the settled areas during the 10th and 9th centuries BCE are susceptible to significant errors. In spite of these limitations, the comparison of the population estimation in Iron I (based on excavations and surveys) to that in the late 8th century BCE enables to presume a gradual increase in population throughout this time duration. A population estimation of about 20,000 people for all of Judah and Benjamin in the Iron IIA (including the Shephelah) seems to be possible, though the methodological difficulties mentioned above should be taken into account. This number, if correct, provides a sufficient demographic basis for an Israelite state in the 10th century BCE.
6. Revival of urban life following demise of urbanism in large parts of the country during the Iron Age I is detected in excavated sites throughout the Israelite territories from Galilee to Judah. This was a gradual process which continued until the late 8th century BCE. Many of the sites remained unfortified and not sufficiently developed as urban centers during the 10th century, while others were fortified (see below). Revival of trade with Cyprus occurred during the Iron IIA.

8 Cf. Sharon et al. (2007; 2008).

9 Cf. Finkelstein/Silberman (2006), 180–182.

10 Cf. A. Mazar/Bronk Ramsey (2008); A. Mazar (2008), 100–105, 112–115.

11 Cf. A. Mazar (2007a; 2008).

7. Tel Reḥov in the Beth-Shean Valley demonstrates continuity of a large 10 ha city throughout the 12th–9th centuries BCE. Yet, while during the Iron Age I (12th–11th centuries BCE), Canaanite material culture is dominant, the 10th century BCE (Iron IIA) sees a considerable change in the material culture (mainly the appearance red-slipped and hand burnished pottery). This change can be detected in many other parts of the country at almost the same time, and may be regarded as reflecting geo-political developments that took place during the 10th century BCE, perhaps related to the emergence of the Israelite state.
8. Yadin's identification of Solomonic cities at Hazor (Stratum X), Megiddo (Stratum IVB–VA) and Gezer (Stratum VIII), thus illuminating 1 Kings 9:15, is still a debated subject. Finkelstein and his followers abandon this theory altogether, yet the current excavators of Hazor and Gezer support Yadin's theory. The new excavations at Megiddo provided two relevant ^{14}C dates from Level H-5, which corresponds to Stratum IVB–VA: one in the 10th century and the other in the 9th century BCE. Dates from the destruction of Megiddo VIA fit the late 11th or early 10th century BCE.[12] These dates suggest that Stratum IVB–VA, with its two ashlar palaces, could have been constructed during the 10th century BCE and thus could have been Solomonic, although additional radiometric dates are required.
9. The discovery of inscriptions with the name *Hanan* at Beth-Shemesh and Timnah (Tel Batash) along the Sorek Valley in Iron IIA contexts recall the name *Elon Beth Hanan* among the places in Solomon's second district, mentioned in 1 Kings 4:9. This adds support to the possible 10th century origin of this biblical administrative list.
10. The small amount of Hebrew epigraphic finds from the 10th century BCE was brought as evidence for lack of literacy during the 10th century and thus for the infeasibility of an Israelite state during this century. However, the number of Hebrew inscriptions from Israel in the 9th century is also very small, and yet there is no debate concerning the existence of an Israelite state in that century. New finds from Tel Zayit and Khirbet Qeiyafa (see below), as well as those mentioned in the previous paragraph, may indicate that during 10th century literacy in Judah was much more advanced than presumed in earlier studies.

---

12 Cf. A. Mazar/Bronk Ramsey (2008); A. Mazar (2008).

Questions related to Jerusalem and several new discoveries are the subjects of the following part of this article.

Jerusalem in the 10th Century BCE

The status of Jerusalem as a city in the 10th–9th centuries BCE has become a major subject of debate. While in the past, archaeological assessment of the United Monarchy tended to ignore the problems concerning Jerusalem, some current authors use the Archaeology of Jerusalem as a major issue in deconstructing the historicity of the United Monarchy. Thus, Ussishkin claimed that Jerusalem was not settled in the 10th century and Finkelstein defined 10th century Jerusalem as a small village.[13] The topography of Jerusalem indeed does not allow to recreate a very large city there prior to its extension to the western Hill during the 8th century BCE. The eastern ridge of the City of David and the Temple Mount comprise about 12 ha, and excluding the temple mount the area is just 4–5 ha. Such a city could not include a population larger than ca. 1000–2000 persons, and such a small city can hardly be imagined as a capital of a large state like the one described in the Bible. However, several exceptional structures that were excavated in this city set it apart from other urban centers of the southern Levant at that time. These include the architectural complex on the summit of the City of David, the possible continued use of the Middle Bronze structures around the spring Gihon, and the temple, known only from biblical descriptions. These real and virtual structures, if correctly dated and understood, may throw light on the power base for rulers such as David and Solomon, providing that we correctly define the nature of their kingship and state.

The 'Stepped Structure' and the 'Large Stone Structure' Complex

The 'Stepped Structure' in Shiloh's Area G and the 'Large Stone Structure' excavated by Eilat Mazar to its west, should be defined as part of one and the same architectural complex.[14] Each of the three excavators of these buildings (Kenyon, Shiloh and E. Mazar) dated them to the

13 Cf. Ussishkin (2003); Finkelstein (2003).

14 Cf. E. Mazar (2008).

Iron I or Iron IIA and related them to the United Monarchy.[15] This date and interpretation were recently challenged by Finkelstein, Ussishkin, Herzog and Avitz-Singer. The importance of this debate for our subject calls for a detailed response, which is the subject of the following paragraphs.[16]

The 'Stepped Structure'[17]

Various parts of the 'Stepped Structure' in the City of David (Fig. 1) were exposed by Macalister, Kenyon and Shiloh, and the excavation of its northern face was recently accomplished by E. Mazar.[18] This is a large structure, about 40–48 m long and ca. 20 m high.[19] It includes several components, the most prominent being the 'mantle wall', a term used by Cahill to describe the outer sloping stepped structure, which in her view was founded on a massive substructure denoted by Kenyon and Shiloh as 'terraces'. The latter are explained as a constructional feature, creating stone 'boxes' filled with stones and intended to support the 'mantle wall' on the steep slope of the hill. In certain places, there are earth layers between the stone 'terraces' and the 'mantle wall', but this is not consistent and in other places the 'mantle wall' was constructed right on top of the stone substructure or, in fact, is bonded to it.

---

15 The 'terraces' below the 'Stepped Structure' were dated by Kenyon (1974) and Shiloh (1984) to the Late Bronze Age, yet they were redated by Steiner (2001) and Cahill (2003) to Iron Age I and defined as the substructure of the 'Stepped Structure', based on a room containing Iron Age I pottery found by Kenyon below the 'terraces', and the Iron I pottery found inside those 'terraces'.

16 The discussion below refers to Finkelstein et al. (2007). My thanks to Eilat Mazar for guiding me several times in her excavation areas during the 2007 and 2008 seasons and discussing with me some of the issues raised in the following discussion. Yet, the views in the following response are mine.

17 This building is usually called 'The Stone Stepped Structure'. Here it is abbreviated to 'The Stepped Structure'.

18 Cf. Shiloh (1984), 15–17; Steiner (2001), 36–39, 43–48, 51–53; Cahill (2003); E. Mazar (2007a; 2007b; 2008).

19 The height of 27.5 m of this structure cited by E. Mazar (2008), 30, is based on including the 'Large Wall' in Kenyon's Trench I as part of the 'Stepped Structure'. Though this is the view of Steiner (2001) and Cahill (2003) as well, I am not confident that this wide wall was part of the same complex (see below). The width of 48 m cited by E. Mazar (op. cit.) is based on adding structural remains exposed by Macalister/Duncan (1926) south of the 'Hasmonean Tower'.

Fig. 1: The remains of the 'Stepped Structure' and the 'Large Stone Building' complex as revealed by the excavations of K. Kenyon, Y. Shiloh and E. Mazar.

Component 1:	The 'terraces' (structural foundations of the 'Stepped Structure')
Component 2:	The 'mantle wall' of the 'Stepped Structure'
Component 3:	A stone structure or fill (probably part of the 'Stepped Structure') in Kenyon's Square AXXIII
Component 4:	'Terraces 4–5' in the upper part of Kenyon's Trench I
Component 5:	The 'Large Wall' in the upper part of Kenyon's Trench I
Component 6:	The 'Large Stone Structure' excavated by E. Mazar

Combined plan based on plans published by Shiloh [1984], Steiner [2001] and E. Mazar [2009a: 38 Fig. 1; 2009b: 64]. Computer work by Y. Shalev.

The following is a list of points raised by Finkelstein et al. concerning this 'Stepped Structure' and the corresponding responses.[20]

1. Finkelstein et al. suggest that the 'Stepped Structure' had two building phases. Its lower part is a later addition, since it was constructed of smaller stones.[21] The stones in the lower 17 courses are indeed 0.20–0.35 m in size while those in the upper 35 courses are 0.35–0.7 m long (a few are up to 1 m long), yet this difference is just a technical matter; the lowest course of large stones was constructed just above the highest course of smaller stones and thus the former could not predate the latter. There is no evidence for two construction phases, and both parts are superimposed by Iron Age II dwellings. The reason for the change in stone size is perhaps related to the challenge faced by the builders when they approached the steep vertical rock scarp behind the upper part of the structure.[22] The purpose of the 'Stepped Structure' was probably to support the foundations of a large building constructed on top of the hill by covering the vertical natural scarp with its inner cavities and karstic features and extending the area to the east. The change in orientation between the lower and upper parts is mentioned by Finkelstein et al. as additional evidence for two construction phases. Yet, this change is gradual: The lower courses of large stones follow the same orientation as the courses of the smaller lower stones, and as we proceed upwards the courses start to turn to the northwest, in accordance with the topography. Thus, the suggestion for two construction phases is intangible.
2. The authors cite Steiner's mention of Iron IIA pottery among the stones of Components 3, 4, 5[23] and suggest (although with reservation) that this pottery provides a *terminus post quem* for the construction of the 'Stepped Structure'. As I have shown elsewhere, this pottery came from unclear contexts above or between the upper stones of 'Component 5' ('The Large Wall') in Kenyon's Trench I.[24] No floor or any other occupation layer related to this wall was ever excavated. I claimed (and Finkelstein et al. agreed) that since Components 4, 5 in Kenyon's Trench I are detached from the main part of the 'Stepped Structure',

20 Cf. Finkelstein et al. (2007), 142–164.
21 Cf. Finkelstein et al. (2007), 151.
22 The latter was clearly revealed by E. Mazar in the 2007–2008 excavation seasons.
23 Op. cit., above n. 20. The numbers refer to Fig. 1 in this paper.
24 Cf. A. Mazar (2006), 263–264.

there is no proof to Steiner's claim (accepted also by Cahill and E. Mazar) that they were part of this structure. In addition, the above mentioned pottery group includes only a few pottery sherds, mostly dating to Iron I but a few undefined sherds. A single almost complete vessel is probably of Iron IIA date, but as said above, it has no chronological value in establishing the date of either the 'Stepped Structure' or even of the 'The Large Wall' itself.[25]

3. Cahill published Iron IIA pottery, including an imported Phoenician Bichrome jug, found on the earliest floor surfaces of the 'Burnt Building' above the lower northern part of the 'Stepped Structure'.[26] According to Cahill, this pottery provides a *terminus ante quem* in the Iron IIA for the construction of the 'Stepped Structure'. Finkelstein et al. claim that the 'floor surfaces' were in fact constructional fills for the late Iron II building.[27] I prefer the interpretation of the excavators as presented by Cahill. If the layers were constructional fills laid in a later period, we would expect some mixture of pottery, and yet these layers contained purely Iron IIA pottery. Even if they were constructional fills, they must have been constructed no later than Iron IIA and thus substantiate the *terminus ante quem* for the construction of the 'Stepped Structure'.
4. The authors claim that the upper part of the 'Stepped Structure' is a rebuild of the Hellenistic period or even a modern reconstruction.[28] As to the latter claim, modern reconstructions were indeed made by the Jordanian authorities before 1967 near the northern corner of the 'Great Tower' of the Second Temple First Wall south of Shiloh's Area G, but not in the latter area, except for some reinforcement with cement of several existing stone courses.[29] As to the former claim, the Second Temple period city wall (Shiloh's Wall 309, E. Mazar's Wall 27) was indeed constructed just above the upper part of the 'Stepped Structure' (E. Mazar's Wall 20) and at places it joined the latter where it was well-preserved. This can be seen, for example, in the southern part of Area G, where the Second Temple period wall continues from Macalister's 'Great Tower' (Shiloh's Wall 310) until the

25 Cf. A. Mazar (2006) for discussion and references.

26 Cf. Cahill (2003), 56–66.

27 Cf. Finkelstein et al. (2007), 152.

28 Cf. Finkelstein et al. (2007), 152–155.

29 Cf. Shiloh (1984), 62, Fig. 27 shows the reconstruction at the corner of Walls 310 and 309.

upper part of the 'Stepped Stone Structure', until it joined the 'Northern Tower' (Shiloh's Wall 308).[30] In his Squares C 1–2, Shiloh excavated the top of the 'Stepped Structure', indicating that the wall was at least 5 m wide, though he did not reach its western face.[31] It was clear to him that this wide wall was the upper part of the 'Stepped Structure' and that it preceded Wall 309 of the Second Temple period. This was further clarified by E. Mazar's excavations: her Wall 20 (which is, in fact, the upper part of Shiloh's Wall 302) was exposed in sections along a total length of 22 m; its width was 5.8 m and its western face was preserved to a height of 1–1.8 m.[32] A 0.8 m thick layer of Iron I occupation debris abutted the western face of Wall 20 at the southern end of the excavation area. Both Kenyon and Shiloh found remains of an earth glacis dated to the Hellenistic period which covered the 'Stepped Structure' and abutted the Second Temple period wall, creating a support for this wall against erosion on the steep slope.[33] Finkelstein et al.'s suggestion that both, the upper part of the 'Stepped Structure' as well as the glacis, were part of a single building project of the Hasmonean era contradicts the facts: These are two different building projects, each with its own function. During 2006 and 2007, E. Mazar dismantled a part of the 'Northern Tower' of the Second Temple period (Shiloh's Wall 308) and found that it was built against the earlier Wall 20 of the Stepped Structure, and its upper part relates to the Second Temple period (Shiloh's Walls 309 equal to E. Mazar's Wall 27).[34] Wall 20 was founded on a rock

30 Cf. Shiloh (1984), 62, Fig. 27; also ibid., 55 Fig. 17; and the photos and drawing in E. Mazar (2009a), 24–25, 27–28; id. (2009b), 37, 58. On the photos one can see how Wall 309 (= E. Mazar's Wall 27), the city wall of the Second Temple period, is founded on the upper part of the 'Stepped Structure' (Shiloh's Wall 320 = E. Mazar's Wall 20). In the southern part of Area G, north of the Southern Tower, the Second Temple Wall 309, preserved 6–7 courses high, abuts the mantle wall of the 'Stepped Structure' which in this place was preserved until the present topsoil, at the same level as the 7th course of the Second Temple Wall. In E. Mazar's excavations the separation between Wall 20 (the upper part of the 'Stepped Structure') and Wall 27 (the Second Temple city wall) became clear; there is a slight difference in their orientation, though they were constructed one on top of the other.

31 Cf. Shiloh (1984), 55–56; Figs. 16–17. The upper part of Wall 302 corresponds to E. Mazar's Wall 20.

32 Cf. E. Mazar (2007b), 15, 21 Fig. 1, 24 Fig. 5; id. (2009b), 56. For isometric drawing cf. E. Mazar (2009a), 28; id. (2009b), 65.

33 Cf. Shiloh (1984), 30, 55 Fig. 17.

34 Cf. E. Mazar (2007a), 71–75, plan on p. 73 and photograph on p. 87, lowest end, and also id. (2009b), 72–79.

scarp and was clearly bonded with the upper courses of the 'Stepped Structure'. Wall 20 and the rock scarp on which it was founded was abutted on its eastern face by thick debris layers; the upper ones contained early Persian/Babylonian Period pottery and other finds, while the lower ones contained rich deposit of finds from the end of the Iron Age, among them several dozens of fragments of inscribed clay *bullae*. This layer appears to have been dumped from a building to the west, apparently the 'Large Stone Structure' which stood at higher elevation (see below). From a structural point of view, there is no doubt that Wall 20 and the 'Stepped Structure' are contemporary. Wall 20 cannot be dated to the Hellenistic period as argued by Finkelstein et al.

The 'Large Stone Structure'

The 'Large Stone Structure' is a term given by E. Mazar to a building which she excavated on the summit of the hill west and northwest of the 'Stepped Structure' (see Fig. 1).[35] Its walls are 2–5 m wide, its width was at least 30 m, and its length is unknown. Since only a few walls and segments of floors of this structure were preserved, and the area was much disturbed by Herodian and later activity, as well as by Duncan and Macalister's excavations, the deciphering of its architecture and date are not a simple task, as explained by E. Mazar in her preliminary publications. Finkelstein et al. present a wholesale denial of the excavator's interpretation of the plan, nature and date of this building. In the following, I will examine their arguments.

1. As explained in the previous section, Wall 20, the eastern wall of the 'Large Stone Structure', is also the upper part of the 'Stepped Structure' and thus cannot be later to this structure, as suggested by Finkelstein et al.
2. The earth layer found above bedrock and below the walls of the 'Large Stone Structure', contained Iron I pottery (as well as Middle Bronze and some Late Bronze sherds). Finkelstein et al. claim that this layer should not be considered when dating the construction of the building.[36] Indeed, in principle, pottery found in earth layers below foundations of buildings can provide just a *terminus post quem* for the construction of the build-

35 Cf. E. Mazar (2007a), and also id. (2009b), 43–65.

36 Cf. Finkelstein et al. (2007), 147–148.

ing above. It should be recalled, however, that establishing a foundation date for an excavated building is a difficult task in most cases. While finds found on floor surfaces provide a date for the final use of a building or to the longevity of its use, its foundation date is always enigmatic, and depends to a large extent on the finds in earlier occupation levels, foundation trenches, constructional fills, etc. Kenyon, for example, argued that "it is commonplace in British archaeology that a building is dated by the latest object in its building deposits", i.e. "foundation trenches, floor make-up and so on."[37] This argument certainly cannot be taken as a general rule, and there are numerous variations: each case should be judged independently. In our case, both Kenyon and Shiloh found that the latest pottery in the constructional fills of the 'Stepped Structure' was Iron Age I and E. Mazar found the same pottery assemblage in the earth layer below the 'Large Stone Structure'. This earth layer abutted the lower parts of the foundation stones of the building and fragmentary floors of the building were found just above this layer. If the 'Stepped Structure' and the 'Large Stone Structure' were constructed at a later date, we would expect to find at least a few post-Iron I sherds in these layers, yet, this is not the case. Since the two structures are bonded (as indicated by Wall 20) and the pottery found by three expeditions in all the constructional fills and layers below the foundations is homogeneous and uncontaminated, it is justified in my view to claim that the Iron I pottery is as close as it can be to the construction date of this large architectural complex.

3. Finkelstein et al. claim that the pottery assemblage in the above-mentioned earth layer is 'as late as 10th–9th century BCE'. However, as mentioned above, this pottery is identical to that found in the constructional layers and foundation 'terraces' of the 'Stepped Structure'[38] and it is similar to Iron Age I contexts at sites like Giloh (12th century BCE) and Shiloh Stratum V (11th century BCE).[39]

---

37 Kenyon (1964), 145.

38 Cf. Steiner (2001), 36–39, 43–48; Cahill (2003), 46–51.

39 The best parallels to the cooking pots from the earth layer are those from Shiloh: Finkelstein et al. (1993), Fig. 6.47:1–5 on p. 165 and Fig. 6.50:1–2 on p. 169 dated by the excavators to the 11th century BCE (ibid., 163, 168). The argument of Finkelstein et al. (2007), 148, that there was "at least one rim which seems to date to the late Iron I or early Iron IIA" was based on an impression from a single visit to the site and from a single photograph of rim sherds. However, the drawings published by E. Mazar (2007a), 50, include only Iron I sherds. Several cooking pot rims have a

4. Finkelstein et al. argue that Wall 107, the main wall of the 'Large Stone Structure', should be divided into an eastern part and a western part, each belonging to a separate structure.[40] Indeed, there is a slight difference in orientation between the eastern and western parts of the wall, yet, this could be due to topographic constraints. The gap between these two parts of the wall was caused by the foundations of a Second Temple vaulted underground room (see below). Although Wall 107 was badly preserved, and most of its southern face is missing, the construction technique of the eastern and western parts are similar, and both were founded above the same earth layer containing Iron I and earlier pottery. On its eastern end, Wall 107 creates a corner with Wall 20.[41] Since the latter served as the western wall of the 'Stepped Structure' (see above), as well as the eastern wall of the 'Large Stone Structure', the two must be contemporary and belong to the same architectural complex. Other walls which corner with Wall 107 (Walls 19, 21, 109) must be a part of the same complex as well.
5. Finkelstein et al. claim that the eastern part of Wall 107 should be dated to the Hellenistic period, since stones of this wall are seen in a photograph above the eastern wall of a vaulted chamber (Walls 69, 72, 71) of the Second Temple period.[42] This argument is flawed, since the chamber was clearly later than Wall 107. The picture was taken after the removal of plaster and other parts of the vaulted chamber. The builders of this Second Temple period underground room left large stones of Wall 107 in place wherever it was not necessary to remove them, utilized these stones as part of their new construction and covered them by plaster. Such plaster was never used in other parts of the 'Large Stone Structure'.
6. Finkelstein et al. claim that a ritual bath (*a miqweh*; Walls 61, 63, 66) should be regarded as belonging to the eastern part of the 'Large Stone Structure' and thus the two should be dated to the Second Temple period.[43] However, this ritual bath is one of sev-

---

molded rounded everted rim, such as E. Mazar (2007a), 50, nos. 12–14. Only a few rims have a concave depression along the outside of the rim such as E. Mazar (2007a), 50, no. 11. However, in all these cases, the rims are everted, indicating an early date in Iron Age I.

40 Cf. Finkelstein et al. (2007), 155–157.

41 Cf. E. Mazar (2007a), 59; plan and photo on p. 87, reproduced in Finkelstein et al. (2007), 158, Fig. 5.

42 Cf. Finkelstein et al. (2007), 154–157. For the photograph see E. Mazar (2007a), 74.

43 Cf. Finkelstein et al. (2007), 154–157.

eral such baths, cisterns and pools, dated to various periods (from the Second Temple period until the Islamic period) which penetrated into the excavation area from higher occupation levels. Finkelstein et al. claim that the bath was part of the 'Large Stone Structure' is based just on its orientation. Yet, even this claim is incorrect: the western wall of the bath (Wall 66) runs on an angle compared to Wall 67 of the 'Large Stone Structure' (unlike in their flawed reconstructed plan).[44] Like in the case of the vaulted chamber, the building technique of the ritual bath differs completely from that of the 'Large Stone Structure': while the former was constructed with plaster typical of Second Temple architecture, the latter was constructed of large, roughly cut stones without the use of plaster.

7. Finkelstein et al. claim that the Iron IIA pottery assemblage published by E. Mazar from Locus 47 in Room C of the 'Large Stone Structure' has no significance, since it was not found on a floor and since it contained also Iron IIB pottery.[45] However, although this pottery group was not on a floor, it was found as a homogeneous deposit, including a few restorable vessels and large sherds of typical Iron IIA horizon, located in a very small space which was enclosed on all four sides by massive walls: Walls 19 and 21 (both abutting Wall 107) and the subsidiary (though massive) Walls 22 and 24. These walls were preserved to a height of 1.2–1.4 m, and the pottery was found close to their lower parts. It is plausible that this pottery was slightly moved from its original place when Walls 22, 24 were added, yet, the group retained its nature as a homogeneous, partly restorable, assemblage.[46]
8. The continuation of Walls 19 and 21 of the 'Large Stone Structure' was found by Kenyon in her Area H1, just a few meters to

44 Cf. Finkelstein et al. (2007), 158–196, Figs. 5–6.

45 Cf. Finkelstein et al. (2007), 149. The assemblage was published in E. Mazar (2007a), 66, with the photo on the left on p. 63.

46 The argument of Finkelstein et al. (2007), 149, that the lower part of Locus 47 contained Iron IIB pottery is based on the basket number of a single bowl rim sherd: E. Mazar (2007a), 70 sherd no. 7. The authors argue that since this basket number is in the same range as the basket numbers of the Iron IIA cache, it must have originated from the same context. Yet, a basket number is just a technical device, and the sherd might have come from an upper level of this locus, regardless of the basket number. E. Mazar (2009a), 37; id. (2009b), 66, argues that the 'Large Stone Structure' continued to be in use until the end of the Iron Age. During its use, changes were made in the building, as evidenced by the additions of walls like Walls 22 and 24 on both sides of the Iron IIA pottery cache. Few Iron IIB sherds could penetrate to lower levels during such building operations.

the north of this building (her Walls 91 and 92, each 2 m wide with 1.3 m space between them; see Fig. 1).[47] Kenyon dated these walls to the 10th century BCE and Steiner writes that although no pottery was found on the plaster floor of the structure, there were 10th–9th centuries BCE sherds in the fill above the floor between the two walls. The pottery from this trench was never published in drawings, but we may suppose that Kenyon and Steiner's dating was based on red-slipped and hand burnished vessels, known to them as typical of the 10th century BCE.

9. Finkelstein et al. argue that Iron IIA pottery was found *below* architectural elements in Room B (west of Locus 47) and thus the 'Large Stone Structure' must be later than the Iron IIA. Yet, E. Mazar wrote that the Iron IIA pottery from this room was found below a bench and a stone pavement, which are attributed to later phases of the building.
10. E. Mazar claims that the 'Large Stone Structure' continued to be in use until the Babylonian conquest of Jerusalem. In fact, very few Iron II remains were found in the excavations, all in disturbed layers or between the collapse of the upper stones of the structure. The contexts of Iron II finds revealed by Macalister and Duncan and cited by Finkelstein et al. are unknown. As the authors admit, Herodian pottery sherds in the stone debris may have infiltrated either during Herodian activity in the area or by Macalister and Duncan's excavations.
11. Finally, Finkelstein et al. published two suggested reconstruction plans of the 'Large Stone Structure', which they attribute to the Second Temple period.[48] The architectural elements in this reconstructed plan belong, in fact, to three different periods: the Iron Age, the Second Temple and the Byzantine period. As explained above, Walls 20 and 107 must be Iron I or Iron IIA, at the latest. Walls 21 and 19 are perhaps an Iron II addition. The ritual bath (Walls 61, 63, 66) is from the Second Temple period, and the southern wall termed in the drawing as *Inner Wall* is Macalister's 'Davidic Wall'; it was exposed by E. Mazar during 2008 and dated to the Byzantine period. Thus, this reconstructed plan should be dismissed.

---

47 Cf. Kenyon (1974), 115 and the photograph on p. 37; Steiner (2001), 48–49; reconstruction in E. Mazar (2007b), 24 Fig. 5, right side. See Fig. 1, walls to the right of Walls 19, 21, 23 and 24.

48 See n. 39 above.

In light of the above, the archaeological arguments presented by Finkelstein et al. are unacceptable. The 'Stepped Structure' and 'Large Stone Structure' should be seen as one large and substantial architectural complex. The former must be explained as a support structure of the latter, which stood on the summit of the ridge to the west, on the narrowest point of the City of David spur, which was naturally bounded by an almost vertical rock cliff on the east. Cahill claimed that the construction date of the 'Stepped Structure' must have been either contemporary or shortly later than the pottery found in its substructure, which is clearly Iron Age I in date, while Kenyon, Shiloh and Steiner suggested a 10th century BCE date for its construction.[49] The same argumentation is valid for the 'Large Stone Structure'.

The magnitude and uniqueness of the combined 'Stepped Structure' and the 'Large Stone Structure' are unparalleled anywhere in the Levant between the 12th and early 9th centuries BCE. Shiloh suggested that the Stepped Structure was intended "to serve as a substructure for the upper structure of the citadel of the City of David, built there over the remains of the Jebusite citadel".[50] E. Mazar suggested that the Canaanite citadel was further to the south (in an unexcavated area), and that the 'Stepped Structure' and 'Large Stone Structure' complex should be interpreted as David's palace, i.e. were constructed during the early 10th century BCE. I suggested to identify the entire complex with *Metsudat Zion* – "the fortress of Zion" – mentioned in the biblical description of David's conquest of Jerusalem. David is said to have changed the name of this citadel to *`Ir David,* "the city of David" (2 Sam. 5:7, 9).[51] This identification is suggested with due caution, since it is based on two rather shaky pillars: the one is the possible Iron Age I construction date of the entire complex. The other is the above mentioned biblical text, the historicity of which may be questioned. We should also note that the Jebusites, the supposed builders of this citadel, are unknown to us from any sources outside the bible, and Archaeology did not provide any particular characteristics of such an independent ethnic group.[52] Finkelstein et al. conclude their paper with

49 Cf. Cahill (2003), followed by A. Mazar (2006).

50 Cf. Shiloh (1984), 17.

51 Cf. A. Mazar (2006), 265.

52 At Giloh, a small Iron I site 7 km southwest of the City of David, I uncovered the remains of a massive square structure dated to the Iron Age I (probably 12th century BCE) which I thought to be a foundation of a tower (Mazar 1990b). The massive structure and its building technique recalls to some extent the large substructure of the 'Stepped Structure'. I identified the site as 'early Israelite' while Ahlström (1984) suggested to identify it as a 'Jebusite' site. The pottery from Giloh resembles the as-

an admonition against such straightforward identifications of structures mentioned in biblical texts which were written much later. Yet, as mentioned in the beginning of this paper, the historicity of the biblical narratives and the relationship between text and Archaeology are subject of continuous debate. There is no absolute truth in this field and we must accommodate pluralism and a wide spectrum of views. I agree with Finkelstein that objective archaeological criteria are essential for examining biblical narratives whenever this is possible. Many scholars argue that the so-called 'Deuteronomistic History', as well as other biblical sources, preserved old memories and knowledge of the past to a certain degree, although these could have been distorted during transmission and editing processes, as noted in the beginning of this paper. In the case of Jerusalem, the preservation and transmission of historical memories during hundreds of years is a feasible possibility, since the city did not suffer from any turmoil between the 10th and 7th centuries BCE. Old inscriptions and other written texts, as well as oral transmission of information, could be preserved over centuries. Finkelstein argued that David's biography as a young leader of a warrior gang is historical, since, in his view, the narrative fits the archaeological background relating to the late Iron I. However, he denies David's biography as a king, since, again in his view, it contradicts the archaeological picture of the 10th century BCE in general, and that of Jerusalem in particular.[53] However, if the Iron Age I or Iron IIA date of the 'citadel complex' (the 'Stepped Structure' and the 'Large Stone Structure') is accepted, then the archaeological profile of Jerusalem before or during the presumed time of David would be very different from that presented by Finkelstein and Ussishkin. Such a profile shows that Jerusalem was a rather small town with a mighty citadel, which could have been a center of a substantial regional polity.[54]

semblage found in the substructure of the 'Stepped Structure' and 'Large Stone Building' in the City of David.

53 Cf. Finkelstein (2003), 89, 91.

54 Cf. Finkelstein (2003); Ussishkin (2003) against A. Mazar (2007a), 152–154.

Additional Discoveries in the City of David

Iron IIA pottery was found in all of the areas excavated by Shiloh on the eastern slope of the City of David.[55] According to the 'Modified Conventional Chronology' which I and many others utilize this pottery may be dated to the 10th–9th centuries BCE, while a more precise distinction needs further research.[56] The fact that almost no Iron IIA architecture was preserved on the eastern slope of the City of David should probably be explained as a result of erosion, the continued use of stone structures over hundreds of years, the 'robbing' of older building materials by later builders, and rock quarrying, all of which caused a distortion of the archaeological picture in Jerusalem. The lack of Late Bronze structures should be explained along the same line, and clearly stands in contrast to the information gained from the Amarna letters from Jerusalem.[57]

Discoveries made by Reich and Shukron in their excavation at the Gihon spring during the last fifteen years include massive structures around and west of the spring that were probably part of a large fortified citadel, a large quarried space in the rock dubbed a 'pool', and the cut of the original (upper level) tunnel known as part of 'Warren's Shaft'.[58] These components were dated by the excavators to the Middle Bronze Age. The fortifications are among the mightiest ever found in any Bronze or Iron Age site in the southern Levant, and thus they are evidence for a central powerful authority and the outstanding status of Jerusalem during the Middle Bronze Age. This special status might have been retained in the local memory until the end of the second millennium BCE and later, and perhaps is one of the main reasons for the choice of Jerusalem as a capital of the newly established kingdom during the Iron Age. We have to ask whether this magnificent architectural system went out of use by the end of the Middle Bronze Age. New discoveries, made in 2008 by Reich and Shukron, have shown that

---

55 For Iron IIA pottery from Shiloh's excavation cf. de Groot/Ariel (2000), 35–42, 93–94, 113–121, Figs. 11–15. The pottery from Area E will be published in a forthcoming volume of 'Qedem' submitted by A. de Groot and H. Greenberg. Iron IIA pottery from Area G was published by Cahill (2003), 59–62.

56 Cf. A. Mazar (2005). Herzog/Singer-Avitz (2004) suggested inner division of the period into an early and late sub-periods, dated to the 10th and 9th centuries BCE accordingly. Yet, the attribution of the assemblage from Jerusalem to one of these periods is still unclear. The substantial finds from this period in Jerusalem excludes their suggestion that Judah emerged as a state in the southern Shephelah and the northern Negev rather than in the hill country.

57 Cf. Na'aman (1996); Millard (2008).

58 Cf. Reich/Shukron (2008).

the two east–west massive walls (about 5 m wide) of the 'tower' west of the Gihon spring continued westwards up the slope until they joined the bedrock scarp close to the horizontal tunnel of Warren's Shaft. The northernmost of these two walls, constructed of incredibly large stones, still stands to a height of over 8 m![59] During the Iron Age II, this system was well-known, as can be learned from three features: 1. Late Iron Age II walls abut walls of the Middle Bronze fortification system at several points. 2. During the Iron Age IIA (9th century according to the excavators), the large rock-cut area (so called 'pool') south of the abovementioned tower was well-known, since it was entirely filled with earth and large stones that served as a constructional fill for an Iron Age II building. This fill contained over 180 unepigraphic seal impressions on bullae dated to the 9th century BCE, as well as thousands of fish bones.[60] 3. The deepening of the 'Warren's Shaft' system and the discovery of the natural karstic shaft occurred, according to Reich and Shukron, sometime during the Iron Age II, but before Hezekiah's tunnel was cut in the 8th century BCE. This indicates that the original upper part of the system was known and probably in use since the Middle Bronze Age through the 9th century BCE.[61] It thus may be suggested that the immense Middle Bronze fortifications and 'pool' were also in continuous use until the Iron Age II, although there is no actual ceramic or other direct proof for this longevity, perhaps due to continued cleaning and renovations of this area throughout this long period.

As to the Temple Mount, if it was indeed part of the city during the time of Solomon, it more than doubled the area of Jerusalem to ca. 12 ha. This new area could provide plenty of space for public buildings as those described in the biblical texts: Temple and palace, and perhaps elite residencies. Yet, the answer to the question whether such buildings indeed stood in Jerusalem during the 10th century BCE depends on one's approach to the biblical text, as no direct archaeological evidence is available. In an earlier discussion of this issue, I asked the question: if Solomon did not built a temple in Jerusalem, who was responsible for the construction of the Jerusalem temple later in the Iron Age?[62] The architectural parallels between the biblical description of the Jerusalem temple to north Syrian temples, like those at Tel Taynat and

---

59 I thank R. Reich and E. Shukron for showing me their recent discoveries.

60 Cf. Reich/Shukron/Lernau (2007).

61 This was already suggested by Cahill (2003). Recall that Kenyon suggested such a continuity in relation to the much scantier Middle Bronze wall which she found higher on the slope.

62 Cf. A. Mazar (2007a), 154; Liverani (2005), 329, who is skeptical concerning the validity of the biblical description, yet, does not exclude a modest Solomonic temple.

`Ain Dara, are telling, and show that the biblical description is rooted in architectural traditions well-known in the Levant before the Assyrian invasions and thus could not be a much later innovation. Notwithstanding this evidence, it is clear that the biblical description of the opulence and grandeur of the temple must reflect later legendary exaggerations. The description of Solomon's palace is too schematic. Attempts to reconstruct it as a Syrian *Bit Hilani* complex or as an Achaemenid *Apadana* is based on insufficient evidence.[63]

Recent Discoveries

Several additional important discoveries made during recent years are related to our subject.

Khirbet Qeiyafa

This 2.5 ha site located 2 km east of Azekah, north of the Elah Valley, became known in 2008 when Garfinkel and Saar discovered a single period fortified settlement there, dated by pottery to the early part of the Iron Age IIA.[64] Four ^{14}C samples provided a date in the first half of the 10th century BCE (in the 1 sigma range), confirming the conventional Iron Age chronology of the pottery found in this site. The town plan of this site consists of a massive stone casemate wall with a four chamber gate. Houses were attached to the wall, using casemate rooms as the inner rooms of the house; a circular street runs parallel to the wall beyond this outer belt of houses. This is the earliest certainly dated example of a town plan which will become characteristic to Judah and Israel in the later Iron Age II (e.g., at Tell en-Nasbeh, Tell Beit Mirsim, Beth Shemesh and Tel Beer Sheba). The magnitude of the fortifications is unrivalled in the later Judean towns and clearly indicates a central administration that enabled such immense public works and technological knowledge. Khirbet Qeiyafa was probably not the only one of its kind. At Khirbet Dawara north of Jerusalem, a fortified site was dated to the same time.[65] At Tell Beit Mirsim, Albright dated the foundation of the casemate city wall to Stratum B3 of the Iron IIA and this date

---

63 For the former cf. Ussishkin (1973), for the latter Liverani (2005), 327–328.

64 Cf. Garfinkel/Saar (2008) [see postscript at the end of the paper].

65 Cf. Finkelstein (1990).

seems now feasible due to the resemblance to Khirbet Qeiyafa.[66] At Beth Shemesh, a similar fortification system was dated by both Wright as well as by Bunimovitz and Lederman to the Iron IIA, and more specifically to the 10th century BCE.[67]

A still unpublished ostracon found at Khirbet Qeyiafa includes about 50 signs written in late Proto-Canaanite script; preliminary publications indicate that it was written in Hebrew, and if this will be confirmed, it would be the earliest known Hebrew inscription to date. Khirbet Qeiyafa is located in the heartland of the inner Shephelah. Na'aman's suggestion that it was an eastern border city of Gath[68] is not feasible, since the pottery differs from that of Gath.[69] The town plan and casemate walls are unknown in Philistia and Hebrew was probably not spoken in Philistia. It thus appears that Khirbet Qeiyafa represents a still largely unknown early 10th century BCE Israelite urban system, which may be related to the rise of the United Monarchy. This discovery may support my assumption that Ekron (Tel Miqne) diminished during the 10th century BCE due to the United Monarchy's domination of the northern Shephelah and the Sorek Valley.[70]

The Copper Industry at Feinan and the Rise of Edom

Excavations and surveys directed by T. Levy at Khirbet en-Naḥas in the Feinan region east of Wadi Arabah in Jordan have revealed an outstanding, large scale copper mining industry dated by ^{14}C dates to the 10th–9th centuries BCE, that perhaps began somewhat earlier. At Khirbet en-Naḥas, architectural remains include a large citadel and administrative buildings, dated by the excavators to the 10th century BCE.[71] Levy claimed that these new discoveries shed light on the emergence of Edom as a centralized polity during this time. It is still impossible to say with confidence what the ethnic affiliation of the initiators of this industry was and how to define the economic system in which they operated. Biblical references to Edom in the David and Solomon narratives may be regarded as later recollections of an outstanding economic and perhaps also political power in this area in the 10th–9th centuries

66 Cf. Albright (1943), 11, 16–17, Fig. 1 and Plate 2.

67 Cf. Wright (1939), 23–24; Bunimovitz/Lederman (2001).

68 Cf. Na'aman (2008).

69 I thank A. Maeir and Y. Garfinkel for this information.

70 Cf. A. Mazar (2003), 93.

71 Cf. Levy et al. (2004); Levy/Najjar (2006); Levy et al. (2008). The latter is a response to the unjustified harsh criticism in Finkelstein (2005).

BCE. The relationship of this 'lower Edom' to the development of the kingdom of Edom on the Edomite plateau (centered at Buseirah) remains an enigmatic question at this stage of research, and only additional excavations at Buseirah and other sites on the plateau may resolve this question.

Conclusions

How should we envisage the United Monarchy in actual historic terms? Various answers are given to this question in recent scholarly literature, as explained in the beginning of this paper. The fluid situation in current scholarship regarding the United Monarchy should be noted. New discoveries of the last few years mentioned in this paper and more to come may change future historical interpretations of this period. Since my views on the issue were recently published, it will suffice to cite those views, with slight omissions.

> "It is certain that much of the biblical narrative concerning David and Solomon is mere fiction and embellishment written by later authors. Nonetheless, the total deconstruction of the United Monarchy and the devaluation of Judah as a state in the ninth century [...] is based, in my view, on unacceptable interpretations of the available data.
>
> In evaluating the historicity of the United Monarchy, one should bear in mind that historical development is not linear, and history cannot be written on the basis of socio-economic or environmental-ecological determinism alone. The role of the individual personality in history should be taken into account, particularly when dealing with historical phenomena related to figures like David and Solomon [...]
>
> Leaders with exceptional charisma could have created short-lived states with significant military and political power, and territorial expansion. I would compare the potential achievements of David to those of an earlier hill country leader, namely Lab'ayu, the *habiru* leader from Shechem who managed during the fourteenth century to rule a vast territory of the central hill country, and threatened cities like Megiddo in the north and Gezer in the south, despite the overrule of Canaan by the Egyptian New Kingdom. [Incidentally, it should be noted that archaeology has revealed no significant finds from 14th century Shechem, as it did not provide any information on Abdi Heppa's Jerusalem.] David can be envisioned as a ruler similar to Lab'ayu, except that he operated in a time free of intervention by the Egyptians or any other foreign power, and when the Canaanite cities were in decline. In such an environment, a talented and charismatic leader, politically astute, and in control of a small yet effective military power, may have taken hold of large parts of a small country like the Land of Israel and controlled diverse population groups under his regime from his stronghold in Jerusalem, which can be identified archaeologically. Such

a regime does not necessitate a particularly large and populated capital city. David's Jerusalem can be compared to a medieval Burg, surrounded by a medium-sized town, and yet it could well be the centre of a meaningful polity. The only power that stood in David's way consisted of the Philistine cities, which, as archaeology tells us, were large and fortified urban centres during this time. Indeed, the biblical historiographer excludes them from David's conquered territories. Short-lived achievements like those of David may be beyond what the tools of archaeology are capable of grasping [...]

Great changes took place in the material culture in many parts of the country during the tenth century (according to the conventional chronology). This new material culture must reflect changes in the social, political and economic matrix, and perhaps also in the self-identity of many population groups. It remains to ask to what extent these changes occured in relation to the emergence of the Israelite state and its neighbours.

The United Monarchy can be described as a state in an early stage of evolution, far from the rich and widely expanding state portrayed in the biblical narrative. Shoshenq's invasion of the Jerusalem area probably came in opposition to the growing weight of this state.

The mentioning of *bytdwd* ('the House of David', as the name of the Judean kingdom in the Aramean stele from Tel Dan, possibly erected by Hazael) indicates that approximately a century and a half after his reign, David was recognized throughout the region as the founder of the dynasty that ruled Judah. His role in Israelite ideology and historiography is echoed in the place he played in later Judean common memory [...]

Rather than accepting a revisionist theory that compels us to discard an entire library of scholarly work, the evidence brought here calls for balanced evaluation of the biblical text, taking into account that the text might have preserved valuable historical information based on early written documents and oral traditions that retained long-living common memory. These early traditions were cast in the mold of literature, legend, and epic, and were inserted to the later Israelite historiographic narrative which is thickly veiled in theology and ideology. Yet many of these traditions contain kernels of historical truth, and some of them can be examined archaeologically, as demonstrated in this chapter. By ridding the texts of their literary, theological and ideological layers and using the archaeological data critically, the Hebrew Bible may be evaluated as a source for the extraction of historical data, yet this has to be evaluated as much as possible in light of external evidence. The results may prevent us—if I may use the colloquialism—from throwing the baby out with the bathwater."[72]

72 Citation from A. Mazar (2007a), 164–166.

Bibliography

Ahlström, G.W. (1984), Giloh: A Judahite or Canaanite Settlement?, IEJ 34, 170–172.

– (1993), The History of Ancient Palestine from the Palaeolithic Period to Alexander's Conquest, JSOT.S 146, Sheffield.

Albright, W.F. (1943), The Excavations at Tell Beit Mirsim 3: The Iron Age, AASOR, 21–22.

Ben-Tor, A. (2000), Hazor and Chronology of Northern Israel: A Reply to Israel Finkelstein, BASOR 317, 9–15.

Bunimovitz, S./Lederman, Z. (2001), The Iron Age Fortifications of Tel Beth Shemesh: A 1990–2000 Perspective, IEJ 51, 121–147.

Cahill, J.M. (2003), Jerusalem at the Time of the United Monarchy: The Archaeological Evidence, in: A.G. Vaughn/A.E. Killebrew (eds.), Jerusalem in Bible and Archaeology: The First Temple Period, SBL Symposium Series No. 18, Atlanta, 13–80.

Davies, P.R. (1992), In Search of 'Ancient Israel', JSOT.S 148, Sheffield.

De Groot, A./Ariel, D.T. (2000), Ceramic Report, in: D.T. Ariel (ed.), Excavations at the City of David 1978–1985: Directed by J. Shiloh, vol. V: Extramural Areas, Qedem 40, Jerusalem, 91–154.

Dever, W.G. (1997), Archaeology and the "Age of Solomon": A Case Study in Archaeology and Historiography, in: L.K. Handy (ed.), The Age of Solomon: Scholarship at the Turn of the Millennium, Studies in the History and the Culture of the Ancient Near East, vol. 11, Leiden, 217–251.

– (2001), What Did the Biblical Writers Know and When Did They Know It? What Archaeology Can Tell Us about the Reality of Ancient Israel, Michigan.

Finkelstein, I. (1990), Excavations at Khirbet ed-Dawwara: An Iron Age Site Northeast of Jerusalem, Tel Aviv 17, 163–209.

– (1996), The Archaeology of the United Monarchy: An Alternative View, Levant 28, 177–187.

– (1999), State Formation in Israel and Judah: A Contrast in Context, A Contrast in Trajectory, Near Eastern Archaeology 62, 35–52.

– (2003), The Rise of Jerusalem and Judah: The Missing Link, in: A.G. Vaughn/A.E. Killebrew (eds.), Jerusalem in the Bible and Archaeology: The First Temple Period, SBL Symposium Series No. 18, Atlanta, 81–102.

– (2005), Khirbat en-Naḥas, Edom and Biblical History, Tel Aviv 32, 119–125.

– (2007), King Solomon's Golden Age? History or Myth?, in: B.B. Schmidt (ed.), The Quest for the Historical Israel: Debating Archaeology and the History of Early Israel, ABSt 17, Atlanta, 107–116.

– /Bunimovitz, S./Lederman, Z. (1993), Shiloh: The Archaeology of a Biblical Site, Monograph Series of the Institute of Archaeology Tel Aviv University, Tel Aviv.

– /Silberman, N.A. (2006), David and Solomon: In Search of the Bible Sacred Kings and the Roots of Western Tradition, New York.

– /Herzog, Z./Singer-Avitz, L./ Ussishkin, D. (2007), Has King David's Palace in Jerusalem Been Found? Tel Aviv 34, 142–164.

Garfinkel, Y./Ganor, S. (2008), Notes and News: Khirbet Qeiyafa, 2007–2008, IEJ 58, 244–248.

Grant, E./Wright, G.E. (1939), Ain Shems Excavations (Palestine): Part V (Text), Biblical and Kindered Studies No. 8, Haverford.

Halpern, B. (1988), The First Historians: The Hebrew Bible and History, San Francisco.

– (2001), David's Secret Demons: Messiah, Murderer, Traitor, King, Grand Rapids.

Handy, L.K. (1997, ed.), The Age of Solomon: Scholarship at the Turn of the Millennium, Studies in the History and the Culture of the Ancient Near East, vol. 11, Leiden.

Herzog, Z./Singer-Avitz, L. (2004), Redefining the Centre: The Emergence of State in Judah, Tel Aviv 31, 209–244.

Jamieson-Drake, D.W. (1991), Scribes and Schools in Monarchic Judah: A Socio-Archeological Approach, JSOT.S 109, Sheffield.

Joffe, A.H. 2002, The Rise of Secondary States in the Iron Age Levant, JESHO 45, 425–467.

Kenyon, K.M. (1964), Megiddo, Hazor, Samaria and Chronology, BIAUL 4, 143–156.

– (1974), Digging up Jerusalem, London.

Kitchen, K.A. (1997), Sheba and Arabia, in: L.K. Handy (ed.), The Age of Solomon: Scholarship at the Turn of the Millennium, Studies in the History and the Culture of the Ancient Near East, vol. 11, Leiden, 127–153.

Knauf, E.A. (1997), Le roi est mort, vive le roi! A Biblical Argument for the Historicity of Solomon, in: L.K. Handy (ed.), The Age of Solomon: Scholarship at the Turn of the Millennium, Studies in the History and the Culture of the Ancient Near East, vol. 11, Leiden, 81–95.

Lemaire, A. (1999), The United Monarchy: Saul, David and Solomon, in: H. Shanks (ed.), Ancient Israel: From Abraham to the Roman Destruction of the Temple, 2nd edition, Washington, 91–128.

Levy, T.E./Adams, R.B./Najjar, M./Hauptmann, A./Anderson, J.D./Brandl, B./Robinson, M.A./Higham, T. (2004), Reassessing the Chronology of Biblical Edom: New Excavations and [14]C Dates from Khirbet en-Naḥas (Jordan), Antiquity 78, 865–879.

– /Najjar, M.N. (2006), Some Thoughts on Khirbet en-Naḥas, Edom, Biblical History and Anthropology – A Response to Israel Finkelstein, Tel Aviv 33, 3–17.

– /Higham, T./Bronk Ramsey, C./Smith, N.G./Ben-Yosef, E./Robinson, M./Münger, S./Knabb, K./Schulze, J.P./Najjar, M./Tauxe, L. (2008), High-Precision Radiocarbon Dating and Historical Biblical Archaeology in Southern Jordan, Proceedings of the National Academy of Sciences 105/43, 16460–16465.

Liverani, M. (2005), Israel's History and the History of Israel, London.

Macalister, R.A./Duncan, J.G. (1926), Excavations on the Hill of Ophel, Jerusalem 1923–1925, Annual of the Palestine Exploration Fund 4, London.

Masters, D.M. (2001), State Formation Theory and the Kingdom of Ancient Israel, JNES 60, 117–131.

Mazar, A. (1990a), Archaeology of the Land of the Bible, 10,000–586 B.C.E., New York.

– (1990b) Iron Age I and II Towers at Giloh and the Israelite Settlement, IEJ 40, 77–101.

– (1997), Iron Age Chronology: A Reply to I. Finkelstein, Levant 29, 157–167.

– (2003), Remarks on Biblical Traditions and Archaeological Evidence concerning Early Israel, in: W.G. Dever/S. Gitin (eds.), Symbiosis, Symbolism, and the Power of the Past: Canaan, Ancient Israel, and Their Neighbors from the Late Bronze Age through Roman Palestina: Proceedings of the Centennial Symposium W.F. Albright Institute of Archaeological Research and American Schools of Oriental Research: Jerusalem, May 29–31, 2000, Winona Lake, 85–98.

– (2005), The Debate over the Chronology of the Iron Age in the Southern Levant: Its History, the Current Situation, and a Suggested Resolution, in: T.E. Levy/T. Higham (eds.), The Bible and Radiocarbon Dating: Archaeology, Text and Science, London, 15–30.

– (2006), Jerusalem in the 10th Century B.C.E.: The Glass Half Full, in: Y. Amit/E. Ben Zvi/I. Finkelstein/O. Lipschits (eds.), Essays on Ancient Israel in Its Near Eastern Context: A Tribute to Nadav Na'aman, Winona Lake, 255–272.

– (2007a), The Spade and the Text: The Interaction between Archaeology and Israelite History Relating to the Tenth–Ninth Centuries BCE, in: H.G.M. Williamson (ed.), Understanding the History of An-

cient Israel, Proceedings of the British Academy 143, Oxford/New York, 143–171.
– (2007b), The Search for David and Solomon: An Archaeological Perspective, in: B.B. Schmidt (ed.), The Quest for the Historical Israel: Debating Archaeology and the History of Early Israel, ABSt 17, Atlanta, 117–140.
– (2008), From 1200 to 850 B.C.E.: Remarks on Some Selected Archaeological Issues, in: L.L. Grabbe (ed.), Israel in Transition: From Late Bronze II to Iron IIa (c. 1250–850 B.C.E.): Vol. 1: The Archaeology, New York/London, 86–121.
– /Bronk Ramsey, C. (2008), ^{14}C Dates and the Iron Age Chronology of Israel: A Response, Radiocarbon 50, 159–180.
Mazar, E. (2007a), Preliminary Report on the City of David Excavations 2005 at the Visitors Center Area, Jerusalem.
– (2007b), Excavations at the City of David (2006–2007), in: E. Baruch/ A. Levy-Reifer/A. Faust (eds.), New Studies on Jerusalem XIII, Ramat-Gan, 7–26 (in Hebrew).
– (2008), The 'Stepped Stone Structure' in the City of David in Light of the New Excavations in Area G, in: E. Baruch/A. Levy-Reifer/A. Faust (eds.), New Studies on Jerusalem XIV, Ramat-Gan, 25–52 (in Hebrew).
– (2009a), The Wall that Nehemiah Built, BArR 35/2, 24–33.
– (2009b), The Palace of King David: Excavations at the Summit of the City of David, Preliminary Report of Seasons 2005–2007, Jerusalem.
Meyers, C. (1998), Kinship and Kingship: The Early Monarchy, in: M.D. Coogan (ed.), The Oxford History of the Biblical World, New York/Oxford, 221–272.
Millard, A.R. (1997), King Solomon in His Ancient Context, in: L.K. Handy (ed.), The Age of Solomon: Scholarship at the Turn of the Millennium, Studies in the History and the Culture of the Ancient Near East, vol. 11, Leiden, 30–53.
– (2008), David and Solomon's Jerusalem: Do the Bible and Archaeology Disagree?, in: D.I. Block (ed.), Israel: Ancient Kingdom or Late Invention?, Nashville, 185–200.
Miller, J.M. (1997), Separating the Solomon of History from the Solomon of Legend, in: L.K. Handy (ed.), The Age of Solomon: Scholarship at the Turn of the Millennium, Studies in the History and the Culture of the Ancient Near East, vol. 11, Leiden, 1–24.
– /Hayes, J.H. (1986), A History of Ancient Israel and Judah, Philadelphia.
Na'aman, N. (1992), Canaanite Jerusalem and its Central Hill Country Neighbours in the Second Millennium B.C.E., UF 24, 275–291.

– (1996), The Contribution of the Amarna Letters to the Debate on Jerusalem's Political Position in the Tenth Century B.C.E., BASOR 304, 17–27.
– (1997), Sources and Composition in the History of Solomon, in: L.K. Handy (ed.), The Age of Solomon: Scholarship in the Turn of the Millennium, Studies in the History and the Culture of the Ancient Near East, vol. 11, Leiden, 57–80.
– (2002), The Past That Shapes the Present: The Creation of Biblical Historiography in the Late First Temple Period and After the Downfall, Jerusalem (in Hebrew).
– (2007), The Northern Kingdom in the Late 10th–9th Centuries BCE, in: H.G.M. Williamson (ed.), Understanding the History of Ancient Israel, Proceedings of the British Academy 143, Oxford, 399–418.
– (2008), In Search of the Ancient Name of Khirbet Qeiyafa, Journal of Hebrew Scriptures 8, art. 21, 1–8.
Niemann H.M. (1997), The Socio-Political Shadow Cast by the Biblical Solomon, in: L.K. Handy (ed.), The Age of Solomon: Scholarship at the Turn of the Millennium, Studies in the History and the Culture of the Ancient Near East, vol. 11, Leiden, 252–299.
Rainey, A.F. (2006), Chapters 1–16, in: A.F. Rainey/R.S. Notley (eds.), The Sacred Bridge: Carta's Atlas of the Biblical World, Jerusalem.
Reich, R./Shukron, E./Lernau, O. (2007), Recent Discoveries in the City of David, Jerusalem, IEJ 57, 153–169.
– /Shukron, E. (2008), Jerusalem, (section 2), in: E. Stern, (ed.), The New Encyclopedia of Archaeological Excavations in the Holy Land, vol. 5, Jerusalem, 1801–1807.
Sharon, I./Gilboa, A./Jull, T.A.J./Boaretto, E. (2007), Report on the First Stage of the Iron Age Dating Project in Israel: Supporting A Low Chronology, Radiocarbon 49, 1–46.
– /Gilboa, A./Boaretto, E. (2008), The Iron Age Chronology of the Levant: The State-of-Research at the ^{14}C Project, Spring 2006, in: L.L. Grabbe (ed.), Israel in Transition: From Late Bronze II to Iron IIa (c. 1250–850 B.C.E.): Volume 1: The Archaeology, New York/London, 177–192.
Shiloh, Y. (1984), Excavations at the City of David: Vol. I: 1978–1982: Interim Report of the First Five Seasons, Qedem 19, Jerusalem.
Stager, L.E. (2003), The Patrimonial Kingdom of Solomon, in: W.G. Dever/S. Gitin (eds.), Symbiosis, Symbolism, and the Power of the Past: Canaan, Ancient Israel, and Their Neighbors from the Late Bronze Age through Roman Palestina: Proceedings of the Centennial Symposium W.F. Albright Institute of Archaeological Research and Ameri-

can Schools of Oriental Research: Jerusalem, May 29–31, 2000, Winona Lake, 63–74.

Steiner, M.L. (2001), Excavations by Kathleen M. Kenyon in Jerusalem 1961–1967: Vol. III: The Settlement in the Bronze and Iron Ages, Sheffield.

Ussishkin, D. (1973), King Solomon's Palaces, BA 36, 78–105.

– (2003), Solomon's Jerusalem: The Text and the Facts on the Ground, in: A.G. Vaughn/A.E. Killebrew (eds.), Jerusalem in the Bible and Archaeology: The First Temple Period, SBL Symposium Series No. 18, Atlanta, 103–116.

Wightman, G.J., (1990), The Myth of Solomon, BASOR 277/278, 5–22.

Williamson, H.G.M. (ed.), (2007), Understanding the History of Ancient Israel, Proceedings of the British Academy 143, Oxford/New York.

Yadin, Y. (1972), Hazor: The Head of All those Kingdoms: Joshua II:10: With a Chapter on Israelite Megiddo, London.

Post Script

Since the submission of this paper the following publications on Khirbet Qeiyafa appeared:

Garfinkel, Y./Ganor, S. (2009), Khirbet Qeiyafa Volume I: Excavation Report 2007–2008. Jerusalem.

Misgav, H./Garfinkel, Y./Ganor, S. (2009), The Ostracon, in: Garfinkel, Y./Ganor, S. (eds.), Khirbet Qeiyafa Volume I: Excavation Report 2007–2008, Jerusalem, 243–257.

Misgav, H./Garfinkel, Y./Ganor, S. (2009), The Khirbet Qeiyafa Ostracon, in: Amit, D./Stiebel, G./Peleg-Barkat, O. (eds.), New Studies in the Archaeology of Jerusalem and its Region, Jerusalem, 111–123 (in Hebrew, followed by responses from A. Yardeni, A. Demsky and S. Ahituv).

Rollston, C. (2009) http://www.rollstonepigraphy.com/?p=56 .

Yardeni, A. (2009), Further Observations on the Ostracon, in: Garfinkel, Y./Ganor, S. (eds.), Khirbet Qeiyafa Volume I: Excavation Report 2007–2008, Jerusalem, 259–260.

Solomon and the United Monarchy: Some Textual Evidence*

ERHARD BLUM

Methodological Considerations

King Solomon's fairy-tale like empire, representing the Golden Age of Israelite history, has long been gone – not only since the archaeological debate about Megiddo IV or the dimensions of Tenth-Century-Jerusalem.

It suffices to recollect the commentary on Kings by Martin Noth,[1] written in the sixties of the last century. According to Noth, the present story of Solomon in 1 Kings 3–11 was mainly formed by his Deuteronomist. This exilic author composed or reworked *inter alia* Solomon's dream at Gibeon (1 Kings 3), the dealings with Hiram of Tyros in 5:15–26, Solomon's great prayer at the inauguration of the temple in 1 Kings 8, the second theophany in 1 Kings 9, and – of course – the report of Solomon's great sin, his violation of the First commandment by building idolatrous cult places for his foreign wives (11:1–13). The deuteronomistic dynastic oracle for Jeroboam ben Nebat, given by the prophet Ahija the Shilonite, finally marks the end of the United Kingdom (11:29–39).

It is true that Noth's Deuteronomist used some pre-exilic 'collection'[2] of Solomon-traditions (perhaps the ספר דברי שלמה mentioned in 11:41[3]), but that does not bring us back to the age of Solomon himself. The tales about Solomon's marvellous wisdom (1 Kings 3; 10), for instance, are mainly haggadic. The same holds true for the descriptions of his extraordinary wealth. Most of the remaining materials are lists or

---

* I dedicate this study to Walter Dietrich, *collegae dilectissimo sexaginta et quinque annorum*, the eminent scholar of the literature and the history of the early monarchy.

1 Cf. Noth (1968).

2 Noth (1968), 148: "eine vordeuteronomistische Zusammenfassung der Salomogeschichte".

3 Cf. Noth (1968), 262–263; id. (1943), 66–67, and for a more recent discussion Dietrich (1997), 224–226 (with bibl.).

short notes, reminiscent of the style of archival records. However, that is no guarantee for their being an old tradition. For example, the description of Solomon's dominion in 1 Kings 5:(1,) 4 forms according to Noth a post-deuteronomistic addition, which betrays itself as such above all through its language: עבר הנהר as designation for the region points to the Persian period.[4] The description of Solomon's daily menu in vv. 2–3 was inserted even later.[5]

Still, in Noth's judgement many traditions concerning the administration and the building activities of Solomon are at least *based* on original records, and, above all, Noth did not have a shadow of doubt about the existence of a 'United Monarchy' in the time of David and Solomon.

In this respect, we are apparently in a different situation.[6] Obviously, many basic assumptions once taken for granted have changed. That might be one reason for the breakdown of established hypotheses in the field of Biblical Studies we have experienced in the last decades. Being part of this process I do not have special reservations in this regard. At the same time, however, I am sceptical if some new presuppositions – readily internalized by a great part of contemporary scholarship – do indeed form a solid basis for future research.

In the scope of this short study I will concentrate on the basic issue of the 'United Kingdom' in the time of David and Solomon. Furthermore, being trained in philological analyses I will take care not to deal with any disputed interpretation of so called 'facts on the ground'[7] and will instead focus on possible exegetical contributions to the topic.

Utilizing biblical texts as historical sources forms a modern and – compared with the aims of exegetical research – a highly restrictive approach. In terms of sound method, however, such an approach has to be based on a comprehensive understanding of the texts in question, their genre, pragmatics, communicative intentions etc., an understanding which in turn requires the determination of the text's primary

---

4 Cf. Noth (1968), 75–76. At the same time he finds in 4:2–6, 7–19 old "documents": "Sie stammen letztlich aus der königlichen Kanzlei in Jerusalem und sind damit primäre historische Quellen." (Idid., 62)

5 Cf. Noth (1968), 76–77.

6 The 'United Monarchy', esp. the 'age of Solomon' has caught remarkable scholarly attention in the last years. A few exemplary references may be mentioned at this place: Handy (1997); Dietrich (1997); Knoppers (1997); Halpern (2001); Gertz (2004); Hendel (2006); Finkelstein/Silberman (2006).

7 Again, it is not my intention to discuss the epistemological state of so called archaeological 'facts' here. Given, however, the controversial debates about central archaeological issues one might get the impression that those 'facts' are not so different from the literary sources – with respect to their interpretative nature.

addressees/readership, their historical context, presuppositions etc. It is for this trivial interrelation that the historical question forms an indispensible part of any exegesis that seeks to explore the proper meaning of biblical texts.

The mentioned reasoning, as trivial as it might seem, proves to be compelling only if two basic data concerning the nature of biblical prose and its relation to history are recognized:[8] Firstly, *Historiography* in a 'western' sense does not exist in the world of (the Ancient Near East and in) Biblical Israel. That means: tradents and primary addressees of Old Testament texts are not acquainted with the concept of *historicity* and the authors do not have the intention to give *historical* information in that sense. This holds true even when comparing the Hebrew Bible with the early Greek prose writers: Herodotus' *historiai* might be highly deficient in terms of historical reliability, but nevertheless the work is representing the basic concepts of historicity (for the first time in European history).

Secondly, the western concept of *literature (= fiction)* does not exist in the world of Biblical Israel. That means: authors and readers do not share the concept of *fictional* narrative which seemingly refers to their own past, but by convention has *no claim* to give a reliable depiction of the 'real' world (as – for instance – novels or drama).[9] As a consequence, many so called 'literary readings' of the Hebrew literature imply an anachronistic projection.[10] To say it the other way around: biblical prose always does imply the claim to give propositional (and often normative) references to its addressees' world – be it concerning the past, present or future.

Unfortunately, a 'historical exegesis' in the sense of reading the texts in their proper historical context remains notoriously difficult. One main reason is that we did not unearth those texts as artifacts preserved by chance, but we have them as part of a living tradition which was formed very often in a quite complex process of transmission. That is why any proper understanding of a biblical text starting with his

---

8 Cf. Blum (2007) for detailed arguments concerning the following distinctions.

9 At the same time we find in the Old Testament – as in many folk traditions – a kind of elementary fictionality in genres such as parables which are semantically marked as depicting an imaginative reality; cf. Blum (2007), 38.

10 Cf. the important discussion of the issues in Sternberg (1985), 1–83. Sternberg offers his own solution for the 'epistemological' difference between Old Testament-prose and the western concept of fiction on the one hand, and historiography on the other hand: the alleged claim of divine inspiration by the biblical authors. Actually, however, this understanding itself forms an anachronistic projection of a late Hellenistic concept onto the literature which arose in pre-exilic or Persian times; cf. Blum (2007), 39–40.

delimitation presupposes a diachronic analysis. The relative or absolute dating of such (hypothetical) units will be possible, only if adequate data as the following are available:

1. significant typological[11] and/or 'stratigraphical'[12] relations to other well dated texts

and/or

2. textual features (for instance: anachronistic or unique elements) which point significantly to or exclude specific historical contexts. Such features are to be expected on the level of
    a. language (vocabulary, morphology, syntax etc.)
    b. form (genre, style, idioms etc.)
    c. content (*realia*, concepts, presuppositions etc.)

and/or

3. compelling evidence showing that the text as a whole or in his very substance was addressing his audience by referring to specific circumstances or constellations which did exist only in a certain historical context or period.

Each of these parameters has its significance and its fallacies. The most specific results, however, are to be expected, if all three options or at least the last one is given. Unfortunately, that is only in a restricted way the case with the pre-deuteronomistic Solomon traditions in 1 Kings 3–11.[13] In my opinion, however, things are different with regard to the larger narrative which tells about Solomon's birth and his accession to the throne and which is usually called 'the Succession Narrative' or 'the Court History'. Therefore, I will focus on some aspects of this highly praised artistic story.

---

11 That means, by comparison of concepts, theological motifs/ideas etc. (in professional terminology that belongs to the realm of *Traditionsgeschichte*) or by determining *inter*textual dependence – a very popular endeavour, but in fact a highly complicated issue.

12 I.e., *intra*textual interrelations such as redactional or compositional dependence on specific literary strata etc.

13 Cf. the sound discussion in Gertz (2004), 22–27. Apparently, there still prevails the tendency to prefer a pre-exilic date for the non-deuteronomistic portions, esp. for the lists in 1 Kings 4 and 9 and the building 'reports' in 1 Kings 6–7. The best candidate for an old document from Solomonic times seems to be the district list in 4:7–19; cf. Alt (1913); Fritz (1995), and recently (with valuable arguments) Kamlah (2001) and Knauf (2001), 127–130. Na'aman (2001) argues for an 8th century BCE dating (based on the inclusion of Judah [v. 19] in the primary list which seems questionable to me).

The Political Setting of the Succession Narrative and the United Monarchy

The stories about King David's family in 2 Samuel 9–20 and 1 Kings 1–2 had been considered as a narrative of its own for a long time.[14] But Leonhard Rost was in 1926 the first to establish thoroughly the thesis of an independent story with a peculiar style and *Tendenz* written during Solomon's reign *ad majorem gloriam Salomonis,* which he called *"Thronfolgegeschichte"*[15]. Nevertheless, in his study Rost felt the difficulty to identify an appropriate beginning for the whole unit, so he argued that the author tied his story to the ark narrative in 2 Samuel 6 and used an ancient oracle for the Davidic dynasty which Rost found in 2 Sam. 7:11b, 16.

Rost's hypothesis gained a prominent role in Old Testament exegesis. In the last decades, however, the *Thronfolgegeschichte* is subjected to so many alterations and modifications that it seems in danger to disappear from the scholarly scene. Time and again multiple redaction-critical stratifications have been proposed.[16] In addition, there is a relatively new trend to dissect the greater story into smaller units like a Bathsheba-Solomon-cycle, an Absalom cycle etc.[17] In my opinion, however, 2 Samuel 9–20 and 1 Kings 1–2 with the exception of a few later additions turn out to be a coherent, marvellous narrative.[18] Its obvious complexity is not a case for redactional multiplicity but for authorial unity. Therefore, even if one advocated for several redactions, one

---

14 Cf. Wellhausen (1899), 255–260; Steuernagel (1912), 325–326, 355 ("Familiengeschichte Davids").

15 Rost (1926).

16 Würthwein (1974) was the first to separate a basic David-critical and a later pro-Solomonic layer. For an excellent, comprehensive review of the intricate *Forschungsgeschichte* until 1993 cf. Dietrich/Neumann (1995), 191–216, and also Seiler (1998), 12–22. Rudnig (2006) takes the redaction-critical approach to the extremes by splitting the story up into 5–12 verbally reconstructed redactions, not to mention numerous glosses etc. See also below.

17 Cf. already Caspari (1926), 509–512; more recently for example: Dietrich (1997), 253ff.; Kratz (2000), 180ff.; McKenzie (2000), though the respective definitions and datings of the narrative units are quite different.

18 It is, for example, impossible to separate 1 Kings 1 neither from the Absalom-story (the depiction of Adonija's behaviour boldly alludes to that of Absalom; moreover, the reaction of his opponents has to be understood in the light of Absalom's rebellion) nor from the Amnon-Tamar-episode (cf. David's reaction in both cases). McKenzie (2000), 129–135, emphasizing such connections, attributes 1 Kings 1–2 as a whole to the Deuteronomist. There are, of course, well known deuteronomistic additions like 1 Kings 2:3–4; 2:27b, but assigning the main corpus of the chapters to deuteronomistic hands would make the distinction between 'deuteronomistic' and 'non-deuteronomistic' almost meaningless.

would have to assume an astonishing congeniality in terms of storytelling which would distinguish these narrator-redactors from any other prose in the Former Prophets. Hence, Rost appears to be basically right, although several questions have still to be settled. That is true especially with regard to the beginning of the story and its diachronic connection with the preceding Saul-David-stories.[19]

Anyway, of greater importance for our present topic is the question of dating. Interestingly, both Rost's and his followers'[20] dating to the Solomonic age has almost unanimously been given up in recent research, at least in Germany. As far as I can see, this is not so much based on specific textual-analytical evidence, as on the general assumption that a literary work of such a scale and standard cannot be ascribed to the early monarchical period, especially not in Jerusalem. But this opinion has to be checked against the available evidence.

Israel Finkelstein and Neil A. Silberman have convincingly demonstrated that several features of the *milieu* found in the David stories fit best the historical patterns and constellations of the 10th century BCE. Thus, the environment and settlement conditions in fringe areas of Judah described in the David story point to the time of the early monarchy.[21] "Another important clue" for an early context of those traditions is "the prominence of the Philistine city of Gath in the David stories"[22] – both in the David-Saul-narratives and in the Succession Narrative (1 Sam. 21:11–16; 27; 28:1–2; 29; 2 Sam. 15:18–22[23]; 1 Kings 2:39–40). As the excavations at Tell es-Safi have revealed, Gath was the predominant Philistine power next to Judah, but only until its destruction by Hazael of Damascus at the end of the 9th century BCE. The rise of Aram-Damascus to the expanding regional power at this time forms also the *terminus ante quem* for an independent 'kingdom' of Geshur playing some role in the plot of the Absalom story (2 Sam. [3:2] 13:37–38; 15:8).[24] At the same time, Finkelstein/Silberman's assumption that

19 Some options are mentioned in Blum (2000), 20–21.

20 Cf. esp. von Rad (1944).

21 Finkelstein/Silberman (2006), 38: "A scribe who lived in Jerusalem in the late eighth century BCE (oder later) would not have described such a reality and had no reason to invent it."

22 Finkelstein/Silberman (2006), 38–39. This point was already made by Halpern (2001), 69.

23 Cf. Rofé (2000) about the significance of "the men of Ittai the Gittite" (and the other 'foreigners' in David's elite) with respect to the historical reliability of the main traditions about David.

24 Cf. Finkelstein/Silberman (2006), 110. According to the authors, the role of Geshur in the "Court History" belongs to "a whole series of historical retrojections in which the founder of the dynasty of Judah in the tenth century is credited with the victories and the acquisitions of territory that were in fact accomplished by the ninth-century

such "uncannily accurate memories of tenth century BCE conditions"[25] go back to oral folk traditions which were written down only in the 7th century BCE is not really convincing: Firstly, I would call into question that prose narratives of this kind shall be orally transmitted over 200 years and more. In any case, if there were some kind of enduring oral tradition, it would be adjusted unconsciously to the changing conditions of the storytellers and their community. Secondly, neither the stories about David's rise nor the Succession Narrative are collections of folk traditions but represent a sophisticated, professional art of storytelling. In fact, at least the author of the Succession Narrative is familiar with the life at the court; his intellectual milieu is the early wisdom (see below).

All the more, we should pay attention to some central features which are *essential* to the given *literary* composition as a whole. I will focus mainly on two topics: on (1) David's conflict with the house of Saul/Benjamin and on (2) the presentation of Solomon.

1. David and the House of Saul/Benjamin

The relations between David and the house of Saul play a significant, actually quite unexpected role in the narrative about David and his sons. First, we have David's favourable treatment of Meribaal son of Jonathan and Ziba his servant (2 Samuel 9). Later on in the Absalom crisis, Meribaal is focused again along with Shim'i ben Gera from the house of Saul. Both appear at David's flight from Jerusalem and at his return. The political implications are always explicitly expounded.[26] Most agitating and moving is the scene with Shim'i who furiously humiliates and curses David as איש דמים and איש בליעל (2 Sam. 16:1–13) and David's humble reaction who prevents Abishai ben Zeruja to kill Shim'i. David keeps this attitude when Shim'i comes to meet the returning king "accompanied by a thousand men from Benjamin", that means: he comes as representative of (or at least supported by) Benjamin (2 Sam. 19:17–24). But despite all indulgence of David the trouble with Benjamin is not settled: another איש ימיני the 'wicked' Sheva ben Bichri calls for a kind of 'passive secession' by denying the Davidic

Omrides." (Ibid., 112) But the Court History neither presupposes Geshur's conquest by David nor do we have evidence for an Omride conquest. Most of the other alleged "retrojections" (ibid.) do not fit the Omride kingdom as well, and most of the texts referred to are not part of the Succession Narrative.

25 Finkelstein/Silberman (2006), 33.

26 Cf. esp. 2 Sam. 16:3, 8; 19:(18, 21,) 28–29.

dominion, without proclaiming an alternative king: ... אין לנו חלק בדוד איש לאהליו ישראל (2 Sam. 20:1). This quiet separatism proves to be effective, but will finally be suppressed by Joab and the men of David.

Seen against this background, it may not come as a surprise that Solomon later on puts Shim'i under open arrest in Jerusalem and let him be killed instantly when his order has been violated. – That's the very end of the story as a whole which concludes: והממלכה נכונה ביד שלמה (2 Kings 2:46b).

Obviously, the Benjamin-topic is not a mere literary motif. Instead, one would expect that such a sensitive matter would have been simply suppressed, if that had been possible. In fact, the bold apologetic[27] presentation of David's behaviour toward Saul and his house proves the political virulence of the issue in the world of the addressees. Especially the Shim'i-scene reflects severe accusations and deep hatred in Benjamin toward the house of David, which forms an imminent danger for the very stability of the Davidic kingdom – as is exemplified by the case of Sheva ben Bichri.

The arguments given here are basically independent from possible redaction-critical stratifications in the story. Nevertheless, I am quite sceptical toward recent attempts to reshape the story substantially in the wake of diachronic analyses. Reinhard G. Kratz, for instance, locates the decisive battle with Absalom (2 Sam. 18:1–17) not in Gilead, but in the Cisjordan mountain region, based on the term יער אפרים in 18:6[28]; thus he transfers the famous scene with the king, waiting for news from the battle, from Mahanaim to Jerusalem.[29] But such a reconstruction does not work, because every narrator (early or late) would know that on this side of the Jordan Ahimaaz' run through the *kikkar* (18:23) would not turn out to be an advantage but actually a foolish endeavour. One could avoid such a consequence by going on with the literary-critical dissection and by attributing the passage of 2 Sam. 18:19–19:9 to secondary layers as well.[30] But this analysis would still leave us with a highly incoherent narrative sequence, 2 Sam. 15:1–6, 13; 18:1–2a, 4b, 6–9, 15b–18[31] (cf. the transition from 15:6 to 13 and Absalom's armed forces in 18:6ff. coming out of nothing). Another solution, the search for an alternative semantic meaning of דרך הככר is advanced by Alexander A. Fischer.[32] But none of the proposed options "Umge-

27 Cf. also McCarter (1980; 1981) and Halpern (2001), 366ff.

28 Cf. Kratz (2000), 181. As seen for long (cf. for instance Stoebe [1994], 398 n. 6a with bibl.) there are, however, several possibilities for the presence of such a name in the region of Gilead, be it with (cf. Judg. 12:4) or without any connection to (the tribe of) Ephraim.

29 The implication is, of course, that the story in 2 Sam. 15:14–17:29 has to be attributed to later addition(s); cf. Kratz, ibid.

30 Cf. Aurelius (2004), 369–402.

31 Cf. Aurelius (2004), 402, and Kratz (2000), 181.

32 Cf. Fischer (2005), 51–52.

bung" (surroundings) or "Bogenweg" (curved way)[33] seems actually convincing.[34]

Apart from the time of David and Solomon itself, I see one period in which such a memory-based, anti-Davidic atmosphere in Benjamin could have had fatal consequences for the Davidic dynasty: that is the first four or five decades after Solomon, when we see an enduring struggle between the two kingdoms for the territory of Benjamin.[35] It is true, Judah managed to control the greater part of Benjamin on the mountain which was evidently of vital interest for Jerusalem, but they could do this only with the assistance of foreign powers. The first one was Pharaoh Shoshenq[36], the second one Benhadad ben Tabrimmon from Damascus (1 Kings 15:16ff.).[37] So much the more, it was crucial for the Davidic kingdom to carry on a struggle for the *hearts* of the Benjaminites. Apparently, our stories serve such an effort in a most subtle (and probably effective) way.[38]

---

33 As evidence for "Umgebung" Fischer can point to Neh. 12:28; "surroundings", however, is hardly fitting as name of a specific route to Jerusalem. "Bogenweg", was proposed already by Caspari (1926), 623. But what should actually be "the (faster?) Bogenweg" from the mountain of Ephraim to Jerusalem?

34 Moreover, Fischer's interpretation of David's retreat to Gilead as a literary anticipation of the Babylonian Exile (Fischer [2005], 65) appears a forced allegoric reading to me.

35 Dietrich (1997), 267, has proposed the period following the fall of Samaria (722 BCE) pointing to the stream of northern refugees into Judah: "Dies erklärte auch die geradezu werbende Apologetik, mit welcher das davidische Herrscherhaus gegen den Verdacht in Schutz genommen wird, den Niedergang des Nordens nicht nur tatenlos verfolgt, sondern aktiv mitbetrieben und sogar bei Königsmorden die Hand im Spiel gehabt zu haben." However, the apologetical *Tendenz* of the David stories is not directed towards the 'North' in general but towards Benjamin, which had long belonged to the Kingdom of Judah.

36 Shoshenq's Karnak-Inscription and the incidental note about Rehoboam's heavy tribute in 1 Kings 14:25–26 form consistent evidence that the Pharao's campaign had no military impact on the central territory of Judah/Jerusalem, but so much the more on the Northern kingdom (cf. Noth [1938] and id. [1968], 330–331). Rehoboam's state as Egyptian vassal and Shoshenq's strokes against the northern territory, including several places in the region of Benjamin and (southern) Ephraim (Ayyalon, Bet Horon, Gibeon, Zemaraim; cf. *int. al.* Noth [1938], 78–81; Mazar [1957], 60–61; Schipper [1999], 125ff., and recently Keel [2007], 339–345; for a different interpretation of the Shoshenq inscription see Wilson [2005]) turned out to be a major advantage for the Southern kingdom with regard to the conflict about the *Kernland* of Benjamin. The argument that the note connecting Shoshenq's campaign with Rehoboam could be due to the Deuteronomist's "retribution theology: Rehoboam sinned and was immediately punished by an invasion of a foreign ruler, who took the treasures of the Temple as ransom" (Finkelstein [2002], 113) misses the specific profile of 1 Kings 14:25–26; cf. again Noth (1968), 330.

37 Cf. also Keel (2007), 350–351.

38 In several respects the place of Benjamin between the house of Joseph and Judah in the tradition (the brotherhood of Benjamin and Joseph) and in history (Benjamin, the

2. The Presentation of Solomon

What is Solomon's role in the narrative? How is he presented? The answer depends mainly on the *syn*chronic reading of 1 Kings 1–2 and on the *dia*chronic analysis of 2 Samuel 11–12.

Besides undisputed deuteronomistic additions to Nathan's speech in chap. 12 there are several redactional-critical proposals for reconstructing the earliest stratum in the Bathsheba episode. Most stratigraphies assume a basic narrative with an anti-Solomonic *Tendenz*. A prominent example forms the analysis proposed by the late Timo Veijola. According to him, the Bathsheba episode originally ended up with the following sequence (2 Sam. 11:27a+12:24bα):

וַיַּעֲבֹר הָאֵבֶל וַיִּשְׁלַח דָּוִד וַיַּאַסְפָהּ אֶל־בֵּיתוֹ
וַתְּהִי־לוֹ לְאִשָּׁה וַתֵּלֶד לוֹ בֵּן
וַ'תִּ'קְרָא אֶת־שְׁמוֹ שְׁלֹמֹה וַיהוָה אֲהֵבוֹ

In this reading, Solomon was Bathsheba's first son begotten in adultery. Bathsheba saw him as "compensation/substitute" for her fallen man Urijah and, therefore, called him שלמה.

Here, I cannot enter the detailed literary-critical arguments of Veijola.[39] But, it is worth to look at the outcome of his analysis: apparently, 2 Samuel 11 is not only a story of brutal criminal power in the realm of kingship, but of criminal power that proves to be successful and without any punishment. The malice with which David tries to cover the offence against his officer and with which he organizes his murder by exploiting Urijah's unlimited loyalty, this royal malice is expounded with an extraordinary strength and narrative skill.[40] Read without the conviction of the king and his humble repentance or at least without the vicarious death of the first child, the story would turn out to exhibit the dominion of chaos in Jerusalem, a world without *ṣedeq* – and with no God. The crucial question, therefore, is not what *really* happened

---

tribe of the first Israelite king, but for the main time part of the Davidic kingdom) causes serious problems to the more or less 'minimalistic' reconstructions of Israelite/Judean tradition and history (cf. also Levin [2004]). Although Edelman (2001) and Davies (2007) recognize the challenge, their failure to give *substantial* data explaining the constellation out of an exilic/post-exilic context actually corroborates the point made here.

39 Veijola (1979), 85–87, bases his analysis on the supposed difficulty that Bathsheba's first child gets no name in the given narrative, an argument that seems, however, quite artificial because this child plays only an elusive role in the story. Giving him a name would lend him an individuality that would be irreconcilable with the narrative logic.

40 Not only in this respect the interpretation of Perry/Sternberg (1968) is highly recommended.

with David, Bathsheba, Urijah and Solomon, but if such a relation does represent a historically possible *story*. In my view, this reconstruction – as similar others – offers a modern anachronistic projection. If there was no first child in reality, it would have to be invented for the story. In this narrative world the name שלמה got in fact a second meaning as "substitution", though not for Urijah but for the nameless child who died. For the same reason, the continuation ויהוה אהבו is essential, not as a sign of divine election, but in order to point out that this second son is no more under God's wrath which means, his life will not be under the shadow of David's sin. The narrator underlined just this crucial difference by an intentional complex *Wiederaufnahme*:

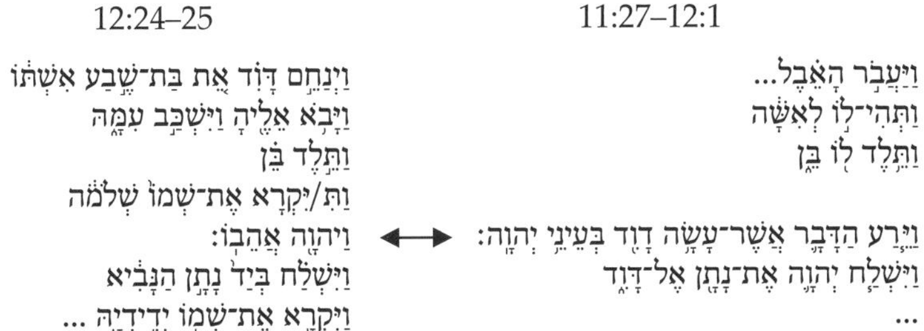

With regard to 1 Kings 1–2 Solomon-critical readings are popular as well. But again, in my opinion the intention of the narrator was different:[41] David is shown as an old man, but not as a demented one. Nathan and Bathsheba are people who know how to act decisively if needed and to say the right word at the right time, whereas Adonijah is paralleled to the hybrid Absalom; he proves the truth of the *mashal* גאות אדם תשפילנו (Prov. 29:23). Conversely, Solomon who never showed personal ambitions for his father's throne gains the crown. After the enthronement Solomon treats his opponents, measured by the normative presuppositions of author and addressees (!), with unusual indulgence and, finally, according to the reason of state. In his statecraft he definitely surpasses his father who failed time and again because he was driven by personal emotions, especially with regard to his sons.

Given this overall pro-Solomonic *Tendenz*, the crucial question remains: why on earth does the narrative connect just the beginnings of the dynasty with such a disastrous display of adultery, betrayal and murder (2 Sam. 11–12)? And one may add: why does the image of the dynastic founder David remain oscillating between disaster-bearing weakness and admirable piety and human greatness? Eduard Meyer

41 For more detailed arguments cf. Blum (2000), 21–26.

and Gerhard von Rad would probably answer: "Weil es wirklich so gewesen ist!" But, that again would be a bold anachronism, because neither Ancient Israel nor the Ancient Near East knew such a 'historical' interest. Instead, the recorded memory was the collectively or politically established and stabilised memory.

As in the case of the hatred in Benjamin the unavoidable conclusion is that the author of our narrative felt a *need* to present the main actors as he did. And as in that case the basic reason for such a need must be that there was some knowledge or memory in the world of the addressees, too virulent and too politically dangerous to be ignored by silence. In the case of Solomon it's not difficult to imagine the very core of such knowledge: the king's marriage with the wife of a fallen officer and the birth of his future successor by that woman. This could give rise *inter alia* to questions regarding Solomon's legitimacy. Is it by chance that David's malicious deeds in the 2 Samuel 11 actually ensure Solomon's royal decent?[42] – Anyway, it is important to have in mind that a basically ambivalent evaluation of the great dynastic founder served in some sense the pro-Solomonic purpose of the Court History as a whole.[43]

In short: Taking into account the milieu of the David stories in general and the special focus on the issue of Benjamin on the one hand and on Solomon's familiar background on the other hand we have to conclude that essential features of the *narrative plot* and of the *overall tendency* fit either the 10th century or the beginning of the 9th century BCE. For certain, the narrative has much to offer to later readers as well; it suffices to call in mind the strong sapiential character of the story which was shown by Roger N. Whybray and Hans-Jürgen Hermisson[44] years ago. Nevertheless, in later periods of the monarchy, not to say after the Exile, I cannot imagine any suitable context for the peculiar profile of our story. Additionally, an early dating is clearly supported by some individual features. I mention for example the episode

42 Cf. Halpern (2001), 401. In this respect the oddly stressed failure of David to cause Urijah to lie with his wife (2 Sam. 11:8–11, 12–13) and other details of the story gain special significance. Nevertheless, it should be emphasized that this aspect *alone* cannot explain the sharp narrative exposition of David's crime. But that issue is beyond the scope of this short study.

43 As a consequence, I would no more prefer whole-heartedly the label *Hofgeschichte* over against *Thronfolgegeschichte* as I did in Blum (2000), 22–23.

44 Whybray (1968); Hermisson (1971); cf. also Blum (2000), 30–36.

with Sheva ben Bichri which would not make sense as a later invention.[45]

According to a widespread opinion, however, all arguments for an early date of the Succession Narrative are in vain, simply because there was no high literature in Israel-Judah before the late 8th or the 7th century BCE.[46] Jamieson-Drake and others made honourable efforts to interpret the archaeological data, especially the epigraphic evidence, in such historical terms. Nevertheless, in some respect those far-reaching conclusions have been reached in a quite uncritical way. The whole issue should be discussed, of course, in greater scale,[47] but I will mention at least some major objections:

1. It is quite reasonable that the significant increase of epigraphic remains since the 7th century BCE indicates an increase in the spread of literacy in Judah.[48] Erroneous, however, is the often assumed direct correlation between general literacy and the production of 'high literature', i.e. texts which go far beyond an everyday usage of writing. I do not see evidence for such a correlation in other Ancient-Near-Eastern cultures, and the case of Ancient Greece points just to the opposite. All the more, the epigraphic evidence in Canaan itself shows a quite different picture: the quasi-literary inscriptions we actually have are almost all (except the Shiloah-inscription) from the *ninth* or the *beginning eighth* century BCE: Mesha, Tel Dan, Kuntillet ʿAjrud, Tell Deir Alla – and none of these elaborated texts comes from a long-established kingdom.[49] Of highest interest are the plaster-texts from Tell Deir Alla and Kuntillet ʿAjrud.[50] The Deir Alla

45 Inventing such a plot while the Davidic kingdom existed would mean: 'talk of the devil and he will appear.' As a later invention after the exile this episode would form a meaningless and superfluous 'doubling' of the Absalom-story.

46 Cf. esp. Dietrich (1997), 229–230 (229: "Das 10. und das beginnende 9. Jahrhundert waren noch keine Epoche breiten literarischen Schaffens und differenzierter Geistigkeit.") with reference to Jamieson-Drake (1991) and Niemann (1993). Cf. also the determined statements in Na'aman (2001), 103; Finkelstein/Silberman (2006), 37 and *passim*.

47 Cf. also the careful considerations in Carr (2005), 126ff., 163ff. (see n. 191), and the arguments in Keel (2007), 153ff.

48 It suffices to recognize the quantitative distribution as reflected in Renz (1995): From the 10th to the mid-8th century BCE: 36 items, second half of 8th century: 129 items, 7th century: 103 items, the first two decades of the 6th century: 65 items.

49 These data seem to be somewhat underestimated in the informative overview of Renz (2009).

50 Comparing the fragments from Kuntillet ʿAjrud written on plaster which are presented on a photography in Ahituv (2005), 241, with the plaster texts from Tell Deir Alla one cannot but find a remarkable similarity in terms of paleography which has

inscriptions, originally threefold in size as the Mesha-stone,[51] contained elaborate sapiential works and belonged apparently to a professional school-context.

2. The correlation between literary education and high urban civilization in the supposed exclusive way is mere theory as well. It suffices to point to the small Late Bronzes-cities like the archaeological almost non existing LB-Jerusalem, where every poor mayor had at least one scribe who was able to communicate in Akkadian with the Egyptian court. Despite the plain character of the letters some prove their scribe's skill in literary language.[52]
3. Last, but not least, we have clear textual evidence for the continuation of scribal traditions from the 2nd millennium down to 1st millennium culture. The most significant examples are based on texts from Ugarit, Amarna-letters and Egypt on the one hand and Tell Deir Alla and the Hebrew Bible on the other.[53] That means: the new political structures emerging in the southern Levant in the first millennium could indeed rely on a well developed literary tradition. Moreover, they had an obvious interest in educating and training their own administrative, political and cultic elite, small as it might have been.[54]

The Greeks had great singers of tale who wrote huge literary compositions only two or three generations after the earliest inscriptional evidence for alphabetical writing in first millennium Greece (ca. 750 BCE).

---

not received much attention so far. – While about 30 years have passed since the discovery of the inscriptions in Kuntillet ʿAjrud it is scandalous that the scholarly community is still waiting for their full publication.

51 Based on a rough estimation according to the average number of signs in a line; cf. Blum (2008b), 34.

52 Cf. de Liagre Böhl (1914) and Alt (1933).

53 Cf. e.g., the late (Hellenistic?) verse Isa. 27:1 with its well-known Ugaritic parallels; Amos 9:2–3; Ps. 139:7–10 and EA 264, 15–16; the hymn to the Aton and Psalm 104; Deir Alla Plaster Texts (DAPT) Combination I,22 and Ps. 46:9; 66:5 and last but not least the layout of DAPT which seems to be based on Egyptian scribal traditions (cf. Lemaire [1986], 89; Blum [2008a], 94–95) and the genre and topic of Combination II; cf. Blum (2008b).

54 Dietrich (1997), 230, seems to have much later historical conditions (of the Hellenistic-Roman period) in mind: "doch fehlte es an den Möglichkeiten und auch an dem Interesse, sie [sc. *Literati*] auszubilden; es fehlte zudem eine Abnehmerschaft für ihre etwaigen Werke, es gab verschwindend wenige Lese- und Schreibkundige, es gab nicht einmal in rudimentärer Form einen Literaturmarkt." The notion of a "Literaturmarkt" is probably anachronistic with regard to the Ancient Near East in general, including the Persian period.

The Israelites had great story-tellers who just could use a quite well established literary medium.

Concluding Remarks

Some final remarks about Solomon and the historical question of the 'United Monarchy': relying on the old narrative traditions about David and Solomon there can be little doubt that both kings reigned on Judah and on the northern tribes called 'Israel' with Jerusalem as residence and capital. Still relying on these narratives, their kingdom was patrimonial,[55] primarily based on personal authority and on loyalty-bonds, be it on the basis of kinship or on patron-client-relations. Its installation and probably its maintenance were not grounded on the material and economical resources of the regions under dominion, but mainly on the military force of several hundred or thousand well trained, efficient fighters: the Judean men of Joab and foreign mercenaries like the Kreti and Pleti or the men of Ittai from Gat. The core of these warriors came from David's gang of outcasts in his early years. As Nadav Na'aman[56] pointed out already, the situation under David resembles structurally the picture one gets from the Amarna-letters concerning the LB-city-states. But apparently, David surpassed Abdi-chepa and fellows in his power as charismatic leader and in the efficiency of his loyal troops. At the end the established 'United Kingdom' proved to be ephemeral and could not survive the charismatic founder more than one generation.

Nevertheless, it has some historical plausibility that Solomon attempted to develop the rudimental administration of the Davidic beginnings and to build persistent state-structures. According to the tradition, he did so by exploiting the resources of the northern tribes, *inter alia* by levying *corvée*. Which of the lists and notes regarding Solomon's political activities etc. go back to primary sources cannot be judged by philological analysis alone. Here, the historical reconstruction needs clear and undisputed archaeological data. Hopefully, we will get this evidence sometime.

55 Cf. Stager (2003).

56 Na'aman (1996); cf. also Finkelstein/Silberman (2006), 40–59.

Bibliography

Ahituv, S. (2005), HaKetav VeHaMiktav: Handbook of Ancient Inscriptions from the Land of Israel and the Kingdoms beyond the Jordan from the Period of the First Commenwealth, Biblical Encyclopaedia Library 21, Jerusalem (in Hebrew).

Alt, A. (1913), Israels Gaue unter Salomo. Alttestamentliche Studien Rudolf Kittel zum 60. Geburtstag dargebracht (1913), BWANT 13, 1–19, wieder abgedruckt in: id., Kleine Schriften zur Geschichte des Volkes Israel, vol. II, München 1953, 76–89.

– (1933), Hic murus aheneus esto, ZDMG 86, 33–48.

Aurelius, E. (2004), Davids Unschuld. Die Hofgeschichte und Psalm 7, in: M. Witte (ed.), Gott und Mensch im Dialog, FS O. Kaiser, BZAW 345/I, Berlin/New York, 391–412.

Blum, E. (2000), Ein Anfang der Geschichtsschreibung? Anmerkungen zur sog. Thronfolgegeschichte und zum Umgang mit Geschichte im alten Israel, Trumah 5, 9–46, (1996), wieder abgedruckt in: A. de Pury/T. Römer (eds.), Die sogenannte Thronfolgegeschichte Davids. Neue Einsichten und Anfragen, OBO 176, Freiburg (Schweiz)/Göttingen, 4–37.

– (2007), Historiography or Poetry? The Nature of the Hebrew Bible Prose Tradition, in: L.T. Stuckenbruck/S.C. Barton/B.G. Wold (eds.), Memory in the Bible and Antiquity, Tübingen, 25–46.

– (2008a), Israels Prophetie im altorientalischen Kontext. Anmerkungen zu neueren religionsgeschichtlichen Thesen, in: I. Cornelius/L. Jonker (eds.), "From Ebla to Stellenbosch": Syro-Palestinian Religions and the Hebrew Bible, ADPV 37, Wiesbaden, 81–115.

– (2008b), "Verstehst du dich nicht auf die Schreibkunst …?" Ein weisheitlicher Dialog über Vergänglichkeit und Verantwortung. Kombination II der Wandinschrift vom Tell Deir ʻAlla, in: M. Bauks/K. Liess/P. Riede (eds.), Was ist der Mensch, dass du seiner gedenkst? (Psalm 8,5). Aspekte einer theologischen Anthropologie, FS B. Janowski, Neukirchen-Vluyn, 33–53.

Carr, D.M. (2005), Writing on the Tablet of the Heart: Origins of Scripture and Literature, Oxford.

Caspari, W. (1926), Die Samuelbücher, KAT 7, Leipzig.

Davies, P.R. (2007), The Trouble with Benjamin, in: R. Rezetko/T.H. Lim/W.B. Aucker (eds.), Reflection and Refraction: Studies in Biblical Historiography in Honour of A.G. Auld, VT.S 113, Leiden/Boston, 93–111.

Dietrich, W. (1997), Die frühe Königszeit in Israel. 10. Jahrhundert v.Chr., Biblische Enzyklopädie 3, Stuttgart.

– /Naumann, T. (1995), Die Samuelbücher, EdF 287, Darmstadt.

Edelman, D. (2001), Did Saulide-Davidic Rivalry Resurface in Early Persian Period Yehud?, in: J.A. Dearman/M.P. Graham (eds.), The Land That I Will Show You: Essays on the History and Archaeology of the Ancient Near East in Honour of J.M. Miller, JSOT.S 343, Sheffield, 69–91.

Finkelstein, I. (2002), The Campaign of Shoshenq I to Palestine: A Guide to the 10th Century BCE Polity, ZDPV 118, 109–135.

– /Silberman, N.A. (2006), David and Solomon: In Search of the Bible's Sacred Kings and the Roots of the Western Tradition, New York.

Fischer, A.A. (2005), Die literarische Entstehung des Großreichs Davids und ihr geschichtlicher Hintergrund. Zur Darstellung der Kriegschronik in 2Sam 8,1–14(15), in: U. Becker/J. van Oorschot (eds.), Das Alte Testament – ein Geschichtsbuch?! Geschichtsschreibung oder Geschichtsüberlieferung im antiken Israel, Arbeiten zur Bibel und ihrer Geschichte 17, Leipzig, 81–101.

Fritz, V. (1995), Die Verwaltungsgebiete Salomos nach 1Kön. 4,7–19, in: M. Weippert/S. Timm (eds.), Meilenstein, FS H. Donner, ÄAT 30, Wiesbaden, 19–26.

Gertz, J.C. (2004), Konstruierte Erinnerung. Alttestamentliche Historiographie im Spiegel von Archäologie und literarhistorischer Kritik am Fallbeispiel des salomonischen Königtums, BThZ 21, 3–29.

Halpern, B. (2001), David's Secret Demons: Messiah, Murderer, Traitor, King, The Bible in Its World, Grand Rapids.

Handy, L.K. (1997, ed.), The Age of Solomon: Scholarship at the Turn of the Millennium, Studies in the History and Culture of the Ancient Near East 11, Leiden et al.

Hendel, R. (2006), The Archaeology of Memory: King Solomon, Chronology, and Biblical Representation, in: S. Gitin/J. Edward Wright/J.P. Dessel (eds.), Confronting the Past: Archaeological and Historical Essays on Ancient Israel in Honor of W.G. Dever, Winona Lake/Ind., 219–230.

Hermisson, H.-J. (1971), Weisheit und Geschichte, in: H.W. Wolff (ed.), Probleme biblischer Theologie, FS G. von Rad, München, 136–154.

Jamieson-Drake, D.W. (1991), Scribes and Schools in Monarchic Judah: A Socio-Archeological Approach, The Social World of Biblical Antiquity Series 9/JSOT.S 109, Sheffield 1991.

Kamlah, J. (2001), Die Liste der Regionalfürsten in 1 Kön 4,7–19 als historische Quelle für die Zeit Salomos, BN 106, 57–78.

Keel, O. (2007), Die Geschichte Jerusalems und die Entstehung des Monotheismus. Teil 1, Orte und Landschaften der Bibel IV,1, Göttingen.

Knauf, E.A. (2001), Solomon at Megiddo?, in: J.A. Dearman/M.P. Graham (eds.), The Land That I Will Show You: Essays on the History and Archaeology of the Ancient Near East in Honour of J.M. Miller, JSOT.S 343, Sheffield, 119–134.
Knoppers, G.N. (1997), The Vanishing Solomon: The Disappearance of the United Monarchy from Recent Histories of Ancient Israel, JBL 116, 19–44.
Kratz, R.G. (2000), Die Komposition der erzählenden Bücher des Alten Testaments. Grundwissen der Bibelkritik, UTB 2157, Göttingen.
Lemaire, A. (1986), La disposition originelle des inscriptions sur plâtre de Deir ʻAlla, Studi Epigrafici e Linguistici 3, 79–93.
Levin, Y. (2004), Joseph, Judah and the "Benjamin Conundrum", ZAW 116, 223–241.
de Liagre Böhl, F.M.T. (1914), Hymnisches und Rhythmisches in den Amarnabriefen aus Kanaan, ThLBl 35, 1914, 337–340 = id., Opera minora, Groningen 1953, 375–379, with Aantekeningen XXII, 516–517.
McCarter, P.K. Jr. (1980), The Apology of David, JBL 99, 489–504.
– (1981), "Plots, True or False": The Succession Narrative as Court Apologetic, Interpr. 35, 355–367.
McKenzie, S.L. (2000), The So-Called Succession Narrative in the Deuteronomistic History, in: A. de Pury/T. Römer (eds.), Die sogenannte Thronfolgegeschichte Davids. Neue Einsichten und Anfragen, OBO 176, Freiburg (Schweiz)/Göttingen, 123–135.
Mazar (Maisler), B. (1957), The Campaign of Pharaoh Shishak to Palestine, VT.S 4, Leiden, 57–66.
Na'aman, N. (1996), The Contribution of the Amarna Letters to the Debate on Jerusalem's Political Position in the Tenth Century B.C.E., BASOR 304, 17–27 (= id., Ancient Israel's History and Historiography: The First Temple Period: Collected Essays 3, Winona Lake/Ind. 2006, 1–17).
– (2001), Solomon's District List (1 Kings 4:7–19) and the Assyrian Province System in Palestine, UF 33, 419–436 (= id., Ancient Israel's History and Historiography: The First Temple Period: Collected Essays 3, Winona Lake/Ind. 2006, 102–119).
Niemann, H.M. (1993), Herrschaft, Königtum und Staat. Skizzen zur soziokulturellen Entwicklung im monarchischen Israel, FAT 6, Tübingen.
Noth, M. (1938), Die Schoschenkliste, ZDPV 61, 277–304 (= id., Aufsätze zur biblischen Landes- und Altertumskunde 2. Beiträge altorientalischer Texte zur Geschichte Israels, Neukirchen-Vluyn 1971, 73–93).

– (1943), Überlieferungsgeschichtliche Studien. Die sammelnden und bearbeitenden Geschichtswerke im Alten Testament, SKG.G 18/2, Königsberg, 43–266 (= Tübingen [2]1958).
– (1968), Könige. 1. Teilband (Kapitel 1–16), BK 9/1, Neukirchen-Vluyn.
Perry, M./Sternberg, M. (1968), The King through Ironic Eyes: The Narrator's Devices in the Biblical Story of David and Bathsheba and Two Excurses on the Theory of Narrative Text, Hasifrut 1, 263–292 (in Hebrew).
von Rad, G. (1944), Der Anfang der Geschichtsschreibung im alten Israel, in: AKuG 32, 1–42 (= id., Gesammelte Studien zum Alten Testament, TB 8, München [2]1961, 148–188).
Renz, J. (1995), Die althebräischen Inschriften. Teil 1. Text und Kommentar, in: J. Renz/W. Röllig, Handbuch der althebräischen Epigraphik, Bd.e 1–3, Darmstadt.
– (2009), Die vor- und außerliterarische Texttradition. Ein Beitrag der palästinischen Epigraphik zur Vorgeschichte des Kanons, in: J. Schaper (ed.), Die Textualisierung der Religion. Konferenz: Die Textualisierung der Religion. Juda und Jerusalem zwischen Kult und Text vom 7. bis 5. Jh. v. Chr. vom 8.–10. Juli 2005 an der Evangelisch-Theologischen Fakultät der Universität Tübingen, FAT 62, Tübingen, 53–81.
Rofé, A. (2000), The Reliability of the Sources about David's Reign: An Outlook from Political Theory, in: E. Blum (ed.), Mincha. FS R. Rendtorff, Neukirchen-Vluyn, 217–227.
Rost, L. (1926), Die Überlieferung von der Thronnachfolge Davids, BWANT 42 (III/6), Stuttgart (= in: Das kleine Credo und andere Studien zum Alten Testament, Heidelberg 1965, 119–253).
Rudnig, T.A. (2006), Davids Thron. Redaktionskritische Studien zur Geschichte von der Thronnachfolge Davids, BZAW 358, Berlin/New York.
Schipper, B.U. (1999), Israel und Ägypten in der Königszeit. Die kulturellen Kontakte von Salomo bis zum Fall Jerusalems, OBO 170, Freiburg (Schweiz)/Göttingen.
Seiler, S. (1998), Die Geschichte von der Thronfolge Davids (2 Sam 9–20; 1 Kön 1–2). Untersuchungen zur Literarkritik und Tendenz, BZAW 267, Berlin/New York.
Stager, L.E. (2003), The Patrimonial Kingdom of Solomon, in: W.G. Dever/S. Gitin (eds.), Symbiosis, Symbolism, and the Power of the Past: Canaan, Ancient Israel, and their Neighbors, from the Late Bronze Age through Roman Palaestina, Proceedings of the Centennial Symposium W.F. Albright Institute of Archaeological Research and

American Schools of Oriental Research, Jerusalem, May 29–31, 2000, Winona Lake/Ind., 63–74.

Sternberg, M. (1985), The Poetics of Biblical Narrative: Ideological Literature and the Drama of Reading, Indiana Literary Biblical Series, Bloomington/Ind.

Steuernagel, C. (1912), Lehrbuch der Einleitung in das Alte Testament, SThL, Tübingen.

Stoebe, H.J. (1994), Das zweite Buch Samuelis, KAT 8/2, Gütersloh.

Veijola, T. (1979), Salomo – der Erstgeborene Bathsebas, in: J.A. Emerton (ed.), Studies in the Historical Books of the Old Testament, VT.S 30, Leiden, 230–250 (= id., David. Gesammelte Studien zu den Davidüberlieferungen des Alten Testaments, SESJ 52, Helsinki/Göttingen 1990, 84–105).

Wellhausen, J. (1899), Die Composition des Hexateuchs und der historischen Bücher des Alten Testaments, 3. Aufl., Berlin.

Whybray, R.N. (1968), The Succession Narrative: A Study of II Samuel 9–20; I Kings 1 and 2, SBT II/9, London.

Wilson, K.A. (2005), The Campaign of Pharaoh Shoshenq I into Palestine, FAT II/9, Tübingen.

Würthwein, E. (1974), Die Erzählung von der Thronfolge Davids – theologische oder politische Geschichtsschreibung?, ThSt(B) 115, Zürich.

Elders or Youngsters?

Critical Remarks on 1 Kings 12

ALEXANDER ROFÉ

The present essay is an additional tentative interpretation of the story in 1 Kings 12:1–16, known as the account of the 'Assembly at Shechem', the failed coronation of Rehoboam over all Israel. In order to shed light upon this story, I shall employ the various tools at the disposal of philology: textual and literary criticism, form-criticism, Hebrew linguistics, history of tradition and history of ideas. It is my hope that a cautious application of these resources will yield a plausible picture of the historical and ideological setting in which this story came into being.

The main contribution of text-criticism in this pericope is the perception that all mention of Jeroboam in vv. 2–3 and 12 is absent from Codex Vaticanus of the Septuagint (LXX^{B}) which can be considered to represent here the Old Greek.[1] The presumed Hebrew *Vorlage* described the exchange at Shechem as taking place only between King Rehoboam and the people. The introduction of Jeroboam into the episode should be considered as interpolated by a later scribe.[2] He probably intended to involve Jeroboam in the assembly at Shechem, thus imputing to him the main responsibility for the secession of the northern tribes.[3] The same tendency is evident in the work of the Chronicler (2 Chron. 10:1–16; 13:6–7).[4]

An additional contribution of text-criticism has significant implications for the extent of this pericope: v. 17 is also not represented in LXX^{B}. Indeed, the contents of this verse and its style resemble the concepts and diction of the Chronicler. The verse runs:

> "But for the Israelites that lived in the towns of Judah, Rehoboam reigned over them."

---

1 Cf. Brooke/McLean/Thackeray (1930), 252–254.

2 Cf. Burney (1903), 166–167; Montgomery (1951), 248–249.

3 Cf. Talshir (1993), 226–228.

4 Cf. also the late Targum to Cant. 8:11–12 as quoted by Talshir (1993), 290.

This kind of attention to people of (northern) Israel living in (the towns of) Judah features in 2 Chron. 30:25 and 31:6. Moreover, the style of the latter is very similar to our verse. It lies at hand, therefore, that 1 Kings 12:17 has been appended to the story of the assembly at Shechem by someone who belonged to the school of the Chronicler.[5]

Once 1 Kings 12:17 is deleted, the conclusion of the story will be established at v. 16b: "And Israel went to their tents". Such is the usual ending of an episode in biblical narrative, with the participants of an exchange going back each to his own place.[6] For this reason, perhaps, one should add v. 18b to the finale: "And king Rehoboam hurriedly mounted his chariot and fled to Jerusalem." On the other hand, the sending of Adoram in v. 18a hardly belongs to the original story. Note that the Israelites have already dispersed; there could be no encounter with them nor stoning. LXX^{B} does not read the name Rehoboam here; did this note originally belong to a story of insurrection during the reign of Solomon? (See below.)

A further surgery is suggested by historico-literary arguments. V. 15 that refers back to the prophecy of Ahijah the Shilonite to Jeroboam is coined in a clear Deuteronomic style: למען הקים את דברו as in Deut. 9:5, and a similar expression in Deut. 8:18. The verse appears to belong to the Deuteronomistic prophecy-fulfillment scheme dominant in the Book of Kings.[7] This series of utterances, however, is not uniform, originating as it does from distinct redactors of the Book of Kings.[8] Moreover, it has been imitated by late scribes. Such is the case of the realization of Joshua's curse on the rebuilder of Jericho. Originally it was related in Josh. 6:26, where it is still extant in the LXX, and then it was clumsily transferred to 1 Kings 16:34, in the midst of the exposition of the Ahab-Elijah epic.[9] The case of 1 Kings 12:15 is similar, as we shall see below. For the time being, suffice it to say that this verse betrays its editorial character and does not belong to the original texture of our story.

The reduced account, 14 verses in all, is 'secular' throughout; it does not hint at any divine intervention in the human realm, all the more so in state affairs. Yet, to what genre does it belong? One notes its indeterminate quality: no names of persons or places occur, save the obvious ones – Rehoboam and Shechem, the first capital of the North-

5 Benzinger (1899), 88, wrote: "Zusatz eines spitzfindigen Lesers ist jedenfalls [v.] 17".

6 Cf. Seeligmann (1962), 307–310.

7 Cf. von Rad (1947), 54–57; id. (1953), 78–83.

8 Cf. Rofé (1988a), 99–105.

9 Cf. Holmes (1914), 37. The verse in 1 Kings 16:34 is not represented by the Lucianic recension nor referred to by Josephus; cf. Fernandez Marcos/Busto Saiz (1992), 56.

ern Kingdom (v. 25). Otherwise, all is vague. This becomes even clearer, if we compare our story with another report of consultation, the one in the privy council of Abshalom in 2 Sam. 17:1–23.[10] There, a multitude of characters are identified: Abshalom, Ahitophel, Hushai, Jonathan, Ahimaaz, David. Moreover, in that story, the choice between the alternative proposals is not so obvious, it is more problematic. Ahitophel's advice seemed reasonable and found approval by the audience, and Hushai was compelled to resort to hard rhetoric in order to dismiss it. In our story, to the contrary, the situation is simplistic: evidently good advice is rejected in favor of bad.[11] The conclusion lies at hand that while 2 Samuel 17 belongs to the realm of history-writing, 1 Kings 12:1–16 is legend. At the same time, one should resist defining 1 Kings 12:1–16 as folktale:[12] the story presents an opposition between two categories of advisers, 'elders' and 'children'. Keeping in mind that the office of counsellor belongs to the realm of wisdom, this account should be considered as a paradigmatic legend emanating from wisdom circles.[13] This genre is well attested in Biblical literature as it occurs more than once in the tales of the prophets.[14]

The literary genre of the story determines its value as evidence for the political institutions of Israel in the 10th century BCE. Even if it were nearly contemporary with the events, as maintained by some scholars,[15] such a legend cannot bear witness to the 'organs of statecraft in the Israelite monarchy',[16] nor to the prerogatives of the people assembly *vis-à-vis* the kingship,[17] nor to the details of possible concessions on the part of the sovereign.[18] Also doubted is the possibility of identifying the 'children' of this story as royal commensals, or as a special group of youngsters raised at court, the sons of officials and courtiers, on the basis of an Egyptian analogy.[19] In reflecting reality every genre

---

10 I have been prompted to this comparison by Prof. Jacques Briend (Paris) who discussed with me 1 Kings 12:1–19 in May 1992. He was preceded by Plein (1966), 8–24.

11 Aliter Zalewski (1986), 51–57.

12 This has been proposed by Debus (1967), 26, followed by Long (1984), 136.

13 Thus rightly Jepsen (1956), 78: "das Kapitel ist daher als Beispielerzählung einer Weisheitsschule zu verstehen". The same position was held by J. Briend (above n. 10): "en récit sapientiel". Cf. also Cogan (2001), 350–351.

14 Cf. Rofé (1988a), 140–182.

15 Cf. Šanda (1911), 347; Plein (1966), 13: "... wahrscheinlich im Kreise der alten salomonischen Beamten entstanden". Cf. further Liver (1967), 75–101; de Vries (2003), 156–157.

16 As maintained by Malamat (1965), 34–65, followed by Halpern (1974), 527–528, in spite of the rebuttal of Evans (1966), 273–279.

17 Cf. Tadmor (1968), 12–14.

18 Cf. Weinfeld (1982), 27–53.

19 Cf. Lipinski (1974), 430–437; Fox (1996), 225–232.

has its own code of expression. This tenet is usually accepted for poetic genres such as the hymn or the dirge. It should be similarly recognized as regards the paradigmatic legend. This genre cannot submit precise data about historical events and situations.

In considering the date of composition, we shall mainly rely on linguistic arguments. Admittedly, in such a short account, which moreover contains not a few repetitions, one cannot expect to find many indicators for dating the language of the narrative. Even so, some tokens of late Biblical Hebrew can be detected. I will hereby present my findings.

A. Verse 8: אשר העומדים לפניו; a similar duplication of the relative pronoun is extant in 1 Kings 21:11: אשר היושבים בעירו. Joüon, in his grammar, observed: "Mais un type אשר היושב est sans doute impossible; 1K 12,8; 21,11 sont alteres", namely "corrupt".[20] In this case I would not opt for correcting the text.[21] I would prefer the possibility that the authors, writing in post-classical times, either during the Exile or after the Restoration, were not proficient in their style. As for the story of the vineyard of Naboth in 1 Kings 21:1–16 which contains the other instance of double pronouns, I hope to have made elsewhere a good case, relying on distinct arguments, for its late date of composition.[22]

B. The consistent use of the pronoun אני (vv. 11, 11, 14, 14) to the exclusion of אנכי indicates a relatively late date. Already by the end of the 19th century CE, scholars observed that "[i]n later books the preponderance of אני is evident".[23]

C. A taste of late diction is given by the use of the verb יעץ 'advise'. It appears here twice in the nif'al construction (1 Kings 12:6, 9). Classical Hebrew mainly uses this verb in the qal, while the Chronicler prefers the nif'al: 1 Chron. 13:1; 2 Chron. 20:21; 32:3 – 'consult'; 2 Chron. 25:17; 30:2, 23 – 'resolve'. Obviously, this piece of evidence alone would not suffice to determine the date. The same applies to the other arguments adduced above.

D. Indicative of late diction is, in my view, the use of ילדים 'children' to denote 'youngsters', 'young men' (vv. 8, 10, 14). This expression features five times in Daniel 1 (vv. 4, 10, 13, 15, 17). A conjecture has been advanced that Daniel 1 preserved the

20 Joüon (1923), 482, n. 3. Muraoka translated: "garbled"; see Joüon-Muraoka (1996), 595, n. 2.

21 Or omitting the whole relative clause; cf. Ehrlich (1914), 244.

22 Rofé (1988b), 89–104.

23 Cf. Brown/Driver/Briggs (1907), 59. They refer to Giesebrecht (1881), 251–258.

> terminology of the royal court which was already used in Solomonic times.[24] This is not very plausible given the span between the tenth and the third second century BCE which is the accepted date for the composition of the introductory story of Daniel.[25] The explanation of the term 'children' lies, I believe, elsewhere. In late Biblical and Rabbinic Hebrew one finds *yaldut*, 'childhood', with the meaning of 'young adulthood'. Instances are in Qoh. 11:9–10, t.Sukka 4:2 (twice). Especially significant is m.Sotah 1:4 where the age of a married woman, suspected of adultery is defined as *yaldut*! The same semantic shift is all the more evident with the designation *tinoq/et*, 'a suckling', extant in Rabbinic Hebrew: t.yoma 1:12 tells about a young priest killed while officiating in the temple and calls him *tinoq*; and in t.niddah 6:3 there is a ruling concerning a *tinoqet* 18 years old![26] This semantic shift, the causes of which escape me, perfectly explains the meaning of *yeladim* in Daniel 1 and in 1 Kings 12 as well: not 'children', but 'youngsters'. At the same time, it helps in establishing the date of our story: nearer to the Book of Daniel than to the reign of Solomon; late in the Persian period would be a sound historical setting.

History of tradition would corroborate this conclusion. Old sources related the revolt of Jeroboam as occurring during the reign of Solomon (1 Kings 11:26–28, 40). A Deuteronomistic writer confirmed this notion, speaking about the reign being torn from the hands of Solomon (vv. 29–31, 33) and his degradation to the rank of נשיא, 'prince' (v. 34), while Jeroboam will be king over Israel (v. 37). A later writer, Deuteronomistic too, introduced the concept that the split of the kingdom took place not in the days of Solomon but of his son (1 Kings 11:12–13, 35–36).[27] This latter trend became dominant in Chronicles, with the omission of the report of Solomon's sins and of the ensuing prophecy of Ahijah.[28] The sole cause of the secession in Chronicles remains Rehoboam's irresponsible behavior towards the people (2 Chron. 10:1–16). Thus, the story of the Assembly at Shechem accords with the views of late scribes. This makes it all the more probable that the story originated with them.

---

24 Cf. Lipinski (1974), 430–437.

25 Cf. Collins (1984), 45–46.

26 Sokoloff (2002), 537–538, lists 'young man' as the 3rd meaning.

27 Alternative analyses of the composite account of the scission of the kingdom are summarized by Würthwein (1985), 139–145.

28 Cf. Peterca (1981), 74–76.

Our conclusions with regard to the late date of composition and the literary genre – paradigmatic legend – suggest looking for an alternative setting, rather than the one usually proposed. The story, as we saw, sets elders and youngsters against each other. It also takes a stand in this opposition. It repeatedly states that Rehoboam "abandoned the advice of the elders who had advised him" (vv. 8a, 13b). And the aftermath is known. Ergo, the author insists on driving home the lesson that abandoning the advice of the elders brings about disaster. A look into the various pronouncements concerning age and wisdom can provide the ideological setting of this tale.

Bildad the Shuhite, one of Job's friends, asserts:

"Ask the generation past, study what their fathers have searched out.
For we are of yesterday and know nothing;
Our days on earth are a shadow.
Surely they will teach you and tell you,
Speaking out of their understanding." (Job 8:8–10 NJPS)

The teaching coming from 'the fathers' is based on their long experience, contrary to the ignorance of those who 'are of yesterday'.[29] And the subject of their teaching is the fate of the wicked, mentioned in v. 13. Job appears to quote this opinion in his third response (Job 12–14) when he says:

"With aged is wisdom
And in the length of days understanding."(Job 12:12)

It seems that Job does not accept this affirmation, but his response to it is not extant. In any case, Eliphaz appears to reiterate the argument in saying:

"What do you know that we do not know
Or understand that we do not?
Among us are gray-haired old men,
Older by far than your father." (Job 15:9–10 NJPS)

A clearer context obtains in Ps. 90:12:

"Declare that we count our days thus,
Then we may gather a wise heart."

The idiom 'to count days', attested by the Ugaritic epic of Aqhat,[30] means 'to live'. With 'thus' the poet refers to the seventy or eighty years, mentioned in v. 10. And the result follows: The long life will al-

---

29 Cf. Dhorme (1926), op. cit.

30 I follow Parker (1997), 61, adapting his translation: "Ask for life, Aqhat the hero, ask for life and I will give you, deathlessness, and I will endow you. I will let you count years with Baal; with the Son of El you will count months."

low the interceders to obtain wisdom. This tenet is not asserted in the psalm, it is just assumed.

However, in postexilic times the accepted truths of traditional wisdom began to be contested. Qoheleth, the great iconoclast, started his dispute by saying:

> "Better a poor but wise youth (ילד [!])
> Than an old but foolish king [...]
> For the former can emerge from a dungeon to become king,
> While the latter, even born to kingship, can become a pauper."
> (Eccles. 4:13–14 NJPS)[31]

The notion of 'old fools', who do 'not know any more how to beware', was well known by Qoheleth. Another late sage, Ben Sira, at the beginning of the 2nd century BCE tries to mitigate the harsh judgment of his predecessor. On one hand, he declares his animosity for "an old adulterous man who lacks intelligence" (Sir 25:2), but in the following verses he praises the discernment of old judges and counsellors (vv. 4–6).[32] Even for conservative Ben Sira age is no guaranty for wisdom!

However, the most fierce rebuttal of the traditional opinion about wisdom of the elders came from a different quarter, the response of Elihu (Job 32–37). Elihu started his speech by asserting:

> "I thought: 'Let age speak:
> Let advanced years declare wise things.'
> But truly it is the spirit in men,
> The breath of Shaddai that gives them understanding.
> It is not the aged who are wise.
> The elders who understand how to judge." (Job 32:7–9 NJPS)

This unequivocal rejection of old age as depository of wisdom does not rely on experience, as done by Qoheleth and Ben Sira. Elihu attributes knowledge to divine inspiration, thus initiating a new trend that will be evident in Daniel, Susanna, apocalyptic and Qumranic literature.[33]

Limiting ourselves, however, to the question of age and wisdom, we note here two propositions that continue Elihu's line of thought, drawing drastic conclusions. The Book of Jubilees declares:

> "And all the generations that shall arise from this time [sc. the death of Abraham] until the day of the great judgment shall grow old quickly, before they complete two jubilees, and their knowledge shall forsake them, by reason of their old age." (Jub. 23:16)[34]

---

31 The ground for this translation was provided by Ehrlich (1914), 71–72.

32 Cf. Segal (1971), op. cit.

33 See a summary in Rofé (2004), 1–11.

34 English translation by Charles (1913), Vol. II, 1–82. Cf. the Hebrew fragment 4Q221, published as '4 Jubilees' by VanderKam/Milik (1994), 70–72.

Old age wisdom is absolutely excluded. Instead, senility or even dementia is the lot of old people. The Damascus Document drew from thence practical conclusions for the organization of the Qumran community:

> "No one sixty years and upward shall stand to judge the congregation, for through the perfidy of man his days have become few, and through the wrath of God against those who dwell on earth, He decreed to take away their knowledge before they complete their days." (CD 10:7–10)[35]

This, it appears, was the opinion dominating the Essenian movement in its various phases, from Jubilees at the beginning to the Damascus Document when a restricted community had come into being.

Our excursus provides a historical setting to the paradigmatic legend in 1 Kings 12:1–16. Two competing lines of thought in Biblical wisdom have been identified: an older, traditional one, upheld the value of seniority, adducing its experience and prudence; a later, revolutionary trend denied the authority of elderly people, on the basis either of a contradicting factuality or of a competing divine inspiration. The story of Rehoboam and his advisers takes a stand on this issue:[36]

"Look what happens when you reject the advice of the elders and follow the suggestions of the youngsters! Once there was a king whose name was Rehoboam ..."

---

35 Cf. Schechter (1910), 109; Broshi (1992), 29; Baumgarten (1996), 159.

36 Cf. Jepsen, Briend and Cogan as quoted above, n. 13.

Bibliography

Baumgarten, J.M. (1996), Qumran Cave 4 XIII: The Damascus Document (4Q266–273) DJD XVIII, Oxford 1996.

Benzinger, I. (1899), Die Bücher der Könige. Mit einem Plan des alten Jerusalem und einer Geschichtstabelle. Erklärt von I. Benzinger, KHC 9, Freiburg i.B. et al.

Brooke, A.E./McLean, N./Thackeray, H.S.J. (1930), The Old Testament in Greek, vol. II/2: I and II Kings, Cambridge.

Broshi, M. (1992, ed.), The Damascus Document Reconsidered, Jerusalem.

Brown, F./Driver, S.R./Briggs, C.A. (1907), A Hebrew and English Lexicon of the Old Testament with an Appendix containing the Biblical Aramaic, Oxford (repr. 1972).

Burney, C.F. (1903), Notes on the Hebrew Text of the Books of Kings: with an Introduction and Appendix, reprinted New York 1970.

Charles, R.H. (1913), The Apocrypha and Pseudepigrapha of the Old Testament in English: With Introduction and Critical and Explanatory Notes to the Several Books, vol. II, Oxford (repr. 1968).

Cogan, M. (2001), I Kings: A New Translation with Introduction and Commentary, AncB 10, New York.

Collins, J.J. (1984), Daniel: With an Introduction to Apocalyptic Literature, FOTL 20, Grand Rapids.

Debus, J. (1967), Die Sünde Jerobeams. Studien zur Darstellung Jerobeams und der Geschichte des Nordreichs in der deuteronomistischen Geschichtsschreibung, FRLANT 93, Göttingen.

De Vries, S.J. (2003), 1 Kings, 2nd edition, Word Biblical Commentary 12, Nashville.

Dhorme, É.P. (1926), Le Livre de Job, Paris 1926. Engl. transl.: A Commentary on the Book of Job, English translation by H. Knight, Nashville 1984.

Ehrlich, A.B. (1914), Hohes Lied, Ruth, Klagelieder, Koheleth, Esther, Daniel, Esra, Nehemia, Könige, Chronik, Nachträge und Gesamtregister. Randglossen zur hebräischen Bibel, Bd. 7, Hildesheim (repr. 1968).

Evans, D.G. (1966), Rehoboam's Advisers at Shechem and Political Institutions in Israel and Sumer, JNES 25, 273–279.

Fernández Marcos, N./Busto Saiz, J.R. (1992), 1–2 Reyes, El texto antioqueno de la Biblia Griega II, Textos y estudios "Cardenal Cisneros" de la Biblia políglota Matritense 53, Madrid.

Fox, N. (1996), Royal Officials and Court Families: A New Look at ילדים (yēlādîm) in 1 Kings 12, BA 59, 225–232.

Giesebrecht, F. (1881), Zur Hexateuchkritik. Der Sprachgebrauch des hexateuchischen Elohisten, ZAW 1, 177–277.

Halpern, B. (1974), Sectionalism and the Schism, JBL 93, 519–532.

Holmes, S. (1914), Joshua: The Hebrew and Greek Texts, Cambridge.

Jepsen, A. (1956), Die Quellen des Königsbuches, 2. Aufl., Halle (Saale).

Joüon, P. (1923), Grammaire de l'Hébreu Biblique, 12th edition Rome, (repr. 1947).

– (1996), A Grammar of Biblical Hebrew, translated and revised by T. Muraoka, SubBi 14/1–2, Rome.

Lipinski, E. (1974), Le récit de 1 Rois XII 1–19 à la lumière de l'ancien usage de l'hébreu et de noveaux textes de Mari, VT 24, 430–437.

Liver, J. (1967), The Book of the Acts of Solomon, Bib. 48, 75–101.

Long, B.O. (1984), 1 Kings: With an Introduction to Historical Literature, FOTL 9, Grand Rapids.

Malamat, A. (1965), Organs of Statecraft in the Israelite Monarchy, BA 28, 34–65.

Montgomery, J.A. (1951), A Critical and Exegetical Commentary on the Book of Kings, ICC 6, Edinburgh.

Parker, S.B. (1997), Aqhat, in: id. (1997, ed.), Ugaritic Narrative Poetry, translated by Mark S. Smith, Writings from the Ancient World 9, Atlanta, 49–80.

Peterca, V. (1981), L'Immagine di Salomone nella Bibbia Ebraica e Greca: Contributo allo studio del "Midrash", Roma.

Plein, I. (1966), Erwägungen zur Überlieferung von I Reg 11,26–14,20, ZAW 78, 8–24.

Rofé, A. (1988a), The Prophetical Stories: The Narratives about the Prophets in the Hebrew Bible, Their Literary Types and History, translated from the 2nd Hebrew edition of 1986 by D. Levy, Jerusalem.

– (1988b), The Vineyard of Naboth: The Origin and Message of the Story, VT 38, 89–104.

– (2004), Revealed Wisdom: From the Bible to Qumran, in: J.J. Collins/ G.E. Sterling/R.A. Clements (eds.), Sapiential Perspectives: Wisdom Literature in Light of the Dead Sea Scrolls: Proceedings of the Sixth International Symposium of the Orion Center for the Study of the Dead Sea Scrolls and Associated Literature, 20–22 May, 2001, STDJ 51, Leiden, 1–12.

Šanda, A. (1911), Das Erste Buch der Könige, EHAT 9/1, Die Bücher der Könige. Übersetzt und erklärt von A. Šanda, Münster.

Schechter, S. (1910), Documents of Jewish Sectaries: vol. 1: Fragments of a Zadokite Work, Cambridge.

Seeligmann, I.L. (1962), Hebräische Erzählung und biblische Geschichtsschreibung, ThZ 18, 305–325.

Segal, M.Z. [Hirsch] (1971), The Complete Book of Ben Sira, 2nd edition, Jerusalem (in Hebrew).

Sokoloff, M. (2002), A Dictionary of Jewish Babylonian Aramaic of the Talmudic and Geonic Periods, Dictionaries of Talmud, Midrash and Targum 3, Publications of The Comprehensive Aramaic Lexicon Project, Ramat-Gan/Baltimore.

Tadmor, H. (1968), The 'People' and the Kingship in Ancient Israel: The Role of Political Institutions in the Biblical Period, Journal of World History 11, 3–23.

Talshir, Z. (1993), The Alternative Story of the Division of the Kingdom: 3 Kingdoms 12:24a–z, JBS 6, Jerusalem.

VanderKam J.C./Milik, J.T. (1994), 4QJubilees, in: H. Attridge et al. (eds.), Qumran Cave 4.VIII: Parabiblical Texts, Part 1, DJD 13, Oxford, 1–186.

von Rad, G. (1947), Deuteronomium-Studien (FRLANT 58), Göttingen.

– (1953), Studies in Deuteronomy, English Translation by D. Stalker, SBT 9, London.

Weinfeld, M. (1982), The Counsel of the 'Elders' to Rehoboam and Its Implications, Maarav 3/1, 27–53.

Würthwein, E. (1985), Das erste Buch der Könige, Kapitel 1–16. Übersetzt und erklärt von E. Würthwein, 2. Aufl., ATD 11/1, Göttingen/Zürich.

Zalewski, S. (1986), Rehoboam and His Advisors (1 Kings 12), Proceedings of the 9th World Congress of Jewish Studies, World Congress of Jewish Studies 9, Jerusalem, 51–57 (in Hebrew).

'What Share Do We Have in David ...?' – Ben Sira's Perspectives on 1 Kings 12[1]

MARKUS WITTE

1. 1 Kings 12 in Modern Research

The story about the division of Solomon's kingdom into two parts upon his death, and the subsequent reign of Rehoboam over Judah and Jeroboam over Israel in 1 Kings 12 has been a key text of recent studies in Old Testament literature. Mainly, eight issues are under discussion.

1. In addition to the usual differences between the Masoretic text and the Septuagint, most manuscripts of the Old Greek text (except the Hexaplaric recension) list an extensive alternative following v. 24, in contrast to what has been narrated before (3 Kings 12:24a–z). The origin of this Old Greek version in 3 Kings 12:24a–z, the history of its composition and its relation to the Masoretic text are still controversial. The question whether 3 Kings 12:24a–z is a midrash on the basis of a source more or less identical with the *Vorlage* of MT[2] or whether it represents an earlier pre-masoretic version of 1 Kings 12*,[3] is still pending.
2. The form-critical differences between a.) the story of Rehoboam and the people (vv. 1–20), b.) the story of Shemaiah, the man of God (vv. 21–24), c.) the different notes on Jeroboam's constructional and cultural measures (vv. 25–33) and d.) the narrator's

---

1 For the compilation of this essay the following editions of Ben Sira were used: Beentjes (1997); Calduch-Benages/Ferrer/Liesen (2003); Vattioni (1968) and Ziegler (1980). With regard to the numeration, the Hebrew text follows the edition of Beentjes, the Greek text the edition of Ziegler; for the problem of varying numerations cf. Reiterer (2003).

2 Cf. Talshir (1993), 260, 277ff.

3 Cf. Schenker (1996), 236.

comments (vv. 15, 19, 30) suggest that 1 Kings 12 does not represent a literary unit.[4]

3. Due to apparent deuteronomistic additions in v. 15b and v. 30, the extent of pre-deuteronomistic and post-deuteronomistic elements in 1 Kings 12 as well as its interrelation with the pre-deuteronomistic, deuteronomistic, and post-deuteronomistic description of the kings of Israel and Judah needs to be verified. This clarification is part of the literary and redaction-historical interrelation of 1 Kings 12 with the texts on statue labour in 2 Sam. 20:24 as well as in 1 Kings 5, of 1 Kings 12 with the narratives on Ahija of Shilo in 1 Kings 11; 13–14, and of 1 Kings 12:16 with the David tradition (cf. 2 Sam. 20:1).[5]
4. 1 Kings 12:28 corresponds clearly to Exod. 32:4, 8. In this regard, the question arises whether one comprehensive editorial revision might have influenced all books from Exodus to Kings. This assumption calls for a further look at the redaction-history of both, the Pentateuch and the *Deuteronomistic History*.[6] As 1 Kings 12 describes events in Shechem, Penuel, Bethel and Dan, our inquiry also seeks to explain the interrelation of 1 Kings 12 with the Shechem passages in Genesis 34, Judges 9 and Joshua 24, the Penuel passages in Gen. 32:23ff. and Judg. 8:8ff., the Bethel passages in Gen. 28:10ff., Genesis 35, Hosea and Amos[7] as well as the Dan passages in Judges 17–18.
5. Based on terminology, style and its overall tendency, the story of Shemaiah in 1 Kings 12:21–24 shows a close connection to another Shemaiah-Rehoboam narrative in the *Sondergut* of Chronicles (2 Chronicles 12).[8] This leads us to the question of an alleged interrelation between 1–2 Kings and 1–2 Chronicles which cannot be explained simply by assuming one common original basis or a dependence of one book upon the other. Instead, recent discussions emphasize differentiated and mutual influences between 1–2 Kings and 1–2 Chronicles.[9]

---

4 For the literary-historical discussion of the last ten years I exemplarily refer to Pfeiffer (1999), 26ff.; Becker (2000), 210ff.; Koenen (2003), 39ff.; Gomes (2006), 17ff.; Köhlmoos (2006), 154ff.; Pakkala (2008), 501ff.

5 Cf. esp. Becker (2000), 217ff.

6 Cf. esp. van Seters (1994), 290ff., 460; Berlejung (1998), 351ff.; Schmitt (2000), 235ff.; Köhlmoos (2006), 185ff.; Pakkala (2008), 519ff.

7 Cf. Pfeiffer (1999), 65ff.; Koenen (2003), 169ff.; Gomes (2006), 141ff.

8 Cf. further 3 Kings 12:24o, where the report of symbolic action narrated in 1 Kings 11:29–31 is not ascribed to Ahija, but to Shemaiah; cf. Talshir (1993), 105, 228ff.; Schenker (1996), 203ff., 225ff.

9 Cf. for 1 Kings 12:1–20 exemplarily Köhlmoos (2006), 158f.

6. The motif of "the day that Ephraim departed from Judah" in Isa. 7:17 prompts to inquire the interrelation of Kings and Isaiah in general and the redaction history of Isaiah in particular (cf. the parallel between Isaiah 36–39 and 2 Kings 18–20). Depending on the literary-historical classification of Isa. 7:17, an answer to the latter question brought forward in this article does not necessarily suggest that 1 Kings 12 is older than Isa. 7:17.
7. A central topic is the character and the value of 1 Kings 12 as a source for the history of Israel[10] and the cult of Yhwh, especially the history of the Exodus-credo and the Yhwh-sanctuaries in Dan and Bethel.[11] Does 1 Kings 12 contain reliable information on the early history of the kings, may it be in the main part, in vv. 1–20, or within the notes of vv. 25–29? Alternatively, does 1 Kings 12 represent a fictional aetiology on the two states, edited throughout the times?[12] Does the note in v. 19, which describes that the house of Israel broke away from the house of David עד היום הזה, refer inevitably to the formation of the narrative in vv. 1–20 before the decline of Israel in 722 BCE? If it does not, does this chapter then reflect the sharp differences between Samaria and Judah as they occurred in the Persian and Hellenistic period?
8. A last question concerns the reception history of 1 Kings 12 in Jewish writings from the Hellenistic-Roman period. Flavius Josephus (37–100 CE) offers an extensive paraphrase of 1 Kings 12 with own comments on the nature of leadership and a long speech by Jeroboam meant as an explanation of 1 Kings 12:26, 28.[13]

Yet, as early as the beginning of the 2nd century BCE, the teacher of wisdom Ben Sira remembers 1 Kings 12 in his 'Praise of the Fathers' (Sir 44–50). This text will be the focus of my essay in which I would like to show how and with which intent Ben Sira reads 1 Kings 12.

10 This applies to the narrated time, i.e. the last third of the 10th century BCE, and to the assumed time of the narrators, which in contemporary research is assumed to comprise roughly 700 years, considering both the earliest text-elements and the latest additions dating to the Hellenistic era.

11 Cf. Berlejung (1998), 326ff.; Pfeiffer (1999), 26ff.; Pakkala (2002), 86ff.; Koenen (2003), 43ff., 165ff.; Köhlmoos (2006); Gomes (2006); Pakkala (2008), 521ff.

12 Cf. Becker (2000), 227; Köhlmoos (2006), 158ff.

13 Cf. Ant., VIII:8, 1–4 (= VIII § 213–229); see for this text Begg (1993), 15ff., 30ff.

2. The Composition of the Portrait of Solomon in Ben Sira 47:12–25

Ben Sira is the first biblical author who connects the Torah and the historiographical, the priestly, and the prophetical traditions of Israel extensively with the wisdom tradition and updates them whilst interpreting them at the same time. On the background of a large gallery filled with heroes of Israel's history beginning with Enoch and ending with the high priest Simon[14] (Sir 44–50), Ben Sira draws his picture of Solomon (47:12–25).[15] This passage has partly remained intact due to the Hebrew manuscript B (H^B). Gaps and v. 16 which is missing in the Hebrew text can be reconstructed with the help of the Greek (G) and Syriac (Syr) versions.[16]

The portrait of Solomon is clearly structured (cf. the table in the appendix). The first section (A) consists of three bicola (vv. 12–13). It describes Solomon as David's successor (v. 12) who reigned at a time of peace granted by God (v. 13a–b) and built "a sanctuary forever" for God (v. 13c–d).[17] The second section (B) is split into two parts (B and B', vv. 14a–18b and vv. 18c–21). Each part consists of five bicola and represents an anastrophe. In direct speech,[18] the entire second section consists of Solomon's praise (vv. 14a–18b), followed by a distinct criticism of Solomon (vv. 18c–21). Both parts (B and B') conclude with a preview of Israel's fate (v. 18b and respectively v. 21b). The third section (C) consists of three bicola (vv. 23a–f), just like the first section (A). However, this section offers a preview of Solomon's death and upcoming succession to the throne (v. 23a–b). This part is then dedicated to Rehoboam and Jeroboam (v. 23c–d, e–f). Two bicola which summarize the history of the Northern kingdom (vv. 23g–25a) lead to Elijah's portrait

---

14 It is Simon II. (218–192 BCE), cf. 3 Macc. 2:1; Josephus, Ant. XII:4, 10 (= XII § 224); Mulder (2003); Schmitt (2004), 885f.

15 Already in his general prologue to the 'Praise of the Fathers', Ben Sira includes allusions to Solomon (cf. 44:3–5 *versus* 47:13a–b, 14–17).

16 V. 16a can be reconstructed according to G (εἰς νήσους πόρρω ἀφίκετο τὸ ὄνομά σου, cf. Isa. 66:19); v. 16b according to Syr (ܘܫܡܥܘܢ ܠܬܕܡܪܬܟ, cf. I Reg 5:14; 10:24): עד איים רחוקים הגיע שמך ויבואו לשמעך. For the reconstructed Hebrew text and the translation see the appendix.

17 Grammatically it is also possible, to understand 'God' himself as the subject of the edification of the temple in Sir 47:13b–c (cf. Ps. 78:69, Mulder [2003], 85). Nevertheless, the construction in G and the parallels in 2 Sam. 7:13, 1 Kings 5:19 and 1 Chron. 22:10 speak in favour of the interpretation of 'Solomon' as the subject. To the deliberate use of words of Ben Sira in 47:13, whereby Exod. 15:17 and Gen. 28:12f. are supplementarily integrated in the recurrence of 1 Kings 8, cf. Hayward (2002), 194f.

18 Cf. Sir 46:2; 48:4; 50:5. Syr underscores this by mentioning Solomon's name explicitly.

in 48:1–14(15–16).[19] By means of this composition Ben Sira offers a recurrence to the events listed twice (v. 21 and respectively in vv. 23–25) in 1 Kings 12. A repeated promise of a dynastic succession to David's throne drawing on 2 Sam. 7:11–16 (cf. Ps. 89:4, 20–30, 34–37)[20] separates the two recursive elements in v. 22, a composition evocative of Josh. 21:45 and its parallels, in which God promises his loyalty with the people.[21] At least, the first two bicola of v. 22 concern future events.[22] Therefore, they are probably not linked to 1 Kings 11:13 (32, 36). They might, thence, more likely represent a messianic commentary here. Isa. 11:1, 10–11, could be the background.[23]

3. Ben Sira's first Resumption of 1 Kings 12 in Sir 47:21

In his first resumption of 1 Kings 12 in 47:21, Ben Sira assumes that the division of Israel into two kingdoms (שבטים) is a negative consequence of Solomon's devotion to foreign women (Sir 47:19–20). Ben Sira's terminology and the motif are derived from 1 Kings 11. He, however, does neither copy the motif of the worship of foreign Gods nor the motif of the erection of foreign cultic places by Solomon. Ben Sira's criticism does not accuse Solomon of breaking the covenant as outlined by deuteronomistic redactors (1 Kings 11:11).[24] He primarily criticizes Solomon's sexual ethics, without pointing to Solomon as a negative example of the mixed marriages portrayed in Neh. 13:26. Corresponding to Ben Sira's statements on the relation between man and woman in 23:16ff. (G), 25:2 (G), 25:21 and 26:1ff., Solomon's behaviour appears to be a sign of foolishness. At this point Ben Sira is very close to Prov. 31:1–3, a passage criticizing Solomon indirectly:

---

19 Cf. Skehan/Di Lella (1987), 529ff., and van Peursen (2007), 409ff., consider v. 23a as the beginning of the Elijah-portrait already.

20 Cf. further Ps. 94:14; 1 Kings 8:57; 2 Kings 21:14; Pietsch (2003), 172–174.

21 Josh. 23:14, 1 Sam. 3:19, 1 Kings 8:56; 2 Kings 10:10; Tob. 14:4 (S). G translates more freely (καὶ οὐ μὴ διαφθείρῃ ἀπὸ τῶν λόγων αὐτοῦ) and therewith dissociates the close connection between Sir 47:22 and the row of God's promises.

22 So does the Greek translation, which in contrast to H^B (בחיריו ... אוהביו) concentrates the promise on the descendants of God's chosen *one* (ἐκλεκτοῦ αὐτοῦ) and the *one* who loved God (τοῦ ἀγαπήσαντος αὐτόν). Peters (1913), 408; Eberharter (1925), 153, and Mulder (2003), 85f., also interpret v. 22e–f future (... ויתן).

23 Cf. Isa. 11:1, 10 with Sir 47:22f (שרש, *conj.*; G: ῥίζαν), and Isa. 11:11 with Sir 47:22e (שארית, *conj.*; G: κατάλειμμα, Sir 44:17), cf. also Ps. 132:17; Segal (1958), 326. For a messianic interpretation of v. 22 cf. Peters (1913), 404ff.; Skehan/Di Lella (1987), 528; Marböck (1995), 132; Corley (2006), 304ff., who still consider this verse original, and Song of Sol. 17:4; 4Q174 Frags. 1 I, 21, 2:10ff.; 4Q252 V,2ff.

24 Against Brown (2002), 215f.

> "The words of Lemuel, king of Massa, with which his mother instructed him: What, my son? What, son of my womb? / What, son of my vows? Do not give your strength to women, / or your ways to those who destroy king."[25]

The historio-theological interpretation of 'God's wrath', which the deuteronomistic author of 1 Kings 11:9 ascribes to Solomon himself, is modified by Ben Sira in the sense that Solomon has drawn God's wrath towards his own descendants (47:20c–d, cf. 2 Kings 13:3; 23:26; 24:20).[26] The lament upon Solomon's bed (47:20d) does not refer to the lament for the people who feel suppressed by Solomon's son Rehoboam (cf. 1 Kings 12:14).[27] Instead, the lament in 47:20d parallels v. 20c and thus refers to the descendants of Solomon and the dissolution of the Davidic-Solomonic kingdom, which for Ben Sira already indicates the catastrophe of 587 BCE and the lament over the downfall of Jerusalem (cf. Lam. 1:22). In G, the lament refers to Solomon's foolishness (ἀφροσύνη), therefore, the relation between the foolish Solomon and his foolish descendants (v. 23c) is underscored (v. 23c) even clearer than in H^B. According to Syr, the 'sons of the sons' of Solomon will lament on their couch because of their father's iniquity (ܥܘܠܐ).

A second point of Ben Sira's criticism concerns Solomon's accumulation of wealth (v. 18c–d).[28] Thence, the *young* Solomon's joyful praise of wisdom (vv. 14–18b, cf. 1 Kings 3:7–12) conflicts with the *older* Solomon's foolishness (vv. 18c–21, cf. 1 Kings 11:4).[29] Ben Sira's yardstick is the Law of the King in Deut. 17:14–20.[30] Deut. 17:17 offers exactly this combination of motifs 'heap of wealth' and 'polygamy'. On the background of the deuteronomic 'Law of the King', we can implicitly deduce the fact that Solomon did not study the Torah (cf. Deut. 17:18–19). For Ben Sira, however, the characteristic of a wise man is the obedience

---

25 For the text-critical problems of Prov. 31:1–3 cf. the apparatus of the BHS and Murphy (1998), 239f.

26 For Ben Sira's use of the motif of the divine wrath as cipher for God's judgement cf. 1:22 (G); 5:7; 7:16; 16:6; 18:24 (G); 33/36:11 (G); 36:7 (H = 33:8 G); 39:27–28; 45:19; 48:10; Witte (2008a), 176ff.

27 Cf. Skehan/Di Lella (1987), 528.

28 Cf. also Bar. 3:16–17; Sir 8:2; 13:24, and for this interpretation of Sir 47:18c cf. Smend (1906), 85 (translation-part); Peters (1913), 407; Hamp (1952), 130; Skehan/Di Lella (1987), 528; Beentjes (2006), 139. In contrast, G understands the gathering of gold and silver as a collection in the name of God for the edification of the temple (cf. 1 Kings 5:20) and therefore appreciates Solomon's wealth (cf. 1 Kings 3:13; 10:27; 2 Chron. 1:15; 9:27). In G, the criticism of Solomon begins only in v. 19; cf. Ryssel (1900), 461; Lee (1986), 17, 214–215; Peterca (1988), 460; Sauer (2000), 323.

29 Cf. Josephus, Ant. VIII:7, 5 (= VIII § 194).

30 Cf. Beentjes (2006), 138–141.

to the Torah.[31] Under this circumstance, we have to assume that Ben Sira's praise of Solomon has to be readjusted according to this new perspective. He consequently holds that Solomon has stained his כבוד / δόξα (v. 20). Consequently, Solomon is not just a negative example of Ben Sira's warning in 33:23 [30:31] ("Be supreme over all of your works / and do not put a stain upon your glory"), but also stands in sharp contrast to Abraham. For Abraham did not stain his כבוד as Ben Sira describes explicitly in 44:19–20. We cannot understand the loss of the undivided reign against the background of 1 Kings 11 and 12 alone. We likewise need to consider a historical verification of the implicit sanctions outlined in the deuteronomic 'Law of the King' (Deut. 17:20):

> "[...] that his heart may not be lifted up above his countrymen and that he may not turn aside from the commandment, to the right or the left, so that he and his sons may continue long in his kingdom in the midst of Israel."

Unfortunately, the beginning of Ben Sira 47:21a has not survived in any of the Hebrew manuscripts. G confirms all remaining pieces in H^B. However, it updates the new political units in a negative manner, evocating a divided τύραννις[32]. This, of course, does not contribute to the reconstruction of the Hebrew version of v. 21a. Instead, Syr underlines the dissolution of Solomon's kingdom by the term ܦܠܓ (Ethpe., "to be divided", cf. Gen. 10:25). If the conjecture להיות העם is correct,[33] Ben Sira emphasizes the separation of the *one* people in his interpretation in 1 Kings 12. V. 23d clearly speaks of *one* people which justifies this interpretation. Here, Ben Sira proves to examine 1 Kings 12 closely, stressing the opposition of king and people in the main part (vv. 3–19). Like Chronicles, Ben Sira adheres to the ideal of the *one* people of Israel. In v. 21b, the qualification stating the "kingdom of violence (ממלכת חמס) deriving from Ephraim" forms a sharp contrast to the initial note, which informs us that Solomon reigned at a time of tranquillity (בימי שלוה in v. 13, cf. 1 Kings 5:4, 18; 1 Chron. 22:9). This opposition is more distinct in G, because the theme of peace (εἰρήνη) forms an essential aspect of the Greek portrait of Solomon (cf. vv. 13a, 16b). However, G mitigates the characterisation of Ephraim, when he calls Ephraim a "disobedient kingdom" (βασιλεία ἀπειθής). According to Syr, the house of Ephraim is the source of "a pagan kingdom" (ܡܠܟܘܬܐ ܚܢܦܬܐ, cf. Sir 16:6 [H^A]; Isa. 10,6). The term ממלכה stems from 1 Kings 12:26. The terminology ממלכת חמס, however, is unique. Ben Sira himself might have inserted this term.

31 Sir 1:26 (G); 6:37; 19:20 (G); 32:15ff.

32 For τύραννις in the sense of a despotic or cruel reign cf. 4 Macc. 1:11; 8:15; 9:30; 11:24; Wisd. of Sol. 14:21.

33 Cf. Vattioni (1968), 259.

4. Ben Sira's second Resumption of 1 Kings 12 in Sir 47:23, 24–25

In the note, explicitly dedicated to Rehoboam und Jeroboam (vv. 23, 24–25), Ben Sira explains the dissolution of the state's unity as a consequence of Rehoboam's foolishness. It is not clear, especially if we consider the gap in H^B, whether v. 23a–b already presents this line of thought.[34] Vattioni reads קצין ("prince", cf. 48:15f.) at the end of the bicolon in a neutral way whereas Smend suggested מנון ("übermütig", i.e. insolent, cf. Prov. 29:21).[35] Reading מנון fits well within the context but considering the background of Ben Sira's use of words, this reading must be considered uncertain.

The *scopus* of v. 23 is enlightened in the following colon. Here, Ben Sira paraphrases the name רחבעם ("broad in people") with the word-play רחב אולת ("broad in folly").[36] Rehoboam, "lacking in understanding" (חסר בינה)[37] stands in sharp contrast to his father Solomon, David's "clever son" (v. 12)[38], who once covered the earth with his "understanding" (בינה cj., v. 15)[39]. Ben Sira, however, does not excuse Solomon

---

34 With regard to v. 23 nearly every commentator offers another conjecture. Smend (1906), 54 (text-part), 86 (translation-part); Hamp (1952), 131, and Beentjes (1997) read מיואש ("in despair", cf. Eccles. 2:20) and understand v. 23a as a statement about the old Solomon; similary Ryssel (1900), 462, מיועש ("abgelebt", cf. Ps. 31:10); Peters (1913), 408, מיושש ("betagt"); Segal (1958), 327ff., משגש ("in error", cf. Job 19:4). Vattioni (1968), 259, reads משריש, which according to Job 5:3 can be understood as "taking root" and can then be related to the descendants of Solomon (cf. v. 22e–f). Sauer (2000), 324, translates "entwurzelt" (i.e. משרש) which does not fit in this context (cf. v. 22f.). G probably already had a corrupted *Vorlage* or did not understand it and uses the standard formula known from the Books of the Kings, Solomon rested with his fathers (μετὰ τῶν πατέρων [αὐτοῦ], cf. 3 Kings 11:43; 12:24a; 14:31; 15:8 etc.).

35 Vattioni (1968), 259; Smend (1906), 54 (text-part), 86 (translation-part); Peters (1913), 408; Hamp (1952), 131. With ἐκ τοῦ σπέρματος G refers to זרע, which Segal (1958), 327ff., takes as a basis for his reconstruction (זרע רך "a weak descendant").

36 G does not include this word-play and already mentions the people in v. 23c: λαοῦ ἀφροσύνην.

37 Cf. also the expression חסר־לב in Sir 6:20; Prov. 6:32; 7:7; 9:4, 16; 10:13; 11:12; 12:11; 15:21; 17:18; 24:30; 11QPs^a XVIII:5.

38 The literary background is 1 Kings 5:21 (cf. 1 Kings 2:3; Jer. 23:5). For the exchange of Solomon's designation in 1 Kings 5:21 as a בן חכם for the formulation בן משכיל cf. Prov. 10:1 *versus* Prov. 10:5. According to the Syriac version of 47:12, Solomon is a "powerful king" (ܬܩܝܦܐ ܡܠܟܐ), cf. the relationship for v. 19a in Syr ("and you gave your strength [ܬܘܩܦܟܝ] to women").

39 Cf. 1 Kings 5:9: Solomon as a man "rich of understanding" (רחב לב); with Segal (1958), 326ff.; Vattioni (1968), 259, and Sauer (2000), 322. In contrast, Smend (1906), 54 (text-part), 85 (translation-part) reads according to G (ἡ ψυχή σου) נפשך, but without changing the subject like Ryssel (1900), 461, reads בתבונתך (cf. Syr and 1 Kings 5:9). Concrete examples of this wisdom of Solomon are his songs, sentences and rid-

but also holds him responsible for the division of Israel into two separate states. Solomon left behind a foolish son. Hence, he was not able to fulfil his obligations as a father, which Ben Sira inculcates in his advices for education continuously.[40] What Ben Sira generally expressed as an admonishment in his speech about children's education in 30:1ff. (G/H^B) had become historically certified:

> "Discipline your son and make his yoke heavy, / so that you may not be offended by his shamelessness (אולת / ἀσχημοσύνη)" (30:13).[41]

Here, we can see how Ben Sira reads 1 Kings 12:1–20 with only a few words against the background of wisdom. This enables him to capture the style of 1 Kings 12:1–20 as a wisdom story quite well.[42]

In v. 23d, we find a typical shift of accent, compared to 1 Kings 12:1–20:

> "Rehoboam, who through his counsel caused the people to riot."

Ben Sira takes the key word "counsel" (עצה, βουλή) from 1 Kings 12.[43] It is new that he omits the *theologumenon* of "God's predestination" (מעם יהוה סבה, μεταστροφὴ παρὰ κυρίου, 1 Kings 12:15),[44] like the Greek version in 3 Kings 12:24s–t.[45] He further does not speak of an independent downfall (פשע) of Israel from the בית דוד (1 Kings 12:19)[46], but of the people's rebellion caused by Rehoboam. In an ironical reversal of his name, Rehoboam does not make wide the people but destroys its solidarity. On this account, the responsibility for the downfall of the kingdom is further shifted to the king. Ben Sira's term פרע (*Hifil*) does

---

dles, with which Ben Sira possibly alludes to the triad of the three canonical works of Solomon (Song of Sol., Prov., Eccles., cf. Goshen-Gottstein [2002], 250). This interpretation is evident in the Syriac version of Sir 47:17, according to which Solomon "explains (ܦܫܩ) sayings of wisdom in a book". This could be a mistake of the Hebrew text, cf. van Peursen (2007), 19f., but fits well with the image of Solomon in Syr. Therefore, an emendation of the Syriac text is not necessary.

40 Cf. Sir 3:11; 11:28; 41:7. To the difference in G see n. 35.

41 Cf. also 7:23–24; 41:5ff. Against this background the irony is to be considered: seeing as Solomon made – against the deuteronomic 'Law of the King' (Deut. 17:16; cf. Becker [2000], 222) – Israel's yoke heavy (1 Kings 12:4, 10, 14; cf. 5:27; 9:15), but not the yoke of his son, which had a fatal consequence.

42 For 1 Kings 12:1–20 as a sapiential narrative cf. the use of the root יעץ (vv. 8, 9, 13, 14, 28) and the contrast between the old and the young counselors (Job 12:12; 32:6–7; Prov. 5:13; 15:1–2; Eccles. 10:16); also Becker (2000), 217, and the article of Alexander Rofé in this congress volume.

43 Cf. 1 Kings 12:8, 13.

44 The word μεταστροφή is only certified here in the LXX and dependent upon 3 Kings 12:15 in 2 Chron. 10:15 LXX (cf. still Job 37,12 [α']) and is also rarely used in the pagan Old Greek, cf. Plato, Resp. 525c5; 532b7; Chrysipp, Fragm. moralia, 221:1.

45 Cf. Talshir (1993), 156, 255ff.

46 3 Kings 12a–z has neither equivalent for 1 Kings 12:19 (MT) nor for 3 Kings 12:19 (LXX), too; cf. Talshir (1993), 156; Schenker (1996), 228.

not come from 1 Kings 12, but it is found in Exod. 32:25. There, פרע describes Israel's lack of restraint caused by Aaron while Moses stayed at Sinai (Exod. 32:1). If we acknowledge the direct literary link between 1 Kings 12:28 and Exod. 32:4, 8, we can assume that the *sôfer* Ben Sira falls back on Exodus 32 for his *relecture* of the Rehoboam-story (1 Kings 12:1–20).[47] This means that Ben Sira stronger parallels Rehoboam's and Jeroboam's fault than 1 Kings 12 does. It can also not be excluded that Ben Sira had Exod. 5:4 in mind, a passage in which the modern exegesis has sometimes seen a parallel to 1 Kings 12.[48] As we can also find in other places of his work, Ben Sira connects different passages from the Hebrew Bible with the help of selective quotations of key words, as it is typical for single pesharim from Qumran and for the later exegesis of the midrash.[49] Ben Sira uses the term פרע precisely. This becomes evident against the background of two other passages in his work. In 46:7, Ben Sira refers to the story of the scouts (Numbers 13–14) and praises Joshua and Caleb for their resistance against the rebel assembly (פרע קהל). Again, Ben Sira does not back up the term פרע by the original in Num. 14:6–10. The actual key to understand Sir 47:23 is found in the aphorism in 10:3 (H^A):

"A wanton (פרוע) king destroys the city."[50]

What Ben Sira describes as a general observation on a possibly precise historical background in 10:3,[51] actually happened after Solomon's death – and might happen again. The strong emphasis on Rehoboam's responsibility corresponds to the judgement regarding this king in the Greek variant of 1 Kings 12:16 in 3 Kings 12:24t:

οὗτος ὁ ἄνθρωπος οὐκ εἰς ἄρχοντα οὐδὲ εἰς ἡγούμενον.

"for this person is not for a ruler or for a leader."[52]

The interpretation of the following stichos (Sir 47:23e–f) becomes difficult because H^B is quite damaged on the one hand but on the other hand contains the sentence עד אשר קם אל יהי לו זכר as a headline in con-

47 However, compare both, the variant to 1 Kings 14:22, in which – like in G, 3 Kings 12:24a and 2 Chron. 12:14 – Rehoboam mentioned in v. 21 is the subject of the sin and not Judah, and the tendency to excuse Rehoboam in 2 Chron. 13:7.

48 Exod. 5:4–5 uses the word פרע – possibly in deliberate assonance to פרעה. To the parallelisation of Exodus 5 and 1 Kings 12 cf. van Seters (1994), 71.

49 Cf. concerning the portrait of Solomon: esp. Peterca (1988), 457ff., and Hayward (2002), 194f.

50 G: βασιλεὺς ἀπαίδευτος ἀπολεῖ τὸν λαὸν αὐτοῦ, cf. 2 Chron. 28:19; Sir 10:8–9; Prov. 29:18.

51 Cf. Sir 47:23c *versus* Prov. 28:16. Finally, the phonetic assonance of פרע and אפרים could also stand in the background of Ben Sira's choice of words.

52 Concerning the origin of this sentence in 3 Kings 12:24t cf. Talshir (1993), 130f., 256.

trast to G. In addition, this stichos is longer than the other stichoi in the 'Praise of the Fathers'. This version of H^B might be derived from a gloss. The wish אל יהי לו זכר proves the assumption that the name ירבעם בן־נבט was added at an earlier stage of the textual transmission (before the production of G).[53] Insofar as the זכר represents a main motif throughout the 'Praise of the Fathers', Jeroboam's non-remembrance marks him as a villain. On the level of the 'Praise of the Fathers', Jeroboam resembles the negative counterpart of Moses (Sir 45:1),[54] the judges (46:11), Josiah (49:1) and Nehemiah (49:13) whose remembrance is a blessing to posterity. Ben Sira remains very close to the deuteronomistic evaluation of Jeroboam's character. The key word זכר succeeds to put Josiah (49:1) in opposition to Jeroboam (47:23) which adheres to deuteronomistic categories (cf. 1 Kings 12:31ff. *versus* 2 Kings 23:15ff.).

Ben Sira illustrates this explicitly in the next colon (v. 23f) when he refers to Jeroboam as a sinner and as Israel's enticer (cf. 1 Kings 14:16). Ben Sira does not explain what the "sin of Jeroboam"[55] consists of. He restricts himself to a formula-like repetition of 1 Kings 12:30a in v. 23f–g and thus connects it with a preview on people being exiled from the Northern kingdom as it is told in 2 Kings 17 (Sir 47:24a–25).[56] Using the term נדח (*Hifil*) in v. 24a, Ben Sira participates in a formula for the banishment of Israel from the Book of Jeremiah[57] and interprets 1 Kings 13:34 and 2 Kings 17:18, 21ff. correctly. In v. 25 (ולכל רעה התמ[כר]),[58] Ben Sira adheres to the phraseology in 2 Kings 17:17b. The term מכשול in v. 23g[59] which does not appear in 1 Kings 12:30 and the structure of his portrait of Solomon in 47:12–25 (cf. the appendix) demonstrate that Ben Sira remembers Jeroboam's installation of the images of the bulls in Dan and Bethel as well as his construction of sanctuaries on the high

53 Cf. Skehan/Di Lella (1987), 530ff. Syr has no equivalent of עד אשר קם. Van Peursen (2007), 327f., holds this for originally.

54 Cf. Witte (2001), 161ff.

55 Cf. 1 Kings 14:16; 15:30; 16:31; 2 Kings 3:3; 10:31; 13:2, 6; 15:9, 18, 24; 17:22.

56 Subject of להדיחם (v. 24a) is still Jeroboam, because נדח *Hifil* has an active resp. causative meaning (cf. G ἀποστῆσαι, and Peters [1913], 405; Eberharter [1925], 153; Skehan/Di Lella [1987], 529). However, Ryssel (1900), 462; Smend (1906), 86 (translation-part), and Sauer (2000), 324, translate להדיחם as a passive.

57 See Jer. 8:3; 16:15; 23:2f, 8; 24:9; 27:10, 15; 29:14, 18; 32:37; 40:12; 43:5; 46:28; cf. also Deut. 30:1.

58 The subject is very likely to be Ephraim, so unequivocal G (ἐξεζήτησαν). Against that Syr relates v. 25a to Jeroboam as perpetrator ("causing them to go into exile from their place / and he multiplied their sins greatly"). The note has a special sharpness because Ben Sira uses the word רעה, which is proved 31 times in the Hebrew fragments, in the context for the 'Praise of the Fathers' only in 47:25.

59 Cf. Ezek. 14:3f., 7; 44:12; 1QS II:12; 4Q372 f.8:7; 4Q428 f.10:9. For the translation in G (ὁδὸς ἁμαρτίας) cf. Sir 21:10 (G); Ps. 1:1 LXX; 145:9 LXX.

places corresponding to 1 Kings 12:28, 31 and 2 Kings 10:29 (cf. 2 Chron. 13:8; Tob. 1:5 [S]). Therefore, the bicolon in v. 23e–f (C.3) corresponds with the bicolon 13c–d (A.3) which talks about Solomon's erection of the temple in Jerusalem.

The following bicolon (vv. 24b–25a) gives a further reason for the downfall of the Northern kingdom. We find it first in the reference to Israel's growing sin, for which Ephraim himself is asked to take responsibility.[60] Ben Sira has compiled the history of the Northern kingdom in just three bicola. We find a comparable condensation of the history in 4QMMT C 19, which is the only non-biblical text found in Qumran to mention "Jeroboam" (4Q398 Frag. 11–13:2).[61] Like the deuteronomistic theology, Ben Sira views the history of the Northern kingdom as a history of sin, from the beginning till the end. Elijah's appearance, Ben Sira remembers in his next passage on the 'Praise of the Fathers' (48:1–14), could not change Israel's sin:

> "But for all of this, the people did not repent / nor did they refrain from their sin, until they were torn from their land / and scattered throughout all the earth. And though but a few were left to Judah / there yet remained a ruler from the house of David." (48:15, cf. Deut. 28:63f.)

In comparison to H^B, Sir 48:15–16 shows characteristic differences in G because of the translator's new historical and cultural situation. According to G, not a small remnant is left for Judah (H^B) but one very small people (ὁ λαὸς ὀλιγοστός) that survives; a ruler does not remain *for* the house of David (לבית דוד), but *in* the house of David (ἐν τῷ οἴκῳ). In line with 47:24, 48:16b states that some of them (i.e. the kings) multiplied sins (ἐπλήθυναν ἁμαρτίας), whilst H^B says that they "committed astonishing wrongs" (הפליאו מעל). The Greek version of v. 25b has an additional colon, which informs about God's retribution that is sure to come (ἕως ἐκδίκησις ἔλθῃ ἐπ᾽ αὐτούς).[62] It puts a further emphasis unto the relation between the note about the history of the Northern kingdom and Elijah's portrait (cf. 48:7b [G]) and corresponds to the ten-

60 With regard to the contents G correctly offers plural-suffixes here, cf. Peters (1913), 409.

61 For the mentioning of Jeroboam beyond the canonical books cf. also VitProph 18:3 (cf. 1 Kings 14:7–14); 19:1 (cf. 1 Kings 13:1–32) and 2 Baruch 62:1–2 (cf. Lied [2008], 88–89); for the "Jeroboam-coins" cf. p. 106.

62 As a translation back into Hebrew shows, the colon could be either the deployed beginning of 47:23 or a doublet to 48:1: cf. עד אשר נקם יבוא עליהם opposite to עד אשר קם אל יהי לו זכר (47:23a) resp. עד אשר קם נביא כאש (48:1a). Beyond that, G shows another order of the stichoi in vv. 23f–25a than does H^B: v. 23g (H^B) corresponds to v. 23f (G), v. 23h (H^B) corresponds to v. 24b (G), v. 24b (H^B) corresponds to v. 25a (G), cf. Reiterer (2003), 232f. H^B represents probably the original sequence of the stichoi, cf. Skehan/Di Lella (1987), 531.

dency of the Greek Sira version which stresses especially God's righteousness.[63]

If we take a look at 1 Kings 12, it is striking that Ben Sira emphasizes the active role of the king, as we have seen in the passage about Rehoboam. Whilst in 1 Kings 12 Jeroboam remains in the background, and the people play an important role to raise him to the throne, Jeroboam stands up himself in Ben Sira (קם, 47:23e). With this word (קום, *Hifil*) Ben Sira takes up the notes concerning the occurrence of Solomon's adversaries in 1 Kings 11:14, 23, especially the note about Jeroboam's revolt in 11:26, and then moves on immediately to 1 Kings 12:25–30. Ben Sira shares this emphasis of Jeroboam's self-contained action with the Greek parallel version in 3 Kings 12:24 (cf. v. 24d–f, 24o).

5. Ben Sira's Image of an Ideal Ruler

The strong focus of the events in 1 Kings 12 on the two kings Rehoboam und Jeroboam is due to the structured 'Praise of the Fathers' as a view on history, orientated to look at a single person, which has its model in the genre of an encomium.[64] Moreover, there is an entirely critical attitude against kingship throughout the Book of Ben Sira (cf. 10:3, 8ff.).[65] Continuing the deuteronomistic assessments of the kings, only David, Hezekiah and Josiah receive a positive judgement by Ben Sira.[66] They alone have kept the תורת עליון (49:4) and proved themselves as Abraham's true descendants (44:20).[67] This proves the above mentioned assumption based on the parallel between Sir 47:18c–19 and Deut. 17:17 that according to Ben Sira's conviction Solomon has despised the Torah. The high priest, Simon, represents Ben Sira's truthful ideal (50:1ff.). He is the pivot of the 'Praise of the Fathers'.[68] Because of his care for Jerusalem and the temple, Simon resembles all those cul-

63 Cf. Sir 2:10–11 (G); 12:6 (G, H[A]); 16:12 (G, H[A]).

64 Cf. the extensive dissertation of Lee (1986); Schmitt (2003), 359–381; id. (2004), 873–896.

65 Cf. the admonition of the leaders of the people (שרי עם, μεγιστᾶνες λαοῦ) in 33:19 (H[E]) / 30:27 (G), the negative design of the kings in 45:3; 46:20; 48:6; 49:4, and the warning of the arbitrariness of the rulers in 4:27; 7:6; 8:1. In 7:5 (H[A]) מלך is likely to refer to God (cf. G, Syr, VL).

66 In 1 Kings 15:11 and 22:43 Asa and Jehoshaphat are still judged positively with reservations.

67 For Abraham as a model of obedience for Jewish religious ethics cf. Mack (1985), 211.

68 Cf. Schmitt (2004), 873–896; Marböck (2006), 155ff.; Beentjes (2006), 141ff., and extensively Mulder (2003).

tural and political virtues which David, Hezekiah and Josiah were praised for. Indeed, the high priest Simon finally appears as the better Solomon and consequently as the better king. He alone can restore Israel's unity, which Solomon, Rehoboam, and Jeroboam have destroyed. He can restore Israel as *one* people gathering around the Torah, coming together around the *one* temple in Jerusalem. According to the covenant which God established with Aaron and Phinehas (cf. Sir 45:15, 24; 50:24 [H^{B}]), only the high priest of Jerusalem might secure Israel's continuity and stability. If we consider that Aaron's task was to teach the Torah to Israel (Sir 45:17, cf. 45:5),[69] we can state that the high priest represents the ideal of the deuteronomic 'Law of the King' (Deut. 17:14–20).

6. Ben Sira's Identification of Ephraim

It is quite remarkable that Ben Sira calls the Northern kingdom by the name of "Ephraim", both in 47:23g and in 47:21b, while 1 Kings 12 uses the terms ישראל or בית ישראל. This could be due to Jeroboam's genealogical characterization as an Ephraimite in 1 Kings 11:26 and the note that Jeroboam had built "Shechem in the hill country of *Ephraim*" (as his residence) in 1 Kings 12:25. However, Ben Sira uses the name "Ephraim" with a negative connotation against the background of the Book of Hosea.[70] In this regard, Ben Sira participates in a special usage of the name "Ephraim" as a cipher for a negative element as it occurs in different scriptures of the Hellenistic-Roman period, e.g. in the Septuagint version of 1 Kings 12:24b,[71] in the Damascus Covenant,[72] in the Qumran-pesher to Psalm 37,[73] and possibly in 4Q381 and in 4Q460.

If the phrase מאפרים ("from Ephraim") is included in the gratitude for the redemption of Judah in 4Q381 Frag. 24:5, we have a negative connotation of Ephraim from a Judean-Jerusalemite perspective as in Sir 47:21. 4Q460 Frag. 5:I:8f. certifies explicitly that "no-one in Ephraim has grasped the precepts" of Yhwh. Because 4Q460 is in a miserable condition, it is difficult

69 Cf. Fabry (2003), 274ff.

70 Cf. exemplary Hosea 4:17; 5:9; 9,11–16; 13:12; 14:9. To the Book of Hosea (in its canonical form) as an anti-Samaritan work cf. Levin (2001), 95f.

71 Therefore, Jeroboam appears here first as an ἄνθρωπος ἐξ ὄρους Εφραιμ, whereby the accent shifts from "the evil Ephraemit" to "the evil Ephraim", and second as a "son of a harlot" (γυνὴ πορνή); cf. Talshir (1993), 51f., 102; Schenker (1996), 217f.

72 CD-A VII:10–14 as a quotation and interpretation of Isa. 7:17; cf. also Zangenberg (1994), 338f.

73 4Q171 II:18f. with a quotation and interpretation of Ps. 37:15; cf. also Zangenberg (1994), 336f.

to decide whether such a verdict of Judah exists. According to Frag. 1:5, Judah might be judged positively.[74]

Like Ps. 78:9 (also cf. v. 67),[75] Ben Sira associates the term "Ephraim" with the Samaritans. Ben Sira shares a perspective which is clearly in favour of Jerusalem. This can be perceived in the passage 1.) where he praises Jerusalem as the Holy city,[76] 2.) of his celebration of the cosmic wisdom, which rests on Zion (Sirach 24), 3.) of his prayer for the salvation of Zion (Sirach 36),[77] and 4.) of his description of the high priest Simon, who practices the worship in favour for Israel's blessings at the temple of Jerusalem and in a continuous line with Aaron and Phinehas (50:13, 24 [H]).[78]

The 'Praise of the Fathers' culminates in Ben Sira's verdict regarding the inhabitants of Seir, the Philistines, and "the foolish people who dwell in Shechem" (50:25–26). The גוי נבל in Shechem is nothing else but the Samaritan congregation and Ephraim's successor. Ben Sira's *literary background* might be the story of the נבלה of the Shechemites in Gen. 34:7. This is explicitly the case in the Testament of Levi 7:2 (2nd century BCE) which benotes Shechem as "City of the Senseless" (πόλις ἀσυνέτων) because of Genesis 34 (cf. Jub. 30:5). 4Q372, a fragmentary historio-theological text (2nd century BCE), mentions נבלים in the land of Joseph with an anti-Samaritan tendency.[79] Finally, the characterisation of the Shechemites as "godless" (ἀσεβεῖς) and as "doers of deadly works" (λοίγια ἔργα) in the work of the Judeo-Hellenistic author Theodotus,[80] who wrote at the time of John Hyrkanus I's destruction of the Samaritan temple on the Mt. Gerizim (ca. 110 BCE) and the destruction of Shechem (107 BCE),[81] and as "doers of violence" (עבדי חמסא) in

74 According to Zangenberg (1994), 335f., 4QpNah 2,1ff. also mention Samaria with a negative connotation. But this interpretation is uncertain.

75 Cf. Witte (2006), 22ff.

76 Cf. 47:11; 48:17, 24; 49:6; 49:12–13; 50:1–4; (51:12g–h [H[B]]).

77 Cf. 36:13(18). The prayer in 36:1–17 (G: 33:1–13a; 36,16b–22) might be an integral part of the Book of Ben Sira.

78 Cf. Sir 45:6ff.; 45:16–17; 45:23. For this and for G's modifications of 50:24 regarding the contemporary historical changes cf. Hayward (1996), 81f.; Mulder (2003), 303f.; Fabry (2003), 272ff.; Brutti (2006), 201ff., 280ff.; Corley (2006), 308; Zsengellér (2008), 147; Boccaccini (2008), 32.

79 Frag. 1:10f. (cf. 4Q371,1:10), cf. Schuller (1990), 360, 371ff. (with dating 4Q372 in the time before John Hyrkanus I); Zangenberg (1994), 332ff.; Zsengellér (1998), 174f. Possibly, the term גוי נבל also refers to Samaria in 11Q14 Frag. 2:1.

80 Frag. IX:22,9, text by Denis (1970), 206, 27ff., translations by Walter (1983), 169f., and by Fallon (1985), 793; cf. also Zangenberg (1994), 35f., and Mulder (2003), 232, 238, 359.

81 For the Samaritan temple on the Mt. Gerizim and its history cf. 2 Macc. 6:2; PsEupolemus (SamaritanAnonymus) 9:17 (text by Denis [1970], 197f.; translation by Walter

the Aramaic Testament of Levi (CTL Cambridge Col. b, 19; 2nd century BCE)[82] belong to this context. Ben Sira's *historical example* is the גוי נבל, who once murmured against God in the desert (cf. Deut. 32:6 as well as Sir 16:6 [גוי חנף] in relation to Num. 11:1–3).[83] According to Ben Sira, Ephraim's next relatives are the Babylonians who destroyed Jerusalem and its temple in 587 BCE (Sir 49:5–6,[84] cf. Deut. 32:21; Ps. 74:18). If the "coins of Jeroboam", minted in the city of Samaria between 350 and 333 BCE, are a witness for the (proto) Samaritan self-consciousness,[85] then Ben Sira's verdict in 47:23 receives an additional historic meaning. On the eve of Antiochus IV Epiphanes' religious crisis, Ben Sira reflects confrontations between the Samaritans and the people of Jerusalem.[86] This becomes clear in the Greek version where "Samaria" substitutes "Seir". This circumstance might be due to a change in the relationship between the inhabitants of Seir/Edom, the Idumeans, and the Judeans respectively between Samaria and Jerusalem at the time of Ben Sira's grandchild after the 38th year of Euergetes (i.e. Ptolemaius II., 132 BCE, cf. Sir prol. 27) and under the rule of John Hyrkan I (134–104 BCE).[87]

Considering the *relecture* in 1 Kings 12, we stick to the fact that Ben Sira has a central interest in Israel's unity.[88] Israel currently finds its unity by receiving instructions from the Torah (45:5, 17) and participating in the worship in Jerusalem as well as in the future instauration of the community of the 12 tribes through Elijah (48:10). Due to the high priest celebrating at the temple of Jerusalem, Israel experiences the saving presence of God who is as the only One (36[33]:5) at the same

---

[1976], 141); Josephus, Ant., XI:8, 4 (= XI § 324); XII:1 (= XII § 10); XII:5, 5 (= XII § 257–264); XIII:3, 4 (= XIII § 74–79); XIII:9, 1 (= XIII § 255f.); Bell., I:2, 6 (= I § 63); bYom 69a, and Kippenberg (1971), 57ff.; Zsengellér (1998), 150ff.; Magen/Misgav/Tsfania (2004), 3ff.; Magen (2007), 157ff.

82 Cf. Beyer (1984), 188ff., 195. That the expression אנשי חמס in 1QpHab VIII:2 also refers to the Samaritans is improbable (cf. Zsengellér [1998], 171).

83 In G, this relationship is more distinct, as the grandchild in 16:6 talks about an ἔθνος ἀπειθές and in 47:21 about a βασιλεία ἀπειθής, cf. Ps. 77(78):8 (σ'); SibOr. 3:668 (the pagans as λαὸς ἀπειθής).

84 G mentions in v. 5 only "a foreign nation" (cf. Sir 29:18; 33(36):3; Song of Sol. 2:2; Bar. 4:3; Josephus, Ant., VIII:7, 5 [= VIII § 191]), in v. 6 Jerusalem is supplementary qualified as the "chosen" city (cf. 1 Kings 8:44, 48; 11:13, 32, 36; 14:21).

85 Cf. Spaer (1979), 218; Spaer (1980), 2f., plate 1; Meshorer/Qedar (1991), 13f., 49, nos. 23–27, plates 3–4; Talshir (1993), 285; Eshel (2007), 230, 233 (Jeroboam as a name of a governor of Samaria?); Magen (2007), 180.

86 Cf. Purvis (1965), 92f.; Kippenberg (1971), 74ff.; Lee (1986), 208–209; Hayward (1996), 62f.; Mulder (2003), 328; Zsengellér (2008), 147.

87 Cf. Zangenberg (1994), 41f.; Hayward (1996), 73–84; Mulder (2003), 221ff., 328, 354–355; Fabry (2003), 278; Marböck (2006), 165f.

88 Cf. Sir 36:11 (33:13); 36:12 (33:17); 36:17(22); 37:25; 44:23; 45:5, 11; 46:14; 48:10; 50:13, 19; (51:12f).

time "all" (הכל, 43:27) and the "Holy of Israel" (קדוש ישראל, 50:17)[89]. This means, according to Ben Sira, that the loss of Israel's unity caused by Solomon, Rehoboam and Jeroboam will be compensated by the *one* Torah, the *one* worship in Jerusalem, and the hope for an eschatological turn through the *one* God.

7. Ben Sira and the Share in David – Sir 47:22

If we combine Sir 47:22, which I have held to be secondary at the beginning of my essay, with the interpretation of Ben Sira's exegesis, we can see, that even 1 Kings 12:16 finds its consideration. Israel's respectively Ephraim's voluntary separation from David (מה־לנו חלק בדוד) appears as a sign of special foolishness if we consider the background of the promised dynastic line to David, which is also evident in Ben Sira (45:25a–b; 47:11–12).[90] To break away from the house of David means to renunciate the participation in the promise given to David. Therefore, Israel surrenders its own existence as 2 Kings 17 and Ben Sira in 47:24–25 and 48:15 confirm. Ephraim is not only a ממלכת חמס but also a גוי נבל. Ephraim has "no share, nor right, nor memorial in Jerusalem" (Neh. 2:20). With this approach, Ben Sira achieved to bring 1 Kings 12 into his own present time.[91] Ben Sira's reception of 1 Kings 12 is not only a remembrance of the past and a subject for his instruction but also a means of his political theology.

8. Conclusions

In his portrait of Solomon, Ben Sira emphasizes the main important points of the description in 1 Kings 3–11. In this process, Solomon's ambivalence, being a wise man in his youth and a foolish ruler advanced in years becomes clearer than in 1 Kings. The authors of 1 Kings illustrate the temple construction in four chapters (1 Kings 5–8). Ben

---

89 G uses the divine title παντοκράτωρ "the Almigthy" here, which the Greek version of Ben Sira employs further in 42:17 (κύριος ὁ παντοκράτωρ; H^B אלהים צבאיו; H^{Mas} אדני) and in 50:14 (ὕψιστος παντοκράτωρ; H^B עליון).

90 Cf. Sir 51:12h. Yet, the originality of the prayer in 51:12a–o (H^B) is disputable; cf. Pietsch (2003), 174f.

91 See also the historiographical sentences about the Philistines (46:18; 47:7) or the references to the exile of Israel and Judah (47:24–25; 48:15–16; 49:4–6), which are transparent to Ben Sira's own time, cf. Marböck (1995), 129ff.; Mulder (2003), 86–87, 273–274.

Sira reduces this theme to one verse because he sees David as the actual founder of the worship at the temple as Chronicles or Psalm 78 describes it,[92] and because the current worship at the temple under Simon is important, too.[93]

In the eyes of Ben Sira, 1 Kings 12 is a wisdom- and sin-narrative. However, he does not consider the note on Ahijah in 1 Kings 12:15 and the story of Shemaiah in vv. 21–24, although he really honours the prophets and their prophecies[94] in favour of a compressed and paradigmatic *relecture* of Israel's history. The centre of Ben Sira's interest on 1 Kings 12 is Israel's unity. The kings of Judah and Israel destroyed this unity. Therefore, Ben Sira reads 1 Kings 12 in the light of criticism of kingship. More rigidly than 1 Kings 12, he marks Ephraim that rebelled against the house of David as a 'reign of violence'. Hence, 1 Kings 12 is an 'anti-Ephraim' and an 'anti-Samaritan'-story for Ben Sira.

How can the questions concerning 1 Kings 12, which I posed in my introduction, be answered from Ben Sira's point of view?

1. Ben Sira's *Vorlage* is a Hebrew text and in its essence corresponding to the Masoretic text. However, there are some remarkable points connecting it to the Greek version in 3 Kings 12:24a–z, e.g. the lack of the theological notices in 1 Kings 12:15, 19 or the emphasis on Rehoboam's and Jeroboam's activity.
2. Ben Sira's grandchild translated the Hebrew text of his grandfather into Greek and did not evidently fall back upon a Greek version of 1 Kings 12. The differences in G (e.g. Sir 47:18) are a result of the translator's specific understanding of his *Vorlage* and of his own historical context.
3. In a literary and redaction-historical perspective Ben Sira obviously considers 1 Kings 12 to be one unit. However, he reads selectively and his omission concerning the story of Shemaiah or the theological interpretation in 1 Kings 12:15, 19 illustrate this.
4. It is remarkable but also a characteristic element of Ben Sira how he presents his intrabiblical interpretation of the scripture

---

92 Cf. Witte (2006), 37ff.

93 For Ben Sira's temple theology in the shadow of Deuteronomy/Deuteronomism and Ezekiel cf. Zsengellér (2008), 145ff.

94 Cf. Sir 36:16(20); 39:1; 46:1, 13; 48:1ff., 22; 49:7ff., and in that regard cf. Goshen-Gottstein (2002), 250ff. According to the Syriac version of 47:17, Solomon signalized himself as well by the prophecy (ܢܒܝܘܬܐ). However, it is disputed whether Syr understood the Hebrew word מליצה (G: ἐν ἑρμηνείαις) as a sapiential term like in Hab. 2:6 and Prov. 1:6 and, therefore, uses the term "prophecy" in a broader sense, so van Peursen (2007), 88f., or whether Solomon is regarded as a prophet in the literal sense of the word, corresponding to Syr's esteem of the prophecy (cf. 36:17; 47:1; 48:12; 48:20, 22).

by means of a carefully chosen lexis. Nonetheless, we have to distinguish between the intrabiblical system of Ben Sira's Hebrew work, the Greek translation of his grandchild as well as the Syriac and the Latin version: Each version of Ben Sira has its own intertextuality and its own canonicity.[95]

5. Ben Sira perceives the narrated events in 1 Kings 12 *historically*. At the same time, he sees them as a *paradigm*, as far as they are a proof for the validity of wisdom-sentences. Finally, Ben Sira looks at the events on a *typological* level as far as they reflect his experience of the opposition between Jerusalem and Samaria.[96]

---

95 Cf. Witte (2008b), 184ff.

96 I warmly thank Christian Becker (Frankfurt a. M.) and Niall Hoskin (Bristol) for their support in translating this paper from German into English.

Ben Sira 47:12–25; 48:1 (H[B])

12a [ו] בעבורו עמד אחריו   בן [מ]שכיל שוכן לבטח :
13a שלמה מלך בימי שלוה   ואל הניח לו מסביב :
<u>13c</u> אשר הכין בית לשמו   ויצב לעד מקדש :
14a מה חכמת בנעריך   ותצף כיאר מוסר :
15a ארץ [כסית בבינת]ך   ותק[לס ב]מרום שירה :
[16a עד איים רחוקים הגיע שמך   ויבואו לשמעך:]
17a בשיר [מש]ל חידה ומליצה   עמים הסערתה :
<u>18a</u> נקראת בשם הנכבד   הנקרא על ישראל :
18c ותצבר כברזל זהב   וכעפרת הרבית כסף :
19a ותתן לנשים כסליך   ותמשילם בגויתך :
20a ו[ת]תן מום בכבודך   ותחלל את יצועיך :
20c [להביא] אף על צאצאיך   ואנחה על משכבך :
<u>21a</u> [להיות העם] לשני שבטים   ומאפרים ממלכת חמס :
22a [ואולם א]ל לא יטוש חסד   ולא יפיל מדבריו ארצה :
22c לא [יכרית לבחירי]ו נין ונכד   [וזרע אוה]ביו לא ישמיד :
<u>22e</u> ויתן ל[יעקב שארית]   ול[דוד ממנו שרש] :
23a וישכב שלמה מ[ ]ש   ויעזב א[חריו קצי]ן :
23c רחב אולת וחסר בינה   רחבעם הפריע בע[צתו] עם :
<u>23e</u> עד אשר קם אל יהי לו זכר {ירבעם בן נבט} אשר ח[טא והחטי]א א[ת ישראל] :
23g ויתן לאפרים מכשול   להדיחם [מ]אדמתם :
24b ותגדל חטאתו מאד   25 ולכל רעה הת[מכר] :

48:1 עד אשר קם נביא כאש   ודבריו כתנור בוער :

V. 15a: cf. 1 Kings 3:12; 5:9; Segal; Vattioni.
V. 15b: קלס II "to praise"; Segal; Vattioni.
V. 16a: G εἰς νήσους πόρρω ἀφίκετο τὸ ὄνομά σου, cf. Isa. 66:19; Segal.
V. 16b: Syr ܘܫܡܥܟ ܠܥܡܡ[ܐ .]ܟܠܗ, cf. 1 Kings 5:14; 10:24. G καὶ ἠγαπήθης ἐν τῇ εἰρήνῃ σου cf. V. 13a (Σαλωμων ἐβασίλευσεν ἐν ἡμέραις εἰρήνης).
V. 20c: G ἐπαγαγεῖν; Segal; Vattioni.
V. 21a: G γενέσθαι δίχα τυραννίδα; Vattioni.
V. 22a: G ὁ δὲ κύριος οὐ μὴ; Segal; Vattioni.
V. 22c: G ἐξαλείψῃ ἐκλεκτοῦ αὐτοῦ; Segal; Vattioni.
V. 22d: G σπέρμα τοῦ ἀγαπήσαντος αὐτόν; Segal; Vattioni.
V. 22e–f: G καὶ τῷ Ιακωβ ἔδωκεν κατάλειμμα´ / καὶ τῷ Δαυιδ ἐξ αὐτοῦ ῥίζαν; cf. Sir 44:17c; Segal.
V. 23a: G μετὰ τῶν πατέρων (αὐτοῦ); Beentjes: מיואש "in despair" (cf. Ws 2:20); Vattioni: משריש "taking root" (cf. Job 5:3); Segal: משגש "in error".
V. 23b: G μετ᾽ αὐτὸν ἐκ τοῦ σπέρματος αὐτοῦ; Vattioni; cf. Sir 48:15f. (H[B]).
V. 23f: cf. 1 Kings 15:30.
V. 25a: G (pl.) ἐξεζήτησαν, cf. 2 Kings 17:17; Segal; Vattioni.
V. 25b: G-Plus: ἕως ἐκδίκησις ἔλθῃ ἐπ᾽ αὐτούς.

Ben Sira 47:12–25; 48:1

A.1 12a [and on] his account there arose after him
12b a clever son, who dwelt in security,
A.2 13a Solomon, ruled as a king in days of peace,
13b for God gave him rest from around,
A.3 13c who established a house for His name
13d and founded a sanctuary forever.

B.1 14a How wise you were in your youth!
14b For you overflowed as the Nile with instruction.
B.2 15a You [covered] the earth with your [understanding]
15b and you sang a song of pra[ise] on high.
B.3 16a [Your name reached distant islands,
16b and they came to hear you.]
B.4 17a With song, [parab]le, riddle, and proverb
17b you astounded the nations.
B.5 18a You were called by the name of the Glorious One,
18b which was called upon Israel.

B′.1 18c But you heaped up gold like iron
18d and multiplied silver like lead.
B′.2 19a And you gave your thighs to women
19b and handed over to them the rule of your body.
B′.3 20a And you [brou]ght corruption upon your glory
20b and profaned your couch
B′.4 20c [to bring] wrath upon your descendants
20d and groaning upon your bed,
B′.5 21a [thus the people came into being] into two tribes
21b and from Ephraim a kingdom of violence.

22a [But G]od will not forsake his faithful love
22b nor will he let any of his words fall to the earth.
22c He will not [uproot] the offspring or posterity [of his choosen ones]
22d nor he will destroy the offspring those who [lo]ve him.
22e And he will give [a remnant] to [Jacob]
22f and [a root of his own (root)] to [David].

C.1 23a But Solomon died [ ]
23b and left [behind him a prince]
C.2 23c broad in folly and lacking in understanding,
23d Rehoboam, who through his coun[sel] caused the people to riot.
C.3 23e Until one arose who should not have a memorial,
23f {Jeroboam, son of Nebat}, who sinned and who caused [Israel] to s[i]n,

23g And he set a stumbling block before Ephraim,
24a to drive them [from] their land.
24b For their sin grew exceedingly
25 and they so[ld] themselves over to all evil.
48:1a Until a prophet arose like fire
48:1b and his words were as a flaming furnance.

Bibliography

Becker, U. (2000), Die Reichsteilung nach I Reg 12, ZAW 112, 210–229.

Beentjes, P.C. (1997), The Book of Ben Sira in Hebrew: A Text Edition of all extant Hebrew Manuscripts and a Synopsis of all parallel Hebrew Ben Sira Texts, VT.S 68, Leiden et al.

– (2006), "The Countries Marvelled at You": King Solomon in Ben Sira 47,12–22*, in: id., "Happy the One who Meditates on Wisdom" (Sir. 14,20): Collected Essays on the Book of Ben Sira, Contributions to Biblical Exegesis and Theology 43, Leuven et al., 135–144.

Begg, C.T. (1993), Josephus' Account of the Early Divided Monarchy (AJ 8, 212–420): Rewriting the Bible, BEThL 108, Leuven et al.

Berlejung, A. (1998), Die Theologie der Bilder. Herstellung und Einweihung von Kultbildern in Mesopotamien und die alttestamentliche Bilderpolemik, OBO 162, Freiburg (Schweiz)/Göttingen.

Beyer, K. (1984), Die aramäischen Texte vom Toten Meer samt den Inschriften aus Palästina, dem Testament Levis aus der Kairoer Genisa, der Fastenrolle und den alten talmudischen Zitaten, Göttingen.

Boccaccini, G. (2008), Where Does Ben Sira Belong?: The Canon, Literary Genre, Intellectual Movement, and Social Group of a Zadokite Document, in: G.G. Xeravits/J. Zsengellér (eds.), Studies in the Book of Ben Sira: Papers of the Third International Conference on the Deuterocanonical Books, Shime'on Centre, Pápa, Hungary, 18–20 May 2006, JSJ.S 127, Leiden/Boston, 21–41.

Brown, T.R. (2002), God and Men in Israel's History: God and Idol Worship in Praise of the Fathers (Sir 44–50), in: R. Egger-Wenzel (ed.), Ben Sira's God: Proceedings of the International Ben Sira Conference, Durham – Ushaw College 2001, BZAW 321, Berlin/New York, 214–220.

Brutti, M. (2006), The Development of the High Priesthood during the pre-Hasmonean Period: History, Ideology, Theology, JSJ.S 108, Leiden/Boston.

Calduch-Benages, N./Ferrer, J./Liesen, J. (2003), La Sabiduría del escriba: Edición diplomática de la versión siriaca del Libro de Ben Sira según ed Códice Ambrosiano, con traducción española e inglesa [= Wisdom of the Scribe: Diplomatic Edition of the Syriac Version of the Book of Ben Sira according to Codex Ambrosianus with Translations in Spanish and English], Biblioteca Midrásica 26, Estella.

Corley, J. (2006), Seeds of Messianism in Hebrew Ben Sira and Greek Sirach, in: M.A. Knibb (ed.), The Septuagint and Messianism, BEThL 195, Leuven et al., 301–312.

Denis, A.-M. (1970), Fragmenta Pseudepigraphorum quae supersunt Graeca, PVTG III, Leiden.

Eberharter, A. (1925), Das Buch Jesus Sirach oder Ecclesiasticus, HSAT vol. VI/5, Bonn.

Eshel, H. (2007), The Governors of Samaria in the Fifth and Fourth Century B.C.E., in: O. Lipschits/G.N. Knoppers/R. Albertz (eds.), Judah and the Judeans in the Fourth Century B.C.E., Winona Lake, 223–234.

Fabry, H.-J. (2003), Jesus Sirach und das Priestertum, in: I. Fischer/U. Rapp/J. Schiller (eds.), Auf den Spuren der schriftgelehrten Weisen, FS J. Marböck, BZAW 331, Berlin/New York, 265–282.

Fallon, F. (1985), Theodotus (Second to First Century B.C.), in: J.H. Charlesworth (ed.), The Old Testament Pseudepigrapha, vol. II: Expansions of the "Old Testament" and Legends, Wisdom and Philosophical Literature, Prayers, Psalms, and Odes, Fragments of Lost Judeo-Hellenistic Works, New York et al., 785–793.

Gomes, J.F. (2006), The Sanctuary of Bethel and the Configuration of Israelite Identity, BZAW 368, Berlin/New York.

Goshen-Gottstein, A. (2002), Ben Sira's Praise of the Fathers: A Canon-Conscious Reading, in: R. Egger-Wenzel (ed.), Ben Sira's God: Proceedings of the International Ben Sira Conference, Durham – Ushaw College 2001, BZAW 321, Berlin/New York, 235–267.

García Martínez, F./Tigchelaar, E.J.C. (1997/98), The Dead Sea Scrolls, Study Edition, vols. I–II, Leiden et al.

Hamp, V. (1952), Sirach, EB.AT 13, 2. Auflage, Würzburg.

Hayward, R.C.T. (1996), The Jewish Temple: A non-biblical sourcebook, London/New York.

– (2002), El Elyon and the Divine Names in Ben Sira, in: R. Egger-Wenzel (ed.), Ben Sira's God: Proceedings of the International Ben Sira Conference, Durham – Ushaw College 2001, BZAW 321, Berlin/New York, 180–198.

Kee, H.C. (1983), Testaments of the Twelve Patriarchs (Second Century B.C.), in: J.H. Charlesworth (ed.), The Old Testament Pseudepigrapha, vol. I: Apocalyptic Literature and Testaments, New York et al., 775–828.

Kippenberg, H.G. (1971), Garizim und Synagoge. Traditionsgeschichtliche Untersuchungen zur samaritanischen Religion der aramäischen Periode, RVV 30, Berlin/New York.

Köhlmoos, M. (2006), Bet-El – Erinnerungen an eine Stadt. Perspektiven der alttestamentlichen Bet-El-Überlieferung, FAT 49, Tübingen.

Koenen, K. (2003), Bethel. Geschichte, Kult und Theologie, OBO 192, Freiburg (Schweiz)/Göttingen.

Lee, T.R. (1986), Studies in the Form of Sirach 44–50, SBL.DS 75, Atlanta.

Levin, C. (2001), Das Alte Testament, München.

Lied, L.I. (2008), The Other Lands of Israel: Imaginations of the Land in 2 Baruch, JSJ.S 129, Leiden/Boston.

Mack, B.L. (1985), Wisdom and the Hebrew Epic: Ben Sira's Hymn in Praise of the Fathers, Chicago Studies in the History of Judaism, Chicago/London.

Magen, Y. (2007), The Dating of the First Phase of the Samaritan Temple on Mount Gerizim in Light of the Archaeological Evidence, in: O. Lipschits/G.N. Knoppers/R. Albertz (eds.), Judah and the Judeans in the Fourth Century B.C.E., Winona Lake, 157–211.

– /Misgav, H./Tsfania, L. (2004), Mount Gerizim Excavations, vol. I: The Aramaic, Hebrew and Samaritan Inscriptions, Judea and Samaria Publications 2, Jerusalem.

Marböck, J. (1995), Davids Erbe in gewandelter Zeit (Sir 47,1–11), in: id., Gottes Weisheit unter uns. Zur Theologie des Buches Sirach, HBS 6, Freiburg et al., 124–132.

– (2006), Der Hohepriester Simon in Sir 50. Ein Beitrag zur Bedeutung von Priestertum und Kult im Sirachbuch, in: id., Weisheit und Frömmigkeit. Studien zur alttestamentlichen Literatur der Spätzeit, ÖBS 29, Frankfurt a.M. et al., 155–168.

Meshorer, Y./Qedar, S. (1991), The Coinage of Samaria in the Fourth Century BCE, Jerusalem.

– /Qedar, S. (1999), Samarian Coinage, Jerusalem.

Mulder, O. (2003), Simon the High Priest in Sirach 50: An Exegetical Study of the Significance of Simon the High Priest as Climax to the Praise of the Fathers in Ben Sira's Concept of the History of Israel, JSJ.S 78, Leiden/Boston.

Murphy, R.E. (1998), Proverbs, WBC 22, Nashville.

Noth, M. (1968), Könige. 1. Teilband (1–16), BK IX/1, Neukirchen-Vluyn.

Pakkala, J. (2002), Jeroboam's Sin and Bethel in 1Kgs 12:25–33, BN 112, 86–94.

– (2008), Jeroboam without Bulls, ZAW 120, 501–525.

Peterca, V. (1988), Das Porträt Salomos bei Ben Sirach (47,12–22). Ein Beitrag zu der Midraschexegese, in: M. Augustin/K.-D. Schunck (eds.), "Wünschet Jerusalem Frieden": Collected Communications to the XIIth Congress of the International Organization for the Study of the Old Testament, Jerusalem 1986, BEAT 13, Frankfurt a.M. et al., 457–463.

Peters, N. (1913), Das Buch Jesus Sirach oder Ecclesiasticus, EHAT 25, Münster.

Pfeiffer, H. (1999), Das Heiligtum von Bethel im Spiegel des Hoseabuches, FRLANT 183, Göttingen.

Pietersma, A./Wright, B.G. (2007), A New English Translation of the Septuagint: And the Other Greek Translations Traditionally Included under That Title: A New Translation of the Greek into Contemporary English – An Essential Resource for Biblical Studies, New York/Oxford.

Pietsch, M. (2003), „Dieser ist der Sproß Davids ..." Studien zur Rezeptionsgeschichte der Nathanverheißung im alttestamentlichen, zwischentestamentlichen und neutestamentlichen Schrifttum, WMANT 100, Neukirchen-Vluyn.

Purvis, J.D. (1965), Ben Sira' and the Foolish People of Shechem, JNES 24, 88–94.

Reiterer, F.V. (2003), Zählsynopse zum Buch Ben Sira, Fontes et Subsidia ad Bibliam pertinentes 1, Berlin/New York.

Ryssel, V. (1900/[4]1975), Die Sprüche Jesus', des Sohnes Sirachs, in: E. Kautzsch (ed.), Die Apokryphen und Pseudepigraphen des Alten Testaments, vol. 4., unveränderter Neudruck, Darmstadt, vol. I, 230–475.

Sauer, G. (2000), Jesus Sirach/Ben Sira, ATD.Apokryphen 1, Göttingen.

Schenker, A. (1996), Jéroboam et la division du royaume dans la Septante ancienne. LXX 1 R 12,24 a–z, TM 11–12; 14 et l'histoire deutéronomiste, in: A. de Pury/T. Römer/J.-D. Macchi (eds.), Israël construit son histoire. L'historiographie deutéronomiste à la lumière des recherches récentes, MoBi 34, Genève, 193–236.

Schmitt, A. (2003), Enkomien in griechischer Literatur, in: I. Fischer/U. Rapp/J. Schiller (eds.), Auf den Spuren der schriftgelehrten Weisen, FS J. Marböck, BZAW 331, Berlin/New York, 359–381.

– (2004), Ein Lobgedicht auf Simeon, den Hohenpriester (Sir 50,1–24), in: M. Witte (ed.), Gott und Mensch im Dialog, FS O. Kaiser, BZAW 345/II, Berlin/New York, 873–896.

Schmitt, H.-C. (2000), Die Erzählung vom Goldenen Kalb Ex. 32* und das Deuteronomistische Geschichtswerk, in: S.L. McKenzie/T. Römer (eds.), Rethinking the Foundations: Historiography in the Ancient World and in the Bible: Essays in Honour of J. Van Seters, BZAW 294, Berlin/New York, 235–250.

Schuller, E.M. (1990), 4Q372 1: A Text about Joseph, RdQ 14/55, 349–376.

Segal, M.Z. (1958), ספר בן סירא השלם. כולל כל השרידים העבריים שנתגלו מתוך הגניה והחזרת הקטעים החסרים, עם מבוא, פירוש ומפתחות. מהדורה שנייה מתוקנת ומושלמת, Jerusalem.

Skehan, P.W./Di Lella, A.A. (1987), The Wisdom of Ben Sira, AncB 39, New York et al.

Smend, R. (1906), Die Weisheit des Jesus Sirach. Hebräisch und Deutsch, Berlin.

Spaer, A. (1979), A Coin of Jeroboam?, IEJ 29, 218.

– (1980), More About Jeroboam, INJ 4, 2–3, plate 1.

Talshir, Z. (1993), The Alternative Story of the Division of the Kingdom: 3 Kingdoms 12:24a–z, JBS 6, Jerusalem.

Van Peursen, W.T. (2007), Language and Interpretation in the Syriac Text of Ben Sira: A Comparative Linguistic and Literary Study, MPIL 16, Leiden/Boston.

Van Seters, J. (1994), The Life of Moses: The Yahwist as Historian in Exodus–Numbers, Contributions to Biblical Exegesis and Theology 10, Kampen.

Vattioni, F. (1968), Ecclesiastico. Testo ebraico con apparato critico e versioni greca, latina e siriaca. Pubblicazioni del Seminario di Semitistica, Testi I, Neapel.

Veijola, T. (2003), Deuteronomismusforschung zwischen Tradition und Innovation (III), ThR 68, 1–44.

Walter, N. (1976), Fragmente jüdisch-hellenistischer Historiker, JSHRZ I/2, Gütersloh, 91–163.

– (1983), Fragmente jüdisch-hellenistischer Epik: Philon, Theodotos, JSHRZ IV/3, Gütersloh 137–171.

Witte, M. (2001), „Mose, sein Andenken sei zum Segen" (Sir 45,1) – Das Mosebild des Sirachbuchs, BN 107/108 (2001), 161–186.

– (2006), From Exodus to David – History and Historiography in Psalm 78, in: N. Calduch-Benages/J. Liesen (eds.), History and Identity: How Israel's Later Authors Viewed Its Earlier History, Deuterocanonical and Cognate Literature – Yearbook 2006, Berlin/New York, 21–42.

– (2008a), „Barmherzigkeit und Zorn Gottes" im Alten Testament am Beispiel des Buchs Jesus Sirach, in: R.G. Kratz/H. Spieckermann (eds.), Divine Wrath and Divine Mercy in the World of Antiquity, FAT II/33, Tübingen, 176–202.

– (2008b), Ist auch Hiob unter den Propheten? Sir 49,9 als Testfall für die Auslegung des Buches Jesus Sirach, Kleine Untersuchungen zur Sprache des Alten Testaments und seiner Umwelt 8/9, 163–194.

Zangenberg, J. (1994), ΣΑΜΑΡΕΙΑ. Antike Quellen zur Geschichte und Kultur der Samaritaner in deutscher Übersetzung, TANZ 15, Tübingen.

Ziegler, J. (1980), Sapientia Iesu Filii Sirach, Septuaginta. Vetus Testamentum Graecum Auctoritate Academiae Scientiarum Gottingensis editum, XII/2, 2., durchgesehene Auflage, Göttingen.

Zsengellér, J. (1998), Gerizim as Israel: Northern Tradition of the Old Testament and the Early History of the Samaritans, Utrechtse Theologische Reeks 38, Utrecht.

– (2008), Does Wisdom Come from the Temple?: Ben Sira's attitude to the Temple of Jerusalem, in: G.G. Xeravits/J. Zsengellér (eds.), Studies in the Book of Ben Sira: Papers of the Third International Conference on the Deuterocanonical Books, Shime'on Centre, Pápa, Hungary, 18–20 May 2006, JSJ.S 127, Leiden/Boston, 135–149.

II. The Cult Centralization in Its Near Eastern Context: Perspectives on Hezekiah and Josia

The Idea of Cultic Centralization and Its Supposed Ancient Near Eastern Analogies

REINHARD G. KRATZ

Lothar Perlitt zum Achtzigsten

1. One God – One Cult

One God – One Cult: This is the central theological message and the main commandment of the Book of Deuteronomy: שמע ישראל יהוה אלהינו יהוה אחד (Deut. 6:5) and במקום אשר יבחר יהוה ... תעלה עלתיך (Deut. 12:14). The idea of cultic centralization is also a central issue in reconstructing the literary history of the Book of Deuteronomy as well as the history of Israelite religion. Therefore, it might be worthwhile paying some attention to this topic at a conference in Jerusalem, one of the two locations that are supposed to be "the place which He has chosen".[1]

It was Julius Wellhausen who first used the idea of cultic centralization as a criterion according to which it was possible to separate the history of Israel into two different epochs: the age of ancient Israel and the age of Judaism.[2] Wilhelm Martin Leberecht de Wette paved the way for this distinction. De Wette identified the law book of Josiah (2 Kings 22–23) with Deuteronomy and introduced the distinction between Hebraism and Judaism.[3] Wellhausen combined both aspects realizing that Deuteronomy must be used when one wants to distinguish both historical epochs within the biblical texts. Wellhausen's analysis is still valid today but seems to aim more at the literary level of the Hebrew Bible than at the history of Israel. From a historical perspective it is impossible to maintain that one epoch simply follows the other. The

---

English Translation PD Dr. Anselm C. Hagedorn (Berlin).

1 On this topic cf. Kratz (2007b).

2 Cf. Wellhausen (1905; 1914).

3 The famous dissertation of de Wette is now re-edited and translated into German by Mathys (2008), and translated into English by Harvey/Halpern (2008). For Hebraism and Judaism cf. Perlitt (1994).

texts from Elephantine and the continuing polemics against ancient Israel within the Hebrew Bible make it seem likely that both types of 'Israel', the historical one and the biblical one from which Judaism derived, existed – from a certain point onwards – next to each other.[4]

Both, de Wette and Wellhausen, arrived at their results with the help of literary-historical criticism, i.e. by using internal criteria. Next to such an approach we also find proposals that operate with extra biblical material, i.e. the so called external evidence. Behind such a preference often lays the intention to form-critically undermine any literary critical hypothesis.[5] Or one wants to confirm the results of literary-historical investigations and, subsequently, place the results on a new religio-historical basis.[6] Since the ground-breaking studies of Deuteronomy and the Deuteronomic school by Moshe Weinfeld from 1972, the discussion tends to focus on certain neo-Assyrian parallels.[7] Today these parallels are not only used to explain the literary history of Deuteronomy but also the origin of the Pentateuch as a whole and many other aspects of the biblical tradition.[8] Here, phrases like 'point of Archimedes' and 'peg in the wall' are used.[9] Thus, the external evidence seems to support a current trend in Hebrew Bible scholarship to date many of the texts, previously thought of having originated during Solomonic times, to the time of Josiah, even though we do not know anything more about Josiah than we do know about Solomon and the pre-monarchic period.[10]

Hopefully the 'peg in the wall' that has to hold all those hypotheses will be spared the destiny of the peg mentioned in Isa. 22:25. In the following I will subject those hypotheses to close scrutiny using the concept of cultic centralization in Deuteronomy and the Deuteronomistic literature as a test-case. Thus, our contribution serves a double purpose: We will discuss the religio-historical place of the cultic centraliza-

---

4 Cf. Kratz (2007a).

5 Cf. Baltzer (1964) on whom see Perlitt (1969).

6 Already Oestreicher criticized the 'isolated method' of de Wette and Wellhausen who 'only knows of an inner-Israelite development' and postulated a 'universal perspective' (*weltgeschichtliche Betrachtungsweise*); cf. Oestereicher (1923), 9–10; id. (1930), 34.

7 Cf. Weinfeld (1992), 59–178; and also ibid., vii, where he notes the significance of Vassal Treaties of Essarhaddon (VTE) for de Wette's hypothesis.

8 Cf. Otto (1996; 1997; 1999; 2000; 2002 etc.); for the broader perspective cf. Otto (1999), 86–87; id. (2000), 237 n. 21; id. (2002), 13 n. 67, followed by Schmid (2008), 73–108.

9 Cf. Otto (1997); id. (1999), 8, 12; id. (2000), 10; id. (2002), 6.

10 Cf. Finkelstein/Silberman (2001), 14 and *passim*; for Hezekiah as Josiah's predecessor see Finkelstein/Silberman (2006). On the methodological incoherence of this position cf. Albertz (2005), 27–29.

tion and, at the same time, address the methodological question which heuristic value ancient Near Eastern parallels can have for the explanation of biblical texts.

2. Subversive Reception

It is scholarly consensus that those laws, which centralize the cult and the stipulations that shape the social and judicial laws in light of the cultic centralization form the basic layer of Deuteronomy.[11] The issue of cultic centralization serves as the motif for the re-working of the older Covenant Code in Exodus 20–23 in Deuteronomy and as the guiding principle for the reception process.[12] This insight provides us with a lucid criterion for any analysis of Deuteronomy. Next to the change in number (*Numeruswechsel*) and the literary dependence on the Covenant Code it is the centralization of the cult that decides the extent of the basic layer of Deuteronomy, the so called *Urdeuteronomium*.[13]

In addition to this analysis, Eckart Otto has proposed that the laws regarding centralization are preceded by an even earlier document that can be found in Deuteronomy 13 and 28 and which he calls – in deviation to traditional terminology – the *Urdeuteronomium*. According to Otto, who follows a proposal made by Paul-Eugène Dion and Hans Ulrich Steymans, this older *Urdeuteronomium* consists of an almost verbatim translation of a neo-Assyrian formulary. He finds this formulary in those texts that are generally classified as the Vassal Treaties of Essarhaddon (VTE) containing a loyalty oath that Essarhaddon imposed on his subjected rulers in favour of his successor Ashurbanipal.[14] In the supposed translation the neo-Assyrian loyalty oath was transformed

---

11 Neglecting any detailed analysis those laws are: Deut. 12:1–28; 14:22–29; 15:1–18; 15:19–23; 16:1–18 as well as Deut. 16:18–20; 17:8–13; 18:1–11; 19:1–13; 19:15–21; 21:1–9; 26:1–16. All other laws do not have a genuine relationship to the theme of cultic centralization. Cf. Reuter (1993); for a wider perspective Hagedorn (2005).

12 Cf. Levinson (1997). In the following I will assume an exclusive exegesis of the formula of centralization. On the problem cf. Reuter (1993), 65–67; Levinson (1997), 23–24 n. 1.

13 Cf. Kratz (2005), 114–133; see also Veijola (2004), 2–3. On the question of the criteria cf. Otto (1999), 10–14. Otto rightly refutes any correlation between Deuteronomy and the 2 Kings 22–23 as a basis for the literary analysis. Unfortunately he only takes the religio-historical comparison into account as an alternative; cf. Otto (1996), 3–4; id. (1999), 13–14, 15–90. Everything else, including the re-formulation of the Covenant Code, is therefore subsumed under this aspect.

14 Text in Parpola/Watanabe (1988), 28–58. On the question whether the documents are a vassal treaty or a succession oath of Essarhaddon cf. Liverani (1995) and Otto (1999), 15–32.

into a loyalty oath of the Judean people in favour of their god YHWH. Otto calls this process a 'subversive reception' and dates it – because of the external evidence, the proposed literary dependence and the supposed anti-Assyrian tendency of Deuteronomy 13 and 28 – to Assyrian times.[15] It is within this chronological and literary frame that Otto is also locating the concept and realization of cultic centralization in Judah. The religio-historical background of this concept and its supposed polemic and anti-Assyrian purpose is called the 'rationality of Assyrian cultic centralization'.[16]

Otto's hypothesis offers a closed and coherent system. Nevertheless, there are quite a number of objections that cause the 'peg in the wall' to wobble.[17] It has often been observed that the hypothesis cannot be reconciled with the literary evidence of Deuteronomy. The laws concerning cultic centralization are not connected to or fitted into the assumed frame of Deuteronomy 13 and 28. Rather, Deuteronomy 13 interrupts the original connection of the laws regarding centralization in Deut. 12:13–28 and 14:22–29.

Additionally, the covenant theology of Deuteronomy 13 and 28 does not mark the beginning of the legal and literary-historical development of Deuteronomy but rather its end. There cannot be any doubt that the covenant in Deuteronomy is inspired by the ancient Near Eastern contract pattern and here especially by the Neo-Assyrian loyalty oaths and their late Hittite predecessors. But, in contrast to the ancient Near Eastern examples neither the Assyrian nor the Judean king takes part in the covenant. It is only a covenant between the people of Israel and the God of Israel. If we had a subversive reception here such a reception would imply that the Judean king (Josiah) terminated his own existence (see Deut. 17:14–20).[18]

15 Cf. Dion (1978; 1991); Steymans (1995; 2003; 2006); Otto (1996; 1997; 1999; 2000; 2002 etc.).

16 Otto (1999), 351: "Wie der assyrische Gott Aššur an nur einem Ort kultisch verehrt wird, so auch der judäische Gott JHWH: Jerusalem steht nicht Aššur nach, und kein Lokalheiligtum in Juda unterminiert die Alternative zwischen dem Gott Aššur und JHWH." Cf. also ibid., 74–75, 350–351, 364–378, and id. (2002), 14–17, 161.

17 Cf. Veijola (2000); id. (2002), 289–298; Köckert (2000); Rüterswörden (2002); Aurelius (2003), 41 n. 77; Pakkala (2006); Koch (2008).

18 The oath from Arslan Taş cannot be used to show that 'the revolt against the Assyrian royal ideology via the covenant theology' is a specific aspect of Deuteronomy 13 and 28; contra Otto (1999), 85–86; (2002), 165–166. The covenant theology of Deuteronomy is neither directed against the god Aššur nor against the Assyrian king but explicitly against 'other gods' (Deut. 13:3, 7 etc.). It goes without saying that also a covenant with Aššur, Marduk or Ahuramazda is excluded here. On Arslan Taş see Koch (2008), 252–253 n. 23.

Finally, the direct dependence of Deuteronomy 13 and 28 on VTE has been questioned since such a linear and mono-causal process does not do justice to the complexity of the ancient Near Eastern literary tradition. Despite the fact that the late Hittite and neo-Assyrian as well as other (Aramaic) parallels provide the general background for the literary development of the Book of Deuteronomy, it is, however, not recommended to accept the hypothesis that a composition of Deuteronomy 13 and 28 is the predecessor and literary frame of the idea of cultic centralization within the original form of Deuteronomy.

Thus, we have to concentrate our investigation on the laws regarding centralization themselves and their relationship to what Otto calls the 'rationality of Assyrian cultic centralization'. Here, Otto depends on information gained from Assyriologists that the god Aššur – according to the sources available to us and with only one exception (during the reign of Tukulti-Ninurta I) – did not have an official temple outside the city of Aššur.[19] Undoubtedly, this is a fact but what does it tell us? Is this fact the 'peg in the wall' we are looking for?

Otto himself has to concede that, as far as the 'programmatic consequence' is concerned, 'the Deuteronomic, pre-Deuteronomistic conception of the sacrificial centralization moves significantly beyond the Assyrian concept'. The same is true for the 'aniconic trait of JHWH-religion' originating in Judah at the same time and equally 'reacting to the power of neo-Assyrian culture'. According to Otto this 'trait of JHWH-religion', too, was inspired by the god Aššur but was turned against him.[20] If we had, however, indeed a process of 'subversive reception' here this reception would have gone so far that its starting point can no longer be recognized. This, in turn, makes it very difficult to construct genetic dependencies from similarities.

If one wants to evaluate the proposed analogy, one has to look at the religio-historical context. The god Aššur always had his cultic centre in the city of Aššur. There was no need for his cult to become centralized, since it was always limited to a single place that was seen in competition to other (Babylonian) cultic centres established earlier. The main point of this rivalry was a question of status of the main god and the capital (i.e. the central cultic place), where the axis of the world was located.[21] Since the god Aššur originally did not have many significant features, he was concerned with acquiring attributes of other powerful

---

19 Cf. Otto (1999), 74–75, 350–351, referring to Mayer (1995), 61–67; id. (1997), 15–17; Maul (1997), 121–124. Cf. also Schmid (2008), 81, 106, who is speaking of an 'Assyrian import'.

20 Otto (1999), 75.

21 Cf. Maul (1997); on the temple of the god Aššur cf. Menzel (1981), Vol. I, 34ff.

gods as well as transferring the significance of their cultic place to his cultic centre of Aššur. The most prominent and brutal expression of this competition can be found in Sennacherib's campaign against the Marduk temple Esangila of Babylon and the rich echo of the events in the literary tradition.[22] Such campaigns are, however, the exception. Normally the rivalry is expressed in rivalling attributes, rites and myths for which Aššur competes with Marduk of Babylon and Enlil of Nippur. These processes cannot be labelled centralization. Rather, they are politically motivated transfers from one centre to another. As far as I am aware we do not know of any prohibition to worship Aššur (or any other god) outside the city of Aššur, although we have to concede that positive pieces of evidence are equally sparse.[23]

The Book of Deuteronomy is quite different. It deals with a deity that was worshipped at different places such as the official temple of the capital and the different local sanctuaries in the cities. The prohibition of any form of offering and the introduction of profane slaughter outside the chosen sanctuary (that is normally identified with Jerusalem, the capital of Judah) do not continue this long-standing tradition. In their original form the laws regarding centralization are not directed against other gods and their cultic places that compete with YHWH. Rather, they are directed against YHWH himself and his own local cultic centres 'in the gates'.

A rivalry between the YHWH of Jerusalem (Judah) and the YHWH of Samaria (Israel) and other manifestations of the same god at other places may have formed the background of the idea of cultic centralization (see Deut. 6:4–5). The rivalry with 'other gods' mainly of the land of Canaan, however, presupposes the first commandment and was only added later – as the supplements in Deut. 12:1–12 or Deuteronomy 13 show. The status of YHWH as the main god of Israel and Judah and the status of Jerusalem as capital of Judah was never questioned if one does not want to think of a rivalry with foreign rule and its capital and gods. Against it, however, the prohibition of sacrifice and the profanation and destruction of local cults would have hardly been a tried and tested measure.

Therefore, any comparison of the Deuteronomic law of centralization with the Mesopotamian concept of a capital lacks a valid point of

---

22 Cf. Vera Chamaza (2002).

23 Cf. Cogan (1974), 49–61, esp. 52–55; Pongratz-Leisten/Deller/Bleibtreu (1992). The fact that there are no extra-biblical attestations for a legal corpus focussing on priestly claims from Mesopotamia is further evidence that not only the Deuteronomic concept of centralization but also the form of it (i.e. a divine law mediated by Moses) is exceptional within the ancient Near East and needs to be explained.

comparison. The only comparative element is the concept of a capital but this is neither a Deuteronomic nor a neo-Assyrian speciality. The concept of a capital is attested in Aššur but also in Babylon and was most likely also prominent – despite the real political constellations – in Israel and Judah and the other small states in Syro-Palestine. As such, the concept represents the common idea that gods of the land ascend to main gods and certain places become capitals, an idea which necessarily includes some rivalry.[24] In all that we find one pre-requisite for the Deuteronomic law of centralization but the two concepts are neither identical nor does one concept simply derive from the other. Above all the common background does not explain any anti-Assyrian polemics, which Otto assumes behind the Deuteronomic programme of centralization.

In fact, it is not the pre-eminence of the city and the god Aššur that leads Otto and those who follow him to the assumption of anti-Assyrian polemics in Deuteronomy but the politics of king Josiah of Judah.[25] In doing so, Otto is trapped in the same circular argument that he rightly criticizes in other places.[26] Issues of methodology make it impossible, however, to simply correlate Deuteronomy with the report of Josiah's reform in 2 Kings 22–23. Such a correlation depends largely on the analysis of both, Deuteronomy and the chapters in 2 Kings, and both are hotly debated subjects. This is not the place to repeat the discussion but we have to remind ourselves that the picture changes depending on the literary reconstruction.

Even if we take the anti-Assyrian measures employed by Josiah that are generally regarded as belonging to the basic layer of 2 Kings 22–23 and compare them – for argument's sake – with the laws regarding centralization in Deuteronomy we realize that both aspects are difficult to reconcile.[27] Neither the dismissal of the *kĕmearim*-priests and the removal of several Assyrian cultic symbols from the Temple in Jerusalem (2 Kings 23:5, 11–12)[28] nor Josiah's encounter with Necho that

---

24 Cf. Mayer (1997) for Ahuramazda who follows the neo-Assyrian and neo-Babylonian examples.

25 Cf. Otto (1999), 74–75.

26 Cf. Otto (1999), 7, 13–14 (with reference to Gustav Hölscher). One gets the impression that placing the 'covenant' and the covenantal document (*Bundesurkunde*) before the 'Law' in Deuteronomy 13 and 28 (Otto [1999], 74) is modelled on the scene of 2 Kings 22–23.

27 Cf. Uehlinger (1995) and the apt remarks by Otto (1999), 12: "Für eine Korrelierung mit einem Urdeuteronomium geben diese Maßnahmen wenig her"; equally Arneth (2001), 206, on the 'anti-Assyrian reform' in 2 Kings 23:4–15: "Von einer Kultzentralisation ist im ursprünglichen Textbestand (noch) nichts zu vernehmen."

28 Cf. Spieckermann (1982), 85–86, 245–256, 271–273, 293–294.

got him killed[29] have anything to do with the Deuteronomic concept of cultic centralization.

On the other hand, the laws regarding centralization of Deuteronomy as well as Josiah's move against the indigenous ('Canaanite') local cults distinctly lack the rationality of anti-Assyrian politics.[30] Already Theodor Oestreicher tried to solve this problem by separating the anti-Assyrian measures of Josiah from his move against the local cults and subsequently interpreted this move as simply being a momentary measure. According to Oestreicher, both aspects as well as the original version of Deuteronomy have nothing to do with cultic centralization. In his view the centralization is an invention of the Deuteronomists based on a misunderstanding.[31] It is quite obvious that such a hypothesis is simply a rationalization of the literary tradition from a universal perspective (*weltgeschichtliche Betrachtungsweise*) – a perspective with numerous problems. Nevertheless, such a hypothesis highlights the difficulties one encounters if one tries to subsume the earliest edition of the Book of Deuteronomy and the report of Josiah's reform in 2 Kings 23 under the aspect of Josiah's anti-Assyrian politics.

Here, it is quite common to assume that one can solve these problems by simply historicizing the statements regarding the high places in the narratives of Hezekiah's (2 Kings 18:4, 22) and Josiah's reign (2 Kings 23:5, 8–9, 13, 15, 19–20). The removal of the high places is then an expression of a Judean (anti-Assyrian) politics of centralization that simply took the historical realities (i.e. the devastation and curtailing of Judean territory after the events of 701 BCE and the assumed opposition of local and official religion) into account.[32] Due to economic, political and religious pressure local cultic places were defamed as being Canaanite (i.e. foreign), and therefore abandoned or deliberately not rebuilt.[33]

---

29 It is difficult to decide whether Josiah approached pharaoh with hostile or friendly intent. Cf. Spieckermann (1982), 138–153; Cogan/Tadmor (1988), 291, 300–301; Würthwein (1994), 464–465.

30 Cf. Otto (1999), 75–76, followed by Arneth (2001), 208, simply ignores both aspects.

31 Cf. Oestreicher (1923), 56, 116–120; id. (1930), 32–42.

32 Cf. Jepsen (1956), 75; Gleis (1997), 177–181. Similarly Fried (2002), 461, who explains Deuteronomy 12 with the situation after 701 BCE but attributes the reforms of Hezekiah and Josiah in total to an exilic Deuteronomist. On the various pictures of Josiah and historical (re-)constructions in light of the Assyrian sources see Handy (2006).

33 Cf. Na'aman (1991), 57; id. (2002), 596–597. Halpern (1991), 27, thinks that the prophets were responsible for such a programme; Barrick (2002), 177–216, refutes any anti-Assyrian tendency and argues for a shift in internal Judean politics. For Albertz (2005) – although the historical evidence is lacking – the Josianic reform just must have happened in Josianic times since the dating of Deuteronomy and the Deuteronomistic History must not be too late.

Methodologically speaking such an approach is highly problematic, since it is, again, based on a combination of Deuteronomy 12 with 2 Kings 23 and fuses the literary level with the historical one. In addition, it is difficult to grasp that Judah would have transformed its despairing situation and the desolate state of its land caused by the Assyrian invasion into a religio-political or even theological programme.[34] Furthermore, it remains unclear who, by defaming the indigenous local cults as foreign cults, should have created an artificial antagonism to the YHWH cult of the capital only for economic profit or in order to fulfil the expectation of a 'subversive reception' and assimilate YHWH to the god Aššur. If Josiah is interpreted by employing any anti-Assyrian tendency it would have been more likely that we find an expansion of the local cults of YHWH rather than their defamation and abolition.[35]

Lastly, it is questionable whether the statements regarding the high places in 2 Kings 23 were ever part of the basic layer of the reform report or whether they were added at a later stage – taking up ideas from later literary levels of Deuteronomy – to transform the anti-Assyrian religious measures of Josiah into an inner-Judean cultic reform.[36] If we use the statements concerning the high places we are in danger of using the judgment of the exilic Deuteronomists to describe the mood of the assumed reform movement active under Josiah or even earlier to explain the origin of the Book of Deuteronomy and of the Josianic reform.[37]

In conclusion, we cannot but state that the idea of cultic centralization neither fits the rationality of neo-Assyrian politics nor any Judean anti-Assyrian political movement. In the light of Moshe Weinfeld's groundbreaking study it remains unquestionable that the Book of Deuteronomy is influenced by the language and social world of the neo-

---

34 Cf. Aurelius (2003), 32 (arguing against Jepsen [1956], 75): "Aber eine solche gewordene, nicht gewollte, geschweige denn einem Programm zufolge durchgeführte (Tendenz zur) Zentralisation wird noch keinem Geschichtsschreiber Maßstäbe für die Königsbeurteilungen, also für das theologische Urteil über die gesamte Geschichte der beiden Reiche geliefert haben."

35 Cf. Kratz (2005), 131–132; Aurelius (2003), 41–42.

36 Cf. Würthwein (1994), 457–458; Kratz (2005), 131, 169. Contrast Aurelius (2003), 44, who, nevertheless, is unable to detect in the statements regarding the high places any political calculation (contra Levin [2003]), nor economic advantage (contra Niehr [1995]), nor theological (contra Spieckermann [1982]) or anti-Assyrian (contra Otto [1999]) intention of King Josiah; cf. Aurelius (2003), 40–42. Also, any action against a YHWH-cult swamped with Canaanite influences does not make sense during Josianic times; contra Hardmeier (2000), 141.

37 Cf. Oestreicher (1930), 41.

Assyrian treaty literature and their Hittite and Aramaic predecessors.[38] However, it is significant that Moshe Weinfeld himself pointed to a very different religio-historical parallel when explaining the law of centralization in Deuteronomy and its realization under Hezekiah.

3. Cultic Reform and Centralization

Moshe Weinfeld himself did not refer to a neo-Assyrian analogy but to one from neo-Babylonian times.[39] Here, Weinfeld is thinking of the transfer of the gods from the Southern Mesopotamian cities to Babylon during the reign of Nabonidus shortly before the conquest of the city by Cyrus II. The events are reported in several documents from the circles of the Babylonian priests of Marduk.[40] This act is interpreted by Weinfeld as a politically and religiously motivated measure to bind the Babylonian cities under threat from Persian invasion to Babylon and to increase their military power. Simultaneously – in Weinfeld's view – this transfer fits well into Nabonidus' reform programme aiming at establishing the cult of the moon god Sîn as the main cult of Babylon. The later inner-Babylonian polemics of the priests of Marduk portrayed this as a sacrilege reversed by Cyrus II.

According to Weinfeld one has to understand the reform of Hezekiah along similar lines, i.e. a political and religiously motivated measure hoping to strengthen the central power in the light of Assyrian pressure and the siege of Jerusalem. Hezekiah was able to refer to the amphictyonic heritage. Weinfeld uses 2 Kings 18:22 as proof that such an act was criticized in Judah, where prophetic circles – especially the pupils of Isaiah – regarded such a measure as a heinous deed. On the other hand the cultic reform of Hezekiah that was supported by the priestly circles of Jerusalem was regarded as a pious act by the authors of Deuteronomy and the Deuteronomistic History (2 Kings 18:4–6). In contrast to Nabonidus, Hezekiah's reform, completed by Josiah, was successful.

---

38 On the condition of such influences cf. Nissinen (1996), 179–182; Steymans (2006); Rüterswörden (2002); the relevant essays in Witte et al. 2006 (303ff, 351ff, 379ff); Koch (2008). Since Hittite traditions were handed down via Syro-Hittite and Aramaic transmission to the 1st millennium BCE, one could assume the same for the Assyrian traditions which were handed down to Persian times via Median and Urartian transmission.

39 Cf. Weinfeld (1964).

40 See Chronicle of Nabonidus III:8–12, 20–21 (Grayson [2000], 109–110); Cyrus-Cylinder 9–10, 33–34 (Schaudig [2001], 550–556); Verse Account V:12–14 (Schaudig [2001], 570, 578).

Weinfeld, too, sees the point of origin of the idea of cultic centralization in a religio-political situation that can be explained against the background of ancient Near Eastern sources. In contrast to the hypothesis of a 'subversive reception' of Assyrian royal ideology, however, Weinfeld does not postulate any direct literary dependence. Rather, the polemic debate about cultic centralization is limited only to the individual culture concerned. Thus, the Nabonidus episode simply serves as a heuristic model to understand the Deuteronomic programme and its realization, reported in the Book of Kings, against the background of the cultural situation of the ancient Near East. An absolute chronology is, therefore, not deduced from such a religio-historical analogy. Following the scholarly consensus at the time Hezekiah, Josiah and the Book of Deuteronomy are dated to the neo-Assyrian period and are thus seen as predecessors to the neo-Babylonian analogy.

It is an advantage of this hypothesis that it does not only take the rivalry between the different capitals into account but also the relationship between capital and hinterland. In doing so, the neo-Babylonian parallel is much closer to the Book of Deuteronomy than the neo-Assyrian material surveyed above. For neither the Assyrian nor the Babylonian concept of a capital city is able to explain sufficiently the concept of centralization in Deuteronomy or the polemics against the high places in the Deuteronomistic History. Another advantage of the material presented by Weinfeld is that both, the biblical and the neo-Babylonian concept is part of a specific situation in which unusual measures are employed to cope with a difficult situation. In both cases, Weinfeld assumes a process of innovation within the framework of an extensive cultic reform that needs to be explained historically.

Despite these obvious advantages, Weinfeld's religio-historical analogy also poses a series of questions, which make it unlikely that we have the desired 'peg in the wall' here. The main problem is the exact meaning of Nabonidus unusual action during the last days of the neo-Babylonian empire. The tendency of the sources is mostly polemical what makes their interpretation difficult. As is the case in the Book of Kings one is faced with the difficult task to discern the historical motifs behind the polemics.

Weinfeld's explanation is heavily influenced by the views put forth by the Babylonian priesthood that expounds a theology centred on Babylon. Since the priests of Marduk lump Nabonidus' actions together with other deeds to denounce them as an offence against Marduk and his cultic place, one gets the feeling that the action has indeed something to do with his religious policy. A centralization of the cults in the name of the moon-god Sîn, however, does not seem to fit Nabonidus' politics of religion and expansion, which was actually more concerned with decentralization.[41] Neither his stay at Teman nor the building project of Ehulul at Harran, pursued by Nabonidus in the last years of his reign, point to a concern with centralization. The accusation of the so called 'Verse Account' (V:18–22) that Nabonidus changed the temple of Marduk at Babylon into a temple of Sîn does not imply a concentration of all cults in one single place but simply fits his religio-political plan to supplant Marduk with Sîn as highest god and to declare the temples of other gods to places of residence for Sîn.[42]

Furthermore, Weinfeld's proposal is not the only possible explanation. Already Mordechai Cogan has pointed to parallels to the behaviour of Nabonidus showing that the dislocation of gods was a protective measure against enemies and served at the same time as reassurance of divine protection.[43] This explanation was excluded by Weinfeld[44] but has recently been revived by Paul-Alain Beaulieu who was able to use newly discovered sources.[45] The documents show that – next to the divine images – cultic personnel, too, was ordered to Babylon and we learn of a lively exchange of goods to support the gods now housed at Babylon. Beaulieu is further able to detect signs that the dates of the transport of the gods and the personnel were connected with the religious policy of Nabonidus in favour of the god Sîn. Only the polemics of the priests of Marduk distorted the true intention to Nabonidus, namely the protection of the gods, in favour of a portrait of Cyrus as the faithful servant of Marduk. Thus, Nabonidus' action was defamed retrospectively as a cultic abomination and an offence happening against the will of the gods brought to Babylon, triggering the wrath of the lord of gods (Marduk).

No matter how we evaluate the process, it is not easy to reconcile it with the Deuteronomic programme of cultic centralization and with the Deuteronomistic portrait of Hezekiah and Josiah. It is possible to understand the election of a cultic place for the main god of the empire against the ancient Near Eastern background, but it is impossible to do so for the flip-side of the coin. In Deuteronomy and the Deuteronomistic History the election of the cultic place is intrinsically linked to the prohibition of cultic deeds and the profanation of slaughter "in your

41 Cf. Beaulieu (1989); Na'aman (2006), 158–162.

42 Cf. Schaudig (2001), 21.

43 Cf. Cogan (1974), 30–34, esp. 33 n. 67, against Weinfeld (1964); see also Cogan/Tadmor (1988), 219.

44 Cf. Weinfeld (1964), 205, and also Galling (1964), 33.

45 Cf. Beaulieu (1989), 219–224; id. (1993).

gates" (Deut. 12:13–18) and with the violation and removal of the "high places" (2 Kings 18:4, 22 and 2 Kings 23:4ff). This aspect cannot be equated with the transfer of the gods and their cultic personnel to Babylon under Nabonidus. Beaulieu has shown that such a measure does not imply any violation or removal of cults in Babylonian cities at all. At the same time, a restitution of these and other defunct cults under Cyrus II does not imply that these cults had previously been forbidden by a higher authority in favour of the capital. Centralization on the basis of the Mesopotamian concept of a state capital and the abolition of local cults in favour of a single legitimate cultic place are simply not the same.

There is, however, a certain similarity on a literary level between the biblical picture of the Hezekiah's and Josiah's reforms and the inscriptional evidence of Nabonidus' cultic reform, his self-presentation in his monumental inscriptions and the later polemics of the priests of Marduk who attribute the violation of cultic places and idolatry to him.[46] These similarities, however, are not too insightful. Nadav Na'aman and others have pointed to similar ancient Near Eastern sources that deal with royal cultic reforms and that contain both, reports of forceful interventions and of restitutions of destroyed cultic centres.[47] It is hardly surprising that the topos of a royal cultic reform and – up to a certain point – also the pattern of representation in texts that all originated in the ancient Near Eastern realm are comparable. But as far as the motivation and aim are concerned the analogies contain significant discrepancies.

All examples are in agreement that the reform "is the attempt to elevate a particular deity to the headship of the pantheon and exalt his status throughout the kingdom."[48] The same can be said of Deuteronomy and the literary presentation of Hezekiah's and Josiah's reforms in the Book of Kings for which the antagonism between YHWH and the 'other gods' is crucial. None of the ancient Near Eastern analogies, however, with the exception of Akhnaten, mentions the destruction of other cults as part of the reform and has the king praise himself for it. The case of Sennacherib might be instructive here: the destruction has a specific aim but is universally condemned in later sources as a cultic violation.

46 On the relationship between self- and outside-perception of Nabonidus cf. Kuhrt (1990) and Kratz (2002).

47 Cf. Arneth (2001), 206–216; Na'aman (2006); cf. also Handy (1995) and on him Barrick (2002), 132–143, who mentions *memorial inscriptions* such as the Mesha stele as parallels.

48 Na'aman (2006), 163.

Thus, neither Weinfeld's nor any of the other analogies provide a convincing reason for the intention to limit any sacrifice to YHWH to Jerusalem and why the other local sanctuaries ought to be profaned, defamed as foreign cults, and subsequently be destroyed. The specific differences of the biblical reports are not simply 'the book' that provides the basis for the reform.[49] The decisive difference is what this book, the Book of Deuteronomy or the Torah of Moses respectively, prescribes and what Hezekiah and Josiah, generally following the example of ancient Near Eastern kings, actually have done on the basis of this book. Here, we have to concede, that "while its theological significance seems clear enough, its exact nature and practical significance as an official governmental action in Josiah's Judah are not."[50]

Finally, literary-historical findings do not support the neo-Babylonian analogy put forth by Weinfeld. As has been the case with Josiah (2 Kings 22–23) also Hezekiah's reform (2 Kings 18:4–7a, 22) was used to find (or invent) historical evidence behind the literary account that fits the historical realities of 701 BCE and can be supported by archaeological evidence.[51] Both arguments, however, are quite uncertain. Hezekiah's anti-Assyrian policy does not necessarily point to a cultic reform, and the factual crisis of Judah does not make the cultic critique of 2 Kings 18:4, 22 a religio-political programme of a Judean king. Additionally, archaeological evidence is sparse and difficult to relate unambiguously to a cultic reform. For these and other reasons Hezekiah's reform has long been regarded as literary fiction of the Deuteronomists and seems to be secondary within the Deuteronomistic reworking. [52]

Further doubts arise in regard to Weinfeld's main evidence, namely the speech of Rabshake in 2 Kings 18:22. As far as the context is concerned, the passage is found within the context of three legendary accounts of the Sennacherib episode and labelled 'Source B1' (2 Kings 18:17–19:9a) by scholars.[53] This source is undoubtedly older than the version in 2 Kings 19:9b–35, called 'Source B2' that is a supplement and

49 Cf. Na'aman (2006), 166–167. For a differentiated view of the role of this book see Ben-Dov (2008).

50 Barrick (2002), 183; cf. also ibid., 171 ("except the closing of the bamoth").

51 Cf. Handy (1988); Finkelstein/Silberman (2006), 269–275; see above nn. 32 and 33.

52 Cf. Spieckermann (1982), 170–175; Camp (1990), 274–287; Na'aman (1995; 2002); Gleis (1997), 149–163; Fried (2002); Aurelius (2003), 30–33; and even Arneth (2006). On the secondary character of the verses in question see Würthwein (1984), 410–412, 421.

53 Cf. Cogan/Tadmor (1988), 240–244; Camp (1990), 38–52, 108ff.; Gallagher (1999), 143–159; and similarly Würthwein (1984), 404–406, 414; Hardmeier (1990), 13–14, 116, 119.

not an independent tradition.[54] Both versions are preceded by 'Source A' (2 Kings 18:13–16) that expands on the short note in 2 Kings 18:7b – either within the frame of an older annalistic source or as part of the Deuteronomistic basic stratum in 2 Kings 18–20.[55] Usually the end of the narrative in 2 Kings 19:36–37 is attributed to 'Source B' but these verses do not only provide the closure for B but for the whole passage in 2 Kings 18:13–19:37 thus including 'Source A'. Since A is older than B, we can assume that originally 2 Kings 19:36–37 – framed by 2 Kings 18:1–3, 7b and 20:20–21 – only formed the closure of A before B was inserted and was finally expanded by the Isaiah-legends in 2 Kings 20.[56]

All this means that Weinfeld's main evidence in 2 Kings 18:22 is handed down as part of a relatively young literary context, in which it is also secondary.[57] The passage stands in a certain contrast to the positive (presumably secondary or at least re-worked) evaluation of Hezekiah's piety in 2 Kings 18:4 and is most likely later than it. No matter how we evaluate 2 Kings 18:22 – as an original element of the text or a secondary addition; as part of an independent narrative or literary supplement to the Book of Kings –, the verse presupposes the centralization of the cult and thus Deuteronomy 12 and most likely also the Deuteronomistic demand for abolishment of the high places as well as the positive ending of the narrative in 2 Kings 19:36–37.

Within the frame of the narrative, however, 2 Kings 18:22 does not want to contradict 2 Kings 18:4. Rather, the verse wants – at a later stage and in its own words and with slightly different accentuation – to align the context in 2 Kings 18:21, 23 with the theological characteristics of the frame in 2 Kings 18:4–6. The cultic reform of Hezekiah placed in the mouth of the enemy rectifies the stigma of the trust in Egypt and in doing so provides the true reason for the factual refutation of the enemy and the deliverance of Jerusalem.[58] Undoubtedly, the Sennacherib

---

54 On this question cf. Gallagher (1999), 156.

55 Cf. Würthwein (1984), 406–409, and Camp (1990), 62–107, for an attribution to an annalistic source, Jepsen (1956), 36, 54, 62, and Noth (1957), 76 n. 6, for an attribution to a Deuteronomistic basic stratum.

56 Cf. Kratz (2005), 169; for the ending of 'Source A' cf. Lewy (1928) followed by Cogan/Tadmor (1988), 241.

57 On the dating of the narrative of 'Source B' to the late period of the monarchy (after 597 BCE) cf. Hardmeier (1990), 169–170. Exegetical reasons for such an evaluation are provided by Hoffmann (1980), 149–150; Würthwein (1984), 421; Gleis (1997), 154–155.

58 Cf. Hoffmann (1980), 149–151; on the different interpretations of the passage cf. Machinist (2000).

narrative and 2 Kings 18:22 breathes an Assyrian atmosphere.[59] This, however, is simply a fictitious argument within the narrative (*erzählfiktives Argument*) and neither a historically reliable reminiscence of oppositional circles during the neo-Assyrian period nor the view of a party during neo-Babylonian times when the narrative was written.[60] Via the detour of enemy polemics and its refutation – quite common in victors' propaganda – the Deuteronomic-Deuteronomistic ideals are powerfully confirmed. It would be rather short-sighted were we to use the atmosphere of a biblical statement for a precise and historical location of the text itself.

4. Conclusion

The result of the religio-historical comparison is quite ambivalent. On the one hand it became obvious that the Mesopotamian concept of a capital as well as other ancient Near Eastern ideas serve as a prerequisite for the origin of the Deuteronomic idea of cultic centralization and its application within the Book of Kings. On the other hand it is not possible to demonstrate a direct dependence on the ancient Near Eastern analogies and thus to date the biblical concept accurately. A religio-historical comparison is important and illuminating but cannot provide the desired 'peg in the wall'.[61]

Here, the main difference is that the concept of cultic centralization in Deuteronomy does not only mean an increase in status of the capital but is intrinsically connected to a radical intrusion upon the local cults 'in the gates' or 'on the high places' of Judah. Every analogy proposed cannot provide a proper explanation for that. Not because the different situation of the sources do not allow it but simply because Deuteronomy itself 'significantly moves beyond' ancient Near Eastern analogies.[62] Thus, we have to note that the concept of cultic centralization "is so special and singular in the world of the ancient Near East that there

---

59 Cf. Gallagher (1999), 160–254, esp. 190–191; Spieckermann (1982), 346–347; Oded (1992), 121–137. Assyrian propaganda continues under Cyrus; cf. Beaulieu (1993), 243.

60 Cf. Hardmeier (1990), 398–399.

61 This is also true for the formula *l^e^šakkēn š^e^mô šām* and its ancient Near Eastern parallels thoroughly investigated by Richter (2002). It is all but scholarly consensus that this expression belongs to the oldest form of the centralization formula; cf. Reuter (1993), 130–138; Kratz (2005), 122 n. 29. And even if it belonged to it the ancient Near Eastern parallels would not allow us at all to date its usage in Deuteronomy to the 7th century BCE or even earlier.

62 Cf. Otto (1999), 75.

must be special reasons for it."[63] Therefore, together with Moshe Weinfeld we have to pose the question: "What was it that prompted the institution of this peculiar reform?"[64]

Answering this question is not at all easy and we have to evaluate the different possibilities quite carefully. Since reasons of foreign policy such as the destruction of the Judean hinterland may have played a role but were hardly responsible for a programmatic destruction of the Judean local cults and the repeated polemics against their continuation we have to look for inner Judean causes.

Here, I see two possibilities that have been debated and it is difficult to reach any certainty.

> "Either the idea of centralization and the no less unusual 'Hear, Israel' in Deut. 6.4f., which is directed against the local differentiation of Yhwh, is a reaction to the downfall of Samaria and is meant to bind the northern Israelites, who have lost a political and religious home, to Judah and Jerusalem. Or the programme is a reaction to the downfall of the kingdom of Judah, the loss of the political and ideological centre of pre-exilic Judah connected with it, and the deportation, and has the purpose of warning against the decentralization threatened as a result [...] creating a substitute for the one place of worship chosen by Yhwh."[65]

When I tend to favour the latter possibility I take into account that it is difficult to explain why Judeans and Israelites had given up their own local sanctuaries. Nevertheless, I would like to stress again that there are equally good reasons to accept the first possibility outlined above and that Deut. 6:4–5 emphasizes the common bond between Israelites and Judeans, a bond first stated by the prophets.

Either way, the idea of cultic centralization remains a valuable criterion for a relative chronology of the history of the literature and theology of the Hebrew Bible, whereas the proposed ancient Near Eastern analogies represent the religio-historical presuppositions to the idea of centralization but cannot be regarded as direct examples. An absolute dating as well as a classifying of the different periods of the history of the literature and theology of the Hebrew Bible remains an object of historical weighing in the light of but not with the exclusive proviso of the ancient Near Eastern sources available.

---

63 Kratz (2005), 132.

64 Weinfeld (1964), 203, similar ibid., 204: "Our question is, then, what was the primary motivation for the action taken to centralize the cult and for the law validating this act?"

65 Kratz (2005), 132; cf. also Aurelius (2003), 40–44.

Bibliography

Albertz, R. (2005), Why a Reform like Josiah's Must Have Happened, in: L.L. Grabbe (ed.), Good Kings and Bad Kings: Library of Hebrew Bible/Old Testament Studies, European Seminar in Historical Methodology 5, JSOT.S 393, London, 27–46.

Arneth, M. (2001), Die antiassyrische Reform Josias von Juda. Überlegungen zur Komposition und Intention von 2 Reg 23,4–15, Zeitschrift für altorientalische und biblische Rechtsgeschichte 7, 189–216.

– (2006), Die Hiskiareform in 2 Reg 18,3–8, Zeitschrift für altorientalische und biblische Rechtsgeschichte 12, 169–215.

Aurelius, E. (2003), Zukunft jenseits des Gerichts. Eine redaktionsgeschichtliche Studie zum Enneateuch, BZAW 319, Berlin/New York.

Baltzer, K. (1964), Das Bundesformular, WMANT 4, 2. Aufl. Neukirchen-Vluyn.

Barrick, W.B. (2002), The King and the Cemeteries: Toward a New Understanding of Josiah's Reform, VT.S 88, Leiden et al.

Ben-Dov, J. (2008), Writing as Oracle and as Law: New Contexts for the Book-Find of King Josiah, JBL 127, 223–239.

Beaulieu, P.-A. (1989), The Reign of Nabonidus King of Babylon 556–539 B.C., YNER 10, New Haven/London.

– (1993), An Episode in the Fall of Babylon to the Persians, JNES 52, 241–261.

Camp, L. (1990), Hiskija und Hiskijabild. Analyse und Interpretation von 2 Kön 18–20, MThA 9, Altenberge.

Cogan, Mordechai/Tadmor, H. (1988), II Kings: A New Translation with Introduction and Commentary, AncB 11, New York.

Cogan, Morton (1974), Imperialism and Religion: Assyria, Judah and Israel in the Eighth and Seventh Centuries B.C.E., SBL.MS 19, Missoula.

Dion, P.E. (1978), Quelques aspects de l'interaction entre religion et politique dans le Deutéronome, ScEs 30, 39–55.

– (1991), Deuteronomy 13: The Suppression of Alien Religious Propaganda in Israel during the Late Monarchical Era, in: B. Halpern/D.W. Hobson (eds.), Law and Ideology in Monarchic Israel, JSOT.S 124, Sheffield, 147–216.

Finkelstein, I./Silberman, N.A. (2001), The Bible Unearthed: Archaeology's New Vision of Ancient Israel and the Origin of Its Sacred Texts, New York (German Translation: Keine Posaunen vor Jericho. Die archäologische Wahrheit über die Bibel, München 2002).

– /Silberman, N.A. (2006), Temple and Dynasty: Hezekiah, the Remaking of Judah and the Rise of the Pan-Israelite Ideology, JSOT 30, 259–285.

Fried, L.S. (2002), The High Places (Bamôt) and the Reforms of Hezekiah and Josiah: An Archaeological Investigation, JAOS 122, 437–465.

Gallagher, W.R. (1999), Sennacherib's Campaign to Judah: New Studies, Studies in the History and Culture of the Ancient Near East 18, Leiden et al.

Galling, K. (1964), Studien zur Geschichte Israels im persischen Zeitalter, Tübingen.

Gleis, M. (1997), Die Bamah, BZAW 251, Berlin/New York.

Grayson, A.K. (2000), Assyrian and Babylonian Chronicles, TCS 5 (1975), Winona Lake.

Hagedorn, A.C. (2005), Placing (a) God: Central Place Theory in Deuteronomy 12 and at Delphi, in: J. Day (ed.), Temple and Worship in Biblical Israel: Proceedings of the Oxford Old Testament Seminar: Library of Hebrew Bible/Old Testament Studies, JSOT.S 422, London, 188–211.

Halpern, B. (1991), Jerusalem and the Lineages in the seventh Century BCE: Kinship and the Rise of Individual Moral Liability, in: B. Halpern/D.W. Hobson (eds.), Law and Ideology in Monarchic Israel, JSOT.S 124, Sheffield, 11–107.

Handy, L.K. (1988), Hezekiah's Unlikely Reform, ZAW 100, 111–115.

– (1995), Historical Probability and the Narrative of Josiah's Reform in 2 Kings, in: S.W. Holloway/L.K. Handy (eds.), The Pitcher is Broken: Memorial Essays for G.W. Ahlström, JSOT.S 190, Sheffield, 252–275.

– (2006), Josiah in a New Light: Assyriology Touches the Reforming King, in: S.W. Holloway (ed.), Orientalism, Assyriology and the Bible, Hebrew Bible Monographs 10, Sheffield, 415–431.

Hardmeier, C. (1990), Prophetie im Streit vor dem Untergang Judas. Erzählkommunikative Studien zur Entstehungssituation der Jesaja- und Jeremiaerzählungen in II Reg 18–20 und Jer 37–40, BZAW 187, Berlin/New York.

– (2000), König Joschija in der Klimax des DtrG (2Reg 22f.) und das vordtr Dokument einer Kultreform am Residenzort (23,4–15*), in: R. Lux (ed.), Erzählte Geschichte. Beiträge zur narrativen Kultur im alten Israel, BThS 40, Neukirchen-Vluyn, 81–145.

Harvey, P.B./Halpern, B. (2008), W.M.L. de Wette's "Dissertatio Critica ...": Context and Translation, Zeitschrift für altorientalische und biblische Rechtsgeschichte 14, 47–85.

Hoffmann, H.-D. (1980), Reform und Reformen. Untersuchungen zu einem Grundthema der deuteronomistischen Geschichtsschreibung, AThANT 66, Zürich.

Jepsen, A. (1956), Die Quellen des Königsbuches, 2. Aufl. Halle (Saale).

Koch, C. (2008), Vertrag, Treueid und Bund. Studien zur Rezeption des altorientalischen Vertragsrechts im Deuteronomium und zur Ausbildung der Bundestheologie im Alten Testament, BZAW 383, Berlin/New York.

Köckert, M. (2000), Zum literargeschichtlichen Ort des Prophetengesetzes Dtn 18 zwischen dem Jeremiabuch und Dtn 13, in: R.G. Kratz/H. Spieckermann (eds.), Liebe und Gebot. Studien zum Deuteronomium, FS L. Perlitt, FRLANT 190, Göttingen, 80–100.

Kratz, R.G. (2002), From Nabonidus to Cyrus, in: A. Panaino/G. Pettinato (eds.), Ideologies as Intercultural Phenomena: Proceedings of the Third Annual Symposium of the Assyrian and Babylonian Intellectual Heritage Project, held in Chicago, USA, October 27–31, 2000, MELAMMU Symposia III, Milano, 143–156.

– (2005), The Composition of the Narrative Books of the Old Testament (transl. by J. Bowden), London/New York.

– (2007a), Temple and Torah: Reflections on the Legal Status of the Pentateuch between Elephantine and Qumran, in: G.N. Knoppers/B.M. Levinson (eds.), The Pentateuch as Torah: New Models for Understanding Its Promulgation and Acceptance, Winona Lake, 77–103.

– (2007b), 'The place which He has chosen': The Identification of the Cult Place of Deut. 12 and Lev. 17 in 4QMMT, in: M. Bar-Asher/E. Tov (eds.), FS D. Dimant, Meghillot 5–6, Haifa/Jerusalem, 57–80.

Kuhrt, A. (1990), Nabonidus and the Babylonian Priesthood, in: M. Beard/J. North (eds.), Pagan Priests: Religion and Power in the Ancient World, London, 117–155.

Levin, C. (2003), Josia im Deuteronomistischen Geschichtswerk, in: ders., Fortschreibungen. Gesammelte Studien zum Alten Testament, BZAW 316, Berlin/New York, 198–216.

Levinson, B.M. (1997), Deuteronomy and the Hermeneutics of Legal Innovation, New York/Oxford.

Lewy, J. (1928), Sanherib und Hizkia, OLZ 31, 150–163.

Liverani, M. (1995), The Medes at Esarhaddon's Court, JCS 47, 57–62.

Machinist, P. (2000), The *Rab šākēh* at the Wall of Jerusalem: Israelite Identity in the Face of the Assyrian 'Other', HebStud 41, 151–168.

Mathys, H.-P. (2008), Wilhelm Martin Leberecht de Wettes Dissertatio critico-exegetica von 1805, in: M. Kessler/M. Wallraff (eds.), Biblische Theologie und historisches Denken. Wissenschaftsgeschichtliche Studien aus Anlass der 50. Wiederkehr der Basler Promotion von Rudolf

Smend, Studien zur Geschichte der Wissenschaften in Basel, Neue Folge 5, Basel, 171–211.

Maul, S.M. (1997), Die altorientalische Hauptstadt – Abbild und Nabel der Welt, in: G. Wilhelm (ed.), Die orientalische Stadt. Kontinuität, Wandel, Bruch. 1. Internationales Colloquium der Deutschen Orient-Gesellschaft, 9.–10. Mai 1996 in Halle/Saale, Colloquien der Deutschen Orient-Gesellschaft 1, Saarbrücken, 109–124.

Mayer, W. (1995), Politik und Kriegskunst der Assyrer, Abhandlungen zur Literatur Alt-Syrien-Palästinas und Mesopotamiens 9, Münster.

– (1997), Der Gott Assur und die Erben Assyriens, in: R. Albertz (ed.), Religion und Gesellschaft. Studien zu ihrer Wechselbeziehung in den Kulturen des Antiken Vorderen Orients, Veröffentlichungen des Arbeitskreises zur Erforschung der Religions- und Kulturgeschichte des Antiken Vorderen Orients (AZERKAVO), vol. 1, AOAT 248, Münster 1997, 15–23.

Menzel, B. (1981), Assyrische Tempel, StP.SM 10, I: Untersuchungen zu Kult, Administration und Personal/II: Anmerkungen, Textbuch, Tabellen und Indices, Rom.

Na'aman, N. (1991), The Kingdom of Judah under Josiah, Tel Aviv 18, 3–71.

– (1995), The Debated Historicity of Hezekiah's Reform in the Light of Historical and Archaeological Research, ZAW 107, 179–195.

– (2002), The Abandonment of Cult Places in the Kingdoms of Israel and Judah as Acts of Cult Reform, UF 34, 585–602.

– (2006), The King Leading Cult Reforms in his Kingdom: Josiah and Other Kings in the Ancient Near East, Zeitschrift für altorientalische und biblische Rechtsgeschichte 12, 131–168.

Niehr, H. (1995), Die Reform des Joschija. Methodische, historische und religionsgeschichtliche Aspekte, in: W. Groß (ed.), Jeremia und die "deuteronomistische Bewegung", BBB 98, Weinheim, 33–55.

Nissinen, M. (1996), Falsche Prophetie in neuassyrischer und deuteronomistischer Darstellung, in: T. Veijola (ed.), Das Deuteronomium und seine Querbeziehungen, SESJ 62, Helsinki/Göttingen, 172–195.

Noth, M. (1957), Überlieferungsgeschichtliche Studien. Die sammelnden und bearbeitenden Geschichtswerke im Alten Testament (1943), 2. Aufl. Tübingen.

Oded, B. (1992), War, Peace and Empire: Justifications for War in Assyrian Royal Inscriptions, Wiesbaden.

Oestreicher, T. (1923), Das Deuteronomische Grundgesetz, BFChTh 27/4, Gütersloh.

– (1930), Reichstempel und Ortsheiligtümer in Israel, BFChTh 33/3, Gütersloh.

Otto, E. (1996), Treueid und Gesetz. Die Ursprünge des Deuteronomiums im Horizont neuassyrischen Vertragsrechts, Zeitschrift für altorientalische und biblische Rechtsgeschichte 2, 1–52.
– (1997), Das Deuteronomium als archimedischer Punkt der Pentateuchkritik. Auf dem Wege zu einer Neubegründung der De Wette'schen Hypothese, in: M. Vervenne/J. Lust (eds.), Deuteronomy and Deuteronomic Literature, FS C.H.W. Brekelmans, BEThL 133, Leuven, 321–339.
– (1999), Das Deuteronomium. Politische Theologie und Rechtsreform in Juda und Assyrien, BZAW 284, Berlin/New York.
– (2000), Das Deuteronomium im Pentateuch und Hexateuch. Studien zur Literaturgeschichte von Pentateuch und Hexateuch im Lichte des Deuteronomiumrahmens, FAT 30, Tübingen.
– (2002), Gottes Recht als Menschenrecht. Rechts- und literaturhistorische Studien zum Deuteronomium, Beihefte zur Zeitschrift für altorientalische und biblische Rechtsgeschichte 2, Wiesbaden.
Pakkala, J. (2006), Der literar- und religionsgeschichtliche Ort von Deuteronomium 13, in: M. Witte et al. (eds.), Die deuteronomistischen Geschichtswerke. Redaktions- und religionsgeschichtliche Perspektiven zur „Deuteronomismus"-Diskussion in Tora und Vorderen Propheten, BZAW 365, Berlin/New York, 125–137.
Parpola, S./Watanabe, K. (1988), Neo-Assyrian Treaties and Loyalty Oaths, SAA 2, Helsinki.
Perlitt, L. (1969), Bundestheologie im Alten Testament, WMANT 36, Neukirchen-Vluyn.
– (1994), Hebraismus – Deuteronomismus – Judaismus, in: ders., Deuteronomium-Studien, FAT 8, Tübingen, 247–260.
Pongratz-Leisten, B./Deller, K./Bleibtreu, E. (1992), Götterstreitwagen und Götterstandarten. Götter auf dem Feldzug und ihr Kult im Feldlager, BaghM 23, 291–356 mit Tafeln 50–69.
Reuter, E. (1993), Kultzentralisation. Entstehung und Theologie von Dtn 12, BBB 87, Frankfurt a.M.
Richter, S.L. (2002), The Deuteronomistic History and the Name Theology: *l^ešakkēn š^emô šām* in the Bible and the Ancient Near East, BZAW 318, Berlin/New York.
Rüterswörden, U. (2002), Dtn 13 in der neueren Deuteronomiumforschung, in: A. Lemaire (ed.), Congress Volume Basel 2001, VT.S 92, Leiden, 185–203.
Schaudig, H. (2001), Die Inschriften Nabonids von Babylon und Kyros' des Großen samt den in ihrem Umfeld entstandenen Tendenzschriften. Textausgabe und Grammatik, AOAT 256, Münster.

Schmid, K. (2008), Literaturgeschichte des Alten Testaments. Eine Einführung, Darmstadt.
Spieckermann, H. (1982), Juda unter Assur in der Sargonidenzeit, FRLANT 129, Göttingen.
Steymans, H.U. (1995), Deuteronomium 28 und die *adê* zur Thronfolgeregelung Asarhaddons. Segen und Fluch im Alten Orient und in Israel, OBO 145, Freiburg (Schweiz)/Göttingen.
– (2003), Die neuassyrische Vertragsrhetorik der "Vassal Treaties of Esarhaddon" und das Deuteronomium, in: G. Braulik (ed.), Das Deuteronomium, ÖBS 23, Frankfurt a.M., 89–152.
– (2006), Die literarische und historische Bedeutung der Thronfolgevereidigung Asarhaddons, in: M. Witte et al. (eds.), Die deuteronomistischen Geschichtswerke. Redaktions- und religionsgeschichtliche Perspektiven zur „Deuteronomismus"-Diskussion in Tora und Vorderen Propheten, BZAW 365, Berlin/New York, 331–349.
Uehlinger, C. (1995), Gab es eine joschijanische Kultreform? Plädoyer für ein begründetes Minimum, in: W. Groß (ed.), Jeremia und die "deuteronomistische Bewegung", BBB 98, Weinheim, 57–89 (English Translation: Was there a Cult Reform under King Josiah? The Case for a Well-Grounded Minimum, in: L.L. Grabbe [2005, ed.], Good Kings and Bad Kings: Library of Hebrew Bible/Old Testament Studies, European Seminar in Historical Methodology 5, London, JSOT.S 393, 279–316).
Vera Chamaza, G.W. (2002), Die Omnipotenz Aššurs. Entwicklungen in der Aššur-Theologie unter den Sargoniden Sargon II., Sanherib und Asarhaddon, AOAT 295, Münster.
Veijola, T. (2000), Wahrheit und Intoleranz nach Deuteronomium 13, in: ders., Moses Erben. Studien zum Dekalog, zum Deuteronomismus und zum Schriftgelehrtentum, BWANT 149, Stuttgart, 109–130.
– (2002–2003), Deuteronomismusforschung zwischen Tradition und Innovation (I–III), ThR 67 (2002), 273–327, 391–424; 68 (2003), 1–44.
– (2004), Das 5. Buch Mose Deuteronomium Kapitel 1,1–16,7, ATD 8/1, Göttingen.
Weinfeld, M. (1964), Cult Centralization in Israel in the Light of a Neo-Babylonian Analogy, JNES 23, 202–212.
– (1992), Deuteronomy and the Deuteronomic School (1972), Winona Lake, Indiana.
Wellhausen, J. (1905), Prolegomena zur Geschichte Israels, 6. Aufl. Berlin (English Translation of the 2nd edition 1883: Prolegomena to the History of Israel, trans. by J.S. Black and A. Menzies [1885], Reprint Atlanta, Georgia 1994).

– (1914), Israelitische und jüdische Geschichte, 7. Aufl. Berlin (Reprint [10]2004).

Witte, M. et al. (2006), Die deuteronomistischen Geschichtswerke. Redaktions- und religionsgeschichtliche Perspektiven zur „Deuteronomismus"-Diskussion in Tora und Vorderen Propheten, BZAW 365, Berlin/New York.

Würthwein, E. (1984), Die Bücher der Könige: 1. Kön. 17–2. Kön. 25. Übersetzt und erklärt von E. Würthwein, ATD 11/2, Göttingen.

Cult Centralization in the Ancient Near East?

Conceptions of the Ideal Capital in the Ancient Near East

HANSPETER SCHAUDIG

1. Introduction

Among the many popular 'first achievements' in human history accomplished by the Mesopotamian civilizations, has there ever been something like a 'cult centralization in the Ancient Near East'? Does asking that question mean taking a too secular, too technical, and too deliberate point of view on the candid religiousness from the days of humanity's 'childhood'? The topic has been presented cautiously with a question mark, and that is quite right, since at first sight there is no period or region in the Ancient Near East which has clearly seen such a harsh cutting down of cults as it is assumed to have been the case at certain periods in ancient Israel and Judah.[1] At second sight however, it becomes quite clear that even if we can not directly observe a deliberate reducing and centralization of cults in Mesopotamia, there must have been a system working, quietly yet efficiently, which prevented the cults of certain gods to proliferate beyond control. And this system in fact produced a situation that was quite close to the 'One God – One Cult' concept known from Jerusalem. As stated, we can not see this system working, via letters of kings or priests or in juridical quarrels, but we can see the results it produced. And that is: certain 'boss gods', the heads of the pantheon, the divine kings of the gods who in turn bestowed kingship on chosen human kings on earth, had only one cult place at a given time in a given region. As we shall see, the topic is tightly interwoven with the concept of the capital city in Mesopotamia. Hence it will also be this topic to be addressed here, rather than the somewhat elusive idea of 'cult centralization'.

---

1 My special thanks go to Jacob L. Wright (Emory Univ.) who kindly commented on an earlier version of this article. – On the situation in Israel and Judah cf. the slaughter of the prophets of Baal by Elijah (1 Kings 18), and the religious reforms of Hezekiah (2 Kings 18:4, 22) and Josiah (2 Kings 23:5–20).

Before we start, let me briefly discuss what is certainly not to be taken as an attempt to centralize Babylonian cults, although it is sometimes adduced in scholarly literature.[2] What I am referring to is Nabonidus bringing the gods of various Babylonian cities into the strongly walled city of Babylon, when the invasion of Cyrus was looming on the horizon. This was, however, only to safeguard them from being kidnapped by the Persians.[3] Yet, after Babylon had been taken by the Persians, Cyrus and his supporters from among the Babylonian priesthood presented Nabonidus' attempt to safeguard the statues of the gods as a sacrilege, which disrupted the gods in their peaceful dwellings:

> "(10a) Arousing Marduk's wrath, Nabonidus even had (the statues of) the gods brought to Babylon (from their proper cities). […] (33–34) And (the statues of) the gods of Sumer und Akkad (i.e. Babylonia), whom Nabonidus had brought into Babylon to the anger of the Lord of the gods, I had them dwell in their beloved sanctuaries in peace again, at the command of Marduk, the great lord."[4]

The precautions Nabonidus took were reproached as sacrilege by his adversaries, but this interpretation is due to their biased point of view. Nabonidus had only employed the same and simple means which had been used time and again by his predecessors.[5] In 625 BCE, when the Assyrian army moved into Babylonia against Nabopolassar who had ascended the throne of Babylon, the gods of the Babylonian cities Šapazzu and Sippar were brought into Babylon for safety.[6] The difference to the case of Nabonidus is only that Nabopolassar succeeded. Marduk-apla-iddinna II had done the same some 150 years earlier, when he was fleeing from the invading Assyrian kings Sargon II and Sennacherib.[7] When Sargon's troops invaded into Babylonia in 709 BCE, Marduk-apla-iddina had brought the gods of various Babylonian cities safely into his heavily fortified home town Dūr-Yākīn, located in the inaccessible swamps in the very South of Babylonia:

> "(The people of) his inhabited cities, and the gods dwelling therein he gathered all together and had them enter Dūr-Yākīn."[8]

2 Cf. e.g. Weinfeld (1964).

3 Cf. Beaulieu (1989), 219–224, esp. 223; Beaulieu (1993).

4 Cyrus on Nabonidus, from the "Cyrus-Cylinder", lines 10 and 33–34, after Schaudig (2001), 554–556.

5 On this tactic of 'safeguarding' the gods, also discussing the other examples given below, cf. Cogan (1974), 30–34.

6 Cf. Grayson (1975), 89, chronicle 2, lines 19–21.

7 Cf. Brinkman (1964), esp. 27 with n. 153.

8 Sargon II on Marduk-apla-iddina, in his 'display inscription' from Khorsabad, l. 126; Fuchs (1994), 226–227, 350.

When Dūr-Yākīn was finally taken by the Assyrians, Sargon II undertook the pious task to return the 'deported' gods to their proper places:

> "I (re-)established the freedom privileges of Ur, Uruk, Eridu, Larsa, Kullaba, Kisik, and Nēmed-Laguda, and I returned their deported gods to their sanctuaries, and re-established their regular offerings which had ceased (by the actions of Marduk-apla-iddina)."[9]

A decade later, Marduk-apla-iddina employed the same 'trick' successfully again. When he was retreating from invading Sennacherib (ca. in 700 BCE), he took his gods and the mortal remains of his ancestors with him:

> "He removed (the statues of) the gods [...] from their dwellings, loaded them into ships and flew off like a bird towards a place which is in the middle of the sea."[10]

This of course was but an attempt to take the gods out of the line of fire, and it was in fact a very successful one. But in saving the gods, the king proved in a way that he would not expect the gods to save him. Furthermore, he in fact did what the enemy was feared to do, that is disrupting the peaceful abode of the gods. If the actions were seen as 'abusing' or 'safeguarding' the gods depended upon the opposing party's points of view. In the cases of Marduk-apla-iddina and Nabonidus, the reports were created by their victorious adversaries. Hence it is hardly surprising that their actions were portrayed as sacrilege. Yet, as indicated above, 'safeguarding' the gods posed a problem in itself. From the very start, the action was quite close to 'abusing' the gods, since in a way they were forced to side the king whom they might have forsaken. But in any case, these acts are not to be considered examples of 'cult centralization'.

2. The Divine Origin of Babylonian Shrines

The issue of 'cult centralization', and the problem of closing down sanctuaries which accompanies it, begins with the decision to understand a particular shrine's character as primarily 'human' or 'divine' – that is, whether we should consider a particular shrine to be set up by humans, or by the gods themselves. In Babylonia the human activity involved in constructing temples posed a very special problem to the ancient mind. Together with the cult statue, temples shared in the primordial and

9 Sargon II, 'display inscription' from Khorsabad, lines 136–137; Fuchs (1994), 229–230, 351.

10 Sennacherib on Marduk-apla-iddina; Luckenbill (1924), 35, iii:65.

transcendent qualities of the deity, yet, in their individual form and existence they were products crafted by humans. They were regarded as built originally by the gods themselves in times primordial, with the actual building being in fact a restoration by humans only, keeping to the original divine layout. After technical completion, these temples had to be purified to make them acceptable for the deity, and thereafter they had to be protected continuously against human pollution and desecration. A Babylonian temple was not a mere brickwork structure where the statue was stored. After inauguration it was considered identical with the original, primeval and transcendent, and sometimes celestial, abode of the deity. Thus, the shrine E'abzu in the city of Eridu was the counterpart of Enki's dwelling in the subterranean ocean. The temple Ebabbar, a building that existed twice on earth in the city of Sippar and Larsa, was the counterpart of the heavenly dwelling of the sungod Šamaš. And the shrine Esagil in Babylon was the representation and successor of the temple built there originally by the assembly of all the gods for Marduk. Fundamental for the understanding of this idea is the ancients' conviction that Enlil, the king of the gods, had placed the gods on the earth, arranging dwellings and cult places for them, which were not to be altered. As early as the 3rd millennium BCE Mesopotamians began to formulate this idea in the opening lines of the 'Temple-Hymns', addressing Enlil's holy city, Nippur:

"City, grown up with the heavens, embracing the heavens,
Nippur, Bond of heaven and earth:
Enlil, the 'Great Mountain',
Enlil, the Lord *Nunamnir*,
The Lord, whose spoken word is to be fulfilled correctly,
not to be reduced, not to be increased,
Enlil has placed the *Anūna*-Gods into their (cult) places,
and thereupon the great gods have sung his praise."[11]

Each god owned a special territory, assigned to him by Enlil, where he had a house – his 'temple'– to live in, and human staff ('priests') to serve him. These territories were not exchangeable and the gods' houses were not to be moved. The cities themselves were property of the gods and thereby holy. In many cases not only the temples, but also the holy cities, were regarded not as human-made, but rather built by the gods.[12] According to this point of view, El built Mari and the as-

11 Biggs (1974), 46, lines 1–14; Krebernik (1994).

12 Also on the following, cf. Hurowitz (1992), 332–334: Appendix 6: "Gods as Builders of Temples and Cities".

sembly of all the gods built Babylon for Marduk.[13] Nippur, the holy city of Enlil, was called "built on its own".[14] In the Ugaritic Baal-cycle, the god Baal has a palace built on the heights of Mount Saphon by the divine craftsman Kothar-wa-Hasis from Crete.[15] Even in the 'West' – the Eastern Mediterranean – we still know this motif from the tales about the walls of Thebes, built by the music of Amphion' lyre – a gift of Hermes, or from the walls of Troy, built by Poseidon and the lyre-playing Apollon.

And here is probably a fundamental difference between the concept of Mesopotamian temples, and the altars, heights or temples of biblical literature. The Mesopotamian sanctuaries were thought to be set up originally by the gods themselves, and not by humans, be their name Abraham, Jacob, or Solomon.[16] In biblical literature, the motif of the god setting up a shrine himself, and "with his own hands", is found only rarely. Apparently, this idea is confined narrowly to two statements in hymnic literature, that is in Psalm 78 and Exodus 15 (the "Song of the Sea").[17] These rare biblical statements display a point of view that was common to Babylonian thought. They elevate the 'divinely made' shrine at Jerusalem over the 'humanly made' sanctuaries throughout the land. We can best appreciate this point by noting the complete lack of Babylonian stories about 'founding heroes' setting up a shrine. In the Babylonian concept, sanctuaries were of divine and primordial nature. A famous epithet of the temple Eninnu[18] at Lagaš – as well as other cities and temples throughout Sumer[19] – runs "founded by (the primeval sky-god) An", i.e. founded by the father of the gods himself in the very beginning of all, and not set up by humans at some time during

---

13 Regarding Mari: cf. Frayne (1990), 605, E4.6.8.2, lines 34–35, and for Babylon: *Enūma elîš* vi:49–73, cf. Talon (2005), 64–65.

14 George (1992), 143.

15 Cf. Pardee (1997), 261.

16 See e.g.: Abram builds the altar at Shechem, and the one between Bethel and Ai (Gen. 12:7–8); Jacob sets up a stone-pillar and calls the place Bethel (Gen. 28:16–22).

17 "He chose the tribe of Judah, his well-loved mountain of Zion; he built his sanctuary like (heavens) on high, like the earth he set firm for ever" (Ps. 78:68–69). And see the same idea, probably retransferred into the "Song of the Sea": "(Mount Zion,) the place which you, Yahweh, have made your dwelling, the sanctuary, Yahweh, prepared by your own hands" (Exod. 15:17). These cases were kindly pointed out to me by Alexander Rofé in the discussion of my paper. They had also been discussed by Hurowitz (1992), 332; Jacob L. Wright (Emory Univ.) kindly pointed out to me that this trope also appears in the 15th century BCE stanza of the Passover song *Dayenu*: "If He had brought us into the land of Israel, and not built for us the Holy Temple – it would have been enough for us!"

18 Gudea Cylinders A 9:11; 27:8; B 20:20; see Edzard (1997), 74, 86, 99.

19 Cf. Sjöberg (1960), 39.

history, just to show that the cosmos could do without it. As a rule, no Babylonian shrine would 'boast' to have been founded by a human king, priest or sage, be it Enmeduranki, Gilgamesh, Adapa the sage, or Sargon of Akkade. Even in the case of Akkade, the city which rose to supremacy as the capital of the Sargonid empire in the third millennium BCE, and which is said to have been 'built', (i.e. established as a royal residence) by king Sargon,[20] the sanctuary of the tutelar deity Ištar of Akkade was considered to have been founded by the goddess herself.[21] Only minor and secondary shrines like that set up by the citizens of Akkade for their deified Akkadian king Naram-Sîn are said to be founded by humans.[22] As opposed to this thoroughly theological and impersonal Mesopotamian concept, the ties between a sanctuary, height, or altar and a family, a clan or tribe seem to have been much closer in some of the biblical traditions.

Of course, this sketch gives the idealistic concept of the philosophy of Babylonian shrines. But however fictitious, this is what the texts set forth. This can be clearly seen in the cases when a shrine was not just restored or rebuilt, but in fact built anew. Even then, the shrine or the cult had to be provided with an ancient tradition to be continued. Many elements of the cults of the first millennium which were said to have been "forgotten" (*mašû* N) or "fallen out of use" (*naparkû*) were in fact newly constructed features which did not exist before. Yet, introducing 'innovations' was no option, and therefore newly established temples and cults were simply presented as 'forgotten' and newly 'restored'. That is why Sennacherib says that the temple of the New Year's festival which he had recently built outside of the city of Aššur in the plain, "had been *forgotten* (*mašû* N) since day of old".[23] In fact, that shrine was of course a newly designed structure, modelled on the temple of the New Year's festival at Babylon. Another beautiful example is the report on an improvement of the fish offerings for Marduk, brought up by Nebuchadrezzar II. Nebuchadrezzar assigned new fishermen to bring in fresh fish to be offered to Marduk. This was in fact an innovation in the cult, yet it was portrayed as an ingenious idea inspired by Marduk himself, and as a most welcome restoration of an old and original custom which only had ceased (*naparkû*) due to human imperfection:

20 As reported in a short note in the *Sumerian King List*: Jacobsen (1939), 110–111, vi:34–35.

21 Cf. Cooper (1983), 50, lines 7–9.

22 Cf. Westenholz (1999), 54. Frayne (1993), 114, E2.1.4.10 (Basetki statue), lines 52–56: for the deified king Naram-Sîn, the citizens of Akkade build a temple which in this case of course did not exist before.

23 Luckenbill (1924), 136, lines 26–27, p. 139, line 2; Frahm (1997), 173–177, 285–286.

"[I lea]rnt [fro]m an inscription of a [for]mer king of ol[d that formerly and up to my reign] fish as an offering gift did not enter Esagil and fresh fish of the same day was [not] offered. But Marduk, my lord, placed into my mind (the idea to bring in) 30 fresh fishes for the regular offering of Marduk, my lord, (a custom) which had ceased since distant days."[24]

Nebuchadrezzar clearly states that this offering did not exist before. Yet, several lines later he describes it as a custom fallen out of use since time immemorial, and restored by him. This contradiction is solved by a recently reconstructed part of the *Esagil Chronicle*,[25] to which Nebuchadrezzar here refers: Although the offering did not exist in historical times, it was considered to have existed in times primordial when Marduk's son Nabû himself took care of it, of course in the most perfect and ideal way. Temples and cults were regarded as parts of the divine layout of civilization as revealed by the gods to humankind at the beginning of history. And any possible flaw could only be taken as a loss in divine perfection caused by human deficiency. The philosophy of this paradox shines up in the stock phrases of Babylonian restoration reports: The pious work was done "exactly like in the olden days" (*kīma labīrimma*), and yet at the same time "greater than ever before" (*eli ša pāni šūturu*).

In Assyria, matters were quite different at times. Aššurnasirpal II (883–859 BCE) founded various temples "which had previously not existed" (*ša ina pān lā bašû*) at Calah.[26] He also created a brand-new cult statue of the god Ninurta "which had previously not existed" either. Furthermore, he appointed a cult and festivals for this new god and his new temple.[27] When Tukultī-Ninurta I (1233–1197 BCE) built his new residence Kār-Tukultī-Ninurta on a greenfield site some miles downstream from the old capital Aššur, he did not present the idea for the new building as bluntly as Aššurnasirpal II did later. Tukultī-Ninurta I referred to an order of his god Aššur who had requested a new cult-centre, and who had commanded the king to build his sanctuary "in the uncultivated plains and meadows, where there was neither house nor [dwelling], where no ruin hills or rubble had accumulated, and no bricks had been laid."[28] In this statement, Tukultī-Ninurta connected the construction programme of his brand new city designed on a draw-

24 Lines 1–8 of the 'fish-episode' from Nebuchadrezzar's Wadi Brisa inscription, according to my reconstruction. For an older version see Langdon (1912), 154–157, Nbc. no. 19, A v:1–10.

25 According to my reconstruction of the text (forthcoming).

26 Grayson (1991), 291, A.0.101.30 ("banquet stela"), lines 53–59.

27 Grayson (1991), 295, A.0.101.31 (slabs from the Ninurta temple at Calah), line 13 (statue), line 15 (festivals).

28 Grayson (1987), 277, A.0.78.25, lines 9–15.

ing board to the ancient idea of building a temple on a pure site, on virgin soil. These examples illustrate the distinctive strength of the king in Assyria, whose foremost function after all was high-priest (*šangû*) of Aššur.[29]

The above reflections demonstrate that in Babylonia temples and cults were regarded as an integral part of the primeval and divine layout of the universe. For the present issue, this means on the one hand that it was not easy to found a temple in just any place. On the other hand, it means an established cultic place was hard to remove. In Babylonia, a 'cultic reform' like those undertaken by Hezekiah and Josiah[30] would seem incompatible with major concepts of the divine. In Babylonia, a ruler could not simply shut some of these holy structures down, just because he might think there were too many of them, and in the wrong places.

3. The Kings of the Gods: Enlil, Marduk, Aššur, and their Cultic Places

According to Babylonian polytheism, which usually arranged the gods in families or divine courts, Enlil was the grand-son of the primeval god Anšar, i.e. "All-Heavens", and the son of the sky-god Anu, who was the father of all the gods. Enlil in turn was considered the king of the gods, the one who determines fates, and the one who chooses the human king. This is the function which matters for the present study. For reasons of state, the priesthood of Enlil and the human king must have shared an interest in ensuring that the choice of the king was legitimate, clear, and undisputed. For Enlil, this meant there could be only one "Enlil", and one priesthood, centered on one temple. It would have been highly disadvantageous to have dozens of Enlils scattered all over the land, with individual priesthoods pursuing their own politics, and with ecstatics rising and delivering prophecies beyond any control.

---

29 See below, with n. 53.

30 See above, n. 1.

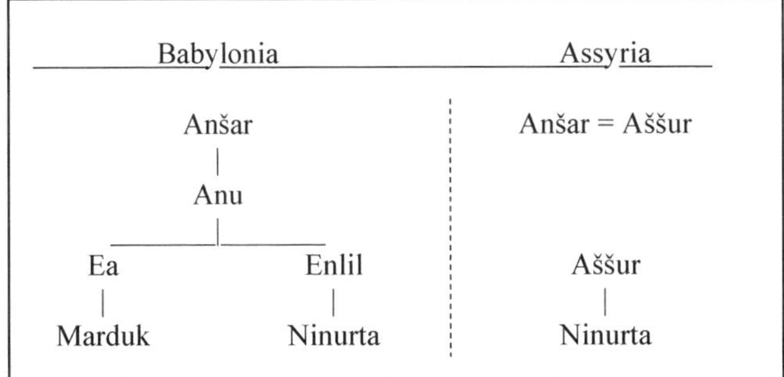

Fig. 1: Sketch of the Babylonian and Assyrian concepts of the positions of Enlil, Marduk, and Aššur.

Enlil had a son, the warrior Ninurta, and a brother, Ea, the god of all wisdom, who in turn had a son, Marduk. Originally, Marduk was only a minor god with some expertise in incantations, but due to Babylon's rise and success from the era of Hammurapi on, he came to be the new king of the gods, eventually dethroning Enlil by the end of the second millennium. Outside of this Babylonian system there was the Assyrian god Aššur, who rose during the second and first millennium from a mere city-god to the position of the "Assyrian Enlil",[31] and in this function he was also provided with Ninurta as his son, as a matter of syncretism. For most of the time, Aššur could be ignored by the Babylonians. It was only in the first millennium BCE when the Assyrians got hold of Babylonia that the role of the "Assyrian Enlil" and that of Marduk, then the "Babylonian Enlil", became an issue. The Assyrians tried to settle this problem by equating Aššur with the primeval god Anšar, grand-father of all the gods. This quite elegant strategy, however, proved unsuccessful since Anšar, together with Anu and Enlil, had also been reduced in his rank by Marduk at that time. Therefore it came to a bitter conflict between Aššur and Marduk in the first millennium, culminating in the destruction of Babylon by the enervated and frenzied Sennacherib in 689 BCE.

In the following, we shall take a quick glance at the cult places of these gods. Enlil, the traditional king of the Sumerian and Babylonian gods, had his main, and in fact sole, sanctuary at Nippur. There are only three major exceptions to this rule: In the 3rd millennium BCE the powerful city state of Lagaš managed to incorporate Enlil with a new temple into its pantheon. Certainly with imperialistic intentions, Lagaš

31 On the syncretism of Aššur with Enlil resulting in the concept of the "Assyrian Enlil", cf. e.g. Mayer (1995), 62; Amar (2002), 39–47: "Ninurta in Assyria".

made its city god Ningirsu the son of Enlil, and accommodated the latter, Ningirsu's new father, in a newly-founded temple called E'adda, "house of the father".[32] When the heydays of Lagaš passed, the temple seems to have fallen into oblivion again. In the Old-Babylonian period, king Hammurapi is reported to have accommodated Enlil in a temple at Babylon, which apparently lasted into the first millennium.[33] And in the Middle-Babylonian period, king Kurigalzu built Enlil a great temple in his new residence at Dūr-Kurigalzu.[34] In all three cases we witness the successful attempt of a strong kingship to take Enlil, the king of the gods, along from Nippur into a royal residence located at another place. Strangely enough, a king never resided at Nippur, or even tried to do so. In the present paper, however, we shall leave this important topic out. This difficult matter is to be addressed in a paper of its own. However, in the cases of Aššur and Babylon we shall see that after Nippur's era the union of the temples of Enlil's successors, Aššur and Marduk, and the palaces of their kings chosen indeed constituted a sort of centralization of divine and royal power in the city sheltering the individual god's sanctuary.

When Marduk was still a minor city god, he had his main temple Esagil at Babylon.[35] In the neighbouring city of Borsippa, he was also worshipped as Tutu in the temple Ezida.[36] Originally, Tutu appears to have been the indigenous tutelar deity of Borsippa. His merging into the overpowering god Marduk-Asarluhi of the neighbouring city of Babylon was probably triggered by Babylon's rising fortunes, and it was supported by his name, Tutu, which could be interpreted as "The One who brings forth the Incantation", matching Marduk's character as a god of incantations. Apart from these main temples he had also some 'seats', chapels, and minor temples scattered throughout Babylonia[37]

---

32 George (1993), 65, no. 40; Selz (1995), 127–128, Enlil §§ 7–9.

33 Enamtila ("House of Life") at Babylon (George [1993], 130–131, no. 849). In the colophon of a Neo-Babylonian copy, Enamtila is given as the place of origin of an inscription attributed to Hammurapi, though looking strangely younger, more like a text from the first millennium (Frayne [1990], 336–337, E4.3.6.3: line 24). Anyway, the temple apparently was still in use in the Neo-Babylonia period. As a further exception from the rule proposed, there is a temple complex at Kish-Hursagkalama dedicated to Enlil and Ninlil, the parents of the city's tutelar deity Ninurta-Zababa, see George (1993), 51.

34 E'umungal "House of the Great Lord", later interpreted as E'ugal "House of the Great Storm"; cf. George (1993), 152, no. 1122.

35 Cf. George (1993), 139–140, no. 967.

36 Cf. George (1993), 159–160, no. 1236. Sommerfeld (1982), 37 on Tutu, table on p. 66: entry no. 1.

37 Cf. e.g. George (1993), 167, no. 1358: a shrine of Marduk at Nippur in the Middle-Babylonian period; ibid., 83, no. 269: a temple in Sippar-Aruru in the first millen-

and even at Aššur due to his increasing importance from the Old-Babylonian period on.[38] But there was no further major and independent cult centre which could rival his temple Esagil at Babylon. After Marduk had become the new king of the gods, we find Marduk's son Nabû being worshipped in Borsippa instead of his father.[39] So, when Marduk had become Enlil, he apparently reduced his foreign commitments and maintained his residence solely at Babylon. The spread of his cult, which went hand in hand with his increasing importance in the early days of his success, seem to have been deliberately halted when he finally achieved the status of the absolute king of the gods.[40]

Aššur originally was a mountain god, and probably the *numen loci* of the city of Aššur, located on a steep cliff overlooking the pastures of the Tigris river.[41] That is why some scholars claim that he was worshipped without a cult statue and firmly fixed at the mountain of Aššur, being in fact that deified rock.[42] Yet, in a report written by the authorities of the Old-Assyrian trading colony at Uršu, we read that thieves had entered the local temple and had robbed it, even taking the golden sun-disc from the breast of Aššur, and his sword.[43] That means of course, that there was a – certainly anthropomorphous – cult statue at Uršu depicting the god Aššur. And since Uršu was by no means a very important colony, any of these Assyrian colonies probably had their local shrine housing a statue of Aššur. This may have also been the case at the city Šubat-Enlil, whose name means "Dwelling of (the Assyrian) Enlil" and which hence likely was home to a shrine of Aššur, inasmuch he was the "Assyrian Enlil". Even if Aššur may have originally been a mountain god, and a *numen loci*, by the time of the Old-Assyrian city-state he had become quite a normal city-god, represented by a statue in human form, which would go as a copy with his colonists abroad. This custom apparently ceased when Aššur changed from trading to imperialism.

---

nium. Sommerfeld (1982), 49, table: temples at Babylon and Borsippa, offerings and priests also in other towns in the Old-Babylonian period.

38 Cf. George (1993), 72, no. 120, and p. 107, no. 564: seats of Marduk, also under his name Asalluhi, in the temple of Aššur; Sommerfeld (1987–1990), 367, § 5.5: Marduk in Assyria.

39 Cf. George (1993), 159–160, no. 1236: Ezida dedicated to Nabû in the first millennium.

40 Cf. in general Sommerfeld (1982).

41 Cf. Lambert (1983).

42 Cf. e.g. Mayer (1995), 62–64.

43 "Thieves have entered the temple of (the god) Aššur and [*have stolen*] the gold sun disk from the breast (of the statue) of Aššur and the dagger of Aššur"; cf. Larsen (1976), 261.

In the Middle- and Neo-Assyrian period, Aššur had only his temple at the city of Aššur. Once again there is an exception to this rule: Tukultī-Ninurta I managed to take him along into his new capital at Kār-Tukultī-Ninurta. But unsuccessfully, Tukultī-Ninurta was killed – probably due to this very sacrilege, as it is often assumed – and the gods of Kār-Tukultī-Ninurta apparently returned to the city of Aššur after his death.[44]

When in the course of military campaigns the Assyrians said they had installed images of the Assyrian gods and of the Assyrian king in foreign temples and had counted them among the gods of those nations, they did not mean full cult statues, but rather royal stelae with depictions of the king and the gods of Assyria.[45] In this way they could avoid the loss of cult statues to the enemy in the case of a rebellion. The cult of royal stelae venerated as deified symbols of the state is amply documented for the Assyrian empire, and the custom continued under Babylonian rule.

4. Concepts of Kingship and the Capital City

In Mesopotamia, the ideal capital city would comprise a combination of temple and palace, of divine and human king.[46] In Assyria, with the Assyrian king being high priest of the god Aššur, this combination could be very close, with god and king dwelling "sill to sill, wall to wall", as Ezekiel (43:8) would have phrased it. In first millennium Babylonia, the king was expected to keep his distance, as we shall see.

A fine example of an ideal capital with a deified king living next to the gods in a palace located in the sacred precinct is found at Ur during the Third Dynasty of Ur. Then, the king was regarded as the protective deity of his country. In exercising his divine office or priestly functions

44 Cf. Eickhoff (1985), 34–35. This assumption rests however on a single statement in a rubrum of a ritual (Müller [1937], 5–6, 16, iii:39–41), probably to be dated to the reign of Tiglath-Pileser I (1117–1077 BCE): "What is listed in the tablet goes to the temples of the gods of Kār-Tukultī-Ninurta. The gods of Kār-Tukultī-Ninurta are present/lodging in the city of Aššur (*ilānū ša Kār-Tukultī-Ninurta ina āl Libbi-Āli usbū* [= **wšb*])." Strictly speaking, we do not know for sure whether this means that the gods were back to Aššur for good or staying there only for the time of the ritual. The results of the excavations however suggest that the temples were in use only for a short time, after which they were abandoned (cf. Eickhoff, above).

45 For a recent discussion of the role of symbols and other representations of the Assyrian state (cult), often in the form of stelae, cf. Holloway (2002), 67–71, 183–193, 198–200.

46 On the concept of the ideal capital city cf. recently Westenholz (1998a and b).

he was sacred and pure.[47] In Mesopotamia, the idea of the divine nature of the king can be traced back to the middle of the third millennium.[48] In the text of the "Stela of the Vultures", E'annatum prince of Lagaš is portrayed as engendered by the city god Ningirsu himself, adopted by Inanna-Ištar, the goddess of war, and nursed by the mother-goddess Ninhursag. That is why he grows up into a giant warrior of 5 cubits' size, able and ready to subdue the enemy country to his lord Ningirsu.[49] Very much the same applies for Gilgamesh, the legendary king of Uruk. Being "two thirds a god" he is famous for his enormous physique, designed by the gods themselves.[50] And the same imagery is still employed in 7th century BCE Assyria, when king Aššurbanipal is presented as nursed and raised by the goddesses of Nineveh and Arbail, when he was a baby.[51] Yet, the phenomenon of "kingly priests" or "priestly kings" that was known in early Mesopotamia continued later only in Assyria where the king functioned as *šangû* "high priest" and *išippu* "purification-priest".[52] In Babylonia, the idea of the priestly or even divine ('deified') king faded in the course of the 2nd millennium BCE, and the priestly offices were fully occupied by professional priests. Evidence for the religious character of the 'Assyro-Babylonian' kingship stems in almost every case from the 3rd millennium BCE, and later from Assyria.[53] At Calah in the Neo-Assyrian period, we see the Assyrian king dwelling next door to Ninurta, "sill to sill, and wall to wall". At Aššur the king dwelt in the "Old Palace" just next to the Aššur temple. "King" (*šarru*) was not the foremost title of the Assyrian king. Above all, he was priest (*šangû*) of the god Aššur, and his appointee (*waklu*), acting as a representative of the god.[54] It is the priestly office of the Assyrian kings and their purity that set them most apart from their Babylonian colleagues. That is why the Assyrian palaces

47 Cf. Sallaberger (1999), 152–154. The divine quality of the king is rather close to the idea of the two bodies of the king in mediaeval Europe, cf. Kantorowicz (1966).

48 On various aspects of the history of divine kingship in the Ancient Near East cf. Sallaberger (2002); Wilcke (2002); Michalowski (2008), and many more contributions in Erkens (2002) and Brisch (2008).

49 Text and translation: Steible (1982), 122–123, no. "Ean. 1", iv:9–V:17; discussion: Selz (1998), 322–323.

50 According to the Standard Babylonian recension from Nineveh (tablet i:48–50), cf. George (2003), 540–541. According to the Hittite version, the gods designed for him a height of 11 cubits and a breast 9 spans wide, cf. Otten (1958), 98–99, obv. i:7–8.

51 From the *Dialogue between Aššurbanipal and Nabû*: Livingstone (1989), 34, no. 13, rev:6–8.

52 Seux (1980–1983), 169–170, §§ 96–100: *šangû/išippu*; Sallaberger/Huber (2003–2005), 624, § 4.1.

53 Cf. e.g. Labat (1939), 131–147: the king as priest.

54 Menzel (1981), 151–159: The Assyrian king as priest (*šangû*); Maul (1999).

were given Sumerian names as the temples were,[55] and it is also why the Assyrian palaces were lavishly provided with baths. These were not least ceremonial baths, set up for the incessant purification of the Assyrian sacred king.[56] The 'toilets' or 'bath-rooms' of Assyrian palaces were costly and elaborate structures, often close to the throne room, where the Assyrian king could be purified over and over again when acting on official occasions. It is no coincidence that these structures are completely absent from Babylonian palaces. It is not because the Babylonian kings would have preferred chamber pots over lavatories, but because they were not regarded as priests and hence did not need these lustration baths. For the inscriptions of his building projects in the Southern Mesopotamian city of Uruk, the Assyrian king Sargon (Šarru-ukīn) II even had the orthographical deification revived which marked the divine status of the kings of Sumer and Babylonia in the third and early second millennium: In the bricks from Uruk his name is written as "*Divine* Šarru-ukīn", using the divine determinative *dingir* "god".[57] Here, Sargon is indeed reviving an ancient Babylonian custom, yet a custom and an idea of kingship which had fallen out of use in Babylonia for nearly a millennium.

The Middle-Assyrian residence Kār-Tukultī-Ninurta (ca. 1200 BCE) provides a good illustration how close the Assyrian king was to his god. This is the only case in which the god Aššur was moved from his main shrine in the days when Assyria was an empire. As noted above, king Tukultī-Ninurta who undertook that innovation was killed, and the gods probably moved back to Aššur. But let us have a look at the names of the palace and the temple which Tukultī-Ninurta I (1233–1197 BCE) picked: The temple of Aššur is called: Ekur-mešarra "Temple of All (divine) Powers", and the palace next to it: Egal-mešarra "Palace of All (divine) Powers".[58] A king could probably not come any closer to his god. God and king of Assyria are displayed as each other's mirror, dwelling side by side in perfect harmony.

As opposed to the sacred Assyrian priest-king, the Babylonian king in the 1st millennium BCE was neither sacred nor priest any more. When approaching the divine, he needed guidance and protection. The

---

55 Cf. the overview given by Postgate (2003–2005), 212–216.

56 Even if lavatories are also found more often in private houses in Assyria than in Babylonia. Examining the pictural programme of hall G of Aššurnasirpal's palace at Calah, just next to the hall H with the lavatories in I–J and N–M, Brandes (1970) proposed that it was used for the ritual purification of the king: "salle de lustration" (ibid., 154).

57 Frame (1995), 150–152, no. 4–6: ^{d}lugal-*ú-kin*.

58 George (1993), 117, no. 687 (temple), p. 171, no. 1444 (palace).

famous scene on the "Sun-God Tablet" of the Babylonian king Nabû-apla-iddina (ca. 888–855 BCE) shows exactly that kind of view of the king:[59] The king is lead by a priest like a protective deity. It is the priest only, to touch the divine table set up in front of the sun god, it is the priest to mediate between the humans – even if kings – and the gods. The scene is inspired by the 'presentation scene' of the late 3rd millennium BCE, but then it were minor protective deities who would introduce an adorer before a higher god. In the 1st millennium BCE, this position had been taken by a priest. The relief of the "Sun-God Tablet" from to the mid-9th century BCE is beautifully matched by a ritual from the Seleucid era describing how the king is allowed to enter the cella of Marduk on occasion of the Babylonian New Year's Festival. In this ritual, the high priest comes out of the cella of Marduk, and takes the king in with him.[60] He lets the king enter before Marduk-Bēl, yet not into the cella, but rather into the court-yard or the pre-cella, since only after the high priest has removed the royal insignia from the king and brought them into the cella, he also lead the king into the cella before Marduk: "He will place [the kin]g behind him and lead him into the presence of Bēl."[61]

5. Nebuchadrezzar II creates a Perfect Centre

When Nebuchadrezzar II built his palace at Babylon, he provided us with an extensive and unique reasoning why doing so. As we shall see, he produced a perfect example of the "one god – one king – one temple – one palace" ideology. Nebuchadrezzar is deeply devoted to Marduk, the supreme god and king of all the gods, and to his city Babylon, thereby the centre of the world. The perfect centre Babylon is characterized by the temple Esagil set up there, being the sole temple of Marduk. Hence it calls for a palace of the Babylonian king to be set up there, only in Babylon, and nowhere else. Nebuchadrezzar rebukes his predecessors to have belittled the status of Babylon by choosing other residences:

59 For a recent and detailed treatment of the tablet, with many fine illustrations, cf. Woods (2004).

60 From the ritual for the Babylonian New Year's Festival (*akītu*) in spring (*Nissān*), lines 415–420, cf. Linssen (2004), 222–223. A new edition and discussion of the New Year's Festival in Hellenistic Babylon is provided by Linssen (2004), 79–86, 215–237. The date of the colophon is lost, but the text can be roughly dated to the Hellenistic period, cf. Linssen (2004), 11.

61 *The New Year ritual* (see above) line 420: [*šarr*]*a ana arkīšu išakkan ana pān Bēl ušerrebšu*; after the copy: Thureau-Dangin (1921), 154, line 420.

"In former times, from times immemorial unto the reign of Nabopolassar, the king of Babylon, (my) father, who begot me, (all those) many kings, who went before me, in their favourite cities, wherever they liked, have built palaces and took them as their residence, have stored their goods therein and heaped up their wealth. (Only) at the New Year's festival, when the Enlil of the gods Marduk rises, did they enter Babylon."[62]

But since Nebuchadrezzar loves Marduk, his lord, he would not turn to any other city but Babylon. Nebuchadrezzar addresses Marduk:

"I do love your lofty figure like (my) precious life, I have not embellished any city in all the world more than your city Babylon, (oh Marduk)!"[63]

This is of course why the *Verse Account*, an invective against Nabonidus likely composed by the priests of Marduk, is so angry at the 'heretic' king Nabonidus, who dared to ignore Marduk in many ways. By leaving for Tayma and taking it as a residence he divided the ideal pairing of god and king, of temple and palace. He turned away from Marduk and set a bad example. Reproaching Nabonidus for honouring Tayma unduly, the *Verse Account* uses the same expressions Nebuchadrezzar had used for embellishing Babylon,[64] sharply contrasting the sacrilege of the wicked king Nabonidus to the pious deed of the model king Nebuchadrezzar:

"He embellishes the city (i.e. Tayma), and builds [a palace]. He builds it just like the palace at Babylon!"[65]

Nebuchadrezzar created a centre for the empire and for the whole world, consisting of a combination of temple and palace. Furthermore, in building his palace in Babylon, he was careful not to change the divinely created layout of the holy city:

"Because my heart did not desire a royal residence in another city, I did not build a lordly abode anywhere else (but in Babylon), I did not scatter the treasure and the regalia all over the lands. (That is why) in Babylon the abode where I had been dwelling had become inadequate as befits my kingship.

But because the fear of Marduk my lord was in my heart, within Babylon, the city sheltered by him, I did not change (the route of) his (sacred) street,

62 Langdon (1912), 114–115, Nbc. no. 14 i:44–49; pp. 134–135, Nbc. no. 15 vii:9–25.

63 Langdon (1912), 140, Nbc. no. 15 ix:52–56: *kīma napšatī(ya) aqarti arâm elâ lānka eli ālīka Bābil ina kal dadmī ul ušāpi āla*. Cf. also Langdon (1912), 114–115, Nbc. no. 14 i:52–53; pp. 134–135, Nbc. no. 15 vii:30–33: same phrase, addressing Marduk and Nabû.

64 A highly literary phrase, using *āla wapû* in the Š-stem: "causing a city to shine forth". The verb (*wapû* Š) is associated with the idea of divine splendour, and applied to buildings in this period it is used regularly only with Babylon, and the temples of Marduk and Nabû, Esagil and Ezida (see e.g. the examples in *CAD* A 2, 203–204, s.v. *apû* Š, 5b).

65 Schaudig (2001), 568, 575; *Verse Account* ii:28'–29': *āla uštāpi ītepuš* [*ekalla*], *kīma ekal Bābil ītepussu*.

> I did not move his shrine, I did not block up his canal in order to enlarge my royal dwelling, but I looked for (more place for) my abode on the outside (of the walls)."[66]

The layout of the city of Babylon is holy, – not only the shrines, but also the canals and streets, which would be used for processions of the gods. Nebuchadrezzar carefully avoids the sin of Nabû-šum-iškun (ca. 760–748 BCE), a former king who was infamous for his many crimes and sacrileges. Among his many misdeeds the Babylonians remembered that he altered the route of the procession of the god Šar-ur, the divine weapon of Ninurta-Marduk, and profaned the place by building his palace there:

> "The 'Wide Street', the processional street of the divine weapon Šar-ur, beloved by his Lord (sc. Ninurta > Marduk), (which he walks) in the month of Ulūl, a street of his (sc. Marduk's) city (sc. Babylon), (that) street of his procession he blocked up and made it into a part of his palace, and he made him (sc. Šar-ur) walk a street that was not his procession(al street)."[67]

Pious Nebuchadrezzar, however, does not follow the bad example set by Nabû-šum-iškun. Respecting the borders set by the sacred canal *Lībil-hegalla* to the South, by the processional street *Ay-ibūr-šabû* to the east, and limited by the river Euphrates in the West, he turns to the North, to the outside of the city for more place for his palace. That is the reason why in the layout of Babylon the palace rides on the city wall. A similar layout is found already in the palace of Sargon II at Dūr-Šarru-ukīn, but this fact has little bearing on our argument, at least as far as the explicit explanation of Nebuchadrezzar is concerned.

66 Langdon (1912), 136–139, Nbc. no. 15 viii:19–41; Nebuchadrezzar says *rapšiš* (viii:40) i.e. "into the wide, the open (land), outside (the walls)".

67 Cole (1994), 230–231, 236 on iii:20'–23'.

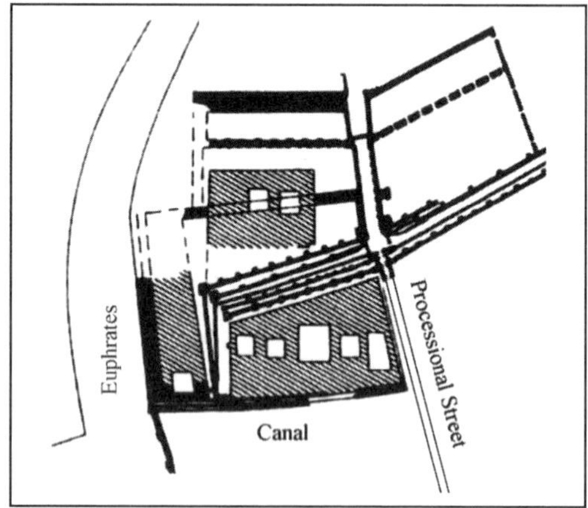

Fig. 2: Schematic plan of the "South Palace" (South of the city walls), and the "Main Palace" (to the North) at Babylon, time of Nebuchadrezzar II (mid-6th century BCE). Sketch by the author after Heinrich (1982), fig. 382.

Although Nebuchadrezzar had taken over Babylon as his residence from his predecessors, he uniquely conceptualized the relationship of the king of Babylon to the god of Babylon. In doing so, he sharpened the focus on an ideology which may well be dubbed "Marduk alone". Nebuchadrezzar's devotion to Marduk is unique among the examples of Mesopotamian kings, in that it moved him to hymnic statements about his love towards Marduk, and to paeans on the physical appearance of Marduk's and his son Nabû's beautiful looks: Nebuchadrezzar extolls their "beautiful and lofty forms".[68] In the relationship between a ruler and the gods his masters, the affection that mattered most was the love of the gods towards the king. The love of the king towards the gods, and his obedience, was taken very much for granted, and rarely became a topic.[69] The examples for "love towards a god" collected by *CAD* are made up nearly completely by the statements of Nebuchadrezzar; there are very few examples from other texts, and some perso-

68 *banâ lānšun* "their beautiful forms", talking about Marduk and Nabû: Langdon (1912), 114 (no. 14 i:52), 134 (no. 15 vii:31); *elâ lānka* "your lofty form", addressing Marduk: Langdon (1912), 140 (no. 15 ix:53).

69 There is a Sumerian phrase among the epithets of the ruler Gudea of Lagaš from the 21st century BCE: *ir₁₁ nin-a-né ki-ág-àm* (statue C, ii:18–19, cf. Edzard [1997], 39), which might be translated as "he who is the servant who loves his lady". Yet, the phrase is ambiguous (literally: "servant: *by/towards* his lady (there is) loving"), and may as well be translated: "he who is the servant whom his lady loves". And since it is the love of the goddess that matters, I prefer the latter translation. Yet, in its unsolvable ambiguity, it is perhaps precisely the mutual love of lady and servant which is expressed in this rather unique phrase.

nal names.[70] A phrase like the following one used by Nebuchadrezzar addressing Marduk is unique among the statements on the relationship between man and god in the Ancient Near East:

> "I do love your lofty figure like (my) precious life!" (*kīma napšatī[ya] aqarti arâm elâ lānka*)[71]

It comes surprisingly close to the characterization and motivation of king Josiah, given in 2 Kings 23:25 as a resumee on his cultic reforms:

> "Before him there was no king like him who turned to the Lord with all his heart and with all his soul and with all his might [...]".

This phrase of course draws on the *shema'* (Deut. 6:5):

> "You shall love (ואהבת) the Lord your God with all your heart and with all your soul (ובכל־נפשך) and with all your might."

It is interesting to observe how "loving" (*râmu*/אהב) a god like "precious life" (*napištu aqartu*), respectively with all the "soul" (נפש, the West Semitic cognate of Babylonian *napištu*), elicited the emergence of a single-minded devotion to a supreme and unrivalled god in two cultures. Among the kings of Babylonia, Nebuchadrezzar's religious-political programme "Marduk alone", – henotheistically focussing on Marduk as the king of the gods, the most important god, and in fact the only god who matters, – produced the closest parallel to the "Yahweh alone" movement in Judah in the 7th and 6th century BCE.[72]

---

70 In *CAD* R, 141, s.v. *râmu* (**r'm*, "to love") A 1c, 2'.

71 See above, with n. 63.

72 On the concept of "convenantal love" meaning loyalty, devotion, and obedience in the Ancient Near East cf. Moran (1963) and Lambert (1987). On the concept of love in Deuteronomy cf. recently Rüterswörden (2006). As it seems, the closest parallel to the commandment of loving God in Deuteronomy from the Ancient Near East which has been hitherto discussed is the passage from the Vassal Treaties of Esarhaddon which commands the people of the Ancient Near East to love (*râmu*) the future king Assurbanipal like their lives (*napištu*): VTE § 24, line 268; edition: Watanabe (1987), 156. The passages from the inscriptions of Nebuchadrezzar which are much closer, since they deal with the submissive devotion of a king to his god, seem to have been skipped attention.

Bibliography

Amar, A. (2002), The God Ninurta in the Mythology and Royal Ideology of Ancient Mesopotamia, SAA vol. 14, Helsinki.

Beaulieu, P.-A. (1989), The Reign of Nabonidus, King of Babylon, 556–539 B.C., YNER 10, New Haven/London.

– (1993), An Episode in the Fall of Babylon to the Persians, JNES 52, 241–261.

Biggs, R.D. (1974), Inscriptions from Tell Abū Salābīkh, OIP 99, Chicago.

Brandes, M.A. (1970), La salle dite 'G' du palais d'Assurnasirpal II a Kalakh, lieu de cérémonie rituelle, in: A. Finet (ed.), Actes de la XVIIe Rencontre Assyriologique Internationale, Ham-sur-Heure, 147–154.

Brinkman, J.A. (1964), Merodach-Baladan II, in: R.D. Biggs (ed.), Studies Presented to A. Leo Oppenheim, June 7, 1964, Chicago, 6–53.

Brisch, N. (2008, ed.), Religion and Power: Divine Kingship in the Ancient World and Beyond, Oriental Institute Seminars 4, Chicago.

CAD: Civil, M./Gelb, I.J./Oppenheim, A.L./Reiner, E. et al. (eds.), The Assyrian Dictionary of the Oriental Institute of the University of Chicago (Chicago/Glückstadt 1956–).

Cogan, M. (1974), Imperialism and Religion: Assyria, Judah and Israel in the Eighth and Seventh Centuries B.C.E., SBL.MS 19, Missoula.

Cole, S.W. (1994), The Crimes and sacrileges of Nabû-šuma-iškun, in: ZA 84, 220–252.

Cooper, J.S. (1983), The Curse of Agade, Baltimore/London.

Edzard, D.O. (1997), Gudea and His Dynasty: The Royal Inscriptions of Mesopotamia: Early Periods, vol. 3/1, Toronto.

Eickhoff, T. (1985), Kār Tukulti Ninurta. Eine mittelassyrische Kult- und Residenzstadt, ADOG 21, Berlin.

Erkens, F.-R. (2002, ed.), Die Sakralität von Herrschaft. Herrschaftslegitimierung im Wechsel der Zeiten und Räume. Fünfzehn interdisziplinäre Beiträge zu einem weltweiten und epochenübergreifenden Phänomen, Berlin.

Frahm, E. (1997), Einleitung in die Sanherib-Inschriften, AfO.B 26, Wien.

Frame, G. (1995), Rulers of Babylonia: From the Second Dynasty of Isin to the End of Assyrian Domination (1157–612 BC): The Royal Inscriptions of Mesopotamia: Babylonian Periods 2, Toronto.

Frayne, D.R. (1990), Old Babylonian Period (2003–1595 BC): The Royal Inscriptions of Mesopotamia: Early Periods, vol. 4, Toronto/Buffalo/London.

– (1993), Sargonic and Gutian Periods (2334–2113 BC): The Royal Inscriptions of Mesopotamia: Early Periods, vol. 2, Toronto.
Fuchs, A. (1994), Die Inschriften Sargons II. aus Khorsabad, Göttingen.
George, A.R. (1992), Babylonian Topographical Texts, OLA 40, Leuven.
– (1993), House Most High: The Temples of Ancient Mesopotamia: Mesopotamian Civilizations 5, Winona Lake.
– (2003), The Babylonian Gilgamesh Epic, vol. I, Oxford.
Grayson, A.K. (1975), Assyrian and Babylonian Chronicles, TCS 5, Locust Valley.
– (1987), Assyrian Rulers of the Third and Second Millennia BC (to 1115 BC). The Royal Inscriptions of Mesopotamia: Assyrian Periods vol. 1, Toronto.
– (1991), Assyrian Rulers of the Early First Millennium BC: Vol. I (1114–859 BC): The Royal Inscriptions of Mesopotamia: Assyrian Periods vol. 2, Toronto.
Heinrich, E. (1982), Die Tempel und Heiligtümer im alten Mesopotamien. Typologie, Morphologie und Geschichte. Unter Mitarbeit von U. Seidl. Deutsches Archäologisches Institut, Denkmäler antiker Architektur 14, Berlin.
Holloway, S.W. (2002), Aššur is King! Aššur is King! Religion in the Exercise of Power in the Neo-Assyrian Empire, Culture and History of the Ancient Near East 10, Leiden.
Hurowitz, V. (1992), I Have Built You an Exalted House: Temple Building in the Bible in Light of Mesopotamian and Northwest Semitic Writings, JSOT.S 115, Sheffield.
Jacobsen, T. (1939), The Sumerian King List, AS 11, Chicago.
Kantorowicz, E.H. (1966), The King's Two Bodies: A Study in Mediaeval Political Theology, 2nd ed., Princeton.
Krebernik, M. (1994), Zur Einleitung der zà-me-Hymnen aus Tell Abū Salābīh, in: P. Calmeyer/K. Hecker/L. Jakob-Rost/C.B.F. Walker (eds.), Beiträge zur Altorientalischen Archäologie und Altertumskunde, FS B. Hrouda, Wiesbaden, 151–157.
Labat, R. (1939), Le caractère religieux de la royauté assyro-babylonienne, Paris.
Lambert, W.G. (1983), The God Aššur, in: Iraq 45, 82–86.
– (1987), Devotion: The Languages of Religion and Love, in: M. Mindlin/M.J. Geller/J.E. Wansbrough (eds.), Figurative Language in the Ancient Near East, London, 25–39.
Langdon, S. (1912), Die neubabylonischen Königsinschriften, VAB 4, Leipzig.
Larsen, M.T. (1976), The Old Assyrian City-State and Its Colonies, Mes.(C) 4, Copenhagen.

Linssen, M.J.H. (2004), The Cults of Uruk and Babylon: The Temple Ritual Texts as Evidence for Hellenistic Cult Practice, Cuneiform Monographs 25, Leiden.

Livingstone, A. (1989), Court Poetry and Literary Miscellanea, SAA 3, Helsinki.

Luckenbill, D.D. (1924), The Annals of Sennacherib, OIP 2, Chicago.

Mayer, W. (1995), Politik und Kriegskunst der Assyrer. Abhandlungen zur Literatur Alt-Syrien-Palästinas und Mesopotamiens 9, Münster.

Maul, S.M. (1999), Der assyrische König – Hüter der Weltordnung, in: K. Watanabe (ed.), Priests and Officials in the Ancient Near East, Heidelberg, 201–214.

Menzel, B. (1981), Assyrische Tempel, StP.SM 10, vol. I, Rom.

Michalowski, P. (2008), The Mortal Kings of Ur: A Short Century of Divine Rule in Ancient Mesopotamia, in: N. Brisch (ed.), Religion and Power: Divine Kingship in the Ancient World and Beyond, Oriental Institute Seminars 4, Chicago, 33–45.

Moran, W.L. (1963), The Ancient Near Eastern Background of the Love of God in Deuteronomy, in: CBQ 25, 77–87.

Müller, K.F. (1937), Das assyrische Ritual. Teil 1: Texte zum assyrischen Königsritual, MVÄG 41/3, Leipzig.

Na'aman, N. (2006), The King Leading Cult Reforms in his Kingdom: Josiah and Other Kings in the Ancient Near East, ZAR 12, 131–168.

Otten, H. (1958), Die erste Tafel des hethitischen Gilgamesch-Epos, IM 8, 93–125.

Pardee, D. (1997), The Baᶜlu Myth, in: W.W. Hallo (ed.), The Context of Scripture, vol. I, Leiden, 241–274.

Postgate, J.N. (2003–2005), Palast. A: V. Mittel- und Neuassyrisch, in: RLA 10, 212–226.

Rüterswörden, U. (2006), Die Liebe zu Gott im Deuteronomium, in: M. Witte (ed.), Die deuteronomistischen Geschichtswerke. Redaktions- und religionsgeschichtliche Perspektiven zur "Deuteronomismus"-Diskussion in Tora und Vorderen Propheten, BZAW 365, Berlin, 229–238.

Sallaberger, W. (1999), Ur III-Zeit, in: W. Sallaberger/A. Westenholz, Mesopotamien. Akkade-Zeit und Ur III-Zeit, Annäherungen 3, ed. by P. Attinger/M. Wäfler, OBO 160/3, Freiburg (Schweiz)/Göttingen, 121–390.

– (2002), Den Göttern nahe – und fern den Menschen? Formen der Sakralität des altmesopotamischen Herrschers, in: F.-R. Erkens (ed.), Die Sakralität von Herrschaft. Herrschaftslegitimierung im Wechsel der Zeiten und Räume. Fünfzehn interdisziplinäre Beiträge zu einem weltweiten und epochenübergreifenden Phänomen, Berlin, 85–98.

– /Huber Vulliet, F. (2003–2005), Priester A: I. Mesopotamien, in: RLA 10, 617–640.

Schaudig, H. (2001), Die Inschriften Nabonids von Babylon und Kyros' des Großen samt den in ihrem Umfeld entstandenen Tendenzschriften. Textausgabe und Grammatik, AOAT 256, Münster.

Selz, G.J. (1995), Untersuchungen zur Götterwelt des altsumerischen Stadtstaates von Lagaš, Occasional Publications of the Samuel Noah Kramer Fund 13, Philadelphia.

– (1998), Über Mesopotamische Herrschaftskonzepte. Zu den Ursprüngen mesopotamischer Herrscherideologie im 3. Jahrtausend, in: M. Dietrich/O. Loretz (eds.), Dubsar anta-men. Studien zur Altorientalistik, FS W.H.Ph. Römer, AOAT 253, Münster, 281–344.

Seux, M.-J. (1980–1983), Königtum B: II. und I. Jahrtausend, in: RLA 6, 140–173.

Sjöberg, A.W. (1960), Der Mondgott Nanna-Suen in der sumerischen Überlieferung, I. Teil: Texte, Stockholm.

Sommerfeld, W. (1982), Der Aufstieg Marduks. Die Stellung Marduks in der babylonischen Religion des zweiten Jahrtausends v.Chr., AOAT 213, Kevelaer/Neukirchen-Vluyn.

– (1987–1990), Marduk. A. Philologisch. I. In Mesopotamien, in: RLA 10, 360–370.

Steible, H. (1982), Die altsumerischen Bau- und Weihinschriften, FAOS 5/1, Wiesbaden.

Talon, P. (2005), Enūma Eliš: The Standard Babylonian Creation Myth, SAA Cuneiform Texts 4, Helsinki.

Thureau-Dangin, F. (1921), Rituels accadiens, Paris.

Watanabe, K. (1987), Die adê-Vereidigung anlässlich der Thronfolgeregelung Asarhaddons, BaghM Beiheft 3, Berlin.

Weinfeld, M. (1964), Cult Centralization in Israel in the Light of a Neo-Babylonian Analogy, JNES 23, 202–212.

Westenholz, A. (1999), The Old Akkadian Period: History and Culture, in: W. Sallaberger/A. Westenholz, Mesopotamien. Akkade-Zeit und Ur III-Zeit. Annäherungen 3, ed. by P. Attinger/M. Wäfler, OBO 160/3, Freiburg (Schweiz)/Göttingen, 17–117.

Westenholz, J.G. (1998a, ed.), Capital Cities: Urban Planning and Spiritual Dimensions: Proceedings of the Symposium held on May 27–29, 1996, Jerusalem, Israel, Jerusalem.

– (1998b), The Theological Foundation of the City, the Capital City and Babylon, in: J.G. Westenholz (1998a, ed.), Capital Cities: Urban Planning and Spiritual Dimensions: Proceedings of the Symposium held on May 27–29, 1996, Jerusalem, Israel, 43–54.

Wilcke, C. (2002), Vom göttlichen Wesen des Königtums und seinem Ursprung im Himmel, in: F.-R. Erkens (ed.), Die Sakralität von Herrschaft. Herrschaftslegitimierung im Wechsel der Zeiten und Räume. Fünfzehn interdisziplinäre Beiträge zu einem weltweiten und epochenübergreifenden Phänomen, Berlin, 63–83.
Woods, C. (2004), The Sun-God Tablet of Nabû-apla-iddina Revisited, JCS 56, 23–103.

Perspectives on Southern Israel's Cult Centralization: Arad and Beer-sheba

ZE'EV HERZOG

Since the discovery of the Arad Temple in Aharoni's excavations, forty-five years ago, its interpretation has remained a heated issue of debate on the archaeological agenda. The history of research on the Arad Temple, coupled with the remains of the horned altar found at Tel Beer-sheba, is a fascinating case within the complex relationship between Archaeology and the Bible. In this review, my aim is to treat the question of the abolishment of cult in the Beer-sheba valley sites during the 8th century BCE and the possibility of relating archaeological finds and biblical statements about demolition of *Bamot* (high places) and destruction of *Massebot* in Judah during the reign of Hezekiah (2 Kings 18:4).

The Layers of Use of the Temple at Arad

Aharoni ascribed the remains of the Arad Temple to five strata (XI to VII), which were dated from Solomon's reign in the second half of the 10th century BCE to Josiah's reign at the end of the 7th century BCE. That is, a period of roughly 350 years.[1] A reassessment of the stratigraphical data shows that such a wide range of levels is not justified. The association of the temple with Stratum XI is incorrect. The remains from Stratum XI antecede the establishment of the temple and present a picture of ordinary buildings totally different from the later temple. In Strata VIII and VII the temple was already buried under thick layer of soil fill. Accordingly, the temple existed only during two Strata: X (see Fig. 1) and IX (see Fig. 2). Hence, it was used for barely a few dozens of years in the course of the 8th century BCE.[2]

1 Cf. Aharoni (1968).

2 Cf. Herzog (1997; 2001a; 2002).

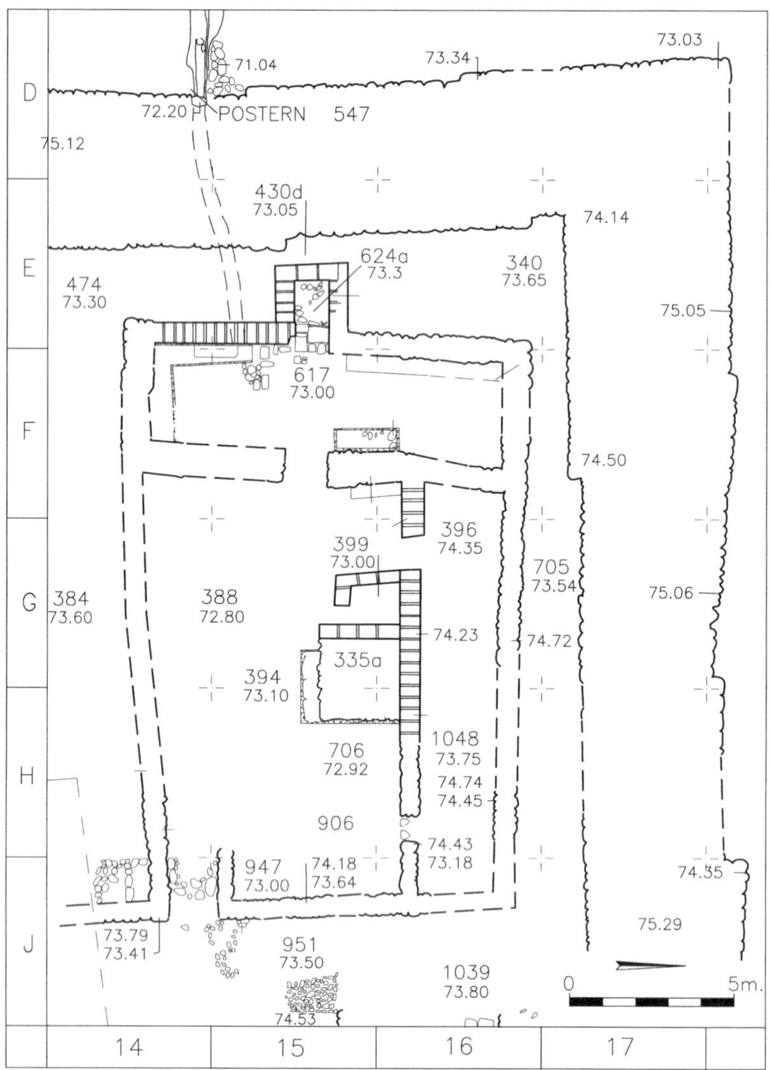

Fig. 1: Plan of Arad Temple, Stratum X.

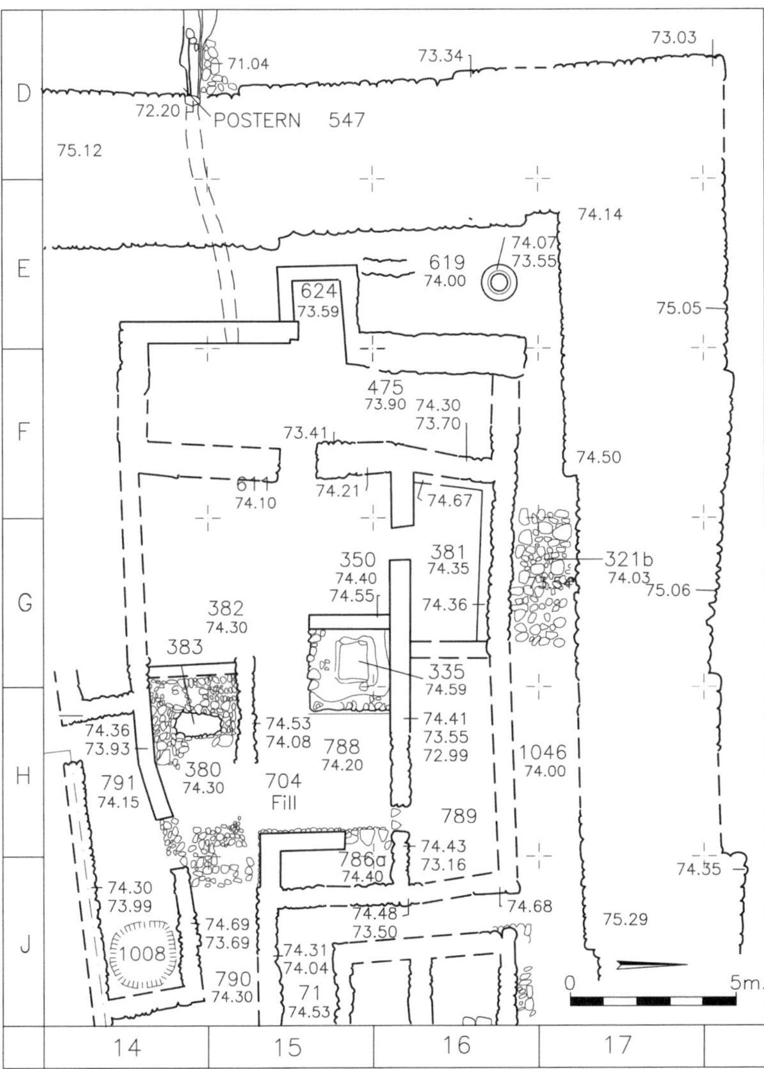

Fig. 2: Plan of Arad Temple, Stratum IX.

Besides discussing the period when the temple was in use, scholars also treated the process of the cessation of its use. Aharoni had a clear answer to this question: The temple was abolished in two stages. In the first stage, after the erection of Stratum VII, the offering altar was abolished, due to the covering of the court by debris. Yet, the temple itself continued to exist. In the second stage, starting with Stratum VI, the temple itself was abolished by the erection of the inner wall of the casemate fortification. At the same time, the incense altars and the *Massebah* (standing stone or stele) in the cella were laid on their sides and covered by debris.[3] Aharoni linked these two stages with the two cultic reforms described in the Bible: The first reform by King Hezekiah in the late 8th century BCE and the second by King Josiah in the late 7th century BCE. The match between the archaeological evidence and the biblical sources – the utmost desire of Biblical Archaeology – allegedly found a perfect example.

However, many scholars disputed Aharoni's conclusions. At first, criticism emerged against the dating of the casemate wall of Stratum VI to the Iron Age. Yadin and Dunayevsky,[4] followed by Mazar and Netzer,[5] objected to the dating of the casemate wall (Stratum VI) to the Iron Age, since this wall included ashlar stones that show combed marks made by a combed chisel. In the reassessment of the stratigraphic data, I have come to the conclusion that the casemate wall, ascribed by Aharoni to Stratum VI, does not belong to this stratum. The wall cuts – without a foundation trench – into remains of Stratum VI and is part of a Hellenistic period fort, which never reached completion. Therefore, it is clear that there is no relation between the abolishment of the temple and the beginning of Stratum VI.[6]

Efforts to relate the temple with Strata VII and VI were made by Ussishkin.[7] In earlier studies I presented detailed arguments against this idea, which I will not repeat here.[8]

---

3 Cf. Aharoni (1968).
4 Cf. Yadin (1965).
5 Cf. Mazar/Netzer (1986).
6 Cf. Herzog (1997), 174–179; id. (2002), 41–49.
7 Cf. Ussishkin (1988).
8 Cf. Herzog (1997), 206–207; id. (2001), 159–162; id. (2002), 69–72.

Evidence for the Cessation of Use of the Arad Temple

By now, the period of the temple's use is clarified, but the mode of its end of use is still debated, which forms the main issue of the present article. Is there evidence for Aharoni's assumption about a gradual, two-phases abolishment of the temple? An analysis of floor levels inside and outside the temple proves that there are only two floors inside the temple (both in the main building and in the court), which can be related to its walls. The lower floor belongs to Stratum X and the upper one to Stratum IX (Fig. 3).

Fig. 3: The Arad Altar and Floors of Stratum X (lower) and Stratum IX (upper).

The Stratum VIII floors covered all the heads of the walls that survived from the temple. This fact rules out the possibility that the court alone was filled with debris, while the main hall and the cella continued to serve the population. If that was the case, the floor of the temple would have been about two meters lower than the floors of the structures surrounding it. Such a situation is illogical, bearing in mind the need for a convenient use of the building, and it is also impossible because of the lack of any walls (to support the assumed fill from collapsing into the temple) and the lack of any stairs (which would have been required for descending into the temple). I have no doubt that Aharoni's supposition of two stages of the temple's abolishment would never have been offered, unless for his ambition to fit the archaeological finds to the biblical evidence that speaks about two events of abolishment of cult in Judah.

What is, then, the evidence for the abolishment of the Arad Temple? The stratigraphic and architectural data is quite clear. The temple existed during Strata X and IX alone and the fortress of Stratum VIII was established without the temple. Following the destruction of the temple and the fortress of Stratum X, the temple was restored in a similar plan in Stratum IX with considerable raising of floor levels – c. 1.3 m at the court and 0.9 m at the main hall. Accordingly, it was necessary to raise the level of the altar, too.[9] The abolishment of the temple is proven on the basis of the floors and walls of the Stratum VIII structures, which covered its area. This situation clarifies that the upper parts of the temple walls of Stratum IX were dismantled and covered by floors of Stratum VIII, with the clear aim of avoiding re-building the temple in this stratum.

The best evidence for the abolishment of the temple comes from the cultic cella (*Debir*), which is located right next to the main hall of the temple. Here, too, we discovered that there is a difference between the treatment of incense altars[10] and that of the rounded standing stone. The incense altars were buried carefully, resting on their side under the Stratum IX floor level and on the stairs of the Stratum X cella. In other words, during the abolishment of the temple, those responsible for dismantling it, took the pains to excavate a pit in the floor of the room and deposit the remains of the altars in it. It is possible that this special kindness was due to the relative softness of the limestone, of which the altars have been made. Traces of plaster, found adhering to the altars, are remains from the plaster of the wall, next to which they have been standing originally. On the other hand, the stone stele was found resting on its side next to the raised stone platform, which had been used in Stratum IX. One may assume that since the stele is made of hard stone, it did not request the same cautionary attitude shown towards the incense altars. Another item that had been removed was the installation – probably of metal – at the head of the sacrificial altar. We can deduce its existence based upon the form of plaster remains at the top of the altar. Lines of plaster descend on the sides of the flat flint stone

9 Cf. in detail Herzog (2002), 53–56.

10 These have been denoted as 'offering tables' by Haran (1993).

that stood at the center of the altar. The vertical plaster remains surround an exposed rectangle free of plaster, indicating that once there was an installation for kindling fire, made surely of metal. This installation was removed during the abolishment of the temple, leaving behind only its 'negative' imprint in plaster.

Beside this evidence, one must stress two facts. Firstly, the floors of the temple were found devoid of any significant artifact. Clearly all the cultic paraphernalia and votive objects that were inside the temple were intentionally removed prior to its dismantling. Secondly, it is significant that – unlike other parts of the fortress that exhibit evidence of destruction in Stratum IX – no evidence of burning or destruction was discovered in the temple itself. The only possible explanation for this fact is that the temple was saved from destruction, because it had been dismantled still within the period of Stratum IX, before the entire fortress was destroyed. It is also clear that the builders of the Stratum VIII fortress left the buried remains of the temple at their place and did not rebuilt it. The structures of Stratum VIII were established above the earth debris that covered the temple.

Since the pottery of the three Strata X, IX and VIII is typologically similar, and since we ascribe the destruction of Stratum VIII to the time of the campaign of King Sennacherib, we have reached the conclusion that the temple was used (within Strata X–IX) for a short period of time – namely only several decades of years. Instead of the 350 years conceived for the temple by Aharoni, we suggest a period of roughly 50–80 years within the 8th century BCE.[11]

Assuming, that the Arad Temple was abolished still prior to Sennacherib's campaign, and since the Old Testament speaks about a reform by King Hezekiah, which included the abolishment of temples throughout Judah, we suggested that the abolishment of the Arad Temple is an archaeological expression of Hezekiah's reform.

11 The range of 50 or 80 years relates to the existing alternatives for the dating of the beginning of the Iron Age IIb period; cf. Herzog/Singer-Avitz (2004).

The Evidence for a Temple and its Abolishment at Tel Beer-sheba

In my view, the evidence from Tel Beer-sheba strengthens the archaeological picture gained at Arad. It is a well-known fact that hewn stones, which can be reconstructed as a horned altar, were discovered at Tel Beer-sheba.[12] Most of the stones were found in secondary use in a wall near one corner of the 'pillared house'; the four stones of the horns were placed in one course at the foundation of the wall. The horn of one of these stones was removed, probably in order to create a leveled threshold at the entrance to the store hall. The removal of the horn was probably necessary to allow passage; but this indicates that the residents of the site no longer felt that this stone has any importance, or even sacredness. The discovery made during the eighth season, of, yet, other four stones that form the upper plane of the temple which unmistakable evidence of burning proved that, indeed, we have parts of an offering altar here. The additional four stones were found in the fill of the rampart that coated the slope of the Tel near the city gate.[13] The 'pillared house', where most of the altar's stones have been found, was used during Strata III and II. Since the line of the fundament of the wall of the 'pillared house' that included the stones was set on a slightly different line than the line of the wall of the earlier phase, we concluded that the stones of the altar were placed inside the wall during the establishment of Stratum II. The end of Stratum II is contemporaneous to the destruction of Arad Stratum VIII and Lachish Stratum III, all related to the Sennacherib's campaign against Judah in 701 BCE.

There is no convincing answer to the question of the original location of the Tel Beer-sheba altar before its dismantling. None of the suggestions made in this regard can be proven.[14] Yet, the finding of stones of the most luxurious altar, so far discovered from Judah, indicates the existence of a cultic installation at Tel Beer-sheba.

We should note that the accepted and widely common reconstruction of the Tel Beer-sheba altar as a structure of roughly 1.5 m in height was made according to the Tel Arad altar. By now, when it is clear that the Tel Arad altar was only 50–80 cm high, one should prefer a reconstruction of a lower (and more convenient in use) altar at Tel Beer-sheba as well. Presumably, the Tel Beer-sheba altar was dismantled and

---

12 Cf. Aharoni (1975); Herzog (2006).

13 Cf. Herzog et al. (1977).

14 Cf. e.g., Aharoni (1968), suggesting the 'basement house' as the original location of the altar, or Yadin (1976), maintaining building 430 'to the left of the gate'.

abolished at the same time when other changes were made at the site, which signify the start of Stratum II at some point within the 8th century BCE. The dismantling of the altar and the placing of the stones inside the wall of a storage building and in the fill of the rampart plainly indicate a decision to change cultic customs at this site.

The Abolishment of Temples at Arad and Tel Beer-sheba and Hezekiah's Reform

The similarity in the date of the abolishment of cultic places in two sites of the Beer-sheba valley at the end of the 8th century BCE – but before the campaign of Sennacherib – is certain. Thus, it could be suggested, that the abolishment of the cultic places at the two sites of Arad and Tel Beer-sheba is due to a conscious decision to change cultic customs, accepted in Judah during the 8th century BCE. It was reasonable and logical to see this phenomenon as fitting the biblical evidence about the activity of King Hezekiah of Judah, dismantling altars and destroying high places (*Bamot*).[15] Nevertheless, there is a place for questioning whether we have found unequivocal proof that at Arad and Tel Beer-sheba the abolishment of cultic buildings was, indeed, performed under the orders of Hezekiah, as told in the Book of Kings. The answer to that is negative, of course. The archaeological finds themselves do not supply such a proof. However, in my view, this is a very likely possibility. Unlike the former traditional attitude, according to which we used to search for a proof of biblical events in the archaeological record, now we analyze the archaeological data independently. I have no doubt that even without the Biblical evidence we would have explained the finds at Arad and Tel Beer-sheba as reflecting a religious revolution. Once, we have reached that conclusion, we must check the biblical data and reach the conclusions required from the comparison of the data of these two disciplines.

Biblical scholars also doubted the reliability of the two traditions of cultic reforms, one under Hezekiah and the other one under Josiah. Have these two reforms really occurred, or perhaps only one, while the second is a copy or duplication of the first? If only one reform occurred, which one is the original and which is its duplication? Since the deuteronomistic tradition, ascribed to the days of Josiah, places the centrality of the cult in Jerusalem as a supreme issue, scholars tended to see the reform of King Josiah as the reliable historical event; while the reform

15 Cf. Herzog et al. (1984); Rainey (1994).

of King Hezekiah was explained as a literary plagiarism that lacks historical reliability.[16] Archaeology came and turned the table upside down: All the archaeological evidences belong to the 8th century BCE, fitting the time of Hezekiah; no archaeological evidence appears for a cultic reform during the 7th century BCE, the time of Josiah.

In fact, the Arad finds contradict the biblical evidence that ascribes the restoration of the high places of Judah to the reign of King Manasseh (2 Kings 21:3). The Arad Temple was abolished in the 8th century BCE and not restored during the 7th century BCE; Tel Beer-sheba was entirely abandoned after its destruction during Sennacherib's campaign. There were no temples or high places at these two sites during the days of King Josiah, which he could have abolished – since they have already been abolished a hundred years earlier and had never been restored. Therefore, although we do not have an archaeological proof that the intentional abolishment of the cultic centers of Arad and Tel Beer-sheba was made under orders from Hezekiah, the combined archaeological and biblical data point in favor of this possibility.

Furthermore, the varied archaeological finds enrich the picture of cultic reality beyond the limited biblical data. The two altars found in these two sites are very different from each other. The Arad altar is built of a mixture of earth coated by fieldstones, probably unadorned by horns in its upper corners. On the other hand, the Tel Beer-sheba altar is made of well-hewn ashlar stones, with horns at the upper corners. These stones originating from the 'Pleshet Formation' were brought from a considerable distance. The formal variation between the two different altars indicates that cultic customs, even in neighboring sites like Tel Beer-sheba and Arad, were not defined by completely standardized rules. Even the way of abolishing the cult was different in the two sites. At Arad the incense altars and the stele were buried in the cella, near their original place of use. At Tel Beer-sheba, on the contrary, the stones of the altar were transferred and disposed of in two locations distant from each other. It seems that rules of cultic behavior, regarding both, establishing and dismantling cultic installations, were not yet fully crystallized and strictly articulated.

16 Cf. Handy (1988); Na'aman (1995).

Support and Criticism of Interpretation of Finds as Evidence for a Cultic Reform

The suggestion to interpret finds related to remains of cult at Arad and Tel Beer-sheba as evidence of cultic reform in general, and the reform of King Hezekiah in particular, has won the support of archaeologists[17] and – at the same time – the sharp criticism mainly of Historians and Biblical scholars.[18]

Despite the clear evidences about abolishment of the cult at Arad and Tel Beer-sheba, criticisms and alternative suggestions have appeared in the literature concerning the finds from these two sites. The criticisms can be divided into three categories:

1. The claim that the finds do testify to intentional abolishment of the cult, but they should not be compared with the Biblical evidence (Knauf).
2. The claim that the abolishment of the cultic centers came out of a desire to protect them from the danger of damage during the Assyrian occupation, not as a result of a cultic reform (Uehlinger, Fried).
3. The claim that the archaeological finds do not testify about a cultic reform at all (Na'aman).

We shall now treat each of these claims and assess their contribution to the interpretation of the data.

1. The Cultic Reform at Arad and Tel Beer-sheba is not from Hezekiah's Days

The first claim accepts the basic interpretation of the archaeological record as evidence of a cultic reform, but does not ascribe this act to Hezekiah. I cannot directly disprove this claim, because the finds support the circumstances but do not directly point to Hezekiah. However, the arguments of the scholars who hold this view seem to me untenable. The view was expressed mainly by Ernst Axel Knauf.[19] In his view, Sennacherib did not destroy the Beer-sheba valley sites at all, and Arad VIII and Beer-sheba II continued to exist at the beginning of the

17 Cf. Borowski (1995) and Finkelstein (2006).

18 Cf. e.g., Na'aman (1995; 1999; 2002); Uehlinger (2005); Knauf (2002; 2005) and Fried (2002).

19 Cf. Knauf (2002; 2005).

early 7th century BCE. He believes that they were destroyed during the 7th century BCE by the Arabs.[20]

Knauf ascribes the abolishment of the Arad Temple to the policy of centrality of cult under Assyrian influence in the days of Manasseh.[21] However, the ceramic similarity between Lachish III, Arad VIII and Tel Beer-sheba II does not allow the postdating of the last two strata to the 7th century BCE.[22] Knauf's claim against an abolishment of cult at Arad is also based on the fact that the incense altars and the stele were found intact; they were not smashed during the abandonment of the temple. In his view, the condition of these cultic objects contradicts the description of Hezekiah's reform in 2 Kings 18:4:

> הוּא הֵסִיר אֶת-הַבָּמוֹת וְשִׁבַּר אֶת-הַמַּצֵּבֹת וְכָרַת אֶת-הָאֲשֵׁרָה וְכִתַּת נְחַשׁ הַנְּחֹשֶׁת אֲשֶׁר-עָשָׂה מֹשֶׁה ...
>
> "He removed the high places, and brake the images [*Massebot*], and cut down the groves [*Asherah*], and brake in pieces the brazen serpent that Moses made." [KJV]

The contradiction between the archaeological evidence of undamaged *Massebah* and altars and the biblical description rules out, in his opinion, any possibility that the abolishment of the Arad Temple was performed by Hezekiah.[23]

This is a peculiar claim from a critical scholar such as Knauf. The fact that the deuteronomistic description stresses the destruction of temples and smashing of the stelae does not prove that demolition was accurately carried out. No doubt the author of the text had a theological and political intention that affected the wording of the verse, which describes the reform. Yet, such a theological description does not have to portray accurately the real act. It is hardly likely that the author had exact and detailed information about the actions as performed in each city of Judah. Here too, the sole authentic evidence for the act of reform comes from the archaeological record. As we have seen, there were significant changes between the handling of the cult installation of the two sites: The Tel Beer-sheba altar was dismantled and transferred elsewhere, while the Arad cultic objects were buried in the same place. If the biblical description was based on a precise and reliable source, then it may portray the style of the orders sent by the King to the administration in the cities of Judah. It is also possible that the author assumed that the orders were strictly obeyed; however, he could hardly

---

20 Cf. Knauf (2002).

21 Possibly also at Tel Beer-sheba, though he does not stress this, Knauf (2005).

22 Cf. Singer-Avitz (2002), 159–182.

23 Cf. Knauf (2005), 184.

have held a detailed report about the performance of these orders in each and every site. The fact that the archaeological picture is varied indicates that the orders were interpreted differently in each site. In my view, the lack of match between the Biblical orders and the archaeological reality strengthens the historical reliability of the reform, rather than weakens it (as Knauf assumes).

Anyway, Knauf accepts the argument that the archaeological finds indicate a cultic reform, related to the centrality of cult in Jerusalem. On this major issue he does not differ from my position.

2. The Abolishment of the Arad and Tel Beer-sheba Temples is not due to a Reform, but comes to protect these Sacred Places

This line of thought is different: It accepts the dating of the Arad and Tel Beer-sheba strata, but holds that the dismantling of the temples and the burial of cult objects was not made as part of Hezekiah's reform, but as an intentional act of site commanders to protect sacred places from the threat of desecration by the threatening Assyrian army. I have also considered this option, since no signs of burning and destruction were found in the Arad Temple,[24] but rejected it – since the temple was not restored once the danger passed.

The claim that the Arad Temple was dismantled in order to protect it from the Assyrians was recently adopted by several scholars. Lisbeth Fried claimed that there is no archaeological evidence for a cultic reform in the days of Hezekiah (or Josiah), therefore, there is no historical basis for the biblical description of these reforms. In her view, the deuteronomistic concept of centrality of Yahweh's cult in the Jerusalem Temple did not derive from reformative decisions of Kings about cultic customs, but from the miraculous saving of Jerusalem from conquest and destruction during Sennacherib's campaign.[25] Fried suggested that Arad Stratum IX was destroyed by Sennacherib, and that the abandonment of the temple of this stratum was made as a preemptive act before the Assyrian campaign.[26] She interprets the finds from Tel Beer-sheba as evidence of contempt towards the sacredness of the temple.

24 Cf. Herzog (1997), 202; Herzog (2002), 66.

25 Cf. Fried (2002).

26 Cf. Fried (2002), 445–447. Fried based this theory on the mistaken assumption that only Arad IX was destroyed, while Arad VIII was not (ibid, 447). However, the destruction of Arad VIII is stressed in the publications and finds evidence in the large quantity of retrieved finds. The similarity between Arad VIII and Lachish III forces the conclusion that Arad VIII, not IX, is the stratum which was destroyed during the campaign of Sennacherib, cf. Herzog (1997), 237.

Since the stones of the Tel Beer-sheba Temple were not carefully buried, but used as building material in the wall of the 'pillared house', here, Fried does not see evidence for intentional abolishment. In her mind, the Tel Beer-sheba Temple was used untill the final destruction of the city during Sennacherib's campaign.[27]

Christoph Uehlinger does not see the process of centrality of cult in Jerusalem as a revolutionary reform, both neither in the days of Hezekiah, nor in the days of Josiah. He thinks that Jerusalem's growth in its political and religious status was a prolonged process, which covered the days of Hezekiah, Manasseh and Josiah.[28] Uehlinger accepts the interpretation that the Arad Temple was abolished intentionally, but favors the idea that this happened as an act of protection when the South of Judah was under military threat. He is ready to accept the possibility that such an act was performed by Hezekiah during Sennacherib's campaign.[29] In his view, there was no reform in a deuteronomistic meaning of abolishment of temples outside Jerusalem even during Josiah's reign, but a change of cultic customs that included abolishment of foreign cultic symbols and especially the removal of the statue of Asherah from the Jerusalem Temple.

I discussed this possibility,[30] but rejected it as an unfitting interpretation. In my view, the idea, that one can protect a structure's sacredness by destroying it, holds an inner contradiction. Any destruction of a sacred structure, including that undertaken by the hands of its owners, damages and desecrates it. The evidence from Arad shows that during the course of abolishment the upper parts of the walls had to be dismantled and the area had to be filled with hundreds of cubic meters of debris, practically making the structure unusable. The idea is even less acceptable for the Tel Beer-sheba evidence. There, the altar was dismantled into pieces, transferred elsewhere, partially buried in a wall and partially in a fill of the rampart. Is this not an act of contempt towards this altar? If the aim was to keep it intact, it would have been much more practical to bury all the parts together in one deep pit nearby. In addition, this interpretation does not answer the main issue: If the aim was to protect the temples, why was the Arad Temple not

---

27 Cf. Fried (2002), 450, ignores the fact that the stones of the altar were buried in the wall of the 'pillared house' of Stratum II, before this house was destroyed. See Aharoni (1974). The abolishment of the temple, therefore, could not come as a result of the destruction of the Stratum II city.

28 Cf. Uehlinger (2005), 291–292.

29 Cf. Uehlinger (2005), 290.

30 Cf. Herzog (1997).

restored when the fortress was rebuilt? That would have been the sole purpose of a protective abolishment!

3. The Archaeological Record does not prove a Cultic Reform at all

The third claim completely negates the interpretation of the archaeological finds as evidence for any cultic reform. This is the recurring view of Nadav Na'aman.[31] Na'aman denies the historical validity of the Biblical description about Hezekiah's cultic reform and claims that the temples and the cultic places of the 8th century BCE were not intentionally abolished, but destroyed during Sennacherib's campaign – and not restored later.[32] In order to deny the possibility that the Arad finds indicate an intentional abolishment of the temple, Na'aman uses a complex set of arguments, in order to doubt the finds of the excavation.

A. Archaeological Finds at Arad and their Contribution to the Question of Abolishment of Cult

In several papers Na'aman develops the claim that the Arad Temple was destroyed during the conquest of the fortress and simply abandoned after the destruction.[33] Na'aman rejects my conclusions about the existence of the temple during Strata X–IX and argues that the temple continued to exist in Stratum VIII. He ascribes the destruction of the temple not to an intentional act of the population, but to the general destruction of the Stratum VIII fortress during Sennacherib's campaign in 701 BCE.

Unfortunately, Na'aman's claims are based on a misinterpretation of the archaeological data and they ignore basic rules of stratigraphic and typological methodology. In the following, I will refute Na'aman's claims; to make things clearer to the readers, I will discuss his claims one by one, following the same order in his articles[34], although these claims hold some contradictions and duplications.

1. In order to prolong the life of the Arad Temple untill Stratum VIII, Na'aman disputes the stratigraphic interpretation that the 'thin walls' built above the temple belong to Stratum VIII, argu-

31 Cf. Na'aman (1995; 1999; 2002).

32 Cf. Na'aman (1995).

33 Cf. Na'aman (1995; 2002).

34 Cf. Na'aman (2002), 587–592.

ing that pottery from the relevant loci was not published.[35] Na'aman refers to one paper,[36] but that paper's title explicitly stresses the fact that this is an interim report. Hence, that paper includes a selection of assemblages, not all the finds. The duration of the temple in Strata X–IX is fixed first and foremost by the floors that adjust to its walls. Only two floors adjust to walls of the Temple- of Strata X and IX, as Aharoni concluded in his preliminary (and correct) observation already in the second season of the excavation.[37] Nowhere in the temple there is a floor of Stratum VIII that can be ascribed to the temple's walls. The existence of only two floors, one of Stratum X and the other of Stratum IX, in relation to the offering altar is especially important.[38] Therefore, Na'aman's assumption that the temple continued to be used untill the end of Stratum VIII is untenable.

2. Na'aman tries to doubt the reliability of the architectural documentation by arguing that the plans of Strata VIII–VII show a mixture of existing and restored walls, in a manner that does not enable their differentiation.[39] This is an argument *ad absurdum*. Every archaeologist experienced in working with excavation reports knows how to read plans of existing walls (showing contours of stones as found in the excavation) and of restored walls (marked by dotted lines). Na'aman could also consult the many marks of heights of exposed walls that appear in the plans in order to verify the difference between existing and restored walls.[40] Instead, Na'aman criticized without justification and created a false picture, which might confuse readers that are not archaeologists.
3. Na'aman tries to shake the stratigraphic reliability of the Arad finds by claiming that loci of Strata IX and VIII should be unified – because of their typological similarity – into one stratum.[41] As proof he cites the ceramic assemblages of loci 429 (VIII) and 462a (IX), found south of the temple area. He claims that the typological similarity between these assemblages demands that both will be ascribed to Stratum VIII. Yet, this shows Na'aman's lack of understanding of the principles of ar-

35 Cf. ibid, 587.
36 Cf. Herzog (2002).
37 Cf. Aharoni (1967).
38 Cf. Herzog (2002), 60 Fig. 27.
39 Cf. Na'aman (2002), 587.
40 Cf. Herzog (2002), 36–39 Figs. 15–16.
41 Cf. Na'aman (2002), 588.

chaeological stratigraphy. Had he made an effort to compare the finds published in the plans, he would have discovered that remains of Stratum VIII (including the foundations of a wall with loci 462 and 418 on its sides) were exposed above the assemblage of Locus 462a of Stratum IX.[42] In view of these facts, one must completely reject the effort to doubt the stratigraphic separation of the Arad strata. One must note that Na'aman does not explain why he chose to ascribe the two loci to Stratum VIII, rather than to Stratum IX. This arbitrary selection originates from his wish to relate the destruction of the temple with Stratum VIII. However, one still wonders how the unification of loci outside the temple affects the dating of assemblages in the temple itself. Na'aman's claim, that in the stratigraphic analysis I have separated loci of Strata IX and VIII by mistake, and that both these strata must form one stratum, has no basis whatsoever. All the Arad loci were carefully studied and their stratum was decided based upon stratigraphic sequence, floor levels and relations between floors and walls of structures. The typological similarity that Na'aman notes between vessels from Locus 429 of Stratum VIII and Locus 462A of Stratum IX is a common phenomenon, typical to all the assemblages of Strata X–VIII. It testifies to closeness in time between these strata, in the second half of the 8th century BCE.[43]

4. Na'aman wonders why rich ceramic assemblages are defined as belonging to Stratum IX, while everyone agrees that the Arad stratum destroyed by Sennacherib Stratum VIII.[44] He does not understand how those, responsible for the publication of the excavations of Arad, relate these assemblages to Stratum IX "although there is a peaceful continuity between stratum IX and VIII"[45].

   There is no basis for this idea. The existence of burning and destruction layers in the fortress of Stratum IX was stressed in the various publications.[46] Perhaps Na'aman confused my words about the lack of signs of burning in the area of the temple and the situation in other parts of the fortress. This contradiction between the fortress destruction in Stratum IX and the situation in the temple forms an important argument in favor of

42 Cf. Herzog (2002), 36f. Fig. 15.
43 Cf. Singer-Avitz (2002), 159–180.
44 Cf. Na'aman (2002), 588.
45 Cf. Na'aman, ibid.
46 Cf. Herzog (1997), 166; id. (2002), 33.

my claim, that the temple was intentionally abolished by the people of the fortress before the destruction of Stratum IX. Hence, Na'aman has no reason to wonder about the rich assemblages of Stratum IX.[47] The loci of Stratum IX that he mentions (460C, 788, 1008) cannot belong to Stratum VIII for the simple fact, that loci of this stratum exist above them.[48] These details are clear in the plans and list of finds published in our interim report.[49] The idea about transferring ceramic assemblages from one stratum to another without checking the stratigraphic sequence betrays a basic lack of understanding of archaeological methodology. In order to test the existence of destruction layer in Stratum IX Na'aman could have simply looked at the data brought by Singer-Avitz about the distribution of ceramic finds from the Arad strata. It expresses the power of the destruction layers of the various strata. From Stratum IX at Arad we retrieved 210 vessels termed 'whole' – just one vessel less than from Stratum VIII, the richest destruction layer.[50] How can one claim that Stratum IX did not end by destruction?

5. Another kind of argument is raised by Na'aman concerning the finds from the temple of Stratum IX. He asks: "...why did not he collect the temple's vessels and put them in *favissa*?"[51] Firstly, it must be stressed out that I have never said that I hold evidence that Hezekiah ordered the abolishment of the cult, but just that this is a reasonable possibility.[52] Secondly, as against the many vessels found in other parts of the fortress, a few finds were retrieved from the temple area. The 'whole' vessels represented in the plates were brought for the sake of ceramic typology and they include also parts of vessels.[53] Indeed, only fragments of vessels were found in the temple, none of them showing a clear cultic usage. On the other hand, from the clear destruction and burning of Stratum X we retrieved clear cultic vessels from the area of the temple, such as the fragments of the

---

47 Cf. Na'aman (2002), 588.

48 Locus 460B of Stratum VIII is located 70 cm above 460C; locus 787 of Stratum VIII is located 80 cm above 788; finally, locus 1008, a pit of Stratum IX, is sealed by the floor of locus 1003. The last is located 40 cm above the tallest vessel in pit 1008.

49 Cf. Herzog (2002); Singer-Avitz (2002).

50 Cf. Singer-Avitz (2002), 111.

51 Na'aman (2002), 588.

52 Cf. Herzog (1999), 65–67.

53 We define a 'half vessel' when at least 2/3 of the profile can be restored in drawing, cf. Singer-Avitz (2002), 110.

cultic stands, the bowls with inscriptions and other finds.[54] The finds from Stratum IX are very meager, and the impression they leave is that the temple's tools were indeed removed. Naturally, Na'aman's argument that assemblages of vessels found in 'nearby rooms' prove that the temple was not evacuated,[55] is not a valid argument. We did not argue that all the structures in the fortress were evacuated when the temple was abolished. Incidentally, Na'aman admits here the existence of a separate destruction layer in Stratum IX outside the temple, contradicting his claim, which we have discussed in the former section.

6. Na'aman misunderstands my words and ascribes to me something that I have never claimed.[56] I have never suggested that Hezekiah performed a cultic reform in the area of the former Kingdom of Israel, ruled by the Assyrians. I explicitly noticed that the abolishment of cult centers in Judah was performed in order to persuade the people of the North to abandon the temples at Samaria and Bethel.[57]
7. Na'aman mentions the difficulties of interpreting the finds from Tel Arad, because it was excavated with methods common in that period.[58] One cannot deny this fact. Although based on experience of years, I can state with satisfaction that the documentation at Arad was as a whole detailed and accurate. Na'aman brings Kenyon's work in Jericho as an example of a more reliable excavation. I assume that he would have avoided this statement, had he carefully checked the publications of Jericho, made mostly after the excavator passed away. Even a casual look at the hundreds of plans and sections from Kenyon's excavations at Jericho reveals dozens of mistakes and amendments, which were required – and marked in almost every plate by the editor Thomas Holland.[59] Aharoni was well aware of methodical differences between various methods of excavation and preferred the method of wide exposure to Kenyon's method of narrow sections.[60] In the excavations of Tel Beer-sheba Aharoni has already adopted the attitude – accepted by most archaeolo-

54 Cf. Singer-Avitz (2002), 110, 164 Fig. 24.
55 Cf. Na'aman (2002), 588.
56 Cf. Na'aman, ibid.
57 Cf. Herzog (1997), 202; Herzog (2002), 67.
58 Cf. Na'aman (2002), 588–589.
59 Cf. Kenyon (1981).
60 Cf. Aharoni (1973).

gists today – that combines the wide exposure with the use of sections.

8. Na'aman is wrong when he claims that those responsible for publishing the Arad finds did not participate in the excavation.[61] I had the right to participate in two seasons of excavation at Tel Arad. During the fourth season (1965) I was responsible, to expose the early layers in the cella (*Debir*), once the upper layers were removed for exhibition in the Israel Museum. In the fifth season (1967) Aharoni agreed to my request to serve as assistant to the surveyor Michael Feist. As a result, I had the chance to become acquainted with the complex of stratigraphic problems raised by the architect Immanuel Dunayevsky and to Aharoni's answers to these.
9. Na'aman uses the sequence of photographs of the Arad cella in order to suggest that the famous photograph, which shows the stele and the two altars resting on their sides[62] was "artificially made by Aharoni".[63] The impression left by such a grave accusation remains even after reading the note in parentheses: "unintentionally, of course". There is no basis for the accusation of fabricating a photograph, wether intentionally or not. The photograph as published represents faithfully one of the phases of the excavation of the cella and testifies about the way the incense altars have been buried. Blaming Aharoni for staging a false presentation is made only because this picture contradicts Na'aman's theory. Furthermore, Na'aman's claim that the altars in the cella of Arad were re-used as building stones for a new wall (in accordance to the burial of the Tel Beer-sheba altar stones inside a wall of the 'pillared house') is not true. The Arad incense altars were laid under the temple's floor and the stones that were placed above them were part of the covering made in order to protect them. The Stratum VIII walls above the temple were located at a higher level, having no connection to the incense altars. The fact that the stele was left in the cella without any connection to a built wall proves that Na'aman's theory has no basis. To use Na'aman's own words, the restoration of the incense altars as secondary building stones in a Stratum VII wall is completely artificial.
10. Na'aman wrongly thinks that signs of burning from Stratum VIII, exposed at the southern side of the cella, are related to the

61 Cf. Na'aman (2002), 589.

62 This photograph as reproduced in Na'aman (2002), 590 Fig. 3.

63 Na'aman (2002), 591.

temple,[64] when in fact they belong to the entrance shaft of the hidden passage near the temple. The same idea was already mentioned by Ussishkin,[65] but Na'aman ignores my answer to it, which includes a detailed stratigraphic analysis, given in various earlier publications.[66] The diagonal band of burning that appears in the photographs at the left side of the cella was clearly caused by collapse and burning (probably of wooden stairs), which had occurred inside the entrance shaft of the hidden passage. This collapse happened with the fortress destruction in Stratum VIII and as part of it, the upper part of the southern wall of the Stratum IX cella collapsed as well. For that reason, the wall was not identified in earlier stages of the excavation, but exposed only at its foundation level when the excavation went deeper at this place. The destruction happened inside the shaft and outside the temple area. At that time, the cultic installations in the cella were already dismantled and covered with earth. This is proven by their state of preservation: the heightened *Bama*, the stele resting next to it, and especially the two offering tables were all made of white limestone. They were all found intact without any mark of damage or signs of burning. The borderline of the fierce fire in the shaft – which did not damage the cella is clear in the photograph of the outer side of the brick wall.[67]

11. Na'aman suggests that the incense altars originally stood at the front of the cella, where in his view the stone bases also stood, which Aharoni saw as bases for two pillars, similar to Yachin and Boas of the Bible.[68] Here, too Na'aman is wrong. Aharoni suggested restoring two pillars at the front of the main hall of the temple,[69] not at the front of the cella. Anyway, a detailed examination of the data shows that the restoration of the stone bases by Aharoni has no basis and should not be trusted.[70]
12. Na'aman assumes that the entrance to the cella was blocked by a wall in order to detach it from the court altar, this allegedly showing that the cella went out of use; or – this is more likely in his view – that the blocking was made since an indirect access

64 Cf. ibid., 591.
65 Cf. Ussishkin (1988).
66 Cf. Herzog (1997); Herzog (2002), 70–72, Fig. 31.
67 Cf. Herzog (2002), 71 Fig. 31.
68 Cf. Na'aman (2002), 591.
69 Cf. Aharoni (1968), 19, p. 23 Fig. 15 and p. 26 Fig. 16.
70 Cf. Herzog (2006), 95.

to the cella was created.[71] Na'aman does not clarify to which stratum he ascribes this indirect access to the cella, and why it was needed once the incense altars had already been buried under the floor. Since he ascribes the destruction of the temple to Stratum VIII, one must conclude that he ascribes this later re-use of the cella to Stratum VII. However, as I have shown, by Stratum VII the temple was already covered by debris and by structures of two strata. Na'aman bases his idea of an indirect access on Ussishkin's claim about the missing southern wall of the cella.[72] However, his claim, as well as Na'aman's claim that this wall was never found, was refuted by myself on the basis of the clear documentation of foundations of the southern wall, exposed in the excavation.[73]

13. Na'aman believes that the offering altar in the court was used till its destruction in Stratum VIII.[74] Again, Na'aman ignores clear stratigraphic data. Two floors alone reached to the offering altar: The lower floor of Stratum X and the upper floor (once the altar was heightened) of Stratum IX. The Stratum VIII walls and floors, which carried ceramic finds of the late 8th century BCE, were found above the altar and cannot be ascribed to Stratum VII, as Na'aman suggested. To remove any doubt from readers' minds, I present here a plate of vessels from Locus 787, found above the offering altar (see Fig. 4).

71 Cf. Na'aman (2002), 591.
72 Cf. Ussishkin (1988), 144–147.
73 Cf. Herzog (1997), 202; Herzog (2002), 72 and 71 Fig. 31.
74 Cf. Na'aman (2002), 592.

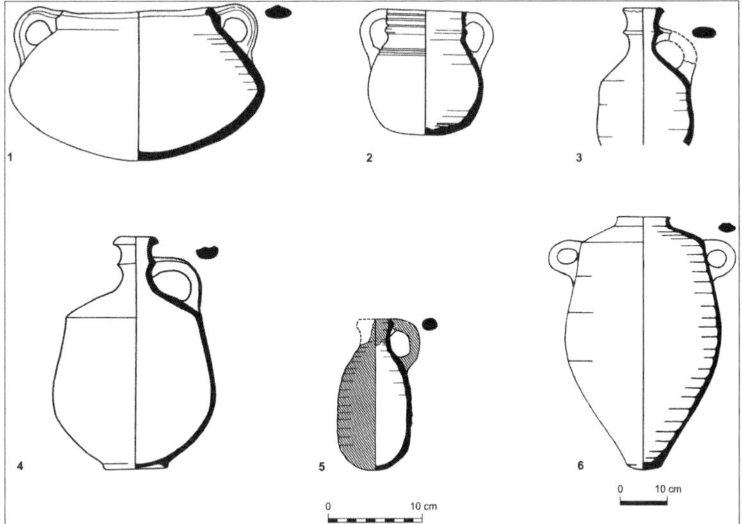

Fig. 4: Pottery from Locus 787 of Stratum VIII found in a Layer covering the Altar of Stratum IX.

14. Once more Na'aman raises the claim – already refuted above – that the cella was destroyed during the burning of Stratum VIII.[75] However, this leads him into contradiction in his argumentation. His claim about a burning inside the temple is contradicted by his quoting of Aharoni's words about finding traces of burning and destruction in the room left of the temple, but not in the temple itself. Furthermore, Na'aman has to admit that: "Finally, the absence of signs of fire on the cella's steps and the two altars is the result of their early covering by a wall."[76] By this, Na'aman admits that the altars were buried before the destruction of Stratum VIII – hence accepting my crucial claim that the incense altars were not destroyed by fire, but dismantled and intentionally buried.
15. Despite admitting the intentional dismantling of the incense altars, Na'aman summarizes his discussion with the statement that the Arad Temple was destroyed by fire during the destruction of the Stratum VIII fortress in the year 701 BCE.[77] The discussion in the present article, as well as Na'aman's own admit-

75 Cf. ibid., 592.
76 Ibid., 592.
77 Cf. ibid., 592.

tance about the lack of marks of destruction on the incense altars, prove that his conclusions do not fit the facts. Not just the lack of traces of fire proves this, but also the careful burial of the incense altars under the floor. Yet, the major flaw of Na'aman's theory is conceptual: he admits that, following the destruction of the temple, the commanders decided not to re-establish it when the fortress was rebuilt. To quote his own words: "I suggest that it was a royal decision not to restore the sacred sites, which reflected the efforts of rulers to centralize power in their hands."[78] This means that on the one hand Na'aman claims that there is no archaeological evidence for cultic reform; but on the other hand that the lack of renewal of cultic sites derived from an explicit order by the royal administration, aimed at centralizing power in their hands. In his view, this was not a religious, but a political decision. Here, I see the main weakness of his entire theory. His effort to create an arbitrary separation between a political-economic and a cultic-religious reform is completely impossible. All scholars agree that cult was an inseparable part of the royal administration in the Kingdom of Judah, where the religious, political and military systems were combined for the Kingdom's needs. Abolishment of temples, even if performed only out of a decision not to rebuild them following a destruction (as Na'aman suggests), forms in itself a cultic reform by all means – since it implies the cessation of bringing offerings and gifts to the local temple. The abolishment of cult was meant, first and foremost, to stop the function of local temples throughout Judah and centralize the cult in the Jerusalem Temple. Na'aman's admittance, that the temples were not renewed based on royal orders, is an admittance of a cultic reform. The finds from Arad and Tel Beer-sheba prove that such a reform took place at the end of the 8th century BCE.

78 Na'aman (2002), 596.

B. Archaeological Finds at Tel Beer-sheba and their Contribution to the Question of Abolishment of Cult

The archaeological evidence from Tel Beer-sheba is clearer than that of Arad, mainly because Tel Beer-sheba II was destroyed in a huge fire. The similarity between the pottery exposed in this destruction and that of Lachish III justified – in the eyes of most scholars – the dating of the end of Beer-sheba II to Sennacherib's campaign in 701 BCE. Based upon the major status of Beer-sheba in the Bible and following the finding of the temple at Arad, Aharoni assumed that a temple would also be found at Tel Beer-sheba. However, despite the wide exposure of this relatively small city, evidence for the existence of a cultic place were uncovered only in the fifth season, when four hewn stones with rounded horns (one of them broken) were found inside a wall of the 'pillared house'.[79] Other stones from the upper part of the altar, showing clear traces of burning, were discovered inside the fill of the glacis that coated the slope outside the city gate.[80] As a result, a discussion started about the original place of the altar, the type of cultic place it served in and the restoration of its original form. Naturally, the circumstance of the end of the cult place were also discussed.[81]

At Tel Beer-sheba the clear stratigraphy does not allow Na'aman to postulate that the altar was abandoned during Sennacherib's campaign (as it was his claim for the Arad Temple). He admits that the altar ceased to be used prior to Sennacherib's campaign, that is, in the second half of the 8th century BCE.[82] Nonetheless, to argue against its abolishment on purpose, Na'aman raises a few points, in order to doubt the common view that the temple's dismantling and burial were related to a conscious decision taken by the city's leaders. Here too, we shall test his arguments one by one.

1. Na'aman[83] attacks Aharoni's reconstruction for the temple in the western part of the city,[84] where building 32 (the so-called 'house of cellars') was built in Stratum II. Indeed, the considerable distance between the place of deposition of the altar stones and the 'house of cellars' is a point against Aharoni's reconstruction, which I do not see as the only possibility.[85] One

79 Cf. Aharoni (1974).
80 Cf. Herzog et al. (1977).
81 For the most recent review, with detailed references, cf. Herzog (2006).
82 Cf. Na'aman (2002), 593–595.
83 Cf. ibid., 593.
84 Cf. Aharoni (1974).
85 Cf. Herzog (2006), 96.

would have expected the stones to be buried in one of the walls of the 'house of cellars' itself. Still, Na'aman's argument is based on a misconception of the excavation data. He claims that the building was deeply built, because it was used as a house that included cellars. However, he ignores the fact that we stressed time and again in our publications, namely, that the three spaces of building 32 were not used as cellars, although they were built approximately to a depth of 3–4 m and then filled by earth. It is a unique phenomenon, which finds no good explanation; Aharoni took it as support for his restoration of the temple's location. Since about a third of the Tel remains unexcavated, the original location of the temple is an open question. This, however, cannot negate the fact that the offering altar was dismantled on purpose.

2. Na'aman stresses the view of those scholars, who deny the identification of Tel Beer-sheba with biblical Beer-sheba.[86] It is hardly the place to discuss the identification issue, but how can it deny the clear reality of the dismantling of the Tel Beer-sheba splendid offering altar?
3. Na'aman[87] quotes Yadin,[88] who argued that there is no need to look for a temple at Beer-sheba;[89] since the altar could have stood in an open place. However, Na'aman avoids referring to the excavators' refutation of Yadin's idea.[90] In any case, this question is also irrelevant to the present debate. Even if the altar once stood in an open place, it was still dismantled and abolished.
4. Na'aman offers alternative scenarios to explain the finding of a dismantled altar, though he admits their lack of probability:[91] perhaps the altar stood outside the city and was dismantled from fear of the Assyrian army? Or, maybe the altar was desecrated by this enemy, and this is the reason for its end of use? The alternatives are proposed in order to show that there is no basis for Aharoni's suggestion, that an order to abolish the altar was sent from Jerusalem.[92] However, this is not logical, since all

86 Cf. Na'aman (2002), 593.
87 Cf. ibid., 593.
88 Cf. Yadin (1976).
89 Here, Na'aman does accept the identification with Biblical Beer-sheba.
90 Cf. Herzog et al. (1977).
91 Cf. Na'aman (2002), 593.
92 Cf. ibid., 594.

his alternatives would have required the same, authoritative royal order.

5. Na'aman points at one real difficulty: My dating of the end of Stratum III and the beginning of Stratum II was influenced by the Biblical source about a reform of Hezekiah.[93] Indeed, nothing in the archaeological record proves that the cultic reform at Tel Beer-sheba was carried during Hezekiah's days. Uehlinger even saw it as an outdated 'Biblical Archaeology' attitude on my side.[94] However, even without the biblical data, the shift from Stratum III to II at Tel Beer-sheba must have occurred during the second half of the 8th century BCE, in view of the similarity to the assemblage of Lachish Stratum III. It must also be dated somewhat prior to Sennacherib's campaign in 701 BCE, when Beer-sheba was destroyed. Still, the claim that there is no archaeological proof that the cultic reform was ordered by Hezekiah does not change a bit of the fact, that the offering altar at Tel Beer-sheba was abolished on purpose and that this happened during the second half of the 8th century BCE, prior to the destruction of Stratum II during Sennacherib's campaign. This is also admitted by Na'aman.[95]
6. Finally, Na'aman compares the Arad and Tel Beer-sheba altars to 14 horned altars from the Ekron/Tel Miqneh excavations, which were found not in cultic, but in industrial contexts.[96] In his view this hints that the altars did not remain sacred once they had been dismantled. This comparison is out of place, since the small incense altars of Ekron are not similar to the large offering altars of Tel Beer-sheba and Arad. The first are completely different from the last in their size, function, period and geo-political association.

93 Cf. ibid., 594.

94 Cf. Uehlinger (2005), 290–291.

95 Cf. ibid.

96 Cf. Na'aman (2002), 594–595.

Conclusion: Is there Archaeological Evidence for Abolishment of Cult at Arad and Tel Beer-sheba?

The detailed discussion about the abolishment of cult at Arad and Tel Beer-sheba shows that one cannot doubt the fact that these cult centers were intentionally abolished. Still, one has to admit that there is, yet, no direct proof that relates this abolishment with the biblical story about Hezekiah's cultic reform.

Are we allowed to suggest that there is, indeed, a relation between the archaeological and the biblical evidence? As one of those who supports the scientific revolution in the Archaeology of Eretz Israel and as someone who called for a separation between the two disciplines,[97] I maintain that such a suggestion is legitimate. The test is the independence of the analysis of the archaeological data, which clearly indicates the existence of a revolution in cultic customs in Judah in the second half of the 8th century BCE. The biblical evidence about Hezekiah's activity is supported by Assyrian chronology, which explicitly mentions the reign of Hezekiah in the late 8th century BCE. This forms a unique, exceptional case of interdisciplinary fit. It justifies the conclusion that the acts of abolishment of cult discovered in the archaeological record of Arad and Tel Beer-sheba are a result of Hezekiah's cultic reform.

Na'aman's position, which tried to deny the interpretation of the archaeological finds as evidence for an intentional abolishment of cultic centers, comes entirely from the traditional attitude of Biblical Archaeology. Since biblical scholarship tries to refute the historical reliability of Hezekiah's reform (based upon assumptions that arise from text-criticism), Na'aman hurries to try doubting the interpretation of the archaeological finds. I have no doubt that, without the existence of this very common attitude since the days of Wellhausen, Na'aman would not have doubted the archaeological evidence about the abolishment of cult at Arad and Tel Beer-sheba.[98]

In my view, *lectio difficilior* holds true here. Especially, in view of the skepticism of textual criticism and historians about the reliability of the biblical description of Hezekiah's reform, the archaeological data should be preferred. Furthermore, the archaeological data raises doubts about the biblical description of the abolishment of temples by King

97 Cf. Herzog (2001b).

98 Münnich (2004), recently published a rejection of Na'aman's suggestion. Münnich's conclusions were independently reached. The present article uses additional data, which was not presented by him.

Josiah. The lack of any archaeological evidence of a cultic reform at the late 7th century BCE may indicate that the reliability of the biblical description of that reform should be examined, and its historicity should be placed in doubt.[99]

The fact that the reform of Hezekiah had political and economic aims, besides the cultic meaning, is self-evident. In Judah's centralized government the economic, military and religious aspects of the state were combined and directed by the royal house. Anson Rainey suggested, as early as 1984, that the centralization of cult in Jerusalem by Hezekiah came in order to crystallize also the population of the (former) Kingdom of Israel around Jerusalem's royal house.[100] A paper by Finkelstein and Silberman stressed, the economic and religious aims of Hezekiah's cultic activity, too,[101] and they accepted my conclusions about the evidence for abolishment of cult at Arad and Tel Beer-sheba.

---

99 I do not see any evidence for proving Josiah's reform. Uehlinger (2005), 290–291, is wrong in thinking that my attitude is a return to the outdated 'Biblical Archaeology'.

100 Cf. Rainey in Herzog et.al. (1984).

101 Finkelstein/Silberman (2006).

Bibliography

Aharoni, Y. (1967), Excavations at Tel Arad: Preliminary Report on the Second Season 1963, IEJ 17, 233–249.

– (1968), Arad: Its Inscriptions and Temple, BA 31, 2–32.

– (1974), The Horned Altar of Beer-sheba, BA 37, 2–6.

Borowski, O. (1995), Hezekiah's Reforms and the Revolt against Assyria, BA 58, 148–155.

Finkelstein, I./Silberman, N.A. (2006), Temple and Dynasty: Hezekiah, the Remaking of Judah and the Rise of the Pan-Israelite Ideology, JSOT 30, 259–285.

Fried, L.S. (2002), The High Places (Bamôt) and the Reforms of Hezekiah and Josiah: An Archaeological Investigation, JAOS 122, 437–465.

Handy, L.K. (1988), Hezekiah's Unlikely Reform, ZAW 100, 111–115.

Haran, M. (1993), "Incense altars" – Are They?, in: A. Biran/J. Aviram (eds.), Biblical Archaeology Today, 1990: Proceedings of the Second International Congress on Biblical Archaeology, Jerusalem, June–July 1990, Israel Exploration Society/The Israel Academy of Sciences and Humanities, Jerusalem, 237–247.

Herzog, Z. (1997), The Arad Fortresses, in: R. Amiran/O. Ilan/M. Sebanne/Z. Herzog (eds.), Arad, Tel Aviv, 113–292 (in Hebrew).

– (2001a), The Date of the Temple at Arad: Reassessment of the Stratigraphy and the Implications for the History of Religion in Judah, in: A. Mazar (ed.), Studies in the Archaeology of the Iron Age in Israel and Jordan, JSOT.S 331, Sheffield, 156–178.

– (2001b), Deconstructing the Walls of Jericho: Biblical Myth and Archaeological Reality, Prometheus 4, 72–93.

– (2002), The Fortress Mound at Tel Arad: An Interim Report, Tel Aviv 29, 3–109.

– (2006), Beersheba Valley Archaeology and Its Implications for the Biblical Record, in: A. Lemaire (ed.), Congress Volume Leiden 2004, VT.S 109, Leiden/Boston, 81–102.

– /Aharoni, M./Rainey, A.F./Moshkovitz, S. (1984), The Israelite Fortress at Arad, BASOR 253, 1–34.

– /Rainey, A.F./Moshkovitz, S. (1977), The Stratigraphy at Beer-sheba and the Location of the Sanctuary, BASOR 225, 49–58.

– /Singer-Avitz, L. (2004), Redefining the Centre: The Emergence of State in Judah, Tel Aviv 31, 209–244.

– /Singer-Avitz, L. (2006), Sub-Dividing the Iron Age IIA in Northern Israel: A Suggested Solution to the Chronological Debate, Tel Aviv 33, 163–195.

Kenyon, K.M. (1981), Excavations at Jericho, III: The Architecture and Stratigraphy of the Tell, ed. by T.A. Holland, British School of Archaeology in Jerusalem, London/Oxford.

Knauf, E.A. (2002), Who Destroyed Beersheba II?, in: U. Hübner/E.A. Knauf (eds.), Kein Land für sich allein. Studien zum Kulturkontakt in Kanaan, Israel/Palästina und Ebirnâri, FS M. Weippert, OBO 186, Freiburg (Schweiz)/Göttingen, 181–195.

– (2005), The Glorious Days of Manasseh, in: L.L. Grabbe (ed.), Good Kings and Bad Kings, Library of Hebrew Bible/Old Testament Studies, European Seminar in Historical Methodology 5, JSOT.S 393, London, 164–188.

Mazar, A./Netzer, E. (1986), On the Israelite Fortress at Arad, BASOR 263, 87–91.

Münnich, M.M. (2004), Hezekiah and Archaeology: The Answer for Nadav Na'aman, UF 36, 333–346.

Na'aman, N. (1995), The Debated Historicity of Hezekiah's Reform in the Light of Historical and Archaeological Research, ZAW 107, 179–195.

– (1999), No Anthropomorphic Graven Image: Notes on the Assumed Anthropomorphic Cult Statues in the Temples of YHWH in the Pre-Exilic Period, UF 31, 391–415.

– (2002), The Abandonment of Cult Places in the Kingdoms of Israel and Judah as Acts of Cult Reform, UF 34, 585–602.

Rainey, A.F. (1994), Hezekiah's Reform and the Altars at Beer-sheba and Arad, in: M.D. Coogan/J.C. Exum/L.E. Stager (eds.), Scripture and other Artifacts: Essays on the Bible and Archaeology in Honor of P.J. King, Louisville, 333–354.

Singer-Avitz, L. (2002), Arad: The Iron Age Pottery Assemblages, Tel Aviv 29, 110–214.

Uehlinger, C. (2005), Was there a Cult Reform under King Josiah? The Case for a Well-Grounded Minimum, in: L.L. Grabbe (ed.), Good Kings and Bad Kings, Library of Hebrew Bible/Old Testament Studies, European Seminar in Historical Methodology 5, JSOT.S 393, London, 279–316.

Ussishkin, D. (1988), The Date of the Judaean Shrine at Arad, IEJ 38, 142–157.

Yadin, Y. (1965), A Note on the Stratigraphy of Arad, IEJ 15, 180.

– (1976), Beer-sheba: The High Place Destroyed by King Josiah, BASOR 222, 5–17.

Why the Cult Reforms in Judah Probably Did not Happen

JUHA PAKKALA

Introduction

The cult reforms of Hezekiah (2 Kings 18:4) and Josiah (2 Kings 22–23) have had considerable impact on Biblical Studies. Especially Josiah's reform has been widely understood as a crucial moment and turning point in the development of Israel's[1] religion.[2] Accordingly, the biblical accounts have been assumed to preserve important historical information from the time of Hezekiah and Josiah. For example, in the last century Hölscher argued that 2 Kings 22–23 is a prime example of authentic history writing.[3] Noth assumed that 2 Kings 23:4–20 was taken from royal annals.[4] Although most scholars nowadays would acknowledge that the biblical accounts are not unbiased historical sources, the kings are usually assumed to have taken at least some measures to renew the cult.[5] Some scholars assume that they purified the cult of foreign elements, whereas others argue that only the location of the cult was at issue.[6] There are also some critical voices that have questioned the his-

1 In this paper Israel's religion denotes the religion of both, Judah and Israel, practiced during the monarchy.

2 According to Albertz (1994) "[t]he most important decision in the history of Israelite religion is made with a dating of an essential part of Deuteronomy in the time of Josiah." (199). Cf. the later discussion about this statement (by Albertz) in Davies (2007), 65–77, and Albertz (2007), 27–36.

3 Hölscher (1923), 208.

4 Noth (1967), 86. Thus also Gray (1963), 663.

5 For example, Lohfink (1987), 459–475; Collins (2007), 86, 150–151; Sweeney (2007), 402–403, 446–449, and Petry (2008), 395 n. 19. Römer (2005), 55, writes: "The Biblical presentation of Josiah and his reign cannot be taken as a document of primary evidence. On the other hand, some indicators suggest nevertheless that some attempts to introduce cultic and political changes took place under Josiah."

6 Hoffmann (1980), 269, has concluded that in almost all details the author of 2 Kings 22–23 presents an idealistic picture of the reform, but that the events have a historical basis in the time of Josiah.

toricity of the reforms altogether, but they still represent the minority.[7] Nevertheless, it is evident that skepticism about the historicity of the reforms has grown in the last decades.[8] It should also be added that the historicity of Hezekiah's reform has been challenged more often than that of Josiah.[9]

The reform accounts have had considerable impact on Biblical Studies and the study of ancient Israel, its history and religion. Many histories of Israel and introductions to the Hebrew Bible refer to the reforms as important events that took place in the late 8th and late 7th centuries BCE.[10] Many central or even defining concepts of later Judaism, such as cult centralization, exclusive worship of Yahweh, idol criticism and law-based religion, would have been introduced by one of the reforming kings. The reforms have also had considerable impact on the study of Biblical books. For example, because of the evident similarities between the Deuteronomy and 2 Kings 22–23, the dating of Deuteronomy is often connected with Josiah's reform.[11] Some scholars who have questioned the historicity of most events in 2 Kings 22–23 have still connected the Deuteronomy with King Josiah or the late 7th century BCE.[12] The Deuteronomy would then be a witness to the religious changes that took place during this time.

The reforms have also influenced the dating of the Deuteronomistic History. Many scholars, traditionally in Anglo-Saxon scholarship, have linked the editorial development of the composition with the reforms. According to the 'Double Redaction Model', one of the main editorial phases of the composition was written during the time of Josiah.[13] One

7 For example, Levin (1984), 351–371; Davies (2007), 65–77.

8 This development can be seen, for example, in recent commentaries and histories of Israel; e.g., Werlitz (2002), 305–311; Grabbe (2007), 204–207.

9 For a review, see Hoffmann (1980), 151–154, who himself assumes that 2 Kings 18:4 contains a memory of a historical event. Similarly also Collins (2007), 148. Earlier scholarship assumed that 2 Kings 18:4 contains an excerpt from the royal annals, e.g., Benzinger (1899), 177.

10 See, for example, Liverani (2005), 175–182; Miller/Hayes (2006), 413–414 (the historicity of Hezekiah's reform is left open; see n. 28), 457–460.

11 Thus many scholars, e.g., Driver (1902), xliii–lxvi; Veijola (2004), 2–3; Römer (2005), 55. In earlier research and already since de Wette (1805), Dissertatio critico-exegetica, the book found in the temple (2 Kings 22:8) was assumed to have been the Deuteronomy or its early edition.

12 Thus, e.g., Levin (2005), 91. According to Schmid (2008), 106, the argumentation about the relationship between 2 Kings 22–23 and the Deuteronomy runs the risk of circular reasoning, but dates the oldest version of the Deuteronomy to the 7th century BCE.

13 Cf. Cross (1973), 274–289, and many following him. Similarly also Lohfink (1987), 459–475. Provan (1988), 172–173, has connected the first edition of the composition with Hezekiah's reign.

has also tried to correlate archaeological data with the cult reforms. Especially in earlier research, the destruction of the cult sites at Arad Tel Beer-sheba was seen as a result or proof of the biblical cult reforms.[14] It has also been discussed whether figurines from Iron Age Judah show any signs of intentional destruction, which could then be used as evidence for Josiah's reform.[15] In more recent scholarly discussion, the decrease in iconographical motives from the 8th century BCE onward has been connected with the reforms.[16]

Confidence in the biblical texts in question as reliable historical sources is problematical, because it is evident that 2 Kings 18 and 2 Kings 22–23 were extensively edited. 2 Kings 23, where the whole discussion about the reforms culminates, may be the most edited chapter in all of 1–2 Kings, if not in the entire Hebrew Bible, and its complicated editorial history is also usually acknowledged. Indicative of the problems is the fact that the scholarly views on its development differ to a great extent, with very little consensus in sight.[17] Nearly any and all parts of the chapter have been variably ascribed to the basic text and to various later editors or to the royal annals. Consequently, the text is, at best, a problematical historical source and thus a poor basis for reconstructions of Israel's history and theories about the development of biblical books.

Even without the problems caused by editing, the texts in question were evidently written from a strongly theological perspective, which means that their historical reliability as a source should be carefully scrutinized. It is hardly possible to use them as such for any historical reconstruction of the monarchic period. The theological profile of the different authors has to be understood before we may even start seeing behind the theology and possibly gain information about historical events. It would be hazardous to neglect the painstaking analysis of the source texts and assume that, despite evident problems, they somehow reflect historical realities during the monarchy. Such an approach to the texts is not uncommon, but can hardly provide a solid historical basis. In this paper, I will try to show that the available texts are not so solid historical sources that we should use them as cornerstones of theories about Israel's religion and the birth of biblical books. The possibility

14 See Aharoni (1968), 233–234; Mazar (1992), 495–498.

15 Kletter (1993), 54–56, has shown that there is no evidence for an intentional destruction of Judean pillar figurines.

16 See Uehlinger (2007), 292–295.

17 See, for example, Benzinger (1899), 189–196; Hoffmann (1980), 169–270; Würthwein (1984), 452–466; Levin (1984), 351–371; Kratz (2000), 173, 193; Hardmeier (2007), 123–163.

that the reforms are projections of later ideals to the monarchic period and thus are completely without any historical basis also has to be taken into consideration or at least discussed. Some features may even indicate that they never happened.

Lack of Evidence for the Reforms

There are several problems with the biblical accounts and thus with the traditional scholarly view that assumes that significant cult reforms, in any form, took place during the times of Hezekiah and/or Josiah. The problems begin with the fact that no other biblical text that is not directly dependent on 1–2 Kings (such as 1–2 Chronicles) makes any reference to the reforms. Without a strong presupposition that the reforms must have happened, it is hard to find even vague allusions to the events described in 2 Kings 18:4 and 2 Kings 22–23.[18] If a significant reform with considerable changes in Israel's religion took place, one would expect that it left at least some traces in the biblical record. Since some biblical texts are usually assumed to have been written in the final decades of Judah, such as parts of Jeremiah and Ezekiel, one cannot ignore the silence, especially over Josiah's reform.

Nevertheless, some scholars maintain that there is evidence of Josiah's reform in Jeremiah. For example, Albertz has suggested that the author of Jer. 5:4–6 and 8:7–8 was aware of the reform.[19] However, a closer look at these passages shows that there is only a reference to a law being written by scribes,[20] but this can refer to many things. There is no reference in these passages to any *indicative features* of Josiah's reform.[21] It is doubtful that the brief references to a law, which the author did not specify further, could be used as any kind of indication of Josiah's reform. In fact, these passages in Jeremiah can be connected with Josiah's reform only with a strong premise that it must have taken place. In addition to these problems, the origin and dating of the heavi-

18 One exception is the Ezra story in Ezra 7–10 and Nehemia 8, which may have been partly modeled after Josiah's reform, see Pakkala (2004), 233, but this is a very late text.

19 Albertz (2007), 43: "The often repeated argument that contemporary texts like the book of Jeremiah do not know anything of the reform is not correct."

20 E.g., Jer. 8:8: אֵיכָה תֹאמְרוּ חֲכָמִים אֲנַחְנוּ וְתוֹרַת יְהוָה אִתָּנוּ אָכֵן הִנֵּה לַשֶּׁקֶר עָשָׂה עֵט שֶׁקֶר סֹפְרִים.

21 In order to argue for a connection one would have to demonstrate that the Deuteronomy was meant, that the text was written in the wake of Josiah's reform and that the Deuteronomy was the legal basis of the reform. All these are disputed and very uncertain.

ly edited and problematical text in these chapters of Jeremiah is hotly debated.

According to Albertz, the apparent lack of reference to the reform by Ezekiel – or even a contradiction with the reform because the prophet accused the Judeans of syncretism during the decades after the alleged reform – may be because "Ezekiel could easily misunderstand or overstate a rumour from Jerusalem."[22] If one discredits the main texts from the period under investigation by assuming that the ancient witnesses' viewpoint may be based on a misunderstanding of a rumor, one can justify almost any theory about the reform. If one assumes that Ezekiel is a witness to the early exilic Judean community, it would appear that the author of this text was not aware of any reform. Further on, Jer. 22:15 speaks positively about Josiah, but instead of referring to any cultic accomplishments, his characterization seems to be based on him having been a just king (וְעָשָׂה מִשְׁפָּט וּצְדָקָה). There is no evidence that the author of this verse connected Josiah with any cult reform, and the same applies to the entire Books of Jeremiah and Ezekiel.[23]

One also does not find any reception history of the cult reforms in the later books of the Hebrew Bible or in the later expansions of earlier books, which is in contradiction with the importance of the events for the author(s) of 1–2 Kings. The heavily edited books of the prophets do not allude to the reforms, although many passages in them share the concerns of 2 Kings 22–23, attacking the other gods and criticizing 'foreign' aspects of the cult. The only exception in the Hebrew Bible is 1–2 Chronicles, which contains a later version of the reforms, but here we are already dealing with a composition that is a further development of the entire 1–2 Kings, written at a much later stage.

In those few extra-biblical sources from the Persian Period that deal with the Jewish community, there is no evidence that the reforms had had any impact on the practice of religion. For example, the Jewish community at Elephantine planned to rebuild a temple for Yahweh at Elephantine, which clearly contradicts the main target of Josiah's reform, the existence of cult sites outside Jerusalem. As late as the late 5th century BCE, this Jewish community did not seem to be aware of any of the restrictions on the location of the sacrificial cult allegedly introduced by the biblical reforms. That the community was also in friendly contact with Jerusalem and Samaria emphasizes the contradiction with

22 Albertz (2007), 43.

23 As noted by Ben Zvi (2007), 64, "[T]he prophetic books do not provide identifiable, independent sources for the reconstruction of the historical circumstances in Josianic Judah."

the biblical account.[24] In other words, the correspondence of the Jewish community at Elephantine does not support the view that the principles of the Josianic reform had been put into practice, or were even known in Jerusalem, Samaria or within the wider Jewish community. This undermines the historicity of the cult reforms, as described in 2 Kings.

The Past as Constant Rebellion

It is very peculiar that the monarchic period is portrayed in 1–2 Kings as a period of constant rebellion of the kings and the people against their own religion, and a period when only some kings fulfilled its demands. The idea that a nation and its kings repeatedly failed the demands of their own religion is exceptional in the Ancient Near East and even absurd. It implies that there is a fundamental contradiction between the reality and the ideals implied by the authors of 1–2 Kings. Of all the kings evaluated in 1–2 Kings only two, Hezekiah and Josiah, received a fully positive evaluation for their cultic standing and they are described as reformers who stood against all others. With the exception of the last four kings of Judah, who are generally assumed to be evil, the others failed in their cult policy.[25] One has to ask whether this picture of Israel's monarchic religion is realistic at all and whether it is possible that there were two kings who had entirely different conceptions of the religion than all the others. What is the background of such a peculiar view of one's own religious past?

Traditionally, one has assumed that Hezekiah or Josiah introduced the new religious ideals, which would have then contradicted the religion practiced by the other kings. However, the traditional theories fail to explain where the new ideas, which in many ways eradicated several parts of the traditionally accepted religion, came from.[26] Such a reorientation and an attack on one's own religion are in many ways so radical that they can only be explained by external influence or a fundamental change in circumstances.

---

24 Cf. Cowley (1923), no. AP 32 (which can be dated shortly after 407 BCE). The communities ask permission to built the temple and receive a friendly reply from Jerusalem and Samaria. The replies are not preserved but a memorandum (AP 35) refers to both replies, which give a permission to build a temple at Elephantine.

25 However, not all kings are characterized as evil, even if they failed in their cult policies.

26 If one assumes that the ideas came from a law book, such as the Deuteronomy, one would still have to explain where it came from and why it criticized the traditional religion in such a radical way.

Many scholars are conscious of the problem and find the reasons in the changed circumstances caused by the collapse of the Assyrian empire. As a vassal of Assyria Judah would have been influenced by Assyrian religious concepts or, as a sign of subjugation, even be forced to accept some religious cult items in the temple of Jerusalem. But does this provide an explanation for criticizing one's own religion? The reforms are primarily targeted against religious phenomena that were common in 9th–7th century BCE Palestine, including the kingdoms of Israel and Judah: standing stones, holy trees, Asherah, Baal, Yahweh's solar aspects and local cult sites. For example, the Asherah, one of the main targets of cult criticism was closely connected with Yahweh and his cult, as shown by the inscriptions from Kuntillet Ağrud and Khirbet el-Qom. The attack on all local cult sites is also a self-evident attack on local religion. Consequently, one cannot avoid the conclusion that the reforms, as described in 2 Kings 18:4; 22–23, were directed against Israel's own religion as practiced during the monarchy.

Moreover, the introduction of radically new religious concepts would have disturbed many traditional structures of the society – religious, political and economic – and challenged the interests of many established groups. For example, if one assumes that the cult centralization is a historical event, the abolition of the local cult sites would have meant an economic catastrophe for many towns where there was an important cult center (such as Bethel, Shiloh or Gibeon). In other words, there would have to be very good reasons for the introduction of such new ideas that would have had the potential to destabilize the entire state and society, and even the monarch's power over the kingdom. It is questionable whether the turbulent times of King Josiah, when the Assyrian empire was collapsing, would have been an ideal time to rock the boat even more. The traditional view leaves many questions unanswered, and the reforms remain an unexplained structural oddity in monarchic times.

Rather than following the biblical account and assuming that the reforming kings introduced the new ideas and represented the turning point in Israel's religion, it is more probable that the fundamental change began only as the result of the destruction of the temple, monarchy and state in 587/6 BCE. From the perspective of long-term historical developments, 587/6 BCE must have represented a crucial turning point in political, religious and economic structures in Judah. It meant a collapse of the main supporting institutions of Israel's religion, the monarchy and the temple. It would be difficult to comprehend how the destruction of the temple would not cause, or force, a radical transformation of the temple-based state religion.[27] The divinity was certainly bound to the temple in some way, as also implied by some vestiges in the Hebrew Bible that refer to him being bound to the Ark of the Covenant (e.g., 1 Samuel 4–6; 2 Samuel 6).[28] If the religion of Judah was at least in some way similar to the better-known religions of the Ancient Near East, the king also must have been an essential part of the official cult of Yahweh. Some of the vestiges in the Hebrew Bible even imply that the king was the son of Yahweh (2 Sam. 7:14; Ps. 2:6–7). Although still relatively little is known about the religion practiced in monarchic Judah and Israel, it is fair to assume that the temple cult of Jerusalem and the king were an integral and crucial part of it. Their destruction in 587/6 BCE would have forced a major reorientation in the religion.

Since the reforming kings represent ideals that were established in Judaism only during the Second Temple period, one has to ask whether it is realistic to assume that these two kings already introduced the new ideas, in the case of Josiah just decades before the destruction and forced reorientation. Instead of assuming the historicity of the controversial biblical texts in question, the reforms may be historically unfounded projections of post 587/6 BCE ideals into monarchic times. This would explain the contradiction that we have between the reforming kings and the religious reality of the monarchic period.

To put it in other words, we know that the religion of Israel in the 9th–8th centuries BCE differed fundamentally from the emerging Judaism of the Second Temple period. Because of the lack of reliable sources from the 7th and 6th centuries BCE, we do not know when and under what circumstances the crucial change took place and whether it was gradual or sudden. Many scholars follow the biblical account and assume that Josiah (or Hezekiah) already introduced many of the new ideas. My point is that the biblical accounts in 2 Kings 22–23 and 2 Kings 18:4 are too uncertain to be used as historical sources. They provide more questions than answers. If we follow the biblical accounts of the reforms, the whole construction of Israel's religion stands or falls on their reliability alone, because it does not receive any support from other sources. The destruction of 587/6 BCE would be a more natural place to seek the turning point in religion, because it meant a forced 'reform' in any case.

---

27 For the sake of the current argument it is not necessary to discuss the nature of the popular religion practiced at private homes and on the local level. 1–2 Kings primarily deals with the 'official' religion of the state.

28 That Yahweh had an image in the temple has become increasingly probable. Cf. the discussion in van der Toorn (1997); esp. Becking (1997), 157–171; Niehr (1997), 73–95; Uehlinger (1997), 97–155.

If the main changes in Israel's religion were the result of the destruction caused by the Babylonians, it is understandable that the biblical authors would have tried to show that the changes were already initiated earlier by pious kings who tried to restore with reforms religious ideals demanded by the divinity in the mythical past. The new religion had to be seen as a restoration of religious ideals that were put into practice before the destruction, because, without some continuity with the monarchic religion, one could easily receive the impression that the new religious ideals were actually the forced result of the destruction caused by Babylonian actions. This would then undermine their credibility and authority. It would not have been in the interests of the biblical authors to emphasize the factual break with the older religion, but instead to try to show at least some continuity with the past. In this scenario it would have been necessary to condemn the past as an almost constant sin, because the past simply did not correspond to the demands of the new religion, but at the same time show that there were some kings who were faithful to the divinity and who represented the ideal.

It is understandable that the later authors would have wanted to eradicate positive references to the older religion, especially in areas where it had proven to be a dead end and where there would be a clear contradiction with the new religious concepts. For example, if we assume that there was an Asherah in Yahweh's temple and it was destroyed in 587/6 BCE, the later authors would have certainly tried to remove all positive references to it and instead interpret it as an illegitimate or foreign element.[29] Rather than referring to the forced destruction of Asherah by the Babylonians, its 'controlled' destruction already before the Babylonians by a pious Judean king, who was executing Yahweh's commandment, would have given much more legitimacy to the new religion that rejected Asherah as a foreign element. Similarly, all references to a pictorial representation of Yahweh would have been highly problematic after his image in the temple had been destroyed. The biblical authors would have had, for obvious reasons, great interest in removing all references to Yahweh's cult image. With slowly increasing archaeological and textual evidence, it has become increasingly evident that the Hebrew Bible mainly contains only vestiges of the monarchic religion and that in most cases they are found in the biased criticism.

---

29 However, some passages may have preserved positive references to a tree, probably an Asherah, growing in Yahweh's temple (Josh. 24:26). The same passage refers to a large stone, evidently a *Massebah*, which Joshua sets inside the temple under the tree.

Dating of the Main Sources for the Reforms

It is probable that both, the Deuteronomy and 1–2 Kings, the main sources for the reforms, were written after 587/6 BCE. The majority of scholars assume that the Deuteronomy is a product of 7th century BCE[30] or of Josiah's time[31] and it is often connected with this period even by scholars who assume that the description in 2 Kings 22–23 is mostly a later literary construction and a pious invention.[32] In view of the book-finding episode in 2 Kings 22:8, 10–11 and/or the parallels between the measures undertaken by Josiah and the laws in Deuteronomy, many scholars have suggested that the oldest version of the Deuteronomy was the basis of Josiah's reform.[33] Although the book-finding episode is now generally accepted as a later addition, many scholars still assume a closer connection between Deuteronomy and Josiah's reform. It is used as a witness to the religious conceptions that emerged during the time of King Josiah.

However, it is very unlikely that the book, even in its earliest forms could derive from the time of Josiah. Several factors suggest that the first edition of Deuteronomy (*Urdeuteronomium*) was written in a context when there was no king, temple or state. I have presented more detailed arguments for dating the *Urdeuteronomium* to a time after 587/6 BCE in another context,[34] and will only provide a summary here:

1. The monarch does not play any role in the *Urdeuteronomium*, which would be exceptional from a legal document in the Ancient Near East. The document implies a setting when there was no king.
2. The Deuteronomy does not imply or refer to any state infrastructure and organization, which one would expect from a document regulating Judah's religion and society.
3. There is no reference to Judah, which one would expect if it was the legal or religious foundation of the state of Judah.
4. The temple is never mentioned, although its main goal was to centralize the sacrificial cult, allegedly to the temple in Jerusalem. This implies a context where there was no temple and the

30 For example, Otto (1999), 364–378; Nelson (2002), 6; Schmid (2008), 106.

31 Veijola (2004), 2–3.

32 Thus Levin (2005), 91; cf. Levin (1984), 351–371.

33 The connection was made already by de Wette (1805), Dissertatio critico-exegetica, in the early 19th century CE. This view has been assumed by many.

34 Cf. Pakkala (2009), 388–401.

author was not even certain that there would ever be one in the future.

5. The Deuteronomy never mentions Jerusalem. To avoid a direct reference to the city implies very special circumstances, or a motivation and background in a narrative context. In this form, the Deuteronomy cannot function as an independent document, as assumed in historical reconstructions that argue for a monarchical dating.
6. Deut. 12:14[35] is dependent on the late concept of Israel consisting of (twelve?) tribes, because it refers to a place in 'one of your tribes' (באחד שבטיך).[36]
7. The Deuteronomy is formally set in the future, which implies a literary context, like its current narrative framework, that justifies the use of the future (see 5 above).
8. According to Deut. 12:21, Yahweh will place his name to live in the place he will choose. The conception that only the divinity's name lives in the temple implies that the temple had already ceased to be the actual dwelling place of his cult image or of his Presence.
9. The Elephantine papyri (see above) imply that the principles of the Deuteronomy were not commonly known in the late 5th century BCE.
10. Many laws in the Deuteronomy are idealistic rather than laws meant to be put into practice. If we connect the Deuteronomy with Josiah or his reform, this implies that the laws were put into practice during his time.

Consequently, several features indicate that the oldest version of the Deuteronomy was written after the destruction of the monarchy, state and the temple in 587/6 BCE. Even if one could question some of the arguments above, the weight of the evidence suggests a dating much after Josiah's reign. This would also mean that the Deuteronomy primarily contains religious conceptions of a post-monarchic setting. The factors presented above imply that the consequences of the destruction had already been drawn and that the authors had already moved away from conceptions that a monarchical setting would necessitate.

As for 1–2 Kings, it is not possible here to go into the debate about the relationship of 2 Kings 24–25 to the rest of 1–2 Kings, which has

---

35 Pakkala (2009), 395, erroneously refers to Deut. 12:13. I am grateful to Robert Whiting for the correction.

36 The late dating of the concept of Israel consisting of twelve tribes has been shown by Levin (1995).

played a central role in the different dating of the composition by the 'Double Redaction Model' and the Göttingen School. If one assumes that the final chapters are part of the oldest version of 1–2 Kings, then the work was obviously written after 587/6 BCE, or 562 BCE if 2 Kings 25:27–30 is also regarded as part of the oldest text.[37] Regardless of the final chapters, some factors imply that the first edition of 1–2 Kings cannot have been written during monarchic times.[38]

The author of the main edition of 1–2 Kings judges the Judean (and Israelite) kings as if he were superior to the dynasty. He is in a position to criticize the kings and to judge many of the kings of the dynasty as evil. This is always possible, but very improbable in circles close to the monarch or within the court, because it would seriously undermine the authority and legitimacy of the entire dynasty, even if the current king were judged to be good, like Josiah. It would mean that the royal house had placed itself not only under the evaluation of scribes, but indirectly of all readers. The dynasty would no longer exist in its own right, but would be under continuous scrutiny and subject to theological evaluation. Therefore, the document could not have been commissioned by the royal house or circles close to the royal house, but rather implies a situation where there was no king or when the king was not in power. In the author's context the theologians appear to be in power.

One could suggest that the document was written by circles critical of or out of the reach of the royal house, but this is improbable, because the authors evidently had access to the royal annals and other royal documents. During the time of the monarchy, this would be possible only if the author(s) were very close to the royal house, because it is very unlikely that the annals were in free circulation to be edited by anyone. Moreover, a book like 1–2 Kings was a major undertaking in the ancient world and would require financial resources and professional expertise, which implies an influential and powerful group at the background. The best solution for this paradox is to assume that 1–2 Kings was written by the royal scribes, or a group representing their followers or pupils, *after* the royal house was no longer in power. In this situation the royal scribes would still be a powerful group, but would be in a position to evaluate the deeds of the royal house. Their

37 Because of the evident contrast between Jehoiakin and Zedekiah, it is probable that 2 Kings 25:27–30 belongs to the same literary layer as 2 Kings 24:18–25:7.

38 Here, it is necessary to distinguish between the royal annals of Judah and Israel, which functioned as the main source for the events during the reigns of each king, and the composition by the history writer, whose perspective was essentially theological.

background in the royal court would also explain why they interpreted and evaluated the past through the actions of the royal house.

Unless one acknowledges that the attack on other gods is a later theme (see below), the criticism of the temple cult also implies a setting after 587/6 BCE. 1–2 Kings effectively undermines the temple as an institution by presenting it as a place of constant sin and rebellion. As with the royal house, the open criticism and style of writing opens the institution to be evaluated by readers. In the author's context the temple and its priests could not have been the center of the religion anymore, whereas it is reasonable to assume that in monarchic times the temple was the highest authority of the religion, which effectively defined it. The author of 1–2 Kings is able to place himself above the temple and criticize it in a way that was possible only after the temple had been destroyed and the temple elite had lost their power in the society.

Consequently, the documents used to argue for the historicity of the cult reforms were written in a time after the destruction of Jerusalem in 587/6 BCE.[39] This does not necessarily mean that they could not preserve any information about events before the destruction, but since their religious context of writing most likely differs essentially from the monarchic one, it is probable that the past was evaluated from a very new perspective. With these considerations in mind, we can now turn to the two passages in question.

Hezekiah's Reform

Hezekiah's reform is restricted to one verse only, 2 Kings 18:4.

הוּא הֵסִיר אֶת־הַבָּמוֹת וְשִׁבַּר אֶת־הַמַּצֵּבֹת וְכָרַת אֶת־הָאֲשֵׁרָה וְכִתַּת נְחַשׁ הַנְּחֹשֶׁת אֲשֶׁר־עָשָׂה מֹשֶׁה כִּי עַד־הַיָּמִים הָהֵמָּה הָיוּ בְנֵי־יִשְׂרָאֵל מְקַטְּרִים לוֹ וַיִּקְרָא־לוֹ נְחֻשְׁתָּן.

Hezekiah is said to have abolished the high places (הוּא הֵסִיר אֶת־הַבָּמוֹת). It is very probable that this was part of the history writer's text, although some scholars, such as *Benzinger* and *Würthwein*, have assumed that this would also be a later addition.[40] Without this comment in 18:4aα^1 it would be difficult to see why Hezekiah was evaluated so positively and likened to David. He was the first, and one of the only two, who removed the high places. Without the high places, the theo-

39 For a detailed discussion, see Noth (1967), 91–95.

40 Benzinger (1899), 177; Würthwein (1984), 406–412. According to Benzinger, only v. 4a is a later addition to v. 4b, which would have been taken from the annals, whereas Würthwein assumes that the entire verse was added after the history writer.

logical profile of the history writer would diminish and it would be difficult to see what his criteria for evaluating the past were. Also, the systematic reference to the high places implies that we are dealing with one of the main theological issues of the history writer. In comparison, most of the other religious phenomena are criticized only irregularly. For example, of all the kings of Judah only Rehabeam and Manasseh are accused of harboring Asherah. There are also no literary critical arguments for removing 18:4aα^1 from the text.

It has traditionally been assumed that the removal of the high places derives from the royal annals,[41] but this seems unlikely because the other probable excerpts from the annals are found in vv. 7b–10, divided from v. 4 by several theological comments about Hezekiah in vv. 5–7a. Moreover, before Hezekiah the verb is always used in connection with the high places when a Judean king is characterized as good:

1 Kings 15:14	Asa	וְהַבָּמוֹת לֹא־סָרוּ
1 Kings 22:44	Jehoshaphat	אַךְ הַבָּמוֹת לֹא־סָרוּ
2 Kings 12:4	Joash	רַק הַבָּמוֹת לֹא־סָרוּ
2 Kings 14:4	Amaziah	רַק הַבָּמוֹת לֹא־סָרוּ
2 Kings 15:4	Azariah	רַק הַבָּמוֹת לֹא־סָרוּ
2 Kings 15:35	Jotam	רַק הַבָּמוֹת לֹא סָרוּ
2 Kings 18:4	Hezekiah	הוּא הֵסִיר אֶת־הַבָּמוֹת

Although the verb is used slightly differently in connection with Hezekiah than with the other kings (qal. vs. hif.),[42] it would be difficult to avoid the impression that its systematic use in this connection is intentional. The regular reference to the high places with the same verb implies that the references were an intentional creation by the editor of the whole composition. The emphasis הוּא before the verb in 2 Kings 18:4aα^1 connects Hezekiah's action with the accounts of the previous kings, where the sin still continued. As an excerpt from the annals the empha-

41 For example Montgomery/Gehman (1951), 481; Hobbs (1985), 251–252 and Fritz (2003), 359. Also Steuernagel (1912), 365 (but with some hesitation). According to Gray (1963), 608, verse 4 "reads like an excerpt from an annalistic source."

42 Whereas Hezekiah is the subject of 2 Kings 18:4, the subject of the verb in the other passages is in the plural and therefore either refers to the high places themselves or to the people. As a consequence the verb must be understood in a slightly different way. Hezekiah removed (הֵסִיר) the high places, but during the time of the other kings, the high places did not stop (from operating) (high places being the subject) or the people did not turn aside from the high places. Neither of the solutions is ideal, and the problems are reflected already in the Greek translations where the subject is changed from the plural to the singular (ἐξῆρεν, e.g., 1 Kings 15:14, 22:44) or the verb is translated in the passive form (μετεστάθησαν, 2 Kings 12:3/4). The author of the original evaluation may have wanted to avoid a direct accusation of the kings, who he regarded as good, and therefore avoided having the king as the subject.

sis would not make much sense. That the author of 2 Kings 18:$4a\alpha^1$ did not specify what was meant by the high places is a further indication that he assumed the readers to have read the preceding text where the problem is specified. Several passages, such as 1 Kings 22:44, tell the reader that sacrifices by the people were meant (עוֹד הָעָם מְזַבְּחִים וּמְקַטְּרִים בַּבָּמוֹת). This had been repeated so many times that the author of 2 Kings 18:$4a\alpha^1$ did not need to repeat it again. As an excerpt from the royal annals, however, the short comment would be puzzling. In other words, v. $4a\alpha^1$ implies that the reader knew what was said about the high places in the rest of 1–2 Kings.[43] The author's viewpoint was the entire history of Israel and Judah, which the authors of the annals, writing in very many different contexts in different centuries, could not have had. This undermines the assumption that the reference was taken from the royal annals or from another source. Several scholars have similarly argued that הוּא הֵסִיר אֶת־הַבָּמוֹת was written by the history writer.[44]

It has been shown by Provan that the rest of v. $4a\alpha^2\beta b$ derives from a later editor.[45] The main technical reason for assuming an interpolation is the cop. perf., which is peculiar and even grammatically incorrect in such a prose context. In other passages that contain lists of further sins that were practiced or removed the verbs are typically expressed with a cons. Impf.,[46] which is also the standard prose form throughout 1–2 Kings. The use of the perfect is probably due to Aramaic influence where the perfect is the usual mode of expression in a prose text.[47] The use of an Aramaic form of expression implies that the expansion was made at a much later stage when the editor already had difficulties with the basic rules of classical Hebrew. In other passages in the Book of Kings the atypical cop. perf. is often regarded as a sign of later expansion or other disturbance.[48] That we are dealing with a very late

---

43 In comparison, 1 Kings 3:4 represents a different editorial phase because the author does not seem to be aware that the high places were forbidden.

44 E.g., Hoffmann (1980), 146–148; Provan (1988), 85–88 (but with a very early dating of the author); Sweeney (2007), 402–403 and Levin (2008), 146.

45 Provan (1988), 85–88; similarly Levin (2008), 146–147. On the other hand, Hoffmann (1980), 146–148, has argued that all of v. 4a derives from the history writer.

46 For example in 2 Kings 21 Manasseh is said to have וַיָּשָׁב וַיִּבֶן אֶת־הַבָּמוֹת . . . וַיָּקֶם מִזְבְּחֹת לַבַּעַל וַיַּעַשׂ אֲשֵׁרָה . . . וַיִּשְׁתַּחוּ . . . Asa is said to have וַיַּעֲבֵר הַקְּדֵשִׁים מִן־הָאָרֶץ וַיָּסַר אֶת־כָּל־הַגִּלֻּלִים אֲשֶׁר עָשׂוּ אֲבֹתָיו (1 Kings 15:12).

47 Levin (2008), 146, and already Gesenius/Kautzsch (1995), § 112 pp.

48 Thus Stade (1907), 201–26. According to Gesenius/Kautzsch (1995), § 112 pp, the cop. perf. in 1 Kings 12:32; 2 Kings 11:2; 14:14; 23:4, 10, 12, 15 may indicate an interpolation.

interpolation is further suggested by the probable dependency of 2 Kings 18:4 on Exod. 34:13 (or Deut. 7:5) and Num. 21:9.

Exod. 34:13	כִּי אֶת־מִזְבְּחֹתָם תִּתֹּצוּן **וְאֶת־מַצֵּבֹתָם תְּשַׁבֵּרוּן** **וְאֶת־אֲשֵׁרָיו תִּכְרֹתוּן**	וְשִׁבַּר אֶת־הַמַּצֵּבֹת וְכָרַת אֶת־הָאֲשֵׁרָה
Deut. 7:5	מִזְבְּחֹתֵיהֶם תִּתֹּצוּ **וּמַצֵּבֹתָם תְּשַׁבֵּרוּ** **וַאֲשֵׁירֵהֶם** תְּגַדֵּעוּן וּפְסִילֵיהֶם **תִּשְׂרְפוּן** בָּאֵשׁ	
Num. 21:9	וַיַּעַשׂ מֹשֶׁה נְחַשׁ נְחֹשֶׁת	וְכִתַּת נְחַשׁ הַנְּחֹשֶׁת אֲשֶׁר־עָשָׂה מֹשֶׁה

It is unlikely that Exod. 34:13 (or Deut. 7:5) and Num. 21:9 could have used 2 Kings 18:4 because then one would have to assume that two editors of the Pentateuch independently adopted two different parts of 2 Kings 18:4 without any overlap. Although one could argue that the references in 2 Kings 18:4 derive from two different editors (v. 4b being a further development), the similar use of the atypical perfect and the use of the Pentateuch suggest that we are dealing with the same late editor who added all additional measures to purify the cult. Consequently, in the history writer's text, Hezekiah's reform is reduced to a short note that he removed the high places.

What remains of the reform for the historical reconstruction of Israel's history? The preserved excerpts from the annals do not contain any reference to a reform or any other measure that was connected to the cult, which means that the only source for the event consists of a couple of words in a theologically oriented composition written at least more than a century after Hezekiah. It is evident that one cannot build any broader historical reconstruction of Israel's history or religion during the monarchic period on this comment. Its background is in the history writer's theological conceptions of a much later time.

The reason for the invention of Hezekiah's cult reform may be the fact that he was otherwise considered as a very able and successful king. During his 29-year reign the economic and political importance of Jerusalem and Judah grew considerably, probably because of the destruction of Israel, which had earlier been the center. The refugees from Israel may have brought in additional technical skill and financial potential. The extensive building activities during his time, which are commonly acknowledged and which have also left traces in the archaeological record, were not left unnoticed by the history writer (see 2 Kings 20:20). That Hezekiah opposed the Assyrians may have been regarded as a positive factor as well, because Judean kings who allied with the Assyrians were regarded as very evil (Ahaz and Manasseh), while those who opposed them received a favorable evaluation (Hezekiah and Josiah).[49] That Hosea, the king of Israel, rebelled against Assyria may have been the reason he was regarded as less evil than other kings of Israel (2 Kings 17:2–4). One should further note that the collapse of Israel was an ideal time to abolish the high places, because the main sin of Israel, the cultic separation of Israel from Jerusalem, ceased to be a problem. That Hezekiah was able to retain independence when Israel was not was perhaps a further positive factor. It is likely that the history writer's conviction that Hezekiah removed the cult sprang up from some or all of these elements. In any case, here we are already in post-monarchic times, where he is building his view of this able king on the basis of late conceptions. There is no reason to assume any cult reform during the time of this king.

Josiah's Reform

Josiah's reform is a puzzle of themes and literary layers, which may have lost so many pieces that it will always remain unsolvable. One cannot exclude the possibility that the available text is partly corrupted and/or rewritten. Even if all the pieces of the puzzle were still present in 2 Kings 22–23, the text is so complicated that one can find problems in all solutions. It is difficult to get a grip on anything that holds. Nevertheless, the nature of the problems is such that any solution has to assume a complicated redaction history where the text was repeatedly corrected and expanded. This is implied by the repetitions, thematic inconsistencies and tensions, as well as several grammatical and other problems.[50] In addition, many parts of the text are literarily connected to other passages of 1–2 Kings,[51] which implies a complicated history of dependence and influence to and from other texts. Further complicating any solution, vocabulary and phrases typical of the attack on foreign cults abounds in this passage. The text has been so heavily edited that, if it is used for any historical purpose, the extent of the later additions has to be understood. We cannot penetrate the theology of the later editors without identifying their contributions. A failure to do so

49 Josiah may have tried to fight the Egyptians who went to help the Assyrians (2 Kings 23:29). The meaning of this verse is disputed.

50 For example, the king is suddenly introduced as the one who removes or destroys the illicit cultic items (in 23:4b, while in v. 4a he commands the priests to do so). The text atypically uses the cop. perf. (for example in 23:4b, 5, 8b, 10, 14). The singular is used when the context clearly would necessitate a plural (v. 5: וְִיִקַטֵּר). There are words that do not seem to fit the context, for example, הִשְׁבִּית (to cause to stop) referring to the killing (?) of priests.

51 E.g., 1 Kings 11:5, 7; 15:12–13; 2 Kings 23:12, 15–17, 19.

would leave us with the theology of the later editors, but would hardly give a reliable picture of what the older textual phases said about Josiah. In other words, without an argued solution to the problems, we do not have a source at all. The countless problems and literary connections of the text are generally accepted, but the consequences are often not seen.

Several scholars have tried to find external fixed points for 2 Kings 22–23 by using archaeological finds[52] but so far one has only been able to show possible broader lines of development that could make sense if there were a reform. Clearly, the nature of the archaeological evidence is such that it would be difficult to find direct evidence for a specific event such as a reform. Archaeological evidence cannot distinguish between the reign of Josiah and 587 BCE, or between the reigns of Manasseh and Josiah. Therefore, much of the discussion about archaeological evidence is tied to attempts to validate or disprove what the Bible says. But the dangers and limitations of this approach have to be acknowledged. For example, if seals from Judah are increasingly aniconic towards the end of the monarchy, should we assume on the basis of 2 Kings 23 that iconographical representations of the divine were banned by Josiah? One cannot exclude this possibility, but 2 Kings 23 does not say anything about Yahweh's iconic representations and it has often been shown that the ban on making an idol or other pictorial representation of Yahweh belongs to the latest editorial phases of Deuteronomy and 1–2 Kings.[53] A cult reform would, for example, not explain why one would not carve a picture of an ibex or a flower, unless one assumes that Josiah's reform included a systematic iconoclasm. In other words, the tendency to increasingly prefer aniconic seals cannot be directly connected with 2 Kings 23.

The main problem with these attempts is that we still know very little about the historical and religious context of the late 7th century BCE in Judah. Much of what is usually assumed about the religious context of the late monarchic period in Judah has been built on Josiah's reform, or on an interpretation of what it is thought to have been. Many of the earlier archaeological attempts to find fixed points about the reform have later been shown as highly unlikely. The archaeological evidence was interpreted in view of the biblical text.[54] Without the biblical text, no archaeological findings or non-Biblical ancient text would have giv-

52 For example, Uehlinger (2007), 279–316. For further discussion, see below.

53 Cf. Köckert (2007), 272–290.

54 For example, Aharoni (1968), 233–234. For review and criticism, see Uehlinger (2007), 287–292.

en any reason to assume a cult reform in Judah.[55] In more recent discussion, parts of the biblical text have been compared with external evidence in the hope of finding connections that could then give indications about the original historical background and dating of the texts in question. For example, it has been discussed whether the reference to the chariots of the sun in 2 Kings 23:11 could correspond to something in the Assyrian religious cult, which would then be used as an argument for the Assyrian origin of the verse (for discussion, see below). Some possible connections may even be established, but one should not lose sight of the fact that such a discussion is bound to 2 Kings 22–23 and about its reliability as a source. Consequently, it is necessary to understand the development and other complexities of the biblical text before we even have a source that can be compared with other evidence. For example, a passage may consist of several additions from different centuries. If we can establish that one part of the passage was very probably aware of an Assyrian cult practice, it does not mean that the whole passage was written during the Neo-Assyrian period.

Of all the countless redaction critical solutions offered to 2 Kings 22–23 that of Levin may be the most convincing.[56] Although often characterized as minimalistic and radical,[57] the reconstructed text corresponds well with what we know about the history writer and the later editorial stages in the rest of 1–2 Kings.[58]

Excursus: The Main Editorial Phases of 1–2 Kings

1–2 Kings is the product of several authors and editors, but three main phases of development can be distinguished: 1. Excerpts from the royal annals, which may provide substantial evidence from the monarchic period. 2. The edition by the history writer, who, by using the annals as source material, created a theological interpretation of the past. 3. Nomistic additions, which represent several successive editors. In addition to these editorial phases, the text contains several individual additions and glosses. Some of the very latest additions attack idols and idol worshippers.

55 As noted about the archaeological evidence by Uehlinger (2007), 279, "'Josiah's reform' […] is essentially a scholarly construct built upon the biblical tradition; without that tradition no one would look out for a 'cult reform' when studying the archaeology of Judah of the Iron Age II C."

56 See Levin (1984), 351–371, reprinted in Levin (2003), 198–216. Some further comments in Levin (2008), 149–150.

57 E.g., by Uehlinger (2007), 298–300.

58 Similarly Niehr (1995), 39–41, who has taken Levin's redaction critical analysis as the basis for his own reconstruction of Josiah's time.

> The most evident differences between the editors are met especially in the conceptions about the divine, which implies that considerable changes took place in the context of the authors or in Israel's religion. One of the main aims of the nomists was to show that the worship of other gods is against Yahweh's will and that it was one of the main sins of the past. These editors were not monotheists, because the main problem was that the Israelites worshipped the gods of other nations. According to them, the Israelites should only worship Yahweh. The worship of other gods, Baal, Asherah and the Host of Heaven was one of the main reasons that led to the destruction of Israel in 722 BCE and Judah in 587/6 BCE. These editors also emphasized the Law as the basis and center of Israel's religion, but the emphasis is particularly evident in the later stages of the nomistic texts. The nomistic editors represent a large editorial phase in 1–2 Kings so that their viewpoint is very dominant in the 'final' edition of the book.
>
> The main aims of the history writer were to provide a history of the Davidic dynasty and to show that Jerusalem is the only legitimate place of worship. All kings of the North were systematically condemned because they 'followed the sins of Jeroboam' and continued to sacrifice outside Jerusalem. Jeroboam's sin only referred to the location of sacrifice and not to the idols or worship of other gods.[59] The golden bulls were added later by editors who wanted to connect Jeroboam with idol worship. The sin for both, Judah and Israel, was in principle the same. Both sacrificed outside Jerusalem, but Israel's sin was more severe because they only sacrificed outside Jerusalem, whereas the Judeans sacrificed in Jerusalem as well. The North had broken all cultic contact with Jerusalem and thus with the Yahweh of Jerusalem, and this was an unforgivable sin, whereas Judah always preserved the cultic connection with the Yahweh of Jerusalem. The location of sacrifice was the main religious criterion by which the history writer evaluated the past. The history writer was not concerned about idols or other gods.
>
> The Davidic dynasty played a dominant role in the history writer's text. He wanted to show that the dynastic succession was unbroken from David to Jehoiakin. The contrast with the North, with its constant *coup d'états* and changing dynasties, is evident. The history writer's message is clear. Jehoiakin would represent the legitimate dynastic line if the dynasty were ever to continue.[60] He wanted to show that Zedekiah could not represent the legitimate line. It is probable that the question of dynastic succession was a central issue in the author's context.

Levin's solution also explains how the text developed later by a chain of associations. It has often been assumed that the oldest text consisted

---

59 For details see Pakkala (2008), 501–525.

60 For details see Pakkala (2006), 443–452.

of a list of more or less independent reform measures,[61] which is always possible, but certainly less convincing than a theory that is also able to explain their interrelationship and development from one to another. Moreover, in trying to find a historical core and some evidence from the time of Josiah, most solutions have neglected how heavy the impact of later editors has been.[62] However, some important alterations to Levin's reconstruction are necessary, as we will see.

It has become evident that the main interest of the history writer in 1–2 Kings is the location of the cult.[63] His main criticism of the kings deals with the high places. Every king from Rehabeam to Hezekiah is criticized for having allowed sacrifices to continue in the high places. Hezekiah removed the high places, but they were rebuilt by Manasseh. If Josiah did not defile them and thus abolish their worship, the problem would remain unsolved. The problem is never mentioned after Josiah, which implies that Josiah solved the problem.[64] If Josiah did not destroy the high places, it would be difficult to comprehend the history writer's main religious conceptions of evaluating the past.

2 Kings 23:8a is the only passage in 2 Kings 22–23 that describes the destruction (or defilement) of the Judean high places. Without this verse, the problem would remain. Moreover, several later additions in the following and preceding text are evidently dependent on v. 8a, which implies that the verse belongs to an early stage in the development of the text. Consequently, any reconstruction of 2 Kings 22–23 should include 23:8a in the basic text of the history writer. Although some scholars have assumed that it is a later addition,[65] it would be hard to see how the chapter could have developed into its present form and scope without v. 8a being at least one of the cores.

---

61 E.g., Gray (1963), 663–677; Hoffmann (1980), 212–270, esp. 264–265. According to Fritz (2003), 406, "[t]he reform includes numerous measures that may have been introduced over a long period of time."

62 Many maximalist solutions have been carefully argued, e.g., by Hoffmann (1980), 212–270, but many histories of Israel and introductions to the Hebrew Bible have adopted a maximalist view without any discussion of the problems and the development of the texts that were used as the basis of the view. E.g., Miller/Hayes (2006), 413–414; Collins (2007), 150–151.

63 It is not possible to discuss here the relationship between 1–2 Kings and the other books of the so-called 'Deuteronomistic History'. It seems increasingly probable that the connection between the different books is much weaker than traditionally assumed. It is probable, however, that 1–2 Kings, at least from 1 Kings 12 onwards, can be treated as a single composition.

64 Israel is also criticized for the same sin because Jeroboam's sin was to build the temples of the high places (1 Kings 12:31 בֵּית בָּמוֹת).

65 E.g., Würthwein (1984), 411–412; Kratz (2000), 173, 193.

By reporting the killing (הִשְׁבִּית) of the priests of the high places, v. 5 partly competes with v. 8a. One could argue that instead of v. 8a, v. 5 is the core of the passage. However, it is more probable that this verse is a later addition. The use of the cop. perf. הִשְׁבִּית suggests that this verse was written by an editor who was uncertain about the rules of classical Hebrew. Moreover, it makes the priests of the high places worshippers of other gods, which was not the history writer's concern. At least there is no evidence in other passages of 1–2 Kings that other gods were worshipped at the high places. Later editors of some passages have made additions that may give such an impression, but these are later (2 Kings 21:3b). In any case, v. 5 would be dependent on v. 8a, because v. 5 does not report the destruction of the high places. Without v. 8a the high places would remain. That v. 5 is not a part of the same literary layer as v. 8a is suggested by the fact that the priests are killed in v. 5, whereas in v. 8a they are brought to Jerusalem. That v. 5 uses an atypical word for the priests (כְּמָרִים vs. כֹּהֲנִים) is not necessarily an indication that v. 5 is early,[66] but certainly implies that different authors are behind the verses.

According to Kratz, the core of the reform should be sought in 2 Kings 23:4a, 11 and 12aα[1], parts of which could also derive from the annals.[67] This reconstruction has the advantage of connecting the removal of the symbols of astral worship with the removal of the horses and chariots of the sun. The main problem with this view is that the high places would play no role in the history writer's text of 2 Kings 22–23. The high places, which were the main problem until Hezekiah, would then remain after Manasseh had restored them in 2 Kings 21:3a.[68] In view of many other passages in 1–2 Kings that clearly show that the high places are the main sin, this, as we have seen, seems very unlikely.

Several technical and thematic considerations suggest that 22:10–23:3 derive from a late stage in the development of 1–2 Kings.[69] That 2 Kings 23:4a originally followed 22:3–7, 9 is seen in the way the verse continues the king's orders to Hilkiah. Moreover, 2 Kings 23:4 is thematically connected with 22:3–7, 9. Both deal with changes made in the

---

66 Nevertheless, according to Uehlinger (2007), 303–305, כמרים may be a sign that the verse is early. For further discussion on the word כמרים, see below.

67 Kratz (2000), 173, 193.

68 Note that Kratz, op. cit., ascribes 2 Kings 18:4aα[1] and 2 Kings 21:3a to the source (but both with hesitation). Without 18:4aα[1], it would be difficult to see the reason for characterizing Hezekiah as the most pious king after David. Similarly, without 2 Kings 21:3a there would be no reason for the extremely negative evaluation of Manasseh.

69 For argumentation see Levin (1984), 355–360; id. (2003), 207–209; Pakkala (1999), 171–175.

temple, whereas the text in between develops the passage towards a reform that was caused by the finding of the Book of the Law. Everything between verses 22:9 and 23:4 was added later, but in several stages. Here, we are already in a stage where the Law had replaced the temple as the center of Israel's religion, and where the cult reform was based on the Law.

Although older than 2 Kings 22:10–23:3, it is unlikely that 23:4–7 is part of the history writer's text. In these verses the foreign cults are the main issue. A similar development where the cult centralization represents the older text, but which the later editors expanded to an attack against illicit cults, idols and other gods is met in other parts of 1–2 Kings[70] as well as in the Deuteronomy.[71] 2 Kings 23:8b–20 contains many interpolations that have added, in several stages, more and more locations where the high places were removed. Levin has shown the literary growth and chain of development in 2 Kings 23. The arguments need not be repeated here.[72] A chart showing the development of the chapter should suffice:

70 For example in 1 Kings 15:12–13; 18:4.

71 Deut. 12:8–12, 13–14, 17–18, 21 represents an earlier literary phase and deals with the location of sacrificial cult, whereas later editors have made several additions (Deut. 12:2–7; 12:28–13:19), which primarily deal with the worship of other gods. Cf. Veijola (2004), 262–293; Petry (2007), 101–103.

72 See Levin (1984), 355–360; id. (2003), 207–209. See also Pakkala (1999), 170–180.

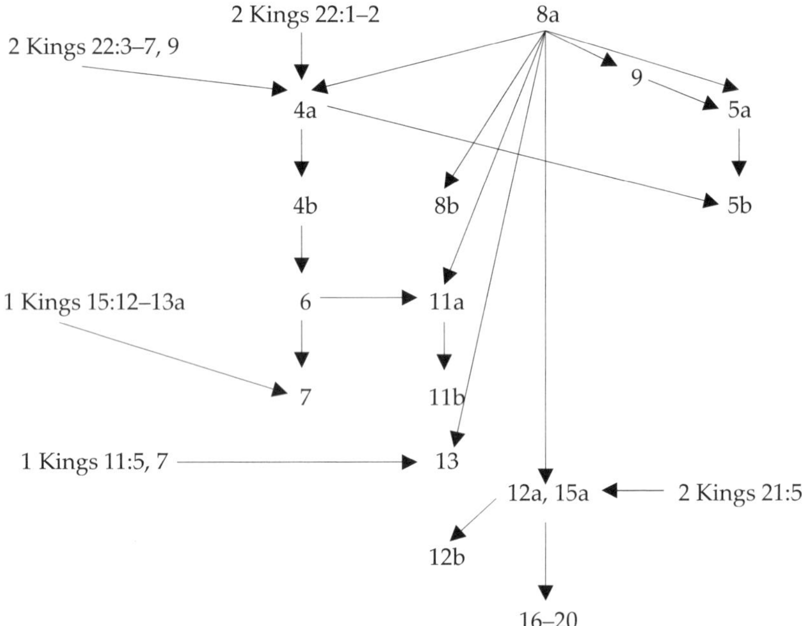

According to Levin, v. 8a is the only core of the reform and "everything else is younger, nothing is from a source."[73] That the original text is so radically shorter than the final text would be surprising, but not impossible. The reigns of many other kings are similarly short reports. It is also understandable that an important turning point in Israel's religion would have attracted considerable attention from later editors. In most cases Levin's argumentation is persuasive. He is able to demonstrate the chains of dependencies and associations.

The main problem with Levin's reconstruction is that it does not provide any explanation why Josiah was made the champion of the cult centralization. If the sources of the history writer did not contain anything that would have given the author a reason to make Josiah the most pious king, one would have to assume that the reform was a pure and calculated invention. This is always possible, but not necessarily probable. Many biblical authors were creative authors, but they were usually inspired by what they found in the older texts.[74] New ideas are often reactions to the older text, which is developed further. The chain

73 Levin (2003), 207. 2 Kings 22:1–2; 23:25a* and 28–30 would also have been part of the history writer's text.

74 For an excellent discussion and examples of the innovative nature of biblical authors and editors, see Levinson (1998).

of associations and additions in 2 Kings 23:4–20 is a prime example of this.

It is surprising that Levin takes out 2 Kings 22:3–7, 9 as an addition to the history writer's text.[75] He assumes that it was a separate fragment from an unknown source or from the royal annals, but not yet part of the history writer's text. The reason for his assumption is that 2 Kings 22:3–7, 9 broke the original connection between 22:1–2 and 23:8a.[76] It is also probable that 2 Kings 22:3–7, 9 and 23:8a were not written by the same author, because in 22:3–7, 9 the king orders Hilkiah the priest to take measures to restore the temple, whereas 2 Kings 23:8a suddenly implies that the king is the executor of the reforms. 2 Kings 23:8a would then be a fitting continuation to 22:2 where the king is similarly the subject. But these problems may only indicate that 22:3–7, 9 was probably written by a different author than 22:1–2 and 23:8a. The question is, which one preceded the other, 22:3–7, 9 or 23:8a.

If we assume that the passage developed by way of associations here as well, a development from 2 Kings 22:3–7, 9 to 23:8a is more understandable than the opposite direction of influence. If we assume that the annals contained a passage about Josiah making repairs in the temple, it would have been logical for the history writer to interpret Josiah as a pious king who cared for the temple. It is only a short step from there to a king who fights for the exclusivity of the temple and who removes the cult sites that competed with the temple. The original idea of cult centralization would not have come from the annals, but from the history writer's own theology, but 2 Kings 22:3–7, 9 would explain why Josiah was made the most pious king and hence became the pivotal figure in the cult centralization. Without 22:3–7, 9 it remains a puzzle what the background of 23:8a was, and there would be no explanation why Josiah, of all kings, was made the cult centralizer *par excellence*. In Levin's reconstruction the annals would not have contained anything that gave a reason to make Josiah the one who removed the high places and one would then have to conclude that Josiah's reform was a calculated fabrication.

If 2 Kings 22:3–7, 9 was a later addition to 23:8a, it would also be difficult to explain why the passage was added. The removal of the high places is only a vague background for repairing the temple, and 22:3–7, 9 does not seem to develop the idea any further. 2 Kings 22:3–7, 9 would remain an isolated passage without a clear function. Additions

75 2 Kings 22:8 is certainly a later addition by an editor who connected the reform with the Law. The passage may contain other additions as well, but they need not concern us here. According to Levin, op. cit., 4b, 5bα, 6, 7 were added later.

76 Levin (2003), 201; id. (2008), 149–150.

usually have a function in the new text. Such an isolated later addition from an external source, which is not integrated to the older text, would be exceptional in 1–2 Kings. Of course, some later editors then used these verses as a background for the finding of the Law, but this is a much later addition, as shown by many. Consequently, it is probable that 2 Kings 22:3–7, 9 was the spark and foundation of Josiah's reform and already an integral part of the history writer's text, most likely taken from one of his sources.

According to Levin, v. 11 is one of the latest additions to the chapter because it may be a further *Fortschreibung* of vv. 4–6, which consists of many phases of late additions. Josiah would not only have removed the priests who sacrificed to the sun, but also destroyed the items used to worship the sun.[77] Verse 5a is already a very late addition (note the cop. perf.), which is then further expanded in v. 5b by a reference to the sacrifices to the sun (and other gods). Verse 11 would then be a further development inspired by at least v. 4 and 5b and thus be one of the latest additions to the chapter.

Levin's conclusions are in manifest contradiction with those of most other scholars because it is usually assumed that this verse may preserve an excerpt from the annals[78] and be the clearest indication that Josiah took some measures to renew the cult. According to Uehlinger, "the removal of the horses and chariots of the sun […] can be traced back to Josiah with great probability."[79] Spieckermann has pointed out that v. 11 does not use vocabulary typical of the attack on other gods and their cults.[80] Horses or chariots of the sun are unknown in the biblical attack on foreign cults. Spieckermann has argued that the Assyrian period in the 7th century BCE is the most probable context for the horses and chariots. He connects the verse with the Assyrian *tāmītu* ritual, where both, living horses and a chariot, have a function. That the horses were kept beside the chamber of the city governor could indicate that the official, as part of the Assyrian administration, had a supervisory function in the cult. Spieckermann further identifies the שֶׁמֶשׁ of v. 11 with the Assyrian god Shamash. Verse 11 would then witness to the Assyrian cult being officially practiced in Jerusalem, possibly in the temple of Yahweh, under Assyrian supervision.[81]

77 Levin (2003), 206.
78 Thus many; for example Würthwein (1984), 453, 459.
79 Uehlinger (2007), 301.
80 Spieckermann (1982), 109.
81 See Spieckermann (1982), 245–251.

Although some of Spieckermann's conclusions may be overdrawn[82] and considerable uncertainties remain as to the exact meaning and background of the horses and chariots, it has become apparent that an Assyrian background of 2 Kings 23:11 is more probable than a later context. It would be problematic to reject the connections with the Assyrian period outright.[83]

Uehlinger has pointed out that since Yahweh himself was probably regarded as a solar deity since the 10th century BCE,[84] it would have been logical that Assyrian religious customs and items with a solar aspect could have found their way into the temple of the Judean solar God in the 8th and 7th century BCE. In other words, an amalgamation of Assyrian practices or influence with Judean beliefs and customs would be quite possible so that one would not have to assume a cult forced and/or supervised by the Assyrians. However, it would require a very good reason, if not a complete catastrophe, for a religion to attack aspects of its own god or to change him into something else. Uehlinger's implication is that Josiah stripped Yahweh of his solar status, but why would he do that and where did the idea come from. The destabilizing aspects would also have to be taken into consideration (see above).

On the other hand, it is not an unreasonable assumption that the collapse of the Assyrian empire and the ensuing liberation of Judah from Assyrian vassalage would have meant the removal of symbols of Assyrian domination from Jerusalem. This would probably happen even if there had been no coercion. The removal of symbols is a powerful and itself a symbolic act. From these two alternatives, acknowledging the very difficult nature of the source text, it is much more probable that it was Assyrian solar symbolism that was attacked rather than the solar aspects of Judah's own God. It is necessary to stop here – before becoming involved in excessive speculation on the basis of a very unclear verse.

If we assume that v. 11 or parts of it were taken from the royal annals, it would explain even better why Josiah was made a pious reformer. With 2 Kings 22:3–7, 9 it would provide an understandable background for the literary development. Not only was Josiah seen as a defender of the temple, but he also made changes in the religion. At the present state of knowledge it seems that the birth of the reformer Josiah

82 For discussion see Uehlinger (2007), 301–303.

83 Thus Levin (2003), 206, who is certain, that the verse is not from the 7th century BCE.

84 See Uehlinger (2007), 302–303; Keel/Uehlinger (1994), 269–306.

is still a post-monarchical phenomenon, although vestiges like 2 Kings 23:11 may have contributed greatly to the process.[85]

In the wake of 2 Kings 23:11 verses 5 and 12a[86] are also brought up in the discussion about potential vestiges and excerpts from the annals. Although in v. 11 we can talk about the probability, in vv. 5 and 12a we can, at most, talk about the possibility. Verse 5 has already been discussed and only one word, כמרים, can be presented as a possible indication of an early origin,[87] but this is not sufficient. We do not know enough about how the word was used in different periods to be able to assume a 7th century BCE dating. Uehlinger appeals to its use in Hosea 10:5 and Zeph. 1:4 and its disappearance in the later books of the prophets, especially Ezekiel and Jeremiah. This would then be an indication that the word was 'typical for the 7th century BCE'. However, it is hardly possible to use these passages for dating. Zeph. 1:4–5 is immersed in Deuteronomistic phraseology and possibly even dependent on 2 Kings 23.[88] The problems, tension with v. 8 and especially the use of the cop. perf.[89] tip the balance to assume a late origin.

Verse 12a is evidently connected with 2 Kings 21:5:

23:12a	21:5
וְאֶת־הַמִּזְבְּחוֹת אֲשֶׁר עַל־הַגָּג עֲלִיַּת אָחָז	
אֲשֶׁר־עָשׂוּ מַלְכֵי יְהוּדָה	
וְאֶת־הַמִּזְבְּחוֹת אֲשֶׁר־עָשָׂה מְנַשֶּׁה	וַיִּבֶן מִזְבְּחוֹת לְכָל־צְבָא הַשָּׁמָיִם
בִּשְׁתֵּי חַצְרוֹת בֵּית־יְהוָה נָתַץ הַמֶּלֶךְ	בִּשְׁתֵּי חַצְרוֹת בֵּית־יְהוָה

At least the second part of the half verse was written in view of 2 Kings 21:5, which suggests that we are not dealing with an excerpt from the

85 This verse is an example of a case that stresses the importance of being open to the possibility of early fragments within heavily edited texts that are mainly late. Any redaction critical analysis cannot live in a vacuum and ignore historical observations. If a context seems probable with the current knowledge, the consequences should be drawn and they should have an impact also on the redaction critical analysis. Or, at least, one would have to challenge the connections argued to exist between v. 11 and the Assyrian background.

86 Because of the evident dependence on v. 6, verse 12b should be regarded as a later addition.

87 Cf. the discussion in Uehlinger (2007), 303–305. According to him, the word may refer to priests involved in astral worship and "probably go[es] back to Aramean influence" (304).

88 Zeph. 1:4–5 refers to the destruction of Jerusalem and Judah, and to their ensuing purification of all vestiges of Baal, Host of Heaven and Moloch/Melech. Contrary to what Uehlinger, op. cit., implies in his argument, it would be very difficult to avoid the conclusion that these verses were written after the destruction of Jerusalem.

89 Admitting that the verse is "rather muddled", Uehlinger (2007), 304, suggests that the use of the cop. perf. "should perhaps express the definite elimination of the כמרים", but such a use of the cop. perf. is atypical.

annals. The author was viewing the whole history and made Josiah remove the altars made by Manasseh. A similar technique is met in 2 Kings 23:13 where Josiah destroys the high places built by Solomon. The first part of the verse may also try to make a connection with the evil Ahaz. Ahaz constructed a new altar after the one he saw in Damascus (2 Kings 16:10–16) and an allusion to the event would have been fitting in 2 Kings 23. On the other hand, v. 23:12a refers to many altars and the עֲלִיַּת אָחָז may be a later addition to the verse. Consequently, the second part of the half verse is very probably late, whereas the first part is potentially an early fragment, especially if one could show a connection with some early religious phenomena that are not met later. However, this does not seem to be the case. Uehlinger reasons that roofs would have been a natural place to worship astral divinities, but concedes that "no primary sources support this hypothesis" and that it does not seem to have been "an Assyrian or Aramean custom."[90] Consequently, verse 12a may be part of the same late addition as v. 12b and, if we follow Levin's argumentation, it is part of the expansion of the reform measures to revoke all sins committed by other kings.

Discussion and Conclusions

Many features in the texts and the broader historical context suggest that the cult reforms, in any form intended by the biblical authors, did not take place. It is more probable that they are literary inventions and projections of later ideals into the monarchic period. The probable excerpts from annals in 2 Kings 22:2–7, 9 and 23:11 are significant fragments, but, solely on their basis, there is no reason to assume that any cult reform took place. Although they should not be used uncritically as authentic documents, perhaps something can be extracted from them about events during the time of Josiah.

According to 2 Kings 22:2–7, 9, Josiah restored the temple. This seems to have been a rather neutral reporting of a restoration of the main state sanctuary and may have a historical background in the time of Josiah. 2 Kings 23:11 is much more difficult to interpret and its authenticity is more uncertain. If authentic, it could be connected to the liberation of Judah from Assyrian vassalage. Cult items and symbols associated with the Assyrian domination would have been destroyed. One would expect some reference to the end of the Assyrian domination – surprisingly missing in the whole composition – but any other

90 Uehlinger (2007), 305.

interpretation faces more problems. The verse remains perplexing as there is no explanation for or reference to the function or meaning of the horses or chariots of the sun in the rest of the Hebrew Bible. The author may have assumed that every reader would know what was meant, or the original context of the fragment is missing. In any case, one needs much more evidence than this verse to assume an attack on the solar aspects of Yahweh took place under Josiah. Without more textual evidence the verse may never be unlocked.

2 Kings 22:2–7, 9 and 23:11 provided an excellent background for making Josiah the great reformer king. Without at least one of these fragments it would be difficult to comprehend why Josiah was made what he is in the 'final' text. The history writer, already convinced that the cult should be centralized to the temple in Jerusalem, probably found these passages in the annals, and was consequently convinced that Josiah was a pious king who took care of the temple. Perhaps he thought that such a king would have certainly defended the temple from the illicit high places. 2 Kings 23:11 gave a further reason to assume that the king was willing to act and remove anything that was not acceptable to Yahweh. Consequently, Josiah was made the centralizer, who removed the high places (23:8a). At this stage, perhaps in the mid to late 6th century BCE, the question was only about the location of the cult. The other gods, foreign cults and vessels connected to these cults were not the target of criticism, but 2 Kings 23:8a became the core and incentive for further development. Later authors ascribed more and more reform measures to the already pious king. In the nomistic texts Josiah was made to attack the Asherah, the standing stones and other gods. Gradually, he was made the one who purged all possible illicit aspects of the religion (2 Kings 23:4–7, 24). These measures were also extended to all possible locations (2 Kings 23:13–20). Finally, the measures were connected with the finding of the Book of the Law (2 Kings 22:8).

In Hezekiah's case the development is much more subtle. The annals gave an impression of a dynamic and able king, who even opposed the Assyrians and saved Judah during a time when the Assyrians defeated and annexed the more powerful Israel. He was made a cult centralizer, although his measures were later canceled by Manasseh, one of the most evil Judean kings. Later some further measures were added to his reform as well, but the development remained much more modest than in 2 Kings 23.

It is fairly evident that the destruction of 587/6 BCE meant a dramatic reorientation in the political, religious and economic structures of Judah. Due to the many gaps in our knowledge, much of the discussion about what 'really' happened – for example, what can be shown to be early in the biblical texts – has to resort to discussions about probabilities and possibilities. Probable is that 587/6 BCE was a turning point in Israel's religion, because the basic fundaments of Israel's religion and society, the temple, Yahweh's temple cult, monarchy and state, had collapsed to the extent that the practice of the old religion would have been impossible except in a radically altered form.

The fragments that we have in 2 Kings 23 do not justify the assumption that the dramatic shift took place under Josiah. The conventional view also does not provide any explanation for why Israel's religion suddenly turned on itself and rejected many traditional conceptions. The coerced reorientation of 587/6 BCE would provide the explanation. With entirely new conceptions rising out of changed circumstances, later authors would have had to turn on Israel's older religion and attack many of its earlier traditions. There would therefore have to be very solid evidence to assume that any significant change in religion, such as an extensive cult reform, took place very shortly, just decades, before the catastrophe, as if anticipating the catastrophe and preparing for a templeless time when there was no monarch, and that such extensive changes came unscathed through the catastrophe.

Bibliography

Aharoni, Y. (1968), Arad: Its Inscriptions and Temple, BA 31, 2–32.

Albertz, R. (1994), A History of Israelite Religion in the Old Testament Period: Vol. 1: From the Beginnings to the End of the Monarchy, OTL, Louisville.

– (2007), Why a Reform Like Josiah's Must Have Happened, in: L.L. Grabbe (ed.), Good Kings and Bad Kings: The Kingdom of Judah in the Seventh Century BCE, T&T Biblical Studies, London, 27–46 (= L.L. Grabbe [ed.], Good Kings and Bad Kings, JSOT.S 393, London 2005).

Becking, B. (1997), Assyrian Evidence for Iconic Polytheism in Ancient Israel?, in: K. van der Toorn (ed.), The Image and the Book: Iconic Cults, Aniconism, and the Rise of Book Religion in Israel and the Ancient Near East, CBET 21, Leuven, 157–171.

Ben Zvi, E. (2007), Josiah and the Prophetic Books: Some Observations, in: L.L. Grabbe (ed.), Good Kings and Bad Kings: The Kingdom of Judah in the Seventh Century BCE, T&T Biblical Studies, London, 47–64 (= L.L. Grabbe [ed.], Good Kings and Bad Kings, JSOT.S 393, London 2005).

Benzinger, I. (1899), Die Bücher der Könige. Mit einem Plan des alten Jerusalem und einer Geschichtstabelle, KAC IX, Freiburg i.Br.

Collins, J.J. (2007), A Short Introduction to the Hebrew Bible, Minneapolis.

Cowley, A.E. (1923), Aramaic Papyri of the Fifth Century B.C., Oxford.

Cross, F.M. (1973), Canaanite Myth and Hebrew Epic: Essays in the History of the Religion of Israel, Cambridge/Massachusetts.

Davies, P. (2007), Josiah and the Law Book, in: L.L. Grabbe (ed.), Good Kings and Bad Kings: The Kingdom of Judah in the Seventh Century BCE, T&T Biblical Studies, London, 65–77 (= L.L. Grabbe [ed.], Good Kings and Bad Kings, JSOT.S 393, London 2005).

De Wette (1805), Dissertatio critico-exegetica qua Deuteronomium a prioribus Pentateuchi libris diversum, alius cuiusdam recentioris auctoris opus esse monstratur. Publice defendet auctor Guilielm Martin Leberecht de Wette, Jena (translated into English by: Harvey, P.B./Halpern, B. [2008], W.M.L. de Wette's "Dissertatio Critica …": Context and Translation, Zeitschrift für altorientalische und biblische Rechtsgeschichte 14, 47–85).

Driver, S.R. (1902), A Critical and Exegetical Commentary on Deuteronomy, ICC 5, 3rd edition, Edinburgh.

Fritz, V. (2003), 1 & 2 Kings: A Continental Commentary, Minneapolis.

Gesenius, W./Kautzsch, E. (1995), Hebräische Grammatik. Völlig umgearb. von E. Kautzsch, 7. Nachdr.-Aufl. der 28., vielfach verb. und verm. Aufl. Leipzig 1909, Hildesheim.

Grabbe, L.L. (2007), Ancient Israel: What Do We Know and How Do We Know It?, London/New York.

Gray, J. (1963), I & II Kings: A Commentary, OTL, Philadelphia.

Hardmeier, C. (2007), King Josiah in the Climax of the Deuteronomic History (2 Kings 22–23) and the Pre-Deuteronomic Document of a Cult Reform at the Place of Residence (23.4–15): Criticism of Sources, Reconstruction of Literary Pre-stages and the Theology of History in 2 Kings 22–23, in: L.L. Grabbe (ed.), Good Kings and Bad Kings, London, 123–163, (= L.L. Grabbe [ed.], Good Kings and Bad Kings, JSOT.S 393, London 2005).

Hobbs, T. R. (1985), 2 Kings, Word Biblical Commentary 13, Waco/Texas.

Hoffmann, H.-D. (1980), Reform und Reformen. Untersuchungen zu einem Grundthema der deuteronomistischen Geschichtsschreibung, AThANT 66, Zürich.

Hölscher, G. (1923), Das Buch der Könige, seine Quellen und seine Redaktion, in: H. Schmidt (ed.), ΕΥΧΑΡΙΣΤΗΡΙΟΝ, FS H. Gunkel, 2 vols., FRLANT 36, Göttingen, 158–213.

Keel, O./Uehlinger, C. (1994), Jahwe und die Sonnengottheit von Jerusalem, in: W. Dietrich/M. Klopfenstein (eds.), Ein Gott allein? JHWH-Verehrung und biblischer Monotheismus im Kontext der israelitischen und altorientalistischen Religionsgeschichte, OBO 139, Göttingen/Freiburg (Schweiz), 269–306.

Kletter, R. (1996), The Judean Pillar-Figurines and the Archaeology of Asherah, BAR International Series 636, Oxford.

Köckert, M. (2007), Die Entstehung des Bilderverbots, in: B. Groneberg/H. Spieckermann (eds.), Die Welt der Götterbilder, BZAW 376, Berlin/New York, 272–290.

Kratz, R. (2000), Die Komposition der erzählenden Bücher des Alten Testaments: Grundwissen der Bibelkritik, UTB 2157, Göttingen.

– (2007), Temple and Torah: Reflections on the Legal Status of the Pentateuch between Elephantine and Qumran, in: G.N. Knoppers/B.M. Levinson (eds.), The Pentateuch as Torah: New Models for Understanding Its Promulgation and Acceptance, Winona Lake, 77–103.

Levin, C. (1984), Joschija im deuteronomistischen Geschichtswerk, ZAW 96, 351–371.

– (1995), Das System der zwölf Stämme Israels, in: J.A. Emerton (ed.), Congress Volume: Papers read at the [14th] congress of the Interna-

tional Organization for the Study of the Old Testament, held July 19–24, 1992 in Paris, VT.S 61, Leiden/New York/Köln, 163–178.
– (2003), Fortschreibungen. Gesammelte Studien zum Alten Testament, BZAW 316, Berlin/New York.
– (2005), The Old Testament: A Brief Introduction, Princeton.
– (2008), Die Frömmigkeit der Könige von Israel und Juda, in: J. Pakkala/M. Nissinen (eds.), Houses Full of All Good Things: Essays in Memory of Timo Veijola, Publications of the Finnish Exegetical Society 95, Helsinki/Göttingen, 129–168.
Levinson, B.M. (1998), Deuteronomy and the Hermeneutics of Legal Innovation, Oxford.
Liverani, M. (2005), Israel's History and the History of Israel, Bibleworld, London/Oakville.
Lohfink, N. (1987), The Cult Reform of Josiah of Judah: II Kings 22–23, in: P.D. Miller/P. Hanson/S.D. McBride (eds.), Ancient Israelite Religion: Essays in Honor of F.M. Cross, Philadelphia, 459–475.
Mazar, A. (1992), Archaeology of the Land of the Bible, 10,000–586 B.C.E., New York/London.
Miller, J.M./Hayes, J.H. (2006), History of Ancient Israel and Judah, 2nd ed., Louisville/London.
Montgomery, J.A./Gehman, H.S. (1951), A Critical and Exegetical Commentary on the Book of Kings, ICC 6, Edinburgh.
Nelson, R.D. (2002), Deuteronomy: A Commentary, OTL, Louisville/London.
Niehr, H. (1995), Die Reform des Joschija. Methodische, historische und religionsgeschichtliche Aspekte, in: W. Groß (ed.), Jeremia und die "deuteronomistische Bewegung", BBB 98, Weinheim, 33–55.
– (1997), In Search of YHWH's Cult Statue in the First Temple, in: K. van der Toorn (ed.), The Image and the Book: Iconic Cults, Aniconism, and the Rise of Book Religion in Israel and the Ancient Near East, CBET 21, Leuven, 73–95.
Noth, M. (1967), Überlieferungsgeschichtliche Studien. Die sammelnden und bearbeitenden Geschichtswerke im Alten Testament, 3. unveränderte Aufl., Darmstadt.
Otto, E. (1999), Das Deuteronomium. Politische Theologie und Rechtsreform in Juda und Assyrien, BZAW 284, Berlin/New York.
Pakkala, J. (1999), Intolerant Monolatry in the Deuteronomistic History, Publications of the Finnish Exegetical Society 76, Göttingen/Helsinki.
– (2004), Ezra the Scribe: The Development of Ezra 7–10 and Nehemiah 8, BZAW 347, Berlin/New York.
– (2006), Zedekiah's Fate and the Dynastic Succession, JBL 125/3, 443–452.

– (2008), Jeroboam without Bulls, ZAW 120, 501–525.
– (2009), The Date of the Oldest Edition of Deuteronomy, ZAW 121, 388–401.
Petry, S. (2007), Die Entgrenzung JHWHs. Monolatrie, Bilderverbot und Monotheismus im Deuteronomium, in Deuterojesaja und im Ezechielbuch, FAT II/27, Tübingen.
Provan, I.W. (1988), Hezekiah and the Books of Kings: A Contribution to the Debate about the Composition of the Deuteronomistic History, BZAW 172, Berlin/New York.
Renz, J./Röllig, W. (1995), Handbuch der althebräischen Epigraphik, 3 Bde., Darmstadt.
Römer, T.C. (2005), The So-Called Deuteronomistic History: A Sociological, Historical and Literary Introduction, London.
Schmid, K. (2008), Literaturgeschichte des Alten Testaments. Eine Einführung, Darmstadt.
Spieckermann, H. (1982), Juda unter Assur in der Sargonidenzeit, FRLANT 129, Göttingen.
Stade, B. (1907), Anmerkungen zu 2 Kö. 15–21, in: ders., Ausgewählte akademische Reden und Abhandlungen, 2. Aufl., Gießen, 201–226.
Steuernagel, C. (1912), Lehrbuch der Einleitung in das Alte Testament, SThL, Tübingen.
Sweeney, M.A. (2007), I & II Kings: A Commentary, OTL, Louisville.
Uehlinger, C. (1997), Assyrian Evidence for Iconic Polytheism in Ancient Israel, in: K. van der Toorn (ed.), The Image and the Book: Iconic Cults, Aniconism, and the Rise of Book Religion in Israel and the Ancient Near East, CBET 21, Leuven, 97–155.
– (2007), Was There a Cult Reform under King Josiah? The Case for a Well-Grounded Minimum, in: L.L. Grabbe (ed.), Good Kings and Bad Kings, London, 279–316 (= L.L. Grabbe [ed.], Good Kings and Bad Kings, JSOT.S 393, London 2005).
Van der Toorn, K. (1997), The Image and the Book: Iconic Cults, Aniconism and the Rise of Book Religion in Israel and the Ancient Near East, CBET 21, Leuven.
Veijola, T. (2004), Das 5. Buch Mose Deuteronomium, Kapitel 1,1–16,17, ATD 8/1, Göttingen.
Werlitz, J. (2002), Die Bücher der Könige, Neuer Stuttgarter Kommentar, AT 8, Stuttgart.
Würthwein, E. (1984), Die Bücher der Könige: 1. Kön. 17–2. Kön. 25, Übersetzt und erklärt von E. Würthwein, ATD 11/2, Göttingen.

III. The Ancient City: Perspectives on the Political and Cultural Interrelations at Beth Shean

Tel Beth-Shean: History and Archaeology

AMIHAI MAZAR

Tel Beth-Shean is one of the most extensively explored biblical sites in the Land of Israel: two expeditions excavated the site over many years, yielding vast quantities of archaeological data. This, together with the limited number of textual sources, makes Beth-Shean an intriguing site for research. The following article provides an overview of the textual sources and archaeological data relating to all periods of occupation at the site through the end of the Iron Age, and a short discussion of the relationship between the textual and archaeological sources.

Beth-Shean in the Written Sources

Egyptian Texts

The earliest reference to Beth-Shean may appear in the Egyptian Execration Texts, although the reading is disputed.[1] The city is mentioned in the topographic list of Thutmose III at Karnak (No. 110: *bt š'ir*).[2] Beth-Shean appears only once in the Amarna letters of the 14th century, referred to as *bit ša-a-ni* in a letter from Abdi-Heba, ruler of Jerusalem (EA 289).[3] After mentioning Gath Carmel as the city ruled by of Tagi, Abdi-Heba notes that the men of Gath comprise the garrison in Beth-Shean, that is, his enemies make up the Pharaoh's protective forces to the north. Further on, Abdi-Heba connects Tagi to the sons of Lab'ayu, the ruler of Shechem, in the context of stirring up hostility against the Pharaoh. A petrographic study of the Amarna letters has revealed that while most of the tablets of Abdi-Heba's letters were made of local hill-country clay, one was made of Jordan Valley clay (EA 285), perhaps

1 Cf. Mazar/Mullins (2007), 1–2 (with references).
2 Cf. Simons (1937), 27–44; Aharoni (1979), 156–166, esp. 163; Redford (1992), 156–160.
3 Cf. Moran (1992), 332–333; Pritchard (1950), 489; Aharoni (1979), 170–176.

produced and written by a scribe at Beth-Shean itself.[4] Beth-Shean is also mentioned six times in topographic lists of Seti I.[5] In a monumental stela of Seti I, found at Beth-Shean, the city is described as besieged by the rulers of Hamath and Pehal, while Reḥob remained loyal to the Pharaoh.[6] Ramesses II refers to Beth-Shean once in a list from Karnak, and Papyrus Anastasi I, probably of the same dating, mentions Beth-Shean in conjunction with Reḥob in relation to crossing the Jordan River.[7] The city is mentioned again in Shoshenq I's list at Karnak, aside Reḥob.[8]

Biblical Texts

The following biblical sources mention Beth-Shean:

- Josh. 17:11: Beth-Shean is mentioned together with other cities in the Jezreel Valley and on the Coastal Plain as Manassite cities in the territories of Issachar and Asher, referring specifically to the Canaanite population that continued to inhabit these regions under Israelite hegemony (vv. 12–13).
- Judg. 1:27: Beth-Shean is mentioned as one of the Canaanite cities in the valley, not conquered by Manasseh. The list of such towns repeats the list in Josh. 17:11, with some changes.
- 1 Samuel 31 and 1 Chron. 10:8–12: following the death of Saul in the battle on Gilboa, the Philistines hung his body and the bodies of his three sons on the walls of Beth-Shean. People from Yavesh-Gilead brought the bodies to their city, burned them, and buried the bones.
- 1 Kings 4:12: Beth-Shean is mentioned as one of the towns in the fifth administrative district of Solomon, governed by Baana Ben Ahilud. The district includes the Jezreel Valley and part of the Jordan Valley.
- 1 Chron. 7:29: Beth-Shean is mentioned among the cities of Manasseh, derivative from Josh. 17:11 and Judg. 1:27.

4 Cf. Goren/Finkelstein/Na'aman (2004), 267–269.

5 Cf. Ahituv (1984), 78–79 (with references).

6 Cf. Rowe (1930), 25–29, Fig. 5 and Pl. 41; Pritchard (1950), 253; Kitchen (1968), 11–12; Higginbotham (2000), 22–24 (with references to earlier literature).

7 Cf. Ahituv (1984), 19, 79; Pritchard (1950), 477. In the Egyptian hieroglyphic texts, the name is always written as *Beth-ŝā'l*.

8 Cf. Ahituv (1984), 79.

The Site

Biblical Beth-Shean is identified with Tel Beth-Shean (Tell el-Ḥosn in Arabic), a steep, prominent mound overlooking the Beth-Shean Valley.

Fig. 1: Aerial view of Tel Beth-Shean during 1994 season (looking west).

The top of the mound is 113 m below sea level, some 12 m above the natural hill on which the site is located. The mound is surrounded on all sides by deep ravines and commands the main road descending from the Jezreel and Harod Valleys to the Beth-Shean Valley that connects the northern Coastal Plain with Transjordan. This latitudinal road intersects with the important longitudinal road that traverses the Jordan Valley and continues northward towards the Sea of Galilee, and from there either to Damascus or the Lebanese Bek'a. These strategic advantages, as well as the abundant water supply and fertile lands nearby, made Beth-Shean an attractive site for a settlement for thousands of years. Although the tell is larger than 4 ha in area, its northern part was not settled for most of the biblical period, and its southern and perhaps western edges were probably cut away during the Roman period.[9] The Hebrew University (HU) excavations have shown that for most of the 2nd millennium BCE, the settled area was limited to the

9 Cf. Arubas (2006), 48–60.

summit of the mound, which is not larger than 1.5–2 ha, inhabited by a community of not more than ca. 500 persons.[10]

The Beth-Shean Valley is strewn with dozens of mounds and ruins of various sizes, the largest of which is Tel Reḥov (Tell eṣ-Ṣarem in Arabic), 5 km south of Beth-Shean. This 10 ha large tell was the location of the city-state of Reḥob in the 2nd millennium BCE.[11] Other sites in the valley are much smaller, evidence for a complex and hierarchical settlement pattern. Subsistence in the valley was most probably based on irrigation agriculture, facilitated by the abundance of springs located at high elevations compared to the fields. The HU investigations at Tel Beth-Shean are part of a regional research project that includes surveys and the long-term excavations at Tel Reḥob.[12]

The Excavations

Extensive excavations were conducted at Tel Beth-Shean by the University Museum of the University of Pennsylvania Expedition (UME) between 1921 and 1933, directed consecutively by Clarence Fisher, Alan Rowe, and Gerald M. FitzGerald.[13] This was one of the first multi-level tells excavated systematically in Palestine, and it provided a sequence of material culture from 18 occupation levels from the late Neolithic through the Medieval period. The framework of the archaeological history of the site was established, and many important buildings and finds were exposed. The excavation methods used during the 1920s and early 1930s, however, were insufficient in terms of modern archaeological research, and in 1983, a three-week excavation season was conducted by Yigael Yadin and Shulamit Geva of the Hebrew University.[14] Subsequently, the present author conducted nine excavation

---

10 This population estimate is based on a coefficient of 250 persons per built-up hectare, cf. Schloen (2001), 169–183. James/McGovern (1993), 238, calculated the town's area as 5 ha, but they included the northern part of the mound, which in my view remained unsettled during the 2nd millennium BCE. Their population estimate was based on a coefficient of 400 persons per hectare, which is too high.

11 Cf. Mazar (2008b).

12 Regional research on the Middle Bronze Age was conducted by A. Maeir as part of his PhD-thesis at the Hebrew University, cf. Maeir (1997). A survey of 120 sq km around Tel Reḥob was carried out by A. Cahn (unpublished M.A. thesis at Hebrew University Jerusalem). Both confirmed the results of earlier surveys of the valley carried out by N. Zori.

13 Cf. esp. Rowe (1930; 1940); Oren (1973); James (1966); James/McGovern (1993).

14 Cf. Yadin/Geva (1986).

seasons on the tell between 1989 and 1996.[15] These excavations took advantage of the fact that the UME excavations had created several large steps on the summit of the mound, in each of which different periods had been exposed.

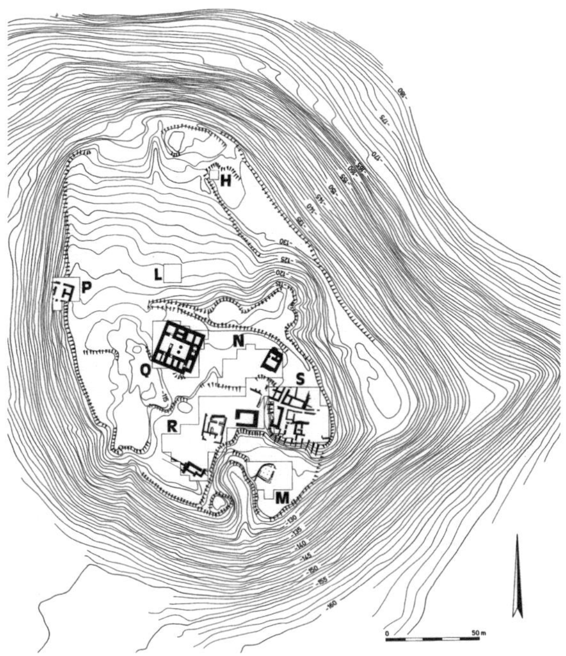

Fig. 2: Topographic Plan of Tel Beth-Shean, with Location of Excavation Areas of Hebrew University Expedition and main Structures, dating to various periods in each area.

We could thus excavate different periods in the 'terraces' left by the UME some 60 years earlier, and were able to study almost the entire stratigraphic sequence of the site using modern methods and to investigate many aspects of this important site (see Fig. 2). Tab. 1 presents correlations between the UME strata (denoted 'Levels' by them) and the various phases in each of the HU excavation areas.

15 The excavations were conducted under the auspices of the Hebrew University of Jerusalem in the framework of a joint expedition coordinated by the Beth-Shean Tourism Development Administration. For additional details on the expedition and the team, cf. Mazar (2006a), 9–25. Special thanks go to Nava Panitz-Cohen and Robert Mullins for their invaluable assistance throughout the field work and publication processes. For summaries of the excavation results, cf. Mazar (1997; 2008a), and for final reports, cf. Mazar (2006); Mazar/Mullins (2007); Panitz-Cohen/Mazar (2009).

Period	Century [BCE]	UME Level	HU Local Strata in Areas R, S	HU Local Strata in Other Areas
Medieval		Ia		P-1
Early Islamic		Ib		P-2; L-1; H-1
Byzantine		II		P-3; H-2; L-2
Roman		III		P-4
Hellenistic		III		P-5
Iron IIB	Late 8th			P-6 (squatters)
Iron IIB	8th until 732	IV and parts of V		## P-7
Iron IIB	9th–early 8th	Parts of V?		P-8a–b
	Mid-9th	Parts of V		P-9 (surface in probe)
Iron IIA	10th	Parts of V	## S-1 (massive buildings)	P-10 (surface in probe)
Iron IB	11th	Temples of V and structures of Late VI	## S-2 (revival of town)	N-2?
Iron IA	12th, Egyptian 20th Dynasty	VI Late VII	## S-3 S-4 S-5?	Q-1; N-3a–b
LB IIB	13th, Egyptian 19th Dynasty	VII VIII		Q-2; N-4 Q-3
LB IIA	14th	IX1	R-1a	
LB IB	Late 15th	IX2	R-1b	
LB IA–B	15th	—	R-2	
Late MB IIB	16th	XA	R-3	
Late MB IIB	Late 17th	XB	R-4	
MB IIB	Late 18th/17th	XB/XI	R-5	
GAP				
Intermediate Bronze Age (EB IV/MB I)	23rd–21st	XI (mixed)	R-6	
EB III	27th–24th	Parts of XI and XII	R-7–R-12	M-1
EB II	29th–28th	Meager remains	GAP	Scattered sherds
EB IB	33rd–30th	XIII XIV		M-2 M-3; L-4
## = destruction by fire				

Tab. 1: Stratigraphic Chart of Tel Beth-Shean

Prior to the Beginning of Egyptian Domination

The Early Bronze Age

The deep sounding excavated down to bedrock by FitzGerald in 1933 was published by Braun more than 70 years later.[16] Seven main strata were identified, encompassing the time-span from the foundation of the settlement on a high rocky hill during the Late Neolithic period (late 6th–early 5th millennia BCE) until the end of the 3rd millennium BCE. During the Early Bronze Age I (henceforth EBI, ca. 3600–3000 BCE), there were two main occupation phases: the earlier EB IA yielded typical 'Grey Burnished Ware' and the later EB IB had typical red-slipped pottery and 'Band-Slipped *pithoi*'. From the latter phase, our excavations in Area M exposed parts of a unique mudbrick building that included two rooms and a large hall (with interior dimensions of 6.5 × 8.3 m). The hall had 14 wooden columns for roof support, benches along the walls, and an unusual grinding installation.[17] In the course of the EB IB, the building was destroyed in a violent conflagration and then rebuilt with a different plan. The finds include many storage vessels, like *pithoi* and various jars, three copper axes, and remains of flint tools workshop. The results of ^{14}C tests on charred seeds date the building mainly to the 31st century BCE. The combined capacity of the storage vessels in this building is estimated at ca. 5400 l, representing the yearly grain consumption of around 20 people. The building must have had an administrative function in the developing complex society of the EB I that eventually led to the emergence of urban societies in the Levant. Many other EB I sites are known in the Beth-Shean and Jordan Valleys, such as Tel Shalem (where fortifications attributed to this period were found), Tel ed-Diaba, Tel Kitan, and Tel Yakush west of the Jordan River and Tell esh-Shuneh to its east. The recent discoveries from this period at Megiddo indicate the existence of complex and hierarchical societies.

Around 3000 BCE, following the second phase of the building, Beth-Shean was almost totally abandoned and not settled during the Early Bronze Age II. There is a similar gap at Megiddo, unlike many other Early Bronze Age cities that continued to flourish during the Early Bronze II, such as Beth-Yerah. In the Early Bronze Age III (ca. 2750–2300 BCE), Beth-Shean became the southernmost settlement of the 'Beth Yerah people', immigrants from the Kura-Araxes region of the Cauca-

---

16 Cf. Braun (2004).

17 Cf. Mazar/Rotem (2009).

sus (modern-day Georgia and Azerbaijan), who brought with them the pottery manufacturing tradition of Khirbet Kerak Ware, which they continued to produce for generations. At Beth-Shean, several occupation phases from this period were excavated, producing some of the best examples of 'Khirbet Kerak Ware' together with local pottery typical of the period.[18] An extensive contemporary settlement was excavated at Tel Iztaba, just opposite Tel Beth-Shean across the Harod River.[19]

The Intermediate Bronze Age

The circumstances that led to the end of the Early Bronze Age III city are unclear: no evidence for a violent destruction was found. In the Intermediate Bronze Age (also known as Early Bronze Age IV or Middle Bronze Age I), the tell was partially inhabited: scant architectural remains were found, possibly the foundations for huts and tents.[20] Dense village settlements from this period were located just north of Beth-Shean, near Tel Iztaba,[21] as well as in other village sites like Tel Yosef and Shaar Hagolan. This pattern has led me to suggest that the villages of the Intermediate Bronze Age unranked communities of farmers and shepherds were deliberately established away from the locations of the earlier cities.[22]

The Middle Bronze Age

Beth-Shean was again abandoned until the Middle Bronze Age, when a permanent settlement was established on the summit of the mound, encompassing an area of ca. 1.2–2 ha.[23] It is unknown whether this settlement was fortified, since the edges of the mound on the south and west are now missing. The three strata observed in our excavations (Strata R-5–R-3) yielded typical late Middle Bronze Age pottery and other artifacts. The excavated parts of the settlement included a street running parallel to the edge of the mound and dwelling houses on both of its

---

18 Cf. Mazar/Ziv-Esudri/Cohen-Weinberger (2000).

19 The excavations were carried out by Gabi Mazor and Rachel Bar-Nathan under the auspices of the Israel Antiquities Authority.

20 Cf. Mazar (2006b).

21 For the northern Cemetery, cf. Oren (1973). A salvage excavation of a large nearby settlement was conducted by E. Yannai under the auspices of the Israel Antiquity Authority in 2009 (oral communication, E. Yannai).

22 Cf. Mazar (2006b).

23 Cf. Mazar/Mullins (2007).

sides. A large paved area and a huge oval pit (18 m long) may have been associated with public activities in the settlement. Several infant jar burials, found below the floors, are also typical of this period; in addition to these, several pit burials of teenagers and adults were excavated. One such burial of a boy contained gold jewelry, which may indicate the high social status of the family. The two later strata, in particular the latest, contained pottery of the 'Chocolate on White Ware' family characteristic of the Jordan Valley in this period. There was no evidence for a traumatic end of the Middle Bronze Age town.

The Late Bronze Age I Temple

The HU excavations below the courtyard of the UME Level IX sanctuary revealed an earlier temple dated to the Late Bronze Age I (or perhaps specifically the Late Bronze Age IA, our Stratum R-2).

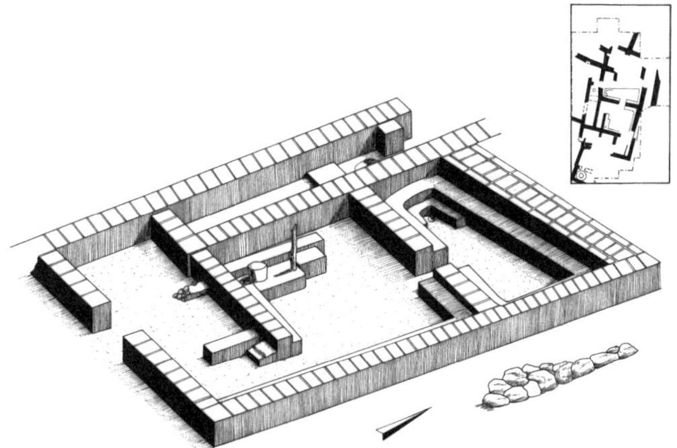

Fig. 3: Isometric Reconstruction of Stratum R-2 Temple (16th–15th centuries BCE).

This is the earliest of a series of temples (Fig. 3) found in the same location by UME.[24] It was a modest mudbrick structure (11.7 × 14.6 m) with an asymmetrical plan, including an entrance vestibule, a central hall, and an inner room. Plastered benches lined the walls of the central hall and inner room. The bench along the western wall of the central hall was widened to form a kind of stepped platform, on top of which were a round stone column and posthole for a wooden pillar, both probably

24 Cf. Mazar/Mullins (2007), 112–138.

related to local cultic practices (perhaps a *massebah* and an Asherah?). Although the temple is unique, it has several features in common with other temples in Canaan, for example, the Fosse Temple at Lachish, the Temple at Tel Mevorakh, and the Temples at Tell Qasile. The Beth-Shean Temple is the earliest of this group of Canaanite assymetrical temples.[25] The building was intentionally abandoned, its remains covered with an artificial fill on which the courtyard floor of the Level IX sanctuary was laid. The temple appears to have been an isolated building – almost no contemporary structures were found around it.

Egyptian Domination

One of the major questions regarding the history of the site is why the Egyptians of the New Kingdom chose Beth-Shean as a garrison town and when this has happened. The answer to the first part of the question is related to the strategic location of the site on the one hand and its status in the previous period on the other. Since Beth-Shean was not the capital of a city-state but rather a small subsidiary town during the Middle Bronze Age, the Egyptians did not have to obliterate a Canaanite city-state in order to turn it into a New Kingdom Egyptian administrative and military center. Indeed, it was the policy of the Egyptian Empire to allow the Canaanite city-state system to continue throughout the Late Bronze Age. As for the second part of the question, although some scholars believe that Beth-Shean became an Egyptian stronghold only from the beginning of the 19th Dynasty,[26] now there is in my view enough textual and archaeological evidence to argue that it acquired this status already during the XVIIIth Dynasty and that it served in this capacity for over 300 years.

The HU excavations demonstrated that throughout this time-span, Beth-Shean remained rather small, at 1.2–2 ha. Three main occupation strata were defined by UME (see Tab. 1 above):

- Level IX: The 18th Dynasty (probably from the reign of Thutmose III through late in the 14th century BCE).
- Levels VIII–VII: The 19th Dynasty (13th century BCE).
- Level VI: The 20th Dynasty (12th century BCE).

In our excavations, at least two sub-strata in each of these occupation levels were defined. The latest of each was violently destroyed, probab-

25 Cf. Mazar (1992).
26 Cf. James/McGovern (1993), 235.

ly in the context of the upheavals caused by the weakness of Egypt at the end of the 18th, 19th, and 20th Dynasties, respectively.

Level IXA–B: The 18th Dynasty

The excavation of the Level IX sanctuary (Fig. 4) first exposed by UME continued in Area R.[27]

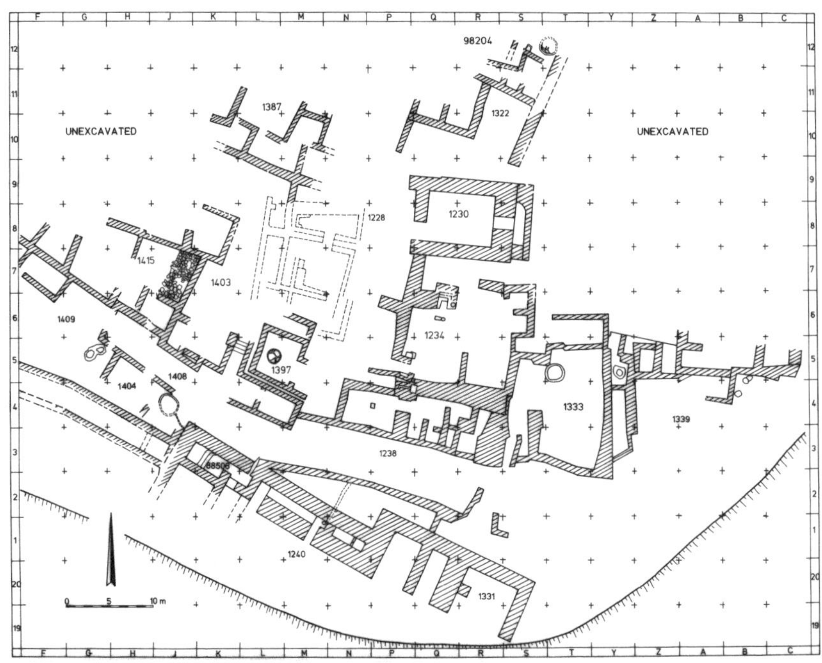

Fig. 4: Plan of the late phase of Level IX (HU Phase R-1a) sanctuary (14th century BCE).

Two architectural phases, Strata R-1b and R-1a, were identified in parts of the sanctuary, while the main structure probably continued to serve in both phases. The principal unit in the sanctuary was rectangular Hall 1230 with massive stone walls; to its south, UME had excavated a cultic room containing raised platforms and cultic objects. Other parts of the sanctuary comprised various rooms and spaces arranged around a

27 Cf. Rowe (1930), 10–17; id. (1940); and also Mazar/Mullins (2007), 23–38, 139–198, and the finds published in various chapters in this volume.

large central courtyard. Four stone-lined circular installations apparently served as roasting pits for animals sacrificed in the sanctuary. Several small rooms contained assemblages of bowls, lamps, and kraters decorated in the local Canaanite style, as well as several typical Egyptian-style vessels produced locally at Beth-Shean, the latter representting the best evidence for an Egyptian presence at the site.

Along the southern edge of the Level IX precinct, UME uncovered a series of rooms bounded by massive walls that they identified as the southern casemate wall of the temple precinct. We found that these rooms in fact belonged to a much larger building, the southern part of which had disappeared due to the cutting away of the mound during the Roman period and erosion. In one of the rooms, UME discovered the renowned basalt orthostat with a relief depicting a struggle between a lion and a dog or a lioness, one of the best examples of Canaanite monumental art. Our excavations of another room in this complex uncovered a bath: it was well plastered with impermeable plaster and had four plastered steps and feeding and drainage channels. These discoveries indicate that the building may have served as a palace or major residence located to the south of the sanctuary, overlooking the valley to the south of the mound. A miniature clay cylinder containing a message from Tagi to Labayu, two well known figures in the Amarna correspondence found at the foot of the mound should be assigned to this period.[28] However, no Egyptian architecture, monuments, or inscriptions were found in the 18th Dynasty town, in clear contrast to the situation in the following Ramesside period.

Levels VIII–VII: The 19th Dynasty (13th Century BCE)

Under the 19th Dynasty, Egypt's hold on Canaan became stronger, as demonstrated by the establishment of citadels, governors' residencies, and headquarters of the Egyptian administration. Beth-Shean was rebuilt according to a new plan (UME's Levels VIII–VII), including a new temple, administrative buildings, and a dwelling quarter.[29] The establishment of the new town may be attributed to the reign of Seti I, who erected two monumental stelae at the site.[30] The planning principles of the new town were maintained until the end of the Egyptian domina-

28 Cf. Horowitz (1966). On the Amarna correspondence see above.

29 For the final report on UME Levels VIII–VII cf. James/McGovern (1993).

30 For the first Seti I stela, found in secondary use in front of the northern Temple of Level V, see above n. 6; for the second stela, found out of context, cf. Rowe (1930), 25–30; Pritchard (1950), 255; James/McGovern (1993), 236.

tion of Canaan in the second half of the 12th century BCE, although considerable changes were made in the transition from the 19th to the 20th Dynasty. Level VIII is not well attested: its plan includes an early phase of a street and residential area and several additional structures.

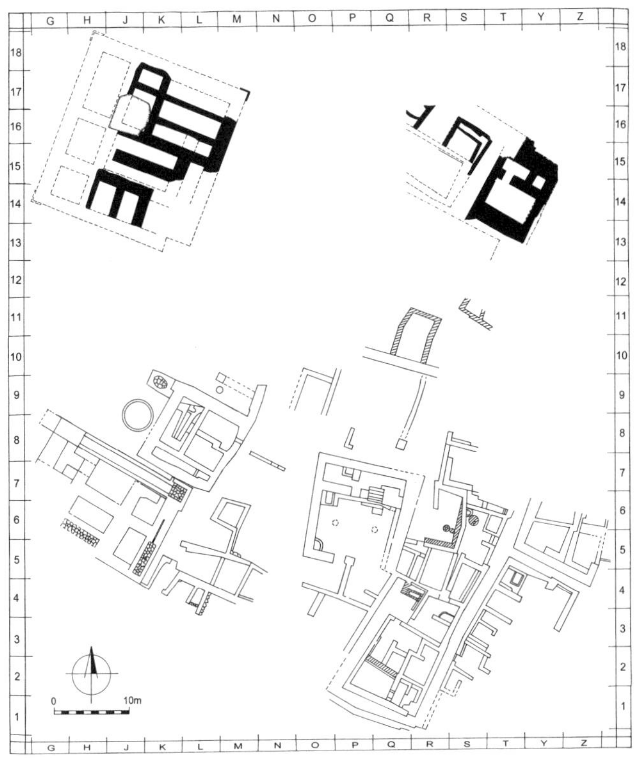

Fig. 5: Plan of Level VII (13th century BCE). In white: walls excavated by UME; in black: walls excavated by the HU expedition.

Level VII (Fig. 5) was a well planned and extensively built town, including a temple, a residential area on both sides of a street to its east, two large structures on the west designated a 'Migdol' and a 'commandant house', a large circular silo to the west of the latter, and a few residences southwest of the temple. The temple combined Egyptian and local traditions, similar to the temple in Area P at Lachish. [31] It has been compared to chapels at Amarna and Deir el-Medineh, but these are

31 Cf. Mazar (1992), 173–177; Ussishkin (2004), 215–281.

considered as inspired by Canaanite forms.[32] Egyptian elements in its architecture are represented by the use of blue paint and Egyptian frieze stones. A phase termed 'Late Level VII', found only in a few locations, represents localized modifications to the Level VII structures.

We excavated 19th Dynasty remains in our Areas Q and N. In Area Q, below the Level VI Governor's Building 1500, an earlier mudbrick public building was exposed in our Stratum Q-2. With dimensions of 20 × 20 m and a plan resembling the 19th Dynasty Egyptian fortress excavated at Deir el-Balah south of Gaza, this building apparently had a military/administrative function.[33] In Area N, a massive mudbrick building containing a large hall and two smaller chambers used for storing grain was excavated. This building and the 'Migdol' represent large administrative buildings with storage facilities used by the Egyptian administration at Beth-Shean. A street and parts of residential buildings were excavated in the western part of Area N.[34] In one of the rooms, five Ramesside scarabs of Egyptian origin were found, one bearing a cartouche of Ramesses II and a rare dedicatory inscription to the god Amun.

Egyptian finds that can be ascribed to Level VII include a stela of Ramesses II and a cylinder seal showing Ramesses II shooting an arrow at a target, both found in a later context in Level V, as well as a private stela of an Egyptian official worshipping the local Canaanite god Mekal, 'Lord of Beth-Shean', and a second stela showing a worshipper in front of a Canaanite goddess Ashtarte.[35] Other Egyptian inscriptions include a hieratic ostracon interpreted as an Execration Text[36] and five faience plaques bearing royal names, four with 'Ramesses' and the fifth with the prenomen of Merneptah.[37] Level VII in general and the temple structure in particular yielded rich finds, including many scarabs, cylinder seals, amulets, jewelry, clay figurines, and imported Mycenaean and Cypriot pottery, all typical to the 13th century BCE.

Although there is no evidence for a general devastation of the 19th Dynasty city, there is sufficient evidence of localized fires and the rapid

32 Cf. Higginbotham (2000), 294–301, for a summary and references to earlier literature.

33 Cf. Mazar (2006a), 61–172.

34 For the final report cf. Panitz-Cohen/Mazar (2009).

35 Cf. Rowe (1930), 19–21, Pl. 48:2; Ward (1966), 171; James/McGovern (1993), 240, 250, no. 10.

36 Cf. Wimmer (1993) and also Higginbotham (2000), 45–46.

37 Weinstein (1993), 221, Fig. 165:1–4, 6. Porter (2008) has challenged this dating, maintaining that one of the plaques should be dated to the reign of Ramesses IV and that the reading of Merneptah is not secure. A reading of Ramesses IV, however, would lead to an impossibly late date for Level VII, comparing to the typical Late Bronze IIB finds from this level and the finds in the succeeding Level VI.

abandonment of buildings at least in parts of the town. These may have been caused by the turmoils and possible attack on the city, resulting from the unstable situation of Egypt at the end of the 19th Dynasty and the transition to the 20th Dynasty. The town was soon rebuilt, retaining it former layout.

Level VI: The 20th Dynasty (12th Century BCE)

Level VI of the 20th Dynasty (the Iron Age IA)[38] was widely exposed in both the UME and the HU excavations (see Fig. 6).[39] Much of the Level VII town plan was retained, including streets, the outlines of residences, and the temple, although substantial modifications were made within all these structures.

Massive governmental buildings were built in the northern part of the town, the most significant of which is Building 1500, constructed on the ruins of and using the same outline as the earlier 13th century BCE building in Area Q.[40] Its plan, pillared central hall, inscribed stone doorjambs, and T-shaped stone doorsills are typically Egyptian in style. This new building can be defined as a small palace, most probably the seat of the governors of Beth-Shean during the 20th Dynasty. It was designed to impress visitors and reflect Egyptian rule and power.

To the east of Building 1500, UME exposed another large building, Building 1700, in which four T-shaped stone doorsills were found, two of which appeared to be *in situ*. Our excavations in Area N showed that this building is later to two phases of 20th Dynasty structures (Strata N-3b and N-3a), and was either added in the late 20th Dynasty or is later than the time of the Egyptian regime (in this case the doorsills must have been in secondary use). Another large building was found in the western part of our Area S and continued westward beyond the excavated area: although we exposed only a single rectangular room of this building, the architecture and elaborate finds indicate that it must have been the residence of high-ranking Egyptian official.

---

38 The term Iron IA used for the period of the 20th Dynasty follows the terminology in Stern (1993). For other terms recently suggested for this period, cf. the discussions in Mazar (2008c) and id. (2009), 1–32.

39 Cf. James (1966), 4–22, 149–151; Mazar (2006a), 61–172; Panitz-Cohen/Mazar (2009).

40 Cf. James (1966), 8–11; Mazar (2006a), 61–82.

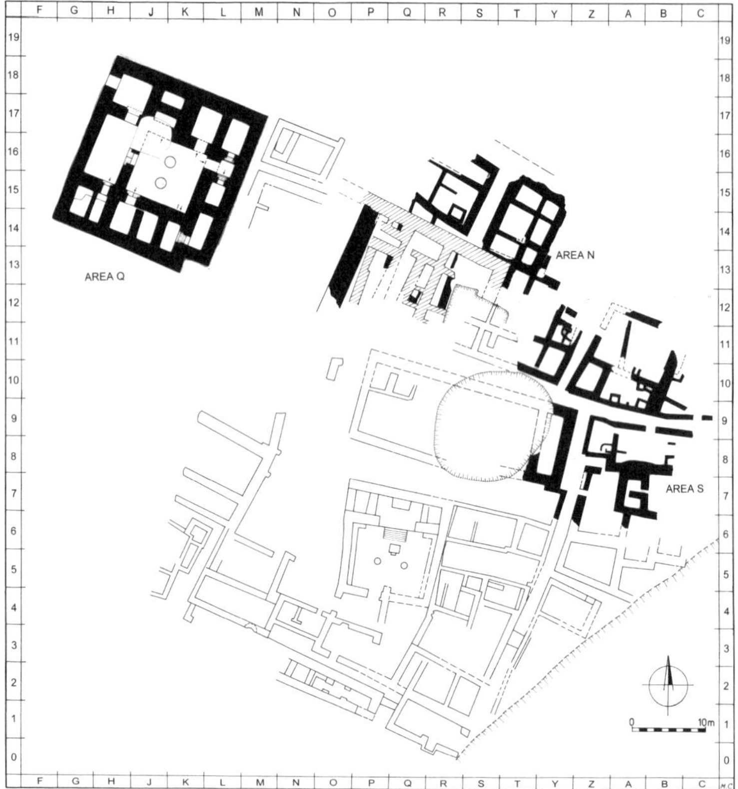

Fig. 6: Plan of Level VI (12th century BCE). In white: walls excavated by UME; in black: walls excavated or re-excavated by the HU expedition; hatched: Building 1700.

In the residential areas excavated in Areas N and S, at least two architectural phases were attributed to the 20th Dynasty (see Tab. 1 above). The houses contained courtyards and rooms in which various grinding, cooking, baking, and storage installations were found. A special feature of the Stratum S-4 houses were the rows of stone bases for wooden posts that divided larger spaces, a feature that disappeared in Stratum S-3. The simple houses cannot be defined as belonging to a specific 'Egyptian' or 'Canaanite' tradition. It is possible that the earlier phase was damaged by an earthquake, as suggested by the two human skeletons found on Stratum S-4 floors.

The quantity of Egyptian inscriptions and monuments found in or attributable to Level VI is exceptionally large and unparalleled elsewhere in Canaan or in earlier levels at Beth-Shean itself.[41] These include the basalt statue of Ramesses III found in front of the northern Temple of Level V which probably originated in Level VI.[42] Inscribed door-jambs and white limestone lintels with prayers and dedications were found in various places in Level VI. Two officials, a father and a son, are each mentioned twice on the Level VI monuments. The father is Thutmose, 'Fanbearer on the right of the king, the captain of the troops, the overseer of foreign countries', and the son is 'Ramesses Weser-khepesh, commander of the troops of the lord of the two lands, great steward'. On one lintel, the latter's name appears aside the royal names of Ramesses III.[43] Level VI also yielded parts of an architectural façade painted in Egyptian style and two relief fragments showing men sitting on folding chairs, which might have belonged to a single lintel.[44] Additional Egyptian monuments found in later contexts may have belonged to either Level VII or VI. These include, among others, a stela of Hesi-Nakht worshipping the goddess Antit and the lower part of a stela with a male figure in Egyptian costume adoring an Egyptian funerary inscription.[45]

While high-ranking Egyptian officials would probably have been able to read the above-mentioned monumental inscriptions, it is inconceivable that local Canaanites or low-ranking Egyptian military personnel could read hieroglyphs. The monuments were probably intended to impress the local population and to symbolize Egyptian hegemony. Knowledge of and the ability to write in hieratic at Beth-Shean during the 13th–12th centuries BCE is demonstrated by two hieratic inscriptions on pottery sherds. One is the above-mentioned Execration

41 For detailed lists cf. James (1966); Ward (1966); Higginbotham (2000), 64– 67; Mazar (2009), 1–32.

42 For a discussion on this statue, cf. Higginbotham (1999). Yannai (1996) has suggested that the Double Temple complex of Level V was constructed in a late phase of Level VI, during the 20th Dynasty, and thus, the Egyptian monuments found in front of the northern Temple were established at a time when there was still an Egyptian presence at Beth-Shean. This is contra to the view of James and myself that the temples of Level V were erected during the Iron Age IB or even later. For the arguments against Yannai's suggestion, cf. Mazar (2009), 1–32.

43 Cf. Ward (1966), 174–176, followed by Singer (1988–1989), suggested that in these inscriptions Thutmose should be identified with the individual of the same name and the titles mentioned in the Megiddo Stratum VIIA ivories hoard. They proposed that Megiddo was an Egyptian administrative center during the 20th Dynasty, but this suggestion has been rejected by Higginbotham (2000), 70–71, and Mazar (2002), 270–271.

44 Cf. Sweeney (1998). For a new reconstruction, cf. Sweeney (2009), 702–707.

45 Cf. Rowe (1930), 34, Fig. 8; 37–38, Pls. 49:1–2, 50:2; Ward (1966), 171.

Text from Level VII and the other, found in our Stratum S-3a, may be read as 'the bow of 'Anat'.[46]

One room in a house in Area S contained the remains of colored wall paintings depicting rosettes and lotus petals, Egyptian motifs known since the 18th Dynasty.[47] The house perhaps belonged to a high-ranking Egyptian official, with the paintings indicating the efforts of such officials to decorate their houses in a way as similar as possible to those in their homeland.

Egyptian experts and craftsmen, working at Beth-Shean permanently or periodically certainly, included scribes, sculptors and engravers of reliefs and inscriptions, potters, wall painters, and perhaps also specialists in faience and glass manufacturing. While some of the Egyptian artifacts were imported from Egypt, most were produced locally. These include duck- or goose-shaped and cobra-shaped clay figurines, faience amulets, stone and bronze objects like fittings, and calcite-alabaster vessels and a bronze razor, although surprisingly, no Egyptian weapons were found. Seal impressions on clay bullae represent evidence of Egyptian administration.[48] The rare commemorative scarab of Amenhotep III describing the arrival of the Mittanian princess Kirgippa is one of only six such scarabs known thus far and the only one found outside Egypt.[49] This must have been a luxury object considered as a valuable heirloom and kept for generations. Some 50% of the pottery was made locally by potters trained in Egyptian pottery-production traditions and technology. Yet, the Egyptian forms were limited to table ware types: bowls, several jar forms, and the enigmatic vessels designated 'beer bottles' that are typical of Egypt. The other vessel types were made in the local Canaanite tradition.[50]

Side-by-side with the Egyptian monuments and artifacts, many objects in the local Canaanite tradition were found. These include about 50% of the pottery (cooking pots, kraters, jars, lamps, etc.), as well as many of the other artifacts like clay figurines, grinding stones, jewelry, spinning and textile manufacture equipment, gypsum vessels, ivory and bone cosmetic boxes, bronze and bone objects.[51] Thus, the majority

46 Cf. Wimmer (1993; 1994); id. (2009), 698–701.

47 David (2009), 708–715.

48 Cf. Brandl (2009), 636–686.

49 Cf. Goldwasser (2002); id. (2009), 687–690.

50 Cf. James/McGovern (1993), 244–245; Martin (2009), 434–477; Panitz-Cohen (2009), 195–433.

51 Cf. Panitz-Cohen/Mazar (2009), 564–596, 721–763; see also James/McGovern (1993), 238.

of the daily-use artifacts were produced by local craftsmen, either locally or brought from nearby Canaanite workshops.

The question raised by these finds is to what extent the Canaanites were part of the population at Beth-Shean and the nature of the interaction between the Egyptians and the Canaanites at the site.[52] Artifacts associated with grinding cereals, cooking, and textile production are all in local Canaanite style, perhaps pointing to the presence of Canaanite women at Beth-Shean. But various other scenarios can be suggested: Canaanite women and their families may have lived at Beth-Shean alongside the Egyptians and cooperated with them; they could have been married to Egyptian officials or military personnel[53] or they could have been inhabitants of nearby local settlements who worked for the Egyptian garrison without actually living at the site. The Canaanite objects could also simply have been purchased in neighboring Canaanite towns. Since it is not possible to distinguish between 'Egyptian' *vis-à-vis* 'Canaanite' households, the proportions of Egyptians and Canaanites among the population at Beth-Shean and the nature of the relationships between the two groups cannot be determined.

The high status of the inhabitants at the site is demonstrated by the elaborate finds like gold foil objects, gold and silver jewelry, and semiprecious stone, glass, and faience beads. But very few objects indicate international trade connections, other than those directly related to Egypt. Some 30 sherds and one restored vessel in the Mycenean IIIC-style came from eastern Cyprus. Such imported pottery is rare in this period in the Levant, and probably reached Beth-Shean under special circumstances, perhaps due to small-scale, privately initiated trade by Cypriots who may have been hired as mercenaries for the Egyptian garrison at the site.[54] Oren suggested the presence of such 'Sea Peoples' mercenaries at Beth-Shean based on the few 'grotesque-style' anthropoid clay coffins found in the northern Cemetery side-by-side with almost 50 naturalistic coffin lids made in the Egyptian style.[55] Three small silver hoards are of particular interest, since they contained 'chocolate bar' silver ingots and used silver objects that had a monetary function,[56] and could have served to pay the wages of Egyptian officials or mercenaries. Analysis of raw materials for various items and of other pro-

52 For a detailed discussion cf. Mazar (2009), 1–32; Panitz-Cohen (2009), 195–433; Martin (2009), 434–477.

53 As suggested by Martin (2009), 434–477, and Panitz-Cohen (2009), 195–433.

54 Cf. Mazar (2007a); Sherratt/Mazar (in press a); Sherratt (2009), 478–499.

55 Cf. Oren (1973), 247, who suggested furthermore that these 'Sea Peoples' are to be identified with the Danuna; cf. also James/McGovern (1993), 247.

56 Cf. Thompson (2009), 597–607.

ducts indicate a wide variety of sources: silver from southeast Turkey and Greece, gold from Egypt; copper from the Timna mines in the Arabah,[57] fish from Egypt and the Mediterranean,[58] and cedar wood from the Lebanese mountains. Stone weights, crucial for trade, indicate the use of the Egyptian dbn unit.

The interaction between Egyptian and Canaanite religion and iconography and religious syncretism at Beth-Shean are reflected in the temple architecture, several monuments, and various artifacts from Levels VII and VI.[59] The above-mentioned Mekal stela from Level VIII or VII and the *ʿAntit* (ʿAnat?) stela indicate the worship of local Canaanite deities by Egyptian officials. Almost half of the pottery figurines and cultic objects were locally produced in the typical Egyptian style, while the other half are Canaanite or unique, again reflecting the mixture of Egyptian and local traditions.

The 'coffin burials' found in the northern Cemetery add important data on the beliefs and customs of the Egyptians at Beth-Shean.[60] The Egyptian character of the burials is demonstrated by the clay coffins, *Ushebti* figurines, and other artifacts paralleled in the cemetery at Deir el-Ballah, which can be attributed with certainty to Egyptian officials or military personnel.

The monuments and statues erected at Beth-Shean during the 20th Dynasty are evidence of extensive Egyptian propaganda and 'showing off'. This does not necessarily indicate strength, but might rather suggest quite the contrary. Throughout this period, Beth-Shean remained a rather small Egyptian stronghold, but it appears to have been one of the few Egyptian strongholds to survive the end of the 19th Dynasty. The Egyptian strongholds at Deir el-Balah, Jaffa, and Aphek (if it was indeed an Egyptian stronghold) were abandoned at or soon after the end of the 19th Dynasty. Apart from Beth-Shean, the few strongholds that continued into the 20th Dynasty are the fort at Haruba in northern Sinai, Tel Sera' Stratum IX, and Tel Mor Stratum VI.[61] Therefore, it ap-

57 Yahalom-Mack/Segal (2009), 589–596.

58 Lernau (2009), 774ff.

59 Cf. Thompson (1970); James/McGovern (1993), 239–244.

60 Cf. Oren (1973), 132–150; James/McGovern (1993), 239.

61 For general surveys, cf. Ward (1966), 174–179; Weinstein (1980). The situation at Tell el-Far'ah (South) is far from clear. For Deir el-Balah, cf. Dothan (1993); for Aphek, cf. Gadot/Yadin (2009); for Haruvit, cf. Oren (1987), 84–97; for Tel Sera', cf. Oren (1993); for Tel Mor, cf. Barako (2007), 242–243. Several scholars consider Lachish Stratum VI and Megiddo Stratum VIIA to have been Egyptian strongholds in the 20th Dynasty, but it seems that both of them rather continued to be Canaanite cities. Tubb and Dorell have suggested the existence of an Egyptian 20th Dynasty stronghold at Tell es-Sa'idiyeh, but this has yet to be substantiated, cf. Tubb/Dorell (1993), 56–58.

pears that the Egyptian hold on Canaan was much weaker during the 20th than during the 19th Dynasty. This would explain the establishment of the Philistine settlements in Philistia, which in the opinion of many scholars occurred during the 20th Dynasty, before the termination of the Egyptian presence in Canaan.[62]

Another important aspect of the excavation data from Beth-Shean is that they provide a solid anchor for an absolute chronology for the 13th–12th centuries BCE in the southern Levant. Even though most of the monuments bearing Pharaonic names were not found *in situ*, it seems that the dating of Level VII to the 19th Dynasty and of Level VI to the 20th Dynasty, together with the equivalent strata exposed in our excavations, is well established and also supported by radiocarbon dates.[63] A scarab of Ramesses IV is the latest New Kingdom object found at Beth-Shean.[64]

The violent destruction of the garrison town apparently occurred at some point between the reigns of Ramesses IV and Ramesses VI. Stratum S-3 houses were destroyed in a severe conflagration, and the collapsed buildings created a thick destruction debris layer up to 1.2 m deep. Beth-Shean could have been destroyed by local Canaanites from neighboring cities, such as Reḥov or Pehal, or by semi-nomadic raiders, who took advantage of the weakness of the Egyptian presence during the late 20th Dynasty (compare the attack of semi-nomadic tribes on the same region described in the Gideon Story Judges 6–7).

The 11th Century BCE

Information on the Iron IB (the late 12th and 11th centuries BCE) at Beth-Shean is based on the few remains attributed to UME Late Level VI, on the Strata 3 and 2 remains excavated by Yadin and Geva, on the results of our excavations in Area S, and on our interpretation of the UME Level V temples.

UME designated ephemeral structural remains above some of the Level VI buildings as Late Level VI.[65] These remains indicate that important Level VI structures went out of use and were replaced by dwellings. A similar picture was seen in our Area S, with Stratum S-2 the equivalent of Late Level VI. The building remains represent the rebuild

62 Cf. Mazar (2007); id. (2008c), 90–95; for a different view cf. Ussishkin (1985; 2008) and Finkelstein (1995).

63 Cf. Mazar/Carmi (2001); Mazar (2009), 1–32.

64 Cf. Weinstein (1993), 221, Pl. 165:8.

65 Cf. James (1966), 19–21.

of the ruined Stratum S-3 city. The street system continued unchanged, with new surfaces laid. Several houses were reconstructed using the same outline as their predecessors, with the outer walls either reused from Stratum S-3 or newly built above the ruined walls of the previous buildings, sometimes with a slight change in orientation.

The pottery recovered from these contexts is typical of the Iron IB in the Jezreel and Beth-Shean Valleys, with close parallels from Megiddo Stratum VI, Yoqne'am Stratum XVII, and other related sites.[66] The lack of Egyptian forms in this assemblage clearly distinguishes it from that of the previous period of Egyptian domination. Clay figurines and cultic objects are either in the local Canaanite tradition or unusual types, and a few may be related to Aegean traditions, like those reflected in Philistine figurines. The continuity in both the architecture and the pottery types indicate that the Stratum S-2 city was built shortly after the destruction of Stratum S-3.[67]

A major question relating to this period is the dating of the Double Temple complex of UME Level V. Although James, following Rowe, attributed it to Level V, she pointed out the mixed nature of the pottery found in the complex that included both Iron I and Iron IIA forms. Ultimately, she opted for the Iron I as the most plausible date for the construction of the temples, and this date is indeed the most plausible in light of the assemblage of ceramic cultic objects found in the southern Temple, elaborately painted in the Canaanite style (see the reconstructed plan in Fig. 7).[68] An impressive collection of Egyptian monuments was found in the courtyard in front of the northern Temple (including the above-mentioned statue of Ramesses III and the stelae of Seti I and Ramesses II) and in the area of the Temple itself (including private stelae, other fragmentary stelae, and inscriptions). Why were so many important Egyptian monuments retained in Level V, at a time when the Egyptians were no longer present at Beth-Shean? It appears that the Canaanite inhabitants of Beth-Shean in the 11th century BCE must have been well acquainted with the special role of their city in the preceding New Kingdom period. The large monuments were probably visible among the ruins of the Egyptian garrison town and perhaps were salvaged and erected in front of the new temples as relics of the

66 Cf. Mazar (1993), 219–223; Panitz-Cohen (2009), 195–433.

67 Contra Finkelstein (1996), who suggested a long gap between Strata S-3 and S-2 and dated the latter to the 10th century BCE based on his 'Low Chronology'.

68 Cf. James (1966), 133–136; Mazar (1993), 219–223; id. (2006a), 34–35. I have suggested that these temples, which may be dated to the Iron Age I, be separated from the well-planned architectural complex of Level V to their north, which can be dated to the Iron Age IIA.

previous 'golden age' of Beth-Shean, and possibly as objects of adoration. It can be assumed that many of the town's inhabitants were descendents of Canaanites who had cooperated with the Egyptians and previously resided at Beth-Shean, and the Egyptian monuments might have held symbolic meaning for them.

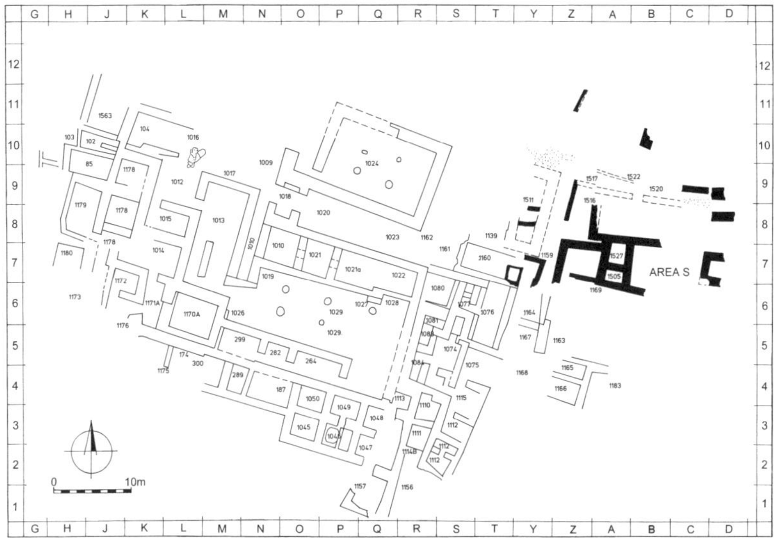

Fig. 7: Reconstructed Plan of Iron IB structures at Beth-Shean. The Double Temple Complex of Lower Level V, excavated by UME (in white) and HU Stratum S-2 (in black).

Canaanite continuity in the plains of Jezreel and Beth-Shean and the Coastal Plain is attested at a good number of other sites, like Megiddo, Yoqne`am, Tel Reḥov, Dor, and Tell Keisan. This fits well to the biblical tradition according to Josh. 17:11, 16 and Judg. 1:27–32, in which these regions are specified as not having been conquered by the Israelites and as where the indigenous Canaanite population resided. The end of this city at Beth-Shean might have come at the same time that the other Canaanite cities on the northern plains were destroyed, like Megiddo Stratum VIA, Yoqne'am Stratum XVII, and Tel Kinarot Stratum V, ca. 1000 BCE.[69]

As for the biblical story of the battle of Gilboa and the hanging of the bodies of Saul and his sons on the walls of Beth-Shean by the Philis-

69 This date, previously based on pottery typology and historical considerations, is now also supported by radiometric data which point to date ca. 1000 BCE with standard deviation of ca. 40 years; cf. Mazar (2008), 102–103, 114; Mazar/Bronk-Ramsey (2008), 164–166; Finkelstein/Piasetzky (2009), 266–267.

tines (1 Samuel 31), if there is any historical truth to it, it cannot be corroborated by archaeology. There is almost no evidence for any 'Sea Peoples' settled at Beth-Shean during the 11th century BCE, perhaps except for a few clay figurines. Although a Philistine raid on the region is not improbable, it left no archaeological evidence, and Beth-Shean certainly was not a Philistine or other 'Sea Peoples' city.

The Iron Age II

Although James presented three Iron II strata at Beth-Shean, designated Lower Level V, Upper Level V, and Level IV, as she herself admitted, it is extremely difficult to interpret the UME results relating to this period. The plans of Level V and Level IV are less than satisfactory: they are schematic and in several places show jumbles of walls from several phases with no clear separation between them.[70] In fact the terms Lower V and Upper V reflect a spatial rather than a vertical stratigraphic division: the southern part of the excavated area, including the Double Temple complex, was attributed mainly to Lower V, while the complex to the north of the temples was attributed to Upper V, or generally to Level V. We tried to gain a better understanding of this period through our excavations in Areas S and P.

Two Iron IIA strata were exposed in Area S. The earlier Stratum S-1b was ephemeral and included only a few building remains, while the later Stratum S-1a included the fragmentary remains of three large structures that must have been public buildings on the summit of the mound.[71] They had wide walls with foundation of basalt boulders and a mudbrick superstructure framed with wooden beams at the bottom, above the stone foundations. These buildings can be integrated with the well-planned architectural complex of Level V excavated by UME to the west (see Fig. 8).

70 Cf. James (1966), Figs. 74–75.
71 Cf. Mazar (2006a), 173–201.

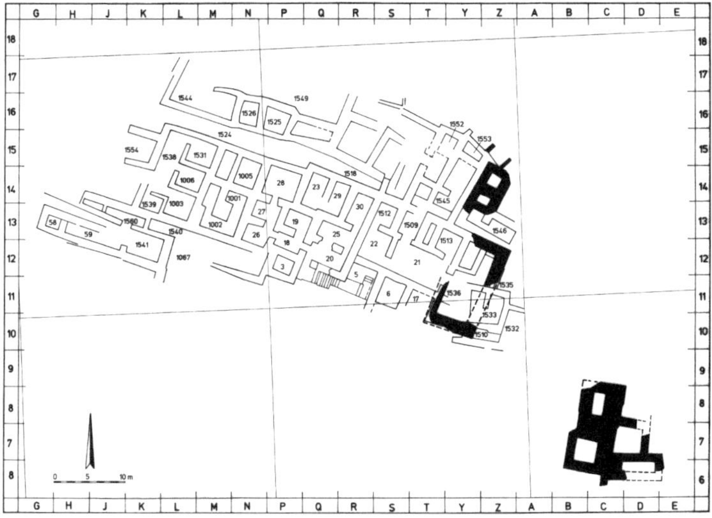

Fig. 8: Reconstructed Plan of Beth-Shean in the Iron IIA, based on Plans of UME Level V (northern block, in white) and HU Str. S-1a (in black).

The architecture as well as a large number of storage jars found in one of these buildings hint that they were administrative buildings, perhaps related to a central administration. The buildings were destroyed in a severe conflagration. Their associated pottery is typical of the 10th–9th centuries BCE and is identical with the pottery from Tel Reḥov Strata V–IV, Tel `Amal, Tell el-Hammah, Megiddo Strata VB and IVB–VA, and Rosh Zayit Strata 2–3.[72] This assemblage is the subject of a current debate. Traditionally, this pottery is dated to the second half of the 10th century BCE, but as demonstrated at Jezreel, Tel Reḥov, and elsewhere, it was certainly in use during the 9th century BCE, until the time of the Aramean Wars ca. 830 BCE. The debate is whether this assemblage was in use already in the second half of the 10th century BCE, as the traditional chronology maintains. My answer to this question is positive, but others are skeptical, and the issue remains unresolved.[73] If this pottery is dated to the 10th century, then Stratum S-1 could be related to the reference to Beth-Shean in the fifth district of Solomon (1 Kings 4:12) and in Shoshenq I's list of conquered cities. However, just as the pottery chronology is debated, so is the date and historicity of Solomon's list of districts: while many scholars credit this list as a reliable histori-

72 For details, cf. Mazar (2006a), 313–384.

73 For recent summaries, with references to other views, of the debate regarding the 'Low Chronology' versus the 'High Chronology' and my suggested 'Modified Conventional Chronology', cf. Mazar (2005; 2007b; 2008c); Mazar/Bronk-Ramsey (2008).

cal source that reflects the time of Solomon, others claim that it was composed in a much later date.[74] The archaeological remains from Stratum S-1 may, therefore, suggest that Beth-Shean was a rather important city and administrative center in the late 10th century BCE, but this equation must be taken with due caution.

In the western part of the northern block of UME Level V, a 'gate structure' was identified.[75] This building was partly built of ashlars with drafted margins, as were other public buildings in Iron Age Israel, but its plan and construction date are uncertain. It may have served as an entranceway to the administrative complex to its east.[76] Two pillared buildings stood to the east of this structure, each with one row of square monolithic pillars. This area was destroyed in a severe conflagration, perhaps at the same time as the destruction of Jezreel and Tel Reḥov Stratum IV during the second half of the 9th century BCE.

UME Level IV, which is not well attested, should be attributed to the rebuilding of the city in the 8th century BCE until its destruction by Tiglath-Pileser III in 732 BCE. Its plan shows a jumble of fragmentary, poorly preserved walls, perhaps representing several building phases.[77] In Area P, close to the western slope of the mound, four successive strata of the Iron Age II city were excavated.[78] The two earlier Strata P-10 and P-9, exposed only in small probes, date to the Iron IIA (10th–9th centuries BCE), while the two upper Strata P-8 and P-7 date to the Iron IIB (ca. 830 BCE until the Assyrian conquest). Stratum P-8 was represented by the remains of substantial buildings that were violently destroyed at some point during the first half of the 8th century BCE. In the following Stratum P-7, parts of a large dwelling were exposed, its plan based on the principles of the 'four-room house', with a central hall surrounded by six rooms on its three sides, albeit without the use of pillars so typical of such houses (see Fig. 9). This is one of the largest Iron Age II dwellings excavated in Israel thus far, and probably served as the residence of a high-ranking family.[79]

74 For a later date, cf. Na'aman (2001), with references to earlier literature.
75 See the plan in James (1966), 31.
76 Cf. the discussion in Mazar (2006a), 35.
77 Cf. James (1966), Fig. 73
78 Cf. Mazar (2006a), 202–286.
79 For the rich finds from this building, cf. Mazar (2006a), 313–504.

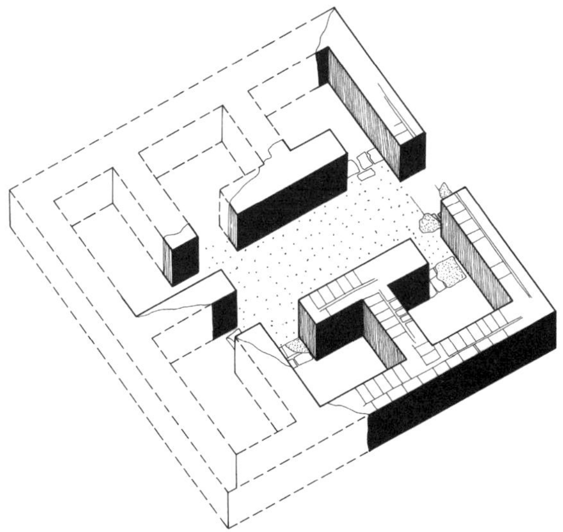

Fig. 9: Reconstruction of Iron IIB Residential Building in Area P.

Several 8th century BCE fragmentary ostraca with lists of names and quantities of commodities were found in our excavations. These are among the few ink inscriptions from northern Israel, apart from the well known Samaria ostraca. The rare name *Zma`* appears three times, once in the combination *`lt zma`* ('The goddess of Zma?').[80]

The combined data from the UME and HU excavations provide some evidence for the town plan of Beth-Shean during the Iron II. The town was built on a steep slope. The 'gate structure' and the buildings to its east on the summit of the mound may have been part of a well-planned administrative complex. The steep step in the mound in all likelihood represents the northern limit of the town, since no Iron II remains were found in Area L to its north. In Area P, a street ran parallel to the slope of the mound at a higher elevation than the elaborate dwelling to its west. Thus, the city appears to have been constructed on a series of terraces on the slope of the mound, descending to the northwest. The buildings in Area P may have been part of a dwelling quarter along the western perimeter of the mound, although it cannot be determined how far this quarter extended further north of Area P. It appears that during the Iron Age, the entire settled area of the town was no more than 1.5–2 ha. No evidence for fortifications was found, either because they did not exist or because the edge of the mound on the west was cut away during the Roman period.

80 Cf. Mazar (2006a), 505–513.

The Iron Age II city at Beth-Shean came to an end in a violent destruction, as evidenced by the fierce fire that destroyed the dwelling in Area P. This destruction can be attributed to the Assyrian conquest in 732 BCE. It was followed by a meager squatters' occupation and then an occupation gap that lasted until the Hellenistic period. The later settlement history of Tel Beth-Shean from the Hellenistic through the Medieval period is outside the scope of the present overview.

Bibliography

Aharoni, Y. (1979), The Land of the Bible: A Historical Geography, transl. from the Hebrew by A.F. Rainey (revised edition), Philadelphia.

Ahituv, S. (1984), Canaanite Toponyms in Ancient Egyptian Documents, Jerusalem/Leiden.

Arubas (2006), B., Excursus: The Impact of Town Planning at Scythopolis on the Topography at Tel Beth Shean: A New Understanding of Its Fortification and Status, in: A. Mazar, Excavations at Tel Beth-Shean 1989–1996. Vol. I: From the Late Bronze Age IIB to the Medieval Period, The Beth-Shean Valley Archaeological Project Publications 1, Jerusalem, 48–60.

Barako, T.J. (2007), Tel Mor: The Moshe Dothan Excavations, 1959–1960, Israel Antiquities Authority Reports 32, Jerusalem.

Brandl, B. (2009), Scarabs, Seals, Sealings and Seal Impressions from Areas N and S, in: N. Panitz-Cohen/A. Mazar, A. (eds.), Excavations at Tel Beth-Shean 1989–1996, Vol. III, The Beth-Shean Valley Archaeological Project Publications 3, Jerusalem, 636–686.

Braun, E. (2004), Early Beth Shan (Strata XIX–XIII): G.M. FitzGerald's Deep Cut on the Tell, University of Pennsylvania Museum of Archaeology and Anthropology 121, Philadelphia.

David, A. (2009), Egyptian 20th Dynasty Wall Paintings From Beth-Shean, in: N. Panitz-Cohen/A. Mazar (eds.), Excavations at Tel Beth-Shean 1989–1996, Vol. III, The Beth-Shean Valley Archaeological Project Publications 3, Jerusalem, 708–715.

Dothan, T. (1993), Deir el-Balah, in: E. Stern (ed.), The New Encyclopedia of Archaeological Excavations in the Holy Land, Vol. I (revised edition), New York/Jerusalem, 343–347.

Finkelstein, I. (1995), The Date of the Settlement of the Philistines in Canaan, Tel Aviv 22, 213–239.

– (1996), The Stratigraphy and Chronology of Megiddo and Beth Shean in the 12th–11th Centuries B.C.E., Tel Aviv 23, 170–184.

– /Piasetzky, E. (2009), Radiocarbon-Dated Destruction Layers: A Skeleton for Iron Age Chronology in the Levant, Oxford Journal of Archaeology 28, 255–274.

Gadot, Y./Yadin, E. (2009), Aphek-Antipatris II The Remains on the Acropolis, Monograph Series of the Sonia and Marco Nadler Institute of Archaeology 27, Tel Aviv.

Goldwasser, O. (2004), A 'Kirgipa' Commemorative Scarab of Amenhotep III from Beit-Shean, Egypt and the Levant XII, 191–193.

– (2009), A 'Kirgipa' Commemorative Scarab of Amenhotep III, in: N. Panitz-Cohen/A. Mazar (eds.), Excavations at Tel Beth-Shean 1989–1996, Vol. III, The Beth-Shean Valley Archaeological Project Publications 3, Jerusalem, 687–690.

Goren, Y./Finkelstein, I./Na'aman, N. (2004), Inscribed in Clay: Provenance Study of the Amarna Tablets and other Ancient Near Eastern Texts, Tel Aviv.

Higginbotham, C. (1999), The Statue of Ramses III from Beth Shean, Tel Aviv 26, 225–232.

– (2000), Egyptianization and Elite Emulation in Ramesside Palestine: Governance and Accommodation on the Imperial Periphery, Culture and History of the Ancient Near East 2, Leiden.

Horowitz, W. (1996), An Inscribed Clay Cylinder from Amarna Age Beth Shean, IEJ 46, 208–218.

James, F.W. (1966), The Iron Age at Beth Shan: A Study of Levels VI–IV, Museum Monographs 28, Philadelphia.

– /McGovern, P.E. (1993), The Late Bronze Egyptian Garrison at Beth Shan: A Study of Levels VII and VIII, Vol. I–II, University Museum Monographs 85, Philadelphia.

Lernau, O. (2009), The Fish Bones, in: N. Panitz-Cohen/A. Mazar (eds.), Excavations at Tel Beth-Shean 1989–1996, Vol. III, The Beth-Shean Valley Archaeological Project Publications 3, Jerusalem, 774ff.

Maeir, A.M. (1997), The Material Culture of the Central and Northern Jordan Valley During the Middle Bronze II Age Period: Pottery and Settlement Pattern, Unpublished PhD Dissertation, The Hebrew University, Jerusalem.

Martin, M.A.S. (2009), The Egyptian Assemblage, in: N. Panitz-Cohen/A. Mazar (eds.), Excavations at Tel Beth-Shean 1989–1996, Vol. III, The Beth-Shean Valley Archaeological Project Publications 3, Jerusalem, 434–477.

Mazar, A. (1992), Temples of the Middle and Late Bronze Ages and the Iron Age, in: A. Kempinski/R. Reich (eds.), The Architecture of Ancient Israel: From the Prehistoric to the Persian Periods, Jerusalem, 161–189.

– (1993), Beth Shean in the Iron Age: Preliminary Report and Conclusions of the 1990–1991 Excavations, IEJ 43, 201–229.
– (1997), Four Thousand Years of History at Tel Beth Shean: An Account of the Renewed Excavations, BA 60, 62–76.
– (2002), Megiddo in the Thirteenth-Eleventh Centuries B.C.E.: A Review of Some Recent Studies, in: E.D. Oren/S. Ahituv (eds.), Studies in Archaeology and Related Disciplines, Aharon Kempinski Memorial Volume, Beer Sheba XV, Beer Sheba, 264–282.
– (2005), The Debate over the Chronology of the Iron Age in the Southern Levant: Its History, the Current Situation and a Suggested Resolution, in: T.E. Levy/T. Higham (eds.), The Bible and Radiocarbon Dating: Archaeology, Text and Science, London, 15–30.
– (2006a), Excavations at Tel Beth-Shean 1989–1996: Vol. I: From the Late Bronze Age IIB to the Medieval Period, The Beth-Shean Valley Archaeological Project Publications 1, Jerusalem.
– (2006b), Tel Beth-Shean and the Fate of Mounds in the Intermediate Bronze Age, in: S. Gitin/J.E. Wright/J.P. Dessel (eds.), Confronting the Past: Archaeological and Historical Essays on Ancient Israel in Honor of W.G. Dever, Winona Lake, 105–118.
– (2007a), Myc IIIC in the Land of Israel: Its Distribution, Date and Significance, in: M. Bietak/E. Czerny (eds.), The Synchronisation of Civilisations in the Eastern Mediterranean in the Second Millennium B.C. III: Proceedings of the SCIEM 2000 – 2nd EuroConference Vienna 28th of May–1st of June 2003, Contributions to the Chronology of the Eastern Mediterranean, Vienna, 571–583.
– (2007b), The Spade and the Text: The Interaction between Archaeology and Israelite History Relating to the Tenth–Ninth Centuries BCE, in: H.G.M. Williamson (ed.), Understanding the History of Ancient Israel, PBA 143, London, 143–171.
– (2008a), Beth-Shean (update), in: E. Stern (ed.), The New Encyclopedia of Archaeological Excavations in the Holy Land, Vol. 5, Jerusalem, 1616–1622.
– (2008b), Rehov, Tel, in: E. Stern (ed.), The New Encyclopedia of Archaeological Excavations in the Holy Land, Vol. 5, Jerusalem, 2013–2018.
– (2008c), From 1200 to 850 B.C.E.: Remarks on Some Selected Archaeological Issues, in: L.L. Grabbe (ed.), Israel in Transition: From Late Bronze II to Iron IIa (c. 1250–850 B.C.E.), Vol. 1, Library of Hebrew Bible/Old Testament Studies 491, New York/London, 86–121.
– (2009), Introduction and Overview, in: N. Panitz-Cohen/A. Mazar (eds.), Excavations at Tel Beth-Shean 1989–1996, Vol. III, The Beth-Shean Valley Archaeological Project Publications 3, Jerusalem, 1–32.

– /Bronk-Ramsey, C. (2008), ^{14}C Dates and the Iron Age Chronology of Israel: A Response, Radiocarbon 50, 159–180.
– /Carmi, I. (2001), Radiocarbon Dates from Iron Age Strata at Tel Beth Shean and Tel Rehov, Radiocarbon 43, 1333–1342.
– /Mullins, R.A. (2007, eds.), Excavations at Tel Beth-Shean 1989–1996. Vol. II: The Middle and Late Bronze Age Strata in Area R, The Beth-Shean Valley Archaeological Project Publications 2, Jerusalem.
– /Rotem, Y. (2009), Tel Beth Shean during the EBIB Period: Evidence for Social Complexity in the Late Fourth Millennium B.C.E., Levant 41, 131–154.
– /Ziv-Esudri, A./Cohen-Weinberger, A. (2000), The Early Bronze II–III at Tel Beth Shean: Preliminary Observations, in: G. Philip/D. Baird (eds.), Ceramics and Change in the Early Bronze Age of the Southern Levant, Levantine Archaeology 2, Sheffield, 255–278.
Moran, W.L. (1992), The Amarna Letters, Baltimore.
Na'aman, N. (2001), Solomon's District List (1 Kings 4:7–19) and the Assyrian Province System in Palestine, UF 33, 419–436.
Oren, E.D. (1973), The Northern Cemetery of Beth-Shean, Museum Monograph of the University Museum of Pennsylvania, Leiden.
– (1987), The "Ways of Horus" in North Sinai, in: A.F. Rainey (ed.), Egypt, Israel, Sinai: Archaeological and Historical Relationships in the Biblical Period, Tel Aviv, 69–119.
– (1993), Sera`, Tel, in: E. Stern (ed.), The New Encyclopedia of Archaeological Excavations in the Holy Land, Vol. 5 (revised edition), 1330–1331, New York/Jerusalem.
Panitz-Cohen, N. (2009), The Local Canaanite Pottery, in: N. Panitz-Cohen/A. Mazar (eds.), Excavations at Tel Beth-Shean 1989–1996, Vol. III, The Beth-Shean Valley Archaeological Project Publications 3, Jerusalem, 195–433.
– /Mazar, A. (2009, eds.), Excavations at Tel Beth-Shean 1989–1996, Vol. III, The Beth-Shean Valley Archaeological Project Publications 3, Jerusalem.
Porter, R. (2008), A Note on Ramesses IV and 'Mernephtah' at Beth Shean, Tel Aviv 35, 244–248.
Pritchard, J.B. (1950, ed.), Ancient Near Eastern Texts: Relating to the Old Testament, Princeton.
Redford, D.B. (1992), Egypt, Canaan and Israel in Ancient Times, Princeton.
Rowe, A. (1930), The Topography and History of Beth-shan, Beth-shan I, Philadelphia.
– (1940), The Four Canaanite Temples of Beth-shan, Beth-shan II:1, Philadelphia.

Schloen, J.D. (2001), The House of the Father as Fact and Symbol: Patrimonialism in Ugarit and the Ancient Near East, Vol. 1, Studies in the Archaeology and History of the Levant 2, Winona Lake.

Simons, J.J. (1937), Handbook for the Study of Egyptian Topographical Lists relating to Western Asia, Leiden.

Sherratt, S./Mazar, A. (in press a), "Mycenaean IIIC" and Related Pottery from Beth Shean, in: A.E. Killebrew/G. Lehman/M. Artzy (eds.), The Philistines and Other "Sea Peoples" in Text and Archaeology, Atlanta.

– (2009), Imported Mycenaean IIIC Pottery, in: N. Panitz-Cohen/A. Mazar (eds.), Excavations at Tel Beth-Shean 1989–1996, Vol. III, The Beth-Shean Valley Archaeological Project Publications 3, Jerusalem, 478–499.

Singer, I. (1988–1989), The Political Status of Megiddo VIIA, Tel Aviv 15–16, 101–112.

Stern, E. (1993, ed.), The New Encyclopedia of Archaeological Excavations in the Holy Land (revised edition), New York/Jerusalem.

Sweeney, D. (1998), The Man on the Folding Chair: An Egyptian Relief from Beit Shean, IEJ 48, 38–53.

– (2009), A Relief Fragment Depicting a Man on a Folding Chair, in: N. Panitz-Cohen/A. Mazar (eds.), Excavations at Tel Beth-Shean 1989–1996, Vol. III, The Beth-Shean Valley Archaeological Project Publications 3, Jerusalem, 702–707.

Thompson, C.M. (2009), Three 20th Dynasty Silver Hoards, in: N. Panitz-Cohen/A. Mazar (eds.), Excavations at Tel Beth-Shean 1989–1996, Vol. III, The Beth-Shean Valley Archaeological Project Publications 3, Jerusalem, 597–607.

Thompson, H.O. (1970), Mekal: The God of Bet–Shan, Leiden.

Tubb, J./Dorrell, P.G. (1993), Tell es-Sa`idiyeh: Interim Report on the Sixth Season of Excavations, PEQ 125, 5–69.

Ussishkin, D. (2004), The Renewed Archaeological Excavations at Lachish (1973–1994), Monograph Series of the Sonia and Marco Nadler Institute of Archaeology 22, Tel Aviv.

– (2008), The Date of the Philistine Settlement in the Coastal Plain: The View from Megiddo and Lachish, in: L.L. Grabbe (ed.), Israel in Transition: From Late Bronze II to Iron IIa (c. 1250–850 B.C.E.), Vol. 1, Library of Hebrew Bible/Old Testament Studies 491, New York/London, 203–218.

Ward, W.A. (1966), The Egyptian Inscriptions of Level VI, in: F.W. James (ed.), The Iron Age at Beth Shan: A Study of Levels VI–IV, Museum Monographs, Philadelphia, 161–180.

Weinstein, J.M. (1980), The Egyptian Empire in Palestine: A Reassessment, BASOR 238, 1–28.

– (1993), The Scarabs, Seals and Rings, in: F.W. James/P.E. McGovern, The Late Bronze Egyptian Garrison at Beth Shan: A Study of Levels VII and VIII, Vol. I–II, University Museum Monographs 85, Philadelphia, 221–225.

Wimmer, S.J. (1993), Ein Ächtungstext aus Israel/Palästina, in: VI congresso internazionale di Egittologia. Atti II, Torino, 571–578.

– (1994), "Der Bogen der Anat" in Bet-Schean?, BN 73, 36–41.

– (2009), A Hieratic Fragment: "The Bow of Anat"?, in: N. Panitz-Cohen/A. Mazar (eds.), Excavations at Tel Beth-Shean 1989–1996, Vol. III, The Beth-Shean Valley Archaeological Project Publications 3, Jerusalem, 698–701.

Yadin, Y./Geva, S. (1986), Investigations at Beth Shean: The Early Iron Age Strata, Qedem 23, Jerusalem.

Yahalom-Mack, N./Segal, I. (2009), Metallurgical Analysis, in: N. Panitz-Cohen/A. Mazar (eds.), Excavations at Tel Beth-Shean 1989–1996, Vol. III, The Beth-Shean Valley Archaeological Project Publications 3, Jerusalem, 589–596.

Yannai, E. (1996), A New Approach to Levels VI–V at Beth-Shan, Tel Aviv 23, 185–194.

Zori, N. (1962), An Archeological Survey of the Beth-Shean Valley, in: The Beth Shean Valley: The 17th Archaeological Convention of the Israel Exploration Society, Jerusalem, 135–198 (in Hebrew).

Nysa-Scythopolis

Ethnicity and Religion

GABRIEL MAZOR

The Beth-She'an Archaeological Project (1986–2000) was conducted by several expeditions of the Israel Antiquities Authority (IAA) and the Institute of Archaeology of the Hebrew University at Jerusalem (IAHU).[1] The large scale excavations revealed, apart from the Beth-She'an mound and the Crusader Fortress, considerable parts of Nysa-Scythopolis, the largest Hellenic polis in the region situated to the west of the Jordan Valley, throughout its Hellenistic and Roman-Byzantine era. Earlier and current researchers revealed the site's magnificent archaeological remains and illuminated the influential contribution of the city of Beth-She'an/Nysa-Scythopolis/Beisan to the region's major historical chapters. The excavations were followed by preservation and reconstruction that turned the site into a tourist attraction and yielded considerable data and many publications.

The rather complicated issues of ethnicity and religious affiliation and their influential impact over culture and history, though not entirely neglected in the past, loomed recently large in the archaeological research. Therefore, as scarce as the accessible evidence might be, its evaluation is undoubtedly crucial for a better understanding of Hellenic culture in its local as well as regional historical expressions. Di-

1 The vast project was conducted by two major and two secondary expeditions. The IAA expedition directed by Gabriel Mazor and Rachel Bar Nathan excavated parts of the Hellenistic period city, the northeastern and northwestern city gates of the Roman-Byzantine periods, the Harod stream bridges and the southern part of the vast Roman-Byzantine civic center. The Expedition of the IAHU directed by Yoram Tsafrir and Gideon Foerster excavated the amphitheater area and the northern part of the civic center. Two other expeditions that of the IAA directed by Jon Seligman excavated the Crusader fortress and that of the IAHU directed by Amihai Mazar excavated the Beth-She'an mound. The excavations were followed by large scale preservation and restoration that turned the site into a major tourist attraction. Recently final reports are gradually published, cf. Hadad (2002; 2005); Mazar (2006; 2007); Mazor/Najjar (2007); Mazar/Mazor/Arubas/Foerster/Tsafrir/Seligman (2008), 1616–1644.

versity of ethnicity throughout the various historical chapters and its interwoven connection with religion and cult were in the past and are still in the present fundamental issues in any research of Nysa-Scythopolis, to which this article intends to open a few windows.

The Hellenistic Polis

Nysa-Scythopolis was first founded on the desolated mound of Beth-She'an by Ptolemy II Philadelphus around the mid-3rd century BCE, as a military stronghold designated to defend the main route from Acco Ptolemais to Philadelphia and served as an important component of the Ptolemaic strategic defensive deployment in the region.[2] Subsequently, it developed into an administrative center, the residence of a growing number of Ptolemaic officials, members of the administrative mechanism. Gradually, a settlement of native services-suppliers developed nearby, resulting in a slow integration of the latter inhabitants with the former. Around 170 BCE a *polis* was founded by Antiochus IV out of the old stronghold-administrative center on the nearby Tel Iztabba, situated to the north of Beth-She'an mound and Harod stream.[3] The newly built and founded *polis* was planned according to the Hippodamian urban planning pattern, characteristic for many Hellenistic period *poleis* all over the east and Asia Minor. Streets and alleys were laid out according to a strict grid while residential and public quarters were separated in preplanned designated insulae, built and decorated ac-

2 Regarding the enigmatic name of the settlement ΣΚΥΘΟΠΟΛΙΣ, Σκυθων πόλις 'City of the Scythians' see Plinius, *Nat. Hist.* V, 74; Solinus, *Collectanea rerum memorabilium* XXXVI; Malalas, *Chronographia* 139–140; cf. Avi-Yonah (1962), 123–134; Lifshitz (1978), 142–144; Rigsby (1980), 238–242; Fuks (1983), 160–165. Avi-Yonah dated the foundation to 254 BCE, regarding it as a possible initiative of Ptolemy II and Paerisides II, king of Bosphorus, on his embassy to Egypt, cf. Avi-Yonah (1962), 127–128, and presumably inhabited by Scythian Archers that served in the Ptolemaic army, cf. Launey (1950), 421–423. Fuks (1983), 44–53, dated it to 260 BCE. Avi-Yonah (1962) argues that the suffix *polis* in its name does not necessarily mean that it was a real polis from the beginning, cf. to Egyptian *nomes*, certainly not cities, that carried the suffix as well Jones (1937), 297, in spite of the fact that in the incident described by Josephus, *Antiquities* 12, 183, concerning the tax collector Joseph the *Comes* some distinguished citizens of the city were termed τούς πρώτους, a term commonly associated with dignitaries of a *polis*, Fuks (1983), 47–49.

3 In contrast to the Ptolemaic policy that minimized new *poleis* foundations, the Seleucids in general and Antiochus IV in particular had a relatively more liberal policy and, therefore, founded out of economic reasons far more *poleis*, cf. Jones (1937), 16–17; Rigsby (1980), 238–242. Rigsby assumes that the city's first name was 'Scythopolis' and her second name Nysa was given when it was re-founded in honor of Antiochus IV niece.

cording to common Hellenistic methods. What kind of evidence does the archaeological data present regarding the ethnic identity and the religious practices of Nysa-Scythopolis' citizens? Avi-Yonah assumed, accepting the name of the city at face value that its first inhabitants were retired Scythian archers (*cleruchy*) from Bosphorus, or units alleged to be Scythian of the Ptolemaic army that did not actually create a *polis* but a *politeuma* (πολίτευμα), whose land was cultivated by native farmers. Fuks rejected those assumptions for lack of supporting evidence and assumed, also with no supporting evidence, that the first inhabitants were most likely of Macedonian, Greek and Thracian origins or Greeks of Asia Minor serving in the army and administrative system of Ptolemy II.[4]

Although the current excavations on the Beth-She'an mound first and at Tel Iztabba later were rather limited in scale, the evidence was quite homogeneous in nature.[5] City planning and building methods, observed at the more recently founded *polis* on Tel Iztabba, clearly indicate Greek urban planning and Hellenistic architectural traditions that were still valid ca. 90 years after the founding of the stronghold-administrative center by the Ptolemaic army and administrative mechanism. Numerous Rodian amphorae, though common in all of the Hellenistic period sites in the region, but rather scarce at Jewish sites in the very same region, together with other *imported* vessels argue for consumption habits of and commercial ties of the Hellenic citizens.[6] A number of bollae (ca. 100) originating from a private archive are comprised exclusively of finger rings with scenes of Greek mythology and did not include even a single oriental origin symbol or scene. All legal or administrative documents that must have been in that archive, the nature and contents of which is regretfully unknown, were clearly stamped by people of Hellenic ethnicity or by deeply Hellenized natives of Syrian origin that must have composed the elite stratum of the city. Furthermore, not even a single find could have attested to remote Scythian origin.

A remarkable marble head of a colossal statue, most probably depicting Alexander the Great, that might have originated from a Hellenistic period temple, the remains of which are still unidentified, was found on the Beth-She'an mound and dated to the 3rd century BCE.[7]

---

4 Cf. Avi-Yonah (1962), 128–129; Launy (1950), 421–423; Fuks (1983), 51.

5 Mazar (2006), 523–625; Mazor/Sandhaus (forthcoming).

6 For the ethnic association of Rodian stamped amphora in Jerusalem cf. Ariel (1990), 13–98; for a contradicting view cf. Finkielsztejn (1999), 21*–36*.

7 Cf. Rowe (1930), 45, Fig. LV. The assumption of Thiersch (1932), 52–76, that it might have been Antiochus IV portrayed as Dionysos is rather questionable.

An inscription found nearby mentions the priests of the Olympian Zeus, the savior Gods and Demetrius II Nicator (at his first reign 145–138 BCE): [Ευβο]υλος Επικράτου [...] [Ηρακλ]είδης Σαραπίωνος. The priests' names are of Greek origin while the father of one of them is most likely Egyptian.[8]

Among the mythological scenes depicted on the bollae one in particular attracts attention by its uniqueness and prominence. It depicts Tyche/Nysa nursing young Dionysos and it might confirm the validity of the city founding myth already in the Hellenistic period. Both, bollae and the above-mentioned inscription mentioning priests of Διός Ολυμπιου, seem to indicate that the gods of the founding triad Zeus, Nysa and Dionysos were the main deities worshiped at Nysa-Scythopolis already during the Hellenistic period. Yet, three of the main components, characteristic of Hellenistic culture and commonly found in all *poleis* of Asia Minor: the Greek theater, gymnasium and temple are absent in all of the Hellenic *poleis* in the region, Nysa-Scythopolis included, as if to make a statement regarding the nature and substance of Hellenization and its cultural influence in the region.

Nysa-Scythopolis was conquered by John Hyrcanus in 108/107 BCE, completely razed and not resettled by the Hasmoneans while its inhabitants were all exiled, most probably seeking shelter in various other *poleis* of the *Decapolis* in Transjordan.[9] The excavations' results clearly indicated a fierce destruction. No Hasmonean resettlement stratum was anywhere found.

A Hellenic Polis under Roman Spell

The conquest of Syria by Pompey (64/63 BCE) established a Roman province in a region that had been densely settled with Greek *poleis* that controlled extensive territories. The Hellenistic *poleis* were liberated from Hasmonean rule, adopted the Pompeian era and were rebuilt or refounded by the governor Gabinius. Nysa-Scythopolis was renamed for a short time *Gabinia Nysa*. Due to the sense of security, later enhanced by the policy of the Roman Empire (*Pax Romana*), the city was now detached from its well-protected mounds and newly constructed in the vast area of the Amal basin and its surrounding hills to the south

8 Cf. Abel/Vincent (1930), 45; Mouterde (1933), 180–182.

9 *Megillat Ta'anit* records that on the 15th and 16th of Sivan the people of Beth-She'an and its valley went into exile.

of the Harod Stream.[10] Although testimony from historical sources for that period is scarce, it seems that the city was included among the territories Anthony granted to Cleopatra, yet, it was not annexed by Augustus to Herod's kingdom after Actium and remained part of *Provincia Syria*. The unique location of Nysa-Scythopolis on the regional junction that linked the flourishing coastal cities (Caesarea, Acco-Ptolemais) with the extensive trade network of Damascus and the wealthy cities of Transjordan, brought about greater importance and economic prosperity for the city.[11] The urban planning of Nysa-Scythopolis in its prime era, the 2nd to 3rd centuries CE, can be best termed "from function to monument"[12], its architecture characterized, as in most other cities in the provinces of the Roman Empire, by the remarkable new architectural design and baroque décor of its colonnaded streets, impressive monuments and vast public buildings.[13]

Ethnicity

Josephus states that the Hellenic cities freed by Pompey and rebuilt and refounded by Gabinius were returned to their lawful inhabitants, joined by steady wave of eager colonizers. The population of Nysa-Scythopolis, the largest Hellenic polis of the *Decapolis*[14], reached at its prime, during the imperial period, an estimated number of ca. 30,000 inhabitants: former citizens and new residents. What do we know about their ethnicity? How many of the descendants of the former Hellenic inhabitants returned, 43 years after a violent exile, to a newly founded and rebuilt city under a new regime? Who were the colonists so glad to relocate? Retired Latin origin soldiers of the Republican legions or native recruits of the auxiliaries, dignitaries of the state administrative system or Hellenic inhabitants from neighboring territories?[15] Prior to the visit of Hadrian in the region (130 CE) a legionary

---

10 Cf. Plinius, *Nat.Hist.* V, 74; Josephus, *Wars* I, VII, 7; Id., *Antiquities* XIV, IV, 2; cf. Barkay (2003), 159; Mazor/Najjar (2007), xii–xiii.

11 Cf. Mazor (2004), 1–12.

12 Segal (1997).

13 Cf. Mazor (forthcoming b); MacDonald (1986); Lyttelton (1974).

14 The term seems to be rather vague and mainly used by foreigners, never mentioned in inscriptions or coins of any *polis* in the region, in which the term *Coele Syria* was preferred, see Parker (1975), 437–441; Schürer (1973–1979), II, 125–127; Fuks (1983), 170–172.

15 Regarding Herod's resettlement of Samaria, cf. Josephus, *Wars* I, XXI, 2, and that of Tiberias, Josephus, *Antiquities* XVIII, 5. It should be pointed out that no Latin inscriptions were found in the city.

camp was built near the city at Tel Shalem.[16] It would be reasonable to assume that relations of various kinds developed between the city and the nearby camp, resulting in marriage, the growth of families and eventually retirement as citizens. Yet, one must point out that all the inscriptions that were found in the city and dated to the Roman period, were written in Greek, not Latin, and carry Greek names. An inscription over a pedestal mounted by a statue of Marcus Aurelius and dedicated to the emperor states the titles of the city: "the people of Nysa also (called) the people of Scythopolis, the holy and of right of sanctuary, one of Coele Syria's Greek cities." The titles are clearly of archaic nature, presumably reborn through the Pan-Hellenic eastern policy of Hadrian.[17] Yet, it is remarkable and most probably significant that 515 years since its first Hellenistic foundation and 234 years after its re-foundation as a *polis* of the imperial Roman *Provincia Syria Palaestina* the citizens of Nysa that was also called Scythopolis declare their ethnicity before the emperor as a "Greek *polis* of Coele Syria". Nysa-Scythopolis is the only *polis* in the region that identified its ethnicity by the title "ΕΛ[ΛΗΝΙΣ] ΠΟΛ[ΙΣ]" on its inscription and its abbreviated version "ΕΛ ΠΟΛ" on its coins. Tsafrir and Foerster viewed it as a "bold cultural acclamation" announced by the city's pagan citizens against growing Jewish and Samaritan minorities in the city, though it seems more plausible that it simply states the citizens' traditional Hellenic origin and ethnicity.[18]

Religion

Scenes of two mythological narratives related to gods of the Greco-Roman pantheon were depicted on Nysa-Scythopolis city coins of the Roman period. The first is the so called founding triad Dionysos, Zeus and Tyche/Nysa, and the second Demeter and Kore-Persephone.[19] Dur-

---

16 Between the years 117–120 CE the province of Judaea was promoted into a consularis province with two legions, cf. Bowersock (1975), 180–185; Isaac/Roll (1979), 149–155; id. (1979a), 54–66. Near the camp, a bronze statue of Hadrian was found, cf. Foerster (1975), 38–40, and an inscription from a triumphal arch commemorating Hadrian's suppression of the Bar Kokhba revolt, see Eck/Foerster (1999), 294–313.

17 Some of the titles are rather common in the region mainly on coins, cf. Foerster/Tsafrir (1986–1987), 53–58; Gatier (1990), 204–206; Gitler (1990–1991), 36–51; Weber (1936), 365–367; Stein (1990), 222–286.

18 Cf. Barkay (2003), 162–163; Millar (1996), 408–414.

19 Cf. Barkay (2003), 111–154. According to Barkay (1994), 147–156, the intensive output of coins bearing Dionysiac motifs is unparalleled by any other city in Syria Palaestina, Asia Minor or Greece, not to mention the founding triad characteristic of Nysa-

ing the earlier excavations on the mound (1921–1923) remains of a temple were revealed. The temple was first erroneously dated to the Hellenistic period and later to the early 2nd century CE, though there might have been an earlier shrine in place.[20] Two inscriptions dated to the mid-2nd century CE mention Zeus Akraios and Zeus Bacchus. A third, carved within a *tabula ansata* over an altar decorated by Dionysiac symbols, mentions Lord Dionysos, the founder (*ktistes*), a title he most probably shared with Zeus.[21] Ascribing the temple on the mound to Zeus Akraios would therefore be reasonable. Although one can positively assume the existence of temples dedicated to Dionysos – presumably the agora western temple – and Tyche/Nysa among the sanctuaries revealed in the city, no clear identification of such candidates within the civic center has been recovered. Demeter (Earth Mother), sister of Zeus and Kore-Persephone, the daughter of Demeter and Zeus, were also worshiped at Nysa-Scythopolis, their shrine was positively identified in the agora's eastern temple. Several inscriptions found over altars in its premises bear witness to their cult practice in the city.[22]

Along with the traditional cults, and in some cases even assimilated within their religious practices and narratives, the imperial cult was also widely embraced by the citizens of Roman Nysa-Scythopolis. Various imperial cult monuments, statues of emperors and dedicatory inscriptions erected during the 1st and 2nd centuries CE were closely related, seemingly immortalizing a monumental political and cultic nucleus within the civic center that was dedicated to and honored the *genius* of the emperor and imagery of the Empire. Built over prominent locations (*caesareum*) or high podia at colonnaded street junctions (*Kalibe, altar, nymphaeum*), they were well distinguished, seen from everywhere and conveniently accessible.[23] Constructed out of superb limestone and imported marble, their Corinthian order columns erected on ornamented pedestals and adorned by a richly decorated entablature,

Scythopolis city coins. For founding legends cf. Lichtenberger (2004), 23–34. Dionysos, son of Zeus and Semele, the daughter of Cadmus, king of Thebas, was the founder (*ktistes*) of the city according to a Mycenaean mythological legend, later attested to by the etiological narrative, mentioned by Roman historians of the 1st and 2nd centuries CE as Plinius and Solinus (see n. 2).

20 Cf. Fisher (1923), 239; Rowe (1930), 44–45; Vincent (1924), 425.

21 Cf. Lifshitz (1961), 186–190; Tsafrir (1987), 282–283; Di Segni/Foerster/Tsafrir (1999), 59–75.

22 One of many versions of Dionysos birth, known from the Orphic account of late Classical writers, states that Dionysos was born to Persephone as she was raped by Zeus, cf. Trip (1970), 203. A column drum found above the mound bears an inscription, most probably of the 1st century CE that mentions a city quarter named Demeter "[A]ΜΦΟΔ[ΟΥ] ΔΗΜΗΤΡ" cf. FitzGerald (1927), 152–154.

23 Mazor/Najjar (2007); Mazor (forthcoming, a).

the monumental imperial cult shrines best reflected the new imperial baroque style architecture of the high Empire.

Early Jewish Community

A Jewish community, that resided (εκεί καθεστωτων) in the city during the Seleucid period, their legal status stated as κάτοικοι (dwelling with), was first mentioned in 2 Macc. 12:29–31 reporting a Jewish delegation to Judas Maccabeus seeking defense for the city and its pagan citizens. Josephus reports a meeting between Alexander Yannaeus and Cleopatra in the city right after its conquest by the Hasmoneans while later he included the city among the desolated cities rebuilt by Gabinius. As the emerging evidence from the excavations clearly points to a total destruction with no Hasmonean resettlement stratum his later statement seems to be confirmed.[24]

In Josephus' detailed report of the Jewish revolt he describes the annihilation of the entire Jewish community of the city by their Scythopolitan neighbors (66 CE). Regardless of the inflated number given by Josephus (13,000 people) that must be regarded with caution – a similar event was reported at Caesarea with an even higher number (20,000 people) – his account seems to confirm that substantial Jewish communities resided in both cities, i.e. Caesarea, the capital of the province, and Nysa-Scythopolis, the largest city of the *Decapolis*.[25] According to Avi-Yonah, Jews returned to the city, mainly from its χωρα during the 2nd–3rd centuries CE, first as a result of the Bar Kokhba revolt and later due to the 3rd century CE crisis that drove farmers to seek economic stability within the wealthy cities.[26] Josephus terms their legal status as ενικος and it seems that they resided in the city not as citizens but rather as a πολίτευμα.[27] During the late Byzantine period, according to Avi-Yonah, the process was presumably reversed, when Jewish vil-

---

24 Cf. Josephus, *Antiquities* 13, 355; 14, 88.

25 Josephus, *Wars* 2, 446–447. Avi-Yonah (1962), 131, assumes that most of them lived in nearby villages and not necessarily in the city. The event points to a rural environment and their legal status was that of 'co-dwellers'.

26 According to Avi-Yonah (1962), 131–132, at that period of time they gradually settled in the city, their economic ties with the pagan community were significantly strengthened as they were mainly connected to the textile industries as stated by the *Descriptio totius orbis*, cf. Schürer (1973–1979), 77 n. 205; Rostovtzeff (1957), 178, 661, n. 24. The local synagogue, not yet revealed, was rebuilt according to the source (yMegilla 73d*)* at the end of the 3rd century CE; cf. Büchler (1956), 210.

27 Applebaum (1974), 420–463. Cf. to Caesarea as stated by Levin (1975), 23.

lages in the Beth-She'an Valley flourished and a number of new synagogues were built in various villages surrounding the city.

Early Samaritan Community

During the 2nd and 3rd centuries CE a gradually rising flow of Samaritans into Nysa-Scythopolis and Caesarea was witnessed. The destruction of the temple at Mount Gerizim and the constant refusal of Roman authorities throughout the centuries to permit its reconstruction indicate, apart from numerous other bans on ritual practices, the Roman policy that sought to prevent any Samaritan national and religious recrystallization. The founding of two Roman cities within Samaria's heartland, Sebaste by Herod in honor of Augustus and Colonia Flavia Neapolis at the foot of Mount Gerizim by the Flavian (72 CE), brought Roman urban culture into the land of the Samaritans, whose clearly delineated ethnicity and religion was never officially sanctioned by the Roman Empire. This ensured Roman domination over the heart of the Samaritan land. Magen states that assimilation of the Samaritans into Roman society and culture was so profound that a distinction between the two in Samaritan or pagan settlements throughout Samaria became more and more blurred through time.[28] Furthermore he points out that the term 'Samaritan' does not necessarily indicate ethnic origin, but rather a regional affiliation and that the two must be carefully distinguished. The Bar Kokhba revolt, in which Samaritans most probably did not participate, had no devastating effect over Samaria. On the contrary, Magen observes an era of flourishing prosperity throughout Samaria during those years. As a result, Samaritans transcended the northern boundaries of Samaria and inhabited Roman cities in growing numbers.[29] There is no surprise that two of the major *poleis* of *Syria Palaestina,* Caesarea and Nysa-Scythopolis, widely favored by Samaritans that fled Samaria were situated on both terminus points of the main connecting artery between the coast and *provincia Arabia,* which also happens to mark Samaria's northern boundary became the main focal points of Samaritan migration into Roman cities outside of Samaria.

28 Cf. Magen (2008), 41–45.

29 Cf. Safrai (1984), 182–214. According to Rabbinic sources, Samaritans entered Jewish towns that were abundant at the "time of anti Jewish persecutions" (yKiddushin 4:65d; yYebamoth 8:9d). Other scholars stated the opposite declaring that harsh economic and security conditions drove Samaritans into Roman cities out of Samaria, cf. Levin (1982), 119–143; Safrai (1982), 252–264; Bar (2002), 43–54.

Byzantine Capital of *Provincia Palaestina Secunda*

Two major events marked the change of an era in the eastern provinces of the Roman Empire. The first, of imperial nature and for some scholar the inception of the Byzantine period in the region, was the declaration of Christianity, the former persecuted religion of a minority, to the official state religion, gradually accepted by the majority. The second, of regional nature, was the establishment of Nysa-Scythopolis as the capital of *Provincia Palaestina Secunda*.

The political victory of Constantine the Great, the first Christian emperor, over his pagan opponent Licinius (324 CE) and the founding of the new imperial capital at Constantinople (324–326, dedicated at 330 CE) shifted the center of power from Rome to the east, whose orthodox Christian affiliation was proclaimed in the council of Nicea (325 CE). The process was thus completed as the empire was divided (395 CE) between the western and eastern emperors.[30]

Around the turn of the century, a new administrative division promoted the status of Nysa-Scythopolis into the capital of *Provincia Palaestina Secunda*. The precise date of that division is somewhat vague, though it must have been later than 385/6 CE, the date of the last known *Proconsol* of *Provincia Palaestina*, and earlier than March 23, 409 CE, the date of Theodosius II rescript that mentions the three provinces (*Prima, Secunda, Tertia*) of *Palaestina*.[31] Di Segni's proposed date for the division (400–404 CE), based on governors' titulature, provides a *terminus post quem* while the rescript of Theodosius II provides a *terminus ante quem*.[32] Based on the Justinian edict of ca. 536 CE (Novel 103),

30 Cf. Tsafrir (1984), 221–223; Dan (1984), 1–12. For different terminology regarding the period cf. Ostrogorsky (1968); Runciman (1961), 14; Jones (1964); Baynes/Set/Moss (1961), xv–xix. Early tendencies of separation and the promotion of the *Orient* can already be seen in Diocletians' act in establishing his capital at Nicomedia and turning his reign into a *dominatio*, i.e. an absolute monarchy. Constantine and his eastern coreagent Licinius' Mediulianic edict of 313 CE granted free Christian practice and banned persecution thus paving the way to Christian state religion.

31 Di Segni (1999), 630, no. 13; Codex Theodosianus, VII, 4, 30. *Palaestina Salutaris* or *Tertia* was probably an earlier creation as Jerom, in his Commentary to Genesis, written *c.* 389–392 CE *Hebraicae quaestiones in libro Geneseos* 1–56, refers to Beersheba as being in a province 'which not long ago' after an administrative split has taken the name of *Salutaris*, cf. Di Segni (1999), 630, no. 14.

32 Di Segni (1999), 625–642, states that since the 80s of the 4th century CE until the division the governor of *Palaestina* held the title of *Proconsul* and the rank *spectabilis*. Once the division was materialized there are three governors of lower ranks: a *consularis* in *Palaestina Prima* (Caesarea) and a *praeses* in both *Palaestina Secunda* (Nysa-Scythopolis) and *Palaestina Tertia* (Petra), all of which held *clarissimus* ranks, sometimes loosely styled as *arcon* and occasionally hard to spot, though they are clearly noted

Mayerson, who researched gubernatorial titular as well, dates the tripartite division somewhat earlier to the years 390–392 CE.[33]

In-between both influential events Nysa-Scythopolis, among other cities of the region, suffered substantial damages in May 19th 363 CE, the result of an earthquake, the heavy toll of which was rather evident in its civic center's monuments.[34] A major reconstruction stage was initiated shortly thereafter, lasting as witnessed by inscriptions until the turn of the century. Among various restored monuments in the civic center the theater's *scaena* frons was rebuilt out of *spolia* and the nymphaeum, as stated in an inscription over its architrave, was rebuilt by Governor Flavius Artemidorus from its foundation. Yet, the most significant change in the landscape of the civic center would have been the disappearance of all temples. Some were presumably damaged by the earthquake, while shortly thereafter all of them were systematically dismantled. In some cases their remains were delicately covered up in a rather respectful manner (*gniza*) presumably by the new Christians, who were still culturally and emotionally attached to their old pagan cultic tradition.[35]

During the 5th and throughout the first half of the 6th centuries CE Nysa-Scythopolis flourished, by then a well established provincial capital, and as evidenced by its monumental renovation stages and attested to by numerous dedicatory inscriptions, a wealthy and powerful economic and administrative center. In spite of all the wide scale reconstruction and renovation, the city kept its Roman Imperial architectural appearance. Its urban plan was hardly altered and its architecture, erected from reused 2nd–3rd centuries CE *spolia*, closely adhered to the deeply rooted Roman Imperial architectural aesthetic that previously as well as now lent the city its magnificent, baroque and monumental scenic appearance. As late as the early 6th century CE the city's colonnaded streets, richly decorated *thermae odeum* and *theaters* were still adorned by a remarkable assemblage of 2nd century CE marble statues of the Greco-Roman pantheon, the sigma by a mosaic floor depicting Tyche, and various inscriptions enriched by Homeric verses and Hellenic terms.[36] It is not easy to evaluate the nature of impact that the still

in the *Notitia Dignitatum Orientis* compiled at ca. 395–413 CE and in Hierocles *Synecdemos* from ca. 527/8 CE. Cf. Di Segni (1999), 630, no. 11.

33 Cf. Mayerson (1988), 65–71; *Novella;* Pharr (1952).

34 Cf. Brock (1977), 267–286; Russell (1980), 47–64.

35 Cf. Foerster/Tsafrir (1987–1988), 27. For the city's administrative mechanism and religious leadership, it was a golden opportunity to dispose all pagan temples, though their dismantling and covering was done with dignified respect.

36 An inscription dedicated by governor Artemidorus commemorates a golden statue to "(Eudocia) queen of the whole earth, the glorious, the gilded one, in far-seen pla-

valid Hellenic culture and traditions held throughout the Byzantine period over the gradually growing Christian culture in a heterogenic Greco-Roman *polis*. Nevertheless, the assessment seems to be crucial if one seeks better understanding of the process in which Christianity in the region gradually gained priority over paganism away from the Ecumenical councils of either Nicea or Constantinople.

Christianity

The Holy Land and its religious sites rapidly gained priority in a christianized empire, mainly due to the decrees and building of churches initiated by Constantine and the holy quest of the cross by his mother Helena. Yet, the spread of Christianity within the region and mainly in its major Hellenic *poleis* was, so it seems, rather slow and gradual. In that respect Nysa-Scythopolis was no exception. Eusebius states that at Diocletian's reign (284–305 CE) a Christian community (of what extent?) already resided at Nysa-Scythopolis, where Procopius, the first Martyr who was executed in Caesarea on June 7th 303 CE, served as a reader, exorcist and translator from Greek to Aramaic.[37] At the council of Nicea (325 CE), Bishop Petropolis – a supporter of Arius – participated as Nysa-Scythopolis' delegate.[38] Epipanius (mid-4th century CE) states that at the time the city's Christian community was mostly Arian and so were its first two bishops after Petropolis, i.e. Philip and Athenasius.[39] Eusebius was exiled to the city (355 CE) by the order of Constantius II and met the *Comes* Josef exiled from Tiberias. Both express their discomfort within an Arian community and gladly welcome the visit of Epipanius of Nora, the Diacon of Syria.[40] In 359 CE the city was chosen as the location of Constantius II special court, whose purpose was to overcome paganism, either because the city was situated half

---

ces" Foerster/Tsafrir (1987–1988), 29. Classical literature so it seems was still essential for the Hellenic citizens of Nysa-Scythopolis and most certainly for the upper classes. A number of notable citizens were lawyers (*scolastikoi*) cf. Di Segni (1999), 637, who acquired their law degrees at Beritus. Gaza and Gadara, cities of great rhetors and philosophers like Procopius, Choricius and John of Gaza and notable poets, play-writers, philosophers and orators from Gadara may exemplify the unique blending of both, new Christian dogma and Hellenic culture and tradition that were strongly rooted in various poleis in the region.

37 Procopius was born at Aelia Capitolina, cf. Eusebius, 9. 6.

38 Cf. Sozomenos, 1:15, 1:19–20.

39 Cf. Epipanius, 30, 4–20.

40 The Christian community of Gaza counted 127 members in 384 CE, when Prophyrius became Episcopus, cf. Marcus Diaconus, 17:56–62.

way between Antioch and Alexandria, or as the result of its growing importance as a provincial capital.[41]

The venerated desert monk Sabas (439–532 CE) visited Nysa-Scythopolis on two occasions (518 and 531 CE), both of which were described by Cyril of Scythopolis who wrote his hagiography (*Vita Sabae*).[42] In the description Cyril mentions various ecclesiastic complexes such as the apostolic shrine of St. Thomas, the Old Church, the Monastery called Enthemaneith, the Church of St. John and the Monastery of the Holy Martyr Procopius. In *Vita Euthymius* (377–473 CE)[43] Cyril mentions the Chapel of the Holy Martyr Basil, presumably the Old Church mentioned in *Vita Sabae*.

The expedition of the Pennsylvania University Museum revealed two ecclesiastic complexes and an inscription of a possible third complex at the city. The remains of a church, a possible monastic compound and a residential quarter were found in the Byzantine period stratum on the mound (level II). The church has a narthex and atrium in the west, a considerably protruding apse in the east and the main body of the church is constructed out of two concentric circular walls, the outer wall consists of basalt masonry and the inner wall contains a columns bearing stylobat, together creating an ambulatory corridor, 4.40 m wide around an open court of 26.40 m in diameter. The *bema* within the apse extends into the ambulatory corridor and was screened by ante pilasters and a chancel.[44] The church was dated by its excavators, based on its Corinthian capitals, which were compared to those of St. Stephan church in Jerusalem, built by Empress Eudocia, to the years 431–438 CE. Yet, the capitals of both churches were reused *spolia* originating from the 2nd century CE cities and can therefore, not date the churches. Fisher mentions in his preliminary reports that remains of an earlier basilica were found under the round church, parts of which were later integrated into the round church.[45] Fisher attributes the construction of the earlier basilica to Bishop Patrophilus who died in 361 CE and was presumably buried in the church that was either burned in the riots of 362 CE or destroyed in the earthquake a year later. The

---

41 Cf. Ammianus Marcellinus XIX 12, 8.

42 Cyril of Scythopolis, Vita Sabae, 61–63:162–164; 75:180.

43 Cyril of Scythopolis, Vita Euthymius, 16:26.

44 Cf. FitzGerald (1931), 18–33.

45 Cf. Fisher (1922), 44; id. (1923), 241; id. (1924), 171–189. FitzGerald (1931), Pls. XXI–XXII, published a few more capitals, part of the *ciborium* which seems to date to the 5th century CE, and have their references in the *Theotokos* Chapel at Mount Nebo, cf. Acconci (1998), 530, no. 159, and bibliography there.

ruins were thus integrated in the round church.[46] The complex, revealed next to the church and identified as a monastery, held among other rooms a bakery, storage rooms and a refectorium with tables and benches.

Avi-Yonah identifies the round church, based on the account of Antoninus of Placentia, as that of John the Baptist, also mentioned by Cyril.[47] Antoninus who visited the city in the 5th century CE states that "Scythopolis was built on a mountain in a place where John the Baptist performed many miracles". Cyril informs us that Sabas, during his first visit, "while passing through the middle of the city, near the apse of St. John" cures a woman with a hemorrhage who was lying in the nearby portico.[48] The IAHU expedition revealed a magnificent *propylaeum* flanking the northern Colonnaded Street adorning a monumental staircase ascending the mound. The apse of St. John – adequately translated as an arch or gateway – seems to refer to the *propylaeum*, most probably named, at the time, after the church to which it led.

From the arch Sabas continues to "a monastery there called Enthemaneith in the district around the church of St. John" where he meets "an anchorite named John" and performs another miracle, banishing the impure spirit out of a little girl possessed by a demon.[49] While the monastery of Lady Mary was being excavated at Tel Izttaba a mosaic floor inscription was accidentally found. Its assumed location, not marked on a map, may be set by FitzGerald's reference "some distance to the east of the cemetery. It lies on the south side of the Jalud (Harod Stream) above an old bridge (Jisr el Maktua)"[50]. The location of the monastery might be identified on the lower terrace over the southern bank of the Harod Stream and the eastern bank of Amal Stream, near the northeastern bridge and the northeastern slope of the mound, where ancient walls and remains were surveyed. The inscription reads as follows: "The Monastery of the Abbot Justin Apocrisarius also, was

46 Bishop Patrophilus represented the church of *Palaestina Secunda* at several church councils. During Julian's reign anti-Christian riots burst (362 CE), in which the pagan mob, still faithful to the dismantled temple on the mound, looted and burned the church and desecrated the tomb of Patrophilus, scattering his bones and using his skull as a lamp, cf. *Chronicum Paschale,* 546. Elements of the church as door handles and lamps, crosses and other metal elements were found scattered around the northeastern lower terrace; FitzGerald (1931), Pls. XXV.4, XXVII.4, XXXVII–III, attributed them to the event.

47 Cf. Avi-Yonah (1962), 133; see also Cyril, *Vita Sabae,* 62:163; Antoninus of Placentia 164, 8.

48 Cyril, Vita Sabae, 163:21–164:10.

49 Cyril, Vita Sabae, 163:15–21.

50 Cf. FitzGerald (1939), 19, Pl. XXII.

founded in the time of the 15th indiction on the 2nd Panaemos of the year 585 (522 CE) and was established in the same year on the [...] September [of the 1st indiction]. An offering of the Scho-lasticus Anoisius. Lord help Anoisius".

On his way from Caesarea, Sabas reached Nysa-Scythopolis, accompanied by an entourage of superiors of the desert monasteries, via the northwestern (towards Caesarea) city-gate. "All the citizens together with the most holy Metropolitan Theodosius came out to meet them at the Apostolic Shrine of St. Thomas" the assumed location of which must have been outside the city-gate. The survey of western Palestine (PEF) marks the remains of a church southwest of Rawahin el Wadi, a tributary of the Harod Stream that runs in-between Tel Izttaba and Tel Naharon, along the way coming from Caesarea. The remains of a monastery were partly excavated in the area in 1959 and they seem to fit the location of St. Thomas monastery.[51]

Once the congregation entered the city they headed to the old church where the liturgy was celebrated. The old church was also mentioned by Cyril in connection with the Laura of St. Euthymius.[52] Among the first monks at the Laura there was Cyrion of Tiberias, a presbyter of the church of the Holy Martyr Basilius from Scythopolis (first half of the 5th century CE). The church, visited by Theodosius between 518 and 529 CE, was described as a *martyrion* erected at the place where the martyr Basilius suffered.[53] Di Segni while researching the role played by the inhabitants of Nysa-Scythopolis in the outbreak of the Samaritan revolt (529 CE) analyzed a report by Malalas regarding an incident in which Christian children were massacred in the church of St. Basilius at Caesarea, an event that, according to Malalas, ignited the revolt, and according to Di Segni most probably happened at Nysa-Scythopolis and not at Caesarea.[54] The incident presumably occurred at Tel Izttaba and involved the Samaritan synagogue and the old church of the Mar-

---

51 Cf. Cyril, *Vita Sabae*, 61, 163; Conder/Kitchener (1882), 109; Tzori (1962); Id. (1971), 18; Ovadiah (1970), 40.

52 Cyril, Vita Euthymius, 16:26.

53 Cf. Theodosius, *De situ Terra Sanctae*, 115. There is little known about Basilius apart from his execution with 70 of his faithful disciples on July 5th, cf. Limor (1998), 175–177; Sauget *Basilio: Bibliotheca Sanctrum*, 2:947. According to an inscription found at the church of the martyr at Tel Izttaba, he seems to have been a native of the city, cf. Meimaris (1986), 119–120. He is mentioned as well in an inscription from the church at Rihab (594 CE) dedicated to the most glorious martyr, St. Basilius, at the time of the archbishop Polyeuctus, cf. Avi-Yonah (1945–1946), 68–72, Pl. XXVIII, 3.

54 Cf. Di Segni (1988), 217–227; Malalas, *Excerpta de insidiis* 44, 171. Out of the three cities mentioned in Malalas report Nysa-Scythopolis is the only city known to have had a church of St. Basilius. The only other known Basilius is the Bishop of Caesarea in Capadocia, cf. Garitte (1958), 30; Di Segni (1998), 222–223, nos. 19–20.

tyr.[55] Two churches in Nysa-Scythopolis mentioned by Cyril were dedicated to martyrs: the old church of St. Basilius and the monastery church of St. Procopius within the bishop's palace.[56] The mosaic medallion inscription found in the Tel Izttaba church does not mention the martyr by name as it was most probably known by all. Basilius was a native of the city while Procopius was a native of Aelia Capitolina. Since the bishop's palace would most likely be close to the civic center it would be reasonable to identify the old church, the church of St. Basilius with the church of the martyr on Tel Izttaba, a short distance away from the city-gate.

That monastic complex contained two churches. The smaller one was built at the last quarter of the 4th century CE. As the city wall was erected in the early 5th century CE, the church was left, due to topographical restrictions, outside of the city wall and was, therefore, entered through a gate in the wall. The earlier church was most probably destroyed during the Samaritan revolt (529 CE) and a new larger and far more elaborate church was built, out of imperial allocation, this time inside the city wall and within a larger monastic compound. At the central apse of the old church an empty tomb was revealed from which the martyr's bones were presumably removed and reburied in a marble sarcophagus that was found within the northern apse of the new church. The old church was a rather small basilica with a single apse, an adjacent chapel and *baptisterium* in the north and a colonnaded narthex in the west. The new church was a considerably larger basilica with a trefoil setting of apses and marble chancel screens. It was adorned by elaborate mosaic floors of geometric carpets and panels adorned by animals' depiction and it had a large colonnaded narthex in the west. Next to the church was a large chapel equipped with a baptisterium. The surrounding monastery had a large number of rooms and a kitchen.

Most of the Christian complexes, mentioned by Cyril and the ones revealed during various excavations, are of monastic nature and situated at the city's outskirts and next to the city-wall. Hardly any public church or basilica, let alone cathedral, were found within the civic center and its neighboring areas that might have served the religious

55 Cf. Tzori (1967), 146–167.

56 Cyril, *Vita Sabae*, 75, 180. According to Eusebius, the bishop of Caesarea, Procopius was a native of Jerusalem. He was widely venerated in Palestine and many churches were dedicated to him including one in Caesarea (484 CE) built by emperor Zeno, one at Nysa-Scythopolis and a third in Jerusalem. He was also mentioned in an inscription from the St. Lot and St. Procopius church at Kh. El Mekhayat, see Saller/Bagatti (1949), 183–184; Meimaris (1986), 133–134.

needs of a gradually growing Christian community at the capital of *Palaestina Secunda* that at the end of the 6th century CE must have reached over 30,000 believers. Compared to other *poleis* in the region the outstanding phenomenon becomes even more enigmatic.[57] The only close parallel seems to be Caesarea, capital of *Palaestina Prima*, in which a similar phenomenon was observed.[58] Both cities were capitals of provinces, powerful administrative and economic centers. They had also composed similar heterogeneous communities of large numbers of Samaritans and Jews residing in the cities along with a gradually growing number of Christians and a rapidly decreasing number of pagans. Both of those phenomena must have had some influence over the integrated relations of *polis* and church in contrast to the earlier separation between state and religion, though to what extent it influenced the location of churches or synagogues within both *poleis* is not entirely clear.

Not less intriguing is the monastic nature of all the ecclesiastic complexes within and around Nysa-Scythopolis. Once all the known monasteries within the city's χωρα are added to the aforementioned a sizeable monastic presence can be clearly posited.[59] Sabas, a distinguished leader of the Judean desert monastic movement, played a major role in the Christian and political life of Nysa-Scythopolis and that of the monastic community that evolved in the city. Sabas visits to the city, reported by Cyril, took place in a rather late part of his life (518, 531 CE) though they were not his first. During his voluntary exile from his Laura (503–506 CE) he built a cell near the Yarmuk Valley, in the vicinity of Gadara where he was later joined by two disciples from Nysa-Scythopolis. The cell, which he left shortly thereafter, as he returned to his Laura, was later known as the coenobium of Eumathius

57 For Gerasa cf. Crowfoot (1938), 171–265; for Pella cf. McNicoll/Smith/Hennesy (1982), 293–304; for Gadara cf. Weber (2002), 126–131; for Bosra cf. Crowfoot (1936), 7–13.

58 Cf. Stroffolino (1965), 293–304. For the history of the church at Caesarea cf. Vann (1992), 261–267.

59 Within the city the expedition of the University Museum of Pennsylvania revealed the 6th century CE monastery of Lady Mary, cf. FitzGerald (1939), and next to it some parts of another were reported, cf. Tzori (1962), 153. At Sde Nahum a monastery of the 5th–6th centuries CE included several rooms, a granary, church and baptisterium, cf. Tzori (1962), 183, Pl. XXV 2–6. Other monasteries were found at Tel Naharon, cf. Tzori (1962), 186, at Tel Basul, cf. Tzori (1962), 190, Pl. XXVI 2–6, along with monastic seclusion cells over the eastern slope of the Gilboa Mountains, cf. Tzori (1962), 197. About 4 km east of the city in the site of Ein Bala (ancient Bella), the remains of a monastery were found. Cyril mentions the priest and Hegumen George that played a part in his monastic education and to whom Cyril dedicates his hagiographies at 555–559 CE, cf. Cyril, *Vita Euthymius* 49, 60; Id., *Vita Sabae* 62, 63, 75; Tsafrir/Di Segni/Green (1994), 75.

the Isaurian. At the time of Cyril's writing Tarasius, an Isaurian as well, was established as the abbot of that monastery.[60] Ties between the city and the desert monks were already previously established during Euthymius' days among whose first disciples were Cyrion, a priest from St. Basilius martyr church and monastery in Nysa-Scythopolis, and Cosmas who later served as the bishop of the city.[61]

Late Jewish Community

The Jewish revolts of the 1st and 2nd centuries CE had their devastating effects over Jewish settlements in Galilee and Judaea and drove some of their inhabitants into the more secure and wealthy Greco-Roman *poleis*, a process that was further developed due to the harsh political and economic conditions of the 3rd century CE. During the Byzantine period, from the late 4th or early 5th centuries, when Nysa-Scythopolis became the capital of *Provincia Palaestina Secunda*, the city and its χωρα (Beth-She'an Valley), at the time densely populated by Jewish villages, flourished. It would be reasonable to assume that a growing sense of prosperity drew to the city increasing numbers of wealthy Jewish manufacturers, merchants and industrialists of the linen industry, for which Nysa-Scythopolis was well known throughout the Byzantine world.[62] As evidence of the prosperity during the Byzantine period, numerous synagogues were built in various villages within the city's χωρα, along with two synagogues revealed within the city.

On Tel Izttaba, about 200 m north of the city wall, a Samaritan synagogue was discovered, shaped as a basilica with an apse directed to the northwest (not towards Jerusalem). In front of the apse its mosaic floor depicts a screened aedicule flanked by two candelabra, ram's horns and incense shovels. Both dedicatory inscriptions are Greek though one was written in Samaritan letters. Next to the citywall in the west a small synagogue was built on the premises of a wealthy Jewish merchant's (Kyrios Leontis) villa. The house included various rooms surrounding a courtyard, among which the prayer room's mosaic floor reveals a medallion, depicting a candelabrum and above the Hebrew word שלום, along with two inscriptions, one in Aramaic and the other in Greek. Another elongated room within the house was paved with a remarkable mosaic floor depicting a scene from the Odyssey and next

60 Cf. Cyril, *Vita Sabae*, 33–34:118–120; Patrich (1995), 161.
61 Cf. Cyril, *Vita Euthymius*, 16, 26; Patrich (1995), 281.
62 Cf. *Descriptio totus orbis* 77, n. 205; Mommsen (1893), 26–28.

to it a Nylotic scene along with a Greek inscription commemorating the house's owner.[63] In spite of both synagogues, that served both Samaritan and Jewish communities, Nysa-Scythopolis, Beth She'an as it was known among the Jews, was considered a gentile city in Jewish sources of the period, exempt from Jewish Sabbatical year restrictions.[64]

Late Samaritan Community

Compared to both, Jewish revolts and their echoing impact on the one hand, and the silence of most Christian sources regarding Jewish residency in gentile *poleis* during the Byzantine period on the other, the Samaritan revolts of the 6th century CE momentarily highlighted the inhabitants of Samaria and their large communities in Christian *poleis* like Caesarea and Nysa-Scythopolis in a way that otherwise might have passed most historical and ecclesiastic sources almost unnoticed.[65] As Procopius describes the events of the Samaritan revolt he outlines the central role played by Nysa-Scythopolis in those events, while Malalas' report seemingly states that they actually started there.[66] Di Segni's work, that analyzed Malalas report on the children's massacre at St. Basilius church, argues that the event was probably erroneously attributed by Malalas or a later interpolator to Caesarea while it actually happened at Nysa-Scythopolis in June 529 CE. Out of various sources Di Segni, then, reconstructs a more accurate timetable of the revolt from April–May 529 to 531 CE.[67] It seems that during the events the Samaritans had the upper hand at Nysa-Scythopolis for a while, in which ecclesiastic complexes were burned down as a result. At the request of the patriarch of Jerusalem, Sabas traveled to Constantinople in order to present the emperor with the Christians' side of the conflict. As a result, a grand sum of money was allocated by the emperor, most of it for *Palaestina Prima* and some of it for Nysa-Scythopolis, for the repairs of damages and the rebuilding of burned churches.[68]

63 Cf. Tzori (1967), 149–167; Lifshitz (1977), 286–292; Bhat (1972), 55–58; Tzori (1966), 123–134.

64 Cf. Sussman (1973–1974), 88–158.

65 For the sources regarding the Samaritan revolt of 529 CE cf. Di Segni (1988), 217–227, n. 1.

66 Cf. Procopius Caesariensis, *Anecdota* XI, 15, 24–30; XXVII, 8–10, 134–138, 320, 352–354; Malalas, *Chronographia*, 445–447, 455f.; id., *Fragmentum* 44; id., *Excerpta historica*.

67 Cf. Di Segni (1988), 217–227.

68 Cf. Cyril, *Vita Sabae*, 73:176–177.

The events of the Samaritan revolt described by both, Procopius and Malalas, mention a certain Arsenius, apparently a notable Samaritan dignitary and Christian convert who was held in high esteem in the emperor's court at Constantinople. Members of his family, his father Silvanus and his brother Salustius, were distinguished lawyers and notable citizens of Nysa-Scythopolis mentioned by Procopius and Malalas.[69] A remarkable link between written sources and archaeological data was revealed when dedicatory inscriptions of various monuments found in the city – as for instance the construction of the *sigma* in 507 CE, a stoa (*basilica*) in 515–516 CE and a street pavement and a water channel near the amphitheater in 522 CE – indicated the projects had been supervised by Silvanus and Salustrius who held high posts (*comes kai protos*) in the city prior to the revolt.[70] Both of them fled from the city once the revolt broke out and were later killed by the Christians as they tried to return.

Early Islamic Beisan: From Polis to Medina

The Arab conquest of the region in 636 CE brought in its wake the fall of Nysa-Scythopolis into Arabs hands, though not its destruction. The city surrendered and signed terms of capitulation that granted a peaceful coexistence between Christian citizens who were allowed to continue their regular daily life and religious practices, and the new Arab settlers, presumably Saracens of the neighboring regions, retired soldiers of the Arab armies and a growing number of administrators and merchants of the new regime. The Byzanto/Arab administrative system with its new leadership still retained its former components presumably maintained by the former Byzantine authorities, adopting the use of Byzantine coins with Arab imprints. The capital of *Jund el-Urdun* was moved to Tiberias, and Beisan, as Nysa-Scythopolis was now called, lost its jurisdiction. At the same time the city continued its bustling commercial and economic coexistence, since linen was still manufactured by Christian artisans but now exported by Arab merchants. Yet, a certain strangeness must have prevailed in a city, whose urban landscape still retained distinct Roman-Byzantine cultural symbols, devoid

69 Cf. Procopius, *Anecdota*, XXVII, 8–10. During his first visit, Sabas is approached by John, a lawyer and notable citizen, which displays his complains against Silvanus, cf. Cyril, *Vita Sabae*, 61:163. They must have fled from the city during the starting events and when they returned on June 259 CE, they were killed by a mob.

70 Cf. Mazor/Bar-Nathan (1994), 116; Tsafrir (1994), 109, 116.

of content, in a city that was now gradually changing from "*polis* to *medina*".[71]

On January 18, 749 CE[72] the Umayyad city of Beisan came to an abrupt end as it was completely devastated by an earthquake and the essence of an earlier magnificent Hellenic *polis* was gradually covered up.

Bibliography

Antique Sources

Ammianus Marcellinus, Rerum gestarum libri qui supersunt, transl. by J.C. Rolfe, LCL, London 1935–1940.

Antoninus of Placentia, Itinera Hierosolymitana saeculi IIII–VIII, rec. et commentario critico instruxit Paulus Geyer, ed. by P. Geyer, CSEL 39, Vienna 1898.

Chronicum Paschale, ed. by L.A. Dindorf, Berlin 1832.

Codex Theodosianus, ed. by T. Mommsen, Berlin 1954.

Cyril of Scythopolis, Vita Sabae; Vita Euthymius, transl. by R.M. Price/ J. Binns, Michigan 1991.

De Situ Terra Sancta, ed. by P. Geyer, Vienna 1965.

Descriptio totus orbis, transl. by E. Schürer, Leipzig 1973.

Epipanius, Panarion, Adversus haeresis, ed. by K. Holl, Leipzig 1915.

Eusebius, The Martyrs of Palestine, transl. by W. Cureton, London 1981.

Hierocles, Synecdemos, ed. by E. Honigman, Brussels 1932.

Jerom, Hebraicae Quaestiones in libro Geneseos, CChr.SL, ed. by P. de Lagarde, Tournhout 1959.

Josephus, Antiquitates Judaicae, transl. by H. Thackerary/J. R. Marcus/ L.H. Feldman, LCL, Harvard University Press, Cambridge 1930–1965.

– Wars, transl. by W. Heineman, LCL, London 1930–1965.

Macc. II, ed. and transl. by A. Jonathan, London 1983.

Malalas, Iohannies Chronographia, ed. by L. Dindorf, CSHB 27, Bonn 1831.

71 Cf. Kennedy (1985), 3–27. It is rather remarkable that after ca. one thousand years of western cultural influence and change of name the ancient city name of Beth-She'an emerges once again as the cultural pendulum swifts back to eastern cultural influence.

72 Cf. Tsafrir/Foerster (1992), 231–235.

– Excerpta historica iussu imperatoris Constantini Porphyrogeniti confecta. Exerpta de insidiis 3, ed. by C. de Boor, Berlin 1905.
– Fragmentum, ed. by C. de Boor, Berlin 1905.
Marcus Diaconus, Vita Porphyrii episcopi Gazensis, ed. by H. Gregoire/M.A. Krugener, Berlin 1885.
Notitia Dignitatum Orientis, ed. by O. Seek, Frankfurt 1876.
Novella, in: Corpus Juris Civilis, Vol. 3, ed. by R. Schöll/W. Kroll, Berlin 1985.
Pharr, C. (1952), The Theodosian Code and Novels and the Sirmondian Constitutions, CRL 1, Princeton NJ.
Plinius, G. Secundus, Naturalis Historia V, 74, ed. by H. Rackham, London 1947–1963.
Procopius, Caesariensis, Procopius: Vol. 6: The Anecdota or Secret History, transl. by H.B. Dewing, London 1954.
Solinus, Collectanea rerum memorabilium XXXVI, 156, ed. by T. Mommsen, Berlin 1895.
Sozomenos, Historia Ecclesistica, ed. by J. Bidez/G.C. Hansen, GCS 50, Berlin 1960.
Yerushalmi, Palestinian Talmud, ed. by J. Neusner 1982–1994, University of Chicago Press, Chicago.

Secondary Literature

Abel, F./Vincent, H. (1930), An Inscription, in: A. Rowe, The Topography and History of Beth-Shean, PPSP 1, Philadelphia, 45.
Acconci, A. (1998), Elements of the Liturgical Furniture, in: M. Piccirillo/E. Alliata, Mount Nebo, New Archaeological Excavations 1967–1997, SBF, Jerusalem.
Applebaum, S. (1974), The Legal Status of the Jewish Communities in the Diaspora, in: S. Safrai/M. Stern (eds.), The Jewish People in the First Century: Historical Geography, Political History, Social, Cultural and Religious Life and Institutions, Compendia rerum Iudaicarum ad Novum Testamentum, Vol. I, Assen, 420–463.
Ariel, D.T. (1990), Excavations at the City of David 1978–1985 Directed by Yigal Shiloh, Vol. 2: Imported Stamped Amphora Handles, Coins, Worked Bone and Ivory, and Glass, Qedem Monographs of the Institute of Archaeology 30, Jerusalem.
Avi-Yonah, M. (1945–1946), Greek Christian Inscriptions from Rihab, QDAP 12, 68–72.
– (1962), Scythopolis, IEJ 12/2, 123–134.

Bahat, D. (1972), The Synagogue at Bet-Shean: Preliminary Report, Qad. 5, 55–58.
Bar, D. (2002), Was There a 3rd-c. Economic Crisis in Palestine?, in: J.H. Humphrey (ed.), The Roman and Byzantine Near East III: Late-Antique Petra, Nile Festival Building at Sepphoris, Deir Qal'a Monastery, Khirbet Qana Village and Pilgrim Site 'Ain-'Arrub Hiding Complex and other Studies, Journal of Roman Archaeology Supplementary Series 49, Portsmouth, Rode Island, 43–54.
Barkay, R. (1994), The Wine God Dionysos on the City Coins of Eretz-Israel, Ariel 102–103, 147–156 (in Hebrew).
– (2003), The Coinage of Nysa Scythopolis (Beth-Shean), Jerusalem.
Baynes, N.H./Moss, H.St.L.B. (1961), Byzantium: An Introduction to East Roman Civilization, OPB 16, Oxford.
Bowersock, G.W. (1975), Old and New in the History of Judaea, JRS 65, 180–185.
Brock, S.P. (1977), A Letter Attributed to Cyril of Jerusalem on the Rebuilding of the Temple, BSOAS 40, 267–286.
Büchler, A. (1956), Studies in Jewish History: The Adolph Büchler Memorial Volume, ed. by I. Brodie, Jews' College Publications N.S. 1, Oxford.
Conder, C.R./Kitchener H.H. (1882), The Survey of Western Palestine: Memoires of the Topography, Orography, Hydrography and Archaeology II, London.
Crowfoot, J.W. (1936), The Cathedral at Bosra: A Preliminary Report, PEQ 68, 7–13.
– (1938), The Christian Churches, in: C.H. Kraeling (ed.), Gerasa: City of the Decapolis, American Schools of Oriental Research, New Haven, 171–262.
Dan, Y. (1984), The City in Eretz Israel during the Roman and Byzantine Periods, Jerusalem (in Hebrew).
Di Segni, L. (1988), Scythopolis (Bet Shean) during the Samaritan Rebellion of 529 C.E. in: D. Yacoby/Y. Tsafrir (eds.), Jews, Samaritans and Christians in Byzantine Palestine, Jerusalem, 217–227 (in Hebrew).
– (1999), New Epigraphic Discoveries at Scythopolis and in Other Sites of Late Antique Palestine: The XI Congresso Internazionale di Epigrafia Greca and Latina, Rome.
– /Foerster, G./Tsafrir, Y. (1999), The Basilica and an Altar to Dionysos at Nysa Scythopolis, in: J. Humphrey (ed.), The Roman and Byzantine Near East II, Journal of Roman Archaeology Supplementary Series 31, London, 59–75.

Eck, W./Foerster, G. (1999), Ein Triumphbogen für Hadrian im Tal von Beth Shean bei Tel Shalem, Journal of Roman Archaeology 12, 294–313.

Finkielsztejn, G. (1999), Hellenistic Jerusalem: The Evidence of the Rhodian Amphora Stamps, in: A. Faust/E. Baruch (eds.), New Studies on Jerusalem, Proceedings of the Fifth Conference, Bar Ilan University, Ramat Gan, 21*–36*.

Fisher, C.S. (1922, 1923, 1924), Beth Shean Excavations, The Museum Journal 3, 14, 15, Philadelphia.

FitzGerald, G.M. (1931), Beth-Shan Excavations 1921–1923, The Arab and Byzantine Levels, Philadelphia.

– (1927), Two Inscriptions from Beisan, PEFQSt 60, 152–154.

– (1939), A Sixth Century Monastery at Beth-Shan, Philadelphia.

Foerster, G. (1975), A Bronze Statue of Hadrian in Armour, Qad. 8, 30–31, 38–40 (in Hebrew).

– /Tsafrir, Y. (1987–1988), Bet Shean Project, ESI 6, Jerusalem.

– /Tsafrir, Y. (1986–1987), Nysa-Scythopolis: A New Inscription and the Titles of the City on its Coins, INJ 9, 53–58.

Fuks, G. (1983), Scythopolis – A Greek City in Eretz Israel, Jerusalem (in Hebrew).

Gatier, P.L.H. (1990), Nouvelles archéologiques: Décapole et Coelé Syrie: deux inscriptions nouvelles, à propos de la Coelé-Syrie, Syr. 67, 204–206.

Gitler, H. (1990–1991), Numismatic Evidence on the Visit of Marcus Aurelius to the East, INJ 11, 36–51.

Hadad, S. (2002), The Oil Lamps from the Hebrew University Excavations at Bet Shean, Excavation at Bet Shean, Vol. 1, Qedem Reports 4, Jerusalem.

– (2005), Islamic Glass Vessels from the Hebrew University Excavations at Bet Shean, Excavations at Bet Shean, Vol. 2, Qedem Reports 8, Jerusalem.

Isaac, B./Roll, I. (1979), Legio II Traiana in Judaea, ZPE 33, 149–155.

– (1979a), Judaea in the Early Years of Hadrian's Reign, Latomus 38, 54–66.

Jones, A.H.M. (1937), The Cities of the Eastern Roman Provinces, Oxford.

– (1964), The Later Roman Empire 284–602: A Social Economic and Administrative Survey, Vols. 1–4, Oxford.

Kennedy, H. (1985), From Polis to Madina: Urban Change in Late Antiquity and Early Islamic Syria, Past and Present 106, Oxford, 3–27.

Launey, M. (1950), Recherches sur les armées hellénistiques II, Paris.

Levin, I.L. (1975), Caesarea under Roman Rule, SJLA 7, Leiden.

– (1982), Eretz Israel in the Third Century, in: Z. Baras/S. Safrai/Y. Tsafrir/M. Stern (eds.), Eretz Israel from the Destruction of the Second Temple to the Muslim Conquest I, Jerusalem, 119–143, (in Hebrew).

Lichtenberger, A. (2004), City Foundation Legends in the Decapolis, Bulletin of the Anglo-Israel Archaeological Society 22, 23–34.

Lifshitz, B. (1961), Der Kult des Zeus Akraios und des Zeus Bakchos in Beisan (Skythopolis), ZDPV 77, 186–190.

– (1977), Scythopolis: l'histoire, les institutions et les cultes de la ville à l'époque hellénistique et impériale, ANRW II/8, 262–292.

– (1978), Scythopolis, ANRW II/8, Berlin/New York, 142–144.

Limor, O. (1998), Holy Land Travels: Christian Pilgrims in Late Antiquity, Jerusalem, 175–177, (in Hebrew).

Lyttelton, M. (1974), Baroque Architecture in Classical Antiquity, Studies in Ancient Art and Archaeology, London.

MacDonald, W.L. (1986), The Architecture of the Roman Empire II: An Urban Appraisal, Yale Publications in the History of Art 35, London.

Magen, Y. (2008), The Samaritans and the Good Samaritan, Jerusalem.

Mayerson, P. (1988), Justinian's Novel 103 and the Reorganization of Palestine, BASOR 269, 65–71.

Mazar, A. (2006), Excavations at Tel Beth Shean 1989–1996, Vol. I: From the Late Bronze Age IIB to the Medieval Period, Jerusalem.

– (2007), Excavations at Tel Beth Shean 1989–1996, Vol. II: The Middle and Late Bronze Age Strata in Area R, Jerusalem.

Mazar, A./Mazor, G./Arubas, B./Foerster, G./Tsafrir, Y./Seligman, J. (2008), Beth Shean, in: S. Ephraim (ed.), The New Encyclopedia of Archaeological Excavations in the Holy Land, Vol. 5, Jerusalem, 1616–1644.

Mazor, G. (2004), Free Standing City-Gates in the Eastern Provinces During the Roman Imperial Period, Ph.D. diss., Bar Ilan University, Ramat Gan (in Hebrew).

– (2010a), Imperial Cult in the Decapolis, Nysa-Scythopolis as a Test Case, in: A. Kilbrew (ed.), FS H. Rachel, (not yet published).

– (2010b), Urban Architecture in the Eastern Provinces and the Image of Empire, in: J.H. Charlesworth (ed.), Methodological Approaches to the Historical Jesus: Second Princeton-Prague Symposium on Jesus Research, Princeton 2007, Princeton, NJ, (not yet published).

– /Bar Nathan, R. (1994), Scythopolis-Capital of Palaestina Secunda, Qad. 107–108, 117–137.

– /Najjar, A. (2007), Nysa-Scythopolis: The Caesareum and the Odeum, Bet She'an I, Israel Antiquities Authority Report 33, Jerusalem.

– /Sandhaus D. (2011), Nysa-Scythopolis: The Hellenistic City, Bet She'an Final Report 5, Israel Antiquities Authority Report, Jerusalem (not yet published).

McNicoll, A./Smith R.H./Hennesy, B. (1982), Pella in Jordan 1: An Interim Report on the Joint University of Sydney and the College of Wooster Excavations at Pella 1979–1981, Canberra.

Meimaris, Y.E. (1986), Sacred Names, Saints, Martyrs and Church Officials in the Greek Inscriptions and Papyri Pertaining to the Christian Church of Palestine, Meletemata 2, Athens.

Millar, F. (1996), The Roman Near East 31 BC–AD 337, London.

Mommsen, T. (1893), Der Maximaltarif des Diocletian, Berlin.

Mouterde, R. (1933), Bibliographie, MUSJ 17, Paris, 180–182.

Ostrogorsky, G. (1968), History of the Byzantine State, Oxford.

Ovadiah, A. (1970), Corpus of the Byzantine Churches in the Holy Land, Theoph. 22, Bonn.

Parker, S.T. (1975), The Decapolis Reviewed, JBL 94, 437–441.

Patrich, J. (1995), Sabas, Leader of Palestinian Monasticism: A Comparative Study in Eastern Monasticism Fourth to Seventh Centuries, DOS 32, Washington.

Rigsby, K.J. (1980), Seleucid Notes, TPAPA 110, 233–254.

Rostovtzeff, M.I. (1957), The Social and Economic History of the Roman Empire, vols. 1–2, Oxford.

Rowe, A. (1930), The Topography and History of Beth-Shan, PPSP 1, Philadelphia.

Runciman, S. (1961), Byzantine Civilization, London.

Russell, K.W. (1980), The Earthquake of May 19 AD 363, BASOR 238, 47–64.

Safrai, Z. (1982), The Samaritans, in: Z. Baras/S. Safrai/Y. Tsafrir/M. Stern (eds.), Eretz Israel from the Destruction of the Second Temple to the Muslim Conquest I, Jerusalem, 252–264 (in Hebrew).

– (1984), The Bar Kokhba Revolt and its Effect on Settlements, in: A. Oppenheimer/U. Rappaport (eds.) The Bar Kokhba Revolt: A New Approach, Jerusalem, 182–214 (in Hebrew).

Saller, S.J.S./Bagatti B. (1949), The Town of Nebo (Khirbet el-Mekhayyat), PSBF 7, Jerusalem.

Sauget, J.M. (1961–1970), Basilio, BSS, Roma.

Schürer, E. (1973–1979), The History of the Jewish People in the Age of Jesus Christ (175 B.C.–A.D. 135), vols. 1–2, revised and edited by G. Vermes and F. Millar, Edinburgh.

Segal, A. (1997), From Function to Monument: Urban Landscape of Roman Palestine, Syria and Provincia Arabia, Oxford.

Stein, A. (1990), Studies on the Greek and Latin Inscriptions on the Palestinian Coinage under the Principate, Ph.D. diss., Tel Aviv.
Stroffolino, G. (1965), Un edificio cristiano, in: A. Frova, Scavi di Caesarea Maritima, Milano, 293–304.
Sussman, J. (1973–1974), A Halakhic Inscription from the Beth Shean Valley, Tarbiz 43, 88–158 (in Hebrew).
Thiersch, H. (1932), Ein hellenistischer Kolossalkopf aus Besan, NGWG.PH Klasse 1, Berlin.
Trip, E. (1970), Dictionary of Classical Mythology, London.
Tsafrir, Y. (1984), Eretz Israel from the Destruction of the Second Temple to the Muslim Conquest II, Jerusalem (in Hebrew).
– (1987), More Evidence for the Cult of Zeus Akraios at Beth-She'an, ErIs 19, 282–283 (in Hebrew).
– (1994), The Hebrew University Excavations at Beth Shean 1980–1994, Qad. 107–108, 93–116.
– /Foerster, G. (1992), The Dating of the Earthquake of the Sabbatical Year of 749 CE in Palestine, BSOAS 55, 231–235.
– /Di Segni, L./Green, J. (1994), Tabula Imperii Romani (Judaea Palaestina): Eretz Israel in the Hellenistic, Roman and Byzantine Periods, Publications of the Israel Academy of Sciences and Humanities: Section of Humanities, Jerusalem.
Tzori, N. (1962) An Archaeological Survey of the Beth-Shean Valley, Jerusalem (in Hebrew).
– (1966), The House of Kyrios Leontis at Beth Shean, IEJ 16, Jerusalem, 123–134.
– (1967), A Ancient Synagogue from Beth Shean, ErIs 8, 146–167.
– (1971), Four Greek Inscriptions from the Beth Shean Valley, ErIs 10, 240 (in Hebrew).
Vann, R.L. (1992), Caesarea Papers: Straton's Tower, Herod's Harbour, and Roman and Byzantine Caesarea, including the Papers given at a symposium held at the University of Maryland, the Smithsonian Institution, and the Jewihs Community Center of Greater Washington on 25–28 March, 1988, Journal of Roman Archaeology, Ann Arbor/MI 1992.
Vincent, H. (1924), Chronique L'année archéologique 1923 en Palestine, RB 42, 425.
Weber, T.M. (2002), Gadara-Umm Qes I. Gadara Decapolitana, BiOr, Wiesbaden.
Weber, W. (1936), The Antonines, in: S.A. Cook/F.E. Adock/M.P. Charlesworth (eds.), CAH, Vol. XI, Cambridge.

Beth Shean/Scythopolis in Late Antiquity: Cult and Culture, Continuity and Change

KATHARINA HEYDEN

1. Introduction: "One of Coele Syria's Greek Cities"

In the late 2nd or 3rd century CE, a time that cannot be called 'Late Antique Period' yet, a statue of the emperor was raised in front of a temple in the centre of Scythopolis.[1] Only the pedestal of the statue is preserved, on which an inscription is engraved that reflects the self-perception of the citizens of Scythopolis:

1 For text and dating cf. Foerster/Tsafrir (1988). There were three Roman emperors with the official name Marcus Aurelius Antoninus: Marcus Aurelius (161–180 CE), Caracalla (211–217 CE) and Elagabalus (218–222 CE). Foerster/Tsafrir incline toward the belief that the emperor on the inscription is Marcus Aurelius.

Ἀγαθῃ τύχῃ	With good fortune
Αὐτοκράτορα Καίσαρα	Imperator Caesar
Μάρκον Αὐρήλιον Ἀντωνῖνον	Marcus Aurelius Antoninus
Σεβαστὸν τὸν κύριον Νυσαέων	Augustus the lord of the people of Nysa
τῶν καὶ Σκυθοπολιτῶν	also (called) the people of Scythopolis
τῆς ἱερᾶς καὶ ἀσύλου τῶν	the holy and of the right of sanctuary
κατὰ Κοίλην Συρίαν Ἑλλη	one of Coele Syria's
νίδων πόλεων, ἡ πόλις	cities, the city
διὰ ἐπιμελητοῦ Θεοδώ	through the curator Theodo
ρου Τίτου	ros son of Titus.[2]

Fig. 1: Stone Pedestal of the Statue of Marc Aurel

What significance the inscription and the name of Scythopolis as 'Greek city' had at the time when the statue was raised is not of concern at this point. Perhaps the term was only used to show that the city belonged to the Decapolis, perhaps the pagan elites wanted to demonstrate the influence they had in the city compared with Jewish or Samaritan citizens.[3] With respect to the Late Antiquity, which is studied here, it is rather interesting to note that the pedestal with the inscription was kept there until its collapse in the earthquake of the year 749 CE[4] – despite the fact that the temple itself was not in use from the beginning of the 5th century, and even though, about 100 years later, most of the Roman statues that had decorated the main streets and places were thrown into the abandoned hypocaust of the eastern bathhouse.[5]

Apparently, for about 500 years, no one took offence at this inscription and the name of the city as one of the Ἑλληνίδων πόλεων. In fact, the citizens of Scythopolis apparently had a special interest in this inscription and chose not to remove it from the main intersection of the city.

It seems that Scythopolis stayed a 'Greek city' in the minds of its citizens during the entire Late Antique period. But what does 'Greek city' mean in the Galilee of this time?

In the following, the history of Scythopolis in Late Antiquity is documented from literary sources. While the archaeological research of Scythopolis has advanced greatly since the excavations of 1980–1996, and while the results are well-documented for the Late Antique or Byz-

2 Transcription and translation: Foerster/Tsafrir (1988), 57.

3 Both interpretations are proposed by the excavators: The first one by Tsafrir (1998), 212, here also with the emphasis, that the Decapolis was "the flagship of Hellenistic culture in the region"; the second one by Foerster/Tsafrir (1986), 58.

4 Cf. Foerster/Tsafrir (1997), 127: "Not only did the columns of the facade survive until they collapsed in the earthquake of 749 AD., but the pedestal of the statue of Marcus Aurelius survived in its original place in front of the temple."

5 For this fact cf. Foerster/Tsafrir (1997), 128–131.

antine Period,[6] a perspective of research based on the texts has not yet been adopted.[7]

The predominance of Christian texts corresponds to the availability of source material, or at least reflects the recent scholarly discussion, since texts on the Late Antique Scythopolis written by pagan, Samaritan or Jewish authors are very rare. They will be considered here when possible.[8] At the same time, the attempt to analyze the religious history of Scythopolis would not be feasible without the results of archaeological excavations. Hence, I will point out important archaeological results in some places, without discussing the findings in detail. The objective is rather to fill the Byzantine city walls with life through the persons and stories we meet in the literary sources.

The 'Late Antiquity'[9] taken into account here covers about three centuries, where the Islamic conquest of Scythopolis 635/636 marks the end of the period. The literary sources are silent from the mid-6th century onward, so that by considering this, the period ends with the beginning of the downfall of Scythopolis after the Samaritan revolt in 529 CE. The starting point of this period is difficult to determine, especially since it has become historically problematic to understand Constan-

6 See Foerster (1993); Foerster/Tsafrir (1997); Tsafrir (1998); id. (2003); Mazar (2006); esp. the article in the recently published supplement to The New Encyclopedia of Archaeological Excavations in the Holy Land by Arubas/Foerster/Tsafrir (2008) and Mazor (2008), as well as Mazor's articles on Beit Shean/Nysa Scythopolis on the homepage of the Israel Antiquities Authority (http://antiquities.org.il).

7 Raynor (1982), in his unpublished dissertation, attempted to make "a synthetic study of the constituent minority communities living in the Bet Shean Valley" (p. xxi), on the basis of architectural/stratigraphic, literary, epigraphic, numismatric, artistic and literary sources concerning Scythopolis in the Roman and Byzantine periods. Raynor points out that he does not want "to outline a consecutive historical account of Scythopolis" (p. xxi). Thus, he cites literary sources without analyzing them, while he neglects some of the texts taken into consideration here. In his recent book on "Palestine in Late Antiquity", Sivan (2008), dedicates two chapters to Scythopolis, one to the supposed Purim festivities (157–167), the other to "Samaritans in Scythopolis" (167–175), both based on literary sources.

8 For methodological considerations concerning the difficulties that raise for the study of Jewish and Samaritan sources, cf. Sivan (2008), 362–365.

9 Some aspects seem to suggest that the term 'Late Antiquity' is more appropriate for the reconstruction of the city's history from literary sources than the term 'Byzantine' that is used by the excavators and that also makes more sense from an archaeological perspective. (1) For Palestine, the Islamic conquest does not lead to a cultural cut – the Christian monks continued to view themselves as 'Byzantines', so that for Palestine the 'Byzantine era' does not end in the 7th century. (2) Already since the mid-6th century, an archaeological stagnation can be discerned that is confirmed by the silence of the literary sources. External factors like the bubonic plague seem to be the reason for this, more than Byzantium itself.

tine's accession as a change of era.[10] When looking at the phenomenon of interculturalism, it makes sense to begin with the establishment of a Christian community in Scythopolis, even though this already took place in pre-Constantinian, i.e. Roman, times. From that time on, Christianity begins to shape the city's history considerably, up to the time of the Islamic conquest.

The Late Antique period was a time of prosperity for the city. Up to the 6th century, its population and with this also the urban area grew continuously. The Byzantine city walls surrounded an area of 134 ha[11], and with a population of 30,000–38,000 citizens[12] Scythopolis was the third largest city of Late Antique Palestine. The excavations of recent decades paint the picture of a prospering city with an environment that was economically and culturally attractive.[13]

2. The 4th Century CE: Plurality and Conflicts

At the beginning of the 4th century, Scythopolis probably contained mostly pagan citizens. So far, there is archaeological evidence for five pagan temples in the city area, whereas there is epigraphic evidence for seven temples.[14] Since Roman times, Scythopolis was famous for the production of textiles, and this lead to prosperity and wealth.[15] A theatre, an odeon, a nymphaeum and bathhouses made Scythopolis a typical affluent Hellenistic city.

The Jewish population mostly settled in the city's back country, while some seem to have returned to the metropolitan area of Scythopolis after the revolt of Bar-Kochba in the 2nd century. The fact, that the Jews of Beth Shean put the question to the wise men of Tiberias

10 Representative for this discussion are the article by Holze (1990) and the volume ed. by Mühlenberg (1998).

11 For the wall cf. Foerster/Tsafrir (1997), 100–103.

12 This estimate follows Foerster/Tsafrir (1997), 118; Mazor (2008), 1632.

13 With regard to economic affairs, Lapin (2001) pointed out the close connection between the city and its surroundings, and with reference to the inscription of Rehov (cf. below) argued that "we should be careful in assuming a sharp distinction between village and urban cultures as mutually autonomous and hostile realms." (177).

14 Cf. Tsafrir (1998), 208–218.

15 Cf. Cod. Theod. 10,20,8, February 16th, 374 (563 Mommsen): *non minore circa eos etiam multae comminatione proposita, qui obnoxios Scytopolitanos linyfos publico canoni in posterum suscipere conabuntur.* The 4th century *Expositio totius mundi et gentium* 31,4 (SC 141, 162,5–164,1 Rougé) mentions Scythopolis at the top of a list of cities that are famous because of their production of textiles (*In linteamina sunt hae: Scythopolis, Laodicia …*); cf. Raynor (1982), 212–222.

whether it was possible to use the stones of a destroyed synagogue to build a new one,[16] points in two directions: on the one hand, there were enough Jews to build a synagogue, on the other hand, they do not seem to have been very wealthy. This impression is confirmed by the statement of a Rabbi at the beginning of the 4th century that describes Jews as living in 'double-floor-houses' on the slopes of the city.[17] The fact that the wise men of Tiberias dealt with the concerns of Scythopolis shows that the city itself did not have an important *Amora* with authority. Although the Talmud mentions *beishana'ei* (ביישנאי), it is not clear whether that term refers to Rabbis or just to Jewish citizens.[18] The Rabbinic prohibition on Jewish citizens of Beth Shean to serve as their own cantors, because of their mispronounciation of the letters of ה as ח and ע as א[19], also underlines their bad reputation. Archaeologically, there is no clear evidence of a Jewish synagogue inside the city walls. Of the two complexes that come into consideration, one is located outside the city walls and was also used by Samaritans,[20] the other one – the 'House of Leontis' – probably belonged to a Judeo-Christian community.[21] Thus, it is also possible that the term *beishana'ei* (ביישנאי) does not designate citizens of Scythopolis, but Jews living in the villages surrounding it.

During the 2nd century CE, a notable number of Samaritans who had been banished from Samaria came into the city. It was probably not just the economic wealth and the convenient location that made Scythopolis attractive for them, but also the fact that, according to several

16 yMeg 3,73d (text and translation cf. Miller [2006], 146): ביישנאי שאלון לר' אימי מהו ליקח אבנים מבית הכנסת זו ולבנות בבית הכנסת אחרת אמ' לון אסור אמ' ר' חלבו לא אסר ר' אימי אלא מפני עגמת נפש. (The Beishana'ei asked R. Immi: What is the law with regard to the taking of stones from this synagogue for use in the building of another synagogue? He said to them: It is prohibited. R. Helbo said: R. Immi only prohibited it because of sorrow [over the destruction of the synagogue whose stones were being used for the reconstruction]).

17 yBM 12c (495 Guggenheimer): אמר רבי יוסי בירבי בון. תיפתר כגון אילין דרייא דבישן דלא יכיל ארעייא באני עד דבני עילייא. (Rabbi Yose ben Rabbi Abun said, explain it, for example, those inhabitants of Bet Shean where the bottom dweller cannot build unless the builder of the upper floor builds). This saying originates either from R. Jose ben R. Abin I, who lived in the first half of the 2nd century or from R. Jose ben R. Abin from the late 4th century CE. Cf. Avi-Yonah (1962), 133.

18 Cf. Miller (2006), 146–157.

19 yBer 2,4d (text and translation cf. Miller [2006], 155): אין מעבירין לפני התיבה לחיפנין ולא בישנין ולא טיבעונין מפני שהן עושין היהין חיתין ועיינין אאין אם היה לשוני ערוך מותרץ (We do not bring to serve as the reader before the ark those from Haifa, those from Beth Shean or those form Tiv'on because they mispronounce the letter *heh* as *heit* and *'ayin* as *'alef*).

20 See below, chap. 4.4.

21 See below, chap. 3.2.

traditions, the Salem of the legendary priest king Melchisedech could be located in or close to the area of Scythopolis.[22]

These three groups were joined by a Christian community in the last third of the 4th century CE at the latest.

2.1 The Establishment of a Christian Community and the Persecution of the Christians

The first Christian from Scythopolis we know by name is Procop. According to Euseb, he was beheaded in 303 as the first Christian martyr of Palestine in the provincial capital of Caesarea.[23] The longer version of Euseb's *On the martyrs of Palestine*, preserved in Syrian and Latin, is interesting with regard to information about the Christian community in Scythopolis:[24] Procop, while living ascetically but also engaging in the profane sciences, occupied a threefold position in the Christian community of Scythopolis. He was lector, translator and exorcist.[25] Especially his second role is interesting: during the service, Procop translated the Greek homilies into Aramaic. Apparently, a part of the community did not understand the Greek language, which suggests that the Christian community also included members from a Semitic background at that time.

Because of his education and his way of life, Procop was certainly an outstanding and, therefore, uncommon member of the Christian community. Euseb characterizes him as an ascetically living philosopher who constantly attended to the study of the Holy Scriptures. Whether he is quoted accurately when refusing the sacrifice for the emperor with the words of Homer, or whether his words are Euseb's literary fiction,[26] cannot be clarified here. But they show Euseb's intention to highlight the outstanding education of the first Palestinian martyr.

---

22 Cf. Raynor (1982), 173–175; Hier., ep. 73,7 (CSEL 55, 20,15–18 Hilberg): *oppidum iuxta Scythopolim, quod usque hodie appellatur Salem. Et ostentatur ibi palatium Melchisedech ex magnitudine ruinarum ueteris operis ostendens magnificentia*; cf. also Itin. Eger. 13–14 (CSEL 175, 54,1–55,24 Franceschini/Weber).

23 Eus., mart. Pal. 1,1 (GCS 9/2, 907,15–21 Schwartz).

24 Text by Violet TU 14/4 (1896), 3–7.

25 Eus., mart. Pal. (TU 14/4, 7,6–9 Violet): *Ibi ecclesiae tria ministeria praebebat: unum in legendi officio, alterum in Syri interpretatione sermonis, et tertium adversus daemones manus impositione consummans.*

26 Cf. Eus., mart. Pal. 1,1 (GCS 9/2 907,21–908,1 Schwartz): οὐκ ἀγαθὸν πολυκοιρανίη, εἷς κοίρανος ἔστω, εἷς βασιλεύς. Cf. furthermore Hom., Il. 2,104.

Another prominent member of the Christian community of Scythopolis was the virgin Ennathas, who was violently brought to Caesarea after the edict of Maximinus of 309 CE and was burned alive there.[27] Procop and Ennathas were the only Christian martyrs from Scythopolis – and both did not die in their home city.[28] Apparently, the imperial edicts were carried out only in the provincial capital, so that the everyday life of Scythopolis was probably largely unaffected.

2.2 The Visit of the Samaritan Leader Baba Rabbah

At the beginning of the 4th century CE, the Samaritan community of Scythopolis seems to have achieved a certain importance which is expressed, for example, by the visit of Baba Rabbah, the charismatic Samaritan leader and reformer, to Scythopolis.[29] According to a Samaritan chronicle, this visit also led him to undertake essential reforms:

> "With the advent of Baba Rabbah, the priest, they were merely called 'Sages' (חכמים); and the priestly title (שם הכהני) was removed from many priests. He likewise removed many people from their priestly rank. The cause of this was that when the priest Baba Rabbah came to Bashan the priests who were there did not come forth to meet him, neither did they fulfil their obligation to accord him honour and glory. However, when he arrived at the city and assumed his rightful position then they came to greet him in their customary manner with all the people. Because of this act he removed them from their positions, because they did not journey out of the city to meet him. In their place he appointed ordinary individuals to discharge their supervisory functions, with the exception of the responsibility (to teach) Holy Scripture."[30]

---

27 Eus., mart. Pal. 9,6–8 (GCS 9/2, 929,7–25 Schwartz).

28 The 6th century archdeacon Theodosius in the report of his pilgrimage *De situ terrae sanctae* 2, mentions a dominus Basilius who died as a martyr in Scythopolis (CSEL 175, 115,15f. Geyer: *ibi dominus Basilius martyrizatus est*), cf. Cyril, Vita Euthymii 16 (GCS 49/2 26,12–14 Schwartz), who mentions a σεβασμός οἶκος τοῦ ἁγίου μάρτυρος Βασιλείου. The only Basilius we know of is the founder and abbot of a monastery from the 5th or 6th century (Cyril, Vita Sabae 34 GCS 49/2 Schwartz 119,15–120,12).

29 Regarding the life and deeds of Baba Rabbah cf. Cohen (1981). It is difficult to determine exactly when Baba Rabbah lived: Cohen (1981), 224–228, suggests 308–328 CE. Crown (1989), 56, places Baba Rabbah in the 3rd century CE, arguing that the events reported by Abū `l Fath lead to the interregnum in Palestine from 235–238 CE.

30 Chronicle II, § 5,5–10 (Cohen [1981], 14, transl. 67):

5 ומיום הכהן בבא רבה נקראו חכמים ויחלף שם הכהני מעל אנשים רבים מן הכהנים.

6 ויסר לאנשים רבים מהם מעל חנותם.

7 והגלל לדבר הזה לעת בא הכהן בבא רבה לבשן הכהנים אשר היו שם לא יצאו לקראתו ולא עשו כאשר הוא חייב עליהם להכבידו ולאיקרו.

It can be reasonably supposed that there was a community with several priests who had administrative duties at the same time. Although the chronicle does not point out a reason for his visit to Scythopolis, it is possible that Baba Rabbah came to implement his administrative and religious reforms.[31] The chronicle justifies Baba Rabbah's reform with a general negligence among the Samaritan priesthood at that time. One might understand the priest's refusal to accept Baba Rabbah as one of theirs, and welcome him in an adequate way, simply as an illustration of this negligence. Certainly, it is more convincing to suppose a willful act of resistance against the appointed Samaritan leader. Therefore, the replacement of the priests with laymen would be a reaction to this disloyalty. Whether it was negligence or resistance, in any case the Samaritans in Scythopolis did not suffer enough to welcome the reformer enthusiastically. None of the seven wise men Baba Rabbah appointed as leaders of the people came from Scythopolis.[32] In addition, the Samaritans of Scythopolis did not seem to take part in the revolt against the Roman powers at that time. The influence of Baba Rabbah and his followers was thus limited.[33] The Samaritans were probably so well integrated into the pluralistic urban society that they did not take part in the nationalist movement led by the Samaritans who lived in the Galilee area.

2.3 Christian Plurality: An exiled orthodox Bishop in the House of a converted Jew amongst a Majority of 'Arians'

After the end of the persecution the Christian community of Scythopolis was engaged in dogmatic conflicts. The main figure was Bishop Patrophilus who had a leading position in a pro-Arian synod in 323 CE

---

8 רק כי כאשר בא העיר ויחן במקום אשר הנכון לו בא שמה וישלמו עליו כפי הסכנתם עם כל האנושים.
9 בגלל הדבר הזה אשר עשו הסירם מעל מקום חנותיהם כי לא יצאו הם לקראתו למחוץ לעיר.
10 ואנשים מן אנשי העם שם תחתיהם ישרתו את משמרתיהם בלתי משא הספר הקדוש.

The chronicle was compiled in 845 CE and is the main source of the 14th century chronicle of Abū `l Fath, Kitāb al-tarīkh 39–65 (transl. Stenhouse 137–206).

31 Abū `l Fath, Kitāb al-tarīkh, 39–51, (transl. Stenhouse 173–186), reports of such 'reform-travels' through Palestine and of the difficulties to implement the reforms of Baba Rabbah.

32 Cf. Chronicle II, § 5, 20–30 (transl. Cohen 68f.).

33 According to Abū 'l Fath, Kitāb al-tarīkh 61 (transl. Stenhouse 183), Baba Rabbah built a synagogue in Scythopolis. The prior chronicle places it in Salem, that is located in the east of Sichem. This shows that Abū `l Fath follows the tradition according to which Salem, the city of Melchisedech (Genesis 14), was located in or near Scythopolis.

and supported the Arian party in Palestine even after the Council of Nicaea (325).[34] During the episcopacy of Patrophilus, the Christian community had a time of prosperity and came to a leading position among the Christians in Palestine. Meanwhile, in the city itself, the influence of the bishop seems to have been limited. This is illustrated by a report of Epiphanius of Salamis, who was born in Palestinian Eleutheropolis and became bishop of Cyprus in 367 CE, in his *Panarion of all haeresies* (ca. 377 CE). He came to Scythopolis between 356 and 361 in order to visit Euseb of Vercelli, who was sent into exile by Constantius II because he kept to his Nicean faith. Together with Euseb of Vercelli, Epiphanius of Salamis dwelled in the house of a wealthy Jewish convert named Joseph.

Joseph[35] was born in Tiberias and had the rank of an ἀπόστολος which means that he was a confidant to the Patriarch Hillel II. While traveling to Cilicia, he converted to Christianity and was, therefore, excluded from the Jewish community. He, then, became *comes imperatoris* of Constantine, and at his behest he built churches in many Palestinian cities. It seems to be an indication of the attractiveness of Scythopolis that Joseph settled there. Possibly, it also means that there was no influential Jewish community in the city, since he justified his going away from Tiberias with his fear of Jewish hostility.

The following passage is enlightening about the city's atmosphere during the episcopacy of Patrophilus:

> "Josephus was not only privileged to become a faithful Christian, but a despiser of Arians as well. In that city, Scythopolis, he was the only orthodox Christian – they were all Arian. Had it not been that he was a count (κόμης), and the rank of count protected him from Arian persecution, he could not even have undertaken to live in the town (οὐκ ἂν ὑπέστη κἂν ἐν τῇ πόλει διατρίβειν), especially while Patrophilus was the Arian bishop. Patrophilus was very influential because of his wealth and severity, and his familiar acquaintance with the Emperor Constantius. But there was another, younger man in town too, an orthodox believer of Jewish parentage. He did not even dare to associate with me in public, though he used to visit us secretly."[36]

34 Cf. Soz., h.e. 1,15,11; 2,20,3 (GCS 50, 34,22–35,7; 76,25–29 Bidez/Hanssen).

35 For further information about Joseph and for an analysis of Epiphanius' reference to him, cf. Perkams (2001); Thornton (1990).

36 Epiph., pan. haer. 30,5,5f. (GCS 31, 340,9–14 Holl): ἦν γὰρ ὁ ἀνὴρ οὐ μόνον Χριστιανὸς πιστὸς καταξιωθεὶς γενέσθαι, ἀλλὰ καὶ Ἀρειανοὺς σφόδρα στηλιτεύων. ἐν γὰρ τῇ πόλει ἐκείνῃ, Σκυθοπόλει φημί, μόνος οὗτος ὀρθόδοξος ὑπῆρχεν, πάντες δὲ Ἀρειανοί. καὶ εἰ μὴ ὅτι κόμης ἦν καὶ τὸ τοῦ κόμητος ἀξίωμα ἐκώλυεν ἀπ' αὐτοῦ τὸν τῶν Ἀρειανῶν διωγμόν, [ἐπεὶ] οὐκ ἂν ὑπέστη κἂν ἐν τῇ πόλει διατρίβειν ὁ ἀνήρ, μάλιστα ἐπὶ Πατροφίλου τοῦ Ἀρειανοῦ ἐπισκόπου τοῦ πολλὰ ἰσχύσαντος πλούτῳ τε καὶ αὐτοῦ Ἀρειανοῦ ἐπισκόπου τοῦ πολλὰ ἰσχύσαντος πλούτῳ

Of course, we have to take into account that Joseph as well as Epiphanius speak polemically about their Arian opponent Patrophilus. But there can be no doubt that Patrophilus did not tolerate Christians who differed from the Arian faith, as illustrated by the example of the other secret orthodox convert. Nevertheless, Patrophilus could not prevent the presence of the Nicean Christians Joseph and Euseb of Vercelli in the city.

2.4 'Theatre of Tortures': The anti-pagan Trial of Scythopolis in 359 CE

In 359, by order of the emperor Constantius, a tribunal was established in Scythopolis in order to accuse "noble as well as unimportant persons from all over the world"[37]. The precise accusations can not be reconstructed anymore. The pagan historian Ammianus Marcellinus mentions as "the slight and trivial occasion"[38] that in the Egyptian city of Abydos written requests to the oracle of the god Bes were found which caused the emperor's distrust. It is difficult to decide whether it concerned the political loyalty or the cultic practices of the suspected persons. Since, in the course of Late Antiquity, oracle requests increasingly gave rise to suspicion of political conspiracy, one cannot disentangle political from religious accusations. [39] Thus, it is not surprising that, even in the report of Ammianus, both aspects are intertwined.[40] He mentions famous public persons who were suspected of high treason as well as common people who wore magical amulets or spent the night in tombs.[41] These latter were, in most cases, sentenced to death and executed, while the four main accused persons – Simplicius, son of a prefect and consul, the former prefect of Egypt Parnasius, the bard Andronikus and Demetrius the philosopher – escaped death and were banned or absolved.[42] Presumably, in his report Ammian exaggerates

---

τε καὶ αὐστηρίᾳ καὶ τῇ πρὸς τὸν βασιλέα Κωνστάντιον γνώσει τε καὶ παρρησίᾳ. ἦν δὲ καὶ ἄλλος τις νεώτερος ἐν τῇ πόλει ἀπὸ Ἑβραίων ὀρθῶς πιστεύων, ὃς οὔτε ἐτόλμα κατὰ τὸ φανερὸν.

37 Amm. Marc., res gestae 19,12,7 (LCL 536 Rolfe): *ab orbe prope terrarum iuxta nobiles et obscuri.*

38 Amm. Marc., res gestae 19,12,3 (LCL 534 Rolfe): *Materiam autem in infinitum quaestionibus extendendis dedit occasio vilis et parva.*

39 Cf. Fögen (1993). The alternative discussed by the older research on whether the trial of Scythopolis was politically or religiously motivated is, therefore, inadequate. Cf. the discussion in Haehling (1978), who mentions the most important positions.

40 In my opinion, Haehling (1978), overemphasizes the fact that Ammian depicts the trial as exclusively political.

41 Cf. Amm. Marc., res gestae 19,12,14 (LCL 540 Rolfe).

42 Cf. Amm. Marc., res gestae 19,12,9–12 (76,28–78,14 Seyfarth) und 9,12,14 (LCL 538–540 Rolfe).

the cruelty of the Christian *notarius* Paulus, who was charged with the preparation and execution of the trial.[43] But Libanius also writes in one of his letters that the tribunal caused shock among the gentiles in Antioch.[44]

It is not the place to reconstruct the historical details of these cases here.[45] Rather, we have to ask why Scythopolis was chosen as the venue for this tribunal. Ammian gives the following reason:

> "As the theatre of inhuman torture Scythopolis was chosen, a city of Palestine which for two reasons seemed more suitable than any other: because it is more secluded, and because it is midway between Antioch and Alexandria, from which cities the greater number were brought to meet charges."[46]

Due to its convenient location Scythopolis became a "theatre of inhuman torture". Ammian seems to suggest that the choice of the "secluded" city was not only motivated by its convenient location, but also by the hope that the population of Scythopolis would not protest against the anti-pagan actions as the citizens of Antioch and Alexandria had done before. Actually, Ammian does not report any immediate reaction of the Scythopolitans.[47]

Only a few years later, however, after Julian had become emperor, the pagans of Scythopolis took advantage of the new politics for revenge. Thus, the Chronicon Paschale notices:

> "They [i.e. the pagans] took the remains of the holy Patrophilus, the bishop of the Scythopolis, out of the tomb and scattered them, insolently hanging up his skull, affixing it as though it were in the form of a lamp."[48]

The public hanging of the skull is at the same time an act of triumph and of desecration. This is the only information we have about anti-Christian actions in Scythopolis during the reign of Julian. In compa-

---

43 In the entire account of Ammian, Paulus appears as the prototype of Christian disposition and cruelty.

44 Cf. Lib., ep. 37,1 (Libanii Opera 1, 35,1 Foerster): τοσοῦτος ἐμέ τε καὶ τὴν πόλιν ἔσεισε φόβος.

45 For that, cf. Haehling (1978).

46 Amm. Marc., res gestae 19,12,8 (LCL II, 536–538, transl. Rolfe): *et electa est spectatrix suppliciorum feralium ciuitas in Palaestina Scythopolis, gemina ratione uisa magis omnibus opportuna, quod secretior et inter Antiochiam Alexandriamque media, unde multi plerumque ad crimina trahebantur.*

47 This can also be explained, however, with Ammian's intention to emphasize the disposition and cruelty of the Christian actors.

48 Chron. pasch. a. 362 (CSHB 546,14–17, transl. Whitby): Ἔτι δὲ καὶ τοῦ ἁγίου Πατροφίλου ἐπισκόπου τῆς ἐν Σκυθοπόλει ἐκκλησίας γενομένου ἀνορύξαντες ἀπὸ τοῦ τάφου τὰ λείψανα τὰ μὲν ἄλλα διεσκόρπισαν, τὸ δὲ κρανίον ἐφυβρίστως κρεμάσαντες ὡς ἐν σχήματι κανδήλας ἐνέπηξεν. (The chronicle was probably compiled in the 7th century CE, basing itself on older sources.)

rison with other Palestinian cities, such as Caesarea and Gaza[49], the retribution against Christians in Scythopolis seems to have been limited. In addition, based on the characterization of Patrophilus' episcopate given by Epiphanius, the bishop was not even favored by all Christians.

2.5 The Earthquake of 363 CE and the Restorations

Excavators of late antique Scythopolis found many traces of demolition on public buildings dating from the middle of the century. In all likelihood, the damages are neither linked to the events of 359 CE nor during the reign of Julian, but were caused by an earthquake that shook the region shortly after his death in 363 CE.[50] The restoration activities in the following decades shed light on the religious situation in the city. The authorities concentrated on the restoration of public buildings such as the monumental porticus in the east, the nymphaeum and bathhouses as well as on the conversion of the hippodrome into an amphitheatre and on the building of a new propylaeum on the southwestern side of Palladius Street, endeavouring to preserve the "classical" appearance of the buildings.[51]

The adherence to classical aesthetics witnesses a cultural continuity. The pagan cult places, however, remained in a state of destruction. This suggests that the pagan population had lost its influence on public issues in the course of the 4th century. Nevertheless, this may not reflect a 'triumph' of Christianity at this time, as Foerster and Tsafrir assumed.[52] Even the Samaritans did not have any interest in restoring pa-

49 Cf. Greg. Naz., or. IV contra Julianum 4, 87.93; 5,29 (SC 309, 218–220.232–234; 350–352 Bernardi); Soz. h.e. 5,9–11 (GCS 50, 204,10–210,22 Bidez/Hansen); Chron. Pasch. a. 362 (CSHB 546,12–548,10 Niebuhr, transl. Whitby), but also Amm. Marc., rer. gest. 22,11 (II, 256–262 Rolfe); for the "battle of the statues" in: Golanide Paneas, cf. Eus., h.e. 7,17 (GCS 9/2, 670,17–672,2 Schwartz); Soz., h.e. 5,21 (GCS 50, 227,24–229,18 Bidez/Hansen). For Gaza and Ashkelon cf. Ambr., ep. LXXIIII (40) (CSEL 82/3, 15,63,175 Zelzer) on Jews burning Christian basilicas, whilst Chron. Pasch. ascribes the rampage to the pagans.

50 Cf. Russell (1980). The most important document of the reconstruction is an inscription that testifies the developments of the metropolite Ablabius, cf. Mazor (1987/1988), 22; Foerster/Tsafrir (1997), 108 n. 104.

51 Cf. Foerster/Tsafrir (1997), 108–116. The authors emphasize that the Roman basilica on the agora was not restored, suggesting that the building had lost its value, and the many small stores as well as Christian basilicas substituted for it. If that is "a most significant expression of the triumph of Christianity and the increasing power of the church and the bishop", according to Foerster/Tsafrir (1997), 116, I doubt anyway.

52 See the more detailed discussion of this topic at the end, chap. 6.

gan temples. Certainly, some of the builders were Christian, such as Artemidoros, whose name appears together with a cross on an inscription at the restored nymphaeum. This does not mean, however, that the elites of the city were predominantly or exclusively Christian.

2.6 Summary

The 4th century is characterized by a relatively equal coexistence of pagans and Christians and only occasional violent conflicts in the middle of the century. The Samaritans seem to have been well integrated, so that they had no interest in the national renaissance sought by the Samaritan leader Baba Rabbah. Unfortunately, we have little information about the Jews.

For the first half of the century we do not have any evidence of violent conflicts. Rather, the Judeo-Christian Joseph who fled, according to his own words, from the harrassment of the Jews of Tiberias, settled unhindered in the city. The other 'orthodox' Christian Euseb of Vercelli was forced to live among the Arians in Scythopolis, and even though Joseph complained about the Arian bishop Patrophilus, neither Joseph nor Euseb seems to have suffered real disadvantages. Probably, the relatively peaceful appearance of Scythopolis was one of the reasons why the city was chosen as the scene of the anti-pagan trials in 359 CE. In this years, the name of the city was famous even in Antioch and was linked to the cruelty of Christian authorities. After the death of Constantius, the pagans all over Palestine took revenge with anti-Christian actions. In Scythopolis they defiled the tomb and the corpse of the venerated bishop Patrophilus, who had been a very influential person within Palestinian Christianity in the first half of the century.

We do not know whether and how Samaritans were involved in the conflicts between pagans and Christians. In any case, after the earthquake of 363 CE the urban elites did not show interest in restoring pagan temples, which obviously does not mean at all that cult practices did not survive even in damaged buildings. Indeed, the authorities were interested in conserving the aesthetic heritage of the city: "The classical character of the restoration proves that the classical tradition was still alive."[53]

53 Foerster/Tsafrir (1997), 108.

3. The 5th Century CE: Provincial Capital with flourishing Surroundings

Around the year 400 the emperor Theodosius made Scythopolis the capital of the newly founded province *Palaestina secunda*.[54] Thus, the city came into competition with the former capital Caesarea, and the connection between the bishop of Scythopolis and the metropolitan of Caesarea remained ambiguous. Information from literal sources concerning the city's history during the 5th century is very rare. Archaeological data, however, document a city in a time of prosperity. The urban area expanded as a result of building the new city-wall,[55] and a new quarter, probably the government district, developed in the south. In the middle of the city, a new commercial centre, the so called 'Byzantine agora' was created. On the tell harbouring the remains of the temple of Zeus-Akraios, a round church was built in the second half of the century – an example of the relatively rare transition of a pagan cult place to a Christian church.[56] This confirms the view that there no longer existed a significant pagan population in this time. Also, the literary sources do not speak of pagans, which does not necessarily mean that there were no 'pagans' at all, but it shows that they did not have an influential lobby anymore.

Religious conflicts marked the relationship not between different religions, but within Christianity. In 452 CE, the bishop of Scythopolis, Severianus, was cast out of the city and killed by charges of the emperor Theodosius II, because after the Council of Chalcedon (451) he had implemented the Chalcedonian faith among Palestinian Christianity. Obviously, the assassins did not came from Scythopolis, but were sent to the city from outside.[57]

---

54 Cf. Jo. Mal., Chron. 13,41 (Thurn 268,19–21, transl. Jeffreys/Scott 188): ὁμοίως δὲ καὶ δευτέραν Παλαιστίνην ἐμέρισεν ἀπὸ τῆς πρώτης καὶ ἐποίησεν ἐπαρχίαν, δοὺς δίκαιον μητροπόλεως καὶ ἄρχοντα τῇ λεγομένῃ Σκυθῶν πόλει. (The emperor Theodosius […] divided off Second Palestine from the First and created a province, giving the status of a metropolis and a governor to the place known as Scythopolis).

55 Cf. Foerster/Tsafrir (1997), 100–102, argue with good reasons for a dating of the Byzantine wall into the end of the 4th or the beginning of the 5th century CE.

56 Cf. Foerster/Tsafrir (1997), 109.

57 Cf. Sivan (2008), 340.

3.1 Purim Marches in Scythopolis?

Since we have no explicit evidence of a Jewish presence inside the city-walls of Scythopolis, it seems to be worthwhile to search for implicit indications. In his recent and illuminative study "Palestine in Late Antiquity" (Oxford 2008), Hagith Sivan argues that the Purim-law enacted on May 29th, 408 CE by the Emperors Honorius and Theodosius[58] was provoked by Purim festivities in Scythopolis around the turn of the century. Sivan's main argument arises from a late antique Purim poet *(piyyut)* that places Haman, the court minister in Persia according to the book of Esther, not in Susa, but in Scythopolis.[59] Sivan assumes that "the reference to Scythopolis was not a fanciful poetic touch" and that "this city provided the catalyst scene evoked the issuance of the imperial law".[60] Even though Sivan's imaginative description of a probable Purim march through the city is very suggestive, I doubt that the reference to Scythopolis in the poem is sufficient to legitimate the supposition of a vivid Jewish festivity inside the city. The appellation of Haman as "the fool of Scythopolis"[61] does not necessarily indicate that the Purim march for which the poem was written was located in the city itself. Being the capital of the province, Scythopolis was a selfevident parallel to Susa in Persia, where the events described in the Book of Esther were happening. Thus, the reference to Scythopolis indicates only the origin of the poet in *Palaestina Secunda*, where many Jewish settlements are proven.[62] Considering that the order to prohibit Purim festivities in the imperial law is directed to all governors of the prov-

---

58 Cod. Theod. 16,8,18 (Mommsen 891, transl. Sivan [2008], 144) from May 29th, 408: *Imperatores Honorius et Theodosius Anthemio praefecto praetorio. Iudeaos quodam festivitatis suae sollemni Aman ad poenae quondam recordationem incendere et sanctae crucis adsimulatam speciem in contemptum Christianae fidei sacrilega mente exurere provinciarum rectores prohibeant, ne iocis suis fidei nostrae signum inmisceant, sed ritus suos citra contemptum Christianae legis retineant, amissuri sine dubio permissa hactenus nisi ab inlicitis temperaverint.* (Emperors Honorius and Theodosius Augusti to Anthemius, Pretorian Prefect: The governors of the provinces shall prohibit the Jews from setting fire to (H)aman in memory of his past punishment during a certain ceremony of their festival, and from burning with sacrilegious intent a form cast in the shape of a holy cross in contempt of the Christian faith, lest they mingle the sign of our faith with their jests. They shall also restrain their rituals from ridiculing Christian law because if they do not abstain from matters which are forbidden they will promptly lose what had been thus fat permitted to them).

59 Piyyut 33, 28: Bet Shean; ibid., 49: Kefar Karnus (Sokoloff-Yahalom); cf. Sivan (2008), 157–167.

60 Sivan (2008), 157.

61 Piyyut 33,28 (Sokoloff-Yahalom).

62 Even Bar Ilan (2001), 179, assigns Scythopolis as the poet's home in his review of Sokoloff-Yahalom. The Samaritans did not celebrate Purim.

inces, the assumption that the law "had been prompted by the situation in Scythopolis"[63] seems to me too daring.

3.2 A Judeo-Christian Community?

The religious plurality of the urban population continued after the disappearance of a public 'paganism'. Although we have no information about the Samaritans of Scythopolis in the 5th century CE, the existence of an influential Samaritan elite at the beginning of the 6th century CE admits the assumption of a continuous Samaritan presence in the city. Because of the lack of archaeological and literary evidence, we can not say whether there was a Jewish community or not. Christianity, however, formed a heterogeneous entity, as the following considerations show. While in the 4th century Joseph of Tiberias and the unnamed convert mentioned by Epiphanius seem to have been the only Judeo-Christians in the city, in the 5th century there apparently existed a Judeo-Christian community with its own assembly room. This is the so-called 'House of Leontis', excavated in 1964.[64] This spacious and noble building was considered a Jewish house with an integrated synagogue for a long time, until Zeev Safrai in 2003 argued on the basis of archaeological and literary indications that the 'House of Leontis' was the centre of a Judeo-Christian community, of which Leontis was a prominent member if not the leader.[65] In the inscription of the assembly room of the house, Leontis calls himself ΛΕΟΝΤΙΣ Ο ΚΑΛΥΒΑΣ. Safrai interprets this as a reference to a Judeo-Christian leader, whose name Epiphanius spells ΚΛΕΟΒΙΟΣ or ΚΛΕΟΒΟΥΛΟΣ.[66] The mosaic pavement of the room combines several iconographic motives that can be interpreted as pagan (Odysseus with Sirens), Jewish (Menora) and Christian (ship and mast).[67]

Another inscription mentions a Nonnos of Kyzikos as the benefactor and, therefore, shows the connections of the circle beyond the city. In the 6th century the assembly room was destroyed and not rebuilt. That indicates probably the end of the existence of the community.

---

63 Sivan (2008), 166.

64 Cf. Zori (1966).

65 Cf. Safrai (2003).

66 Epiph., pan haer. 51,6,6 (GCS 31, 255,17, ed. K. Holl): Κλεόβιον εἴτ' οὖν Κλεόβουλον.

67 Although, in my view, one has to exercise the interpretation of these motives more thoroughly than Safrai actually does. Ship and mast *may* be interpreted as Christian symbols, but this is not compelling. The Jewish background, however, is clear not only because of the Menora, but also due to the Jewish name the Leontis' brother, Jonathan.

Although the precise religious identity of Leontis and his circle cannot be reconstructed definitively, it seems plausible to suggest the existence of a vivid Judeo-Christian circle that was independent from the Orthodox church.

3.3 Christian Monks in the Surroundings of Scythopolis

At the beginning of the 5th century CE, a new social form within Christianity emerged in the surroundings of Scythopolis. Shortly after the outbreak of the Origenist conflicts in Egypt, a group of about 80 monks arriving from the Nitrian desert settled in the region. According to the report of Sozomenus, they choose Scythopolis for economic reasons:

> "The group of Dioscurus and Ammonius noticed the intrigue (of Theophilus) and withdrew to Jerusalem. From there they went to Scythopolis, which they considered suitable because of the many palm trees, whose leaves they used for the monastic handwork."[68]

In search of an alternative to the Egyptian desert the monks first went to Jerusalem, but then preferred Scythopolis as the scene of their monastic life. Given the monastic custom to settle outside the cities, there can be no doubt that "Jerusalem" and "Scythopolis" do not refer to the cities here, but to the rural landscape surrounding the cities. From the palm leaves the monks produced baskets and ropes. Along the way there emerged a rural monastic Christianity as a counterbalance to the cosmopolitan Christianity in the city. In the course of time, bishops also arose from this monastic movement to Scythopolis,[69] the first of whom was Cosmas, a pupil of Euthymius.[70]

3.4 Jews in the Surroundings of Scythopolis

More important was, however, the Jewish population in the fertile valleys of Scythopolis. The synagogues of Maᶜoz Hayim and Rehov, built in the late 4th or early 5th century CE and their mosaic pavements testify to the vivid Jewish life and the participation in Hellenistic culture.[71]

---

68 Soz., h.e. 8,13,1 (FC 73/4, 996,4–9): Αἰσθόμενοι δὲ τῆς ἐπιβουλῆς οἱ ἀμφὶ Διόσκορον καὶ Ἀμμώνιον ἀνεχώρησαν εἰς Ἱεροσόλυμα κἀκεῖθεν εἰς Σκυθόπολιν ἧκον ἐπιτηδείαν ἡγησάμενοι τὴν ἐνθάδε οἴκησιν διὰ τοὺς πολλοὺς φοίνικας, ὧν τοῖς φύλλοις ἐχρῶντο πρὸς τὰ εἰωθότα μοναχοῖς ἔργα. εἵποντο γὰρ αὐτοῖς ἀμφὶ ἄνδρες ὀγδοήκοτα.

69 Cf. Cyr. Scyth., Vita Euthymii 16, 37 (GCS 25,13–26,5; 55,20–56,3 Schwartz, 52).

70 Cf.. Cyr. Scyth., Vita Euthymii 16, 37 (GCS 25,13–26,5; 55,20–56,3 Schwartz, 52).

71 Cf. Tsaferis (1981), 86–89; Vitto (1981), 90–94; Sivan (2008), 255–263.

Of special interest is a halachic inscription that was placed in the narthex of the synagogue of Rehov in the 6th or 7th century CE, but contains an older text that is passed on also in the Jerusalem Talmud and gives us an impression of the situation of the Jews in the region.[72] According to the inscription, the city of Bet Shean is not a part of Eretz Israel in its narrow definition as the region where the repatriates of the Babylonian exiles settled. This region was subjected to very strict laws such as the contribution of the tenth or the prohibition on harvesting certain fruits during the Sabbatical year. The exemption of certain regions from Eretz Israel reflects the endeavour of the Rabbis to safeguard the economic situation of the Jews.[73] But some restrictions also applied to the exempted region of Bet Shean: for example, it was forbidden to sell certain fruits produced in Eretz Israel during the Sabbatical year. The inscription contains also an exact geographical description of the city borders in order to mark the area where the laws applied, and is, therefore, a useful source for reconstructing the topography of late antique Scythopolis.

3.5 Summary

Since we have little information about Scythopolis in the 5th century CE from literary sources, we can only assume with an *argumentum e silentio* and on the basis of archaeological data that the new provincial capital underwent a time of prosperity and tranquillity. The urban authorities reinforced the development of the city, preserving its classical appearance. It is illuminating to observe that antique statues decorated the streets and places up to the beginning of the 6th century CE, but in many cases were decapitated – apparently in order to expel the demons who were supposed to live inside the statues.[74] Who were the authorities that governed the issues of city administration? It is not easy to answer this question on the basis of archaeological or literary data. Anyway, in my opinion, it would be misleading to assume that the authorities must have been predominantly Christians. We have to state that the sources do not prove this assumption. The only citizens of 5th century Scythopolis known by name are the Christian bishops (Theodo-

72 Cf. Sussmann (1981), 146–153, for the translation and the explanation of the inscription; cf. Lapin (2001), 169–173.

73 Foerster/Tsafrir (1997), 102, suppose that as a result of the exemption of Scythopolis from Eretz Israel, Jews settled inside the city in order to profit from the economic liberty. This is possible, but there is no evidence to prove this assumption.

74 Cf. Foerster/Tsafrir (1997), 129.

sius, Severianus, Olympius and Cosmas)[75] and the likely Judeo-Christians Leontis and his brother Jonathan, who presumably belonged to the urban elites. In addition, the existence of an influential Samaritan elite at the beginning of the 6th century admits the assumption of a continuous Samaritan presence in the city. Being monotheistic, all of them would deal with the city's classical heritage in the way described above. In the surroundings of the city Christian monks lived side by side with Jews influenced by Hellenism.

The population in and around the "Greek city" Scythopolis, therefore, remained pluralistic in the course of the 5th century. After the disappearance of paganism, the plurality no longer includes polytheism, but continues with regard to the three monotheistic religions of late antique Palestine and their fragmentations.

4. The 6th Century CE: Rivalry and Violence between Samaritans and Christians

The expansion of the city, its demographic growth and the building activity reach their peak in the first half of the 6th century, in the times of Anastasius (491–518) and Justin I (518–527)[76]. The urban area expanded to the south, the walls were renovated. At the beginning of the century the Palladius Street was renewed, and the so-called *Sigma*, a luxurious commercial centre including taverns and shops, was constructed by the governor of *Palaestina Secunda*, Theosevius. The rooms of the *Sigma* were decorated with magnificent mosaics, among them a medallion depicting the city goddess Tyche (see Fig. 2). Somewhat later the governor Flavius Theodorus built a basilica in the western wing of the western bathhouse. At the same time the Byzantine agora was reconverted. The theatre, the odeon, the amphitheatre and the western bathhouse continued to be used by the citizens.

75 Cf. Fedalto (1988), 100.1.3.

76 Cf. Foerster/Tsafrir (1997), 116–125.

Fig. 2: Mosaic of Tyche in the Sigma

All population groups seem to have benefited from this recovery, but at the same time – and probably for the same reason – hostilities emerged between Samaritans and Christians. The literary sources only reflect the hostilities between the citizens of the town, while archaeological data show a flourishing Jewish life in the surrounding region.

The main source for the history of this time is the *Lifes of the Monks of Palestine* composed by Cyril, a citizen of Scythopolis. Cyril originated from the urban Christian elite, his father John was a lawyer and assistant to the metropolitan bishop Theodosius.[77] Early in his life Cyril became pupil of the charismatic and prominent monk Saba. Cyril's *Vita of Saba* is a hagiographical monument that sheds light on the history of Scythopolis. Compared to the 5th century, the relationship between the cosmopolitan and the monastic Christians is much closer in this time. While the Christians emerge more and more as a homogeneous group, another conflict appears: the hostility between Christians and Samaritans.

4.1 Sabas and Silvanus

Cyril reports that around the year 500 CE Sabas withdrew to the region of Scythopolis and stayed for a short time in a cave where a lion lived. When the lion returned and found the monk sleeping, Sabas began to sing psalms and calmed the beast.[78] Quickly he became famous in the region and inspired many Christians of the upper classes to retreat and

77 For John, the life of Cyril and the cultural milieu of the family cf. Flusin (1983), 11–32; Rorem/Lamoreaux (1998), 23–39.

78 Cf. Cyr. Scyth., Vita Sabae 33 (GCS 49/2, 118,21–119,14 Schwartz, 127f.).

live as ascetics in the vicinity of the town.[79] Twice, Sabas visited the town. In 518 he came by order of the archbishop John of Jerusalem to promulgate the return of all Chalcedonians exiled by Justin I after the death of Anastasius and to reactivate the dogma of Chalcedon.[80] Sabas and his legation were received by the citizens and their metropolitan Theodosius with a service in the 'ancient church', that is the round church which was constructed above the ruins of the temple of Zeus-Akraios.[81] He spent only one night in the city,[82] healed a woman with a haemorrhage and a girl possessed by a demon,[83] visited the bishop's palace and received the citizens in audience there:

> "There was at Scythopolis a lawyer called John, the son of the collector of tax arrears, a wise man inspired in soul, who came to see saint Sabas in the bishop's palace and spoke at length about Silvanus the Samaritan, who at that time exercised some authority as an imperial dignitary (παραδυναστεύοντος ἔν βασιλικοίς ἀξιώμασιν) and was plotting against the Christians (τοῖς Χριστιανοῖς ἐπιβουλεύοντος), describing his wickedness and war against God. On hearing this, our sainted father Sabas was filled with the Holy Spirit and said to the bishop and those present, 'Behold, the days are coming, says the Lord, when the fifty-first Davidic psalm shall be fulfilled in the case of Silvanus by his being consumed by fire in the middle of the city.' This was the prophecy he made about Silvanus."[84]

79 Cf. Cyr. Scyth., Vita Sabae 34 (GCS 49/2, 119,15–20 Schwartz, transl. Price 128): Αὐτοῦ δὲ ἐν ὀλίγαις ἡμέραις ἐπισήμου αὐτόθι γεγονότος ἤρχοντο τινὲς πρὸς αὐτὸν τῶν Σκυθοπολιτῶν καὶ τῶν Γαδαρηνῶν, ἐν οἷς νεώτερός τις Σκυθοπολίτης ὀνόματι Βασίλειος προσγενὴς ὑπάρχων Σευήρου καὶ Σωφρονίου τῶν αὐτόθι περιβοήτων θείαι κινηθεὶς κατανύξει ἦλθεν πρὸς αὐτὸν καὶ ἀπετάξατο καὶ τὴν ἀσκητικὴν ἐπαιδεύετο ἀκρίβειαν. (In a few days he became famous there, and received visits from some of the people of Scythopolis and Gadara, including a young man of Scythopolis, Basil by name, a relative of the local celebrities Severus and Sophronius, stirred by divine compunction, he came to Sabas, made his renunciation and received instruction from him in strict ascetism).

80 Cf. Cyr. Scyth., Vita Sabae 61 (GCS 49/2, 162,19–23 Schwartz, transl. Price 172).

81 Cyr. Scyth., Vita Sabae 61 (GCS 49/2, 162,25–163,3 Schwartz, transl. Price 172): καὶ πληρώσαντες ἐκεῖσε τὰ ἐντεταλμένα ἦλθον εἰς Σκυθόπολιν καὶ ἐξῆλθον ἅπαντες οἱ πολῖται ἅμα τῶι ἁγιωτάτωι μητροπολίτηι Θεοδοσίωι εἰς συνάντησιν αὐτοῖς εἰς τὸ ἀποστολεῖον τοῦ ἁγίου Θωμᾶ. καὶ εἰσελθόντες μετὰ ψαλμῶν, γέγονεν ἡ σύναξις ἐν τῆι ἀρχαίαι ἐκκλησίαι καὶ ἐμφανίζεται τὸ θεῖον γράμμα καὶ ἐντάσσονται τοῖς ἱεροῖς διπτύχοις αἱ τέσσαρες σύνοδοι. (They went to Scythopolis, where all the citizens together with the most holy metropolitan Theodosius came out to meet them at the apostolic shrine of Saint Thomas. They made their entry with psalms, the liturgy was celebrated in the ancient church, the imperial letter was read out, and the four councils were inserted in the sacred diptychs.) It is also interesting that there apparently existed a shrine in Scythopolis that kept the remains of the Apostle Thomas.

82 This results from Cyr. Scyth., Vita Sabae 75 (GCS 49/2 179,26–182,2 Schwartz, 188–190).

83 Cf. Cyr. Scyth., Vita Sabae 62f. (GCS 49/2, 163,14–164,28 Schwartz, 173f.).

84 Cyr. Scyth., Vita Sabae 61 (GCS 49/2, 163,3–13 Schwartz, transl. Price 172f.): ἦν δέ τις ἐν Σκυθοπόλει σχολαστικὸς Ἰωάννης ὁ τοῦ ἐκσπελλευτοῦ, ἀνὴρ σοφὸς καὶ τὴν ψυχὴν πεφω-

The report shows, that the impression of a predominant Christian population in Scythopolis is misleading, even if Cyril himself suggests that "all citizens came" (καὶ ἐξῆλθον ἅπαντες οἱ πολῖται)[85] to receive the legation of Sabas. Besides the Christians there were rich and influential Samaritans that were a thorn in the Christian's flesh. So John asked the help of abbas Sabas against the Samaritan Silvanus, who had the protection of the emperor. Apparently, Sabas did not have the influence to put things right in favour of the Christians. So he left it at consoling them with the approaching death of Silvanus. Actually, this does not mean that the assassination of Silvanus was arranged by Sabas. Being a *vaticinium ex eventu*,[86] the announcement of the death is merely used by the hagiographer Cyril to demonstrate the prophetical charisma of Sabas. The episode shows, however, that Silvanus was more influential than the Christians around the lawyer John. This leads to the conclusion that there was a group of Samaritan elites in Scythopolis that either acted as a counterpart to the Christians (seen then as a uniform group) or cooperated with certain Christians in a way that scandalized another Christian group surrounding John and Sabas.

There is archaeological evidence that illustrates the influence of Silvanus on public affairs of Scythopolis: in the years 516/517 CE, a magnificent street and a hall of impressive dimensions (60 m x 28.7 m) were built in the eastern quarter, near the bathhouse. Two inscriptions mention the scholasticus Silvanus and his brother Sallustius, sons of Arsenius, as developers.[87] There can be no doubt that this Silvanus is identical with the Samaritan of whom the Christian John complained at Sabas. It is all the more interesting to note that one of the inscriptions

---

τισμένος, ὅστις ἐλθὼν πρὸς τὸν ἐν ἁγίοις Σάβαν ἐν τῶι ἐπισκοπείωι περὶ Σιλουανοῦ τοῦ Σαμαρείτου τὸν λόγον παρέτεινεν τὸ τηνικαῦτα παραδυναστεύοντος ἐν βασιλικοῖς ἀξιώμασιν καὶ τοῖς Χριστιανοῖς ἐπιβουλεύοντος, ἐξηγούμενος τὰς τούτου πονηρίας τε καὶ θεομαχίας. καὶ ἀκούσας ὁ ἐν ἁγίοις πατὴρ ἡμῶν Σάβας καὶ πνεύματος ἁγίου πλησθεὶς εἶπεν τῶι τε ἐπισκόπωι καὶ τοῖς παροῦσιν· ἰδοὺ ἡμέραι ἔρχονται, λέγει κύριος, καὶ πληρωθήσεται εἰς Σιλουανὸν ὁ Δαυιτικὸς πεντηκοστὸς πρῶτος ψαλμὸς πρὸς τὸ αὐτὸν ἐν μέσηι τῆι πόλει πυρίκαυστον γενέσθαι. καὶ ταῦτα μὲν περὶ Σιλουανοῦ προεφήτευσεν·

85 Cyr. Scyth., Vita Sabae 61 (GCS 49/2, 162,26f. Schwartz), cf. also Vita Sabae 75: ἐξῆλθεν ὁ μητροπολίτης Θεοδόσιος μετὰ παντὸς τοῦ λαοῦ εἰς ἀπάντησιν αὐτου (GCS 49/2, 180, 3f. Schwartz).

86 The realization of the murder is mentioned Cyr. Scyth., Vita Sabae 70 (GCS 49/2 172,18–22 Schwartz), cf. note 90.

87 Description of the inscriptions by Foerster/Tsafrir (1997), 124. The first one runs: "From a gift of Lavius Anastasius, imperator Augustus, the basilica was made together with the ceiling and the ceramic, through the brothers Sallustius and Silvanus, the Scythopolitan lawyers, children of the lawyer Arsenius of Scythopolis, in the ninth year of the indiction, at the time of the most magnificent governor Entrichius." In the second, yet unpublished metric inscription, the building itself praises the work and art of its constructor Silvanus.

begins with the sign of a cross: was this "the price that Sallustius and Silvanus had to pay for the right to record their names together with the name of the emperor", as Tsafrir supposes?[88] Or does the cross testify to a certain religious negligence by the Samaritan elites of Scythopolis?

According to Procop of Caesarea, after the anti-Samaritan legacy of 527 CE many Samaritans in the towns succeeded in shaking off the danger arising from the law by adopting names of Christians, because they "regarded it as a foolish thing to undergo any suffering in defence of a senseless dogma" (παρὰ φαῦλον ἡγησάμενοι κακοπάθειάν τινα ὑπὲρ ἀνοήτου φέρεσθαι δόγματος).[89] This comment probably reflects precisely the attitude of the Samaritan elite in the great cities like Caesarea and Scythopolis.

Some years after the construction of the Silvanus hall and the Silvanus street, in 529 CE, Silvanus was assassinated by a Christian mob in the centre of Scythopolis:

> "At this juncture Silvanus, mentioned above, coming as if peaceably to Scythopolis without an imperial order, was seized by the Christians and burnt in the middle of the city, fulfilling the prophecy concerning him made in the bishop's palace to John son of the compulsor by our sainted father Sabas."[90]

What had Silvanus done to incur the wrath of the Christians, besides sponsoring public buildings? Cyril cites the Christian lawyer John to the effect that Silvanus was plotting against the Christians. In his *Historia arcana* Procop defends the assassination of Silvanus more explicitly. He states that the son of Silvanus, Arsenius, who had the rank of an *illustris* at the imperial court, in order not to loose the power he held, adopted the name of a Christian. Under the guise of Christianity, he supposedly acted against the Christians through his father Silvanus and his brother:

> "His father and brother, however, relying upon this man's power, had continued on in Scythopolis, preserving their ancestral faith, and, under instructions from him, they were working outrageous wrongs upon the

---

88 Foerster/Tsafrir (1997), 125.

89 Procop., hist. 11,25 (LCL 290, 136–139 Dewing): ὅσοι μὲν οὖν ἔν τε Καισαρείᾳ τῇ ἐμῇ κἀν ταῖς ἄλλαις πόλεσιν ᾤκουν, παρὰ φαῦλον ἡγησάμενοι κακοπάθειάν τινα ὑπὲρ ἀνοήτου φέρεσθαι δόγματος, ὄνομα Χριστιανῶν τοῦ σφίσι παρόντος ἀνταλλαξάμενοι τῷ προσχήματι τούτῳ τὸν ἐκ τοῦ νόμου ἀποσείσασθαι κίνδυνον ἴσχυσαν.

90 Cyr. Scyth., Vita Sabae 70 (GCS 49/2 172,18–22 Schwartz, transl. Price 182): τότε δὴ Σιλουανὸς ὁ ἀνωτέρω μνημονευθεὶς ὡς ἐπὶ εἰρήνηι ἐν Σκυθοπόλει ἐλθὼν χωρὶς κελεύσεως βασιλικῆς ἁρπαγεὶς ὑπὸ τῶν Χριστιανῶν εἰς τὸ μέσον ἐκαύθη τῆς πόλεως καὶ ἐπληρώθη ἡ περὶ αὐτοῦ πρὸς Ἰωάννην τὸν τοῦ ἐκσπελλευτοῦ ῥηθεῖσα ἐν τῶι ἐπισκοπείωι προφητεία τοῦ ἐν ἁγίοις πατρὸς ἡμῶν Σάβα.

> Christians. Consequently the citizens rose against them and killed them both with a very cruel death, and many evils came to pass for the people of Palestine from that cause."[91]

Procop calls Arsenius "an utter scoundrel"[92] (μιαρώτατος ὤν) and "the chief cause of all the difficulties" (αἰτιώτατον γεγονότα δυσκόλων ἁπάντων) in Palestine.[93] Thus, in keeping with the thrust of the work as a whole, Procop uses Arsenius to underscore the corrupt reign of Justinian I, who privileged a Samaritan masked as a Christian and abandoned him only because of persistent intervention of the Christians.[94]

According to Cyril, it was only after the assassination of his father that Arsenius successfully tried to turn the emperor Justinian and his wife Theodora against the Christians of Scythopolis. Only the intervention of the old Sabas in Constantinople avoided an act of revenge. Sabas managed to change the emperor's mind and focused his anger on the Samaritans, so that Justinian enacted laws that strictly limited the rights of Samaritans.[95] Finally, Sabas is claimed to have converted even Arsenius and his family to Christianity.

With regard to Scythopolis, the story of Silvanus and his family illustrates the great influence that the Samaritans had at the beginning of the 6th century. The fact that the inscription of the Silvanus hall was covered with a cross reveals that the will of the Samaritan elite to participate in city issues was stronger than the pursuit of religious correctness.

On the other hand, reading the Byzantine chronicler Johannes Malalas, we get another impression of the situation in the city at that time, regarding probably people of lower ranks. In his *Excerpta*, Malalas describes a children's ritual that illustrates the intensifying mutual animosities and violence between Christians and Samaritans:

---

91 Procop., hist. 27, 8f. (LBL 290, 320, transl. Dewing): ὁ μέντοι πατήρ τε καὶ ἀδελφὸς τῇ τούτου δυνάμει θαρσοῦντες διαγεγόνασι μὲν ἐν Σκυθοπόλει, περιστέλλοντες τὴν πάτριον δόξαν, γνώμῃ δὲ αὐτοῦ ἀνήκεστα τοὺς Χριστιανοὺς εἰργάζοντο πάντας. διὸ δὴ οἱ πολῖται σφίσιν ἐπαναστάντες ἄμφω ἔκτειναν θανάτῳ οἰκτίστῳ, κακά τε πολλὰ ξυνηνέχθη Παλαιστίνοις ἐνθένδε γενέσθαι.

92 Procop., hist. 27,6 (LBL 290, 320, transl. Dewing).

93 Procop., hist. 27,10 (LBL 290, 320, transl. Dewing).

94 Procop., hist. 27,10 (LBL 290, 320, transl. Dewing): τότε μὲν οὖν αὐτὸν οὔτε Ἰουστινιανὸς οὔτε βασιλὶς κακόν τι ἔδρασαν, καίπερ αἰτιώτατον γεγονότα δυσκόλων ἁπάντων, ἀπεῖπον δὲ αὐτῷ ἐς Παλάτιον μηκέτι ἰέναι· ἐνδελεχέστατα γὰρ τούτου δὴ ἕνεκα πρὸς τῶν Χριστιανῶν ἠνωχλοῦντο. (And at that time neither Justinian nor the Empress did Arsenius any harm, though he had been the chief cause of all the difficulties, but they did forbid him to come to the Palace any longer: for they were being harassed most persistently by the Christians on account of this matter).

95 Cf. Cod. Iust. I, 5,20 *De Haereticis et Manichaeis et Samaritis* (Krüger 85f.).

> "Every Sabbath, after reading the Gospels, Christian children used to proceed from the church in the direction of Samaritan synagogues, jokingly stoning their homes, since the Samaritans were accustomed to isolate themselves at their homes on that day. Once the Samaritans could no longer tolerate yielding to Christians, and when the children left the church after the reading of the Gospel and walked to the synagogues of the Samaritans, starting to pelt them with stones, the Samaritans went out against the children with ready swords and killed many. Some of the children escaped to the holy altar of the church of holy Basil, whence they were pursued by some Samaritans who killed them under the very altar."[96]

That this occurred in Scythopolis is evident from the mention of the church of Holy Basil, which is attested by the Christian pilgrim Theodosius in the 6th century CE.[97] The Samaritan synagogue was only a few steps from the Church of Basil, both were located outside the city wall. Probably, the gruesome murder of Silvanus in 529 was also an act of revenge for the massacre of the Christian children.[98]

Altogether, these events illustrate the increasing Christian-Samaritan hostility in the first half of the 6th century CE.

4.2 The Samaritan Revolt of 529 CE

Do the reports of Cyril, Procop and Malalas permit the conclusion that the Samaritan revolt of 529 CE that affected the entire region of Pales-

96 Jo. Mal., Excerpta (CFHB 35, 374,5–16 Thurn): τῇ σαββάτου ἡμέρᾳ μετὰ τὸ ἀναγνωσθῆναι τὸ εὐαγγέλιον ἐκ τῆς ἐκκλησίας ἐξήρχοντο τὰ παιδία τῶν χριστιανῶν καὶ ἤρχοντο παίζοντα εἰς τὰς συναγωγὰς τῶν Σαμαρειτῶν καὶ ἐλίθαζον τοὺς οἴκους αὐτῶν. εἶχον γὰρ ἔθος τῇ αὐτῇ ἡμέρᾳ ὑπαναχωρεῖν καὶ ἰδιάζειν. καὶ τῷ χρόνῳ ἐκείνῳ οὐκ ἠνέσχοντο δοῦναι τόπον τοῖς χριστιανοῖς, καὶ ἐξελθόντα τὰ παιδία μετὰ τὸ ἅγιον εὐαγγέλλιον ἀπῆλθον εἰς τὰς συναγωγὰς τῶν Σαμαρειτῶν καὶ ἐλίθαζον, ἐξελθόντες δὲ οἱ Σαμαρεῖται κατὰ τῶν παιδίων μετὰ ξιφῶν πολλοὺς ἀπέκτειναν. καὶ πολλὰ παιδία ἔφυγον ἐν τῇ ἁγίᾳ τραπέζῃ τοῦ ἁγίου Βασιλείου τοῦ ὄντος ἐκεῖσε, καὶ κατεδίωξαν αὐτά τινες τῶν Σαμαρειτῶν καὶ κατέσφαξαν ὑποκάτω τῆς ἁγίας τραπέζης.

97 Cf. Theodosius, *De situ terrae sanctae* 2 (CSEL 175, 115 Geyer). For the placement in Scythopolis (instead of Caesarea), cf. di Segni (1988), 223; Sivan (2008), 168, with reference to further Hebrew literature.

98 Sivan (2008), 170, surmises that the burning of Silvanus might have fallen on a Purim and would have been "a sinister-re-enactment of the burning of Haman on a cross. [...] Christian vengeance in the sixth century reached a climax with the execution by fire of a live Samaritan. From a theatre of the ridicule which integrated various groups, the ideology of Purim was appropriated by Christians to make brutally clear the sharp boundaries, historical and physical, that separated Christians from Samaritans. More than the deliberate demolition of pagan temples or of Samaritan and Jewish synagogues, this mode of applying violent rituals to reality encapsulated the tipping of the balance in favour of Christianity." In my view, this interpretation of the burning of Silvanus is too speculative as it is based on the supposition of a vivid Purim-tradition in Scythopolis until the 6th century. That this is precarious even for the late 4th/early 5th century, I tried to show above, chap. 3.1.

tine started as a conflict between religious communities in Scythopolis?[99] In my view, we have to evaluate the historical plausibility of the sources with caution. Procop suggests – as Cyril does in the above-mentioned Book 27 of the *Vita of Sabas* – that the anti-Samaritan legacy of Justinian was caused by anti-Christian actions of the Samaritans. But elsewhere, in chap. 11 of the *Historia arcana*, Procop describes the course of events in a different and more plausible way as protest against the legislation of 527 CE that broke out in Neapolis, the city with the largest Samaritan population in Galilee.[100]

The revolt seems to have started simultaneously in various regions and cities with a Samaritan population, being a reaction to the legislation of 527 CE as well as an expression of the increased animosity between Christians and Samaritans.

The dimension of the damages caused by the revolt in Scythopolis we can only infer from a note of Cyril about the money provided by local authorities for reconstruction.[101] In April 530 CE, the archbishop of Jerusalem Petrus sent the aged Sabas to Constantinople to request a remission of taxes in favour of the reconstruction in Palestine. 12 centenaries were conceded to Palestine and Samaria, whereof only one centenarium was distributed to Scythopolis. Even though Malalas declares that "many parts of Scythopolis were set on fire", the damages do not seem to have been as heavy as in other places of the region. This view is confirmed in writing by Cyril, who states that "not much devastation had occurred there"[102], and archaeologically by missing evidence

99 Thus argues di Segni (1993). For a detailed study of the Samaritan revolts cf. Winkler (1964) and Meier (2003), 209–215. In my opinion, Meier overemphasizes the eschatological motivation of the revolt. Explicitly, John Malalas seems to place the outbreak of the revolts in Scythopolis, writing in Jo. Mal., Chron. 18, 35 (Thurn 373, 46–49, transl. Jeffrey/Scott 260): Τῷ δὲ ἰουνίῳ μηνὶ τῆς ἑβδόμης ἰνδικτιῶνος ταραχῆς γενομένης ἐθνικῆς, συμβαλόντων γὰρ τῶν Σαμαρειτῶν μεταξὺ χριστιανῶν καὶ Ἰουδαίων, πολλοὶ τόποι ἐνεπρήσθησαν ἐν Σκυθοπόλει ἐκ τῶν Σαμαρειτῶν. (In the month of June of the 7th indiction a riot broke out among the local people when the Samaritans fought with the Christians and Jews, and many parts of Scythopolis were set on fire by the Samaritans).

100 Procop., hist. 11, 24–30 (LCL 290, 136–139 transl. Dewing): ὅσοι μὲν οὖν ἔν τε Καισαρείᾳ τῇ ἐμῇ κἀν ταῖς ἄλλαις πόλεσιν ᾤκουν, παρὰ φαῦλον ἡγησάμενοι κακοπάθειάν τινα ὑπὲρ ἀνοήτου φέρεσθαι δόγματος, ὄνομα Χριστιανῶν τοῦ σφίσι παρόντος ἀνταλλαξάμενοι τῷ προσχήματι τούτῳ τὸν ἐκ τοῦ νόμου ἀποσείσασθαι κίνδυνον ἴσχυσαν. (Now all the residents of my own Caesarea and of all the other cities, regarding it as a foolish thing to undergo any suffering in defence of a senseless dogma, adopted name of Christians in place of that which they then bore and by this pretence succeeded in shaking off the danger arising from the law).

101 Cyr. Scyth., Vita Sabae 75 (GCS 49/2 181,18–182,2 Schwartz, 190).

102 Cyr. Scyth., Vita Sabae 75 (GCS 49/2, 181,21–23 Schwartz, transl. Price 190): "In the territory of Scythopolis, since not much devastation had occurred there, the bishops

of demolition in the first half of the 6th century CE. However, for the time after the revolt, we have neither archaeological[103] nor literary evidence for the existence of a sizable Samaritan population in Scythopolis.

4.3 A vivid Jewish Presence inside and outside the City

We do not know how the Jews responded to the Samaritan revolt.[104] But we can observe a revival of the Jewish community of Scythopolis in the second half of the 6th century CE. Near the house of Leontis, a synagogue was built and covered with mosaic and Aramaic inscriptions.[105] Whether this synagogue was actually situated in a "Jewish quarter", as Bahat assumed,[106] we can not reconstruct. But the new construction of a Jewish synagogue supports the view that the Jews, who fought side by side with the Christians according to Malalas, profited by the defeat of their Samaritan brothers.

Even in the surroundings of Scythopolis we have indications of a revival of Jewish communities. The synagogue of Beth Alpha was constructed in the time of Justin I (518–527 CE) or Justin II (565–578 CE) and was covered with mosaics that reflect the intercultural character of this community impressively: Hebrew inscriptions and biblical motives (such as the Binding of Isaac) appear next to Greek inscriptions and images of Helios and the Zodiac.[107]

In the synagogue of Rehov, during the 6th century CE, the abovementioned halachic inscriptions were installed on the architrave. This indicates close economic connections between the urban population of Scythopolis and the Jews in the surrounding areas. It seems that the religious leaders thought it necessary to restrict the economic and cultural contacts.

---

decided to grant remission of only one hundred pounds." (τοῖς δὲ ὁρίοις Σκυθοπόλεως ὡς μὴ πολλῶν αὐτόθι γεγονότων ἀφανισμῶν ἑνος καὶ μόνου κεντηναρίου συγχώρησιν δοθῆναι συνεῖδον οἱ ἒπίσκοποι).

103 Cf. Foerster/Tsafrir (1997), 126. Given the missing archaeological evidence of demolition I cannot understand why Tsafrir and Foerster suppose "that the city was rather severely damaged."

104 Malalas (chron. 18, 445) pits Samaritans against Christians and Jews, while other Christian historians (Theophanes and Cedrenus) pit Jews with Samaritans against Christians.

105 Cf. Bahat (1981), 82–85.

106 Cf. Bahat (1981), 82–85.

107 Cf. Avigad (1993).

4.4 Summary

The economic revival led to greater competition between Christians and Samaritans in the first decades of the 6th century CE. This is illustrated by the conflict between the Christian group of the lawyer John and the monk Sabas on the one side and the Samaritan family of Silvanus on the other. The Samaritans represented a wealthy, influential and educated elite that was, at least in the case of Silvanus' family, under the emperor's protection. A 6th-century Greek inscription in Samaritan letters in a synagogue located north of the wall is an example of cultural autonomy and interaction at the same time.[108] The cross in the inscription of the Silvanus hall attests to the readiness to adapt the Christian symbol and is simultaneously an indication of the Christian dominance. Likewise, the *pro-forma* conversion of many Samaritans as a reaction to the anti-Samaritan legislation of 527 CE gives the impression that, for the urban Samaritan elites, cultural integration was much more important than religious confession. On the other side, the custom of Christian children to stone Samaritan houses while their parents listened to Christian preachers is an outcome of ritualized violence.

The focus on national identity and religious purity during the Samaritan revolt apparently originated with the population of lower ranks. It is likely that most of the Samaritan elites of Scythopolis either converted to Christianity, at least *pro forma* to avoid legal discrimination, or abandoned Palestine. However, the result of literary or archaeological evidence is that the history of the Samaritans in Scythopolis came to an end by the middle of the 6th century. The Jews seem to have profited by the downfall of the Samaritans and possibly took their place within the urban society.

5. The Deterioration of the Byzantine City from the second Half of the 6th Century CE

For the time after the Samaritan revolts we do not have any literary sources about the religious history of Scythopolis, apart from Christian works that witness the involvement of the Christian authorities in the inner-Christian conflicts of that time.[109] There seem to be several exter-

108 Cf. Crown (1989), 143f.; Naveh (1981).

109 For instance, John of Scythopolis, bishop of Scythopolis from 536 to 553 CE, published the works of Dionysius of Areopagita with a commentary, cf. Irmscher (1986); his successor Theodor of Scythopolis was involved in the Second Origenist Controversy, cf. Hombergen (2001).

nal reasons for the deterioration of the city, as for the whole region of Palestine, in the course of the 6th century. In the years 541/542 CE the bubonic plague devastated the population of Palestine.[110] The conquest of Palestine by the Sassanids in 614 and the Arabs in 635/636 CE was already a result of the interior collapse of the region. The Umayyads transferred the administration of the province Al-Urdunn – the Arab equivalent of *Palaestina Secunda* – to Tiberias. In 660 CE an earthquake had a dramatic effect on the city's appearance, destroying the Silvanus hall, the porticoes of the Byzantine agora and the *Sigma*.[111] It would be premature, however, to infer a downfall or decline of the city at this point. A magnificent market erected in the ruins of Silvanus Hall by order of Caliph Hisham in 738 CE speaks of a certain interest among the new rulers in the development of the city. But another earthquake totally destroyed the city on January 18th, 749 CE.[112]

6. Conclusion: Cult and Culture, Continuity and Change in the "Greek City" Scythopolis in Late Antiquity

Scythopolis had always been and remained a Greek city, in accordance with the pedestal inscription that was cited at the beginning of our discussion. But what does 'Greek' mean in late antique Palestine?

The excavators of Byzantine Scythopolis detected a "radical religious and cultural change" in the city that came with the "triumph of Christians over pagans" in the course of the 4th century CE. "A study of the process of Christianization of Scythopolis", they argue, "reveals a deep change in political and social life of the city and in the daily behaviour of the urban city."[113] But is it really possible to find any proof for changes in political life and in the daily behaviour of the citizens of Scythopolis? On the one hand, the archaeological data document only the abandonment of pagan temples and the building of churches. It is important to point out, however, that most of the churches were built outside the city walls, the rounded church at the top of the acropolis being the only one that was constructed within the borders of the city's civic centre.[114] No Christian basilica or cathedral has been found in the

110 Although we have little information about the plague and its impact on Palestine, it seems to have been devastating, cf. Conrad (1986).

111 Cf. Foerster/Tsafrir (1997), 143–146.

112 Cf. Foerster/Tsafrir (1992).

113 Foerster/Tsafrir (1997), 106.

114 This aspect, missing in the argument of Foerster/Tsafrir (1997), is correctly pointed out by Mazor (2008) and Kennedy (2000). There was another Church dedicated to

city. The location of the palace of the bishop with the church of Procop mentioned by Cyril is still unknown. The most important known church is the monastery of the Virgin Mary, sitting isolated in a remote location on the northern fringes of the walled area. The other churches, too, probably belong to monastic complexes.[115]

In addition, we have to note an almost complete absence of ecclesiastical patronage. In contrast with other Palestinian cities, such as Gerasa, the public buildings were paid for by the governors, not by bishops. While this can be explained by the fact that Scythopolis, being the provincial capital, had the patronage of the governors, it is even more surprising that most of the building works were entirely secular in character. Considering that the pagan temples were closed at the beginning of the 5th century CE, at the latest, we can indeed expand on Mazor's statement that "the civic centre of Nysa-Scythopolis retained its secular character and Hellenic appearance"[116]. While in the Hellenistic and Roman periods various cults were present in the city centre, after the emergence of Christianity the cultic aspect seems to have disappeared from the public urban life. Thus, the civic centre did not maintain, but rather assumed a secular character in Late Antiquity. In contrast with other cities in Palestine, the governors apparently did not transform Scythopolis into a 'Christian city'. Religion seems to have been a mostly 'private affair', religious assemblies taking place on the outskirts of the urban centre. It seems that the rise of Christianity did not cause the 'Christianization' but the secularization of the cityscape of Late Antique Scythopolis.[117]

On the other hand, even with regard to the literary sources, I doubt that it is at all adequate to speak of a 'triumph' of Christians in Palestine. Nevertheless, paganism in its cultic sense seems to have disappeared from the public life of the city. But the presence of an influential Samaritan elite in the city and the multifaceted Jewish life in the surrounding areas acted as a counterbalance to the Christians. In addition, Christendom itself was so variegated, and the Christians were so involved in their own dogmatic and church-political affairs, that we cannot characterize them as a homogeneous group. Thus, the religious plurality contradicts the assumption of 'triumph' and 'radical changes'.

Procopius, which is mentioned by Cyril and was inside the bishop's palace, whose location is not known.

115 Cf. Mazor (2008), 1634–1636.

116 Mazor (2008), 1634.

117 Therefore, it does not seem to me adequate to speak of "The Christianization of Beth Shean (Scythopolis)" as Tsafrir (2003) did.

Certainly, I would not deny that the disappearance of the official pagan cults altered the life in the city in a perceptible way. However, in order to define the historical changes more precisely, it seems helpful to me to differentiate between *cultic* and *cultural* changes. The official cultic life of Scythopolis was shaken as a consequence of the earthquake in 363 CE, that is for external reasons. In the decades of reconstruction, the influence of the Christians in city affairs increased, so that they could prevent the restoration of the temples. In this regard, the rise of Christianity in Scythopolis has indeed caused a change in the city's appearance and life. But this does not mean that Christianity became a kind of dominant culture. Christianity itself grew on the soil of the Hellenistic culture of Scythopolis and was Hellenistic in cultural terms. Therefore, we cannot separate Christianity from its Hellenistic background. The pagans who converted to Christianity in the course of the 4th and 5th centuries changed – if at all[118] – their cultic habits. A specific Christian cultural alternative to the Hellenistic urban life in the city does not appear until the 5th century, when the Origenist monks founded a *laura* nearby Scythopolis. But even monastic Christianity did not become the predominant culture in the city. The survival of the theatre suggests civic tenacity which transcended religious confessions.

Given the ethnic and religious plurality and the resulting potential for conflict, it is astonishing to see that Late Antiquity was a largely peaceful age in Palestine. We do not hear of any war-like conflicts between 363 and 529 CE. The quarrels occur within the religious communities (mostly between different Christian groups), not between them.

The historian G.W. Bowersock explained the "miracle" of the "relative tranquillity of the region"[119] with the survival of the pagan culture based on polytheism and plurality. Bowersock finds proof for this (not only cultural, but even cultic) survival during Late Antiquity in the Byzantine mosaic pavements in Scythopolis, showing Helios and Selene, Tyche and Orpheus with Sirens. I doubt whether the existence of vital pagan cults was the "precondition" for this survival of Hellenistic culture, as Bowersock believes.[120] The ease in the adoption of Greek

118 All we can say on the basis of archaeological and literary evidence concerns the official pagan cults. We have no information about the private piety of Scythopolitans, apart from a Byzantine Magical Amulet of Jewish origin, cf. Khamis (2006), 675f.

119 Bowersock (1997), 8.

120 Bowersock (1997), 8: "A precondition of this realm of culture is that at the same time there really were other people for whom this culture was still alive and meaningful. Pagan cults belonged now to the minority, but without them the majority would have lacked any interest in them." This assumption leads Bowersock to the thesis, that "in the Palestine that fell to the prophet Muhammad, Jews and Christians to-

mythological motives by Jews, Christians and Samaritans shows that the common Hellenistic culture of the 5th and 6th centuries was liberated from its cultic origins. Therefore, Jews, Christians and Samaritans did not perceive this culture as competition for their cults. Thus, the Hellenistic culture was available to adherers of various cults. The image of the city goddess Tyche in the 6th century mosaic pavement in the region of the Sigma and the images of Helios and Selene in the Monastery of the Lady Mary (middle of the 6th century) are only two examples of this non-cultic, but cultural, Hellenism.

Fig. 3: Mosaic of Helios and Selene
(Monastery of the Lady Mary)

Late antique Scythopolis remained a Greek city until Islamic conquest. But it remained a Greek city only in cultural, not in cultic respect. After the disappearance of official pagan cults, the urban Hellenistic culture in late antique Scythopolis was the common ground on which every religious community (Christians, Jews, Samaritans) could practice its own cult. The conflicts that broke out between Samaritans and Christians in the first half of 6th century are a consequence of – and therefore a proof for – the fact, that until this moment Scythopolis offered a space for development for both groups. The demolition of this plurality and balance, forced by the imperial legislation in the age of Justinian, heralds the decline of the Greek city Scythopolis. In this sense, we may conclude that the very diversity of its population and the 'secular appearance' of the urban city were the cause and also the effect of the flourishing of late antique Scythopolis.

gether inhabited a land where the majority had been, until relatively recently, what the Greek-speakers of the time called Hellenes, meaning pagans or polytheists" (p. 1). There is neither archaeological nor literary evidence to support this hypothesis. In my opinion, the distinction between cult and culture offers a better way to explain the relatively peaceful co-existence of Christian, Jews and Samaritans in late antique Palestine.

Bibliography

Antique Sources

Abū ʹl Fath, *Kitāb al-tarīkh*, transl. with Notes by P. Stenhouse, Studies in Judaica 1, Sydney (Mandelbaum Trust) 1985.

Ambr., ep. 40: Ambrosius, *epistula 40,* CSEL 82/3, ed. by M. Zelzer, Vienna 1982.

Amm. Marc., res gestae: Ammianus Marcellinus, *Res gestae,* with an English translation by J.C. Rolfe, LCL, Aberdeen 1935.

Chron. Pasch.: *Chronicon Paschale,* CSHB 14, ed. by B.G. Niebuhr, Bonn 1832.

Cod. Iust.: *Codex Iustinianus,* ed. by P. Krüger, Berlin 1877.

Cod. Theod.: *Codex Theodosianus,* ed. by T. Mommsen, Berlin 1954.

Cyr. Scyth.: Cyril of Scythopolis, *Vitae,* GCS 49/2, ed. by E. Schwartz, Leipzig 1939. Transl.: Lives of the Monks of Palestine by Cyril of Scythopolis, transl. by R.M. Price, with an Introduction and Notes by J. Binns, Michigan 1991.

Epiph., pan. haer.: Epiphanius von Salamis, *Panarion omnium haeresium,* GCS 31, ed. by K. Holl, Leipzig 1915. Transl.: F. Williams, The Panarion of Epiphanius of Salamis: Book I (sects 1–46), NHS 35, Leiden 1987.

Eus., h.e.: Eusebius, *Historia ecclesiastica,* GCS 9, ed. by E. Schwartz, Leipzig 1908.

Eus., mart. Pal.: *De martyribus Palaestinae,* GCS 9/2, ed. E. Schwartz, Leipzig 1908, 905–950. Recensio longior: TU 14/4, ed. B. Violet, Leipzig 1896.

Expositio totius mundi et gentium: SC 141, ed. by J. Rougé, Paris 1966.

Greg. Naz., or.: Gregor Nazianzenus, *Orationes contra Julianum,* SC 309, ed. by J. Bernardi, Paris 1983.

Hier., ep.: Hieronymus, *Epistulae,* CSEL 55/2, ed. by I. Hilberg, Wien 1996.

Itin. Eger.: *Itinerarium Egeriae,* CSEL 175, ed. by A. Francheschini/ R. Weber, Turnhout 1965, 25–103.

Jo. Mal., Chron.: John Malalas, *Chronicon ecclesiasticum,* CFHB 35, ed. by J. Thurn, Berlin 2000. Transl.: The Chronicle of J. Malalas. A Translation by E. Jeffreys/M. Jeffreys/R. Scott, Australian Association for Byzantine Studies, Byzantina Australiensa 4, Melbourne 1986.

Lib., ep.: Libanios, *Epistulae,* Libanii Opera, ed. by R. Förster, Hildesheim 1963.

Piyyut: ed. by M. Sokoloff/J. Yahalom, (1999), Jewish Palestinian Aramaic Poetry from Late Antiquity: Critical Edition with Introduction and Commentary, Jerusalem (in Hebrew).

Procop., hist.: Procopius of Caesarea, *Historia arcana anecdota,* LCL 290, with an English Translation by H.B. Dewing, London/Cambridge 1969.

Samaritan Chronicle: ed. by J.M. Cohen, A Samaritan Chronicle: A Source-Critical Analysis of the Life and Times of the great Samaritan Reformer, Baba Rabbah, StPB 30, Leiden 1981.

Soz., h.e.: Sozomenos, *Historia ecclesiastica,* GCS 50, ed. by J. Bidez/G.C. Hanssen, Berlin [3]1960.

The Jerusalem Talmud, ed. by H.W. Guggenheimer, SJ 45, Berlin 2008.

Theodosius, *De situ terrae sanctae,* CSEL 175, ed. by P. Geyer, Turnhout 1965, 113–125.

Secondary Literature

Arubas, B./Foerster, G./Tsafrir, Y. (2008), Beth Shean: The Hellenistic to Early Islamic Periods at the Foot of the Mound: The Hebrew University Excavations, in: E. Stern (ed.), The New Encyclopedia of Archaeological Excavations in the Holy Land 5, Supplementary Volume, Jerusalem/Washington DC, 1636–1641.

Avi-Yonah, M. (1962), Scythopolis, IEJ 12, 123–134.

Bahat, D. (1981), A Synagogue at Beth-Shean, in: L.I. Levine (ed.), Ancient Synagogues Revealed, Jerusalem, 82–85.

Bar Ilan, M. (2001), Review of Sokoloff-Yahalom, Aramaic Poems from Eretz Israel, Mahut 23, 167–188 (in Hebrew).

Bowersock, G.W. (1997), Polytheism and Monotheism in Arabia and the Three Palestines, DOP 51, 1–10.

Cohen, J.M. (1981), A Samaritan Chronicle: A Source-Critical Analysis of the Life and Times of the great Samaritan Reformer, Baba Rabbah, StPB 30, Leiden.

Conrad, L.I. (1986), The Plague in Bilad al-Sham in Pre-Islamic Times, *Proceedings of the Symposium on* Bilad al-Sham 2, Amman, 143–163.

Crown, A.D. (1989), The Samaritans, Tübingen.

Di Segni, L. (1988), Scythopolis (Bet Shean) during the Samaritan Rebellion of 529 CE, in: D. Jacobi/Y. Tsafrir (eds.), Jews, Samaritans and Christians on Byzantine Palestine, Jerusalem, 217–227 (in Hebrew).

– (1993), Julianus ben Sabar, in: A.D. Crown/R. Pummer/A. Tal, A Companion to Samaritan Studies, Tübingen, 140.

Fedalto, G. (1988), Hierarchia Ecclesiastica Orientalis. Series episcoporum ecclesiarum christianarum orientalium II, Padova.
Flusin, B. (1983), Miracle et histoire dans l'œuvre de Cyrille de Sythopolis, EAug, Paris.
Fögen, M.T. (1993), Die Enteignung der Wahrsager. Studien zum kaiserlichen Wissensmonopol in der Spätantike, Frankfurt/Main.
Foerster, G./Tsafrir, Y., (1988), Nysa-Scythopolis – A New Inscription and the Titles of the Cities on its Coins, INJ 9, 53–58.
– (1992), The Dating of the Earthquake of the Sabbatical Year of 749 CE in Palestine, BSOAS 55/2, London, 231–235.
– (1997), Urbanism at Scythopolis-Beth Shean in the Fourth to Seventh Centuries, DOP 51, 85–146.
Fuks, G. (1982), The Jews of Hellenistic and Roman Scythopolis, JJS 37, 407–416.
Haehling, R. von (1978), Ammianus Marcellinus und der Prozess von Skythopolis, JAC 21, 74–101.
Holze, H. (1990), War die "Konstantinische Wende" tatsächlich ein Umbruch? Beobachtungen zum vorkonstantinischen Gemeindeleben am Beispiel Karthagos, ThBeitr 21, 78–97.
Hombergen, D. (2001), Cyril of Scythopolis and the second Origenist Controversy, StMon 43, 31–46.
Irmscher, J. (1986), Teodoro Scitopolitano, "De vita et scriptis", Aug. 26, 185–190.
Kennedy, H.N. (2000), Gerasa and Scythopolis: Power and Patronage in the Byzantine Cities of Bilad al-Sham, BEO 52, 199–204 (re-published in: id. (2006), The Byzantine and Early Islamic Near East, Variorum Collected Studies Series 860, Aldershot, 199–204).
Khamis, E. (2006), Chapter 23B: A Byzantine Magical Amulet, in: A. Mazar (ed.), Excavations at Tel Beth-Shean 1989–1996: Vol. 1: From the Late Bronze Age IIB to the Medieval Period, The Beth-Shean Valley Archaeological Project Publication 1, Jerusalem, 675f.
Lapin, H. (2001), Economy, Geography, and Provincial History in Later Roman Palestine, TSAJ 85, Tübingen 2001.
Levine, L.I. (1981, ed.), Ancient Synagogues Revealed, Jerusalem.
Mazar, A. (2006, ed.), Excavations at Tel Beth-Shean 1989–1996: Vol. 1: From the Late Bronze Age IIB to the Medieval Period, The Beth-Shean Valley Archaeological Project Publication 1, Jerusalem.
Mazor, G. (2008), Beth Shean: The Hellenistic to Early Islamic Periods: The Israel Antiquities Authority Excavations, in: E. Stern (ed.), The New Encyclopedia of Archaeological Excavations in the Holy Land 5, Supplementary Volume, Jerusalem/Washington DC, 1623–1636.

Meier, M. (2003), Das andere Zeitalter Justinians. Kontingenzerfahrung und Kontingenzbewältigung im 6. Jahrhundert n. Chr., Hyp. 147, Göttingen.

Miller, S.S. (2006), Sages and Commoners in Late Antique 'Erez Israel: A Philological Inquiry into Local Traditions in Talmud Yerushalmi, TSAJ 111, Tübingen.

Mühlenberg, E. (1998, ed.), Die Konstantinische Wende. Tagung der Wissenschaftlichen Gesellschaft für Theologie (Berlin 1996), Veröffentlichungen der Wissenschaftlichen Gesellschaft für Theologie 13, Gütersloh.

Naveh, J. (1982), A Greek Dedication in Samaritan Letters, IEJ 32, 220–222.

Perkams, M. (2001), Der Comes Josef und der frühe Kirchenbau in Galiläa, JAC 44, 23–32.

Podolak, P. (2007), Giovanni di Scitopoli interprete del "Corpus Dionysiacum", Aug. 47, 335–386.

Raynor, J.T. (1982), Social and Cultural Relationships in Scythopolis/Beth Sehan in the Roman and Byzantine Periods, Ph.D Duke University, University Microfilms International, Ann Arbor.

Rorem, P./Lamoreaux, J.C. (1998), John of Scythopolis and the Dionysian Corpus: Annotating the Areopagite, Oxford Eearly Christian Studies, Oxford.

Russell, K.W. (1980), The Earthquake of May 19, A.D. 363, BASOR 238, 47–64.

Safrai, Z. (2003), The House of Leontis 'Kaloubas' – a Judaeo-Christian?, in: P.J. Tomson/D. Lambers-Petry (eds.), The Image of the Judaeo-Christians in Ancient Jewish and Christian Literature, WUNT 158, Tübingen, 245–266.

Sivan, H. (2008), Palestine in Late Antiquity, Oxford.

Sussmann, J. (1981), The Inscription in the Synagogue at Rehob, in: L.I. Levine (ed.), Ancient Synagogues Revealed, Jerusalem, 146–151.

Thornton, T.C.G. (1990), The Stories of Joseph of Tiberias, VigChr 44, 54–63.

Tsaferis, V. (1981), The Synagogue at Ma'oz Hayim, in: L.I. Levine (ed.), Ancient Synagogues Revealed, Jerusalem, 86–89.

Tsafrir, Y. (1998), The Fate of Pagan Cult Places in Palestine: The Archaeological Evidence with Emphasis on Bet Shean, in: H. Lapin (ed.), Religious and Ethnic Communities in Later Roman Palestine, Studies and Texts in Jewish History and Culture 5, 197–218.

– (2003), The Christianization of Bet Shean (Scythopolis) and Its Social-Cultural Influence on the City, in: G. Brands/H.-G. Secerin (eds.), Die spätantike Stadt und ihre Christianisierung. Symposion vom 14. bis

16. Februar 2000 in Halle/Saale, Kunst im ersten Jahrtausend 11, Wiesbaden, 275–284.
Vitto, F. (1981), The Synagogue at Rehob, in: L.I. Levine (ed.), Ancient Synagogues Revealed, Jerusalem, 90–94.
Winkler, S. (1965), Die Samaritaner in den Jahren 529/30, Klio 43–45, 434–457.
Zori, N. (1966), The House of Kyrios Leontis at Beth Shean, IEJ 16, 123–134.

Figures

IV. The One and The Only: Perspectives on the Development of a Divine Concept

God and His People: The Concept of Kingship and Cult in the Ancient Near East

HERMANN SPIECKERMANN

1. Definition of the Problem

The title and subtitle combined may evoke astonishment. 'God and his People' could be regarded an issue for which sufficient evidence is available only in Israel. The strong relationship between one god and his people is commonly considered to characterize a situation unique to the Northern and even more to the Southern monarchy. However, the title I gave this paper is not relevant merely for the two pre-exilic kingdoms. The ideology of the Ancient Near Eastern empires, namely the Assyrian, Babylonian and Persian, provides similar evidence for a special relationship of the leading deity of the national pantheon with the ruler. The god Ashur holds such a position in the Assyrian pantheon, Marduk in the Babylonian, and Ahuramazda in the Persian. According to Ancient Near Eastern imperial ideology, one god predominates, while others form a duo or triad covering additional duties or simply lightening the chief god's burden of responsibility. In pre-exilic times, the situation of Yhwh was not entirely different. Asherah or Baal may have shared Yhwh's burden as the *summus deus* of the Northern as well as the Southern kingdom. Such a monolatric concept of the divine can hardly be distinguished from a polytheistic concept, tending toward a downsizing of the major deities to an extended family.[1]

The true problem of the title of the lecture rather centres on the term 'people'. Here it is used to indicate a special relationship between a certain deity and a certain 'whatever'. Using 'people' demands defining the very essence of the term. Does it imply an ethnic identity, or is it characterized by other identity markers of a cultural, social or regional

* I would like to express my gratitude to Judith H. Seeligmann and Franziska Ede for making my English palatable for readers.

1 Cf. Smith (2001), esp. 54–80; Nunn (2009), 267–281; Spieckermann (2009), 283–301.

kind? Can we differentiate between 'people' and 'nation', often serving as parallel terms in the Hebrew Bible, at least in several translations? What are the equivalents for 'people' and 'nation' in the Semitic languages of the Ancient Near East? And what happens when the Hebrew terms are translated into Greek and Latin?

The first step in my study will be to explore the ideas inherent to the terms 'nation' and 'people'. The investigation includes the Ancient Near Eastern context in general and the relation between a special deity and a certain nation/people in particular. The second step is devoted to kingship as the prevalent order of dominion in the Ancient Near East – among deities as well as among humans. It needs to be investigated what significance is ascribed to the ideas of nation, people, and land in the given religio-political frame predominated by kingship. The third step focuses on the representations which royal dominion prefers to constitute corporate identity. I will examine prayers and cultic practices in order to delineate in what way they contribute to generate and to preserve corporate identity and how this is related to the ideas of nation, people, and land. As last step, the question will be raised whether any insights pertaining to Israel can be attained from the investigations performed regarding the Ancient Near East.

2. 'Nation' and 'People' in the Ancient Near East

In Biblical Studies the term 'nation' is often used *promiscue* with the term 'people'. Given that one can find several or no equivalents for each term in the major Semitic languages, each of the terms needs a close examination in order to grasp the idea of its specific use. I will concentrate primarily on the term 'nation' used to render the Hebrew words gôy and lĕʾôm.[2] It appears to be a quite problematic term to denote the kind of rule which prevailed in the Ancient Near East as it is connected with the quite different semantic and cultural setting of the Latin language.

The Vulgate uses *natio* nearly a hundred times for Hebrew gôy and lĕʾôm.[3] *Natio* is, however, not the regular translation. The Vulgate usu-

2 The Hebrew term ʿam is attested 1868 times, including 229 references for the plural ʿammîm, while the term gôy is attested 561 times comprising the plural gôyîm 438 times; cf. Hulst (1976), 290–325, 293–294; Clements (1973), 965–973; Lipiński (1989), 177–194. The term lĕʾôm – far less frequent than gôy (34–36 times) – is also primarily attested in the plural lĕʾummîm; cf. Preuß (1984), 411–413.

3 Cf. Fischer (1977), 2213–2225 s.v. *gens*, 3262–3264 s.v. *natio*, 3858–3885 s.v. *populus*, 5243–5248 s.v. *tribus*.

ally renders gôy into *populus*, rarely into *gens* or *tribus*. *Populus* is not used exclusively for gôy; it covers a wide range of Hebrew equivalents. In Latin literature, *populus* is the term denoting a complex political entity. *Gens* is regularly used as the more general term designating tribes, communities or peoples. *Gens* may incorporate several *tribus* or *nationes*. *Natio* is not confined to tribal organisations only; it can also signify a certain pedigree of horses and donkeys. Applied to groups, *natio* may at times have ironic overtones.[4] It goes without saying that in Latin literature *natio* is not regarded as applicable to the Romans. *Imperium Romanum, res publica* or *populus Romanus* are the usual and official self-designations which the Romans proudly use. In ancient Rome, it would never have occurred to anybody to call the Roman empire *natio grandis – la grande nation*.

It is obvious that the Vulgate uses the term *natio* neither in the common Latin sense nor in the sense of our understanding today, which is predominantly influenced by legislative and national ideas of the past two centuries. 'Nations' in Antiquity are not characterized by the will to form a political unit defined by a specific kind of reign or government, constitution, laws and institutions, and sometimes also by a certain degree of ethnic identity (nationality) as well as a common cultural and religious heritage. 'Nations' could not have been gathered into an assembly of 'states' called 'United Nations'. Such a view of 'nation' is characteristic of an altogether modern constitutional understanding overlapping considerably with the designation 'state', a term far less apt to designate political entities in Antiquity, except for the Greek πόλεις and the Roman *res publica*. The term 'nation', or more precisely 'nations', has been significantly introduced through the Vulgate. Rendering primarily the Hebrew terms gôyîm and lĕʾummîm as well as the Greek terms ἔθνη, λαοί, and φυλαί in the Septuagint[5], it is used to denote political entities, characterized by sovereignty, connected with a certain cultural and religious identity, military power and law. Aspects of legitimacy of reign may only be relevant within the religio-political sphere of the cult, warfare, legislation, and administration as far as the king is concerned. The Vulgate mirrors all those Ancient Near Eastern aspects in using the term 'nation' in a more or less interchangeable manner with 'people'.

It is noteworthy that there are similarities in the Akkadian literature, where the use of mātu 'land', *in sensu lato* also 'nation', and nišū, 'humankind, humans' is almost interchangeable. Nišū can also mean

4 Cf. Georges (1976), 1099–1100 s.v. *natio*.

5 The linguistic usage of the most prominent terms ἔθνος and λαός in the Septuagint is analyzed by Bertram (1935), 362–366; Strathmann (1942), 29–39.

'people', yet not primarily in the sense of an ethnic identity, rather in the sense of inhabitants of all the regions under the dominion of a certain king. It can be interchanged and combined with the 'dark-headed' (ṣālmāt qaqqadi).[6] This is significantly different in the Hebrew Bible where the singular 'people' (ʿam and sometimes gôy) is the predominant designation for Israel, while the plural 'peoples' and 'nations' (gôyîm, lĕʾummîm) exclusively refers to foreign nations under whose supremacy Israel – the pre-exilic kingdoms as well as the post-exilic diaspora – had to suffer.

3. God, King, and People in the Ancient Near East

The precise distinction between population and people, between territory and nation is not significant for Ancient Near Eastern cultures. Ethnic, cultural and religious identity is related to fairly small units, be it urban or rural areas. There is no word in the Akkadian language that may be regarded an appropriate equivalent to the Hebrew ʿam, denoting the people of Israel in a quite characteristic way, as it is at least the case in the Prophetic and Deuteronomistic literature. The Akkadian word nišū denotes 'humankind, humans' as well as 'inhabitants, population, subjects' of a king, and not the people belonging to a certain nation.[7] A god can be praised as being the "lord who guides all mankind, every living being" (bēlu muštēšir kiššat niši gimir nabnīti)[8]; likewise a goddess is praised as "the sun to her people" (šamaš nišīša).[9] The same metaphor is used by Adadnirari II (911–891): "I am the sun of all mankind" (šamšu kiššat nišē anāku).[10] The expression kiššatu "totality, the entire inhabited world"[11] leaves no room for doubt that an imperial and not a special national perspective is predominant. Consequently, Adadnirari I (1307–1275) claims that he "takes over all mankind/peoples, extends the border/territory and the boundary stone/boundary (of his kingdom)" (ṣābit kiššat nišē/ī murappiš miṣri u kudurri).[12] The text uses the same term nišū for other peoples and for the "people of Assyria" (nišē māt Aššur). The kingdom of Assyria is more aptly distinguished by the borders of the territory than by the

6 Cf. CAD Ṣ (1962), 75–76, and AHw, 1077–1078 s.v. ṣalmāt qaqqadi.
7 Cf. CAD N/II (1980), 283–289 s.v. nišū; AHw, 796–797 s.v. nišū.
8 King (1896), no. 1:53.
9 Zimmern (1912–1913), n. 215:1.
10 Schroeder (1922), no. 84:10.
11 Cf. CAD K (1971), 457–459 s.v. kiššatu A; AHw, 492 s.v. kiššatu(m) I.
12 Ebeling/Meissner/Weidner (1926), 60:14.

inhabitants. However, both are insufficient to define what Assyria really is. Assyria as a kingdom is identified by the ruling king and subsequently everything that belongs to his reign. To design the identity of such a kingdom, ideological, military and administrative issues are interrelated and focused on the king. He is the one who embodies what Assyria as a nation stands for: not the people, nor the territory, or a certain cultural heritage. All those are means to the same end: to establish the king as the central figure of political representation. King and dominion, respectively king and empire, are the appropriate terms to conceptualize how political units are perceived in the Ancient Near East. Assyria is no more than a striking example for political conditions which can be found almost everywhere.

It goes without saying that a certain idea of cultural identity of the population and of international recognition of a certain territory with vaguely defined borders belongs to the criteria of an Ancient Near Eastern political unit. However, the king is the decisive figure in this respect as well. Nebuchadnezzar I (1125–1104) is praised as the one "who safeguards borderlines, establishes cords (i.e. measures)" (nāṣir kudurrēti mukinnu aplê).[13] To safeguard the borders belongs to both, the royal as well as to the divine duties. Several deities claim again and again to establish the boundaries. The boundary stone itself can bear the name "Establisher of permanent boundaries" (mukīn kudurrī dārâti) as divine and royal power will make sure that the name will protect what is announced.[14] The acts of the gods and of the king are closely related. Though it is not said explicitly, it is obvious that the king defends the territory because the gods have entrusted him with the task.

Using the plural 'gods' in this context distorts the picture, seeing that the texts, in most cases, mention only one deity. This is illustrated by an inscription of Tiglathpileser I (about 1114–1076) in which he is characterized as the one "who exercised his rule over mankind, the subjects of Enlil" (ša ... nišē baʾūlāt Enlil ultašpiru).[15] It is the god Enlil who endows the king with the rule over nišē, not only over the people of Assyria, but rather over all mankind. A specific god transfers the dominion over mankind to a certain king, regardless how restricted the territory may have been in fact.[16] The basic scheme is pretty much the same even in the famous prologue of the Codex Hammurapi where

13 King (1912), no. 6 i 5; cf. CAD K (1971), 495–496 s.v. kudurru A.

14 King (1912), no. 7 superscript and ii 40.

15 King (1902), 32 i 32.

16 The ideology is not affected by the knowledge formulated by Ben Sira: mlkwt mgwy ʾl gwy; *regnum a gente in gentem transfertur* (Sir 10:8); cf. Oppenheim (1964), 143–170.

many gods are mentioned.[17] The E/Illilūtu "the honour/rank of Ellil/Enlil, the highest executive power (among the deities)"[18] is conferred on Marduk by the highest gods Anu and Enlil, who allotted supreme power over all peoples (nišī), made the city of Babylon predominant within the regions of the world, and established everlasting kingship (šarrūtum darītum) for Marduk.[19] At the same time, they appoint a ruler on earth to act accordingly. They install Hammurapi "to rise like the sun(-god) over the dark-headed (people) and to illuminate the land, to care for the welfare of the people".[20] Hammurapi acts as the benefactor of all deities and temples in Southern Mesopotamia, including cities in the North such as Ashur and Ninive in order to lay claim also to those territories. Hammurapi declares himself "the chief of kings" (etel šarrī)[21], "the first of kings" (ašarēd šarrī)[22], and even "god among kings" (ilu šarrī).[23] His intention is not to deify himself, rather to establish a position as close to the gods as possible. A remarkable number of deities and temples, located in the respective cities, is listed in the prologue to underscore Hammurapi's claim to dominion. Peoples in the sense of particular national identities are not a significant issue in the prologue. It is the relationship between gods, kings, cities and their important temples.[24] Nearly all of them are called 'centre of the universe' in other texts. With regard to Hammurapi, there can hardly be any doubt that not all deities listed in the prologue are equally important. Most of them demonstrate Hammurapi's imperial claim. Only two of them are essential for his kingship: Enlil[25] conferring the mighty rank of his E/Illilūtu on Marduk in order to endow him with everlasting

---

17 Transcription: Borger (2006), 5–10.113–115; Roth (1995), 76–81; translations: Borger, TUAT I/1, 40–44; Roth, COS II, 335–337.

18 Cf. CAD I/J (1969), 85–86 s.v. illilūtu; AHw, 204 s.v. Ellilūtu, Illilūtu.

19 Codex Hammurapi i 1–26.

20 Codex Hammurapi i 40–48.

21 Codex Hammurapi iii 70.

22 Codex Hammurapi iv 23.

23 Codex Hammurapi iii 16.

24 Within the interplay of forces the temples deserve due attention. They are centres not only of religious but also of economical, juridical, and political importance. The evidence available is abundant. I only mention two publications which, each in its own right, testify to the influence of temples in Mesopotamia: George (1993), temple lists; Menzel (1981), cult, administration, staff.

25 Anu, Enlil's inherited companion, is here as nearly everywhere *summus deus* and *deus otiosus*. It is obvious that Enlil has already occupied all important universal functions. He is "lord of heaven and earth", Codex Hammurapi i 4–5.

kingship, and Marduk transferring the kingship to Hammurapi, "the sun(-god) of Babel" (^{d}Šamšu Bābilim).[26]

Though polytheism is clearly presupposed, a kind of monarchical monolatry is the striking profile of the ideology of kingship. The core of the relationship between god(s) and king is royal dominion. As the idea of kingship on earth is closely connected to divine kingship its universalistic claim is predominant in both spheres. The texts adduced mirror the royal ideology of the 2nd millennium BCE, i.e. the time prior to the fully elaborated ideology of the great empires of the 1st millennium BCE. Obviously, the vast dimensions of an empire are not needed to grasp the idea of universalistic kingship. Though the ideological roots of kingship on earth are divine without deifying the human ruler, pretentious divine metaphors for the king are not excluded. He can even be called "flesh of the god, the sun-god of his people" (šīr ili ^{d}Šamši ša nišēšu)[27], "the son of his personal god, who sustains the life of the country like the luminary, the Moon god" (mār ilīšu ša kīma nannari Sîn napišti māti ukallu).[28] The very close connection of the reigning king with the divine sphere is the reason why the king's deeds and his acting in the cult play such an important part in the royal ideology. It is precisely the king's performance of cultic duties that conveys the idea of the very essence of kingship. Not the correlation between god and his nation is regarded crucial, but the give and take between the king and his god(s). This is the way to establish the welfare of people and land.

4. King and Cult – Religious and Political Identity in the Ancient Near East

The king acts as intermediary between the divine and human realm, not primarily perceived as the Assyrian or Babylonian people or empire. Rather, the human realm designates the sphere where the Mesopotamian gods and subsequently the ruling kings are supposed to exercise supremacy. Being aware of the danger to underestimate the military and administrative duties of a king, the extensive field of royal activities associated with the cult deserve due attention. Building and

---

26 Codex Hammurapi v 4–5; cf. iv 67–v 24. Inscriptions from the time of Hammurapi witnessing the same royal ideology can be found in Frayne (1990), 333–336, 340–342; id., COS II (2000), 256–257.

27 Lambert (1960), 32:55; cf. 40:31; for further evidence cf. CAD I/J (1960), 91–92 s.v. ilu 1a1'; CAD Š/II (1992), 86–87 s.v. šarru 1c1'–2'.

28 CT 16 21:184–185 according to CAD Š/II (1992), 86 s.v. šarru 1c1'.

restoring temples, making statues for deities, offerings and votive gifts, attending processions and especially performing or participating in rituals:[29] All those cultic services of the king can only be properly understood as being meaningful in order to rule the land and to ward off danger of any kind. The great commitment of the king to cultic activities is subject to the conviction that both, the well-being and affliction of the palace and the land, depend upon the king exercising his reign in accordance with the divine will. The royal care for the land includes the people, without them being particularly in view. The cultic duties address a far larger dimension. They are meant to preserve the order of the world in so far as this is up to the king's power according to divine will. The cult provides the king with the essential means to identify and to combat any lurking evil which threatens the whole and its parts. Kingship requires a kind of religion, which mirrors the complementary structures in heaven and on earth. To achieve this goal, all kinds of divination are applied. It is the very essence of Mesopotamian religion. Divination has been underestimated ever since its predominant character in Mesopotamia became more and more apparent. Not until quite recently research has shifted toward evaluating the high standard of divinatory thinking. It is no less than the very origin of scholarly work in the Ancient Near East, resulting in comprehensive collections of omens and in comprehensive works commenting upon their respective understanding and applicability. Though all the people of Mesopotamia hope for personal benefit through divinatory practices, it is first and foremost the king who is expected to act, more precisely, to react according to the relevant divinatory observations. It belongs to his most important religious and political duties to safeguard the kingdom according to the diviners' expertise.

In 1964, A. Leo Oppenheim in his famous work "Ancient Mesopotamia"[30] advanced a provocative thesis: "One obtains the impression – confirmed by other indications – that the influence of religion on the individual, as well as on the community as a whole, was unimportant in Mesopotamia. No texts tell us that ritual requirements in any stringent way affected the individual's physiological appetites, his psychological preferences, or his attitude toward his possessions or his family. His body, his time, and his valuables were in no serious way affected by religious demands, and thus no conflict of loyalties arose to disturb or to shake him. Death was accepted in a truly matter-of-fact way, and the participation of the individual in the cult of the city deity was re-

29 The entries in CAD Š/II (1992), 76–114, and AHw, 1188–1190 s.v. šarru, provide ample evidence for all aspects mentioned.

30 Oppenheim (1964).

stricted in the extreme; he was simply an onlooker in certain public ceremonies of rejoicing or communal mourning. He lived in a quite tepid religious climate within a framework of socio-economic rather than cultic co-ordinates. His expectations and apprehensions as well as his moral code revolved within the orbit of a small urban or rural society."[31] Without evaluating every word of this quotation, Oppenheim characterizes *grosso modo* the essence not only of Mesopotamian, but of any Ancient Near Eastern religion, including pre-exilic Israel and Judah. Due to Oppenheim's continental background, which was strongly influenced by ideas of enlightenment, he was not prepared to call the Mesopotamian concentration on cult and divination a religion. However, it would rightly be characterized as one. In a way, Oppenheim puts together all criteria on which Ancient Near Eastern religion is focused.

The contrast between personal religious requirements and public cultic performance observed by Oppenheim is not all compelling. The individuals, more or less, make use of the same divinatory practices for their personal needs as does the king who finds himself accountable for the welfare of the land (mātu) and his subjects (nišū). When he performs cultic duties, especially in all areas of divination, he acts as intermediary between gods and subjects *and* as a corporate personality representing the entire community he is responsible for. It is necessary to understand the king's strong involvement in divinatory rites as a substantial and indispensable part of his daily duties to exercise kingship. Celestial and terrestrial omens as well as other phenomena of divinatory impact have to be observed carefully to ensure that nothing portentous for the order and welfare of the land is neglected. The diviners are among those court-officials who control the daily life of the king to a remarkable degree. They are experts of the ritual calendar, and they are held in high esteem as they "guard the secrets of god and king" (nāṣir pirišti ili u šarri).[32] Consequently, it is they who decide when the days are favourable or unfavourable for the king to perform any actions.[33]

Prayers are an outstanding example to demonstrate how closely royal sphere and cult are interrelated. I will confine myself to the example of šu-ila-prayers.[34] The prayers of the 'Lifting of the hand' refer

---

31 Oppenheim (1964), 176; cf. the entire section 172–183: "Why a 'Mesopotamian Religion' should not be written".

32 Winckler (1894), 52 K 4730:14 = Tadmor (1958), 150–163.*93, 155; for further evidence cf. CAD P (2005), 398–401 s.v. pirištu.

33 Cf. Spieckermann (1982), 229–306.

34 Cf. King (1896); Ebeling (1953); Mayer (1976); id. (1990), 449–490; Zgoll (2003).

to individual laments in the Sumerian tradition, while they draw on incantations in the Akkadian tradition. The prayers are generally superscribed with én, šiptu 'incantation'. Praying a šu-ila is not only a divinatory act subject to a concomitant ritual. The prayer itself is, as the title indicates, a proper part of the incantation rite. In the religion of Mesopotamia prayer and incantation are just as inseparable as are magic and religion. A šu-ila will not be spoken, but 'recited', literally: 'counted' (manû).[35] When the king makes use of those incantations it goes without saying that he does not act as an individual, rather as a corporate personality. Though this might be perceived in every single prayer where the name of a king has been introduced instead of the usual *N(ullum) N(omen)*, it becomes even more obvious with the incorporation of prayers in larger incantation rituals. Such a ritual would be represented by bīt rimki 'bath-house, house of the washing ritual', a ritual starting in the palace and ending in the bīt rimki. It is a provisional building probably made of reed, where the exorcist recites prayers of the Shamash cycle (ki-ᵈutu-kam), and the king, on his part, recites prayers of the šu-ila series accompanied by different offerings, purification ceremonies and apotropaic rites in order to reconcile the deity.[36]

Evidence of other rituals and prayers could easily be provided. It is all too obvious that the king's cultic activities are an integral part of exercising kingship. Being involved in rituals and prayers the king's position as a corporate personality functioning as an intermediary between the divine and the political sphere comes to the fore. He is the personification of the kingdom, and his kingdom is the image of heavenly dominion; accordingly, the king is seen as the "perfect likeliness of the god" (kal muššuli ša ili).[37] The interrelationship of heaven and earth is revealed by the institution of kingship. Dominion takes its concrete shape in the form of one king and regularly no more than one or two gods as his direct divine counter-parts and many others who expect to be venerated as individual divine personalities. It is the first duty of a king to balance divine and demonic powers, especially with regard to their benevolent and malevolent effects on dominion on earth by applying those divinatory means, which the gods themselves have established through the cult. The king acts for the benefit of his land and his subjects. However, the texts do not infer that the subjects – hardly ever called 'people' or 'nation' – are the primary concern of royal dominion.

35 Cf. Kunstmann (1932), 3–6; CAD M/I (1977), 223 s.v. manû 3a; CAD M/II (1977), 99 s.v. minûtu 3.

36 Cf. Seux (1976), 21–32.215–464.

37 Harper (1892–1914), n. 652 r. 12; cf. Parpola (1970), n. 145.

It has to be proved in the temples, at court, and in impressive deeds of warfare and building activities.

5. What is the Benefit for Israel?

I have concentrated my investigation on how god, king, and cult are interrelated in Mesopotamian culture and religion. Israel was, however, the starting point of my inquiries, trying to clarify why and to what extent 'people' and 'nation' may be regarded as useful notions to grasp Israel's self-perception of her relation to God. The concentration on Mesopotamia did not result in losing sight of Israel. On the contrary, studying Mesopotamia more closely shed light on concepts and conditions in Israel: First on the situation during the time of the two monarchies, and subsequently on Israel's self-image as God's people and God's nation in post-exilic times. Focusing on Mesopotamia allowed for an investigation of the political and religious interrelation of god(s), king, and cult on the basis of plenty of source material obtained from different genres of texts, which for their greater part can be dated exactly.

The study undertaken yields a quite coherent picture. Kingship is closely linked with divine will which aims at establishing dominion, order, and welfare for the land and the "four regions" (kibrāt erbetti/arbāʾi) of the world.[38] Endowed with kingship by the leading god of the divine assembly, a king needs a land and cities, above all a capital, equipped with temples, palace, royal institutions, and – no less – people, subjects to serve the king. Pondering all these entities essential for royal dominion, one cannot avoid the conclusion that the king's responsibility for a people or a nation does not hold an influential position neither under the ideological aspect of kingship nor in reality. Subjects are necessary to exercise kingship. However, they are not the primary concern of royal dominion. They testify to the fact that a king has been bestowed with dominion according to divine will. This is far more significant for Mesopotamian kingship than any other aspect.

Kingship in Mesopotamia has proved to be a successful venture through centuries, even through millennia. It coordinates religion, ideology and political reality in a system predominated by divine decree which is the indispensable basis and – by means of divination – the

38 The image of the four regions is referring to the entire inhabited world; cf. CAD K (1971), 331–334 s.v. kibrātu. The word is also used in epithets of deities. It is no accident that divine and royal dominion of the entire world is formulated by the same imagery.

daily guidance to make ordinary decisions and to meet every extraordinary political challenge.[39] Not least due to the strong authorization and to the manifold ways of divinatory safeguarding involving numerous leading groups in administration, army, and temples kingship in Mesopotamia has proved the capacity to link a long-term institutional stability with a remarkable adaptability to changing conditions. Deities, kings, and areas of dominion change, kingship lasts – in heaven and, consequently, on earth.

Notwithstanding the many divergences of mental, political, and religious preconditions, I dare to maintain, that the concept of kingship in pre-exilic Israel and Judah was by and large similar to the Mesopotamian – perhaps a little less characterized by divination, but even this is hard to be certain of. The view on kingship has been fundamentally changed in the late 8th century BCE. The pre-exilic monarchies shaken by the expanding power of the Neo-Assyrian empire were confronted with the phenomenon of prophecy, not unknown to the Assyrian empire either[40], yet in Israel from a religious angle, which proved to be far more influential than in any other culture in the Ancient Near East. Presupposing the special relationship of Yhwh with his people in the North and South, prophets utter in God's name the threat of judgement against 'my people' (ʿammî)[41] – even to a degree that Yhwh is prepared to annul the relationship (Hosea 1:9; Amos 7:8; 8:2). In the wake of prophecy, in the 7th and 6th century BCE, the Book of Deuteronomy formulates the positive reply. Using the fiction of Moses' farewell speech right before his death, it characterizes the people before entering the land as 'holy people' (ʿam qādôš) and a 'treasured possession' (sĕgullâ), chosen by Yhwh out of love (Deut. 7:6–8).

At roughly the same time, critical voices were raised against kingship. The idea of a chosen people replaced the king installed according to divine will. The destruction of Jerusalem in 586 BCE, the loss of the Davidic dynasty and the exile fostered the idea of the one God choosing and guiding his people without any intermediary. Only exceptional intermediaries such as Abraham, Moses, and the Servant of the Lord are welcome. It is the Priestly Code, which (re)installs the Aaronite priesthood in early post-exilic times to exercise the regular intermedi-

39 From a comparative point of view cf. Launderville (2003).

40 Cf. Parpola (1997); Nissinen (2003).

41 Cf. Hosea 4:6, 8, 12; 11:7; Isa. 3:12, 15; 5:13; Mic. 1:9; 2:4, 8, 9; 3:3. The problem to which literary layer of the growing prophetic books these references may be ascribed need not be discussed in this context. It is obvious that, generally speaking, Yhwh's menacing utterances against his people have shaped the specific character of prophetic literature in the Old Testament prior to salvation oracles which belong in most cases to later literary layers.

ary function of the cult. The post-exilic Book of Ezekiel confirms the programmatic ideas of the Priestly Code. Moreover, it dares to express hope for a new future shepherd (Ezekiel 34). Such a position can be held either by God alone (34:1–16) or together with a new David (34:23–31), who acts as a 'servant' (ʿebed) and a 'prince' (nāśîʾ, 34:24), yet not as king.

Promoting the idea of a new shepherd, the Book of Ezekiel demonstrates involuntarily that the notion of kingship, tightly associated with the epithet shepherd in the Ancient Near East, can hardly be avoided. Post-exilic concepts continue to concentrate on kingship as an indispensable theological notion and political reality. This is true for Yhwh (Psalms 96–99, 145; 1 Chron. 17:14), for his people – be it in taking on the role of David (Psalm 89), be it in hoping for a *David redivivus* (Ps. 78:68–72; 132) – and, finally, for the nations whose kings and kingdoms are under Yhwh's dominion (2 Chron. 36:22–23 par. Ezra 1:1–3; Dan. 2:21). Facing the permanent change of dominion, post-exilic Judaism gradually elaborates its understanding of election. It no longer claims the special term ʿam, to stress Israel's election. All peoples may be called ʿammîm, and accordingly Israel may be termed 'nation' (gôy). Israel has come a long way towards-regarding herself as 'a great nation' (gôy gādôl, Gen. 12:2) among all nations of the ancient world. Gôy gādôl in this sense does, of course, not refer to political power, rather to a status of a different kind. Being chosen is one way of expressing it, being an intermediary of Yhwh's blessing for the world another, echoing royal overtones this way (Psalm 72). Deut. 4:7–8 chooses a third ambitious option. The text links Israel's exceptional status as gôy gādôl with God's accessibility and the law: "For what (other) great nation has god(s) so near to it as Yhwh our God whenever we call to him? Or what great nation has statutes and rules as just as this entire law that I am setting before you today?" This is exactly what makes Israel a gôy gādôl. Deut. 4:7 is the only instance where the Vulgate translates gôy gādôl by *'natio grandis'*. Israel is a *'natio grandis'* because of having a God so near and having the law. The good theological judgement documented in this translation should be appreciated.

Bibliography

AHw: Soden, W. von (ed.), Akkadisches Handwörterbuch. Unter Benutzung des lexikalischen Nachlasses von B. Meissner, bearb. von W. von Soden, vols. 1–3, Wiesbaden 1965–1981.

Bertram, G. (1935), Art. ἔθνος, ἐθνικός A., ThWNT II. In Verbindung mit O. Bauernfeind et al. hrsg. von G. Kittel, Stuttgart, 362–366.

Borger, R. (2006), Babylonisch-assyrische Lesestücke. Die Texte in Umschrift, AnOr 54/1, 3. Aufl., Rom.

CAD: Civil, M./Gelb, I.J./Oppenheim, A.L./Reiner, E. et al. (eds.), The Assyrian Dictionary of the Oriental Institute of the University of Chicago (Chicago/Glückstadt 1956–).

Clements, R.E. (1973), Art. gōj, in: ThWAT I. In Verbindung mit G.W. Anderson et al. hrsg. von G.J. von Botterweck/ H. Ringgren, Stuttgart/ Berlin/Köln/Mainz, 965–973.

COS: D.W. Thomas et al. (eds.), Cambridge Oriental Series, London 1950–1953.

Ebeling, E. (1953), Die akkadische Gebetsserie "Handerhebung". Von neuem gesammelt und hrsg. von E. Ebeling, Deutsche Akademie der Wissenschaften zu Berlin, VIOF 20, Berlin.

– /Meissner, B./Weidner, E.F. (1926), Die Inschriften der altassyrischen Könige, Altorientalische Bibliothek 1, Leipzig.

Fischer, B. (1977), Novae concordantiae Bibliorum Sacrorum iuxta Vulgatam versionem critice editam, vols. 1–5, Stuttgart/Bad Cannstatt.

Frayne, D.R. (1990), Old Babylonian Period (2003–1595 BC): The Royal Inscriptions of Mesopotamia: Early Periods, vol. 4, Toronto/Buffalo/ London.

George, A.R. (1993), House Most High: The Temples of Ancient Mesopotamia: Mesopotamian Civilizations 5, Winona Lake.

Georges, H. (1976), Ausführliches Lateinisch-Deutsches Handwörterbuch. Aus den Quellen zusammengetragen und mit besonderer Bezugnahme auf Synonymik und Antiquitäten unter Berücksichtigung der besten Hilfsmittel. Ausgearb. von K.E. Georges, Nachdr. der 8., verb. und verm. Aufl. H. Georges, 14. Aufl., Hannover.

Harper, R.F. (1892–1914), Assyrian and Babylonian Letters Belonging to the Kouyunjik Collection of the British Museum I–XIV, London/ Chicago.

Hulst, A.R. (1976), Art. ʿam/gôj, THAT II. Hrsg. von E. Jenni unter Mitarb. von C. Westermann, München/Zürich, 290–325, 293–294.

King, L.W. (1896), Babylonian Magic and Sorcery: Being "The Prayers of the Lifting of the Hand", BMS, London.

– (1902), Annals of the Kings of Assyria: The Cuneiform Texts with Translations, Transliterations, etc. from the Original Documents in the British Museum, ed. by E.A. Wallis Budge and L.W. King, London.
– (1912), Babylonian Boundary-Stones and Memorial Tablets in the British Museum, London.
Kunstmann, W.G. (1932), Die babylonische Gebetsbeschwörung, LSSt Neue Folge 2, Leipzig.
Lambert, W.G. (1960), Babylonian Wisdom Literature, Oxford.
Launderville, D. (2003), Piety and Politics: The Dynamics of Royal Authority in Homeric Greece, Biblical Israel, and Old Babylonian Mesopotamia, Grand Rapids/Cambridge.
Lipiński, E. (1989), Art. ʿam, ThWAT VI. In Verbindung mit G.W. Anderson et al., begründet von G.J. Botterweck und H. Ringgren, hrsg. von H.-J. Fabry/H. Ringgren, Stuttgart/Berlin/Köln, 177–194.
Mayer, W.R. (1976), Untersuchungen zur Formensprache der babylonischen "Gebetsbeschwörungen", StP.SM 5, Rome.
– (1990), Sechs šu-ila-Gebete, Or.NS 59, 449–490.
Menzel, B. (1981), Assyrische Tempel, vols. 1–2, StP.SM 10, Rome.
Nissinen, M. (2003), Prophets and Prophecy in the Ancient Near East, ed. by P. Machinist, with Contributions by C.L. Seow and R.K. Ritner, Writings from the Ancient World 12, Atlanta.
Nunn, A. (2009), Aspekte der syrischen Religion im 2. Jahrtausend v. Chr., in: R.G. Kratz/H. Spieckermann (eds.), Götterbilder – Gottesbilder – Weltbilder, Bd. 1, FAT II/17, 2. Aufl., Tübingen, 267–281.
Oppenheim, A.L. (1964), Ancient Mesopotamia: Portrait of a Dead Civilization, Chicago/London.
Parpola, S. (1970), Letters from Assyrian Scholars to the Kings Esarhaddon and Assurbanipal: Part I: Texts, AOAT 5/1, Kevelaer/Neukirchen-Vluyn.
– (1997), Assyrian Prophecies, SAA 9, Helsinki.
Preuß, H.D. (1984), Art. leʾom, ThWAT IV. In Verbindung mit G.W. Anderson et al. hrsg. von G.J. Botterweck/H.-J. Fabry/H. Ringgren, Stuttgart/Berlin/Köln/Mainz, 411–413.
Roth, M.T. (1995), Law Collections from Mesopotamia and Asia Minor: With a contribution by H.A. Hoffner, Jr., volume ed. by P. Michalowski, Writings from the Ancient World 6, Atlanta.
Schroeder, O. (1922), Keilschrifttexte aus Assur historischen Inhalts (KAH), in: F. Delitzsch (ed.), Ausgrabungen der Deutschen Orient-Gesellschaft in Assur. Inschriften. Zweites Heft: autographiert, mit Inhaltsübersicht, Nummern- und Namenlisten versehen von O. Schroeder, WVDOG 37, Leipzig.

Seux, J.-M. (1976), Hymnes et prières aux dieux de Babylonie et d'Assyrie, LAPO 8, Paris.

Smith, M.S. (2001), The Origins of Biblical Monotheism: Israel's Polytheistic Background and the Ugaritic Texts, Oxford.

Spieckermann, H. (1982), Juda unter Assur in der Sargonidenzeit, FRLANT 129, Göttingen.

– (2009), "Des Herrn ist die Erde". Ein Kapitel altsyrisch-kanaanäischer Religionsgeschichte, in: R.G. Kratz/H. Spieckermann (eds.), Götterbilder – Gottesbilder – Weltbilder, Bd. 1, FAT II/ 17, 2. Aufl., Tübingen 283–301.

Strathmann, H. (1942), Art. λαός A.–C., ThWNT IV. In Verbindung mit O. Bauernfeind et al. hrsg. von G. Kittel, Stuttgart, 29–39.

Tadmor, H. (1958), The "Sin of Sargon", ErIs 5, 150–163.

TUAT: Kaiser, O. et al. (eds.), Texte aus der Umwelt des Alten Testaments, Gütersloh 1982–.

Winckler, H. (1894), Sammlung von Keilschrifttexten, vol. II, Leipzig.

Zgoll, A. (2003), Die Kunst des Betens. Form und Funktion, Theologie und Psychagogik in babylonisch-assyrischen Handerhebungsgebeten zu Ištar, AOAT 308, Münster.

Zimmern, H. (1912–1913), Sumerische Kultlieder aus altbabylonischer Zeit, VAS 10, Heft 2, Leipzig.

YHWH in the Northern and Southern Kingdom

MATTHIAS KÖCKERT

For Erhard Blum (23rd February 2010)

1. Point of Departure, State of the Question and Sources

1.1

From its beginnings the history of Palestine was defined by profound contrasts. Already in the second half of the 2nd millennium BCE the West-Jordan mountain range was ruled by two disparate city-states.[1] Topographical factors and climatic conditions favoured the North; additionally the major international trade routes were easier to reach from here.[2] The differences between both states as well as the predominance of the North increased during the 1st millennium BCE, when the expanding regional rule of Lab'ayu of Shechem had long become the Northern kingdom under Omride rule.[3] Its territory not only encompassed the middle-Palestinian mountain range but also the plain of

My sincere thanks to PD Dr. Anselm C. Hagedorn who was kind enough to help to transform my German lecture as well as the expanded article into acceptable English.

1 The situation is reflected in the Amarna letters written by the Palestinian regional rulers to the Egyptian central power at El-Amarna. While Shechem was already the centre of a larger territorial entity that a certain Lab'ayu endeavoured to enlarge, Jerusalem during the late Bronze Age simply appears to be a small, fortified town surrounded by several smaller hamlets. Its ruler, however, seemed to control a significant, though sparsely populated area. On Labaiah of Shechem cf. EAT no. 245, 247, 248, 250, 289; on Abdi Heba of Jerusalem cf. EAT no. 285–291. On the Amarna Letters in general cf. the translation with commentary in Moran (1992).

2 Both, Megiddo and Hazor, were located at the cross-roads of important trade routes. Cf. the map in Aharoni (1979), 45.

3 According to EAT the regional rule of Lab'ayu of Shechem roughly corresponds to the later core of the Northern kingdom.

Jezreel and Galilee towards the North as well as Gilead and Moab East of the Jordan river and extended from Bethel to Dan. The cultivation of corn, especially in the plain of Jezreel, and of olives and wine in the hill country added to the economical power of a country that entertained a lively cultural and economic exchange with Syria and Phoenicia. All this required a tight state organisation and administration. This structure pervaded the whole country in the form of functional places and public buildings, especially in urban settlements. And it increased during the Assyrian period.

In comparison the Southern kingdom was relatively small and economically inferior to the North. It consisted of the Judean hill country, of parts of the Shephelah in the West, and of the Negev in the South. All in all hardly more than a quarter of the territory of the North. In relation to the Northern kingdom the remote South was far more homogeneous and mainly agrarian. In contrast to the North that was often rocked by usurpations and changes in the dynasties, the South remained faithful to the Davidic dynasty. The biblical texts only mention a few times that the dynasty was under threat in Judah. Here the *ᶜam ha'āræṣ* is always mentioned as a stabilizing element that in the end ensured the continuation of Davidic rule. A comparable institution is apparently missing in the North. Additionally, the symbiosis of Temple and palace in Jerusalem has probably contributed significantly to political stability, while in the North the capital Samaria and the sanctuary at Bethel were separated geographically.

Despite several similarities we can detect differences in the material culture. Burial caves with cleared benches and niches are probably limited to Judah.[4] In a similar way rosette stamp seals and stone weights can be seen as markers of Judean culture in the 7th century BCE.[5] Also the clay figurines are mainly from Judah.[6]

Vice versa, the craftwork of the North displays a larger degree of independence and originality in utilizing foreign motifs as part of iconography than is the case in indigenous and Egyptian-influenced Judah.[7] This is undoubtedly connected to the different geo-political location and the different cultural integration of both states.

On the other hand, the North significantly influenced the South culturally. Here, one only needs to look at the diffusion of so-called proto-Aeolian capitals that are found as part of monumental architecture in

4 For a description of the special Judean tomb types during Iron II cf. Yezerski (1999), 253–270.

5 Cf. Kletter in Yezerski (1999), 261.

6 Cf. Kletter (1996).

7 Cf. Keel/Uehlinger (1998), 220–223, 282–298.

Palestine since Iron IIa. They first adorn royal representational buildings in Hazor, Megiddo and Samaria before they become fashionable in Jerusalem and Ramat Rahel and are integrated as a motif into Judean glyptics.[8]

After these few and rather random insights into the multi-facetted and very differentiated relationship between the Northern and Southern kingdom it is impossible to dismiss the question of the different divine concepts in Israel and Judah. Of course and in contrast to Ammon, Moab and Edom, YHWH was worshipped as the state god in both states. But was his profile the same in Israel and Judah? Were the same beliefs and ideas connected to him in the North and in the South?

1.2

The significant differences between the Northern and the Southern kingdom have long been noted and to stress them has become a *ceterum censeo* in the guild. If one looks for recent studies of the different divine concepts in Israel and Judah, however, one quickly reaches a dead end.[9] Recent reference works limit themselves to investigate the origin of the god of Israel and to evaluate his relationship to El and Baal.[10] Or they simply offer a sketch of the representations of the divine in Judah without even mentioning Israel.[11]

These accusations cannot be leveled against a well-known introductory work: here, Angelika Berlejung offers a survey of the "History and Religion of Israel" by mainly using archaeological and material remains.[12] Biblical texts, however, simply play a marginal role in her presentation. On the basis of the different conditions in Northern and Southern Palestine, Berlejung argues for two quite distinct local shapes of YHWH and his worship. While the official cult in the North mainly found its expression in the non-urban sanctuaries, the cult in Judah was from the beginning tied to the city-kingship and to its central sanctuary in Jerusalem. The different contours of the profile of YHWH remain, however, pallid:

8 Cf. Schmitt (2001), 77–89, and Keel/Uehlinger (1998), 413–414.

9 See here the "older" studies of Ahlström (1984), 117–145, and Davies (1992), 60–74.

10 Cf. van der Toorn, DDD ^{2}1999, 910–919.

11 Cf. Janowski (2006), 25–28, 229–230.

12 Cf. esp. § 4,2.2 ("Religion und Kult" in the Iron Age) in Berlejung (2006), 117–144.

> "Vielleicht war der Jhwh des Nordens [...] stärker als Baal/Baal-Šamem konzipiert, während der Jhwh des Südens Züge des Jerusalemer Stadtgottes (evtl. Sonnengottheit) rezipiert hatte."[13]

The postulated differences are never fleshed out and they are not documented by reference to the material culture. This is hardly surprising because the main tendencies of the Northern cult also appear in Judah, though with a slight delay.

Fritz Stolz accentuates the different profiles of YHWH more clearly.[14] He limits his presentation mainly to the concepts of the official state-cult but does not only use the so-called 'primary sources' but also takes the biblical texts into account. According to Stolz YHWH in the North and the South is an 'El-figure'. In the South he develops YHWH's profile by looking at the identification of the state-god of Judah with the hitherto dominant city-god of Jerusalem especially on the basis of the Jerusalem cult. He derives this concept from the design of the Temple and from the cult-lyric as reflected in the Psalms. The god of Jerusalem is therefore similar to the state-preserving gods of other states such as Ba'al in Ugarit or Marduk in Mesopotamia.[15] In great similarity to these gods, YHWH guarantees the cosmos of Israelite living space and defends this against its enemies with the help of the king who mediates the divine world-order. Additionally, it is highly likely that in Jerusalem YHWH had a female consort in the figure of Asherah. As far as the profile of YHWH in the North is concerned Stolz derives its main contours from the cultic legends of Bethel in Genesis 28 and 1 Kings 12. Bull-god and the god of the Exodus are fused in Num. 23:22; 24:8. In the North too, YHWH was considered an El-figure but – as the bull testifies – he was at the same time envisaged as a storm-god. The obvious reservations against such a concept are countered by Stolz by stating that the apparent alternative storm-god or El as an explanation for the bull is irrelevant: both gods embody potency in the true sense of the word and the same potency is represented by YHWH in Bethel and Dan as well as in Jerusalem.[16] Additionally, the mentioning of ʿAnat-Bethel and Asham-Bethel in the papyri from Elephantine suggests that YHWH had two female consorts. Nevertheless, according to Stolz, we cannot assume a differentiated pantheon in the North.

13 Berlejung (2006), 133 with reference to Keel/Uehlinger (1998).

14 Cf. Stolz (1996), 114–120.

15 Cf. Stolz (1996), 115.

16 Cf. Stolz (1996), 119: here he cloakes the problem and this cannot explain the antagonism of an El-godhead and a storm-god.

Herbert Niehr also offered a short sketch of the problem.[17] On the basis of the biblical notes regarding the building of the palace and Temple in 1 Kings 5–8 he assumes a strong Phoenician influence. This influence is not limited to architecture but can also be detected in the way YHWH was worshipped in the Temple of Jerusalem. He finds support for this in the representation of YHWH as sitting on a cherub-throne (*yošeb hakᵉrubîm*). "Yahweh was modeled in the image of a supreme god of the contemporary Phoenician religion."[18] In Samaria, however, YHWH was worshipped as Baalshamem. At least in the two latter points we seem to approach a consensus, when we look at the contributions of Berlejung, Stolz and Niehr.

A last work deserves to be mentioned here, because it unites all the important and significant finds from archaeology, epigraphy and especially iconography. Here, we think of the seminal compendium by Othmar Keel and Christoph Uehlinger.[19] The following presentation owes a great deal to this work.

Next to these few mostly sketchy overall presentations we find numerous specialist studies of individual aspects. A detailed exploration and a comparison of the two divine concepts in Israel and Judah is, however, still lacking.

1.3

This lack is mainly due to the difficult nature of the sources. This poses several problems of which a few need to be highlighted here:

1. The number of sources relevant for a reconstruction of the preexilic period is limited. The selection of archaeological artefacts is the result of historical coincidences, the biblical texts the result of canonical censorship. The respective texts from the Hebrew Bible and archaeology were not written to satisfy our religio-historical curiosity. This is the reason why many of the questions we pose cannot be answered on the basis of the sources but only by analogies, combinations and a good deal of speculation. This forces us to be modest and to refrain from sweeping statements.
2. In comparison to Judah, for the Northern kingdom we have significantly less sources at our disposal. The biblical texts are

17 Cf. Niehr (1995), 45–74.

18 Niehr (1995), 54.

19 Cf. Keel/Uehlinger (1998).

written from a certain perspective. They place reading glasses on our nose and these glasses give us a certain, i.e. Judean or Jerusalemite perspective. Authentic and non-polemical sources for the religious practices of Israel are difficult to find in the Hebrew Bible and are mostly reported in their Judean adaptations. If one identifies several *Fortschreibungen* in the Book of Hosea as Judean actualizations one should probably also count on such processes and adaptations in parts of the Psalter.[20]

3. We have to remind ourselves that only very few – if any – texts describing the period of kingship were written by eye-witnesses. The time of the narrator very often differs significantly from the time narrated. As a result a significant part of the texts reflects later times. Without a detailed analysis these texts cannot be used for the reconstruction of the religious history of the monarchic period. Limited space does not allow for such analyses here and thus we have to presuppose many of the results.
4. The biblical text was written with special intentions in mind. The Hebrew Bible presents the god of Israel, if not as the one and only god, at least as the highest one who was from beginning worshipped without a cult-statue. In the retrospective of several texts differing realities are simply seen as witnessing to the rejection of the pure faith in YHWH and as a violation of the stipulation regarding foreign gods and images. By using this simple and effective way of explanation, the Deuteronomists, for example, were able to explain the exile as a well-deserved punishment of God. Any religio-historical analysis has to take such tendentious presentation into account.
5. For some of our questions archaeological finds are more important than the texts from the Hebrew Bible. Occasionally, we are in the lucky position to be able to check the biblical view of things against the archaeological remains. This then can sometimes lead to its correction. Archaeological finds present their own problems that we can ignore here. Epigraphic material is part of these archaeological artefacts and this material makes it possible for us to take up the outside position, i.e. to look at Israel and Judah from the perspective of its neighbours and to relate this perspective to the events reported in the Hebrew Bible. Here too, we have to take the tendentious character of the sour-

20 After the fall of the North refugees brought several Northern traditions to Judah where they were adapted for Judean readers.

ces into account and this material has to be subjected to the same critical analysis as the biblical text.

6. When we speak about religious concepts we can take up insights from Manfred Weippert and use his ideal-type distinction of three levels.[21] For the single individual, the level of family and clan is most important. Here he feels safe under the protection of his god. The expressions of personal piety do not need a temple. At the same time, the individual lives together with other families in a common settlement. Therefore, local religion is equally important to him and his family. This religion finds its expression in the many local sanctuaries or – as the Hebrew Bible observes polemically – 'on every hill and under every green tree'. Finally, there is the level of kingship and the state. The royal state cult of the god of the royal dynasty is administered in Jerusalem and at Bethel. This cult, however, does not play any significant role in the day to day routine of the individual, even though his weal and woe is dependent on it. These different levels of religious communication have to be taken into account when interpreting the different sources. Here, we have to ask: on which level do we encounter YHWH and can we trace developments? It is simply impossible to transfer the findings from one level to another.
7. The period of the monarchy ended in the North in 722 BCE and in 587 BCE in the South. The Bible places its beginnings to the 10th century BCE, while archaeologists such as Israel Finkelstein argue for the 9th century and the 8th century BCE respectively. No matter when we date the beginnings of the monarchy, the institution was subject to historical change. The same is true for religious symbolic systems though we have to state that here conservative forces tended to be stronger than on other levels. The complex nature and the manifold difficulties of the sources should dampen the optimism to be able to trace theological changes in detail. We can at best hope to uncover basic traits and tendencies. Nevertheless the iconographic material adds important facets to the portrait of God presented in the literary texts.

Profound changes only occur during the 7th, the 6th and during the 2nd century BCE. Their causes, however, such as the 'Josianic reform', the end of the state of Judah and the destruction of the Temple and the struggle with Hellenism, lay outside the period under scrutiny here.

---

21 Cf. Weippert (1997), 1–24.

The same has to be said of questions regarding the beginnings or the origin of the God of Israel and they will expressly be excluded from the discussion. A comparison of the different divine concepts in Israel and Judah does not force one to add yet another hypothesis regarding the origin of YHWH. Instead we will take the topic posed seriously and limit ourselves to the period of the monarchy of both kingdoms.

2. YHWH in the Northern Kingdom

2.1

Outside the Hebrew Bible, Israel is first mentioned on the stele of king Mesha of Moab.[22] The stele was discovered in 1868 in the vicinity of Dhiban and is housed today in the Louvre. It can be dated to the middle of the 9th century BCE and its original place probably was the cultic height of Karchoh (l. 3).[23]

The stele can be characterized as a royal building report. As part of it king Mesha reports that his Israelite colleague Omri and his successor had conquered large parts of Moabite territory. The inscription mentions Madeba, Ataroth, Nebo and Jahas. King Mesha blames the anger of Kemosh, the state and dynastic god, for the loss of the land (l. 5). This anger is now abated. Therefore, Mesha was able to recover the territories lost to Israel. The inscription, however, describes the military victory of the king as the act of the god who apparently is the actual war-lord: "But Kemosh restored it in my days" (l. 9).[24] Naturally the spoils are dedicated to him (l. 11–12, 16–17). Even though the king conquered the city of Nebo, it is his god who had ordered him to do so: "Go, take Nebo from Israel" (l. 14).[25] In lines 17–18 we read:

> "And from there, I took the vessels of YHWH and hauled them before the face of Kemosh."

Likewise, after the conquest of Ataroth, Mesha hauls the fire-hearth of her (= Ataroth) DWD before the face of Kemosh in Kerioth (l. 12–13).[26]

---

22 Text according to KAI no. 181, translation according to COS II, 137–138 (Smelik). See also TUAT I/6, 646–650 (Müller).

23 Lines 21–25 suggest that Qeriho (Karchoh) could have been a new quarter of the city and possibly denotes the acropolis of the capital Dibon.

24 Thus the proposal of Smelik in COS II, 137. Contrast Donner/Röllig in KAI II, 168 who assume a verb *yšb* here instead of *šwb* and translate: "Aber es wohnte Kamoš darin während meiner Tage".

25 See 1 Sam. 15:3.

26 The term DWD, i.e. "beloved" is probably the epithet of a god. See Isa. 5:1.

If the designation DWD refers to YHWH, YHWH functions in Ataroth as the god of the city.

The inscription depicts YHWH as analogous to Kemosh. What Kemosh is for Moab, YHWH is for the Omrides in the North. In king Mesha's eyes, YHWH was the state and dynastic god of his Israelite neighbours. As Kemosh assisted king Mesha, so does YHWH assist the Northern kingdom. He wages war. He gives victory. Spoils are dedicated to him. Finally, the conquered land is put under his control. Therefore, YHWH is worshipped in the conquered regions of Eastern Jordan, outside the heartland of Israel. The inscription of king Mesha assumes the existence of sanctuaries with corresponding installations dedicated to YHWH when it mentions the "vessels of YHWH" (l. 17–18) and the "fire-hearth of her DWD" (l. 12). For now, Kemosh returned them to Moab (l. 9, 33).

2.2

Despite all polemics against the Northern kingdom, the Hebrew Bible, too, knows that YHWH was the state and dynastic god of the Omrides. Ahaziah and Joram, the sons of Ahab, bear theophoric names formed with elements of the divine name YHWH (1 Kings 22:52; 2 Kings 3:1).

Apparently YHWH had a sanctuary in the new capital Samaria founded by Omri. 1 Kings 16:32 mentions that Ahab "erected an altar for Baal in the house of Baal, which he built in Samaria". That a house of Baal also contained an altar of Baal is self-evident and does not need to be mentioned. We can assume, therefore, that the text originally mentioned a "house of God" (*bêt ʾ^ælohîm*), i.e. a YHWH-Temple.[27] In antiquity it is fairly common to extend hospitality in the temple to other gods. Only the Deuteronomists start to find this problematic. For them such a temple cannot be a sanctuary of the God of Israel but only a house of idols, i.e. a "temple of Baal".

The Nimrud prisma D containing the report of Sargon II about the conquest of Samaria, too, allows to assume the existence of a Temple of YHWH in Samaria. Here we read:

> "I counted as spoil 27,280 people, together with their chariots, and gods, in which they [i.e. the Samarians] trusted."[28]

YHWH undoubtedly belonged to these gods. Since the removal of gods can only happen by removing their cultic images, the text suggests that

27 Cf. Timm (1982), 32–33.
28 COS II, 295.

there was a cultic image of YHWH in the Temple in Samaria.[29] The image of YHWH, however, was in the company of other gods and together with them taken to Assur. This implies that YHWH was indeed the state and dynastic god of the North but by no means a loner. At least in Samaria, other gods were worshipped next to him. But we should not picture the Samarian pantheon as too densely populated.

2.3

This corresponds to the distribution of theophoric personal names in the more than 100 ostraca that were found in two rooms of a repository in immediate vicinity to the royal palace in Samaria and which can be dated to the first half of the 8th century BCE.[30] As far as contents and form are concerned the ostraca can be classified as entry lists registering the deliveries of natural produce for the palace registry.[31] Amongst the fifty different personal names we find several shortforms that are composed without using any theophoric elements. Others are using kinship elements. All these cannot be connected to a certain deity. Of the remaining names, eleven contain the shortform (of YHWH) *yw*. These names show that the state god of the Northern kingdom was popular at least in realm of elite personal piety during the first half of the 8th century BCE. There are, however, also six names formed with *bʿal*. Here, these names do not differ from the ones using YHWH. Since 'Baal' is an epithet it cannot be excluded that this name refers to YHWH as 'lord'. The image of YHWH probably did not differ too much anyway from that of Baal during the monarchic period. This is, however, not the case for the names using Bes and Horus: *qadbeś* and *'eśḥor*. These names reveal Egyptian influence that was probably mediated via Phoenicia. Since names only disclose information about the personal piety of the parents or maybe witness to certain trends it is impossible to derive any reliable facts about the state cult from them.

---

29 The extensive discussion of this problem by B. Becking and Chr. Uehlinger significantly helped to clarify the situation, offering a certain degree of interpretative security; cf. Becking (2001), 151–163, and Uehlinger (1998), 739–776.

30 See HAE I, 79ff., 135ff., and the index in HAE II/1, 55–87; Tigay (1986).

31 Thus the classification of Renz in HAE I, 80.

2.4

More light on the problem is shed by the often discussed storage jar inscriptions found in a building at the site of Kuntillet ʿAjrud. These inscriptions can be dated to the first half of the 8th century BCE.[32] The building complex is situated at the crossroads of two trade routes and is, therefore, often described by scholars as being a trade centre or caravanserai. Other scholars, however, think of a cultic place because the large number of unusual finds and inscriptions is unlikely for a caravanserai. Recently, Nadav Na'aman and Nurit Lissovsky tried to link the site to the cult of Asherah that was connected with a holy grove or a tree.[33] The site is located in the far South of Palestine between Gaza and Elat but due to the theophoric names and the multi-lingual nature, the inscriptions are generally attributed to travelers from the North. The texts can be characterized as requests or wishes for a blessing, making them attestations of personal piety.

The key sentences on jar 1 read: "I bless you by Yahweh of Samaria and his Asherah."[34] On jar 2 we read: "I bless you by Yahweh of Teman and his Asherah. May he bless you and keep you, and may he be with my lord."[35] On jar 2 we find further inscriptions, again mentioning "Yahweh of Teman and his Asherah."[36]

A YHWH of Teman side by side to a YHWH *Šomᵉrôn* let it appear likely that *Šomᵉrôn* has to be understood as Samaria. Since the official state cult of the Northern kingdom was located in Bethel, YHWH of Samaria probably denotes a local manifestation of YHWH in Samaria. To both expressions we can add the "God (of/in) Dan" (Amos 8:14). These epithets allow for the conclusion that the YHWH in the North did not only function as a state and dynastic god but was also envisaged in several local manifestations.

What is meant by Asherah here? As a result of the extensive discussion of the topic we can record the following: Asherah does not denote a cult symbol here but is the name of a goddess. Apparently YHWH in the North was not a loner but had a partner called Asherah. She is not

32 On the site, the inscriptions and the interpretation of the complex findings cf. HAE I, 47–64; Keel/Uehlinger (1998), 237ff. For a dating of the site to 795–730/720 BCE cf. Finkelstein/Piasetzky (2008), 175–185.

33 Cf. Na'aman/Lissovsky (2008), 187–208. Such an interpretation – in connection with 2 Kings 23:7 – would then explain the large number of textiles found at the site. The main building could then be described as "a storehouse for the sancta of the goddess Asherah, her dedications and treasures".

34 COS II, 171.

35 COS II, 172.

36 COS II, 172.

simply his companion ("his Asherah") but clearly subordinate to him as indicated by the syntactical position of the word. Above all it is YHWH, not Asherah, whom the suppliant of pithos 2 addresses. Nevertheless, he does not want to do without Asherah. Therefore he mentions "YHWH and his Asherah." Apparently, Asherah plays an important role in personal piety, maybe as a mediator of blessing and benediction requested of YHWH.

It appears that Asherah was not only part of personal piety but also played a role in the state cult of the Northern kingdom. The deuteronomistic accusation of 1 Kings 16:33 that Ahab made an Asherah refers to the manufacturing of a cultic symbol or an image of the goddess. Despite the note in 2 Kings 10:26 this image continued to exist even under Jehu's son Joahas as the Deuteronomist complains in 2 Kings 13:6. The accusation presupposes the historical reality of Asherah as the consort of YHWH even in the cult of the temple. The practice that was considered normal during the monarchic period becomes an apostasy in the eyes of the Deuteronomists and they transform the hated king into a religious villain.

2.5

As we know from Amos 7:13 the main sanctuary of the Northern Kingdom, however, was not located in Samaria but at Bethel.[37] The Bible provides us with some information about this sanctuary: Genesis 28 traces its origins back to Jacob and in 1 Kings 12 it is connected to the cultic and religious innovations of Jeroboam I. Archaeology has yet failed to unearth such a sanctuary at Bethel.

1 Kings 12:25ff. illuminates the concept of YHWH as the state god clearly. In its current form the text has been heavily reworked by the polemics of the Deuteronomists but it is nevertheless possible to isolate an older kernel – formulated quite unpretentiously – that could derive from historical annals:[38]

37 On the tradition and history of Bethel cf. Koenen (2003) on the one hand and Köhlmoos (2006) on the other.

38 For literary-critical analysis cf. Pfeiffer (1999), 21–31. Koenen (2003) attributes the vv. 25, 26–29, 30b, 32* to his basic layer and argues – despite v. 27 – for a pre-dtr. and pre 722 BCE origin. Köhlmoos (2006), 154–182, in contrast attributes the oldest kernel (including the bulls but without the formula of presentation!) to the dtr. layer of the Book of Kings and dates it to the 6th century BCE. Recently Pakkala (2008), 501–525, voiced some opposition to the interpretative mainstream and regarded the notes on the bulls in 1 Kings 12,28aβ–30 as a later addition to the basic layer 1 Kings 12:26–27aαb*, 28aα, 31a; 13:33b*, 34a. For him, these notes and all the allusions to them in

(25) And Jeroboam built Shechem in the hill country of Ephraim and resided there.
He went out from there and built Penuel.

(28*) And he made two calves of gold:
'Here is your God, Israel, who brought you up from the land of Egypt!' He set one in Bethel and the other he put in Dan.

This note does not report the foundation of new sanctuaries but a change of status initiated by the king of older, already existing sanctuaries. Also it appears that the golden cultic images must be connected to YHWH. The Deuteronomists report in 2 Kings 10:28–29 that Jehu eradicated "Baal", i.e. the worship of foreign gods but at the same time it is stated that he did not turn aside from the "sin of Jeroboam". These sins are especially mentioned when reference is made (maybe by a later addition?) to the golden bulls at Bethel and Dan. As far as 2 Kings 10:28–29 is concerned these golden bulls were images of YHWH. The cult connected to them was not regarded as a foreign cult, even though it was suspicious for other reasons. The description of the cultic images as "bulls" is certainly not of polemical nature.[39] It seems that we have here an official title of the cultic image of YHWH.

The formula of presentation in 1 Kings 12:28 has its place in the cult of these state sanctuaries. It may have been the cultic formula of Bethel, which was proclaimed "when the image of Yahweh left the temple to be carried around in procession."[40] The following factors determine the concepts connected with Bethel (and Dan):

1–2 Kings are simply later additions and constructions. Originally, the sin of Jeroboam in the Deuteronomistic History simply referred to the establishment of cultic heights. The topic of sacrifice is the primary concern of the text and for this only the cultic heights are necessary. Pakkala does not realize that the bulls are symbols of the deity and therefore – as addressees of the cult – naturally include the topic sacrifice. He further overlooks that the topic of cultic heights in the North in 1–2 Kings only appears in the Jeroboam narrative and in the general back references in 2 Kings 17:9, 11; 23:15, 19–20. All the other statements refer to Judah and belong to the standard repertoire of the evaluation of the Judean Kings. It appears that the cultic heights were later transferred from Judah to Jeroboam (cf. Gleis [1997], 121–126). The objection that we hardly have any references to the bulls and the few we have appear to be secondary can also be levelled against the cultic heights of Jeroboam. If there is indeed some older tradition from the monarchic period lurking behind 1 Kings 12:25ff. it cannot be found in the layers reconstructed by Köhlmoos (2006), 156, and Pakkala (2008), 522, since both include 1 Kings 12:27, a verse that already presupposes the 'Josianic reform' and Jerusalem as the only legitimate cultic place.

39 This view finds support in Ezek. 1:7 where the same expression is used to denote the animal that carries the throne of YHWH; Lev. 9:3 and Mic. 6:6 mention the bull calf as part of the sacrificial animals and in Gen. 15:9–11 it is part of a treaty ritual.

40 van der Toorn (2001), 124.

1. The cultic presence of the deity is represented at Bethel and Dan by a golden bull (*ʿgl*). Within ancient Near Eastern iconography the bull is mainly connected to the storm-god. Especially in the rain fed agricultures of Syria and Anatolia it is hardly surprising that a storm-god should be the highest god.[41]
2. There are no indications that the bulls have functioned as carriers of an otherwise invisible deity. Instead, the mode of proclamation shows that the bulls were regarded as symbols representing YHWH. This relationship between the god and his image can be illuminated by a cylinder seal from Ebla.[42] Here, we find a bull on a pedestal between the worshipper and the storm-god who is pictured wearing a crown of horns and carrying a club/mace. The bull brokers the presence of the deity. When encountering the bull the worshipper encounters the god.[43]
3. In the royal proclamation in front of the bull (v. 28), YHWH appears as the "God of Israel", i.e. as the national god who bases his special relationship to "Israel" on the Exodus from Egypt. However, it remains open what is meant by the phrase "[…] brought you up from the land of Egypt."
4. If we assume – as proposed here – that the formula in 1 Kings 12:28 is an old official cultic formula associated with Bethel we would have here the earliest attestation for the Exodus in the biblical text. This formula, then, could no longer be regarded as the concentrate of multi-facetted narrative traditions but these – in turn – would be younger expansions of the cultic formula. If that is the case the phrase "brought you up from the land of Egypt" would then refer – in the context of the Northern Kingdom – to "Canaan" as a former Egyptian province. The tribes of Middle-Palestine from which Israel emerged were autochthonous groups that lived in close economic and cultural symbiosis with the Canaanite city-states. Only at a later stage then and under the impression of the demands of a new time did one interpret the Exodus from Egypt as an Exodus from the land of the Nile.[44] No matter how one understands the term "Egypt" in the cultic formula of Bethel, every explanation has to stress that

41 The extensive material is collected in Schwemer (2001).

42 Cf. Keel (1984), no. 290.

43 See the discussion in Pfeiffer (1999), 43–47, and Koenen (2003), 101–110.

44 See the careful evaluation of all Egyptian data contained in the Exodus narrative in Redford (1992), 98–122. He is able to show that they can be explained best when dating them to the 7th century BCE.

the presence of the Northern Kingdom is connected to an act of the past of its god YHWH. Here, the cultic formula of Bethel transcends the way how king Mesha speaks of his god Kemosh.

5. By choosing the verb to "bring up" (*ʿlh* hi.) the proclamation accentuates the possession of the land and not the liberation from slavery. The *Sitz im Leben* of the proclamation is the cult of the sanctuaries. In this concrete form it aims at safeguarding the possession of the land and thus at protecting the national existence of the Northern kingdom – an existence that has to be secured again and again in the cult: "... who brought you (sg.!) up ..."
6. It is hardly surprising that the monarchy of the Northern kingdom is closely tied to the sanctuary at Bethel. Amos 7:13 calls Bethel a royal sanctuary and a temple of the kingdom (*miqdaš mælæk* and *bêt mamlakah*), even though the king resides in Samaria, which had its own sanctuary of YHWH.
7. The choice of place of Bethel in the South and Dan in the North emphasizes the territorial aspect: YHWH is the god of the whole land. He does not only protect it against enemies from the outside but he is also responsible for the thriving of the fields, the cattle and the people.

Since Dan and the whole of the Northern part fell to the Assyrians in 733 BCE, the Deuteronomists focus solely on Bethel.[45] The sanctuary at Bethel survived the fall of the Northern Kingdom but the image of the bull did not as the allusions to its surrender to the Assyrians in Hos. 10:5 shows. Maybe it was replaced by the massebah that is connected to the sanctuary in Genesis 28 via the patriarch Jacob.

2.6

Texts from the Book of the prophet Hosea offer support for our observations above, since these texts allude to the calf.[46] I will limit my remarks to Hosea 8, a text containing numerous literary-critical problems so that no reconstruction can expect to be accepted universally.

---

45 Comp. 2 Kings 15:29; only since the time of Omri did Dan (like Galilee as a whole) belong to the Northern kingdom. From 840–800 BCE it was separated from Israel by the Arameans under Hazael and in 733 BCE finally lost to the Assyrians. On the archaeological data see NEAEHL 5 (Suppl. Vol.), 1686–1689.

46 The texts are Hosea 8:5–6; 10:5–6; 13:2. For literary-critical analysis cf. Jeremias (1983) and Pfeiffer (1999), 101–170.

The small but very complex pericope Hosea 8:4–6 consists of a statement indicating Israel's guilt in v. 4 that provides the reason for the doom described in vv. 5–6. This clear structure is encroached by several additions which are indented and set in italics:[47]

(4) They have made kings but not with my sanction;
they have made officers[48] without my knowledge
Their silver and gold they made into idols for themselves –
to the end that it will be lost.
(5) He rejects your calf, Samaria.
My anger has flared up against them.
How long will they be incapable of purity?
(6) *What has Israel to do with that?*
The craftsman fashioned it,
It is no God.
No, the calf of Samaria
shall be reduced to splinters.[49]

The passages set in italics put an emphasis on the material from which the calf was fashioned and – by referring to "their gold" – deny him and the cultic images any numinous character since it is simply the work of craftsmen. The verses call to mind the polemics against any manufacturing of cultic statues in Deutero-Isaiah and interpret the calf as a completely useless idol. Therefore, the underlined passages – connected by the common theme of the calf – have to be older than their interpretation. I have no problem attributing them to the prophet Hosea himself, although we have to note that the different address in v. 5a creates a certain literary tension with the rest of the passage. Be it as it may, kingship (v. 4a) and calf (vv. 5a.6b) are embraced with each other in the current literary composition.

Both aspects form a meaningful correlation because the monarch of the Northern kingdom receives his dignity from the calf as the representative of the state god located at Bethel. In our text, Samaria most likely refers not to the city of the same name but to the Northern kingdom as a whole since – after 733 BCE – its territory hardly extended beyond the city itself and its hinterland.[50]

It is a major innovation of the prophet Hosea to separate the divine presence from its cultic representation in the calf of Bethel and to connect it instead to the deeds of the addressees. If the calf is reduced to splinters nothing will remain of the king. As such Hosea does not attack the calf as an illegitimate idol. Rather, by announcing his destruc-

47 For literary-critical analysis cf. Pfeiffer (1999), 129–142.

48 Hi. of *śrr* (GK § 67v).

49 The word has to be derived from *šb'* (HAL).

50 The continuation at least has understood Samaria in the next two lines like that.

tion he withdraws the sacred authority of the monarchy.[51] He simply uncovers what king and officials with their bloody deeds have long started. They were undoubtedly kings and officials "but not with my sanction"! Therefore, the servants of the calf vanish with the calf.

2.7

The bull as the symbolic animal of the storm-god and YHWH represented by the image of the bull preceded the Northern kingdom and they too survived it, since the bull was not limited to the official cult. Rather he was present on every level of Israelite religion.

Bull-images representing the deity were not an iconographic innovation of the Northern kingdom. Just north of Samaria and east of Dothan on the summit of a ridge, archaeologists excavated a cult place with the statue of an attacking bull.[52] The bull is generally dated to the 11th century BCE. Since the open-air sanctuary was located outside any of the late bronze-age cities it might have been a regional cultic place of several surrounding early Israelite settlements. Bull-image and open-air sanctuary with a large stone that was probably more mazzebe than altar and maybe even a sacred tree[53] belong to the oldest realities of a "local religion" in the geographical region of the later Israel.[54]

Additionally the bull left traces behind in the realm of personal piety. In the ostraca from Samaria from the first half of the 8th century BCE we encounter the personal name of *ʿglyw*.[55] Unfortunately, it is not clear whether the name has to be understood as a construct-state (i.e. bullock YHWH's [is the child]) or as a nominal sentence (i.e. YHWH is a bullock). In the context of the naming of a child the first possibility appears to be more likely.

Finally, Hosea 13:2 indicates that small figurines of the bullock of Bethel were manufactured as devotional objects:

51 Thus Pfeiffer (1999), 152–155 and 222–226.

52 Cf. Mazar (1982), 27–42.

53 Thus the interpretation of a stone circle proposed by Mazar (1982), 35, in the vicinity of the entry to the sacred site.

54 Ben-Ami (2006), 121–133, connects the Bull-site to two open-air cult places from the 11th century BCE at Hazor that were used successively. Both cult places were decorated with a massebah and with stones for offerings. As part of the pottery of the cult place in area A we find "a horned head of a zoomorphic vessel, most probably a bull" (Ben-Ami [2006], 125).

55 Samaria 41 (Ostracon) = Dobbs-Allsopp/Roberts/Seow/Whitaker (2005), 463.

"They make for themselves molten images,
idols skilfully[56] made of silver
– all of them the work of craftsmen."

This sacral handiwork was possibly venerated in the domestic cult – a view that is supported by the last sentence of the verse:

"They are wont to kiss calves."

In the current context the accusation refers to the time after the fall of Samaria, since Hosea 13:1 is formulated retrospectively: "Ephraim [...] incurred guilt through Baal, and so he died."

2.8

Thus far all of our considerations were centred around Samaria and the bull-image of Bethel. In the following I would like to broaden the interpretative horizon a bit.

Our sparse knowledge of the theological ideas connected with YHWH in the Northern kingdom can maybe expanded by looking at some expressions of cultic poetry. I think it likely that the fugitives from the North carried with them not only the words of Hosea but also hymns. Already Hermann Gunkel proposed a Northern setting and origin for Pss. 29; 81:2–5.6b; 89:2, 3, 6–19.[57] In the final form of the text, of course, we only have them in their Jerusalem *Gestalt*. Here I will simply mention some aspects.

Psalm 29 – one of the oldest pieces of the Psalter – reflects a distinct Canaanite mythological flavour, well known to us from the texts from Ugarit. Additionally, the Psalm is oriented northwards due to the references to Lebanon and Anti-Lebanon (*śiryon*). Only its Judean adaptation interprets the "holy desert", known from the Ugaritic myth of *Shahar and Shalim*, as the wilderness of Kadesh.[58] The Psalm joins aspects that are allocated to El and Baal in the texts from Ugarit in the figure of YHWH. In vv. 1–2 and v. 9c that frame the Psalm we encounter YHWH as king sitting on his throne in his palace surrounded by his court. In contrast to that the main body of the Psalm (vv. 3–9b) sings the praises of the sevenfold thunderous voice of the storm-god that commands the mighty waters, shatters the cedars of Lebanon, makes Lebanon skip like a calf (!), kindles flames of fire, convulses the wilderness and that

---

56 Irregular form, cf. GK § 91e.

57 Gunkel (1975), 90. Equally the basic layer of Psalms 80 and 83 could derive from the North.

58 KTU 1.23 Rs. l. 65. On the translation of *qdš* and on the further Canaanite associations of Ps. 29:6–9a cf. Spieckermann (1989), 166 and 176 with n. 24.

causes hinds to calve. In v. 9c the heavenly court does what is commanded of it in the introit – they pay homage to this God: "in his palace all say 'Glory!'." The vv. 10–11 leave this frame and speak of the consequences. They possibly stem from the Judean authors who adapted the Psalm.[59] If we are correct in postulating a Northern origin of the Psalm, it shows that – from very early on – YHWH of the Northern kingdom united features that were otherwise attributed to Baal and El. It is not surprising that motifs related to Baal and Hadad form the centre. Reinhard G. Kratz has demonstrated that the corpus of the Psalms can in fact be read as being an abbreviated version of the Baal-cycle from Ugarit.[60] The concept of the kingship of YHWH in Psalm 29 fuses the kingship of Baal and El.

Things are slightly more complicated when looking at Psalm 89.[61] There is a certain degree of scholarly agreement that vv. 2–3, 6–19* contain older material from the period of the monarchy even if it is not quoted directly.[62] The mentioning of Tabor and Hermon as well as Zaphon and possibly Amanus (?) in v. 13 nurture the assumption that the piece originated in the Northern kingdom. Due to the scanty evidence this can, of course, only be an assumption. In the vv. 6–9, YHWH is praised as the highest god and portrayed using features and contours of El: YHWH resides in the midst of his court, called 'the assembly of the holy ones.' But none of the 'sons of God' are equal to him: "Who is a mighty one, like you? Mighty is YHWH!" In vv. 10–13 YHWH is furnished with characteristics of Baal who sustains the cosmos by keeping the waters of chaos in check. Thus heaven and earth became his property. YHWH's kingship is based on his victory over the waters of chaos as is the case with Baal in Ugarit. Therefore, "Tabor and Hermon rejoice in Thy name." Vv. 14–15 add additional titles to the unrivalled king of gods. This time, imagery from the palace of the solar god is used: "Righteousness and justice are the foundation of Thy throne." Here we have arrived in Assyrian times. Vv. 16–19 continue within this cultural milieu but add – after the heavenly court, earthly property and just rule of this king of the gods – the aspect of the people. V. 19 mentions "our king" and "shield" as being part of the property of the unrivalled heavenly king.

---

59 Thus Kratz (2004), 38–39. Spieckermann only regards v. 11 and the middle colon in v. 3 as later additions.

60 Cf. Kratz (2004), 40.

61 On the Psalm cf. Hossfeld/Zenger (2000), 576–601. They regard vv. 4–5, 36–38, 48–49 as a later addition and date the Psalm to the period after 515 BCE.

62 On the history of scholarship cf. Veijola (1982), 11–21.

2.9

The solarization of YHWH in Psalm 89 does not happen out of the blue. Othmar Keel and Christoph Uehlinger have long observed an increase of solar elements in the iconography of the Northern kingdom since the 9th century BCE.[63] Such iconography originated in Egypt and reached Israel via Phoenician mediation.

First we encounter Samarian ivory carvings depicting a youthful solar god in a lotus flower. Then we find seals and bullae representing a winged sun or scarabs with two or four wings.

Finally, we have to mention in this context depictions of a figure on scrimshaw that can be identified with Baal (because of its youth) and seems to be – because of its two or four wings – a heavenly being.[64] Keel and Uehlinger interpret it as a solar lord of heaven, i.e. Baalshamem.[65] The names on the seals do not exclude an Israelite attribution but we cannot prove that the carriers of these seals regarded the figure as YHWH. Since we are dealing with items of personal piety here it may equally be possible to speak of expressions of religious pluralism here.

2.10

Time and again one reads that YHWH was worshipped as Baalshamem of Phoenician character in the Northern kingdom and that he has to be distinguished from the YHWH of the South. The careful analysis of all available epigraphic and biblical data by Herbert Niehr makes such a distinction impossible. Niehr arrives at the insight that all evidence from the time before 720 BCE can only be regarded as "quite hypothetical".[66] Only after the downfall of the Northern kingdom and as part of the reception of uranian symbols of Mesopotamian and Aramaic provenance is the concept of Baalshamem taken up and added – via the Aramaic "god of heaven" – to the epithets of YHWH. Niehr finds the earliest literary attestation of the epithet first in the Elephantine papyri.

63 Cf. Keel/Uehlinger (1998), 228–229.
64 Cf. Keel/Uehlinger (1998), no. 210–213.
65 Cf. Keel/Uehlinger (1998), 223.
66 Niehr (2003), 188.

3. YHWH in the Southern Kingdom

When looking at the Southern kingdom of Judah we can hardly speak of a lack of sources (at least from the Bible). However, the exact dating of them creates problems.

3.1

As in the Northern kingdom, Judah had more than one sanctuary. Thus far, archaeology has excavated only Arad in the Negev for the 8th century BCE. Ze'ev Herzog undertook fresh a detailed and careful excavation and his precise interim report buried several wild theories.[67] The sanctuary only existed during the 8th century BCE and was used merely for 50 years. It was not destroyed as part of the Assyrian military campaigns. Rather we find "clear evidence of intentional cancellation." The whole temple of stratum VIII was covered by a 1 m thick layer of earth so that "the temple no longer existed."[68] Herzog assesses the archaeological data "as pointing to wilful cancellation a short time before the destruction of the fortress [...] to protect the sacred components of the temple from damage and mutilation by an enemy besieging the fortress."[69] The sanctuary consisted of a courtyard, which housed an altar for burnt-offerings and a broad-room temple with an elevated adyton in the West. In a chamber next to the altar an incense burner was found.[70] The broad-room, the *hekal*, had benches made from stone and earth. It is possible that these were used to deposit offerings.[71] The adyton, the *debir*, contained two stone altars and a stone stele (*massebah*). In stratum IX a new one replaced this stele.[72] We learn

67 Cf. Herzog (2002), 3–109.

68 Herzog (2002), 65. Stratum VIII of Arad can be dated to ca. 734–701 BCE.

69 Herzog (2002), 66. All parts of the cult place used in rituals were carefully buried and their place marked with stones so that they can be found and used again. All removable objects were previously removed so that one did not find any cultic instruments or votive offerings. The reasons for such a cancellation of a sanctuary remain speculative. Maybe it was a move to protect the sanctuary from defilement during the conflict with Assyria – a conflict Hezekiah must have expected. In any case, the sanctuary was never used again. Herzog explains this with a reference to the cult reforms of Hezekiah but this is simply one possible explanation.

70 Cf. the similar incense burners on the Lachish reliefs.

71 Pillar figurines, often mentioned in the literature (cf. Berlejung [2006], 134–135), were not found by Herzog.

72 The old *massebah* was not destroyed but carefully placed on the ground of the *debir* and thus made obsolete.

that in Arad there was never more than one *massebah* in use.[73] The *massebot* were completely aniconic but traces of red paint were found on the stele from stratum X. The sanctuary of Arad was undoubtedly connected to the official cult of YHWH. Here it is remarkable that YHWH was represented in the form of a *massebah*.

The preserved stones of a burnt-altar allow us to assume that a sanctuary existed at Beer-Sheba. The bas-reliefs depicting the conquest of Lachish by Sennacherib from his palace in Nineveh show amongst other things how the Assyrians carry away spoils from the city.[74] Here we find two Assyrian soldiers who carry large incense burners probably made from bronze. Cultic utensils of such format and material were probably not used in the private cult but rather part of a public sanctuary so that we too can postulate the existence of such a sanctuary for Lachish.[75]

Since Arad was a royal garrison and Lachish the centre of royal administration in the Shephelah it is likely that in both places YHWH was worshipped as the state and dynastic God of Judah. This cannot be proven for Beer-Sheba but it appears likely. To these we have to add several cult places (*bāmôt*[76]) – partly in the gate[77] – as part of Judean border-fortresses of the 7th century BCE: Horvat ʿUza, Horvat Radum, Vered Jericho, Mezad Michmash were certainly connected with the cult of YHWH.[78]

3.2

Otherwise the official Judean state cult happened in Jerusalem. Unfortunately we are unable to translate the report of the construction and dedication of the Temple in 1 Kings 6–8 into historical realities. The oldest part of the chapters can be found in 1 Kings 8:12–13, i.e. the dedicatory formula of the Temple. Admittedly, the Septuagint has a different text here. Using this version Othmar Keel argued for the worship of a solar god already in Jebusite Jerusalem and its relation to

73 Therefore speculations can be dropped whether YHWH and his Asherah were worshipped in Arad in the form of two *massebah*. Sometimes one finds reference within the literature to a third *massebah* but this turned out to be a larger stone of the wall.

74 The bas-reliefs are easily accessible in the beautiful volume edited by Ussishkin (1982).

75 See the detailed argument in Na'aman (1995), 192–193.

76 On these cf. Gleis (1997).

77 Comp. the cult places in the gate on the territory of the Northern kingdom in Dan and Bethesda. Cf. Bernett/Keel (1998).

78 Cf. the description in Stern (2001), 134, 138, 151–152, 202–203.

YHWH.[79] We cannot repeat the discussion here.[80] YHWH's profile is determined by the undisputed verse 12b:

"YHWH has said he will abide in a thick cloud (*ʿrpl*)."

In Jerusalem too, YHWH is introduced as a storm-god and comparative texts such as Pss. 18:10–12 and 97:2–5 support such a view.[81] The reference to the thick cloud-darkness indicates that YHWH's mythical dwelling place reaches into the earthly Temple. Here, it is symbolized by a windowless and therefore dark *debir*. As a shrine, it enshrouds the presence of YHWH represented by the cherub-throne as cult image. The second line of the dedicatory verse provides the storm-god with a royal palace and throne:

"I have surely built you an exalted house,
a pedestal for your throning forever."

The whole Temple appears as a pedestal of the throne that extends into cosmic heights. Isaiah 6 comes to mind. In this chapter the Temple is only able to accommodate the hem of the royal cloak of YHWH. The tricolon of Jer. 17:12 – apparently a remnant of pre-exilic Temple theology – fits very well here:[82]

"A glorious throne,
set on high from the beginning,
is the place of our sanctuary."

The phrase "glorious throne" alludes to the cherub-throne in the holy of holies of the Temple. The formulation "set on high from the beginning" (*mrwm*) connects the divine mountain and Ur-hill with which the creation began. Together with divine throne, divine mountain and creation the decisive cues of Temple theology are mentioned.

Within the Temple of Jerusalem YHWH is depicted as a deity of the type of Baal-Hadad (1 Kings 8:12) who sits enthroned as king (Isaiah 6; Jer. 17:12).

---

79 In several studies O. Keel has revised his position and connected it to extensive religio-historical theses; cf. most recently Keel (2007), 267–272.

80 For a critical evaluation of the philological basis of the formula cf. Hartenstein (2007), 53–69, and Rösel (2009), 402–417, who reaches the following conclusion that it is impossible "die kaum zu sichernde Rückübersetzung von III Reg 8,53 zur Grundlage einer Aussage über alte Vorstellungen über den Tempel zu machen. Für die Frage nach der Gottheit, die vor JHWH in Jerusalem verehrt wurde, sollte die Septuaginta künftig nicht mehr herangezogen werden" (416).

81 On these texts cf. Köckert (2001), 209–226.

82 On Jer. 17:12 cf. Metzger (1991), 237–262.

3.3

Several installations within the Temple precinct allude to the storm-god imagery such as the molten sea that stood upon twelve oxen (originally probably bulls) and had the shape of a gigantic lotus flower.[83] Here, the storm-god as the victorious combatant is associated with the theme of creation and its maintenance. We encounter said theme again in the decorations of the walls and gates by palms protected by cherubs. Similarly the numerous floral elements signify life, regeneration, and maintenance.

YHWH's cultic representation fits the concept of the Temple as a royal palace very well. Here, Jerusalem is quite distinct from Bethel. The windowless chamber of the holy of holies is filled with two enormous sculptures – the cherubim. We know from passages such as Ezek. 41:18–19 and several ancient Near Eastern analogies that these cherubim were winged hybrid creatures. They stood next to each other in such a way that their inner wings formed the seat of a throne.[84] Such thrones are well known from Phoenicia. What is remarkable of the throne of Jerusalem is its enormous measures and the absence of a statue sitting on it. In the Hebrew Bible the throne is empty – hardly surprising if one takes the measurements into account. Uehlinger has pointed out that we encounter such empty thrones of deities only in Persian times.[85] It is, however, unlikely that the cherubim-throne as an important feature of the cultic inventory was only invented during the Achaemenid period. Rather, the missing cultic statue that enables the retrospective monumentality of the throne is an innovation of the Persian period. During the monarchic period there probably was a cultic image of YHWH sitting enthroned on the cherubim-throne. The argument used to support the ban on images in Deuteronomy 4 supports such a view.[86]

It is stated that under the cherubim the small ark was placed.[87] After its transfer to the Temple it is not mentioned again. In the literature of deuteronomistic provenance the ark becomes the container for the two tablets with the ten words. Priestly texts envisage it as the carrier of the numinous *kapporæt*. If we assume the presence of a cultic image in the Temple the disappearance of the ark is easily explained. Cultic im-

---

83 Inventory and installations of the Temple in Jerusalem are collected – with comparative material and reconstructions – in Zwickel (1999), and Keel (2007), 294–330.

84 Cf. Keel (1977), 15–45.

85 Cf. Uehlinger (1997), 149.

86 Cf. Köckert (2008), 21–37, and id. (2009), 371–406.

87 On the ark and its literary history cf. Porzig (2009).

ages are never placed directly on the ground but on a pedestal and they are generally moved around during processions at festivals. For doing so one needs corresponding litters. Maybe the ark was once a portable pedestal for the deity sitting enthroned on the cherubim during processions of the image of YHWH.[88] After the destruction of the Temple both items disappeared.

Independent of the currently open question whether or not an anthropomorphic statue of YHWH existed in the Temple of Jerusalem during the period of the monarchy we have to observe – on the basis of the material remains from Arad – that the official state cult outside Jerusalem was simply connected to *massebot*.

3.4

The profile of YHWH discernible from the fittings of the Temple is made even clearer by the older cultic poetry. I will simply use Psalm 93 as an example since the kernel of the Psalms can be dated to the monarchic period. Other facets from additional Psalms will supplement the picture.

Jörg Jeremias has shown how well Psalm 93 is acquainted with the cultural milieu known to us from the Ugaritic texts about Baal.[89] The oldest kernel of the Psalm, that can be dated to the monarchic period, consists of the superscription and the three tricola in vv. 1, 3, 4. The superscription states the theme of the Psalm:

"YHWH rules as king."

The first tricolon presents this king exercising his royal functions. Therefore he is robed in grandeur, i.e. in regalia, and girded with strength, i.e. ready for combat:

"He is robed in majesty,
YHWH is robed,
he is girded with strength."

What follows in vv. 1–2 interrupts the context with v. 3 both stylistically and content-wise:[90]

88 Full particulars in Köckert (2009), 396–398.

89 Cf. Jeremias (1987), 15–29.

90 The interpretation follows the astute analysis of Pfeiffer (2008), 38–50, whose proposal displays a high degree of clarity.

(3) The ocean sounds, o YHWH,
the ocean sounds its thunder,
the ocean sounds its pounding.
(4) Above the thunder of the mighty waters,
more majestic than the breakers of the sea
is YHWH majestic on high (JPS).

The lord of the Temple is girded with strength because he seems to return victoriously from a struggle with his adversaries; these are called – as is the case in Ugarit – oceans and mighty waters. They rose up and will do so again but the majesty of YHWH is greater than the thunder of the mighty waters and the breakers of the sea. He has the first and the last word of the Psalm – at least in the oldest version of it. YHWH appears as king and his rule manifests itself especially in maintaining the world against the forces of chaos.

The younger additions (vv. 1b–2, 5) emphasize what was apparent for the older Psalm: the steadfastness of the earth as the result of YHWH's kingship, which is based on the steadfastness of his throne, and the beauty of his Temple. These verses seem to offer a definition of God's steadfastness (from "eternity" v. 2d to "endurance" v. 5c) that otherwise only occurs in the late Psalm 90 and Psalm 102. Additionally, they add the aspect of the Torah (v. 5a being a quotation from Ps. 19:8b). Obviously these are signs of a new era.

In the first part of Psalm 24 the earth and all that it holds is declared YHWH's property:[91]

(1) The earth is YHWH's and all that it holds,
the world, and its inhabitants;
(2) for he founded it upon the ocean,
and set it on the nether-streams (JPS).

The Psalm justifies God's ownership of the earth, since "he founded it upon the ocean" and "set it on the nether-streams." Like Baal,[92] YHWH appears as the maintainer of the world and therefore as its possessor and Lord. The third part of the text changes to whatever holds the world together in its inmost folds – YHWH's presence in his Temple.

---

91 The Psalm is a relatively late composition consisting of three parts. Here, the middle part (vv. 3–6 with the additions in vv. 4–6, which are easily determined due to the change in person) is the youngest. Whether the first part was connected to the third part from the beginning does not need to concern us here. However, the change in style (bicola) and topic gives reason for suspicion, since the recollection of the foundation of the earth envisages the *creatio prima*. In any case, the tricola of the last part can derive from the monarchic period. On the Psalm in general cf. Spieckermann (1989), 196–208.

92 See KTU 1.3 I 2–4; 1.5 VI 9–10; 1.6 I 41–43.

(7) Lift up your heads, O gates!
    and be lifted up, O ancient doors!
        that the King of glory may come in.
(8) Who is the King of glory?
    YHWH, strong and mighty,
        YHWH, mighty in battle.

Here, attributes of Baal ("strong and mighty" and "mighty in battle") are placed alongside those of El ("King of glory"). Here, it is possible that the poet quotes an existing liturgy from Temple worship written in tricola.

In the same way, Psalm 47 presupposes a festive celebration in the Temple. Already the kernel of the Psalm connects the kingship of El with the one of Baal and transfers both to YHWH:[93] YHWH is the most high, who seated himself on his throne and is now king over all the earth.

The enduring presence of king YHWH in the sanctuary of Jerusalem became the foundation of the theological concept that will later be called Zion-Theology.

3.5

The heavenly king is present in his Temple in Jerusalem. But he rules via the king from the house of David, his son (Ps. 2:7) who is seated at his right hand and is thus literally sitting on God's throne.[94] Ps. 110:2 describes the relationship between the two as follows: The king carries the mighty sceptre, which means he is ruling but YHWH has to be asked to send out the royal sceptre from Zion. Only then is the king able to rule over his enemies. The king is not only the receiver of blessings but also the distinct mediator of them (Psalms 21, 72). In the South, the symbolism as well as the royal ideology reveal a noticeable Egyptian[95] but also Assyrian[96] influence. The god who resides in the Temple is first and foremost the god of the Davidic dynasty. In contrast to the

---

93 I attribute vv. 2–3, 6 and vv. 7–8a, 9b to the oldest kernel. The additions introduce national tones (vv. 4–5) and ponder upon the question how this God can rule over the nations (v. 8b, 9a, 10); cf. Zenger (1989), 413–430, and Kratz (2004), 18–20.

94 Comp. Ps. 110:1 with the adyton of the great temple in Abu Simbel where Ramses II is enthroned between Ptah, Amun and Re (Roeder [1961], 364) and the double sculpture of Haremhab to the right of Horus (Keel [1984], no. 324a).

95 Comp. Psalm 2 and Psalm 110 with the material collected in Brunner (1964).

96 Cf. Otto/Zenger (2002).

Northern kingdom, YHWH carries a distinct royal profile in Judah.[97] His rule on Zion is designed as being universal but it is nevertheless connected to the king on the throne of David as an earthly mediator.

3.6

When looking at the Jerusalemite Temple-, royal and Zion-theology one could get the impression that the ring around throne and altar was forged for eternity. This, however, has not been the case. Yahwistic religion in the South also becomes a fertile ground for prophetic opposition during the 8th century BCE.

The most impressive figure of this opposition was the eloquent prophet Isaiah. Isaiah may have simply announced doom for the Syro-Ephraimite coalition (Isa. 8:1–4) but things did not stop there. In the following verses he sees Jerusalem being flooded with Assyrian troops. Along the same lines we encounter in the throne room vision of Isaiah 6 a lord of Temple and Zion who is prepared for judgment and who terminates all salvific contact with him.[98] If one regards the base stock of the vision of Isaiah as authentic (even without the so-called hardening of the people), one has to assume an Isaianic announcement of judgement against Zion, king and people.[99] Isa. 1:21–26, then, speak of a cleansing judgment. In doing so the verses leave the possibility of a future existence beyond the judgment open. The *Fortschreibungen* of the text during and after the exile make – despite several objections – the existence of an older kernel likely.[100] The destruction of the Northern kingdom in 720 BCE must have created a crisis as far as national-religious self-evidence was concerned. Texts like Isa. 9:7–10 indicate an intellectual reflection on these trenchant events and the fatal consequences drawn from it.

---

97 We have to admit, however, that we know next to nothing about the royal ideology of the Northern kingdom. The "son" and the "man of your right hand" in Ps. 80:16b, 18 probably belong to a Judean edition of a Psalm that originated in the cultural milieu of the Northern kingdom and reflected the situation after its diminishment in 732 and its demise in 722 BCE.

98 This view of the vision has been put forward convincingly by Hartenstein (1997).

99 Contrast Becker (1997), 61–123.

100 For a kernel dating to the 8th century BCE see the arguments in Blum (1996), 563–568; id. (1997), 12–29; Steck (2003), 97–103 and recently Schmid (2008), 98–99.

3.7

Thus far we have only looked at the realm of official religion where YHWH functioned as the God of state and dynasty. The numerous and typical Judean horned altars that were discovered in many buildings with oil-presses at Tel Miqne/Ekron, however, belong to the sphere of the domestic cult.[101] They were probably used by Judean forced labourers for burnt offerings. The small altars do not allow to deduce which godhead was worshipped in the work place (the goddess of Ekron *ptgyh*? Asherah? YHWH?).

The epigraphical evidence is more conclusive here. The evidence shows that in Judah, too, YHWH was no soloist but had a female partner. In a funerary inscription from Khirbet el-Qom (about 13 km west of Hebron) dating to the 8th century BCE the owner of the grave reflects on his life:

> "Uriah the rich commissioned it.
> Blessed was Uriah by YHWH,
> and from his enemies by his (YHWH's) Asherah he has delivered him."[102]

The dead person does not hope for a salvation from death,[103] but he ascribes his deliverance from his enemies to YHWH who acted via the mediation of his Asherah. Apparently in Judah, too, Ashera was venerated as the mediator of blessings and called upon in a variety of private distresses.

The so-called pillar figurines from the 8th to the 6th century BCE belong into this context. Thus far roughly a thousand of these figurines have been found. Apart from a few from the Northern kingdom most of them stem from Judah and here from every part. 400 of such figurines have been found in Jerusalem alone. Recently, Kletter has studied them in great detail and he identified them as representing the goddess Asherah.[104] The archaeological context of the findings (*houses and tombs*) support an interpretation of Asherah as mediator of blessings and as a protective deity within the environment of the private (house) cult and family piety.

Similarly in the Bible we have some passages where Asherah refers to a deity.[105] She even had her own cultic image in the Temple of Jerusa-

101 Cf. Gitin (2002), 95–124.

102 Qom 3. Translation according to Dobbs-Allsopp/Roberts/Seow/Whitaker (2005), 409.

103 The inscription cannot be used to argue for a belief in a hope beyond death. Such a belief would be unique in pre-Maccabean times.

104 Cf. Kletter (1996).

105 See Judg. 3:7; 1 Kings 18:29; 2 Kings 23:4.

lem and is thus part of the official cult.[106] Again, the Deuteronomists did not invent the story but simply distorted it polemically. It is remarkable, however, that the prophets of the 8th century BCE polemicize against 'Baal' but never against Asherah.

3.8

During the 8th century BCE and therefore a little later than in the Northern kingdom the first solar symbols appear in Judah. Especially during the time of Hezekiah the winged sun-disc or scarabs with four wings on jar handles are popular at royal demesnes.[107] Similarly, we encounter solar motifs on private seals.[108] This popularity corresponds to the transfer of solar symbols and functions to YHWH in the Hebrew Bible: He sends forth his light and truth (Ps. 43:3); he is sun and shield (Ps. 84:12); like the sun god he issues judgment every morning, as unfailing as the light (Zeph. 3:5). YHWH appears by shining forth like the sun.[109] Finally, solar motifs move into the realm of personal names.[110]

Under Assyrian influence and mediated by the Arameans we can detect an increasing astralization and lunarization of the religious symbols in Judah. Especially the moon-god Sin of Haran is very popular in the whole Assyrian empire. Equally YHWH receives lunar traits: He is praised as a "lamp [...] that lights up my darkness" (Ps. 18:29). Several seals depict the crescent moon standard or an anthropomorphic moon-god on a stool or in a boat.[111] Some owners can be identified as YHWH worshippers because of their names. They clearly imagine and worship YHWH as a moon-god.

---

106 See 2 Kings 21:7; comp. 1 Kings 15:13.

107 Cf. Keel/Uehlinger (1998), 314–317 with illustrations no. 275–276.

108 Cf. Keel/Uehlinger (1998), 311–312 with illustrations no. 273–274.

109 See Deut. 33:2; Pss. 50:2; 80:2; 94:1; Hab. 3:3–4.

110 Zeraiah (Ezra 7:4) and Jehozarach on three seals from the 8th/7th century BCE (HAE II/2).

111 Cf. Keel/Uehlinger (1998), 340–455 with illustrations no. 305–307 and esp. no. 296 and no. 306a.

3.9

In the ante-room of a grave in Khirbet Beit Lei (8 km east of Lachish) one reads the following inscription from the 7th century BCE:

"YHWH, the God of all the earth,
the mountains of Judah belong to the God of Jerusalem."[112]

The inscription connects in both chiastic parts the universality of YHWH with the concentration of the same godhead on Jerusalem. The first line can be compared to Baal's title "lord of the earth", while the second line corresponds to the declaration of property encountered above in Ps. 24:1. The god of all the earth appears in his local manifestation as the God of Jerusalem. All this is quite similar to expressions such as "YHWH in Zion" (Ps. 99:2); "YHWH in Hebron" (2 Sam. 15:7).[113] A local concentration does not impede on the universality of this god YHWH.

Unlike the gods Assur and Marduk who simply had one sanctuary at Assur and Babylon respectively, YHWH was also worshipped outside Jerusalem in local sanctuaries. In the context of the Ancient Near East this is a peculiarity, and perhaps it has something to do with YHWH's origin in being a storm-god.

3.10

The *Sh^{e}ma*ʿ (Deut. 6:4) documents a fundamental change. It does not state anything self-evident but utters a profession. It is the programmatic statement that introduces the reform-programme of the deuteronomic movement during the time of Manasseh. It explicitly replaces the manifold local manifestations of YHWH with the one god in Jerusalem and transforms YHWH to the exclusive god – at least for those who can join in this profession. 'Monojahwism' and 'YHWH-Monolatry' are not succeeding, but two sides of the same coin. This will later lead to the demand of cultic unity and cultic purity, to use a slogan of a didactically skilled interpreter of Deuteronomy. But this moves us outside our frame of reference.

---

112 HAE I, 246.

113 This use corresponds to the title "Dagon in Ashdod" (1 Sam. 5:5) but is also related to the northern manifestations of Yahweh of Samaria or Teman at Kuntillet ʿAjrud and the "god at Dan" (Amos 8:14 and on a dedicatory inscription from Hellenistic times cf. Qadmoniot 10 [1977], 14–15).

4. Comparison

The comparison can be summarized in one single sentence: as far as we are able to recognize divine concepts they hardly differ as far as the subject is concerned but they do so in their concrete realizations.

If we look at the differences of both state-systems not the differences are surprising but the similarities. Economically speaking the Northern kingdom was much more prosperous but it had in Samaria a political centre with no religious tradition that lasted roughly 150 years. Additionally, continuous change on the throne and in the dynasties created permanent unrest. Further, the main sanctuary was disconnected from the capital.[114] In contrast to that Judah was blessed with the Temple in Jerusalem and a long Davidic dynasty. The great similarities can be explained by the fact that Israel and Judah were small monarchies with rain fed agricultures. As such they are also similar to other small states in Syria. In all of these monarchies – Sam'al, Bit-Agusi, Hamath or Damascus – the storm-god Hadad or one of his local manifestations heads the Pantheon.[115] Divine concepts are thus tied to certain functions. These functions, however, tend not to differ too much. All this explains the striking similarities.

In both kingdoms YHWH is the royal as well as the state god. He possesses the stature of a storm-god of the type of Baal-Hadad. Cultic poetry praises him as a divine king in whom the attributes and concepts of El and Baal are united. He is surrounded by a heavenly court consisting of other divine beings. Here, only Asherah has any distinctive features who is subordinate to him but his female consort. YHWH's rule manifests itself in his maintenance of the world expressed by keeping the waters of chaos in check. Therefore, the earth and especially the individual kingdom are the property of this god. The heavenly king exercises his rule via the earthly king, his agent on earth.

---

114 We find a similar constellation in Urartu. Pfeiffer (1999), 31–34, was the first who evaluated the contribution of the Urartian texts for an analysis of 1 Kings 12:26ff. Musasir, the sanctuary of the Urartian state god Haldi, was also the place of the investiture of the Urartian kings. It was located outside the territory of Urartu. On Urartu cf. M. Salvini (1995), 37–47, 183–192.

115 One simply has to peruse the relevant inscriptions: At Sam'al we find different manifestations of Baal, among them Hammon, the "lord" of Amanus, i.e. a local storm-god; additionally there is Rakibel. Hadad, however, is in the fore. At Bit-Agusi (Aleppo and Ain Dara) Melqart was the god of the king Bar-Hadad (!); the stategod, however, was the far more prominent Hadad of Aleppo. Baalshamin and Baalat were worshipped at Hamat but the personal god of king Zakkur was Iluwer, a storm-god. Hadad and Ramman form the spearhead of the Pantheon at Damascus; the inscription from Tel Dan, too, mentions Hadad as the god of king and state. Even in the far South, in Edom, Qaus – a storm-god – appears as state and royal god.

The official cult is closely connected to the king and takes place in front of the cultic images at the corresponding sanctuaries.

Next to that YHWH is also worshipped at other sanctuaries in his many local manifestations. He is not only a state-god but also a local god. Additionally and possibly via the mediation of the state officials the dynastic god and the protector of the king enters the realm of personal piety. Personal piety then is the home of Asherah who mediates blessings and protects from all evil.

These basic features of YHWH are expanded in Israel and Judah by two things that are connected to the prevalent tendencies in the Syro-Mesopotamian area during the 1st millennium BCE: Firstly, we can detect a solarization via Egyptian influence since the time of Hezekiah and secondly, there is a lunarization via Assyrian influence that can only be grasped after the end of the Northern kingdom.

Finally, Yahwistic religion gives rise to prophetic opposition that dissolves the automatism of a national-religious connection of God, king and sanctuary. Salvation is now tied to actual deeds and no longer to the cult.

One main difference between Israel and Judah concerns the representation of YHWH within the official cult. The bull-image of the North is the traditional symbol of the storm-god and widely distributed in the Syro-Mesopotamian realm. The cherub-throne, however, originated in Phoenician city culture. Both items are symbols of the presence of the divine that are specifically connected with the king. Nevertheless, the presentation of the bull at Bethel stresses the territorial aspect while the cherub-throne carries the distinct flavour of a city-state. It is probably not a coincidence that only Judah and not Israel developed a royal ideology comparable to the other states in the ancient Near East.

Since Judah outlived the Northern kingdom it also becomes the place of new developments that took shape in the Book of Deuteronomy. In the end they moved beyond those aspects that connected Israel with Judah: YHWH became the one and only god.

Bibliography

Aharoni, Y. (1979), The Land of the Bible: A Historical Geography, Translated from the Hebrew by A.F. Rainey, London.

Ahlström, G.A. (1984), An Archaeological Picture of Iron Age Religions in Ancient Palestine, StOr 55/3, 117–145.

Becker, U. (1997), Jesaja – Von der Botschaft zum Buch, FRLANT 178, Göttingen.

Ben-Ami, D. (2006), Early Iron Age Cult Places – New Evidence from Tel Hazor, Tel Aviv 33, 121–133.

Berlejung, A. (2006), §4, 2.2 Religion und Kult, in: J.C. Gertz (ed.), Grundinformation Altes Testament. Eine Einführung in Literatur, Religion und Geschichte des Alten Testaments, UTB 2745, Göttingen, 117–144.

Bernett, M./Keel, O. (1998), Mond, Stier und Kult am Stadttor. Die Stele von Betsaida (et-Tell), OBO 161, Freiburg (Schweiz)/Göttingen.

Blum, E. (1996), Jesajas prophetisches Testament. Beobachtungen zu Jes 1–11 (Teil 1), ZAW 108, 547–568.

– (1997): Jesajas prophetisches Testament. Beobachtungen zu Jes 1–11 (Teil 2), ZAW 109, 12–29.

Brunner, H. (1964), Die Geburt des Gottkönigs. Studien zur Überlieferung eines altägyptischen Mythos, ÄA 10, Wiesbaden.

COS: Cambridge Oriental Series, London 1950–.

Davies, P.R. (1992), In Search of "Ancient Israel", JSOT.S 148, Sheffield.

DDD: Dictionary of Deities and Demons in the Bible, ed. by K. van der Toorn/B. Becking/P.W. van der Horst, Leiden 1995; 2nd ed. 1999.

Dobbs-Allsopp, F.W./Roberts, J.J.M./Seow, C.L./Whitaker, R.E. (2005), Hebrew Inscriptions: Texts from the Biblical Period of the Monarchy with Concordance, New Haven.

EAT: Die El-Amarna-Tafeln, ed. by J.A. Knudtzon, vols. 1–2, Leipzig 1915 (reprint: Aalen 1964).

Finkelstein, I./Piasetzky, E. (2008), The Date of Kuntillet ʿAjrud: The ^{14}C Perspective, Tel Aviv 35, 175–185.

Gitin, S. (2002), The Four-Horned Altar and Sacred Space: An Archaeological Perspective, in: B.M. Gittlen (ed.), Sacred Time, Sacred Place: Archaeology and the Religion of Israel, Winona Lake, 95–124.

GK: Wilhelm Gesenius' Hebräische Grammatik, völlig umgearbeitet von E. Kautzsch, 28th ed., Leipzig 1909 (reprint. Hildesheim 1962).

Gleis, M. (1997), Die Bamah, BZAW 251, Berlin/New York.

Gunkel, H. (1975), Einleitung in die Psalmen. Die Gattungen der religiösen Lyrik Israels, 3rd ed., Göttingen.

HAE: Handbuch der Althebräischen Epigraphik, ed. by J. Renz/W. Röllig, vols. 1–3, Darmstadt 1995–2003.

HAL: Hebräisches und Aramäisches Lexikon zum Alten Testament, ed. by L. Köhler/W. Baumgartner, vols. 1–5, Leiden 1967–1995.

Hartenstein, F. (1997), Die Unzugänglichkeit Gottes im Heiligtum. Jesaja 6 und der Wohnort JHWHs in der Jerusalemer Kulttradition, WMANT 75, Neukirchen-Vluyn.

– (2007), Sonnengott und Wettergott, in: J. Männchen (Hg.), Mein Haus wird ein Bethaus für alle Völker genannt werden (Jes 56,7). Judentum seit der Zeit des Zweiten Tempels in Geschichte, Literatur und Kult, FS T. Willi, Neukirchen-Vluyn, 53–69.

Herzog, Z. (2002), The Fortress Mound at Tel Arad: An Interim Report, Tel Aviv 29, 3–109.

Hossfeld, F.-L./Zenger, E. (2000), Psalmen 51–100, HThKAT, Freiburg i.Br.

Janowski, B. (2006), Art. "Gottesvorstellungen" and: "Gottesbilder", in: A. Berlejung/C. Frevel (eds.), Handbuch theologischer Grundbegriffe zum Alten und Neuen Testament, Darmstadt, 25–28, 229–231.

Jeremias, J. (1983), Der Prophet Hosea, ATD 24/1, Göttingen.

– (1987), Das Königtum Gottes in den Psalmen. Israels Begegnung mit dem kanaanäischen Mythos in den Jahwe-König-Psalmen, FRLANT 141, Göttingen.

KAI: Kanaanäische und Aramäische Inschriften, hg. von H. Donner u.a., 2nd ed. vols. 1–3, Wiesbaden 1967–1969.

Keel, O. (1977), Jahwe-Visionen und Siegelkunst. Eine neue Deutung der Majestätsschilderungen in Jes 6, Ez 1 und 10 und Sach 4, SBS 84/85, Stuttgart.

– (1984), Die Welt der altorientalischen Bildsymbolik und das Alte Testament. Am Beispiel der Psalmen, 4th ed., Zürich.

– (2007), Die Geschichte Jerusalems und die Entstehung des Monotheismus. Teil 1, Orte und Landschaften der Bibel IV/1, Göttingen.

Keel, O./Uehlinger, C. (1998), Göttinnen, Götter und Gottessymbole. Neue Erkenntnisse zur Religionsgeschichte Kanaans und Israels aufgrund bislang unerschlossener ikonographischer Quellen, QD 134, 4th ed., Freiburg.

Kletter, R. (1996), The Judean Pillar-Figurines and the Archaeology of Asherah, British Archaeological Reports International Series 636, Oxford.

Koenen, K. (2003), Bethel. Geschichte, Kult und Theologie, OBO 192, Freiburg (Schweiz)/Göttingen.

Köckert, M. (2001), Die Theophanie des Wettergottes Jahwe in Psalm 18, in: Th. Richter et. al. (eds.), Kulturgeschichten. Altorientalische Studien für Volkert Haas zum 65. Geburtstag, Saarbrücken, 209–226.
– (2008), Suffering from Formlessness – The Prohibition of Images in Exilic Times, JNWSL 34, 21–37.
– (2009), Vom Kultbild Jahwes zum Bilderverbot. Oder: Vom Nutzen der Religionsgeschichte für die Theologie, ZThK 106, 371–406.
Köhlmoos, M. (2006), Bet-El – Erinnerungen an eine Stadt. Perspektiven der alttestamentlichen Bet-El-Überlieferung, FAT 49, Tübingen.
Kratz, R.G. (2004), Reste hebräischen Heidentums am Beispiel der Psalmen, Nachrichten der NAWG.PH 2004/2, Göttingen.
KTU: Die keilalphabetischen Texte aus Ugarit. Einschließlich der keilalphabetischen Texte außerhalb Ugarits, ed. by M. Dietrich et al., Kevelaer 1976 (= AOAT 24/1).
Mazar, A. (1982), The "Bull Site" – An Iron Age I Open Cult Place, BASOR 247, 27–42.
Metzger, M. (1991), "Thron der Herrlichkeit". Ein Beitrag zur Interpretation von Jer 17:12f., in: R. Liwak/S. Wagner (eds.), Prophetie und geschichtliche Wirklichkeit im alten Israel. FS S. Herrmann, Stuttgart, 237–262.
Moran, W.L. (1992), The Amarna Letters, Baltimore/London.
Na'aman, N. (1995), The Debated Historicity of Hezekiah's Reform in the Light of Historical and Archaeological Research, ZAW 107, 179–195.
NEAEHL: The New Encyclopedia of Archaeological Excavations in the Holy Land, ed. by E. Stern, Jerusalem 1993.
Niehr, H. (1995), The Rise of YHWH in Judahite and Israelite Religion: Methodological and Religio-Historical Aspects, in: D.V. Edelman (ed.), The Triumph of Elohim: From Yahwisms to Judaisms, Contributions to Biblical Exegesis and Theology 13, Kampen, 45–74.
– (2003), Baʿalšamem. Studien zu Herkunft, Geschichte und Rezeptionsgeschichte eines phönizischen Gottes, OLA 123, Leuven.
Otto, E./Zenger, E. (2002, eds.), "Mein Sohn bist Du" (Ps 2,7). Studien zu den Königspsalmen, SBS 192, Stuttgart.
Pakkala, J. (2008), Jeroboam without Bulls, ZAW 120, 501–525.
Pfeiffer, H. (1999), Das Heiligtum von Bethel im Spiegel des Hoseabuches, FRLANT 183, Göttingen.
– (2008), Gottesbild und Kosmologie – ein Korreferat, in: C. Markschies/J. Zachhuber (eds.), Die Welt als Bild. Interdisziplinäre Beiträge zur Visualität von Weltbildern, AKG 107, Berlin, 38–50.
Porzig, P. (2009), Die Lade Jahwes im Alten Testament und in den Texten vom Toten Meer, BZAW 397, Berlin/New York.

Redford, D.B. (1992), Egypt, Canaan and Israel in Ancient Times, Princeton.

Roeder, G. (1961), Ägyptische Religion in Texten und Bildern, vol. 4: Der Ausklang der ägyptischen Religion mit Reformation, Zauberei und Jenseitsglauben, BAW.AO, Zürich.

Rösel, M. (2009), Salomo und die Sonne. Zur Rekonstruktion des Tempelweihspruchs I Reg 8,12f., ZAW 121, 402–417.

Salvini, M. (1995), Geschichte und Kultur der Urartäer, Darmstadt.

Schmid, K. (2008), Literaturgeschichte des Alten Testaments. Eine Einführung, Darmstadt.

Schmitt, R. (2001), Bildhafte Herrschaftsrepräsentation im eisenzeitlichen Israel, AOAT 283, Münster.

Schwemer, D. (2001), Die Wettergottgestalten Mesopotamiens und Nordsyriens im Zeitalter der Keilschriftkulturen. Materialien und Studien nach den schriftlichen Quellen, Wiesbaden.

Spieckermann, H. (1989), Heilsgegenwart. Eine Theologie der Psalmen, FRLANT 148, Göttingen.

Steck, O.H. (2003), Zur konzentrischen Anlage von Jes 1,21–26, in: I. Fischer u.a. (eds.), Auf den Spuren der schriftgelehrten Weisen, FS J. Marböck, BZAW 331, Berlin/New York, 97–103.

Stern, E. (2001), Archaeology of the Land of the Bible, vol. 2: The Assyrian, Babylonian, and Persian Periods (732–332 B.C.E.), AncB Reference Library, New York.

Stolz, F. (1996), Einführung in den biblischen Monotheismus, Darmstadt.

Tigay, J.H. (1986), You Shall Have No Other Gods: Israelite Religion in the Light of Hebrew Inscriptions, Harvard Semitic Studies 31, Atlanta.

Timm, S. (1982), Die Dynastie Omri. Quellen und Untersuchungen zur Geschichte Israels im 9. Jahrhundert vor Christus, FRLANT 124, Göttingen.

Uehlinger, C. (1997), Anthropomorphic Cult Statuary in Iron Age Palestine and the Search for Yahweh's Cult Images, in: K. van der Toorn (ed.), The Image and the Book: Iconic Cults, Aniconism, and the Rise of Book Religion in Israel and the Ancient Near East, Contributions to Biblical Exegesis and Theology 21, Leuven, 97–155.

Ussishkin, D. (1982), The Conquest of Lachish by Sennacherib, Publications of the Institute of Archaeology 6, Jerusalem.

van der Toorn, K. (2001), The Exodus as Charter Myth, in: J.W. van Henten/A. Houtepen (eds.), Religious Identity and the Invention of Tradition. Papers Read at a Noster Conference, Soesterberg, January 4–6, 1999, Studies in Theology and Religion 3, Assen, 113–127.

Veijola, T. (1982), Verheißung in der Krise. Studien zur Literatur und Theologie der Exilszeit anhand des 89. Psalms, AASF Ser.B 220, Helsinki.

Weippert, M. (1997), Synkretismus und Monotheismus. Religionsinterne Konfliktbewältigung im alten Israel, in: id., Jahwe und die anderen Götter. Studien zur Religionsgeschichte des antiken Israel in ihrem syrisch-palästinischen Kontext, FAT 18, Tübingen, 1–24.

Yezerski, I. (1999), Burial Cave Distribution and the Borders of the Kingdom of Judah toward the End of the Iron Age, Tel Aviv 26, 253–270.

Zenger, E. (1989), Der Gott Abrahams und die Völker. Beobachtungen zu Ps 47, in: M. Görg (ed.), Die Väter Israels, Beiträge zur Theologie der Patriarchenüberlieferungen im Alten Testament, FS J. Scharbert, Stuttgart, 413–430.

Zwickel, W. (1999), Der salomonische Tempel, Kulturgeschichte der antiken Welt 83, Mainz.

From Many Gods to the One God: The Archaeological Evidence

EPHRAIM STERN

The following discussion is based in its entirety on the archaeological finds and is, therefore, limited to the presentation of this data. I realize that my interpretation of the finds may be oversimplified. Nevertheless, I believe that the issue is of singular importance because it dates to the biblical period, and as such is worthy of our attention.

I will begin with a discussion of the finds of the 7th century BCE, the last century of the independent Judean kingdom. At that time, not less than eight nations were settled in Palestine. These include the Arameans of the kingdom of Geshur, who lived on the northeastern border of Israel; the Phoenicians, who inhabited the northern coast and the Galilee; the Israelite kingdom; the late Philistines, who prospered in their four cities, Ashdod, Ashkelon, Gaza and Ekron; and the three nations of East Jordan, the Ammonites, the Moabites and the Edomites; and, finally, the Judean kingdom.

In this period each of these nations had its own independent cult, consisting of the worship of a pair of major deities. Each of the male gods of these nations had its own distinct name: the Arameans had Haddad as their chief deity, the Phoenicians had Ba'al, Dagan or Ba'al Shmem, was the chief god of the Philistines, Milcom of the Ammonites, Chemosh of the Moabites, Qos of the Edomites and YHWH of the Israelites and the Judeans. It is interesting to observe that among all of them, including the Philistines and even the Judeans, the chief female deity was Ashtoret (Ashtart) or Asherah.[1] Also that each of these many nations created the images of their gods in a form, different from that of the others.[2] By the 7th century BCE the representation of the different deities had been clearly consolidated and it is easy for any experienced archaeologist or specialist in ancient art to attribute at first glance a

1 Cf. Stern (1999; 2006).

2 Cf. Stern (2001).

figurine to a Phoenician[3], a Edomite[4], Moabite[5] or that of the Judean cult. At the same time one of the strange results of the study of the cult objects is that, despite these differences of deities and cults, there exists a large amount of unity, too. The various nations used the same cult objects, the same types of incense altars, made of stone and clay, bronze and clay censers, cult stands and incense burners, chalices, goblets and bronze and ivory sticks, adorned with pomegranates etc. It was easy to take cult vessels of one deity, for example from the sanctuary of Arad, and place them in the service of another one, as is described in the famous stele of Mesha, the king of Moab, who delivered the vessels of YHWH taken from the conquered Judean city of Nevo to the Temple of Chemosh.[6] Archaeological excavations in Judah had uncovered many sanctuaries dedicated to the national god. These sanctuaries had been erected at various sites. Such a sanctuary was called: 'The house of YHWH'. The most important and central one was, no doubt, the sanctuary on the Temple Mount in Jerusalem. But the Bible itself testifies to the existence of additional sanctuaries at Dan, Shechem, Bethel, Shilo and Beersheba. Others had been found in various excavations of which the best-known example is that of Tel Arad. In one of the Arad ostraca, for example, it is written that "He sits in the house of YHWH".[7] Aharoni also believed that the plan of the house and its contents justified the assumption that it was 'a Yahwistic-Judean temple'.

Apart from the sanctuary at Arad others had been excavated by Beit-Arieh at Judean fortresses at 'Uza and Radum near Arad. Another one, previously reported by Aharoni, was near the gate of Tel-Sheba, where a large four-horned stone altar has also been found.

A similar cult center has also been uncovered in the Judean fortress of Vered-Jericho near modern Jericho and at Mesad-Michmash, on the kingdom's northern border.[8]

These new finds have strengthened Aharoni's assumption that almost all border-fortresses of the Judean kingdom had cult centers. It should also be mentioned that in a large number of these fortresses numerous figurines, altars, and other types of cult objects have been recovered.

We may assume that a sanctuary for YHWH also existed in Lachish, the second city in importance in Judah, as in the Lachish relief in

---

3 Cf. Stern (2001), 54–55, 77–78.
4 Cf. Beit-Arieh (1995).
5 Cf. Davaiau/Dion (2002).
6 Cf. Cooke (1903), lines 17–18.
7 Cf. Aharoni (1981), 35–39.
8 Cf. Stern (2001), 200–212.

Nineve a pair of large cultic stands are depicted as war spoil, taken out by Sennacherib's soldiers after they had sacked the city. These stands belong to a type of which smaller ones have been unearthed in many of the country's towns.[9]

Other sanctuaries dedicated to 'YHWH' in various settlements outside Jerusalem are known. Mention should be made of the famous cult site in Kuntillet-Ajrud, dating to the end of the 9th century BCE and dedicated to "Yahweh of Samaria and his Asherah" or "Yahweh of Teman" and his Asherah.[10] Another one is mentioned in the Mesha stele which was even earlier, where the Moabite king claims to have taken (from the city of Nevo) the vessels of YHWH and had laid them in front of Chemosh. This means that there was also a sanctuary dedicated to YHWH in the Judean city of Nevo, before it had been plundered by the Moabites.[11]

We may, therefore, conclude that a 'house of YHWH' may have been located in every settlement in Judah or in any area settled by the Judeans.

Who served in these sanctuaries? In this respect we should add that on ostraca in the sanctuary of Arad itself, the names of two well known Jerusalemite priestly families, Meremot and Pashur, have been found, who probably served in the local Arad sanctuary.[12]

Generally, the priests who served in the YHWH sanctuaries received their positions within their families, from father to son. We do possess a few seals in which only the title "Cohen" (priest) is added to the name. One of them published that of "Hanan the son of Helqiah the priest", who may have been the father of a high priest in Jerusalem.[13] Other seals mentioned the place name of the sanctuary such as: "Zechario the priest of Dor" (cf. "Amaziah, the priest of Bethel", Amos 7:10). Another seal refers to "Miqnayahu, servant of YHWH"[14], which means that Miqnayahu served in the cult of one of the many YHWH temples. Based on this data it may be concluded that someone who had the title of a priest, could serve in any of the country's temples.

There is, yet, another inscription from Judah and from the same period, mentioning the name of the divine couple, who were worshipped by the locals: YHWH and the Asherah. This matches their occurrence in

9 Cf. Ussishkin (1982), 84–85.

10 Cf. Meshel (1979); Dever (1999).

11 Cf. Cooke (1903), lines 17–18.

12 Cf. Aharoni (1981), 85, nos. 50, 52.

13 Cf. Avigad/Sass (1997), 59, no. 28.

14 Cf. Avigad/Sass (1997), 60, nos. 27, 29, 59.

the inscriptions in the early Israelite sanctuary at Kuntillet-Ajrud and their worship by the Israelites at that time.[15]

Another inscription was found in a tomb at Khirbet el-Qom near Hebron. The inscription says, "blessed will be Ariyahu to YHWH and his Asherah".[16] In the nearby site of Beit Loyah a Judean tomb inscription has been uncovered which mentions YHWH as the lord of Jerusalem and the mountains of Judah.

Now we must turn to another common and important archaeological find, that is the frequent appearance of cultic objects, unique to Judah, namely the hundreds of clay figurines which are divided into female and male types. The pagan cult in Judah, whether being of foreign origin (either Egyptian or Phoenician) or of national Judean origin, in the shape of the deities YHWH and Asherah (or Ashtart) is represented by quite a rich assemblage of finds, distributed over all the Judean settlements from Benjamin to Beersheba and mainly in Jerusalem. R. Kletter, who surveyd all these finds, sums up: "If we adopt the heartland of Judah concept (i.e. Judah within the borders described above), then 822 figurines (ca. 96%) were found within this area. This number is so high that there is only one possible conclusion: *these pottery figurines are Judean.*"[17]

In Judah, as in other kingdoms of Palestine, most of the figurines represent females, and they belong to the type known as 'pillar figurines'. This is the type with the molded heads that are similar to each other in their expression. They look somewhat stylized. The body usually is solid and handmade, in the shape of a small column, to which the exaggerated breasts supported by the goddesses' hands were added. This type of deity is usually identified with Ashtart, the fertility goddess.

Another popular type are the Ashtart figurines with 'pinched' heads, sometimes called 'bird head figurine' (see fig. 1).[18]

The *male figurines,* even though they are found by dozens in all sites of Judah which have been enumerated above, including Gibeon and Jerusalem (see figs. 2–3), are not well represented in the reports and in the academic literature.[19] With regard to the results and statistical data from the cults, practiced in the other parts of the country, namely from the Phoenicians, the Ammonites, the Edomites and the Philistines, it seems that among those nations the male deities also constitute an im-

15 Cf. Meshel (1979).

16 Cf. Dever (1969–1970; 1999); Zevit (1984); Shea (1990); Hadley (1994).

17 Kletter (1996); see also Amr (1988); Stern (1999; 2006).

18 Cf. Gilbert-Peretz (1996), Pl. 2.

19 Cf. Gilbert-Peretz (1996), Pl. 1.

portant part of the finds. In this respect, Judah also did not differ from its neighbors.

Fig. 1: Judean Astarte Pillar Figurines from Jerusalem

Fig. 2: A Judean Warrior Deity from Lachish

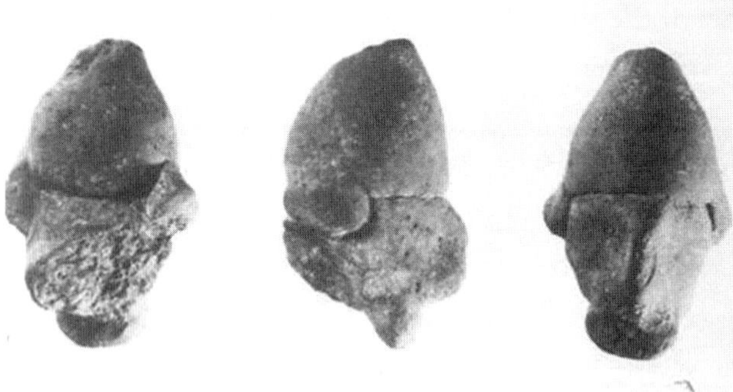

Fig. 3: Judean Head of a Male Deity
from Jerusalem

Which Judean deities are represented by these clay figurines? We may only guess. They might represent one of the foreign deities whose cult was also practiced in Jerusalem, perhaps that of the Phoenician god Ba'al. But, it is also possible, that they are pagan representations of the national Judean god, Yahweh and his consort Ashtart or Asherah, for all these figurines – as we have seen – are Judean and only Judean. The combination of the archaeological finds, namely the mention of the name 'YHWH' (and of his Asherah/Ashtart) in the ostraca and other Judean inscriptions of the period, and the fact that many clay figurines are only typical for Judah, brings us to the inevitable conclusion that a cult existed between the foreign pagan practices and the pure monotheism of Jerusalem, which may be called 'Yahwistic Paganism', common to all other Judean settlements.

From the archaeological point of view, we know almost nothing about the cult of the Babylonian period which lasted from the destruction of the first Temple in the year 586 down to 539 BCE. Here, I do not intend to deal with this period but I want to stress my conclusion that this period means a clear and objective vacuum. The Babylonians did not only destroy Judah but also the rest of the country. They exiled many nations, among them the Philistines who never returned, and many regions of the country were left completely devastated by them, including the previously prosperous sea coast.[20]

In the beginning of the Persian period, however, when the curtains are lifted again, the archaeological picture is completely different. Instead of a separate national pagan cult, unique to each of the individual nations of the country, new types of clay figurines appear which reflect a certain 'Koine'. This 'Koine' develops along the entire eastern coast of

20 Cf. Stern (2000).

the Mediterranean Sea. The new types of clay figurines, which now appear, are henceforth produced in two styles: (a) the Phoenician style that preserves eastern elements, and (b) the western Greek style that becomes increasingly dominant throughout pagan Palestine.

From now all the figurines are only found in areas outside the region settled by the returning Judean exiles – in Indumea, Philistia, Phoenicia and Galilee – that is, in those parts of the country which are still dominated by pagans. At the same time, in the areas of the country occupied by Jews, not a single cultic figurine has been found! This in spite of many excavations as well as surveys that have been conducted in Judah, and the same holds true for Samaria.[21] Also, archaeologists failed to locate any sanctuary for this period within Judah and Samaria while many have been found elsewhere. There are, of course, two exceptions, namely the Temple in Jerusalem and the huge complex of the Samaritan Temple uncovered on the top of the sacred mountain: the mountain of Gerizim being excavated in recent years by Y. Magen.[22] Now, the beginning of this complex has been established by hundreds of coins from the Persian period. The plan of this temple highly resembles that of the temple in Jerusalem as it is described by Ezekiel and it, in fact, was also called (according to the local inscriptions) by the Samaritans: "The House of YHWH".[23]

How can we explain the complete absence of sanctuaries and, even more significantly, the complete absence of these cultic figurines in areas of the Judeans (and the Samaritans)? Apparently, pagan cults ceased to exist among the Judeans, who purified their worship, and Jewish monotheism was at last consolidated. And from this newly established monotheism also sprang the Samaritans. In any case, it seems that this development occurred among the Babylonian exiles and was transferred to the land of Israel by the returning exiles such as Zerubbabel, son of Shealtiel, and Joshua, son of Jehozadak, who rebuilt the second Temple in Jerusalem, or by Ezra and Nehemiah. Certainly not by the local Jews or the Jews from Egypt, for in Egypt the situation was different. From biblical sources we know that there was an Egyptian Diaspora even before the Babylonian destruction of 586 BCE. In Egypt, unlike in Babylon, the Jews continued their pagan customs and even built their own temple and adopted Egyptian and Canaanite names, as we know from papyri found on the island of Elephantine.

21 Cf. Stern (1989).

22 Cf. Magen (2008).

23 Cf. Meshorer/Qedar (1999); Magen/Misgav/Tsfania (2004), 254, no. 383, Pl. 3; Magen (2008), 194–199, Pls. 7–9.

To sum up: the change from many gods to one god in Judah was established by the Jews in Babylon, and from there it was brought back to Judah.

Bibliography

Aharoni, Y. (1981), Arad Inscriptions, Judean Desert Studies, Jerusalem.

Amr, A.-J. (1988), Ten Human Clay Figurines from Jerusalem, Levant 20, 185–196.

Avigad, N./Sass, B. (1997), Corpus of West Semitic Seals, Publications of the Israel Academy of Sciences and Humanities, Section of Humanities, Jerusalem.

Beit-Arieh, I. (1995), Horvat Qitmit: An Edomite Shrine in the Biblical Negev, Monograph Series of the Sonia and Marco Nadler Institute of Archaeology Monograph – MSSMNIA 11, Tel Aviv.

Cooke, G.A. (1903), A Text Book of North-Semitic Inscriptions: Moabite, Hebrew, Phoenician, Aramaic Nabataean, Palmyrene, Jewish, Oxford.

Daviau, P.M.M./Dion, P.-E. (2002), Moab Comes to Life, BArR 28/1, 38–43, 46–49.

Dever, W.G. (1969–1970), Iron Age Epigraphic Material from the Area of Khirbet El-Kom, HUCA 40–41, 139–204.

– (1999), Archaeology and the Ancient Israelite Cult: How the Kh. el-Qôm and the Kuntillet 'Ajrûd "Ashera" Texts have Changed the Picture, in: B.A. Levine et al. (eds.), Frank Moore Cross Volume, ErIs 26, Jerusalem, 9*–15*.

Gilbert-Peretz, D. (1996), Ceramic Figurines, in: D.T. Ariel/A. De Groot (eds.), Excavations at the City of David 1978–1985, Vol. IV, Qedem 35, 29–134, Jerusalem.

Hadley, J.M. (1987), The Khirbet el-Qom Inscription, VT 37, 50–62.

– (1994), Yahweh and "His Asherah": Archeological and Textual Evidence for the Cult of the Goddess, in: W. Dietrich/M.A. Klopfenstein (eds.), Ein Gott allein? JHWH-Verehrung und biblischer Monotheismus im Kontext der israelitischen und altorientalischen Religionsgeschichte, 13. Kolloquium der Schweizerischen Akademie der Geistes- und Sozialwissenschaften, im Januar 1993 in Bern, OBO 139, Freiburg (Schweiz)/Göttingen, 235–268.

Kletter, R. (1996), The Judean Pillar-Figurines and the Archaeology of Asherah, British Archaeological Reports International Series – BARIS 636, Oxford.

Magen, Y./Misgav, H./Tsfania, L. (2004), Mount Gerizim Excavation, Vol I: The Aramaic, Hebrew and Samaritan Inscriptions, Judea and Samaria Publications 2, Jerusalem.
– (2008), Mount Gerizim Excavation, Vol. II: A Temple City, Jerusalem.
Meshel, Z. (1979), Did YHWH Have a Consort? The New Religious Inscriptions from the Sinai, BArR 5, 24–35.
Meshorer, Y./Qedar, S.H. (1999), Samarian Coinage, Numismatic Studies and Researches 9, Jerusalem.
Naveh, G. (1963), Old Hebrew Inscriptions in a Burial Cave, IEJ 13, 74–92.
Shea, W.H. (1990), The Khirbet el-Kom Inscription, VT 40, 50–63.
Stern, E. (1989), What Happened to the Cult Figurines?, BArR 15, 22–29, 53–54.
– (1999), Religion in Palestine in the Assyrian and Persian Period, in: B. Becking/C.A. Korpel (eds.), The Crisis of Israelite Religion: Transformation of Religious Tradition in Exilic and Post-Exilic Times, OTS 42, Leiden.
– (2000), The Babylonian Gap, BArR 26/6, 45–51, 76.
– (2001), Archaeology of the Land of the Bible: The Assyrian, Babylonian and Persian Periods, 732–332 BCE, Vol. 2, The Anchor Bible Reference Library, New York.
– (2006), The Religious Revolution in Persian Period Judah, in: O. Lipschits/M. Oeming (eds.), Judah and the Judeans in the Persian Period, Conference, "Judah and the Judeans in the Achaemenid Period", that took place in Heidelberg on 15–18 July, 2003, Winona Lake/Indiana, 199–205.
Ussishkin, D. (1982), The Conquest of Lachish by Sennacherib, Publications of the Institute of Archaeology 6, Tel Aviv.
Zevit, Z. (1984), The Khirbet el-Qôm Inscription Mentioning a Goddess, BASOR 255, 39–48.

Monotheism and Angelology in Daniel

MICHAEL SEGAL

The Book of Daniel, which reached its final form in the 2nd century BCE, lies on the boundary between biblical and postbiblical literature. It is the latest book included in the Hebrew Bible, and perhaps for that reason, contains numerous ideas and beliefs that differ fundamentally from earlier biblical notions. As it is well known, the book can be divided into two parts based upon literary genre, with the first six chapters presenting stories about Daniel and his companions, and the final six chapters containing four apocalyptic visions. Each part has its own compositional history, and each presents unique challenges in the analysis of these theological issues. This article addresses two topics in Daniel, monotheism and angelology, which taken together, form a coherent whole. It will attempt to show that the study of these fundamental notions in Daniel can be best appreciated through an awareness of the textual and literary development of the book. Only by means of an integrative approach which takes these processes into account, one can arrive at an accurate description of these fundamental theological notions throughout Daniel.

Since the book is comprised of materials of varying genres and origins, it is necessary to analyze each on its own merits. Different sections of the book perhaps reflect different approaches and ideas. Only after investigating each section it is possible to assess their independent significance, and the interrelationships within the larger context of the Book of Daniel.

Doxologies

In the first half of the book a number of passages put doxologies or theological proclamations regarding the supremacy of the Israelite God into the mouths of the foreign kings Nebuchadnezzar and Darius (Dan.

2:47; 3:28–29, 31–33; 4:31–32; 6:27–28).[1] In these cases, one has to keep in mind that these are literary texts, and hence, the words placed in the mouths of these characters are often intended for literary or rhetorical purposes, and are not intended to be nuanced theological assertions. In almost all instances, they merely declare that the God of Daniel and his companions is superior to their own, but do not address the theological implications of such statements. Thus for example, in Dan. 2:47:

> עָנֵה מַלְכָּא לְדָנִיֵּאל וְאָמַר מִן-קְשֹׁט דִּי אֱלָהֲכוֹן הוּא אֱלָהּ אֱלָהִין וּמָרֵא מַלְכִין וְגָלֵה רָזִין דִּי יְכֵלְתָּ לְמִגְלֵא רָזָא דְנָה.
>
> The king said to Daniel, "Truly, *your God is God of gods and Lord of kings, and a revealer of mysteries,* for you have been able to reveal this mystery."

The statement in the MT does not discount the existence of other gods. In fact, Daniel's god is referred to as the God of gods, which could be understood as standing at the head of a pantheon of others.[2] However, the pronouncements from the mouths of the gentile kings were primarily intended to emphasize Daniel's success *vis-à-vis* the non-Jews in the story. The context of Daniel 2, in which Daniel successfully competes against the Babylonian magicians and sorcerers, and both reveals and interprets Nebuchadnezzar's dream, lends itself to such a conclusion. The clear relationship to the story is expressed in the reference to Daniel's god as a "revealer of mysteries". This description is most appropriate in this case where He did indeed bring to light knowledge that was unattainable through earthly means. While this verse in its original form did not express a coherent cosmological worldview, the translator of the Old Greek version either interpreted it that way, or was concerned that it could be by others, and therefore offered a small correction to Nebuchadnezzar's description of Daniel's god.

> And the king cried out to Daniel and said, "It is certain; your God is God of gods [and Lord of lords][3] and Lord of kings who alone brings to light hidden mysteries (ὁ ἐκφαίνων μυστήρια κρυπτὰ μόνος), because you have been able to disclose this mystery!" (Dan. 2:47 OG)

1 According to Kratz (1991), 156–160, these hymnic passages are an essential aspect of the redactional process by which the stories were combined into a theologically coherent collection in the first half of the Book of Daniel.

2 At the same time, one could argue that the possibility of other gods is not even indicated by that epithet, since it appears elsewhere, including Deut. 10:17; Ps. 136:2–3, which do not seem to hint at that meaning. However, in light of the competition motif throughout the chapter, it seems to be plausible that it is indeed intended to compare Daniel's God to Nebuchadnezzar's.

3 According to the reading of Pap. 967; Syh and MS 88 omit this phrase. Cf. my discussion in Segal (2009), 130–132.

He is no longer "*a* revealer of mysteries", but he "*alone*" is the "revealer of hidden mysteries". This sort of theological correction is well attested in the history of textual transmission of biblical texts.

Another more complex example from the first half of the book, in which literary considerations perhaps outweigh theological concerns, can be found in Daniel's prayer in Dan. 2:20–23:[4]

> [20] Daniel spoke up and said: "Let the name of God be blessed forever and ever, for wisdom and power are His. [21] He changes seasons and times, removes kings and installs kings; he gives the wise their wisdom and knowledge to those who know. [22] He reveals deep and hidden things; knows what is in the darkness, and light dwells with Him. [23] I acknowledge and praise You, O God of my fathers, you who have given me wisdom and power, for now You have let me know what we asked of You; You have let us know what concerns the king."

In this prayer, which can be shown to be part of a secondary addition to Daniel 2, Daniel praises the "Most High" (OG; "God of Heaven" in MT) for revealing the mystery of Nebuchadnezzar's request. Of further significance for the current discussion are the praises of God that do not directly relate to the surrounding story. These refer to His involvement in the world and its history, including His establishment of and control over the seasons and time, as well as His enthronement and deposing of monarchs. However, here too, I would suggest that these descriptions are not necessarily intended to paint a comprehensive cosmological portrait of the place of God in the world, but they were rather added in order to serve as a contrast between God and the brazen, blasphemous King Antiochus IV, who is accused in Dan. 7:24–25 of changing times and laws, and of usurping the throne from his predecessors, based upon the following parallels (or contrasts). The description of God's ability to instate and remove kings (v. 21aβ) stands in opposition to the portrayal of Antiochus in Dan. 7:24, causing the downfall of the three kings before him.

4 For a more detailed analysis of this passage, cf. Segal (2009), 145–149.

God – 2:21	Antiochus – 7:24, 26
מהעדה מלכין ומהקים מלכין ...	ותלתא מלכין יהשפל ... ושלטנה יהעדון
Removes kings and installs kings [...]	He will bring about the downfall of three kings [...] and his dominion will be taken away

While Dan. 7:24 describes the perceived political perspective, the author of the prayer stresses that the rise and fall of kings is the result of one cause alone, God's intervention in the workings of the world:

Dan. 2:21aα presents another interesting contrast between Antiochus and the actions of God, as can be seen by aligning the two descriptions:

God – 2:21	Antiochus – 7:25
והוא מהשנא עדניא וזמניא	ויסבר להשניה זמנין ודת
And He changes seasons and times	He will think to change times and law

While these verses each refer to very different notions, they both use the same verb שני in the *aphel* conjugation ("change") and a compound direct object, one of which is the plural of זמן ("time"). While Antiochus will plan to change the laws and calendar but will ultimately fail, God has the ability to bring about actual change in the passage of time and seasons. The power of Antiochus in the vision in Daniel 7 is thus contrasted with the true sovereign in the world – God is the one who installs and removes kings, and he is the one who establishes the world order. Dan. 2:21 thus serves a *foreshadowing foil* to Dan. 7:24–25. When viewed in this way, it is more difficult to extrapolate developed theological notions from this passage.

The Apocalyptic Section

In contrast to the doxologies, in the apocalyptic section of the book there appears to be a more clearly defined cosmological perspective. One of the prominent characteristics of these passages is the interpretation of Daniel's visions by an angelic intermediary, a primary feature of apocalyptic literature (Dan. 7:16ff., 23ff.; 8:15ff.; 9:21ff.; 10–12).[5] More interesting are passages that ascribe a salvific role to the angels, who intervene on behalf of individuals or the Israelites/Jewish people. For

5 This interpretive role is found in other prophetic books of the Second Temple period, such as in Zechariah 1–6.

example, within the same apocalyptic section, Daniel 10 records a vision in which Daniel alone sees:

> " [...] a man dressed in linen, his loins girt in gold of Uphaz; his body was like beryl, his face had the appearance of lightning, his eyes were like flashing torches, his arms and legs had the color of burnished bronze, and the sound of his speech was like the noise of a multitude." (Dan. 10:5–6)

Subsequent to this vision, the human-like angelic being informs Daniel that he and Michael, the prince of Israel, were battling on behalf of Israel against the princes of Persia and Greece (Dan. 10:13, 20). The entire scenario of angels fighting on behalf of nations exists in a parallel and unseen heavenly reality that does not pose a clear and present danger to the common observer. At the same time, the threat is real, and the efforts of the heavenly princes cannot be overestimated. This passage is often cited as reflecting a similar theological conception to that found in Deut. 32:8–9 (according to the original reading as preserved in LXX and 4QDeut[j]); Sir 17:17 and Jub. 15:30–32. However, while Daniel 10 shares with these compositions the belief that each nation in the world has a divine representative in heaven, the other works posit that the Lord himself rules over and protects the Israelites directly, without any intervention by other divine beings. In contrast, Daniel 10 has at least two divine intermediaries, Michael and Gabriel (according to the identification of the speaker in Dan. 11:1), with the former referred to as "your prince" in Dan. 10:21, and the "great prince" in Dan. 12:1. This difference perhaps suggests a less particularistic perspective in Daniel, since although they do seem to have highly regarded divine representatives on their side, there does not seem to be a suggestion of exclusive, direct divine favor for Israel from the head of the pantheon.[6]

Daniel 10:20–11:1

This scheme appears to lie at the root of the frame of the fourth apocalypse in Daniel 10 and 12, enveloping the apocalypse itself in Daniel 11. However, I would like to analyze a difficulty that appears in the text of Dan. 10:20–21, the central description of the national, divine representa-

6 For a discussion of the biblical theological background of this passage, cf. e.g. Hartman/Di Lella (1978), 273; Collins (1993), 374–375. It is perhaps more similar to the perspective reflected in the contemporaneous Book of Jubilees, which in Jub. 15:30–32 seems to reflect a position similar to Deuteronomy 32, but at the same time emphasizes the mediating role of the 'Angel of Presence' throughout the book.

tives. This difficulty has already been noted by interpreters of the text.[7] Dan. 10:20–11:1 read as follows:

A	Then he said: Do you know why I have come to you?	10:20 וַיֹּאמֶר הֲיָדַעְתָּ לָמָּה־בָּאתִי אֵלֶיךָ	A
B	Now I must go back to fight the prince of Persia. When I go off, the prince of Greece will come in.	וְעַתָּה אָשׁוּב לְהִלָּחֵם עִם־שַׂר פָּרָס וַאֲנִי יוֹצֵא וְהִנֵּה שַׂר־יָוָן בָּא.	B
C	However/Indeed, I will tell you what is recorded in the book of truth.	10:21 אֲבָל אַגִּיד לְךָ אֶת־הָרָשׁוּם בִּכְתָב אֱמֶת	C
D	No one is helping me against them except your prince, Michael.	וְאֵין אֶחָד מִתְחַזֵּק עִמִּי עַל־אֵלֶּה כִּי אִם־מִיכָאֵל שַׂרְכֶם.	D
E	In the first year of Darius the Mede, I took my stand (4QDan[c] עמדתי) to strengthen and fortify him.	11:1 וַאֲנִי בִּשְׁנַת אַחַת לְדָרְיָוֶשׁ הַמָּדִי עָמְדִי לְמַחֲזִיק וּלְמָעוֹז לוֹ.	E

Dan. 10:20 opens with a question from an angelic being (presumably to be identified with Gabriel according to the date presented in MT of 11:1) – "Do you know why I have come to you?" (line A). The answer to this question does not follow immediately, but is rather found in line C, "(Indeed)[8] I will tell you what is recorded in the book of truth." This is clearly the ultimate purpose of the angelic intermediary's visit, as can be demonstrated by the opening of the apocalypse itself in Dan. 11:2 –

7 Cf. esp. Montgomery (1927), 416–418, who suggests a similar direction to that suggested here.

8 Here, the word אֲבָל is generally translated by modern lexicons, commentators and translations as "but, however". This is based upon a general distinction between the meanings of the word in classical and late biblical Hebrew, with either asseverative ("indeed") or adversative ("but") force respectively; cf. e.g. BDB, s.v. אֲבָל, 6; HALOT, s.v. אֲבָל, 7), who list Gen. 42:21; 2 Sam. 14:5; 1 Kings 1:43 (HALOT offers more than one option for the meaning of this instance); 2 Kings 4:14 as examples of the first meaning (both classify Gen. 17:19 as possibly reflecting both meanings), while Daniel is placed in the latter category. In fact, a clear example of adversative אבל can be found in v. 7. However, I would suggest that this meaning is not appropriate for the context of v. 21, which does not seem to indicate a contrast to the previous statement. This was recognized by the Old Greek translation, καὶ μάλα, "and indeed, certainly", which corresponds to the LXX translations of 2 Sam. 14:5; 1 Kings 1:43; 2 Kings 4:14 (these are the only four instances in which this Greek word has a Hebrew equivalent according to the Hatch-Redpath concordance). In Gen. 42:21, the LXX translator used a different Greek word, but with the same affirmative meaning, ναί (see also LXX Gen. 17:19). As this example demonstrates, late biblical texts can employ both classical and late language.

ועתה אמת אגיד לך, "And now I will tell you the truth", since Daniel 10 serves as the introduction to the apocalypse in Daniel 11, which reflects this "truth" (cf. also Dan. 10:1 – ... ואמת הדבר). In between the question and the answer, we find the often-quoted reference to the heavenly battle with the "princes" of Persia and Greece, which interrupts the flow between question and answer. Moreover, if we search for the natural continuation of sentence B, it is found in sentence D – "(B) Now I must go back to fight the prince of Persia. When I go off, the prince of Greece will come in. (D) No one is helping me against them except your prince, Michael." In light of this discontinuity, for example, Marti suggested that clause C is actually a doublet of Dan. 11:2a, and therefore removed it from in between B and D, allowing for the natural continuous progression between them.[9] In less radical textual operations, Charles inverted clauses B and C (unifying A with C, and B with D),[10] while the New Jewish Publication Society translation rearranged clauses C and D, uniting B and D as a sensible progression (but distancing A from C).[11] However, all of these scholarly rearrangements point to the complexity of the issue.

I would suggest that the problematic order in vv. 20–21 is the result of the textual growth of the chapter. Specifically, I suggest that the clauses B and D (and E), those that are significant for the discussion here, interrupt the natural flow of the chapter, which is intended to introduce the final apocalypse of the book. In fact, if one skips over vv. 20aβ–b and 21b, then the chapter reads smoothly as a classic introduction to an apocalyptic revelation.

10:20aα	Then he said: Do you know why I have come to you?
10:21a	Indeed (אבל), I will tell you what is recorded in the book of truth.
11:2	And now I will tell you the truth: Persia will have three more kings [...]

While Marti and others viewed Dan. 10:21a and 11:2a as a doublet, and therefore essentially removed 10:21a from the passage, it seems best to interpret them as an example of resumptive repetition. This technique serves to highlight the material that falls between the two clauses as a secondary addition (in essence, the completely opposite claim of development of Marti's suggestion that the doublet itself is the addition).[12] In this instance, when the clauses about the divine emissaries were

9 Cf. Marti (1901), 77; similarly rearranged by Hartman/Di Lella (1978), 256, esp. n. i.

10 Cf. Charles (1929), 265.

11 Cf. NJPS, ad loc., n. c–c: "Order of verses inverted for clarity".

12 The use of resumptive repetition to enable the integration of secondary passages has been noted frequently in biblical scholarship; cf. esp. the insightful study of Seeligmann (1962), 314–324.

added to the introduction to this apocalypse, they were woven into an existing text, and the stitches of these threads are still visible.[13]

Daniel 10:12–14

The suggestion that clauses B and D are an addition also calls for a reexamination of v. 13, which refers to the same cast of characters: the prince of Persia, Michael, and the angelic narrator: "The prince of the Persian kingdom opposed me for twenty-one days; now Michael, a prince of the first rank, has come to my aid, after I was detained there with the kings of Persia." Within the immediate context of the surrounding material, this verse appears to serve a specific function. According to Dan. 10:2–3, Daniel "mourned" for three weeks before receiving a revelation. The purpose of these mourning rituals was most likely to catch the attention of God and prepare himself for the subsequent divine revelation, and not as mourning over the destruction of the Temple.[14]

In v. 12, following these mourning rituals, the angel informed Daniel, "Have no fear, Daniel, for from *the first day* that you set your mind to get understanding, practicing abstinence before your God, your prayers were heard, and I have come because of your prayer." The alert reader will read v. 12 and wonder immediately – if Daniel's prayers were already heard at the beginning of the 21 days, then why was he made to suffer for the remainder of the period? In v. 13, the angel attempts to explain this delay: during the entire three-week period, he was locked in a heavenly battle with the prince of Persia, and therefore could not get away to respond to these prayers. This parenthetical explanation is enclosed by a *Wiederaufnahme*, since v. 12 ends with ואני באתי בדבריך and v. 14 opens with ובאתי להבינך. Similar to the argument made above, the natural continuation of v. 12 is in v. 14, in

13 The difficult order has been noted by Goldingay (1989), 292, who describes the structure as "an a-b-a-b-a arrangement". Interestingly, he also notes the similarity to vv. 12–14, which he refers to as an "a-b-a" arrangement (see my discussion in the next section). What he takes as a literary or poetic device is described as related to the textual growth of the chapter here. Whether it be original to the text (as suggested by Goldingay) or secondary (as proposed here), the net result is the same: "the effect is to tie the delivering of the earthly message and the reality of the heavenly conflicts closer together." (ibid.)

14 For the use of mourning rituals in preparation for the reception of divine revelation, see esp. 4 Ezra 5:13; 9:24–25; 2 Bar. 9:1–10:1; 12:5–13:1; 20:5–6; cf. Charles (1929), 255; Collins (1993), 372. For a more complex perspective on the purpose and meaning of fasting rituals in the Bible, cf. Lambert (2003), 490–491.

which the purpose of the angel's visit is specifically expressed: "So I have come to make you understand what is to befall your people in the days to come [...]".

Returning to the question of the three weeks of mourning in vv. 2–3, I would like to propose that this motif was originally unrelated to the angel's 'reaction time', since it can be found in a related apocalyptic text in the same context of rituals that attract the attention of God. In 4 Ezra, the same three-week period of mourning rituals is used by the pseudonymous author in order to arouse divine interest. Note especially 4 Ezra 6:35: "And it came to pass after this I wept again and fasted seven days as before, in order to complete the three weeks as I had been told"[15] (cf. also 4 Ezra 5:13; 5:20; 6:31).[16] I suggest that only after this extant motif of three weeks was compared to the "first day" of v. 12 it raised an exegetical issue for a later scribe. Therefore, v. 13 was added, presumably by the same author as the additional clauses in the latter part of the chapter, since they share both expressions and ideas, in order to solve this very same problem. In this case, the use of resumptive repetition hints to this process.

Daniel 12:1

One final argument needs to be made in order to complete this proposed textual development of the frame of the final apocalypse in Daniel 10–12. At the end of the apocalypse, we hear once again of the prince Michael:

---

15 The text according to the translation of Stone (1990), 176.

16 Most commentators have suggested that this three-week period in 4 Ezra is based upon the period in Daniel 10, and we would, therefore, not be able to use the later passage as independent evidence for this phenomenon. However, there does not seem to be any direct influence of Daniel 10 in the text (other than the three-week total). Many scholars have noted the discrepancy between this three-week total "that I had been told", and the record of only two seven-day periods prior to this in the book. The most plausible suggestion to solve this discrepancy is to assume that an additional such period originally preceded the first vision at the beginning of chap. 3 thus bringing the sum total to 21 days (cf. Stone [1990], 176). It is unclear at what stage in the transmission or literary development of the book this omission transpired. As noted by Stone (1990), 373f., if one includes this missing seven-day period, then Ezra abstained from food and drink (to some degree) for a sum total of 40 days, creating a parallel between him and Moses. This parallel to Moses does not negate the parallel to Daniel's fast, but it does suggest that Daniel was not necessarily the source for the length of Ezra's fast as generally assumed. On the theme of Ezra as a second Moses in 4 Ezra, cf. Stone (1990), 301–302, 373–374, 410–414.

(11:45 וְיִטַּע אָהֳלֵי אַפַּדְנוֹ בֵּין יַמִּים לְהַר־צְבִי־קֹדֶשׁ)
A וּבָא עַד־קִצּוֹ וְאֵין עוֹזֵר לוֹ.
B 12:1 וּבָעֵת הַהִיא יַעֲמֹד מִיכָאֵל הַשַּׂר הַגָּדוֹל הָעֹמֵד עַל־בְּנֵי עַמֶּךָ וְהָיְתָה עֵת
צָרָה אֲשֶׁר לֹא־נִהְיְתָה מִהְיוֹת גּוֹי עַד הָעֵת הַהִיא
C וּבָעֵת הַהִיא יִמָּלֵט עַמְּךָ כָּל־הַנִּמְצָא כָּתוּב בַּסֵּפֶר.
(12:2 וְרַבִּים מִיְּשֵׁנֵי אַדְמַת־עָפָר יָקִיצוּ אֵלֶּה לְחַיֵּי עוֹלָם וְאֵלֶּה לַחֲרָפוֹת לְדִרְאוֹן עוֹלָם.)

(11:45 – He will pitch his royal pavilion between the sea and the beautiful holy mountain,)

A and he will meet his doom with no one to help him.

B 12:1 At that time, the great prince, Michael, who stands beside the sons of your people, will appear/arise. It will be a time of trouble, the like of which has never been since the nation came into being until that time.[17]

C At that time, your people will be rescued, all who are found inscribed in the book.

(12:2 Many of those that sleep in the dust of the earth will awake, some to eternal life, others to reproaches, to everlasting abhorrence.)

Dan. 11:40–45 are almost unanimously accepted by scholars as the turning point in the historicity of the apocalypse, since from v. 40 onwards, the events described contradict external data describing the final days of Antiochus' life. The events detailed in these verses relate to the further military exploits of the King of the North, at this point in the historical apocalypse referring to Antiochus IV. This description culminates in v. 45, in which he sets up his royal pavilion near הר צבי קודש, an apparent reference to the Temple Mount. Let us examine the order of the clauses at this juncture in the text once again. The erecting of the pavilion opposite the holiest of shrines is intended to indicate the seriousness of the assault on Israel. It is exactly at this peak of tension in the series of events that the apocalypse informs the reader that Antiochus will meet his doom and be left without any assistance. This verse predicts his demise, and in doing so, asserts that the threat posed to Israel will disappear. It is, therefore, surprising when one continues to read in Dan. 12:1 that at that point Michael will arise, and there will be a time of trouble such as never happened from the dawn of Israel's existence (clause B). Only one verse earlier, the reader was informed that the threat to Israel had been removed! Furthermore, while Michael has presumably come to save Israel, it is not clear at this juncture, and

17 Note that these final words are not represented in the NJPS translation.

subsequently, how he performs this role.[18] The salvation of Israel is actually described in clause C, and there it is not described as the work of Michael, but rather using a passive *niphal* form of the root מלט ("to be rescued"). Finally, note that both clauses B and C open in an identical fashion, בעת ההיא, "at that time" (and similarly the end of clause B). The reference to a specific time appears to refer to the עת קץ ("the time of the end") in Dan. 11:40, according to which Israel was in danger of being destroyed (vv. 40–45).[19] The repetition of the expression בעת ההיא has generally been understood as an indication that all of the events took place at the very same point in time. However, I would suggest that here too, similar to the previous two passages, the placement of the clause about Michael's appearance, and the difficulties it creates in the sequence of events, particularly the note that this point in time, following Antiochus' death, was more troubling than any other in the history of the Israelite nation, hints to its secondary status in this context. The conclusion of the apocalypse originally culminated in a description of the demise of Antiochus (clause A), and was immediately followed by the salvation of those recorded as righteous in the book (clause C), and these two events reflect the two aspects of Israel's deliverance from this foreign dictator.

The repeated use of בעת ההיא at the beginning of both clauses B and C seems to point to this process of this development. The original בעת ההיא was found at the beginning of clause C, and referred to the same point in time as the end of clause A – when Antiochus was no longer a clear and present danger for Israel, the righteous individuals recorded in the book will be saved. When the sentence about Michael was added, it was the scribe's intention to assert that he arrived on the scene at that very same moment of impending disaster, and thus he did so using the same phrase בעת ההיא, the same technique of resumptive repetition noted above. In this instance, the marking of the additional passage through this scribal-literary technique is even more pronounced due to

18 Collins (1993), 390, notes that "Michael's exact role in Dan. 12:1 is not specified", but suggests that he acts "as judicial advocate or executor of the judgment or both", based upon the use of the verb from the root עמד. However, this verb is too common in Biblical Hebrew for the purpose of determining its precise meaning, and should be understood with the general meaning "arise, appear". Montgomery (1927), 472, suggests that the verb עמד here connotes protection as in the English idiom "stand by" or "stand over" (citing the example of Esth. 8:11; 9:16). Although he is probably correct about the general meaning of the verse in Daniel, based upon the general context, it does not appear to be the meaning of the verb itself, which indicates Michael's arrival at this stage.

19 As noted e.g. by Goldingay (1989), 305–306; Collins (1993), 390; HaCohen/Kil (1994), 294*.

the bracketing of clause B in its entirety with the expression ב/העת ההיא at its beginning and end. These considerations support the suggestion that a later scribe was responsible for the addition of clause B – perhaps the same scribe who added Michael to Daniel 10 sought to do the same here, but this addition left its traces. However, as in other examples of interpolations into the biblical text, it was inserted in the wrong place, at the beginning of v. 1, after the suspense of the moment had already passed.[20]

Influence of the Apocalypses upon Each Other

If the analysis presented until now is correct, then it has fundamental implications for the description of angelology and monotheism in Daniel. The notion of national, heavenly princes fighting on behalf of each of the peoples of the world, including Israel, Persia and Greece, finds no parallel in Daniel outside of Daniel 10–12, and as just suggested, perhaps they also did not include this notion either in their earliest form.[21] Why, then, was it added to the frame of the final apocalypse?

Daniel 7

The passage in Daniel most frequently discussed with respect to the issue of monotheism is found in Daniel 7, the vision of the four beasts. In that passage, Daniel describes a judgment scene in which the final beast (representing Greece) was punished for its behavior. The portrayal of the judgment scene and the role of each of the characters are of interest to the present discussion:

> [9] "As I looked, thrones were placed and one that was ancient of days took his seat; his raiment was white as snow, and the hair of his head like pure wool; his throne was fiery flames, its wheels were burning fire. [10] A stream

20 In contrast to the interpretation of the evidence proposed here, the alternative is to suggest that the oscillation between the heavenly and earthly realms in each of these passages is a stylistic-rhetorical device in order to indicate the simultaneity of these two planes of existence (cf. e.g. Collins [1973], 55–58, and n. 13 above). While this approach is perhaps convincing in the analysis of 10:12–14, the difficulties in sequence that this technique created in 10:20–11:2 and in 11:45–12:1 support the option of textual development in these passages.

21 It is interesting that these divine princes do not play any role in the apocalypse itself in Daniel 11, perhaps an additional indication that they are not an original element of the vision.

of fire issued and came forth from before him; a thousand thousands served him, and ten thousand times ten thousand stood before him; the court sat in judgment, and the books were opened [...]"
13 "I saw in the night visions, and behold, with the clouds of heaven there came one like a son of man, and he came to the Ancient of Days and was presented before him. 14 And to him was given dominion and glory and kingdom, that all peoples, nations, and languages should serve him; his dominion is an everlasting dominion, which shall not pass away, and his kingdom one that shall not be destroyed." (Dan. 7:9f., 13f.)

The major issue of interpretation in this passage relates to the relationship between the Ancient of Days, who sits in judgment with myriads serving him, and the one "like the son of man", presented before him, who receives everlasting dominion and glory, and whom will be served by all nations and peoples.[22] This chapter creates a picture of a head God, the Ancient of Days, with a subordinate divine figure, who arrives with the clouds of heaven, in addition to the thousands serving before the former in the heavenly court. Of course scholars have compared this to the Canaanite pantheon, relating Daniel 7 to the images of ʾEl and Baʿal in Ugaritic texts, and the hierarchical relationship reflected in those works.[23] Based upon the continuation of the chapter, the one "like the son of man" is a heavenly representative of the "people of the holy ones of the Most High" (vv. 18, 27), who receive an everlasting kingdom and dominion (vv. 14, 18, 22, 27), after the destruction of the previous four kingdoms. In the context of the vision, and of the book as a whole, this promise for an eternal kingdom is made to Israel, and therefore "one like a son of man" acts as Israel's representative.[24] If so, it would appear that there is some relationship between the depiction of the "one like the son of man" in Daniel 7, and the prince of Israel, Michael, depicted in Daniel 10 and 12, who acts as a heavenly representative of Israel, parallel in his position to the princes of Persia and Greece. In fact, numerous commentators have equated the two figures.[25] However, if one accepts the analysis proposed above, that these references to princes for each of the nations were secondarily added to Daniel 10 and 12, perhaps then we can offer now a plausible explanation for the origins of these additions – they were added based upon

22 This question has been discussed extensively by scholars, and it is beyond the scope of this discussion to review all of their suggested interpretations. For an extensive survey of opinions, with important analysis, cf. the excursus on "One Like a Human Being" in Collins (1993), 304–310.

23 Cf. the seminal discussion of Emerton (1958).

24 This point has been emphasized extensively by Collins: cf. Collins (1973), 61–66; id. (1977), 99–101; id. (1993), 304–322.

25 Cf. e.g. the many studies quoted by Collins (1993) 310, nn. 288–291; Goldingay (1989), 172 (and the literature quoted there); HaCohen/Kil (1994), 176*.

the theological and cosmological worldview expressed in Daniel 7. The Lord renders judgment on the nations of the world, including Israel. Each of these nations is depicted by a supernatural being, and in the case of Israel, by a divine entity second in rank only to God himself.

Daniel 8

While the theological underpinnings of the national princes are found in the vision in Daniel 7, the language of these additions is based upon the vision in Daniel 8. Specifically, the word שר in reference to heavenly beings is found twice in that chapter (vv. 11, 25). Furthermore, the chapter refers explicitly to the kings of Persia and Greece (vv. 20–21). In Dan. 8:11, the small horn, representing Antiochus IV, vaunts itself against the heavenly "Prince of the Host", ועד שר הצבא הגדיל, while in v. 25, it is similarly told that he will rise up against the "prince of princes", ועל שר שרים יעמד. These epithets refer to the same divine character whom is assaulted by Antiochus, and commentators have debated his identity. Two primary possibilities suggest themselves – either שר שרים is God himself, the preferred option of the medieval Jewish exegete Rashi and most modern commentators (which I also take as correct),[26] or as suggested by the medieval exegete Abraham Ibn Ezra, שר שרים in chap. 8 is identical with השר הגדול, the great prince Michael, in Daniel 12.[27] A primary argument for this latter option is the presence of the common construction in which a substantive in construct state is placed before the plural of the same word (שר שרים), generally used to express the superlative.[28] The adjective הגדול found in Dan. 12:1 often serves the same function in Biblical Hebrew.[29] The equivalence of שר שרים and השר הגדול is further bolstered by the use of the epithet שר הצבא in v. 11, reminiscent of the term used for the divine emissary who appeared before Joshua with a drawn sword, שר צבא ה' "the prince of the Lord's Host" (Josh. 5:14–15). I suggest that the scribe responsible for the addition of the heavenly princes in Daniel 10 and 12 also understood the שר שרים in Daniel 8 in this fashion, and not as God himself, allowing for the use of this term to describe the heavenly representatives of each of the nations in the interpolations into Daniel 10 and 12. This would be an instance in which this later scribe has inter-

26 Cf. e.g., Montgomery (1927), 351; Hartman/Di Lella (1978), 236; Goldingay (1989), 210–211, 218; Collins (1993), 333, 341; HaCohen/Kil (1994), 209*–210*.

27 Cf. similarly Lacocque (1979), 172.

28 Cf. GKC §133i.

29 Cf. GKC §133g.

preted the apocalypse in Daniel 8, and has perhaps done so incorrectly, taking the terms referring to God himself as referring to his divine emissaries.[30]

Conclusion

While the presence of similar ideas in Daniel 7 and 8, and 10 and 12 could theoretically be used to argue for their common authorship, this study suggests that Daniel 7 and 8 influenced the scribe who added the verses to Daniel 10–12. The similarity in the theological worldview of these passages would, therefore, be the result of a secondary process in which the apocalypses were altered and updated in order to unify the perspective presented throughout the second half of the book.[31] In general, I suggest that more caution needs to be exercised before assuming an identical provenance of the four visions in the second half of the book.[32] Some of the similarities among them might be the result of a process of contamination, assimilation or homogenization of the various visions in order to align them more closely with one another. It is our role, however, to unravel this process in an attempt to identify the unique worldview presented in each passage, and thus perceive their particular perspective on fundamental issues of ideology and theology.

30 Alternatively, if ibn Ezra's reading of Daniel 8 is correct, then the scribe in Daniel 10 and 12 has also read and been influenced by that apocalypse and its original meaning and context.

31 A similar editorial process can be identified in the first half of the book as well, in which originally disparate stories have been combined together secondarily through various redactional techniques; cf. e.g. Kratz (1991), sections A and B; Collins (1993), 35–37, 242 passim; Segal (2009), nn. 8, 48, 52.

32 Such an approach in general has already been put forth by Ginsberg (1948), 29–38; Hartman/Di Lella (1978), 13–14.

Bibliography

Charles, R.H. (1929), A Critical and Exegetical Commentary on the Book of Daniel, Oxford.

Collins, J.J. (1973), The Son of Man and the Saints of the Most High in the Book of Daniel, JBL 94, 50–66.

– (1977), The Apocalyptic Vision of the Book of Daniel, HSM 16, Missoula.

– (1993), Daniel: A Commentary on the Book of Daniel, Hermeneia, Minneapolis.

Emerton, J.A. (1958), The Origin of the Son of Man Imagery, JTS 9, 225–242.

Ginsberg, H.L. (1948), Studies in Daniel, TSJTSA 14, New York.

Goldingay, J.E. (1989), Daniel, Word Biblical Commentary 30, Nashville.

HaCohen, S./Kil, Y. (1994), The Book of Daniel, Jerusalem (in Hebrew).

Hartman, L.F./Di Lella, A.A. (1978), The Book of Daniel: A New Translation with Introduction and Commentary, AncB 23, New York.

Kratz, R.G. (1991), Translatio imperii. Untersuchungen zu den aramäischen Danielerzählungen und ihrem theologiegeschichtlichen Umfeld, WMANT 63, Neukirchen-Vluyn.

Lacocque, A. (1979), The Book of Daniel, transl. by D. Pellauer, Atlanta.

Lambert, D. (2003), Fasting as a Penitential Rite: A Biblical Phenomenon?, HThR 96, 477–512.

Marti, K. (1901), Das Buch Daniel, KHC 18, Tübingen.

Montgomery, J.A. (1927), A Critical and Exegetical Commentary on the Book of Daniel, ICC, Edinburgh.

Seeligmann, I.L. (1962), Hebräische Erzählung und biblische Geschichtsschreibung, ThZ 18 (1962), 305–325; repr. in: id. (2004), Gesammelte Studien zur Hebräischen Bibel, ed. by E. Blum, FAT 41, Tübingen, 119–136.

Segal, M. (2009), From Joseph to Daniel: The Literary Development of Daniel 2, VT 59/1, 123–149.

Stone, M.E. (1990), Fourth Ezra: A Commentary on the Book of Fourth Ezra, Hermeneia, Minneapolis.

Justice, the King and the Gods: Polytheism and Emerging Monotheism in the Ancient World

CHRISTOPH AUFFARTH

1. Authority and Individual Responsibility: Monotheism and 'Remembered History' in the Current Debate

Along with the questioning of authorities in the revolution of May 1968, in the revolt of the angry younger generation against the generation which had been raised to trust in an authoritarian state, a dispute was launched about monotheism. Praise of polytheism as the way of life of a permissive society, as opposed to monotheism as typical of an authoritarian society, was expressed. Up to then (and one still hears this widely asserted) monotheism had been seen as a major achievement, which mankind had attained in the course of its evolution.[1] Since then, the dispute on the legitimacy and implications of monotheism gained force, not least in 1979 with the religious monotheistic revolution in Iran, and again with 9/11 and the 'war on terror'. Terrorism was portrayed as having its deeper roots in overdone monotheism in Islam – as was argued, e.g. in the Regensburg speech of pope Benedikt XVI.[2] Monotheism is, thus, accused of generating not only authoritarianism and intolerance, but also violence. With respect to some particular violent Muslims, perhaps many would agree. But in the prolific writings of Assmann, the argument turns against 'the Mosaic destinction'.[3] On his account, not so much Islam or Christianity are to blame for any intolerant implications of monotheisms, but rather the founder of Ju-

1 Cf. Schäfer (2008), in an excellent book on the ability of monotheism to split the divinity into persons and to integrate gods and godly powers and competences again.

2 Regensburg, 12th Sept. 2006, recurring on Manuel II. Palaiologos, Diologues with a Muslim, 7, 1.4–7.

3 Cf. Assmann (1998; 2003).

daism, Moses. Assmann posits what he calls the Mosaic distinction, or Moses's invention of a counter-religion as opposed to the true religion, for which there is only one god, one fundamental principle, one legitimate teacher of the only correct interpretation. Every divergent understanding in other religions, but especially within the own true religion, are pagan and heretical, and their proponents should be annihilated.

Assmann relies especially on the famous monograph which Freud published under the title *Der Mann Moses* (1938) one year before his death. In this view, Freud qualified his previous criticism of religion (esp. in *Totem und Tabu* 1912/13). Whereas, for Freud, religion is a neurotic behaviour, consisting in the obsessive-compulsive repetition of prescribed actions, with the rise of monotheism religion gradually became sublimated and spiritualized (*Vergeistigung*). Mankind made a step towards coping with fears and hopes in a rational manner which was free from illusions. On Freud's view, however, many further steps have to follow from that point onwards.[4]

<table>
<tr><th colspan="2">The Current Debate on Monotheism</th></tr>
<tr><td>Monotheism generates Violence
by creating a Counter-Religion
• exclusive,
• no alternative,
• intolerance</td><td>Praise of Polytheism
Odo Marquard, Jan Assmann
• capacity for inclusiveness,
• translation,
• tolerance</td></tr>
<tr><td colspan="2">recurring in 'remembered history'
in Sigmund Freud's Der Mann Moses (1939)
and Erich Voegelin Die politischen Religionen (1938)
and beyond in the study of the History of European Religion</td></tr>
</table>

Fig. 1

Many of the constructions in Freud's book are hazardous assumptions when seen from the point of view of historical methodology. It is impossible to accept that there were two 'Moseses', the Egyptian one and the Midianite, which led to the invention of two different monotheisms, the Egyptian one of Akhenaten (Echnaton) and the Arabian one, the religion of the desert.[5] But Assmann builds a line of defense for this view which saves both Freud and himself from the assault of historical arguments by retreating to the stronghold called 'remembered history'.

4 Cf. Stroumsa (2006).

5 This is the famous imagery of Ernest Renan.

In doing so, however, he does not get to grips with several presuppositions, three of which I might set out here.

1. Freud came nearer to his parent's religion through his praise of monotheism, but only in a restricted way. He found that monotheism is a step towards sublimation of religion. Religion, however, in itself, as he had pointed out in his *Totem und Tabu* (1912/13), is a mental illness, an obsessive repetition of the same irrational actions. In his old age Freud found monotheism to be a sublimation (*höhere Geistigkeit*), but even monotheistic religion tends to prevent mankind from becoming an adult personality, so that any fundamental change in his attitude toward religion apparent in his views on monotheism cannot really be identified.
2. Assmann, like Freud, constructs a primordial situation in which the desease of religion first broke out. In a cultic revolution Akhenaten destroyed all the other gods of Egypt. But the 'primordial sin' of Akhenaten did not have the effect of burdening every following generation in the same way, because Akhenaten's revolution was reversed at his death and polytheism reestablished. The primordial sin (*Ursünde*) of monotheism became the hereditary sin (*Erbsünde*) only with the appearance of the 'Mosaic distinction'.
3. Once invented, this mode of thought becomes a matter of history, not just of remembered history. Assmann's argument often switches to a historical one, though he asserts that he is speaking only of remembered history. This ambivalence arises out of the fact that he is concerned to identify a construct which can be observed throughout ancient and European history, which he sees as traces of a memory. Not only does identifying a construct with a memory blur the line between the positivist and the interpretive, but the construct he identifies motivates and creates actual historical events, so that more than merely remembered history is in play.

Though Assman persistently refers to remembered history, what he treats is one historical institution of religion as opposed to another institutionalized type of religion, and not the constructed past of a religious community. But in the European History of Religion[6] the two ideal types of historical fact and historical construct were invented as

6 On the methodological and historical particularities of a *Europäische Religionsgeschichte* (in contrast to religions in the geographical space of Europe), cf. Gladigow (1995); Auffarth (1999; 2009); Kippenberg/Rüpke/von Stuckrad (2009).

opposed to each other in an intellectual debate,[7] which has become part of the European History of Religion insofar as critique of religion, atheism, and disputes among intellectuals are all part of religious history specifically in Europe. Monotheism is, in the first instance, a discourse among intellectuals, including theologians:[8] a systematic rational definition in contrast to a field of terms of negative types of religion like magic, fetishism, totemism etc., reduced to the immaterial god.[9] In the pragmatics of religion, however, in the history of European religion one can find two corresponding evolutions: the one is institutionalized religion with a central authority: the Bible, a centrally institutionalized church, centralized professionals like bishops and priests, instructed and controlled by theology. The original agent of all of this is god as interpreted and given voice by the professionals. The other evolution (which is also found within the church) posits the individual and his religion (the term 'religiosity' is used instead of religion) as the agent of religion.[10] The advocates of religion as institution often defined religiosity as standing outside or at the margins of prescribed religion, such as Baptism, Pietism, Paganism, Monism, Esotericism, but also every individuation of religion.

Accordingly, monotheism is a kind of meta-religion, a claim by intellectuals and theologians about what religion should be, the prescribed religion, a program and a utopia existing in tension with individualized religiosity. But monotheism has also consequences for practical religion, especially in a highly professionalized and institutionalized religion where conclusions drawn by intellectuals and theologians can, by means of the institution, be applied to the broader practice of religion by ordinary people. This can be observed especially in Christianity during the age of reformation and the development of multiple Protestant confessions, in contrast to the Middle Ages, when the cult of the saints formed a 'secondary polytheism'.

The type of absolute monotheism began with Plato, not with Moses – whoever Moses might be, and whenever he might have lived – as an intellectual auctorial action in opposition to the religion which Greek people practiced at that time, and it became a leading idea in the philo-

7 Monotheism is introduced by Henry More 1660 in contrast to polytheism, invented by Jaen Bodin in 1580. Cf. also Bendlin (2001).

8 Hailer (2006), 191–243, divides the debate by conceiving 'Polytheismus als Theologiekritik'.

9 Cf. Auffarth (2007b).

10 The term religiosity is often used pejoratively in contrast to belief. In German the terms are sharply distinguished between *Glaube* (with positive and Protestant connotations) vs. *Dogma* (with negative and Catholic connotations), cp. French *foi/croyance*. Cf. Auffarth (2000).

sophical (and theological) debates in late antiquity in the formative period of Christian theology. This conference, however, has chosen as the focus of discussions a Pre-Platonic (or pre-Socratic) monotheism in the 'Earliest Antiquity' and concentrates on historical inquiries into a change of world view.

2. One among Others: Relative Monotheism in Polytheistic World Models

2.1 Polytheism as a Mode of Thought

On the topic of this 'historical' pre-Platonic monotheism, I quote three conclusions which West has proposed. West is the great scholar of Greek philosophy, literature and religion who has also mastered the Akkadian, Hebrew and Ugaritic languages. His expertise has been demonstrated in a massive volume entitled *The East Face of Helicon* (1997), on the modes of thought, metaphors, and literary genres which the Greeks inherited from the cultures of the Ancient Near East and changed and integrated into their own.[11] The three conclusions he draws are as follows:

1. The sophisticated monotheisms of the so-called world religions "are not survivals from a primitive monotheism".
2. "Among the ancient civilizations polytheism was the norm."[12]
3. "Monotheism may seem a stark antithesis to polytheism, but there was no abrupt leap from the one to the other."[13]

With the first two points I agree; the last one, I hope to show, is not the case (and, incidentally, contradicts the first one). There is, indeed, a distinct change in principles from relative monotheism which can be thought of within a polytheistic framework (how this is possible, I will show in the following parts) and the absolute monotheism which Plato invented.

11 After a long time, in which Greek and Classical culture was thought of as the decisive step in the history of cultures, 'le mirage grecque' without precedent (see my article [1999b = 2006b], or Cancik (1998), 536–542, after World War II the strong ties of Greece to Ancient Near Eastern cultures were detected more and more. Cf. Burkert (1984; 2003); Auffarth (1991); West (1997); Ribichini/Rocchi/Xella (2001).

12 Both quotations in West (1999), 21.

13 West (1999), 24.

2.2 Is Monotheism a Consequence of Empire-Building? The King is God

In the discussions on ancient Israelite monotheism, most biblical scholars tend to use as a model what they consider the common model of Near Eastern cultures, from Egypt to Babylonia, from Ugarit to Tyre. This model fits together (unlike the title 'One God – One Cult – One Nation') in terms of a different identification, namely 'one king in heaven – one king on earth – one cult in or nearby the palace of the king'. In the articles by Schaudig and Kratz, the problems of this identification have already been clearly formulated, establishing that the model mentioned should be better differentiated or even rejected as the common Ancient Near Eastern model.

I would like to present another different model. My evidence is taken from Early (Geometric and Archaic) Greece, comparing it with the society and social regulations of Israel in the time before the institution of the kingdom and, as an alternative to this form of regulating a society,[14] in the tradition of prophecy. The reasoning behind and justification for this comparision is, first, that the ecological, social and economic circumstances of life in the mountains of Israel and Judea are comparable with those of the Greeks much more than with the empires at the great rivers and a society based on irrigation. Second, in Greece, we frequently find a reception of Ancient Near Eastern ideology and modes of thought borrowed from the East (hence, the designation for this epoch as Orientalizing). But the reception is realized in a very different society, which refuses to be commanded by a king, and accordingly stresses different points in the symbols, metaphers, and images which it receives. These points are present in the Ancient Near Eastern ideology as well, but are differently interpreted. I call these alternative models:

- The king claims to be God's representative on earth.
- God himself is ruling.[15]

In the latter model, God himself does not give the (written) laws, which could be defined and administrated only by a human king, but he en-

14 Cf. Crüsemann (1978).

15 The term 'theocracy' is reserved for a social movement which strictly rejects monarchy and refuses to be ruled by a king. But it is connected with the rule of the priests, instead of monarchy. The first occurence should be restricted to the revolt of the Maccabees.

sures justice.[16] The lack of laws doesn't end in anarchy, but rather in a 'regulated anarchy', meaning that each individual member of this society can do what he decides to do, but still feels obliged to stop himself doing what is contrary to justice. With this model as a contrasting model to 'One God – One King – One Cult in the Palace/Temple' applied to Israel and Judea, we come especially nearer to the position of the prophets and their criticism of the evils of kingdom: war, radical inequalities in the distribution of wealth, and a cult which reduces god to a friendly sponsor of the king.

The King's Rule is Salvation[17]	God is Ruling
Power centralized in the king's palace in continuity	Many powerful houses no firm hierarchy from time to time a charismatic ruler
The ruler defines the laws according to topicality/situations (according to his own interests)	God defines justice absolutely (without respect to human interests)
Palace cultures in the Ancient Near East	Polycracy/regulated anarchy
Cult-religion/priests confirm power and vice versa	Prophetic criticism of war/wealth/cult

Fig. 2

This conference has undertaken to re-evaluate the rise of a particular type of monotheism on the basis of our current knowledge of the sources. On the one hand, the sources include the interpretation of archaeological finds, and, on the other hand, 'Remembered History' from the time of the Babylonian exile and afterwards, with the hope of accessing sources from before the exile. I do not consider it my task to take up the current debate on monotheism in full and compare it with the historical debate. With regard to the historical material, this essay is based on the comprehensive analysis in an earlier monograph which was concerned with investigating an alternative to the centralised type of ancient oriental monarchic ideologies which was not based on the

16 The Hebrew term *malkut JHWH* and the Greek βασιλεία θεοῦ (τῶν οὐρανῶν) are the corresponding terms in the prophetic tradition.

17 An excellent survey of these problems can be found in Assmann (2000).

perspective of palace culture and its adaptation to smaller aspiring palaces. Instead, the comparison with early Greece opened up a society which was not centralized or ruled by a monarch, but still takes on patterns and images from Ancient Near Eastern ideologies of kingship, but reinterprets them with a view to equality among all citizens.[18] In doing so, the issue of monotheism is removed from its entanglement as an image of the divine reflecting Ancient Near Eastern monarchic ideologies, as a projection of earthly monarchies onto a higher, more powerful world, and back (as apparent in the term 'monotheistic kingship').[19]

In the Greek world, then, the image of god no longer serves the purpose of ideologically propping up the ruler, but instead provides an alternative to the monarchy, a world of values which is not subject to the vicissitudes of everyday affairs. As such, the Early Greek, anti-monarchic framework of values is very close to the criticisms expressed by the prophets of Israel and Judah regarding power, wealth, and cult.

King and Citizens in mutual Responsibility face to face with God

As an example I take 'The king's oath'[20], which relies on Ancient Near Eastern models:[21]

If	*Then*
The king is ruling with justice	Black Earth brings plenty of fruits
But in reality	
There is (seems to be) no lord. The enemies sitting in the lord's house dream of becoming the new lord of the house by marrying his wife	the suitors are devouring the fruits stored in Odysseus' house
Δίκην παρεκβαίνουν They step out of the circle of justice	Δίκην τεκμαίρεται … Ζεύς Justice is allotted by Zeus[22] i.e. Zeus punishes the evil doer

18 Cf. Auffarth (1991).

19 Al-Azmeh/Bak (2004) looks from Carl Schmitt's 'political theology' backwards into the Middle Ages, esp. in Eastern Europe. The authors combine monotheism and monarchy without respect to the alternative combinations like polytheistic monarchy or monotheistic democracy.

20 Odyssey 19, 107–114, and Hesiod, *Erga*, 224–247.

21 A detailed analysis of the ANE evidence and the Early Greek reception is given in Auffarth (1991), 524–558.

22 Hesiod, *Erga*, 226/239.

If kings are not successful and there is famine or defeat in a battle, that is a divine sign that the god has not kept up his part of the bargain to even the scores in response to shortcomings in the king's commitment to justice. This indicates that *dike* is an absolute value, which Zeus, any other god, and the kings, have to respect.

From this perspective, there is a principle higher than the individual persons of gods with proper names, their own individual characters, preferences and abhorrences, envy and anger. Every god is bound to fulfil justice, though not every action of every god must mete out a fair share to every human being. Gods are thus free to punish, to harm people or to engage in favoritism, divine wrath and mercy.[23] But in sum, at the end, the account must balance and justice must be the result.

Kings may call themselves friends of or beloved by god. But if they do not practice justice among their people, they will destroy the order of society as well as the natural order. Not an individual god, (sometimes Zeus as the highest god in charge) has to restore order, but order herself forces the individual men and gods back to justice. In some respect this idea is close to the concept of Ma'at in Egypt,[24] and *sedaqah* in Israel or in the Ancient Near East.

In polytheistic modes of thought this relative monotheism can be expressed in terms of the transpersonal order behind the vices and virtues of the individual god-persons and their free actions. The more difficult question is how polytheistic modes of thought provide a transpersonal principle of religion, when religion becomes the authority for ethical conduct in a civic society, which is binding for every member. In other words, this type of format requires 'monotheism' in a polytheistic framing. There are a set of models, borrowed from everyday experiences, in which the transpersonal principles could be formulated, such that they are binding for both men and gods: the family of gods attributes to each member his or her duty and a restricted freedom to act independently. The assembly of gods disputes about the destiny of men, but in the end the god-fearers must be rewarded. The pantheon as a whole is responsible for the luck of a city or nation, but is led by a presiding god on duty.

---

23 Cf. Kratz/Spieckermann (2008).

24 Cf. Assmann (1990); Fischer-Elfert (2005).

2.3 Model 1: Family, Genealogy, Megatheism

One of the plausible models according to which one can imagine the invisible world of gods by comparing it with the experiences among men is to portray the gods as members of a familiy with parents, grandparents, uncles and aunts, extramarital lovers, husband, children, brothers and sisters, younger and older, even including favorites among the children or problem-children, those eager to get their inheritance, or rebellious offspring planning a revolution to overcome the ruling god. The members which form the family unit can represent:

- Social groups within an ethnic body like peasents, women, girls, warriors, strangers, etc., which all together form the nation. The partition into ressorts of a healing god, a warrior god, one god for the merchants and another for the sailors, mirrors the interests and the special needs of every professional group. The reconciliation of differences and conflicts must happen within the group.
- One city or one nation for each family member, so that the family is the international concert of political communication between nations.

The family model makes clear that there is a given unit, within which each member has to find its role by negotiating his or her own interests in the larger framework and achieving consensus or at least organising the feasibility of a particular plan with the other members of the family. The god as an individual cannot act independently or arbitrarily, but functions as a member of a divine kinship-group.[25]

The family can be organized either as a 'house' or even a king's house (palace) in the strict form of patriarchal hierarchy, or the family is in loose contact from time to time when the father, for example, hosts a dinner but has no particular prerogatives. I will discuss this problem in the section on the assembly of gods and on pantheon (see below 2.6). The formula 'Father of men and gods'[26] does not mean that Zeus is anyone's biological father nor that he is defined by any of the elements of authority or responsibilty which would be attached to fatherhood. It is just a title, borrowed from the Ancient Near East. The same is true for the titles like 'the highest of the rulers' (Odyssey 1, 45 and *passim*). Cult-

25 For the level beneath (social groups within the society of a city-state) and above (regional and federal alliances) the city-state or nation in Early Greece, cf. Auffarth (2006a); Gladigow (1983).

26 Odyssey 1, 28, and in many instances elsewhere.

titles like these belong to a phenomenon which I treat in the following paragraph as 'megatheism'.

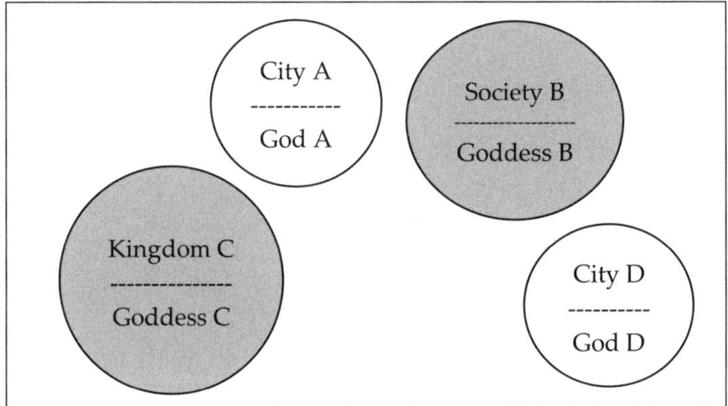

Fig. 3: Genealogy and Megatheism

If City A and Kingdom C build a coalition in order to make war against City D, God A and Goddess C are tied together in form of family bonds: 1. as a genealogical bonding, 2. e.g., as 'father' and 'daughther', 3. as opposed to a jealous brother, 4. or other oppositions in a society of gods. If the coalition has become kingdom, these bonds may also be those between 'Queen' goddess and 'King' god.

Megatheism is a term coined recently by Chaniotis as a result of the need for an expression for divinities who may be one of many, but are characterized as 'the outstanding god' or even 'the only one' – in a polytheistic pantheon. As a formula applied to men, it is used in inscriptions for winners in sport competitions in the pan-hellenic games. The winner of the prize is the first one and he has become the only one to win the competition. Hence, the same formula can be used for gods and for humans who have distinguished themselves in some way, especially in the literary genre of hymns and prayers. There it is expressed as 'Our God is the greatest', 'is the best', 'the only one'. I have treated this formula εἷς καὶ μόνος, as Paul uses in his letter to the Corinthians 1 Cor. 9:6, elsewhere.[27] It indicates an outstanding position or status, as recognized by those who honor that particular god, but not by everybody. Award of such predicates suggests a triumph over the other gods, but within the structures of existing polytheism. Other terms which have been suggested for this are not wholly satisfactory, because using terms

27 Cf. Auffarth (2003); Chaniotis (2009).

like 'Hochgott'[28] or henotheism[29] interpret this format as a step in a linear evolution towards monotheism.

2.4 Model 2: Succession – The Temporal Model of Transpersonal Continuity

A second mode of thought which the Greeks learned and received from the Ancient Near East is the Myth of the 'Kingship in Heaven' or succession myth. In many variants this myth is told and reflected in the whole Ancient Near East and Mediterranean region, among the literary versions one can count the Atramhasis epos of Babylonia, the Hittite succession myth, the Baal-cycle of Ugarit, and also Hesiod's *Theogony* in Greece. Also in the Biblical canon we find this myth in versions like that of Gen. 6:1–4, Isaiah 14, Ezechiel 28. Its most influential reception arose outside of the canon in the apocalyptic literature of the Henoch-Tradition, including the canonical Apocalypse of John.[30]

The myth tells of the always impending danger that the existing order could be overthrown (*Der drohende Untergang*[31]). In two earlier generations of the order of the world and its guardians a revolution happened. How can the next revolution be avoided? The model is conceived in a society with one central palace, from where the irrigation, which in effect means the society as a whole, must be organised in order to provide food and prevent sabotage. Especially in Atramhasis and the biblical story of the flood, the ruling gods try to annihilate mankind, which is going to revolt against the ruling class of gods, by opening the weirs of the irrigation-chanels. Men on the other hand can put the gods under pressure by starving them: they refuse the gods food by boycotting sacrifices.[32] The cult of the god/gods is the guarantee of the world order: men give food and honour to the gods; the gods provide the conditions for a good harvest, blessing a god-fearing human society.

Qualifying as god-fearing also requires that rulers and subjects, citizens and fellow-citizens, all correctly maintain their mutual rights and honours. The succession myth is not only an apeal to accept the ruling class and the ruler, whatever he does, but also a threat of divine sanc-

28 Cf. Elsas (1993).

29 Cf. Auffarth (1993).

30 Cf. Auffarth/Stuckenbruck (2004).

31 This title *Impending Doom* I chose for my monograph, cf. Auffarth (1991).

32 With the Ancient Near Eastern models I have analysed three Greek versions and rituals; cf. Auffarth (1994).

tions against those who might attempt to transcend or subvert the order of justice. The King's oath (see above 2.3) is an example of that mutual obligation.[33]

Generation 1	Generation 2	Generation 3
Primordial powers like love, strife, ocean and water;	The (elder) Gods of the Golden Age,	Our (Young) God
the primordial beast, devouring every life, has been killed and thus space[34] is created for life.	are deposed, retired, or tied up in a jail, but still alive.	overcame his father/ king by a revolution and castrated him

Fig. 4: The Succession Myth

There will be no further new order of the world. The order of the younger god, who is now ruling, will last in all eternity. The way to guarantee the order in the society and in the kosmos is thus (1) the cult of the god and (2) the upholding of justice.

Here it is both, ironic and significant, that the current god, whose order has to be upheld to keep the world from falling apart, is himself a god who has disrupted previous orders. This makes the suggestion that the current god is capable of allowing chaos or a breakdown of order, and thus requires appeasement, more plausible.

2.5 Model 3: Dividing the World – the Spatial Model

Another model attributes the various experiential realms, which human beings have to cope with, to different gods. Neither of two gods is allowed to act in the realm of the other god, but men have to live in each of them, though temporarily. The world is divided into three realms, each of them is ruled by one mightiest god. In the conflict between Odysseus and Polyphemus, the son of Poseidon, the Odyssey tells how conflicts arise if a god-fearing man from Zeus' realm has to cross the sea and the underworld in order to sail home.

33 The following diagram should be read comparatively from left to right.

34 Gen. 1:6 raqia[c] *Feste* (Luther), *expanse* (JPS).

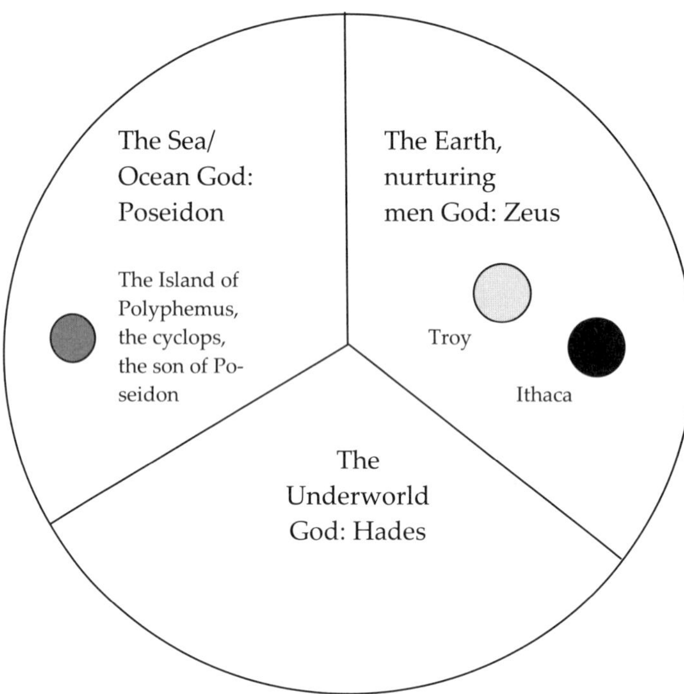

Fig. 5: The World is divided into three Spaces or Realms

Sailing home from Troy to Ithaca, Odysseus had to cross the realm of the sea, Poseidon's world. On the island of Polyphemus[35] Odysseus encounters a giant, who did not pass through the evolution of human culture; he is still in the natural phase, more a beast than a man. As his hospitality gift, he promises that his guest Odysseus will be the last one he will eat. Against the man-eating primordial man, Odysseus invokes Zeus as the protector of strangers/guests, Ζεὺς ξείνιος. But in vain: Polyphemus, the son of Poseidon, continues to devour his guests. In the realm of Poseidon, Zeus cannot help, he's outside of his jurisdiction. Thanks to the skills of human civilization the clever but hopelessly weaker Odysseus can escape from the island, but he is now burdened with the spell of Polyphemus and his father Poseidon: He will never be able to escape from the realm of Poseidon. The solution for the god-fearing man will be found later – in the course of the epic narration this is, however, the opening scene – in the assembly of gods.

35 Odyssey 9, 105–565.

2.6 Model 4: The Assembly of the Gods

The twelve gods (of the younger generation according to the time model), however, are not hermits but act as a group. They gather on the mountain in the North (that is Mt. Zaphon in Ugarit, Mt. Olympus in Greece).[36] There, they like to dine together, but it is also an opportunity to discuss and solve problems. After dinner Athene stands up in the assembly and complains that Odysseus is still the only one of the Greek warriors of the Trojan war who has not yet come home. The opportunity is well chosen because Poseidon, who hates Odysseus, is absent from the table this time. He is on a trip to see his friends to take part in the Poseidonia-festival among the African people far away. So it is possible for Athene and Zeus to take care of Odysseus' return home. They convince the assembly that it is time to end the trials of the god-fearing man Odysseus (who carries the same name as Job – the hated man[37]).

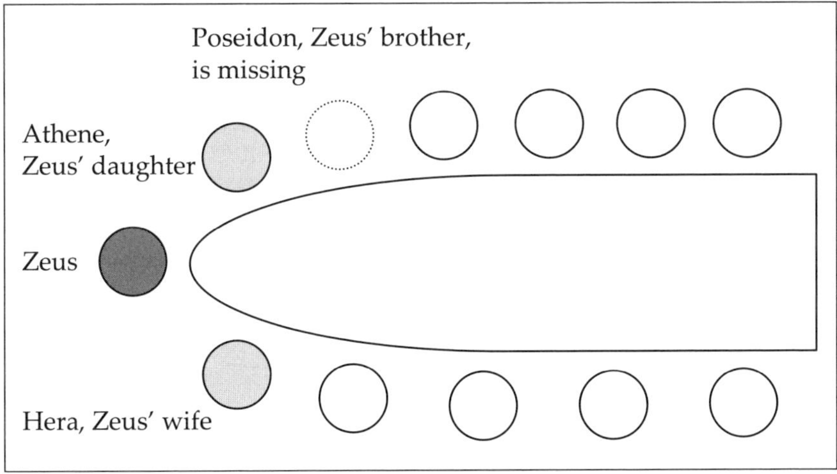

Fig. 6: The Assembly of Gods

The similarity to the scene sketched in Psalm 82 (or the reverse situation painted in Job 1) is striking: In the assembly of gods, one god complains about the state of affairs: Wicked people are doing well whereas the humble and poor cannot get justice. It is the task of the gods to re-

36 On the Ancient Near Eastern image of the assembly of the gods, cf. Mullen (1980).

37 Cf. Odyssey 1, 11–95.

medy this situation and provide for a fair balance in society, otherwise, they are neither gods nor kings; the order of the world is shaken.[38]

In the context of the evolution of monotheism I have to discuss an interpretation of West, who sees in the assembly of gods an instrument for implementing the will of Zeus.[39] He sees a form of the throne-council in it. But the Ugaritic, Hebrew and Greek assembly of the gods is structured as a democratic, not monarchic institution. No one in it has the authority to impose his will upon any other god. Zeus is the one who opens and guides the discussion, but he is not the god of gods. He has just one vote in decision making, just like all the others.[40]

West exaggerates the authority granted to the role of Zeus in the round table, referring to 'the will of Zeus' (Διὸς βουλή) in the *Cypria*[41] and also to one famous myth, that of the Golden Chain (*aurea catena Homeri*) recalled in the *Iliad* 8, 18–27.[42] In this episode, Zeus forbids the other gods to interfere in the battles of the Trojan war. There, he stresses that he is stronger than all the other gods together. But in the end every goddess and god interferes in each battle, so that the story, taken as a whole, shows that Zeus' claim is rhetorical and boastful, rather than a statement of fact. The counterpart to his claim, put forward in another episode, is the cheat of Zeus (Διὸς ἀπάτη), when Hera seduces her husband in order to distract him from playing at commanding the war.[43] Zeus underlines his claim of superiority by an image of a rope:

---

38 Among biblical scholars a short indication of the background of this view may be sufficient. I follow the religious-historical connections argued by Oswald Loretz, Herbert Niehr and others. A justification of the interpretation in comparision with Odyssey 1 is promising.

39 Cf. West (1999), 22–24.

40 For the analysis of a similar scene in the Iliad cf. Flaig (1994).

41 Scholion D commenting Ilias 1, 5 Διὸς δ' ἐτελείετο βουλή. The late antique comment takes from the epic *Cypria*, that it was the will of Zeus, to solve the problem of over-population of the earth. Cf. West (2003), Cypria F 1 = 1.7 Bernabé. See the dicussion on 'Zeus' will' (as the blue-print for the whole epos of the Iliad) in Latacz (2000), 20, who rejects this interpretation: besides the word 'Zeus' will', there is no further hint in the whole rest of the epic of any divine wish to kill (the greater part of) the mankind.

42 As possible models for the rope or chain, West (1997), 371, recalls the rope *seretu*, by which the kings in Babylonia catch and pull captives behind them.

43 Cf. Iliad 14, 147–360. Cp. also Iliad 1, 396–406, the other gods tried to tie up Zeus, but in vain.

εἰ δ' ἄγε πειρήσασθε θεοὶ ἵνα εἴδετε πάντες:
σειρὴν χρυσείην ἐξ οὐρανόθεν κρεμάσαντες
πάντές τ' ἐξάπτεσθε θεοὶ πᾶσαί τε θέαιναι
ἀλλ' οὐκ ἂν ἐρύσαιτ' ἐξ οὐρανόθεν πεδίονδε
Ζῆν' ὕπατον μήστωρ', οὐδ' εἰ μάλα πολλὰ κάμοιτε.
ἀλλ' ὅτε δὴ καὶ ἐγὼ πρόφρων ἐθέλοιμι ἐρύσσαι,
αὐτῇ κεν γαίῃ ἐρύσαιμ' αὐτῇ τε θαλάσσῃ:
σειρὴν μέν κεν ἔπειτα περὶ ῥίον Οὐλύμποιο
δησαίμην, τὰ δέ κ' αὖτε μετήορα πάντα γένοιτο.
τόσσον ἐγὼ περί τ' εἰμὶ θεῶν περί τ' εἴμ' ἀνθρώπων.

Come, you gods, make this endeavour, that you all may learn this. Let down out of the sky a cord of gold (σειρὴ χρυσειή seirè chruseiè); lay hold of it all you who are gods and all who are goddesses, yet not even so can you drag down Zeus from the sky to the ground, not Zeus the high lord of counsel, though you try until you grow weary. Yet whenever I might strongly be minded to pull you, I could drag you up, earth and all and sea and all with you, then fetch the golden rope about the horn of Olympos, and make it fast, so that all once more should dangle in mid air. So much stronger am I than the gods, and stronger than mortals.[44]

In later philosophical speculation on theology this text was widely commented upon, as in Plato's *Theaitetos*, 153 C (the Golden Chain as a metaphor for the sun); Aristotle thought that this passage might be the first mythical evidence for his unmoved mover (*De animalium motione* 4. 699 b 32) and the Stoics understood it as the necessary equilibrium of the four elements, without which the world would be destroyed by the apocalyptic fire.[45] Not earlier than in the 4th century AD the term *Aurea Catena Homeri* is found in Ambrosius Theodosius Macrobius as the Great Chain of Being, the cosmic hierarchy and interdependence (*connexio*) from the highest god down to the last bit of muck (*ultima faecem*) of the universe.[46]

This is, however, later speculation after the invention of principal monotheism. According to Homer the role of Zeus is not that of the highest and mightiest god, but in the assembly of gods he is just the host, speaker, sometimes a charismatic leader, but not the ruler and monarch among the other gods. In this form, the same principle was realized in organizing the order of society as democracy and the republic in Greece and Rome. In the manner of counting the vote of each person, one per head, not counting noblemen more than peasents, the

44 Transl. by James Huddleston in the Chicago Homer.

45 Cf. Eustathii (1828), 184. Cp. Lévêque (1959), 17.

46 Macrobius, *Comm. in Somnium Scipionis*, 14. It is astonishing that the founder of the 'History of Ideas', Lovejoy (1936), ignored the Homeric origin of the allegory. For it was Alexander Pope, the famous translator of the Iliad in 1720, whose poetic formulation is Lovejoy's prime evidence.

decision according to the majority as a fundamental principle of democracy was installed. The assembly of the gods served as a model for this innovation.[47]

3. The Gap between Relative and Absolute Monotheism: From Aischylos' Zeus to Plato's *summum bonum*

3.1 Aischylos' Zeus as the Highest Authority and the Pantheon of Gods

The stage nearest to monotheism, yet, still totally different to the Platonic construction of an absolute monotheism, can be found in Aischylos,[48] the eldest of the three classical authors of Greek tragedies (ca. 525–456/445 BCE). In the tragedies of this author, more archaic in tone than his two younger rivals Sophocles and Euripides, an eminent role is attributed to Zeus. Among his attributes Aischylos created many previously unheard-of epikleseis combined with the praefix *pan-* or all.[49] By these cult-names he asserts for Zeus (1) a paragone position among the other goddesses and gods and (2) extraordinary power which surpasses the capacities of any other god besides him.

Even a kind of cosmotheism can be found in Aischylos' frg. 70, a part of his dramatical work, which survived because a Christian theologian saw a pagan knowledge of Christian monotheism in this stance before the advent of Christ.

> Ζεύς ἐστιν αἰθήρ, Ζεὺς δὲ γῆ, Ζεὺς δ' οὐρανός,
> Ζεύς τοι τὰ πάντα χὤ τι τῶν ὑπέρτερον.
>
> Zeus is the aether (day-light), Zeus is the earth, Zeus is the heaven;
> Zeus, I say, is all things and whatever is higher than these.[50]

In contravention of the view that Zeus was generally regarded as the one truly omnipotent god, I might analyse just one stanza from Aischylos, *Eumenides* 1045–1046:[51]

---

47 Cf. Flaig (1994). A monograph by the same author is still awaited.

48 I prefer this spelling, which is rendered in America often as Aiskhulos, whereas in English still the Latin form is rendered as Aeschylus.

49 A full list and analysis can be found in Kiefner (1965).

50 *Tragicorum Graecorum fragmenta* 3, F 70 Radt, from Eusebios, *Praeparatio Evangelica* 13, 13, 41. Tr. Lloyd-Jones (1983), 86.

51 The edition of the text by Martin L. West in the Bibliotheca Teubneriana, Stuttgart 1990, presents a new text, very different to the textus receptus since Wilamowitz' edition. The translation is taken from West (1999), 28.

Παλλάδος ἀστοῖς Ζεὺς παντόπτας	With the citizens of Pallas
οὕτω Μοῖρά τε συγκατέβα.	Zeus (the all-seeing)
	and Fate have thus come to terms.

The word συγκατέβα I would prefer to render with 'came down to earth together with (the other ones)'. Three gods are involved here:

- Pallas Athene, the city goddess of Athens
- Zeus, the all-seeing.
- Moira, goddess of fairness

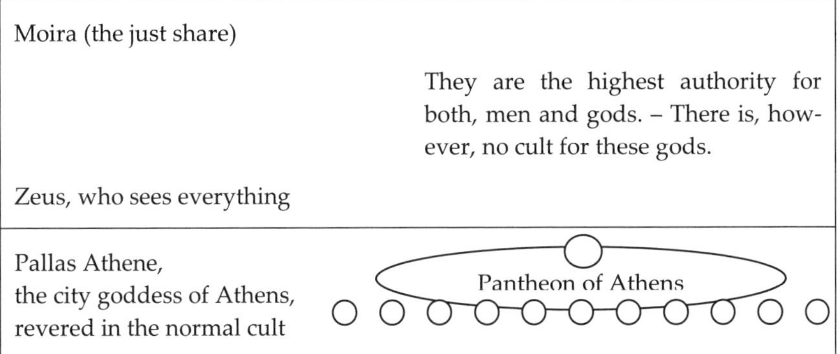

Fig. 7: Pantheon

We have to distinguish between two realms of religion:

1. The level of cult with distinguished individual god-persons who have a name, cult-title in hymns, rituals, cult-place, myth, genealogical ties to other gods.
2. The level of religion where every god but also other divine powers interact in favour of the polis (city-state) and every individual living in the city, repelling evil powers from the faithful servants of gods, both, enemies coming from outside and enemies of the order inside society.
3. In the case of the polytheistic systems, the interaction of gods called pantheon (the twelve gods within the city) represents the different parts of the society beneath the local level of the city as a whole, like citizens and slaves, men and women, young males/females and adults, warrior and shepherds, etc.
4. But also on the social and political level above the city a unity can be represented by gods, as shown above in the case of Zeus *xeinios*.

Martin West gives the following constituents for the first level:

> "An ancient god is a complex entity, a compound made up from some or all of the following: a name, or rather a cluster of names and titles, a poetic persona, a mythology, a doxology, an iconography, a constituency, defined by geographical, or social factors; a set of prompts, I mean situations, and occasions when the god is brought to mind; a 'dromenology', that is a repertory of cult activities. That is all at the synchronic level. Each of those bundles was subject to historical change and development through time either with or without influence from outside."[52]

Back to Aischylos' prayer: On the level of cult Athena is the city-goddess with the most prominent temple on the Akropolis, and other sanctuaries. The specific cult-name of the goddess *Pallas* is invoked, by which she is called upon as dwelling in her 'maidens' chamber', the *Parthenon* on the Akropolis.

Concerning Zeus, Aischylos uses an epiklesis (cult-name): the *all-seeing* πανόπτας.[53] Zeus is revered at Athens in some smaller sanctuaries – but not as prominent as Athena's sanctuaries – in the city and in the countryside, in the following manifestations:[54]

1. on the Agora (central political place), the great Altar of Zeus *Agoraios*,
2. as Zeus *basileus* (king) and *boulaios* (council) and *phratrios* (local community) and *herkeios* (of the correct oath), each for his functions as the god of political decisions, which would not harm any other citizen of Athens either by false testimony asserted with an oath or an evil intention,
3. often as *meilichios* for deceased people,
4. and especially interesting (in the context of a study on monotheism) is the evidence for veneration as Zeus *hypsistos*.[55]

But nowhere in Athens the Epiklesis Zeus *panoptes,* the all-seeing, is attested in cult. There is only one piece of evidence for this epiklesis as a cult-name, namely in Argos in the sanctuary of Apollo Pythaios,

---

52 A very British answer to the question 'what is a god?' in West (1997), 54, down to earth, but very useful descriptively.

53 Cf. Schwabl (1972), 349f. The Doric form (instead of Attic πανόπτης) is typical for hymnic passages in Greek Drama.

54 Catalogues of every sanctuary and every *Epiklesis* (cult name) of the Greek Gods are only available for Zeus by Schwabl (1972; 1978); for Aphrodite by Pirenne-Delforge (1994); for Poseidon on the Peleponnese Mylonopoulos (2003). But for many others there is no relyable data-base. – For Zeus in Athens and Attika cf. Schwabl (1978), § 29, col. 1063–1078.

55 Before Roman times, cf. Schwabl (1978), 1074f., in the broader context of the Highest God, and also Colpe/Löw (1994); Wischmeyer (2005); Belayche (2005); Teeter (2007); Mitchell (in print).

where it is a reference to the guardian-god Argos *Panoptes* with his hundred eyes, who takes care of the pregnant Io, who will give birth to the son of Zeus and father of the Danaides, founders of the city of Argos.[56]

That means that this particular usage of this epiklesis is a creation of the dramaturgist. The hymnic evocation is part of an hymnos (epi-) *kletikos*,[57] a prayer to a specific god begging that she or he may come down among people, a prayer that the god might dwell among the citizens – *shekhina* in Hebrew, *parousia* in Greek, *adventus* in Latin. The godesses of revenge came down to dwell among men, but together with them came Zeus. Revenge is turned into justice. This hymn is not a fiction or even a parody of a cult hymn, but the form of cult which is in this specific festival, both, service to the god and part of the drama.[58] And it diverts the potentially destructive forces of revenge towards wielding peaceful power in the service of social cohesion.

The same is true for *Moirai*, a personification as a group[59] of the fair share, the part alloted to someone, or destiny – also to the gods. In cult they are revered, but remain marginal.[60] Already in the Homeric epic, it is stated that Gods are helpless against the *Moira* and/or that they are the agents of the superior destiny.[61]

Even in early Greece (which as I take as the period from Homer to Aischylos), there was a concept of monotheism beyond cultic polytheisms, the oneness of god. Here I'm referring to an archaic way of thought, prior to Plato and his equivalence of god and the good τὸ θεῖον = τὸ ἀγαθόν, thus creating a fundamentally different philosophical foundation on which Jewish, Christian, and Islamic monotheisms were then built.

This means that even in a non-centralized, non-monarchial culture, amidst cultic polytheism, it is perfectly possible to conceive of the oneness of god, and to do so not only as a mere thought experiment which is then put forward as dogma. Rather, this type of monotheism constitutes a canon of values which is non-negotiable, which is not open to the arbitrary and situational changes which it would be exposed to if it merely served to bolster up and legitimate contemporary rulers. A non-

56 Cf. Wernicke (1895), esp. no. 19 (col. 791–795). Auffarth (1995), 88–116; id. (1999a).

57 Cf. Furley (2000).

58 For cult, ritual, literary form and literature, cf. Bierl/Lämmle/Wesselmann (2007), among them my paper on the Older Attic Comedy, see Auffarth (2007a).

59 For groups of divine persons in Greek religion, often nameless or euphemistic as the instance in Eumenides or Maends, satyroi, cf. Henrichs (1991).

60 Cf. Henrichs (2000), (excellent, brief, and comprehensive).

61 Cf. Fränkel (1976), 58–70 with Index A 5.8 on pp. 616–617.

cultic, but personified entity can stand for such a non-negotiable and unchangeable canon of values, but a cultic figure can also stand as the embodiment as the highest and universally valid values. This latter format can be observed in the epithets used of Zeus by Aischylos, the eldest of the three classical dramatists of Athens.

4. Absolute Monotheism as conceived by Plato

Before I come to the last stage with regard to monotheism evolving from polytheism, I present a diagram of the totally different monotheism Plato has constructed, which constitutes a leap which cannot be conceived as an evolutionary step from 'primitive' to 'principal' or 'absolute' monotheism (see Fig. 8).

Plato criticised the normal practice of religion of his time fundamentally in his utopian programs *Politeia* (constitution of the ideal state) and *Nomoi* (laws given in order to realize the ideal state). His own construction of religion in the ideal state needed a world outside this world as authority. This 'Other World', as part of the divine realm and participating with the eternal being, has its place both, inside men and outside the material world.

By inventing the 'Other World' beyond the visible and sensual experiences of men in this world, Plato found an authority which could not be contested or evaluated. The better or real life in that 'Other World' only appeared later as eternal life as a tempting reward which could be gained after death. That there was not the mass of gods, one fighting against the other, bringing harm or good fortune to men, but only one principle as identical with one god, the principle the *summum bonum*, the Good *per se*, was an innovation on the part of Plato. Among the church fathers there was a tradition according to which Plato had gone to Egypt for beeing a pupil of Moses himself, or heard the prophet Jeremiah.[62] Early Christian intellectuals perceived Plato as one of us, who conveniently invented and philosophically developed absolute monotheism prior to the Church requiring it. Plato had presented a model for the new system of thinking of god as absolutely different from this world, as an entity to whom no anthropomorphic behaviour could be attributed.

62 Cf. Ridings (1995); Pilhofer (1990); Fuhrer (2006), esp. 108–109.

	Polytheism	Monotheism
Spatial Model	divided realms for various gods	unbounded jurisdiction of the god
Chronological Model	one generation of gods follows the other	eternal
Epistemological Model	this world is just appearance (Plato's simile of the cave)	the realm inhabited by the divine is true reality
Theodicy	evil arises from lack of knowledge of what is good	only *philosophoi* get the knowledge of τὸ θεῖον as identical with τὸ ἀγαθόν
Cult religion	Mystery religion	Plato's monotheism presupposes the invention of • an eternal 'Other World' • the Inner World of the eternal soul Philosophical religion

Fig. 8: Plato's Monotheism

The Justice of God in a Society without Kings

Let us turn back to the alternative model presented above, namely the society in which god is in charge of ensuring justice, but is not represented by a king.

In the semi-arid landscapes of the Mediterranean, with its triple crops of olives, grapes and wheat, no central authority was needed for organizing and controlling irrigation and all the hierarchy, bureaucracy, storage houses etc. necessary to allow a substantial human population to prosper in the desert. After a time, when Greece experimented with palace culture (i.e. the Minoan and Mycenean cultures), Greeks decided to live in *poleis*, dividing up power in time (rulers in charge only for one year), and among competing rivals (colleagues), mediating wealth (the rich citizens had to finance communal projects like feasts and building ships for wars), voting of non-noble magistrates, no dynastic accumulation of power and wealth, a genealogy (presented by means of commemorative luxury, family cult for the ancestors).[63] The Greeks were hostile to monarchy. In Israel, also a Mediterranean culture, we can see that after an intitial period of hostility against the kingdom, the institutionalizing of the kingdom with palace, bureaucracy, standing military, a temple with daily cult took place. But the older aversion to living in a kingdom left its legacy: from time to time people came into public and pronounced 'the word of the Lord' as critique against the politics of the kings and the élite: the prophetic resistance.

In order to find a common and indisputable principle for justice and the ethical conduct of life, the models I analyzed above could show that even if evildoers can live prosperously for a time and boast that a god is on their side, in the long run justice will prevail. The advantage a god might have given to a man must be equalized because every god is bound to justice as the superior principle either represented by *Moirai* or by all-seeing Zeus. In Israel, JHWH became the personal name and representative of Justice, especially after the fundamental crisis of the exile in Babylon. The prophetic tradition explained that the deeper causes of this crisis lay in the institution of the kingdom.

In both cases montheism is an instance on a level beyond manipulation neither by men nor by individual gods and their cult-group. Nobody can dispute these values and even a king or a war-lord has to accept it. The ultimate authority of justice is not the prophet, not a judge. The power to punish wrongdoers is not immediately at hand in any human institution, but can be depended on nonetheless. God's punishment of the unjust and righting of wrongs will eventially take place, even if one must wait for generations: "For I, JHWH, Your god, am an impassioned god, visiting the guilt of the parents upon the children, upon the third and upon the fourth generations of those who reject Me." (Exod. 20:5 [JPS]) Or in Herodotean Greek: "Don't praise any one before his end!"[64]

63 Auffarth (1995) shows that this process began in the last phase of the Mycenean palaces LH III C, before the destruction.

64 Herodotus 1, 30–33.

Conclusion

To come to the conclusion of this comparision between Israel and Greece: There are tendencies in the history of both cultures towards a monotheism which assumes that there are other gods, that is, a relative monotheism. This can be observed both, in cult and in the conception of god as one god only. In cult, the worshippers turn to their god exclusively, especially in the communicative situation and the literary genre of prayer and hymn. But these tendencies did not remove the cultic reality of a plurality of gods, neither within a pantheon, whose highest or city god enjoyed extraordinary honours above the other gods of the same pantheon, nor as a specific relationship between men and god or still better: one god and his people, one nation and her god/goddess. This all remains in a framework in which other gods exist apart from this exclusive relationship.

That means that there is no historical evidence for an evolution towards monotheism having actually occurred such that it leads to absolute monotheism. Even a cult reform like that of king Josiah in Israel (as reported in 2 Kings 22–23, but in the archaeological evidence hard to confirm) could not eradicate the attendance of other cults; there are still other gods outside Israel, the gods of the other nations, but also inside Israel and Jerusalem (e.g., Ezekiel 8 – after the cult reform).

In Greek cultural history absolute monotheism was constructed by Plato by inventing two worlds outside this world, namely the transcendent world or the other world and the inner world of the divine soul. This absolute monotheism is the model in which the church fathers constructed the absolute monotheism of Christianity and which was also used by the rabbis in Judaism.

In Israel, thinking about monotheism became possible and necessary due to the fact that traditional cultic behaviour had been destroyed and its practice prevented by the destruction of the temple by the Babylonians. That may be the destruction of the *bamot* during the so called cult reform of King Hezekiah and of King Josiah in 622 BCE or the temple at Jerusalem by the Babylonians in 586 BCE. That means this new form was a matter of fact first in the countryside as early as the time of centralization of cult, but became much more urgent in the time of exile. The lack of cult encouraged a new form of non-cultic religion. Especially during the Babylonian exile, the lack of cult provoked the movement of the Deuteronomistic school and in the long run also the essential control over only one cult centre. Monotheism and the establishment of just one cult center constituted the most radical forms of a relative monotheism, but never evolved into an absolute monotheism.

In Greece, there could have been a similar result if the Persians had destroyed not only the Athenian Acropolis but also sanctuaries in Sparta and Corinth. The central sanctuary of Plataiai was a common temple for all Greeks; there they swore an oath to Zeus to go together into battle against the Persians or to die. But they overcame the Persians. Polytheism prevailed. Plato was a singular philosopher who became an influential figure in religion not earlier than in Hellenistic and Roman times and his utopian religion led to consequences in the image of god and in cult performance. Modern monotheisms are the result of the Platonic invention of an 'Other World' as the totally different world of pure principles which no human being can realize during the life of this world.

Therefore, it is not at the point of any 'Mosaic destinction' that an exclusive religion began generating expulsion, excommunication and censorship of thought, or even the execution of men accused of thinking false thoughts. Instead, it was the cooperation between imperial power and the Platonic superhuman monotheism during the Roman Empire which formed the basis of absolute monotheism, but also found ways of mitigating the absolute, utopian and unhuman radicalism of Plato's construct, so that monotheism becomes a great vision of justice.[65]

---

65 I would like to thank Blossom Stefanie for her assistance concerning this essay.

Bibliography

Al-Azmeh, A./Bak, J.M. (2004), Monotheistic Kingship: The Medieval Variants, Annual Interdisciplinary Workshop held in Feb. 2002 at Central European University, Central European University medievalia 7, Budapest.

Assmann, J. (1990), Ma'at. Gerechtigkeit und Unsterblichkeit im alten Ägypten, München (repr. with a postface 2006).

– (1998), Moses the Egyptian: The Memory of Egypt in Western Monotheism, Cambridge/Mass. (German title: id., Moses der Ägypter. Entzifferung einer Gedächtnisspur, München 1998, and reprints).

– (2000), Herrschaft und Heil. Politische Theologie in Altägypten, Israel und Europa, München.

– (2003), Die mosaische Unterscheidung oder der Preis des Monotheismus, Edition Akzente, München.

Athanassiadi, P./Frede, M. (1999, eds.), Pagan Monotheism in Late Antiquity, Oxford (reprint 2002).

Auffarth, C. (1991), Der drohende Untergang. "Schöpfung" in Mythos und Ritual im Alten Orient und in Griechenland am Beispiel der Odyssee und des Ezechielbuches, RGVV 39, Berlin/New York.

– (1993), Art. Henotheismus/Monolatrie, in: Handbuch religionswissenschaftlicher Grundbegriffe, Hrsg. von H. Cancik/B. Gladigow/M. Laubscher (ab Bd 4: K.-H. Kohl), 5 Bde, Stuttgart u.a. 1988–2000, HRWG 3, 104–105.

– (1994), Der Opferstreik. Ein altorientalisches "Motiv" bei Aristophanes und im homerischen Hymnus, GrB 20, 59–86.

– (1995), Hera und ihre Stadt Argos. Methodische und historische Untersuchungen zur Polis-Religion im frühen Griechenland, Tübingen (unpublished Habilitation).

– (1999a), Constructing the Identity of the Polis: The Danaides as "Ancestors", in: R. Hägg (ed.), Ancient Greek Hero Cult: Proceedings of the Fifth International Seminar on Ancient Greek Cult, organized by the Department of Classical Archaeology and Ancient History, Göteborg University, 21–23 April 1995, Skrifter utgivna av Svenska Institutet i Athen 8, Stockholm, 39–48.

– (1999b), Art. Antike, in: Metzler Lexikon Religion. Gegenwart – Alltag – Medien, hg. v. C. Auffarth/J. Bernard/H. Mohr, Bd. 1, Stuttgart/Weimar, 63–70.

– (2000), Art. Religiosität/Glaube, in: Metzler Lexikon Religion. Gegenwart – Alltag – Medien, hg. von C. Auffarth/J. Bernard/H. Mohr, Bd 3, Stuttgart/Weimar, 188–196

– (2003), Herrscherkult und Christuskult, in: H. Cancik/K. Hitzl (eds.): Die Praxis der Herrscherverehrung in Rom und seinen Provinzen. Tübingen, 283–317.

– (2006a), Das Heraion von Argos oder das Heraion der Argolis? Religion im Prozeß der Polisbildung, in: K. Freitag/P. Funke/M. Haake (eds.), Kult – Politik – Ethnos. Überrregionale Heiligtümer im Spannungsfeld von Kult und Politik, Historia-Einzelschriften 189, Stuttgart, 73–87.

– (2006b), Art. Antiquity, in: The Brill Dictionary of Religion, vol. 1, 81–106.

– (2007), Ritual, Performanz, Theater. Die Religion der Athener in Aristophanes' Komödien, in: A.F. Bierl/R. Lämmle/K. Wesselmann (eds.), Literatur und Religion 1: Wege zu einer mythisch-rituellen Poetik bei den Griechen, MythosEikonPoiesis 1, Berlin/New York, 387–414.

– (2007b), Theologie als Religionskritik in der Europäischen Religionsgeschichte, Zeitschrift für Religionswissenschaft 15, 5–27.

– (2008a), Religio migrans. Die 'Orientalischen Religionen' im Kontext antiker Religion. Ein theoretisches Modell, in: C. Bonnet/S. Ribichini/ J. Rüpke (eds.), Religioni in Contatto nel Mediterraneo Antico: Modalità di diffusione e processi di interferenza, atti del 3. colloquio su "Le Religioni Orientali nel Mondo Greco e Romano", Loveno di Menaggio (Como), 26–28 maggio 2006, Mediterranea 4, Rom, 333–363.

– (2008b), Teure Ideologie – billige Praxis. Die 'kleinen' Opfer in der römischen Kaiserzeit, in: E. Stavrianopoulou/A. Michaels/C. Ambos (eds.), Transformations in Sacrificial Practices: From Antiquity to Modern Times, Proceedings of an International Colloquium, Heidelberg, 12–14, July 2006, Performanzen 15, Münster, 147–170.

– (2009), Europäische Religionsgeschichte, in: R. Faber/S. Lanwerd (eds.), Aspekte der Religionswissenschaft, Würzburg, 29–48.

– /Stuckenbruck, L.T. (2004, eds.), The Fall of the Angels, Symposium held 19–21 January 2001 in Tübingen, Themes in Biblical Narrative. Jewish and Christian Traditions 6, Leiden u.a.

Belayche, N. (2005), Hypsistos, Une voie de l'exaltation des dieux dans le polythéisme gréco-romain, Archiv für Religionsgeschichte 7, 34–55.

Bendlin, A. (2001), Art. Polytheismus, Der Neue Pauly 10, 80–83.

Berner, U. (2008), Verlauf und Ertrag der Monotheismusdebatte aus religionswissenschaftlicher Sicht, in: L. Bormann (ed.), Schöpfung, Monotheismus und fremde Religionen. Studien zu Inklusion und Exklusion in den biblischen Schöpfungsvorstellungen, BThSt 95, Neukirchen-Vluyn, 37–61.

Bierl, A.F./Lämmle, R./Wesselmann, K., (2007, eds.), Literatur und Religion 1: Wege zu einer mythisch-rituellen Poetik bei den Griechen, MythosEikonPoiesis 1, Berlin/New York.

Bormann, L. (2008, ed.), Schöpfung, Monotheismus und fremde Religionen. Studien zu Inklusion und Exklusion in den biblischen Schöpfungsvorstellungen, BThSt 95, Neukirchen-Vluyn.

Burkert, W. (1984), Die orientalisierende Epoche in der griechischen Religion und Literatur, Sitzungsberichte der Heidelberger Akademie der Wissenschaften, Philosophisch-Historische Klasse 1984/1, Vorgetragen am 8. Mai 1982, Heidelberg.

– (2003), Die Griechen und der Orient. Von Homer bis zu den Magiern, München.

Cancik, H. (1998), Art. Antike, in: RGG, Bd. 1, 4. Aufl., Tübingen, 536–542.

Chaniotis, A. (2009), Megatheism: The Search for the Almighty God and the Competition of Cults, in: S. Mitchell/P. van Nuffelen (eds.), One God: Pagan Monotheism in the Roman Empire (in press).

Colpe, C./Löw, A. (1994), Hypsistos (Theos), in: Reallexikon für Antike und Christentum. Sachwörterbuch zur Auseinandersetzung des Christentums mit der antiken Welt, bearb. im Franz-Joseph-Dölger-Institut der Universität Bonn. Hrsg. von G. Schöllgen et al., begr. von F.-J. Dölger et al., RAC 16, Stuttgart 1941– , 1035–1056.

Crüsemann, F. (1978), Der Widerstand gegen das Königtum. Die antiköniglichen Texte des Alten Testamentes und der Kampf um den frühen israelitischen Staat, WMANT 49, Neukirchen-Vluyn.

Elsas, C. (1993), Hochgottglauben, in: Handbuch religionswissenschaftlicher Grundbegriffe, Hrsg. von H. Cancik/B. Gladigow/M. Laubscher (ab Bd 4: K.-H. Kohl), 5 Bde, Stuttgart [u.a.] 1988–2000, HRWG 3, 155–160.

Eustathii, A.T. (1828), Eustathii Archiepiscopi Thessalonicensis Commentarii ad Homeri Iliadem, Leipzig.

Fischer-Elfert, H.-W. (2005), Abseits von Ma'at. Fallstudien zu Außenseitern im alten Ägypten, Wahrnehmungen und Spuren Altägyptens 1, Würzburg.

Flaig, E. (1994), Konsensprinzip im homerischen Olymp. Überlegungen zum göttlichen Entscheidungsprozess Ilias 4,1–72, Hermes 122, 13–31.

Förster, H. (2007), Die Anfänge von Weihnachten und Epiphanias. Eine Anfrage an die Entstehungshypothesen, Studien und Texte zu Antike und Christentum 46, Tübingen.

Fowden, G. (1993), Empire to Commonwealth: Consequences of Monotheism in Late Antiquity, Princeton.

Fränkel, H.F. (1976), Dichtung und Philosophie des frühen Griechentums. Eine Geschichte der griechischen Epik, Lyrik und Prosa bis zur Mitte des fünften Jahrhunderts, 3. Aufl., München (Engl. transl.: Early Greek Poetry and Philosophy: A History of Greek Epic, Lyric, and Prose to the Middle of the Fifth Century, Oxford 1975).

Freud, S. (1939), Der Mann Moses und die monotheistische Religion. Drei Abhandlungen, in: Fragen der Gesellschaft. Ursprünge der Religion, Studienausgabe, hg. v. A. Mitscherlich et al., vol. 9, Frankfurt/Main 1974, 457–581.

Fürst, A. (2006), Monotheismus und Monarchie. Zum Zusammenhang von Heil und Herrschaft in der Antike, ThPh 81, 321–338.

Fuhrer, T. (2006), Stoa und Christentum, in: A. Fürst, Der apokryphe Briefwechsel zwischen Seneca und Paulus. Zusammen mit dem Brief des Mordechai an Alexander und dem Brief des Annaeus Seneca über Hochmut und Götterbilder, Sapere 11, 108–125.

Furley, W.D. (2000), Komplementäre Erinyen-Hymnen in den aischyleischen Eumeniden, in: A. Haltenhoff/F.-H. Mutschler (eds.), Hortus Litterarum antiquarum, FS H.A. Gärtner, BKAW II/109, Heidelberg, 143–151.

Ginsburg, R./Pardes, I. (2006, eds.), New Perspectives on Freud's "Moses and Monotheism", Conditio Judaica 60, Tübingen.

Gladigow, B. (1983), Strukturprobleme polytheistischer Religionen, Saeculum 34, 292–304 (repr. in: Religionswissenschaft als Kulturwissenschaft, ed. by C. Auffarth/J. Rüpke, Stuttgart 2005, 125–137).

– (1995), Europäische Religionsgeschichte, in: H.G. Kippenberg/B. Luchesi (eds.), Lokale Religionsgeschichte, Marburg 1995, 21–42.

– (2001), Polytheismus, in: H.G. Kippenberg/M. Riesebrodt (eds.), Max Webers 'Religionssystematik', Tübingen, 131–150.

– (2002), Polytheismus und Monotheismus. Zur historischen Dynamik einer europäischen Alternative, in: M. Krebernik/J. von Oorschot (eds.), Polytheismus und Monotheismus in den Religionen des Vorderen Orients, AOAT 298, Münster, 1–20.

Hailer, M. (2006), Gott und die Götzen. Über Gottes Macht angesichts der lebensbestimmenden Mächte, FSÖTh 109, Göttingen.

Henrichs, A. (1991), Namenlosigkeit und Euphemismus. Zur Ambivalenz der chthonischen Mächte im attischen Drama, in: H. Hofmann/A. Harder (eds.), Fragmenta dramatica. Beiträge zur Interpretation der griechischen Tragikerfragmente und ihrer Wirkungsgeschichte, Göttingen, 161–203.

– (2000), Art. Moira, Der Neue Pauly 8, 340–343.

Keel, O. (2008), Die Geschichte Jerusalems und die Entstehung des Monotheismus, Orte und Landschaften der Bibel 4/1, Göttingen 2008.

Kiefner, W. (1965), Der religiöse Allbegriff bei Aischylos. Untersuchungen zur Verwendung von pān, pánta, pántes und dergleichen als Ausdrucksmittel religiöser Sprache, Spudasmata 5, Hildesheim.

Kippenberg, H.G./Rüpke, J./von Stuckrad, K. (2009, eds.), Europäische Religionsgeschichte. Ein mehrfacher Pluralismus, 2 vols., Göttingen.

Kratz, R./Spieckermann, H. (2008, eds.), Divine Wrath and Divine Mercy in the World of Antiquity, A Symposium held on November 8th–10th 2006 in Göttingen, FAT II/33, Tübingen.

Krebernik, M./van Oorschot, J. (2002, eds.), Polytheismus und Monotheismus in den Religionen des Vorderen Orients, AOAT 298, Münster.

Latacz, J. (2000), Homers Ilias. Gesamtkommentar I, auf der Grundlage der Ausgabe von Ameis-Hentze-Cauer (1868–1913), Sammlung wissenschaftlicher Commentare, München.

Lévêque, P. (1959), Aurea Catena Homeri. Une étude sur l'allégorie grecque, ALUB 27, Paris.

Lloyd-Jones, H. (1983), The Justice of Zeus, Sather Classical Lectures 41, 2nd ed., Berkeley.

Lovejoy, A.O. (1936), The Great chain of being, The William James Lectures delivered at Harvard University, Cambridge (German transl. by D. Turck: Die grosse Kette der Wesen. Geschichte eines Gedankens, stw 1104, Frankfurt/Main 1993).

Markschies, C. (2002), Heis Theos – Ein Gott? Der Monotheismus und das antike Christentum, in: M. Krebernik/J. van Oorschot Polytheismus und Monotheismus in den Religionen des Vorderen Orients, AOAT 298, Münster, 209–234.

Marquard, O. (1979), Lob des Polytheismus. Über Monomythie und Polymythie, in: H. Poser (1979, ed.) Philosophie und Mythos. Ein Kolloquium, Berlin, 40–59, wiederabgedruckt in: O. Marquard (2003, ed.), Zukunft braucht Herkunft. Philosophische Essays, Stuttgart 2003, 46–71.

Mitchell, S. (2010), Further Thoughts on the Worship of Theos Hypsistos, in print.

Mullen, E.T. (1980), The Divine Council in Canaanite and Early Hebrew Literature, HSM 24, Chico/CA.

Mylonopoulos, J. (2003), Peloponnêsos oikêtêrion Poseidônos. Heiligtümer und Kulte des Poseidon auf der Peloponnes, Kernos Suppl. 13, Liège.

Peterson, E. (1926), Heis theos. Epigraphische, formgeschichtliche und religionsgeschichtliche Untersuchungen, FRLANT 24, Göttingen, als Reprint vorgesehen in: Ausgewählte Schriften, vol. 8, ed. by C. Markschies, Würzburg (forthcoming).

Petry, S. (2007), Die Entgrenzung JHWHs. Monolatrie, Bilderverbot und Monotheismus im Deuteronomium, in Deuterojesaja und im Ezechielbuch, FAT II/27, Tübingen.

Pilhofer, P. (1990), Presbyteron Kreitton. Der Altersbeweis der jüdischen und christlichen Apologeten und seine Vorgeschichte, § 3 Philon, Tübingen, 173–192.

Pirenne-Delforge, V. (1994), L'Aphrodite grecque. Contribution à l'étude de ses cultes et de sa personnalité dans le panthéon archaïque et classique, Kernos Suppl. 4, Liège.

Ribichini, S.R./Rocchi, M./Xella, P. (2001, eds.), La questione delle influenze vicino-orientali sulla religione greca, atti del Colloquio internazionale, Roma, 20–22 maggio 1999, Monografie Scientifiche, Roma.

Ridings, D. (1995), The Attic Moses: The Dependency Theme in Some Early Christian Writers, SGLG 59, Göteborg.

Schäfer, P. (2005), Geschichte und Gedächtnisgeschichte. Jan Assmanns "Mosaische Unterscheidung", in: B.E. Klein/C.E. Müller, Memoria – Wege jüdischen Erinnerns, FS M. Brocke, Berlin, 19–39.

– (2006), The Triumph of Pure Spirituality: Sigmund Freud's Moses and Monotheism, in: R. Ginsburg/I. Pardes (eds.), New Perspectives on Freud's "Moses and Monotheism", Conditio Judaica 60, Tübingen, 19–44.

– (2008), Weibliche Gottesbilder im Judentum und Christentum, Frankfurt/Main (American Original: Mirror of His beauty: Feminine Images of God from the Bible to the Early Kabbalah, Princeton 2002).

Schwabl, H. (1972), Art. Zeus. I. Epiklesen, in: Paulys Realencyklopädie der classischen Altertumswissenschaft, PRE vol. 10A, 253–376.

– (1978), Art. Zeus. II. (mit Beiträgen zur Sprachgeschichte von J. Schindler und zu mykenischen Texten von S. Hiller), und Art. Zeus, Nachträge und Korrekturen, in: Paulys Realencyklopädie der classischen Altertumswissenschaft, PRE.Suppl. 15, 993–1411 und 1441–1481.

Simon, E. (1978), Art. Zeus III. Archäologische Zeugnisse, in: Paulys Realencyklopädie der classischen Altertumswissenschaft, PRE.Suppl. 15, 1411–1441.

Stolz, F. (1996), Einführung in den biblischen Monotheismus. Die Theologie, Darmstadt.

– (2001), Wesen und Funktion von Monotheismus, EvTh 61, 172–189.

Stroumsa, G.G. (2006), Myth into Novel: The Late Freud on Early Religion, in: R. Ginsburg/I. Pardes (eds.), New Perspectives on Freud's "Moses and Monotheism", Conditio Judaica 60, Tübingen, 203–216.

Stuckenbruck, L.T. (2004, ed.), Early Jewish and Christian Monotheism, JSNT.S 263, London.

Teeter, T.M. (2007), Theos Hypsistos in the Papyri, in: Akten des 23. Internationalen Papyrologen-Kongresses. Wien, 22.–28. Juli 2001, ed. B. Palme, Papyrologica Vindobonensia 1, Wien, 675–678.

Wallraff, M. (2001), Christus verus sol. Sonnenverehrung und Christentum in der Spätantike, JAC.E 32, Münster.

– (2003), Viele Metaphern – viele Götter? Beobachtungen zum Monotheismus der Spätantike, in: J. Frey/J. Rohls/R. Zimmermann (eds.), Metaphorik und Christologie, TBT 120, Berlin, 151–166.

– (2004), Pantheon und Allerheiligen. Einheit und Vielfalt des Göttlichen in der Spätantike, JAC 47, 128–143.

– (2007), Tendenzen zum Monotheismus als Kennzeichen der religiösen Kultur der Spätantike, in: Religionsgeschichte der Spätantike. Themenheft, hg. v. M. Wallraff, VF 52/2, 65–79.

Wernicke, K. (1895), Art. Argos, in: PRE 2,1. Neue Bearbeitung. Unter Mitwirkung zahlreicher Fachgenossen, hg. v. G. Wissow et al., 790–798.

West, M.L. (1990, ed.), Aeschylus, Tragoediae, BSGRT, Stuttgart.

– (1997), The East Face of Helicon: West Asiatic Elements in Early Poetry and Myth, Oxford.

– (1999), Towards Monotheism, in: P. Athanassiadi/M. Frede (eds.), Pagan Monotheism in Late Antiquity, Oxford (reprint 2002), 21–40.

– (2003, ed.), Greek Epic Fragments: From the Seventh to the Fifth Centuries BC, LCL 497, Cambrigde/Mass. et al.

Wischmeyer, W. (2005), Theos Hypsistos. Neues zu einer alten Debatte, in: Zeitschrift für Antikes Christentum 9, 149–168.

Index of Subjects

List of Contributors

AUFFARTH, Christoph, is Professor for Comparative religion at Bremen University. His main research interests are Religions in the Ancient world, especially Greek and Early Christian, and Relgions in Europe especially concerning the multi-religiosity of the Age of the Crusades in the Middle Ages and religion in Modernity, 19th century.

BLUM, Erhard, is Professor for Old Testament at the Eberhard Karls Universität Tübingen, Germany. His main research interests concern the history of the OT literature, *inter alia* of the Pentateuch and the prophetic literature, including the issues of philological-exegetical methodology.

FINKELSTEIN, Israel, is Professor of Archaeology at the Department of Archaeology and Ancient Near Eastern Civilizations, Tel Aviv University. His main research interests are the archaeology and history of the Levant from the Bronze Age through the Iron Age until Hellenistic times, Biblical History and the contact between archaeology and the exact sciences.

HERZOG, Ze'ev, is Professor of Archaeology at the Department of Archaeology and Ancient Near Eastern Cultures at Tel Aviv University, Israel. He also serves as the Director of the Sonia and Marco Nadler Institute of Archaeology at Tel Aviv University. He is the co-editor of Salvage Excavations Reports and member of the Editorial Board of the Monograph Series published by the Institute of Archaeology. His main fields of interest are: Social Archaeology, Ancient Architecture and Field Archaeology.

HEYDEN, Katharina, is Assistent for Church History and Patristics at the Faculty of Theology, Georg-August-University of Göttingen. Her main research interests are religious history of Late Antiquity, the importance of Palestine as the 'Holy Land' within ancient Christianity, and Christian archaeology and art.

KÖCKERT, Matthias, is Professor for Old Testament studies/Hebrew Bible emeritus at the Humboldt-University zu Berlin. His areas of research are the religions of Ancient Israel, the temple and his history, the books of Genesis, and the Minor Prophets.

KRATZ, Reinhard G., is Professor for Old Testament Studies at Georg-August-University of Göttingen. His main fields of research are the history of literature and theology of the Hebrew Bible, Ancient Near Eastern and Israelite prophecy, Judaism in the Persian and Hellenistic periods, including Qumran studies.

MAZAR, Amihai, is Professor of Archaeology at the Hebrew University of Jerusalem, Israel. His main fields of research are the archaeology of the Levant in the Bronze and Iron Ages; the relationship between archaeology and Old Testament history; the art and architecture of the Ancient Near East. He has directed excavations in several sites in Israel including Tell Qasile, Tel Batash, Tel Beth Shean and Tel Rehov.

MAZOR, Gabriel, is Director of Beth She'an Archaeological Project and Final Publications Research, Senior Archaeologist and Researcher, Israel Antiquities Authority, Jerusalem, Israel. His main research fields are Hellenistic, Roman and Byzantine periods in the region of the Eastern Provinces of the Roman Empire: architecture, culture, religions and ethnicity in the Hellenic *poleis* of the region.

PAKKALA, Juha, is Docent and Lecturer for Hebrew Bible and Biblical Studies at the University of Helsinki. His main research interests are Editorial Processes of the Hebrew Bible, Ezra-Nehemiah, Deuteronomy, 1-2 Kings, 1-2 Chronicles and the Archaeology of the Southern Levant.

ROFÉ, Alexander, is Emeritus Professor of Bible at the Hebrew University of Jerusalem. His main interest is the history of the biblical text, literature and religion. His 'Introduction to the Literature of the Hebrew Bible' has been published by Simor Ltd., Jerusalem 2009.

SCHAUDIG, Hanspeter, is Assistant Professor for Assyriology at the 'Seminar für Sprachen und Kulturen des Vorderen Orients' at University of Heidelberg, Germany. He focusses on the intellectual sphere of Babylonia in the first millennium BCE, and on its transmission to neighbouring cultures.

SEGAL, Michael, is a Lecturer in the Department of Bible at the Hebrew University of Jerusalem and co-editor of the Hebrew University Bible Project. His research interests include biblical literature of the Persian and Hellenistic periods, Apocrypha and Pseudepigrapha, textual criticism of the Hebrew Bible, and early biblical exegesis.

SPIECKERMANN, Hermann, is Professor for Old Testament Studies at Georg-August-University of Göttingen; his main research interests are: theology of the Old Testament, Psalms, wisdom literature, and Ancient Near Eastern history of religion.

STERN, Ephraim, is Emeritus Professor of Biblical Archaeology in the Institute of Archaeology at the Hebrew University of Jerusalem, Israel, specializing in the Assyrian, Babylonian and Persian periods and the Phoenician material culture. He has directed many excavations, among them at En-Gedi, Tel Meorakh and at Tel Dor, and published many books and articles in these subjects.

WITTE, Markus, is Professor for Exegesis and History of Old Testament Literature at Humboldt-University, Berlin. His major fields of research are the Pentateuch, the book of Job, the wisdom literature, the Septuagint and the connections between Israel and Greece in the Hellenistic Age. He is co-editor of the BZAW and member of the international advisory panel of the 'International Society for the Study of Deuterocanonical and Cognate Literature' and member of the international advisory board of the 'Biblische Notizen. Aktuelle Beiträge zur Exegese der Bibel und ihrer Welt'.